EDITION 4

Conducting Research in Psychology

Measuring the Weight of Smoke

Brett W. Pelham

National Science Foundation

Hart Blanton

University of Connecticut

WADSWORTH
CENGAGE Learning·

Australia • Brazil • Japan • Korea • Mexico • Singapore • Spain • United Kingdom • United States

WADSWORTH
CENGAGE Learning·

Conducting Research in Psychology: Measuring the Weight of Smoke, **Fourth Edition**

Brett W. Pelham and Hart Blanton

Senior Publisher: Linda Schreiber-Ganster

Executive Editor: Jon-David Hague

Acquisitions Editor: Tim Matray

Assistant Editor: Paige Leeds

Editorial Assistant: Lauren K. Moody

Media Editor: Mary Noel

Marketing Manager: Sean Foy

Art Direction, Production Management, and Composition: PreMediaGlobal

Cover Direction: Pamela Galbreath

Manufacturing Planner: Karen Hunt

Rights Acquisitions Specialist: Tom McDonough

Cover Designer: Lisa Langhoff, One Good Dog Design

Cover Image: © Yellowj/Shutterstock.com

For product information and technology assistance, contact us at **Cengage Learning Customer & Sales Support, 1-800-354-9706.**

For permission to use material from this text or product, submit all requests online at **www.cengage.com/permissions.** Further permissions questions can be e-mailed to **permissionrequest@cengage.com.**

Library of Congress Control Number: 2011935082

Student Edition:

ISBN-13: 978-0-495-59819-0

ISBN-10: 0-495-59819-4

Wadsworth
20 Davis Drive
Belmont, CA 94002-3098
USA

Cengage Learning is a leading provider of customized learning solutions with office locations around the globe, including Singapore, the United Kingdom, Australia, Mexico, Brazil, and Japan. Locate your local office at **www.cengage.com/global.**

Cengage Learning products are represented in Canada by Nelson Education, Ltd.

To learn more about Wadsworth, visit **www.cengage.com/wadsworth** Purchase any of our products at your local college store or at our preferred online store **www.cengagebrain.com.**

Printed in the United States of America
1 2 3 4 5 6 7 16 15 14 13 12

About the Authors

BRETT PELHAM grew up as the second of six children near the small town of Rossville, Georgia. Brett received his B.S. from Berry College in 1983 and received his Ph.D. from the University of Texas at Austin in 1989. He wrote the first edition of this book while working as an associate professor at UCLA, and he is currently a program officer in social psychology at the National Science Foundation. The bulk of his research focuses on automatic social judgment and self-evaluation. He teaches courses in social psychology, research methods, statistics, social cognition, and the self-concept. In his spare time, he enjoys juggling, sculpting, listening to alternative rock music, cooking, and traveling. His two favorite activities while completing the latest revision of this textbook (in late July of 2011) were spending time with his 2.9-year-old daughter Brooklyn and his 8.5-year-old son Lincoln. Along with his wife LJ Pelham, he is co-inventor of the recently released card game *PRIME*. Along with his son Lincoln, he is co-inventor of the soon-to-be-released card game *Cliff-Hanger*. Along with his daughter Brooklyn, he is co-inventor of the not-so-soon-to-be-released card game *It's a Hat. You Like It?* His most recent writing project is a novel tentatively entitled *Elvis 2.0*, which focuses on problems associated with the apparent resurrection of Elvis Presley.

HART BLANTON grew up as the second of three children in a small town in Appalachian Virginia. Hart received his B.A. from Virginia Tech in 1990 and received his Ph.D. from Princeton University in 1994. He worked on the second edition of this book while at SUNY, Albany, and the third edition while at the University of North Carolina, Chapel Hill and the fourth edition while at the University of Connecticut. The bulk of his research is on social influence and social communication. He has taught courses in research methods, social psychology, statistics, the self, social comparison, and social influence. Most recently, he has become interested in what he terms "negative psychology." This he conceptualizes as the formal study of social structural and individual emotional factors that lead people to die before their time. He hopes to finish his work on this new research area very quickly because, well, one never knows.

Brief Contents

Contents

APPENDIX 2   Methodology Exercises   416

APPENDIX 3   How to Describe the Results of Statistical Analyses   429

APPENDIX 4   XXX-Box: The Effect of Sexualized Video Games on Players' Rape Supportive Responses   446

Preface

Before you begin this book, we would like to make a simple observation: most undergraduate students dread courses in research methods. This fact was brought home by one of our own students, who (as part of a class exercise) wrote that he anticipated that "few things could be more boring, useless, intimidating, or impenetrable than research methods." We find opinions such as this disturbing, not only because we each teach courses in research methods but also because we firmly believe that few things could be more interesting, useful, inviting, or intuitive than research methods. If this belief strikes you as strange, that is fine with us. However, we take it upon ourselves to convince you in this book that most students' dread of research methods has much more to do with how the topic is presented than with the nature of research methods.

To make this point in a different way, we suspect that, with a little effort, we could write a boring, useless, intimidating, and impenetrable book about such topics as skydiving, juggling, or romantic trysts. The key to doing so would be to focus heavily on the rules and technical details of skydiving, juggling, or trysting without much attention to the actual experience of these inherently interesting activities. Unfortunately, common approaches to research methods frequently focus too much on the rules and technical details. In our opinion, this is a major reason why research methods courses have such a bad reputation. In contrast, the approach we adopt in this book takes you behind the scenes of psychological research. In this text, of course, we do describe and explain the technical skills you need to conduct solid research. However, we also try to communicate some of the excitement and pleasure that comes from actually conducting research. Along the way, we point out many interesting and surprising things scientific research methods reveal about human nature. To these ends, we generally pursue a hands-on, common sense approach to research, supplementing lively examples and stories with hands-on exercises that will give you a sense of what it is like to conduct your own research. In summary, our approach to this book is based on two important premises. First, research methods become easy to understand when you can relate them to things that you already know. Second, research methods become interesting when you can use them to discover things you never would have known otherwise. Although the study of survey development, experimental design, and inferential statistics can be exceptionally difficult and boring when viewed in isolation, these same procedures can come alive when they help us learn about human nature.

Because we both happen to be social psychologists, another important aspect of this text is that we emphasize what is social about psychological research methods. Being a good experimental psychologist requires the use of the same methodological rules that apply to all other scientific disciplines. However, the fact that people are social beings generates some practical dilemmas that are not likely to plague researchers in astrophysics, metaphysics, or psychophysics (a branch of perceptual psychology). The most ubiquitous of these problems is that when people know that their behavior is being studied, they often behave unnaturally. The challenge of experimental psychology is to study "natural" behavior in unnatural (laboratory) situations. The clever solutions psychologists have developed to deal with this problem make experimental research methods in psychology a little different, and perhaps a little more interesting, than experimental research methods in general. Because of the human element in psychological research, good experimental psychology is not just good science; it is also good art. It takes a good scientist to generate precise tests of psychological theories, but it takes a good artist (and occasionally a good con artist) to translate these tests into laboratory experiences that are psychologically real to research participants.

New in the Fourth Edition

Now that this book is in its fourth edition, we will avoid the temptation to review all of the many ways in which it has evolved over time. Instead we will focus on (a) the most important revision and (b) the most recent revision. Let's begin with the most important. The first author wrote the first edition of this textbook after he had been teaching research methods at UCLA for about five or six years. He wanted to create a book that was fun, accessible, and highly sophisticated. The first edition of this book was, in fact, both fun and accessible. However, it was not until Brett convinced Hart to become his co-author on the second edition of the book that it became at all sophisticated. Another way of saying this is that Hart is one of the three or four people on the planet whom Brett admits is more knowledgeable than he is. Luckily for readers, Hart is also one of the 34 people who have ever been in Brett's kitchen who are all patently funnier than he is. At the cost of a devastating blow to Brett's fragile self-concept, that is, the benefits Hart brought to this book were too numerous to mention. If you come away from this book appreciating EGWA scales, cluster sampling, conceptual validity, or patching you can thank Hart. If you come away with a greater repertoire of jokes to tell to your 11-year-old nephew, you can thank us both.

This brings us to the most recent revision. Although it has been only six years since we penned the third edition of this book, research methods in psychology have been evolving at a very rapid rate, and there have been thousands of fascinating, methodologically rigorous studies that complement the many studies we cited in the third edition of the book. To try to give readers a better feel for this recent work, we have provided updated examples of contemporary research in nearly every chapter of the book. Perhaps even more important, we added a new chapter to the book (Chapter 12) that emphasizes the most important methodological improvement we have seen in psychology in the past decade, which is the increasing reliance on multi-method approaches to research. Chapter 12 also serves as a useful reminder of how real researchers have applied many of the principles we emphasized in the first 11 chapters of the book. We hope readers of the book will find this new chapter to be as enlightening as it is entertaining. If nothing else, we hope this new chapter will enrich your psychological perspective on topics as diverse as alien abductions, police officers' shooting decisions, topless dancers, and stinky t-shirts.

Acknowledgments

Marianne Taflinger, senior acquisitions editor, convinced Brett Pelham to write the first edition of this book. In addition, she gave him a great deal of excellent advice about how to do so—at all stages of the book's development. She continued to work with us through the second edition. As we have already told her, Tracy DeHart also contributed in a myriad of ways to the second edition. The third edition benefited from the editorial guidance of Vicki Knight, and the fourth benefitted from the editorial guidance of both Tim Matray and Greg Johnson. We also thank Diane Giometti Clue for her extremely careful copyediting of the fourth edition. She caught many short-comings in the new and old sections of the text.

We also are indebted to the outside reviewers of the manuscript who have made many insightful and constructive suggestions that allowed us to improve the book. The reviewers of the first edition were: Bernard C. Beins, Ithaca College; Brian C. Cronk, Missouri Western State College; Joel S. Freund, University of Arkansas–Fayetteville; Thomas E. Nygren, Ohio State University; and Carl Scott, University of Saint Thomas. The reviewers of the second edition were: Janet Andrews, Vassar College; Wendy Francis, The University of Texas at El Paso; Matthew Johnson, Binghamton University, State University of New York; Doug Matheson, University of the Pacific; Dawn McBride, Illinois State University; and Celia Reaves, Monroe Community College. The reviewers of the third edition were: David Campbell, Humboldt State University; Jim Eck, Rollins College; David Haaga, American University; Steve Haase, Shippensburg University; Robert Hessling, University of Wisconsin–Milwaukee; Andy Karpinski, Temple University; Michael Mallen, Iowa State University; Dawn McBride, Illinois State University; Monisha Pasupathi, University of Utah; Kristen Salomon, University of South Florida; and Annette Taylor, University of San Diego.

Brett, the first author, also thanks his dad, who first taught him to be a critical thinker, and his mom, who first taught him to be patient with his dad. Brett also thanks Daniel McBrayer, Robert McCrae, David McKenzie, Dennis Selvidge, Julian Shand, and Edward Vatza, who taught him to love science. Brett also thanks his graduate advisers, Dan Gilbert and Bill Swann, who patiently taught him to be a psychological scientist, along with Janet Spence, who taught him to be patient with Gilbert and Swann.

During Brett's ten years at UCLA, he benefited enormously from the wit, warmth, and wisdom of Paul Abramson, David Boninger, Marilynn Brewer, John Hetts, Anne Peplau, Jim Sidanius, Shelley Taylor, Heidi Wayment, and Bernie Weiner. Bernie Weiner was the wittiest. The rest of you, as you all know, were all the warmest and wisest. Brett also thanks those who helped him learn to teach research methods at UCLA: Khanh Bui, Tom DeHardt, Pam Feldman, Marie Helweg-Larsen, Paul Mallery, and Eve Rose. While at SUNY, Buffalo, the first author also learned a great deal about research methods from Mauricio Carvallo, Shira Gabriel, John T. Jones, Sandra Murray, Gretchen Sechrist, Mitsuru Shimizu, and Derek Taylor. Finally, it should go without saying that the person to whom Brett can only tip his cap, the person from whom he has learned more about science than anyone else, is the ever-thoughtful Curtis Hardin.

Hart, the second author, also wishes to thank many people. Unfortunately, the first author has used up so much space that Hart has to be more discriminating. He thanks the two undergraduate advisers who turned him into a budding psychologist: Caryn Carlson, who convinced an engineering dropout to try a different major, and Danny Axsom, who inspired Hart's love of social psychology. Hart also thanks the teachers of his graduate methods and statistics courses, Dale Miller and Debbie Prentice. Hart hopes that this book will reveal that he usually listened to their lectures, even though he offered no outward signs at the time. He also thanks his methodologically savvy postdoctoral advisers, Jenny Crocker, Meg Gerrard, and Rick Gibbons. Without them, Hart would have had to abandon psychology and become a miserable, bitter, and wealthy man. He also thanks Norbert Schwarz. Norbert invited Hart to team-teach a graduate course with him at the University of Michigan, and much of Hart's input for this book was inspired by Norbert's wise and thoughtful lectures. Hart also thanks his former colleague, current collaborator, and longtime friend, Jim Jaccard. Much of the wisdom in this text (Hart's part at least) was stolen directly from casual comments Jim Jaccard happened to make while in Hart's company. Finally, Hart joins Brett in tipping his cap to the ever-thoughtful Curtis Hardin, who has been incredibly thoughtful and supportive to Hart at several key points in Hart's career.

A Brief Note to Students

For both aesthetic and pedagogic reasons, we do not include any definitions in the margins of this text. However, to help you identify crucially important theoretical and technical terms, these terms appear in boldface type (**like this**) throughout the text. In addition, when introducing crucial terms, we provide an explicit definition, description, or summary of the term in the text. These explicit definitions of key terms are summarized more formally in the glossary that appears at the end of the book. Theoretical and technical terms that are important but secondary to the crucial terms are typically printed in italics (*like this*), and they, too, are almost always accompanied by an explicit definition. Finally, to help you organize your knowledge of research methods, we have organized the material in each chapter by using major and minor subheadings. Paying attention to these headings will help you organize your knowledge of the major themes in each chapter.

Brett Pelham
Hart Blanton

How Do We Know?

For if we show that what follows from the thing in question is not the case, we shall have demolished the thing in question....
—Aristotle *(in Barnes, 1984)*

Thus I arrived, by the end of 1919, at the conclusion that the scientific attitude was the critical attitude, which did not look for verifications but for crucial tests; tests which could refute *the theory being tested, though they could never establish it.*
—Karl Popper *(1974/1990)*

INTRODUCTION: WHAT THIS TEXT IS ABOUT

It is said that in the late 16th century, Sir Walter Raleigh made a very audacious bet. In an effort to impress Queen Elizabeth I, he bet a young courtier that he could *measure the weight of smoke*. The courtier considered Sir Walter's claim ridiculous and eagerly accepted the bet. After establishing the details of the wager, Sir Walter produced two identical cigars and weighed them on a very precise scale. He then lit one of the two cigars and placed it back on the scale. After the cigar burned away, Sir Walter weighed the remaining ashes and announced that the weight of the smoke was to be found in the ashes. Specifically, it was the *difference* between the weight of the intact cigar and the weight of the ashes. The courtier had to agree and reluctantly paid the bet.

It is highly unlikely that this story is true. For one thing, when cigars aren't continually puffed on, they typically do not remain lit. For another, it wasn't until the late 18th century that Antoine Lavoisier demonstrated (by means of some very careful experiments) that the part of a burning object that seems to disappear when burned continues to exist but goes elsewhere (Harré, 1981). Although this story may not be very accurate, it is very scientific. For one thing, it illustrates that seemingly immeasurable things can sometimes be measured very well. For another, this story illustrates that it often takes a good deal of creativity, and a small leap of faith, to figure out *how* to measure the seemingly immeasurable. If Sir Walter Raleigh had actually made a bet about measuring the weight of smoke, he could have won the bet only if the young courtier possessed an intuitive appreciation of the law of conservation of matter. That is, Sir Walter's argument about the cigars is valid only if one takes it as a given that matter can neither be created nor destroyed.

In psychology, we are in the business of measuring things even more fleeting and ephemeral than smoke. The objects of our research attention are elusive concepts such as passion, perception, prejudice, and persuasion. We cannot directly observe any of these psychological concepts, but we can often make reasonable inferences about them by making *indirect* observations. This is why, when asked what he does for a living, one of the authors sometimes tells people that he is in the business of measuring the weight of smoke. When asked what this book is about, we are tempted to give the same answer. It is about how to answer some elusive questions about people by making use of careful, albeit typically indirect, observations.

A Few Quick Tips for Using This Text

Now that you know why we chose the subtitle for this text, we'd like to draw your attention to a few key features of the text—so that you can use it as wisely and efficiently as possible. Just as we have done in this chapter, we begin most chapters of the text with a story or anecdote that serves as a simile for getting a grasp of that particular chapter. A **simile** is a saying or description in which the communicator explicitly uses one concept to help people understand or appreciate another—typically by using words such as "like" or "as." A nice example of a simile is "This textbook is like an oasis in an intellectual desert." A not-so-nice example is "This textbook is like an anchor that is tied to my neck, while I struggle to remain afloat in a sea of despair." Incidentally, we are making such a big deal about similes for two reasons. The first reason is that in addition to opening most chapters with a simile, we also make liberal use of similes throughout the book—to make the point that many important methodological concepts have parallels in real life. The second reason we emphasize the word "simile" is that doing so allows us to define the word and thereby point out another important feature of this book that students sometimes overlook. When we introduce important terms, we always print them in **bold font** (as we did with the decidedly non-methodological word "simile"). We include a glossary of these terms at the end of the text, and we urge you to consult this glossary if you forget the meaning of an important term. At this point, the only other important thing you should know about this book is that we close each chapter with a brief summary to reinforce basic concepts and help you focus on the key themes of the chapter. In other words, we hope that each chapter summary will feel more like an oasis than an anchor.

Preamble for Chapter 1

In this first chapter, we set the stage for the chapters that follow by familiarizing you, in both formal and informal ways, with the nature of the scientific method. We consider this a very important goal. By specifying the basic underpinnings of science, we hope to prepare you to think about psychology as an enterprise that is just as scientific as physics or chemistry. By showing how the basic underpinnings of science are reasonable and intuitive, we also hope to introduce you to the idea that you can translate your common sense—things that you know tacitly or implicitly—into formal knowledge of scientific research methods. Believe it or not, we introduce you to the basic principles of science by doing something that strongly resembles a palm reading.

Imagine that you now have in your hands the world's first custom-designed textbook. We wrote this particular version of the book with you and you alone in mind, tailoring the content and presentation to your own unique personality. As ridiculous as this may sound, try to keep an open mind while you read our professional evaluation of your personality:

> You feel good when other people like and admire you. However, you sometimes have a tendency to be self-critical. You have some personality weaknesses, but you are generally able to compensate for them. Though you try not to appear this way to others, you tend to be worrisome and insecure on the inside. You have a great deal of unused energy that you have not turned to your advantage. At times you have serious doubts about whether you have made the right decision or done the right thing. You prefer a certain amount of change and variety and become dissatisfied when hemmed in by restrictions and limitations. You pride yourself on being an independent thinker and do not accept other opinions without satisfactory proof. You have found it unwise to be too frank in revealing yourself to others. At times you are introverted, wary, and reserved; at other times you are extroverted, affable, and highly sociable. Though you have weaknesses that sometimes bother you, you have many talents and are above average at many things. Where character is concerned, two of your biggest strengths are your ability to get along with others and your self-insight. You have a clear and balanced sense of your strengths and weaknesses. Most of all, you rarely deceive yourself; you are in touch with the real you.

You should now be having at least two reactions to this description. First, you should find it surprisingly accurate. Second, you should be curious to know *how* it could be so accurate. To address the second reaction first, what you have just read is a *Barnum description*, aptly named after the famous circus promoter P. T. Barnum. Like many psychics and astrologers, Barnum knew that most people readily confuse statements that are true of *people in general* with statements that are true of *them in particular* (see Forer, 1949; McKelvie, 1990). When Bui (1997) gave a description very much like this to undergraduates at UCLA, she found that the typical student reported that it was highly accurate. When asked how well this personality profile described them on a 9-point scale whose upper endpoint was labeled *extremely well*, the large majority of students responded with 7s, 8s, or 9s. (The mean was 7.5, and the most common response was 8.)

To appreciate how truly *un*informative a Barnum description really is, consider how you would have felt about the description if it had been a little more obvious that it describes virtually everybody: "You dislike being publicly humiliated, and you enjoy it when important people tell you that you

"I was hoping you could tell me something mildly favorable—yet vague enough to be believable."

are wonderful. You strongly prefer typing with your hands over typing with your feet. You hate waiting in long lines, having root canals, contracting serious illnesses, and getting into motor vehicle accidents...."

But what do Barnum descriptions have to do with psychological research methods? For starters, your curiosity about the apparent accuracy of our original Barnum description is an example of your general curiosity about human nature. Nothing, absolutely nothing, is more interesting to people than people, and this has probably been true for as long as people have existed. For finishers, Barnum descriptions are also good reminders of the difference between intuitive and scientific ways of understanding behavior. More specifically, Barnum descriptions are not scientific. Instead, they closely resemble some of the earliest ways that human beings explained human behavior. To fully appreciate the kinds of explanations for human behavior that psychologists currently offer, one should place them in historical context. From this perspective, the story of how people's explanations for human behavior have changed over time is a story of great progress. It is also a testament to the power of systematic research methods to uncover truths that would be difficult if not impossible to uncover through intuition or casual observation. We hope that we will not sound overly enamored of scientific research methods if we say that the 100 or so years in which people have conducted systematic research on human behavior have taught us more than we learned in the hundreds of centuries that preceded the last 100 years.

A BRIEF HISTORY OF HUMAN KNOWLEDGE

Metaphysical Systems

The earliest explanations for human behavior (and for the physical world as well) appear to have been **metaphysical** or supernatural explanations. Metaphysical explanations are explanations that violate what scientists now consider to be established physical laws, primarily by attributing behavior or experiences to nonphysical forces such as spirits or deities. The earliest category of metaphysical explanations for human behavior was probably **animism,** the belief that natural phenomena are alive and influence behavior. The common members of many prehistoric bands of hunter-gatherers, along with the distinguished members of many ancient civilizations, appear to have endorsed a wide variety of animistic beliefs. For example, a common belief among many ancient people was that possessing parts of certain animals (e.g., a buffalo's hide, an eagle's feathers) would endow the owner with some of the psychological properties of the animal in question. Similarly, among ancient people almost everywhere, natural phenomena such as the wind, sun, and rain were often assumed to have wills or temperaments. Even early scientists and philosophers sometimes explained natural phenomena in animistic terms. For example, Plato apparently believed that the universe was literally alive and had a soul at its center. According to at least some interpretations, Aristotle argued that gravity reflects the desire of physical objects to return to "mother earth" (Rensberger, 1986).

More subtle versions of animistic thinking appeared in Aristotle's analysis of human personality. In his *Physiognomics*, Aristotle heartily endorses the idea that people who possess the *physical* attributes of certain animals possess the habits and dispositions of those same animals. According to Aristotle, just as people with thick necks were strong in character and fierce tempered (like bulls), people with long, thin necks were backward and cowardly, like deer. Similarly, it seemed self-evident to Aristotle that "men with small *ears* have the disposition of monkeys" and that "those with large ears [have] the disposition of asses." And speaking of asses, Aristotle did not limit his analysis to facial features. He also argued that "*Buttocks* pointed and bony are a mark of strong character" and that curved toes and nails "on the evidence of birds with curved claws" are a sign of disrespect or rudeness (Aristotle, in Barnes, 1984). (Though we hate to quibble with Aristotle, we should note that we have never met a disrespectful sparrow.)

Animistic explanations such as these seem naive by today's standards, but the natural appeal of animistic and anthropomorphic explanations has not completely disappeared from modern thought. Any car lover who has ever assumed that his reliable old Dodge Dart will not be as good to its new owner as it was to him, any cat lover who has ever assumed that his tabby genuinely loves and admires him, and any PC lover who has ever commented that her aging laptop "is still thinking" about a command (or that her out-of-date software program "is temperamental") has engaged in highly animistic ways of thinking. In fact, researchers who appreciate our predisposition to infer that machines have wishes and dispositions have begun to capitalize on this predisposition to create user-friendly robots that can get people to trust them (e.g., see Brazeal, 2005, 2007). Further the specific knowledge of what physical, social, and emotional cues we use to make automatic inferences about the likeability or trustworthiness of a robot may play in role, for example, in how effectively robots can be used as tutors (Desteno, 2011, personal communication).

A second very old category of metaphysical explanations shares many of the features of animism but is still a potent force in the lives of millions of people everywhere. This second category of metaphysical explanations includes **mythology and religion**. In the U.S. about 65 percent of adults say that religion is an important part of their daily lives. In less affluent countries this figure is considerably higher. In both Sri Lanka and Bangladesh, for example, fully 99 percent of adults say that religion is an important part of their daily lives (Crabtree, 2010).

Mythological and religious systems make the assumption that deities (who exist in a spiritual rather than physical plane) play an important role in human behavior. Religious explanations for behavior are typically much more sophisticated and comprehensive than animistic explanations, but they share the basic assumption that nonphysical, even magical, forces determine much of what people do. We include religious systems in this historical sequence not because they are right or wrong relative to scientific explanations, but because they are different. Religious systems are built on a different set of assumptions than those upon which scientific systems are built (though scientists, too, make plenty of assumptions). As you will see later, religious and scientific systems of thought are also built upon very different sources of evidence. For now it may be instructive to remember that, in addition to being an important part of the lives of people everywhere, religions are also systems of understanding and explaining human behavior.

A third very old category of metaphysical systems is **astrology**. Astrology appears to have been first practiced by the ancient Egyptians, who, like modern advocates of horoscopes, made the assumption that human behavior is determined by the activity of celestial bodies. An interesting aspect of astrology is that, despite its demotion to a form of entertainment for many, it does adopt some scientific practices in trying to explain human behavior. For example, serious astrologers are very focused on accuracy and precision in measurement. They believe that to give a person the most accurate astrological reading possible, it is necessary to know the exact year, month, day, and time of day of that person's birth, along with the exact latitude and longitude of the person's birth location (Candlish, 1990). Thus, according to *some* of the criteria of good science, astrologers are scientific in the same way astrophysicists are. Of course, according to many other criteria, they are the perfect model of decidedly *un*scientific ways of thinking. We will return to this topic later. For now, suffice it to say that metaphysical systems such as animism, mythology, and astrology were eventually abandoned by scientists in favor of explanations based on an entirely different approach to knowledge.

Philosophy

One of the earliest systems of thought to compete with metaphysical systems was **philosophy**. As it is practiced today, philosophy refers to the study of knowledge, behavior, and the nature of reality by making use of logic, intuition, and empirical observations. However, early philosophers often borrowed concepts from less scientific ways of thinking. Many early European philosophers worked hard to make sure that their ideas were consistent with the Bible or with the works of Aristotle or Plato—both of whom, as you may recall, endorsed some highly animistic beliefs. As late as the 17th century, the brilliant philosopher Descartes, who almost single-handedly transformed thinking about human behavior into a scientific enterprise, accepted the argument that nerves were hollow tubes through which "animal spirits" flowed to the brain. As philosophy matured, however, its practitioners increasingly came to rely on logic and empirical observation. Among contemporary philosophers, arguing for an idea or opinion solely on the basis of authority is considered a sign of weakness.

The focus on logic among philosophers had its roots in early Greek philosophers such as Plato and Aristotle, and it has never really fallen out of favor. In contrast, the focus on empirical observation, though championed by Aristotle himself, never really caught on until the concept got a big jump start from Descartes in the 1600s. After Descartes, the value of making empirical observations grew in popularity during the days of British empiricists such as Locke, Hume, and Hartley. This principle reached its philosophical heyday after August Comte convinced most 19th-century philosophers that a comprehensive theory of knowledge and human behavior should follow the principle of **positivism** (Schultz, 1981). That is, it should be based only on observations that can be made with absolute certainty. By the middle of the 19th century, the concept of **empiricism**—the idea that the best way to learn about the world is to make observations—not only took firm hold in philosophy but also became one of the core assumptions of the scientific method. Because psychology emerged as an independent field of study in the mid- to late 19th century, and because it emerged partly in the wake of philosophy, it should come as no surprise that psychologists, especially experimental psychologists, place a great deal of stock in systematic observation. Before we discuss psychology, however, it is useful to remind ourselves that psychology owes only about half of its genealogy to philosophy. Psychology also grew out of physiology and the physical sciences.

Physiology and the Physical Sciences

Although philosophers believe in empirical observation, very few philosophers gather data to test their theories and hypotheses. Psychology probably owes its current emphasis on systematic observation to its roots in the physical sciences, especially **physiology**. Physiology is the study of the functions of and interrelations between different parts of the brain and body. Physiologists study topics as diverse as how voluntary and involuntary muscle tissues differ and whether different areas of the brain can perform the same basic cognitive or emotional functions. Virtually everything we know about physiology has been discovered using the experimental method. Before William Harvey's landmark experiments on the circulation of blood in 1628, scientists had little or no idea that blood is pumped throughout the body by the heart. Similarly, the tenacious belief that nerves were Lilliputian (i.e., tiny) pipelines for animal spirits was put to rest once and for all by means of the **experimental method**. A few simple experiments conducted by biologists like Luigi Galvani and Alessandro Volta demonstrated that an electrical rather than a spiritual charge must be applied to a frog's nerves to produce muscle movements. Finally, only when researchers began to experimentally destroy certain parts of the brains of animals were they able to determine that different areas of the brain performed different physical and psychological tasks. For example, Marshall Hall's experiments with decapitated animals in the early 1800s provided some of the first convincing evidence that reflex movements are determined by the spinal cord and not the brain. (We said that experimental physiology was enlightening, not that it was always beautiful to behold.)

What a super genius like Descartes could never quite resolve in a lifetime of careful speculation, a regular genius like Volta all but proved with a battery and a single, freshly severed frog leg (see Asimov, 1964). And what Volta left unfinished, subsequent generations of smart folks with a little training in experimental physiology proved beyond the slightest doubt (Schultz, 1981).

We are making two distinct points. The first point is that the experimental method is a powerful way to answer research questions—whether they are physical questions about quantum mechanics or social psychological questions about Quattro mechanics. The second point is that experimental psychologists owe a great deal of what is good about their discipline to the traditions and methods developed and refined by physiologists and other physical scientists.

Now that we have paid some tribute to the metaphysicians, philosophers, and physiologists who preceded scientific psychology, let's take a brief look at the development of scientific psychology. Although it would be a mistake to equate science with experimentation (many scientific studies are not experiments), most historians of psychology would probably agree that psychology first became a science when psychologists first began to conduct experiments. Thus, we begin with an account of when psychologists first seized upon the experimental method.

Experimental Psychology

Most historians of psychology agree that experimental psychology was invented in Germany sometime around the mid- to late 1800s. The only point of disagreement is whether the German scientist who invented it was named Fechner, von Helmholtz, Weber, or Wundt.[1] Although most people have bestowed this honor on Wundt, one could easily make an argument for almost any of these visionary researchers. To a greater or lesser extent, they all studied perceptual and sensory processes in the mid- to late 1800s, and they all made use of experimental methods. However, Wundt was the most psychologically minded one in the bunch. His desire to break consciousness down into its component parts as well as his heavy emphasis on experimental methods reflected his extensive training in physiology. On the other hand, Wundt was also quite interested in higher-order mental processes. In fact, in one of his earliest and most important works (the *Beitrage*, published in 1862), he expressed a keen interest in creating a field he called *social psychology*, and he eventually published a ten-volume book entitled *Folk Psychology* between 1900 and 1920. Surprisingly, however, Wundt felt that the experimental method that was so crucial to understanding basic psychological experience was ill-suited to the study of complex cognitive and social processes. Of course, a major theme of this text is that nothing could be further from the truth.

In the past 120 years or so, **psychology** has become both decidedly experimental *and* decidedly scientific. In fact, like many other researchers, we define psychology as the scientific study of human behavior. That brief definition warrants an entire textbook on research methods because of the single word "scientific." In a nutshell, this book is about how to go about the business of psychology scientifically. Your brief foray into the history of how people have understood their physical and social worlds should have given you some appreciation for how scientific approaches to understanding human behavior differ from other approaches. To gain a fuller appreciation of what it means to study human behavior scientifically, it is probably useful to give some additional thought to exactly how scientists go about their business. The first thing to know about scientists is that, like pastors, politicians, and pastry chefs, scientists make some very important assumptions. Knowing what scientists take for granted can help make us better methodologists because many of the specific principles that are dear to the hearts of methodologists can be derived from the general principles that almost all scientists take for granted. Fundamental principles that are more or less accepted on faith are often referred to as **canons**. At least four such fundamental principles appear to be accepted by almost all scientists.

THE FOUR CANONS OF SCIENCE

Determinism

One hallmark of scientific thinking is the assumption of **determinism**. This is the doctrine that the universe is orderly—the idea that all events have meaningful, systematic causes. Even animistic and astrological systems of thought are partly deterministic. Astrologers appear to believe that something about the motions and positions of celestial bodies causes people to behave in certain predictable ways. They can't (or won't) tell us exactly what it is about Neptune's rising or Venus's falling that caused Serena to have bad luck last Wednesday, but it is presumably *something* systematic. Otherwise, why not assign people to astrological signs at random? Whereas there may be some deterministic slippage in astrological systems, there is no room for such slippage in science.[2] Some psychologists have even argued that people (and perhaps many other animals) are predisposed to think in causal terms. Whether or not we are predisposed to do so, plenty of evidence suggests that we are wont to do so. As an example of the power and utility of causal thinking, consider the following problem (adapted from Tversky & Kahneman, 1982):

A cab was involved in a hit-and-run accident at night. Two cab companies, the Green and the Blue, operate in the city. You are given the following data:

1. 85 percent of the cabs in the city are Green and 15 percent are Blue.
2. A witness identified the cab as Blue.

The court tested the reliability of the witness under the same circumstances that existed on the night of the accident and concluded that the witness correctly identified each one of the two colors 80 percent of the time and failed 20 percent of the time. What is the probability that the cab involved in the accident was Blue? If you are like most people, your intuitions are telling you that it is about .80, which corresponds very well to the reliability of the witness. In numerous studies, this is exactly what Tversky and Kahneman (1982) found. The median (middle) and modal (most common) answer for a large group of participants was .80.

Now, if you can somehow cleanse your cognitive palate, consider a slightly different version of the same problem. In this version, you learn exactly what you learned above, except that the information about the cab companies is a little different. Specifically, replace statement (1) in the original problem with the following statement:

1. Although the two companies are roughly equal in size, 85 percent of cab accidents in the city involve Green cabs and 15 percent involve Blue cabs.

Now think again about the accident, the reliability of the witness, and the probability that the cab involved in the accident was Blue. What is this probability?

Although the correct answer hasn't changed, your intuitions about the answer may have. When Tversky and Kahneman gave this logically equivalent version of the problem to a different group of participants, the median answer changed to .60, which indicates that participants in this second group were making at least partial use of information about *base rates*. Base-rate information is information about the proportion of things in a target population—in this case, either the proportion of Green and Blue cabs in the city, or the proportion of Green and Blue cabs involved in accidents.

The main point of the cab problem is that people find it easier to think in terms of causality than not. Thus, when you were provided with both base-rate information and some kind of subjectively useful competing information (in this case, a witness's report), you probably did not make very good use of the base-rate information. However, if you revised your answer downward once you realized that most accidents in this city are *caused* by Green cabs, you improved the accuracy of your judgment by being more sensitive than usual to base-rate information when it was expressed in causal terms (see Ajzen, 1977, for additional evidence along these lines). The correct answer to the cab problem, by the way, is .41. In light of the facts that (1) Green cabs are 5.67 times as likely to be involved in accidents as are Blue cabs and (2) the witness's judgment was pretty poor (only 30 percent better than the chance performance level of 50 percent), you should have adjusted your answer *quite a bit* in the direction of Green cabs (see Tversky & Kahneman, 1982, for a more detailed explanation). The fact that most people come a lot closer to the correct answer when the base-rate information is framed in causal terms attests to the tendency that people prefer to think, and are possibly predisposed to think, in causal terms.

Further evidence that people may be predisposed to think in causal terms comes from research that deals more directly with how people perceive covariation. Consider the information about glorks and zarks presented in Table 1.1. Based on the information in this table, decide which of the two groups, zarks or glorks, you find more likable. Please make this judgment before you read any further! If you are like most people, you probably found the glorks at least a little more likable than the zarks. If you did in fact

Table 1.1   Prosocial and antisocial behavior of zarks and glorks

Group	Who Harmed the Nems?	Who Helped the Nems?
Zarks	T, a zark, harmed the nems.	E, a zark, helped the nems. N, a zark, helped the nems.
Glorks	R, a glork, harmed the nems. O, a glork, harmed the nems.	A, a glork, helped the nems. S, a glork, helped the nems. L, a glork, helped the nems. P, a glork, helped the nems.

conclude that you'd prefer to invite a glork rather than a zark to your next dinner party, you probably fell prey to a common judgmental bias known as the **illusory correlation** (Hamilton & Gifford, 1976). In a number of judgment situations very much like this one, Hamilton and his colleagues found that people falsely infer a connection or correlation between group membership and the likelihood of engaging in nice versus nasty behavior. More specifically, they typically judge small groups like the zarks to be less likable than large groups like the glorks.

If you were careful enough to resist the illusory correlation, consider the simple and highly concrete information that you see in Figure 1.1. Which of these obnoxious guys grabbed your attention? It's probably the same one that you're more likely to remember in ten minutes. The combination of statistical minority status and noteworthy (i.e., statistically unusual) behavior is very hard to resist.

The perceived correlation between group membership and likeability is referred to as illusory because in the preceding examples (and in many others like them) there is no connection between group membership and behavior. In the case of glorks and zarks, both groups are exactly twice as likely to help the nems as they are to harm them. There just happen to be twice as

Figure 1.1

Minority and majority faces: which of these guys will you remember best in a few minutes?

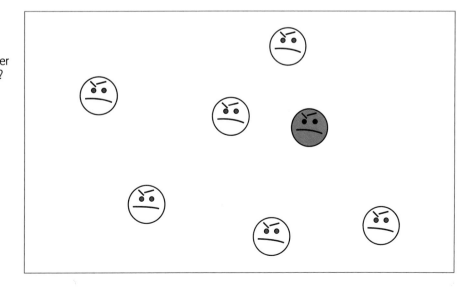

many glorks as zarks. If we consulted Tversky and Kahneman to help us describe this situation, they would probably remind us (1) that base rates for helping are twice as high as they are for harming, (2) that base rates for glorks are twice as high as they are for zarks, and (3) that in this case, there is no need to adjust anything for base rates—except perhaps in the sense that, in light of base rates, there is no reason to be impressed by the fact that four different glorks helped the nems. Helping is simply popular; glorks are simply populous.

Presumably, the fact that people often perceive connections where none truly exist plays an important role in the development and maintenance of stereotypes (see Hamilton & Rose, 1980). Did you notice, for example, that in most people's eyes, the statistical minority group (the much maligned zarks) was judged more harshly than the statistical majority? The well-established finding that people often perceive connections between things that aren't really connected also suggests that people may be a little too ready to see the world in terms of causes. If this is true, people do not appear to be alone in this tendency. Behaviorists who condition animals such as rats and pigeons have identified an animal analogue of this judgmental bias. More specifically, B.F. Skinner demonstrated that if you place an animal in a box and drop reinforcements in a food tray at random intervals (irrespective of what the animal is doing), the animal will often behave as if there is a contingency (i.e., a causal connection) between some behavior it may have spontaneously emitted during the "training" session and the delivery of the reinforcement. For example, if a pigeon happened to be standing on one foot prior to the (random) delivery of a food pellet, the pigeon might engage in this behavior several times again. Of course, if the pigeon does this long enough, another pellet will eventually be dropped into the food tray. The exact behavior that is "falsely conditioned" in this way will differ from one pigeon to the next, but conditioning will often occur nonetheless. Skinner (1948) referred to this false conditioning process as **superstitious conditioning**. At the risk of anthropomorphizing, the pigeon appears to have formed an illusory correlation between the arbitrarily produced behavior and the arbitrarily delivered food pellet. If pigeons could invite people to dinner parties, they too might prefer the company of glorks.[3]

The principle of determinism has a close corollary. This is the idea that science is about **theories**. A theory is simply a statement about the causal relation between two or more variables. It is typically stated in abstract terms, and it usually has some degree of empirical support (though many people would quibble with this final part of the definition). Theories wouldn't be very useful in the absence of determinism, because in the absence of determinism, orderly, systematic causes wouldn't exist. Although many people think of psychology as a "soft" science that may not be as theoretical as "hard" sciences like physics or biology, theories play exactly the same role in psychology that they play in physics or biology. They identify abstract, hypothetical constructs that presumably tell us something about how the world operates. From this perspective, psychological constructs such as "relative deprivation" or "selective attention" are just as scientific as physical and biological constructs such as "relativity" or "natural selection" (see Hedges, 1987).

Just as laypeople tend to think deterministically, they also tend to think theoretically. Most people have well-elaborated "theories" about things as diverse as police officers, baseball games, and golden retrievers. Moreover, much like scientists, people often learn these theories from their ancestors, and they are often reluctant to part with them. Social psychologists have a host of terms for these naive (untrained) causal theories; they include terms such as causal schema, script, stereotype, self-concept, and working model. In fact, when Fritz Heider (1958) wanted to summarize the way in which common people understand their social worlds, he referred to people as "naive scientists." By this he meant that people have little or no formal training in explaining the social world but go about doing so in much the same way that scientists typically go about explaining the physical world.

In this regard, it could be argued that scientists are just as likely as laypeople to make assumptions about how the world works. Most scientists would probably like to think of themselves as completely fair and impartial, and in a sense, when practiced properly, science pursues fair and impartial answers to questions. But there is an important difference between a system that seeks impartiality and a system that is free of assumptions. Many scientists and philosophers have argued, in fact, that no form of knowledge can exist in the absence of assumptions. If one assumption is chief among those endorsed by scientists, it is probably the assumption that the universe is chock full of orderly causes (that are just waiting to be discovered by scientists who think themselves impartial). Scientists accept this canon largely on faith, in much the same way that a rabbi accepts the Torah largely on faith. To be anti-Torah in any serious way would probably mean being something other than a rabbi. Similarly, to be devoutly anti-deterministic would probably mean being something other than a scientist. However, being enamored of determinism isn't the only thing that makes a person a scientist. You probably need to believe in at least three other things if you want to be a card-carrying scientist.

What horses think about while philosophers count teeth.

Empiricism

Scientists not only assume that the universe obeys orderly principles; they also assume that there are good and bad ways of *figuring out* these orderly principles. The best method, according to scientists, is to follow the canon of **empiricism**, that is, to make *observations*. Of course, you are already familiar with the concept of empiricism because, as we noted earlier, it is one of the favorite tools of modern philosophers. It is an even more favorite tool of scientists, and psychologists are no exception. Like astrophysicists and psychophysicists, psychologists assume that the best way to find out how the world works is to make observations. It may seem patently obvious to you that making observations is a great way to find things out, but this is a relatively modern assumption—even among philosophers and scientists.

This point should be brought home for you anytime you hear someone use the phrase "I got it straight from the horse's mouth." What people typically appear to mean by this is "I got it straight from the source" (often an expert source)—meaning that they are reporting firsthand rather than secondhand information. Like many other common phrases, this one has been around for so long that it has come to take on a subtly different meaning from the one originally intended. Apparently, the phrase originated when a group of philosophers were debating the number of teeth that a horse should have (see Rensberger, 1986). We don't know exactly how many teeth a horse should have, and apparently the philosophers didn't either. If we may take a little creative license to re-enact this discussion, a biologically inclined philosopher may have argued that as a member of the family *Equidae*, a horse should, like a quagga or a zebra, have exactly 34 teeth. A more theologically inclined philosopher may have retorted that, as a scripturally unclean, non-cloven-hoofed grazer, the horse should have fewer teeth than a cow and should therefore have somewhere in the neighborhood of 28 teeth. Of course, we have no idea *exactly* what logical or intuitive arguments the philosophers debated, but the point is that the debate was extremely long and extremely speculative. Eventually, one of the philosophers put an abrupt end to the debate by posing a simple but profound solution. He suggested that if everyone really wanted to know how many teeth a horse has, they should just go out, find a horse, look it in the mouth, and count its teeth (unless, perhaps, it proved to be a gift horse, but that's a different story). In other words, he suggested that *making an observation* is a good way to find things out about the world.

This second canon of science is probably the least controversial of the four. After all, throughout human history, there have been plenty of empiricists. As we noted earlier, one of the things that distinguished Aristotle from many of his contemporaries was his emphasis on systematic observation. Similarly, Galileo's biggest claim to fame is a legendary experiment in which he simultaneously dropped a heavy and a light cannonball from the Leaning Tower of Pisa. As the famous story goes, the two balls obligingly fell at precisely the same rate, invalidating the Aristotelian theory that the rate at which objects fall is directly proportional to their weight. This is an excellent example of Galileo's extreme faith in empiricism. However, this example has a serious problem. The problem is that Galileo *never performed* this celebrated experiment (see Asimov, 1964; Glenn, 1996; Rensberger, 1986). Moreover, the reason he never did so is quite interesting. Galileo *did* place a great deal of faith in empiricism. However, he apparently placed an even greater deal of faith in himself (or, to be more precise, in his powers of reasoning). Galileo solved this gravitational puzzle logically, and then he *challenged his detractors* to perform the crucial experiment.

Galileo's logic took the form of a thought experiment that went something like this: Imagine that we held a heavy object directly underneath a light object and simultaneously dropped the two objects. According to Aristotle, the heavy object should outpace the light object in its descent toward the earth, leaving it behind. Fair enough. Now imagine that we reversed the situation by holding the light object directly *underneath* the heavy object before releasing them. According to Aristotle, the light object should actually slow the heavy object down! To Galileo this seemed ridiculous. By combining arguments such as these with some additional arguments about wind resistance, Galileo convinced himself that if one could eliminate the problem of wind resistance, all objects would fall at the same rate. Apparently, Galileo convinced his detractors as well. When he challenged them to prove him wrong by performing the much acclaimed experiment with cannonballs, they declined the invitation. The point is that Galileo was so confident of his prediction that he challenged *others* to test it empirically.

Because empiricism has become one of the guiding assumptions of modern science, you shouldn't be too surprised to learn that many other famous scientists have placed a great deal of faith in it. However, you might be at least a little surprised to learn that many laypeople, and at least a few famous religious thinkers, have also placed a great deal of stock in empiricism. For example, when someone says "the proof of the pudding is in the eating" or tells someone else to "put up or shut up," this person is expressing an intuitive appreciation of empiricism. Similarly, when the much maligned "doubting Thomas" said that he could not truly believe

that Jesus had risen from the dead unless he could be allowed, among other things, to place his finger in the holes in Jesus' hands, he was identifying himself as an empiricist. Of course, this hasn't done much for Thomas's popularity with followers of Christianity. For at least one famous Christian, however, preaching the merits of empiricism never caused much of a ruckus. When the apostle Paul wrote that "faith without works is dead," part of what he appears to have been saying is that works count for something special because works, unlike faith, are readily observable. If Paul had been addressing a group of cooks rather than a group of disciples, he might have said that the proof of the pudding is in the eating. If he had been addressing a group of athletes or gamblers, he might have reminded them that talk is cheap and asked them to put up or shut up.

Parsimony

A third basic assumption of most scientific schools of thought is a sort of scientific tiebreaker. It is a pragmatic recommendation about the kind of theory or explanation that a good scientist should prefer. Virtually all scientists agree that if we are faced with two competing theories that do an equally good job of handling a set of empirical observations, we should prefer the simpler, or more *parsimonious*, of the two. As the word "parsimony" is commonly used by nonscientists, it refers to extreme stinginess or frugality. This is good to remember because the canon of **parsimony** says that we should be extremely frugal in developing (or choosing between) theories—by steering away from unnecessary concepts. Mechanics and engineers would probably appreciate parsimony because it is a sort of theoretical analogue of the mechanical idea that it is preferable to make machines that have the smallest possible number of moving parts (because this leaves fewer parts to break down).

Because people often confuse science with closely related fields like technology and higher mathematics, parsimony is probably the canon that is least consistent with most laypeople's intuitions about science. When people see a "scientific" figure or diagram that resembles the wiring schematic for a telephone dispatch system—full of circles, boxes, arrows, and cryptic labels—they tend to think "How scientific! I wish I could understand it!" The point of parsimony is that if something is good science you *should* be able to understand it. If forced to choose between two pretty good theories that both explain the results of your experiment, choose the one that your great-aunt Josephine will understand better. Unless your great-aunt Josephine is a retired electrical engineer, it will almost never be the one that looks like a wiring diagram. Arnold Buss (1988) has appropriately labeled the tendency for psychologists to be intrigued by models with lots of boxes and arrows "boxology." And he has noted that boxology is very *un*scientific—because it is very unparsimonious.

One of the first people to make a potent argument for parsimony was the medieval English philosopher William of Occam, and for this reason the principle of parsimony is sometimes referred to as "Occam's razor." To paraphrase Occam, the principle of parsimony states that it is intellectually inappropriate to make more assumptions than you absolutely have to (Duffy, 1993). In the late 1800s, another famous Englishman, the animal psychologist C. Lloyd Morgan, made a very similar point. Morgan argued that we should avoid making too many assumptions when we try to understand the behavior of animals. He is best known for the version of this point that he emphasized in his debates with the famous animal psychologist George Romanes. Morgan was very frustrated with Romanes's elaborate (and typically anthropomorphic) explanations for animal behavior. For example, Romanes (1882) frequently assumed that animals possess complex ideas, engage in reasoning by analogy, and make use of the "logic of feelings" in pretty much the same way that human beings do (see Figure 1.1). Morgan's recommendation to animal psychologists was that whenever one can explain animal behavior in terms of simple mental activities such as conditioned associations, it is inappropriate to explain these behaviors in terms of higher mental functioning. In the early days of scientific psychology, behaviorists such as John B. Watson and B. F. Skinner took "Lloyd Morgan's Canon" a step further by assuming that we should strive to explain human as well as animal behavior using a small set of relatively simple principles. From this perspective, Watson and Skinner were even bigger fans of parsimony than the two men whose names have become virtually synonymous with this basic tenet of science.[4]

At the risk of undermining our basic argument about the canon of parsimony, it is worth noting that it may not *always* be parsimonious to explain human and animal behavior using different theories. In the case of explaining how a housecat opens a door, for example, we agree that it is inappropriate to assume that a cat's thoughts and feelings about doors are as complex as a carpenter's. But what if you were trying to explain why chimpanzees do some of the amazing things they do? For example, like people, chimpanzees easily learn to recognize themselves in mirrors. Chimpanzees also make and use tools, and they appear to engage in strategic deception as well as strategic cooperation. For instance, the Dutch primatologist DeWaal (1996) once observed an amorous but low-ranking male chimpanzee display his erect penis to a desirable female (to protect the chimp's identity we'll call him C. H.). C. H. expressed his affection for this beautiful female chimp by simply facing her, sitting upright, and spreading his legs. However, when the alpha male in this troop wandered by, C. H. quickly and strategically placed his hand over his penis—and casually looked away. Is it more parsimonious to explain this behavioral sequence using the principles of operant conditioning or to describe it using words such as fear, jealousy, and deception? Considering the fact that chimpanzees share about 98 percent of their genetic information with human beings (Diamond, 1992), DeWaal suggests that it would sometimes be more parsimonious to explain similar behaviors in human beings and chimpanzees using a single theory rather than two completely different theories. This controversial example should illustrate that whereas there is a great deal of consensus concerning the basic canons of science, there is somewhat less consensus regarding exactly how and when to apply these canons.

A final perspective on parsimony is to consider it an extension of the idea that science is a very theoretical enterprise. One of the most important things a good scientific theory does in the first place is to simplify and organize a great number of otherwise disparate observations—by tying them together into some kind of coherent causal story. A good theory about why people fall in love, for example, can simplify and organize a great number of otherwise unrelated observations about romantic attraction. The idea behind parsimony is that as long as we are at the business of simplifying and organizing, we might as well *keep* at it until we have made things as simple as possible. When it comes to scientific journeys, most scientists believe in traveling light.

Testability

The final, and perhaps the most important, canon of science is the assumption that scientific theories should be testable (confirmable or disconfirmable) using currently available research techniques. The canon of **testability** is

Figure 1.2

At the time this photo was taken, Devon was a 2-year-old housecat. In this series of photos, Devon is opening a door to get to some tuna the first author placed on the other side (and his housemate, Tasha, is capitalizing on his efforts). The animal psychologist George Romanes (1882, pp. 421–422) observed a cat very much like Devon and described the cat's behavior as follows: "Cats ... have a very definite idea as to the mechanical properties of a door.... First the animal must have observed that the door is opened by the hand grasping the handle and moving the latch. Next, she must reason.... If a hand can do it, why not a paw? ... the pushing with the hind feet after depressing the latch must be due to adaptive reasoning." How parsimonious is this explanation?

closely related to the canon of empiricism because the techniques that scientists typically use to test their theories are *empirical* techniques. It is hard to be a believer in empiricism without also being a believer in testability (and even harder to be a believer in testability without also being a believer in empiricism). After all, empirical tests of an idea often reveal that the idea is not as correct as its proponents had originally assumed. In addition to being closely related to the canon of empiricism, the concept of testability is even more closely associated with the more specific philosophy of **falsifiability**. The idea behind falsifiability is that scientists should go a step beyond putting their theories to some kind of test by actively seeking out tests that could prove their theories *wrong* (see Abramson, 1992). During the period of tremendous scientific advancement that occurred in the early to middle part of the 20th century, Karl Popper became very famous for espousing this idea.

During his youth, Popper had been an ardent devotee of Marxism, but as he thought about how Marxism compared with some alternate schools of thought, he began to realize that most Marxists accepted Marxist doctrines uncritically—going about their lives as if all the predictions of Marxism were self-evident truths. His feeling was that if he were to devote himself to a school of thought, it would have to be one that could survive some kind of critical test.

In the early portion of his book *Unended Quest*, Popper (1974/1990) described his conversion to a philosophical and scientific school of thought known as **logical positivism**. Logical positivists believe that science and philosophy should be based solely on things that can be observed with absolute certainty. Many of them also believe that the way to go about testing scientific theories and hypotheses is to actively try to disconfirm them. Popper (1974/1990) described a crucial step in his conversion to this critical school of thought by explaining his delight at the way Einstein wrote about his general theory of relativity:

> But what impressed me most was Einstein's own clear statement that he would regard his theory as untenable if it should fail in certain tests. Thus he wrote, for example: "If the red-shift of spectral lines due to the gravitational potential should not exist, then the general theory of relativity will be untenable." ... This, I felt, was the true scientific attitude.

Among psychologists, concepts such as testability and falsifiability are extremely important because many early psychological theories (e.g., the work of Freud and other psychoanalysts) were difficult to put to any kind of objective test. Prominent behaviorists such as E. C. Tolman and Clark Hull improved this state of affairs when they followed the example of many physicists and popularized the idea of operationism, or **operational definitions**. Operational definitions are definitions of theoretical constructs that are stated in terms of concrete, observable procedures. It is a thorn in the flesh of psychologists that much of what we wish to understand (e.g., hunger, fear, attention, prejudice, etc.) is not directly observable. Operational definitions solve this problem by connecting unobservable traits or experiences to things that *can* be observed. For example, researchers such as Tolman and Hull operationally defined hunger in terms of hours of food deprivation or proportion of normal body weight after extended food deprivation (Schultz, 1981). Unlike the nebulous experience of hunger, things like time and weight can be readily observed or measured. Of course, there is no way to know with absolute certainty that a rat (or a person) that hasn't eaten in two days is experiencing hunger, but it is an extremely reasonable assumption. More important, it is an assumption that makes theories involving internal states such as hunger the objects of empirical investigation.

Operational definitions also lend themselves well to precise quantification. An elephant that hasn't eaten in 48 hours should be somewhat hungrier than one that hasn't eaten for 36, and should be much, much hungrier than an elephant that has just eaten. It would be highly presumptuous to assume that an elephant that hasn't eaten for 48 hours is *twice* as hungry as an elephant that hasn't eaten for 24 hours, but if we plot hours of food deprivation against a quantitative, operationally defined measure of learning (e.g., the number of wrong turns taken prior to reaching a goal box in an enormous maze), we can begin to say something precise about how hunger relates to learning in elephants. And if we are in the business of theory testing, we might be able to say that a particular theory of hunger and learning is in need of revision.

Operational definitions are so much a part of scientific ways of thinking that most modern scientists probably take them for granted. However, if we define both science and operational definitions pretty loosely, it could be argued that operational definitions have been around as long as science has. A case in point has to do with an operational definition of intelligence that was (somewhat begrudgingly) adopted by the Greek philosopher-scientist Thales. Thales was one of the first people recorded in history to address questions about the basic nature of the universe without falling back on magical or metaphysical explanations. Although Thales cared little for money, he apparently cared a great deal about being viewed as intelligent. After becoming legendary for his intellect, Thales was apparently insulted by jealous critics who asked him (if we may translate loosely from the Greek), "If you're so smart, why ain't you rich?" In short, Thales found himself oppressed by a questionable operational definition of intelligence that he himself probably did not endorse. Though he may have cared little about money, Thales apparently cared enough about his reputation for being smart that he decided to play by the rules of his critics. Thales happened to have an excellent understanding of weather, and according to Asimov (1964), he responded to his jealous critics by buying up olive presses in a year in which his meteorological observations told him it would be an excellent year for olives. During that year's bountiful olive harvest, Thales charged bountiful rates for the use of his olive presses. Thales thus became an instant olive oil baron and, having met the critics' operational definition of intelligence, went back to his genteel life as an intellect.

The fact that psychologists must rely so heavily on operational definitions points to an uncomfortable fact about our discipline. We cannot ever directly observe internal psychological states such as hunger, anger, or frustration. This does not mean, however, that psychology is not a science. After all, astronomers cannot directly observe black holes, and physicists cannot directly observe the tiniest subatomic particles. Like psychological scientists, physical scientists appreciate the fact that operational definitions make the unobservable observable. To some degree, laypeople also appreciate this fact. Long before Tolman and Hull were imploring their fellow psychologists to convert the unobservable into the observable, rabbis and referees were doing much the same thing—and for much the same reason. They wanted observable answers to important but elusive questions having to do with things like the will of God or the relative skill of two soccer teams. In the case of religious figures, ancient Jewish prophets, when faced with difficult decisions about the will of God, used to place "prayer cloths" on the ground around dusk and consult these cloths the next morning to ascertain what they assumed were God's wishes. Most frequently, the presence or absence of dew on the cloth would be taken to indicate which of two potential courses of action was to be taken. Of course, prophets who made use of such prayer cloths were making some pretty big assumptions about the connection between dew and their chosen deity, but the issue is not that they did or didn't make good decisions this way. It is that even people with no training in scientific methods can appreciate the logic of operational definitions.

Most sports and games provide more familiar examples of operational definitions. In fact, to our knowledge, there is no such thing as a competitive sport or game that does not make use of operational definitions. In basketball, for example, the operational definition of scoring a basket is propelling the ball from a legal position on the court so that it falls downward through a metal hoop that is suspended ten feet in the air on some kind of backboard. Nothing else players do, no matter how spectacularly athletic, will score a basket for their team. Of course, the ability to do this while following all the other rules of the game is one good, solid indicator of the abstract, hypothetical construct most people call basketball-playing ability. To appreciate the utility of operational definitions, imagine trying to play a complex game like basketball, football, or chess *without* operational definitions. It is hard to know how winners and losers would be decided, and it is quite possible that there would never *be* any losers. If we asked the members of opposing baseball teams to introspect on their skills and decide who should be declared victorious, we strongly suspect that both teams would typically decide that they were superior. Operational definitions play a similar role in science. If we simply asked proponents of a theory what they think of their theory's chances of being correct, we would find that very few theories ever got disconfirmed.

Because operational definitions are so important, it is useful to consider some concrete examples. Table 1.2 summarizes at least two distinct ways in which psychologists might operationally define constructs as varied as cognitive load and interpersonal attraction. Whereas no one way of operationalizing any of these constructs is perfect, they all share the positive trait of making abstract hypothetical concepts measurable (and thus testable). To flesh out one of these examples in more detail, consider the two operational definitions of "memory." The first definition, the number of words from a list that a participant can recall after a delay, is very intuitive. If we want to know how well you learned the words in a list, we can simply ask you to recall the words and count up the number of words you listed correctly. However, unless you happen to know a lot about memory, the second definition, the specific word a participant makes when presented with a word fragment such as "ele_____," may not make much sense. How could you test people's memory by asking them to complete a word fragment?

Let's begin by considering how *you* completed this word fragment. What was the very first word that came to mind for you? If you made the word "elephant," we suspect it is because you were exposed to this word a few minutes ago—when you were reading about operational definitions of hunger.

Table 1.2 Some abstract psychological concepts and some potential operational definitions for them

Concept	Operational Definition
Depression	1. Total number of symptoms a person reports having experienced (e.g., sadness, loss of appetite, sleep disturbance) in a structured interview 2. A person's true-false responses to an anonymous, 20-item pencil-and-paper survey (e.g., "During the past four weeks, I have had serious thoughts of harming myself.")
Cognitive load	1. Whether participants are given five seconds or 50 seconds to estimate the answer to a problem 2. Whether participants are instructed to keep a running total of a series of 1-digit numbers that appear in the center of a computer screen (while they are listening to a story)
Attraction	1. How close participants sit next to a confederate who is always seated at the end of a row of chairs 2. Whether a person is married to someone
Memory	1. The number of words from a list a participant can recall after a delay 2. The specific word a participant makes when presented with a word fragment such as "ele _____"

If we hadn't mentioned elephants in this example (or if you had just taken the *elevator* from your *elementary* calculus class on the *eleventh* floor), we suspect that you'd be way more likely to have made a different word.

As it turns out, word fragment tasks are excellent measures of certain kinds of memory. When a person cannot recall a specific word, but this word nonetheless influences how the person completes a word fragment task (or some other cognitive task), memory researchers would say that the person has an implicit (i.e., unconscious) memory for the word (Schacter, 1996). To frame this a little differently, everyone knows that people can sometimes *recognize* words that they cannot *recall*. Measures of recognition memory (e.g., "Did you see the word 'apple'?") are often more sensitive than measures of recall memory (e.g., "List all the words you can remember."). Memory researchers happen to know that word fragment measures are sometimes even more sensitive than measures of recognition. Having a cool operational definition can sometimes allow researchers to learn things they never could have learned without it. Judging from research using measures of implicit memory, we have learned that people sometimes "know" things that they themselves do not realize.

Speaking of memory, you may recall that we said operational definitions are important because they make theories testable or disconfirmable. What, exactly, makes a theory disconfirmable? In addition to operational definitions, things like clear and parsimonious statements of what the theory predicts can make a theory disconfirmable. One additional thing to keep in mind is that testability and disconfirmability refer as much to the attitude of a theory's proponents as they do to the nature of a theory itself. For example, very few voters would consider conducting an experiment to decide whether to become a Republican or a Democrat. Similarly, if Zeke tells you that there is no kind of empirical evidence that could persuade him to change his opinion of shellfish or Zen Buddhism, you can be pretty sure that he did not arrive at his opinions scientifically. Thus, the cornerstone of the scientific perspective is openness to criticism and revision. In fact, Popper has argued that openness to criticism and revision, rather than the use of any specific methods or procedures, is what makes a field of study scientific (Popper, 1974/1990). The degree to which a belief system is open to revision is an important determinant of the kinds of evidence or support that advocates of the belief system are typically most interested in scrutinizing. For example, scientists place very little stock in authority, but popes and presidents typically consider authority to be the bottom line. To gain a final bit of perspective on how scientific belief systems differ from other common belief systems, it is useful to consider four different kinds of support for beliefs and see how advocates of the different belief systems typically view each kind of support.

FOUR WAYS OF KNOWING ABOUT THE WORLD

One of the best ways to learn about a person's thinking style is to ask a difficult question and then ask the person to explain how he or she arrived at the answer. For example, consider the proposal that there is a gravitational attraction between the tip of your left thumbnail and the quasi-planet Pluto. Is there? Use any reasonable method that is currently at your disposal, but do not read any further until you have come up with an answer.

If you guessed that there is no such attraction, you might have come to this conclusion in several different ways. First of all, your **intuition** may have simply told you that such an idea seems far-fetched. Second, you may have tried to make use of **logic**, reasoning that if the tip of your left thumbnail is attracted to things as bizarre and distant as a dwarf planet, then you'd have some noticeable difficulties keeping it in your possession. Though it is less likely, you may have also consulted some sort of **authority** figure. If your roommate, the physics major, was handy when you were reading this question, you may have simply asked him or her for the answer to the question. Finally, although it would have been desirable to do so, it is extremely unlikely that you made any kind of empirical **observation** to test this idea because doing so would be virtually impossible. The correct answer, by the way, is that there is indeed a gravitational attraction between the tip of your left thumbnail and the quasi-planet Pluto. The universal law of gravitation states (and empirical research has thus far confirmed) that there is a gravitational attraction between all the matter in the universe. One reason you are at little risk of having a tiny piece of your thumbnail wrenched from your thumb in a meteoric descent toward Pluto is that gravitational attraction falls off as a squared function of the distance between the objects in question.

As long as you stay close to Earth and far away from other celestial bodies, you will save a lot of money on manicures.

As far as we can tell, the four methods of "knowing" you may have consulted when trying to answer this question—namely, authority, intuition, logic, and observation—come pretty close to exhausting all the basic ways in which people decide what they believe. Although each of these ways of knowing plays a role in almost all kinds of belief systems, the relative emphasis placed on each varies dramatically from one belief system to the next. Consider authority. Authority refers to status or prestige, typically based on things like expertise or legitimately acquired power. Laypeople appear to place a great deal of emphasis on authority or expertise when making day-to-day decisions. In fact, the tendency to do so is prevalent enough that it has been labeled the *expertise heuristic* by researchers who study attitudes and persuasion (e.g., see Chaiken, Liberman, & Eagly, 1989; Hovland & Weiss, 1951; Petty & Cacioppo, 1986; Smith & Mackie, 1995). Whereas scientists and philosophers claim to place little stock in authority, believers in virtually all governments or religions consider authority (e.g., the president, the Buddha, the Torah, the Constitution) the final word on many important beliefs and decisions.

Governments and religions are also similar in that both systems appear to consider intuition an important way of understanding the world. The U.S. Declaration of Independence makes the bold, intuitively appealing statement, "We hold these truths to be self-evident...." As another example, most religions and governments take the intuitively appealing position that people are free to make all their own choices in life. Many philosophical and scientific views call this intuitive claim into question because it is potentially at odds with the canon of determinism (see Skinner, 1971). Debates about topics like freedom versus determinism, which have taken on great importance among philosophers and scientists, are not nearly so important to ministers and prime ministers. One reason this is true is that religious and political thinkers place great faith in intuition. In contrast, scientists and philosophers place greater faith in logic and may become deeply troubled by logical paradoxes. Politicians are more likely to put paradoxes to a vote. Ministers are more likely to leave them in the hands of a higher power.

Although the typical scientist and the typical philosopher might both prefer logical rather than intuitive solutions to a debate, scientists and philosophers differ somewhat in the relative emphasis they place on logic. To the typical philosopher, logic is likely to take preeminence even over observation as the touchstone against which all other things are judged. Philosophers as a group devote an enormous amount of their intellectual efforts to discerning the correct and incorrect rules of reasoning (Copi, 1978). Philosophers seem to have learned that they cannot always believe their eyes. To the typical scientist, logic can be incontrovertible, but it can also be impenetrable—and thus take a back seat to observation as the primary mode of figuring out the world. Whereas the philosopher finds comfort in the use of contrapositives, the scientist finds more comfort in the use of counterbalancing. Scientists prefer experimentation over argumentation.

Table 1.3 Relative importance of different ways of knowing to different belief systems

Religion	Government	Philosophy	Science
1. authority	1. authority	1. logic	1. observation
2. intuition	2. intuition	2. observation	2. logic
3. logic	3. logic	3. intuition	3. intuition
4. observation	4. observation	4. authority	4. authority

Note: Rank orderings are from (1) most to (4) least important.

The relative importance of authority, intuition, logic, and observation for religion, government, philosophy, and science is shown in Table 1.3. Although it is possible to quibble with the exact rankings, a gross analysis of the table should clarify an important distinction between scientific and nonscientific belief systems. Scientists and nonscientists prefer different ways of knowing about the world.

Three additional notes are in order about the four ways of knowing. The first note is that there is no guarantee that one way of knowing will be superior to others across all possible situations. Observation compels scientists to create particle accelerators; intuition compels people to create families, sculptures, and governments. If the Declaration of Independence had been written by political scientists rather than politicians (e.g., "Recent research in public policy suggests a number of useful generalizations about self-governance...."), we suspect that it would have generated a bit less enthusiasm among colonists struggling with their allegiances to the British Crown.

The second note is that Table 1.3 describes the ways in which science is *supposed* to be carried out. Because scientists are human beings, they sometimes fall back on other ways of knowing that do not represent the ideals of the discipline. For instance, because scientists often share the same powerful intuitions as laypeople, they sometimes rely on their intuitions when they should not. As an example, clinical psychologists once believed that they could make solid inferences about a person's character or mental health by using the "Draw-A-Person" test. Patients who drew figures that had large eyes, for example, were thought to be paranoid or delusional. As it turns out, this is not the case. Thus, when clinicians were kept blind to a person's diagnostic status, they could not rely on a person's responses to the Draw-A-Person test to determine who did or did not suffer from schizophrenia. In the case of this particular projective test, scientists and laypeople alike shared some powerful intuitions about how the features in a drawing might reflect the psychopathology of the artist. These intuitions led at least a few clinically inclined researchers down some blind alleys. In other words, intuition probably plays a slightly bigger role in the day-to-day business of science than it ideally should. At times, scientists also rely more heavily on authority than they would probably like to admit. When ideas are proposed by well-known researchers or published in highly prestigious journals, they are usually accepted more readily than they might be otherwise. Thus, a young researcher who writes a paper challenging the validity of Dr. Bogg's Draw-A-Person test might have trouble getting this piece into a high-prestige journal. When his criticism subsequently appears in a lower-prestige journal, other researchers might at first infer that the criticism in the article is not valid. Although inappropriate reliance on intuition or authority sometimes gets scientists in trouble, scientists hold the view that facts eventually will win out. Thus, bad ideas should have a relatively short "shelf life" in the literature.

The third additional note about the ways of knowing is that different ways of knowing summarized here are convenient simplifications. In fact, true genius often consists of finding the balance between different ways of understanding the world. For instance, Thomas Jefferson was a scientist as well as a politician, and his scientific side often influenced his political arguments. Unlike many of his contemporaries, for example, Jefferson argued that systems of government, like scientific theories, should change with the times on the basis of new evidence. When asked, in 1816, whether the Virginia constitution should be revised, Jefferson remarked:

> I am certainly not an advocate for frequent and untried changes in laws and constitutions.... But I know also, that laws and institutions must go hand in hand with the progress of the human mind. As that becomes more developed, more enlightened, as new discoveries are made, new truths disclosed, and manners and opinions change with the change of circumstances, institutions must advance also, and keep pace with the times. We might as well require a man to wear still the coat which fitted him when a boy, as civilized society to remain ever under the regimen of their barbarous ancestors.

(Letter to Samuel Kerchreview, July 12, 1816)

Good thinkers rarely limit themselves to a single way of understanding the world. As a very different example, when Galileo finally got around to doing some empirical studies of gravity, he was plagued by the inaccuracies of the current technology of measurement. Instead of waiting a couple of hundred years for the invention of a good stopwatch, he slowed things down by studying the behavior of bodies *rolling down inclined planes* (Asimov, 1964; Harré, 1981). By doing so, Galileo was able to demonstrate quite convincingly that heavy and light objects "fell" at the same rate. In addition, he was able to show something more subtle, and perhaps more important. Things don't simply fall at a constant rate: they constantly accelerate. Of course, accepting Galileo's conclusions requires us to make some logical inferences about the compatibility of rolling and falling, but this is exactly the point. Galileo was not simply a good logician or a good observer. One of his unique talents was his ability to blend logic and observation into a seamless set of arguments that could knock someone's socks off (and predict how quickly they would fall to the floor).

To further your appreciation of the four ways of knowing, we draw your attention to Appendix 1. Hands-On Activity 1, Galileo's Dice, presents a class exercise that can help you better understand the distinctions between these approaches to knowledge and their relative strengths and weaknesses.

SUMMARY

Human beings attempt to understand the physical and psychological world in many ways. Throughout history humans have tried to understand their world by such means as animism, mythology, and philosophy. By comparing these different ways of understanding the world, we can see how psychology evolved out of such disciplines as philosophy and physiology. The four canons of science, that is the four basic assumptions about the world that virtually all scientists take as a given, are determinism, empiricism, parsimony, and testability. The four distinct "ways of knowing," that is, four ways of trying to figure out what the world is like are intuition, logic, authority, and observation. Whereas political and religious systems place great emphasis on authority and intuition as ways of knowing, scientific systems place more stock in logic and observation. This explains, for instance, why scientific beliefs are revised much more frequently than religious beliefs. Although the basic rules of science are highly stable, this stable system of methods and procedures facilitates the revision of beliefs based on new observations and discoveries.

STUDY QUESTIONS

1. What are positivism and empiricism? Why would a typical research psychologist (i.e., a scientist) view these philosophical traditions as progress away from metaphysical ways of knowing?

2. Raphael has a theory that adults who grew up as first-born children are more likely to be outgoing than those who grew up as later-born children. To test his theory, he gives a questionnaire to 200 students at his college and asks them to report (a) whether they were first-born children or later-born children and (b) the degree to which they consider themselves outgoing. Is Raphael's approach to acquiring knowledge scientific? In answering this question, consider each of the four canons of science and evaluate how Raphael's approach measures up on each of these dimensions. Can you think of any ways for Raphael to make his birth-order analysis more scientific?

3. Gloria has a theory that people who are born between July 23rd and August 22nd (i.e., "Leos") are more likely to be outgoing than people who are born at other times of the year. In support of her theory, she notes (a) that most of the Leos she knows are outgoing and (b) that she is very good at correctly guessing the astrological sign of Leos when she meets them. Is Gloria's approach to knowledge acquisition scientific? In answering this question, consider each of the four canons of science and evaluate how Gloria's approach measures up on each of these dimensions. Can you think of any ways for Gloria to make her astrological analysis more scientific?

4. Although one of the tenets of science is that theories should be based on observable events (empiricism), most of the constructs that psychologists study are not visible to the naked eye. For instance, we can't directly observe a person's true attitudes, beliefs, or thoughts. How, then, can psychology be considered scientific? In answering this question, carefully consider the role of logic, theory testing, and operational definitions. (*Note:* Your answer to this question will become more sophisticated after you read Chapter 2.)

NOTES

1. For a more detailed discussion of this issue, see Schultz (1981, pp. 56–57). Schultz notes, for example, that Wundt was the only one in this distinguished group to set himself the explicit task of founding a new discipline.

2. Actually, proponents of chaos theory might argue that the universe isn't completely deterministic. For an interesting discussion of this topic, see Stewart (1989).

3. The best evidence that people may be predisposed to think in ways that reflect some kind of belief in systematic causes comes from developmental studies of infants (for example, see Spelke, 1991). Even evidence that very young infants possess certain kinds of causal knowledge, however, is open to multiple interpretations (see Baillargeon, 1994). For our purposes, suffice it to say that scientists are not alone in their assumption that the world operates on the basis of systematic, predictable causes.

4. Of course, an even more important reason why Watson and Skinner didn't like to speculate about higher-order mental processes is their belief that that these processes are impossible to observe. (They did not, however, argue that they don't exist.) In other words, behaviorists like Watson and Skinner were big fans of empiricism. Although we are big fans of behaviorism, we feel that the devotion of many behaviorists to empiricism may have been misguided. Physicists cannot *directly* observe black holes, subatomic particles, or radio waves, but they can test theories about them empirically by making indirect observations—that is, by examining the consequences of these hypothetical entities for things that we *can* observe.

How Do We Find Out? The Logic, Art, and Ethics of Scientific Discovery

[L]aws haven't the slightest interest for me—except in the world of science, in which they are always changing; or in the world of art, in which they are unchanging; or in the world of Being in which they are, for the most part, unknown.
—Margaret Anderson

If a man will begin with certainties, he shall end in doubts; but if he will be content to begin with doubts, he shall end in certainties.
—Francis Bacon

When the first author's oldest nephew, Sean, was three years old, the first author asked him a few questions about cars, driving, and traffic laws. Because Sean had always been fascinated with cars and driving, he demonstrated an impressive knowledge of cars. For example, at the tender age of three, Sean knew that a Chevy Camaro was a *lot* cooler than a typical sedan. He also seemed to have a keen appreciation of his parents' driving behavior. Consider his answers to the following questions about traffic lights. "What do you do at a *red* light?" "Stop," answered casually. "What about a *green* light?" "Go!" he answered with a bit more emotion. "And what about a *yellow* light?" "Go *faster*!" he responded enthusiastically. Sean's third answer illustrates the difference between descriptive and prescriptive laws (i.e., the difference between what people *ought to do* and what people *actually do*). We think this story serves as a fitting introduction to this chapter, which focuses heavily on psychological laws and scientific discovery. In a sense, Sean's lack of preconceived notions about what was right and wrong meant that he provided an empirical, scientific answer ("Here is what people do.") to what his uncle had intended as a legal question ("What are people *supposed* to do?"). The fact that Sean had no preconceived notion of the rules of the road is also relevant to this chapter because, as we will see, scientists and laypeople alike often have preconceived notions about the best way to discover what is true. Moreover, these preconceived notions sometimes get in the way of accurate scientific discoveries. Perhaps anthropologists from a distant planet would learn more about human driving behavior by interviewing small children than they would learn by interviewing adults. Better yet, of course, they could use records from those annoying cameras that sometimes take your picture when you are blowing a red light.

In this chapter, we build on the foundation laid in Chapter 1 by discussing the process of scientific discovery. The chapter is broken into three sections. In the first section, we discuss the logic of scientific discovery. We begin by arguing that the primary goal of any science is to establish laws of nature, and we distinguish laws from theories and hypotheses. We then examine the role of observation and reasoning in science, and in so doing we distinguish between inductive and deductive approaches to scientific thinking. Next, we identify three distinct approaches to scientific hypothesis testing and discuss some of the ways in which each approach is compatible or incompatible with the basic goals of science. In the second section, we discuss the art of scientific discovery. We review a set of inductive and deductive techniques that will help you generate exciting ideas that merit the kind of attention to methodological detail that you will learn about in subsequent chapters. In the final section of the chapter, we discuss the ethics of scientific discovery. As we show, exciting and insightful ideas are of no use unless you can find an ethical way of testing these ideas.

THE LOGIC OF SCIENTIFIC DISCOVERY

Laws, Theories, and Hypotheses

If you are a psychology major, you probably take it as a given that psychology is a science. However, you probably won't be surprised to learn that many *non*-psychologists (including some scientists) assume that it is impossible to study human behavior scientifically. Some people even react with annoyance or indignation when they learn about psychologists' latest efforts to understand important phenomena such as love, morality, or altruism. To some people, it is disturbing to imagine that wonderful things like love are subject to orderly laws. As the poet e. e. cummings put it, "he who pays any attention to the syntax of things will never wholly kiss you." By this, he seemed to mean that it is easy to ruin a wonderful experience by overanalyzing it. We couldn't agree more with this opinion. In fact, we agree with it because scientific research has confirmed it! For example, taste testers who think too much about the basis of their preferences while sampling jellies have a lot of trouble telling the difference between really succulent and really sucky jellies (Wilson & Schooler, 1991; see also Albrechtsen, Meissner, Susa, & 2009; Dijksterhuis, 2004). However, this does *not* mean that we shouldn't seek scientific explanations for important experiences such as love, altruism, and the taste of strawberry jelly. It just means that we shouldn't allow what we learn about the nature and causes of these important experiences to get in the way of the enjoyment these experiences can bring us. In principle, psycholinguists (i.e., syntax experts) can enjoy kissing just as much as poets and artists can. We don't have to be afraid of knowledge.

Of course, critics come in many shapes and sizes, and some critics argue that although it would be highly *desirable* to understand things like infatuation or gustation, it simply is not possible. Such critics correctly point out that no one can ever predict *exactly* what another person will do. However, this criticism doesn't hold up to close scrutiny. The fact that psychologists cannot predict the behavior of one specific person is no more troubling than the fact that meteorologists often cannot predict the behavior of one specific cloud. Meteorologists *can*, however, predict the weather (loosely speaking, the behavior of large groups of clouds), just as psychologists can predict the behavior of large groups of people. Researchers who study interpersonal attraction couldn't tell you *for sure* whether Rupert is going to fall in love with Rita tomorrow, but they could identify a long list of conditions that would make this much more likely than usual. The fact that prediction is imperfect doesn't mean that rules don't govern human behavior. On the basis of scientific studies of interpersonal attraction, for example, we know that people gravitate toward other people who (1) are physically attractive, (2) are familiar rather than unfamiliar, and (3) are highly competent (but not *too* competent). The same kind of research also shows that we are strongly attracted to others whose earlobe shapes closely resemble our own! If you throw a large group of Ruperts and Ritas together at a dance, researchers who know about things like this can predict reasonably well who ends up dancing together.

In short, like vulcanologists and virologists, psychologists are in the business of seeking out laws that allow them to make precise predictions of human behavior. The fact that such predictions are rarely perfect is no reason to give up hope. From this vantage point, the goal of every branch of science, from anthropology to zoology, is to discover *laws*. Although the search for scientific laws is as old as science itself, the scientist who did the most to draw attention to the importance of laws was Sir Isaac Newton (1642–1727). Newton was probably the most important scientist who ever lived. When he wasn't busy inventing calculus or the reflecting telescope, he was busy developing his three famous "laws of motion." In his second law of motion, Newton asserted that the "acceleration of an object is directly proportional to the net force acting upon it and inversely proportional to its mass." Roughly speaking, this means it's a lot easier to throw a rock at a barn than to throw a barn at a rock (unless the rock happens to be the Rock of Gibraltar). However, this rough translation does little justice to the beauty, precision, and utility of this law. Knowledge of this law, for example, has allowed scientists to put telecommunication satellites into orbit around the earth, and thus you wouldn't be able to text your friend Rita about how much you love research methods if scientists didn't understand this law. It's important to realize that Newton proposed this law without *any qualification* because he was confident that it would predict the acceleration of *any object in any circumstance.* This law applies whether the accelerating object in question is a soccer ball, a human cannonball, or a giant ball of gas better known as a star. That is the beauty of a law. A **law** is a universal statement of the nature of things that allows reliable predictions of future events.

As we have already noted, psychologists are often unable to predict the future, and so we can only feel humbled by Newton's laws. Does this mean psychology is not a science? Nope, not at all. Like the goal of any science, the goal of psychology is to try to develop laws. It is not the fault of psychology that it has not yet mastered the practice. If this sounds like a cop-out, it shouldn't. Even if we could identify laws of human behavior, we would not necessarily be able to predict every detail of a person's behavior. In fact, even Newton's laws of motion would fail if held to this high standard. To illustrate, imagine that you go to a baseball game and discover that the person seated next to you is none other than Sir Isaac Newton. You compliment him on looking so young for a man born in the early 1640s, and he compliments you on your mastery of the absurdly complex rules of baseball. He deftly answers a couple of difficult questions about your upcoming calculus exam, and you deftly explain the difference between a breaking ball and a slider. In short, you are both having a wonderful time. Just as you are about to explain the concept of a change-up, the batter makes contact with a blazing fastball. Do you suppose Newton will be any better than you are at predicting whether this hit will be a home run? Probably not. You probably feel just as capable as old Isaac when it comes to everyday prediction. Of course, Newton would be excellent at this sort of prediction if he were given all the relevant "data" (e.g., the speed and mass of the ball, the speed and mass of the bat, the angle of contact of the bat and ball, etc.). Newton is not to be blamed for developing laws that are hard to apply in complex situations.

The same is true for psychologists. A psychologist will not always be able to predict the specific actions of your roommate Jennifer. Nevertheless, a well-trained psychologist should be able to make some predictions that untrained people would be unable to make. Furthermore, the psychologist's ability to make correct predictions about Jennifer should increase (1) to the degree that the behavior in question was well studied (e.g., psychologists know more about human memory than they do about human taste in music) and (2) to the degree that the psychologist was given a great deal of relevant data about Jennifer (e.g., her nickname is J-Lo, she has a lesion in the ventromedial portion of her hippocampus). It might be unrealistic to think that we will ever succeed in developing psychological laws or that we will ever get our hands on all the data we'd need to do so, but these are just two of the many challenges that make psychology exciting.

To say that the goal of psychology is the establishment of laws is not to overlook the fact that a great deal of psychology focuses on less grandiose pursuits. We can't all be Sir Isaac Newton. Most contemporary psychologists are content to try to develop and test *theories.* As mentioned in Chapter 1, a theory is a general statement about the relation between two or more variables. Good theories share all the features of good science emphasized in Chapter 1. First, they should be deterministic. Thus, they should be logical and orderly, emphasizing the systematic *causal* relations between variables. Next, they should be empirically grounded. This means that they should generate predictions about readily observable events. Next, they should be parsimonious. A good theory is a simple and concise statement that allows you to predict a wide variety of conceptually similar behaviors (e.g., feelings of closeness among siblings, the strength of commitment between marriage partners, cohesion among the members of a junior high school debate team). Finally, a good theory should be testable. As we explain later in more detail, theories do much more to advance scientific understanding when they prove to be wrong than when they prove to be untestable.

Taking all this into account, how do theories differ from laws? The main difference between laws and theories is their breadth or universality. Laws are comprehensive, fundamental statements about reality. In contrast, theories have *boundary conditions;* there are plenty of times when they do not apply. Even the best of theories offers accurate prediction only in certain circumstances. A psychologist who develops a theory of aggression, for instance, usually knows that this theory will not predict all forms of aggression in all situations. If the theory is a good one, however, it will offer reliable prediction of aggression under a reasonable, and specifiable, set of circumstances. For instance, a theory may apply well to physical aggression among boys, but it may need some careful revision to explain the aggressive behavior of girls (see Ostrov & Godleski, 2009).

Because theories have boundary conditions, it is possible for more than one theory to be true. This occurs, for instance, when one theory predicts behavior in one set of circumstances (or for one group of people) and another theory predicts the same kind of behavior in a different set of circumstances (or for a different group of people). To illustrate, each of the following theories enjoys a good deal of support under at least some circumstances: "alcohol produces aggression," "frustration produces aggression," and "exposure to violent media images produces aggression." Each of these theories is correct a good deal of the time, but none is valid for everyone under every possible circumstance. As a result, a good theory not only states specific relations between specific variables, but it also states the conditions under which these relations do and do not apply. Furthermore, two or more correct theories will sometimes cancel one another out. For example, if a person grew up watching a lot of violent TV but never drinks alcohol and is not currently frustrated, this person's nonviolence does not invalidate the theory that exposure to violent TV causes aggression.

This analysis of theories helps to address a response we sometimes encounter when we tell friends (or unfortunate strangers) about some new and exciting psychological theory. Sometimes, the friend or stranger will criticize the theory by noting that they know someone who does not usually behave in the manner suggested by the theory. ("You say frustration leads to aggression, but whenever my friend Leonard is frustrated, he just goes shopping.") Although exceptions such as this are interesting, they do little to invalidate a theory.

Instead, they simply remind us that the theory falls short of being a law. Incidentally, this explains why very few people refuse to believe in basic laws of nature. ("You say gravitational forces exist everywhere, but whenever my friend Leonard is dropped from a high place, he floats magically in the air.") Another way to say this is that human behavior usually has multiple determinants. This is known as the principle of **equifinality**—the notion that the same behavior is often produced by many different causes (McKearney, 1987–1988). Because of equifinality, psychologists sometimes disagree about the conditions favoring one theory over another, and so good theory testing will often take the form of determining each theory's proper domain of application (Greenwald et al., 1986). This sort of theory testing is especially important when different theories lead to contradictory predictions. For instance, some have argued that "alcohol consumption causes aggression" (Taylor & Gammon, 1975), whereas others have argued that "alcohol consumption causes helping" (Steele, Critchlow & Liu, 1985). Clearly, both theories are sometimes true. However, to determine whether your inebriated friend Leonard is going to help or hurt you in a specific situation, you will need to know which theory applies. For example, if Leonard is inebriated enough to think he can fly, he might hurt you while trying to help you.

To bring this general point about behavioral prediction even closer to home, we'd like to make an important announcement. As soon as this fourth edition of our text is published, the first author of the text is going to begin sending free, postage-paid decks of a new card game (PRIME) to the first 100 readers of this book who simply ask for a deck. Will you yourself respond to this news by yawning, rolling your eyes, or requesting a deck? The answer is that *we don't know*. More specifically, we don't know because we don't know (a) whether you love or hate playing card games, (b) whether you actually read the footnotes in research methods textbooks,[1] (c) whether you care about getting things for free, (d) whether you are chronically distrustful of "free" offers, and (e) whether you believe this offer is real or hypothetical (i.e., made just for the sake of argument). The fact that it is hard to predict your behavior in this specific situation just means that *numerous* factors (including some we surely did not think of) may contribute to this specific decision. But that does not mean that your behavior doesn't follow meaningful rules.

As it turns out, laws and theories do not account for every kind of statement scientists can make about the relation between two or more variables. A third category of research statements is **hypotheses**. To test a theory, a person should use that theory to derive specific predictions that can be readily tested. Hypotheses are thus predictions about specific events that are derived from one or more theories.[2] For hypotheses to serve as tests of specific theories, they must follow in a clear and logical fashion from the theories in question, preferably under conditions clearly specified by the theory. Many times, a theory clearly and obviously leads to a specific hypothesis in a given circumstance. In these instances, hypothesis testing boils down to theory testing. A lack of support for the hypothesis translates into a lack of support for the theory that produced it. More often, researchers may be uncertain about the conditions under which the theory applies. Thus, they test hypotheses in specific circumstances to see whether these circumstances fall within the boundary conditions of the theory. At other times, two different theories might make opposing predictions in the same conditions, and researchers might then outline two rival hypotheses. If the results support one theory to the detriment of the other, the theory that lost out *may* prove to be false. However, it is quite possible that this particular set of circumstances simply favored the theory that seemed to win out. A creative researcher (i.e., a fan of the losing theory) might be able to identify a different set of circumstances that would provide much stronger support for the losing theory.

Through the benefit of extensive hypothesis testing, researchers can determine exactly when (if ever) specific theories are true. If a wealth of research on relevant theories accumulates, researchers might be able to integrate this knowledge and propose a law. In truth, because psychology is a young science, psychological research has not yet produced any hard and fast laws. For the time being, however, it appears that what psychology lacks in laws it has more than made up for in theories. In fact, psychological theories are almost as plentiful as psychologists. Most of these theories (especially the good ones) can be used to generate dozens of specific hypotheses about human behavior.

The Science of Observation

As we noted in Chapter 1, one of the most important concepts distinguishing science and nonscience is empiricism—basing knowledge on observations. The notion that we should base what we know on what we observe now seems pretty obvious, but development of this concept represents a major advance in the history of science. But how did some ancient philosopher's advice about counting horses' teeth evolve into one of the cornerstones of the scientific method? How, exactly, did scientists come to appreciate the value of observation? Furthermore, how do scientists make the difficult trip from scientific observation to scientific conclusions? Although there are many answers to these two closely related questions, it is clear that Francis Bacon deserves a great deal of the credit. In the early part of the 17th century, Bacon boldly proclaimed that scientists can uncover hidden truths from everyday observation. However, Bacon appreciated just how hard it is to do this, and so he made some very specific recommendations about how to make and interpret scientific observations.

To benefit from careful scientific observations, Bacon argued, you must apply the **method of induction**. Making use of induction means making many observations under controlled conditions and arriving at a general statement about how things are. Induction, then, is reasoning from specific instances to general principles. We engage in induction all the time. After observing dozens of incidents in which specific cats and dogs always fight like, well, cats and dogs, we might come to the general conclusion that cats and dogs always hate each other. Similarly, after observing hundreds of individual birds that can all fly, we might boldly assert that all birds can fly. In scientific circles general conclusions drawn in this way (e.g., "dropped objects always fall toward the earth") usually come to be known as theories, and these theories can often be tested against new observations that are made in a variety of new situations. If the new observations are consistent with the statement, then the statement survives. If not, the statement is either discarded or revised. If the statement is revised, it is then tested against new observations, and the whole process starts over again. With the benefit of continuous revisions, the general statement should become more and more accurate. Eventually, it may become so precise and well supported that it evolves into a law. To put this in a nutshell, the inductive technique Bacon supported requires careful, systematic observation, and in scientific circles it usually leads to a more or less continuous cycle of revisions based on precisely these observations. Careful induction is much more of a pain in the butt than casual observation, but the idea is that it eventually pays off (no pain, no gain, you might say).

Bacon was one of the first people to appreciate the merits of learning from systematic observation. Like a bold explorer, he pushed scientific frontiers to new limits. Like a bold explorer, Bacon was also one of the first people to be attacked when other people realized where he was headed. (Fortunately for Bacon, he was dead and gone by the time the attack reached its climax.) In the 18th century, the method of induction came under vigorous attack by the British philosopher David Hume, who felt that Bacon was dead wrong. Hume argued that observation is *not* the appropriate dividing line between science and nonscience. He identified what is now called the **problem of induction**. The problem of induction is simple. Careful induction requires scientists to make a great number of observations. Scientific progress is a long journey that contains many steps. This seems reasonable enough. After all, it shouldn't be child's play to develop laws of nature. But how do you know when you've made *enough* observations to be sure that your law is true? According to Hume, you never *do*. Even if you have made hundreds of observations, all of which are consistent with your general conclusion (i.e., your law or theory), it is always possible that the very *next* observation you make will prove you wrong by violating your conclusion (see Taleb, 2007, who applies a modern version of the problem of induction to everything from economics to terrorist attacks).

The history of science is full of examples of seemingly well-established theories that were later proven to be wrong. For instance, we now know that earth is not at the center of the universe, that the heart is not the seat of human emotions, that you cannot determine a person's character by reading the bumps on his or her head, and that people are not the only animals to create and use tools. To pick a slightly more controversial example, social psychologists who study person perception once believed that there is a fundamental human tendency to attribute a person's actions to that person's enduring personality (rather than attributing the actions to situational factors). This is, in fact, a pretty potent and pervasive tendency. Consider the last time another driver cut you off on the freeway or drifted erratically into your lane. We suspect that you leapt to the conclusion that your fellow commuter was an incompetent driver. Perhaps you were right. However, why not leap to the conclusion that this person must have been sick with worry over an ailing parent, must have spilled a drink in his or her lap, or must have been rushing a sick orphan to the hospital? People *do* seem to be predisposed to explaining other people's behavior in terms of these other people's enduring character traits.

Lee Ross (1977) was so impressed with this tendency for people to favor dispositional ("He's a lousy driver.") over situational ("He's distracted.") explanations that he labeled this tendency the *fundamental attribution error*. Many researchers subsequently embraced this label. Ross's use of the word "fundamental" suggested that this attributional tendency was a basic feature of human social judgment. Moreover, at the time, this was a very reasonable conclusion. But here's the rub. Not long after this label took hold, Miller (1984) collected cross-cultural data suggesting that people from India do not make the fundamental attribution error.[3] Social psychologists thought that they had uncovered something basic to human judgment because they had run numerous carefully designed studies showing this effect. Miller's findings changed the whole picture.

This example illustrates the problem of induction. Like politicians whose personal lives have not been closely scrutinized, scientific assertions that are strongly supported today might be strongly rejected tomorrow. But let's imagine that Miller had observed a very robust fundamental attribution error in India. Would this have settled things once and for all? We hope you can see that it wouldn't have. As Hume correctly noted, the fact that all our observations to date have been consistent with a law or theory does not mean that this will always be the case in the future. Someone might run a study tomorrow showing that one of psychology's most cherished theories is incorrect (see Montoya, Horton, & Kirchner, 2008, for example, who argue that the seemingly powerful connection between similarity and attraction may not be as powerful as we once thought). Because we can never know if this will happen, induction does not allow us to uncover unwavering laws of human nature. Induction is always probabilistic.

So how can we resolve this dilemma? The most popular answer is probably that we can complement our use of induction by making use of **deduction** as well. Deduction refers to reasoning from the general to the specific. In science, deduction thus occurs when a general statement (a theory) is used to develop predictions (hypotheses) that are then tested against observations. Karl Popper (the same guy who promoted logical positivism; see Chapter 1) was particularly fond of the deductive method. Recall that Popper argued that good theories have to be falsifiable, which means being open to empirical tests. Popper also noted that empirical tests can never prove that a theory is correct. Thus, Popper was a big fan of subjecting theories and laws to empirical tests even though he strongly believed that no theory or law can ever be *proven*. Why is it impossible to prove a theory or law? For precisely the reason that Hume mentioned: you can never be sure that you have subjected the idea to every possible test. In this sense, a scientific law strongly resembles a governmental law. Obeying a law hundreds of times does not prove that Tracy will never break it. In contrast, breaking the law only once permanently establishes Tracy's guilt.

As this example shows, it is possible to prove that a theory is false, but it is not possible to prove that it is true. But if scientists can never, ever prove their theories correct, why should they bother to test them in the first place? Why continue to court rejection when acceptance is unattainable? One answer to this question is that folks like Popper and Hume may have overstated their cases. Of course, we can never prove anything with absolute certainty, but we can sometimes show that a general idea is supported under a wide variety of circumstances. As philosophers interested in debunking the notion of absolute truths, Hume and Popper may have set the bar a bit too high for scientists. If we're willing to live with a little bit of uncertainty and trust science to correct itself, we don't need to worry about the fact that very few, if any, scientific statements are ever *completely* true. A second way of responding to the uncertainty of the scientific method is to realize that a great deal may be learned from failure (from falsifying a theory). Popper himself made this very point. Sometimes it is more useful to know what is *not* true than to know what is true. From this viewpoint, scientists do not travel forward toward truth so much as they walk backwards away from falsehood. In other words, the debate over what is scientifically knowable is partly a matter of how you choose to frame things.

Consider an analogy from the world of art. Word has it that Michelangelo was once asked by what method he was able to carve masterpieces such as his statue of David. He replied that it was easy. All he did, he said, was get a big block of marble and then remove everything that was not David. In this same way, psychology starts with a big block of possible truths and then it slowly, methodically, removes the ones that are not true. Does this ever leave anything good behind? Ever seen Michelangelo's *David*?

So what's the bottom line on induction and deduction? Our position is that even scientists who make careful use of both induction and deduction live in a tenuous world where their most beloved theories may be discarded when they prove to be wrong. Nonetheless, most scientists also realize that their erroneous theories, if they receive attention from other scientists, will serve as the inspiration for the superior theories that someday replace them. The goal of science is not to get things right so much as it is to be a part of making things righter. Finally, it is worth noting that scientists do not let go of their theories quite as quickly as you might hope. Clever experiments that fly in the face of existing theories *sometimes* inspire people to abandon old theories, but at other times, they merely inspire people to fly off the handle and attack the researchers who collected the new data! This reaction is not entirely unhealthy, and if it is done well, it does not involve personal attacks (physical or otherwise). Instead, the healthy skepticism that is a natural part of scientific thinking often translates into a healthy sense of skepticism regarding novel and provocative findings. Old theories do not always die easily. But when they are wrong enough, they do usually die.

Three Approaches to Hypothesis Testing

The processes of induction and deduction provide a partial answer to the question of how scientists go about the business of deciding what is true. However, a different way to address this same question is to ask how scientists test

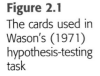

Figure 2.1

The cards used in Wason's (1971) hypothesis-testing task

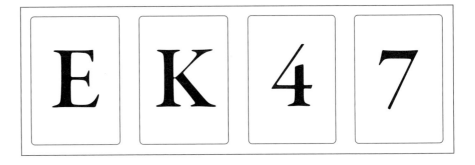

hypotheses. From our perspective, scientists seem to test hypotheses in three basic ways. But before we discuss the details of scientific hypothesis testing, we would like to ask you to test a couple of hypotheses yourself. Let's begin with a very simple hypothesis about a set of cards containing letters and numbers. Imagine that you are presented with the set of cards depicted in Figure 2.1 and told that every card has a letter on one side and a number on the other. You may take this as a given (e.g., no cards contain letters on both sides). Having established this much, you would like to test a proposed hypothesis about the cards. That is, you would like to determine for certain whether the hypothesis is correct or incorrect. The hypothesis is that *every card containing a vowel must have an even number on the other side*. If this is not true, then the hypothesis is wrong. Of course, one approach to testing the hypothesis would be to turn over all four of the cards, but this isn't very efficient. Not all cards need to be turned over to test the hypothesis. Your goal is to carry out a complete and accurate test of the hypothesis while turning over *only the cards necessary* to do so. Given this constraint, which cards would you turn over?

Most people report that they would turn over two cards: the card showing the E and the card showing the 4. Let's do this. In this case, the E has a 2 on the other side, and the 4 has an A on the other side. The obvious conclusion would appear to be that the hypothesis is correct. After turning over the E and the 4, this was certainly the first author's conclusion when Bill Swann (the professor who would eventually become his dissertation adviser) asked him to test this hypothesis many years ago. It was also the conclusion of the large majority of participants who were given this same problem by Wason (1971) in his studies of hypothesis testing. The problem with this common approach to hypothesis testing is that it is wrong. First of all, there was no need to turn over the 4 at all. The stated hypothesis was that every vowel *had to have an even number on the other side*. This could still be completely true if some or even all of the consonants *also* had an even number on the other side. The rule simply didn't say anything about consonants. If you are at all like the first author, you probably looked at the other side of the card with the 4 because you were somehow hoping or expecting to see a vowel. Strike one. If you are even more like the first author, you are now saying to yourself, "So big deal, I turned over a card I could have left unturned. I still drew the right conclusion. After all, every vowel *does* have an even number on the other side." Does it? Let's turn over the 7 to make sure. As it turns out, the 7 has a U on the other side. U is definitely a vowel, and unless you are very, very liberal in rounding numbers upward, 7 is definitely *not* an even number. Strike two. As it turns out, the hypothesis is false. If you are even *more* like the first author, you are now struggling to find a way to feel rational about your choice of the E and the 4. Perhaps you are complaining that the question was vaguely worded or misleading. Strike three. Don't be so defensive! Unless Bill Swann is standing in front of you right now and smiling because you were so predictably wrong, you still have one up on the first author.

Wason and his colleagues referred to the systematic bias they observed in this and several other studies as the **positive test bias**. This refers to the tendency for people who are evaluating hypotheses to attempt to *confirm* rather than to *disconfirm* these hypotheses. Of course, this intuitive approach is highly inconsistent with the logic of good science. However, it probably does not surprise you to learn that laypeople do not usually concern themselves with behaving scientifically. More often than not, people who are asked to test a hypothesis look long and hard for evidence that would support the hypothesis while looking past equally important evidence that could disconfirm it. Although Popper would certainly disapprove of this bias toward confirmation, the tendency for people to adopt a confirmatory approach to hypothesis testing is pretty pervasive. For instance, research in social psychology also suggests that when people are testing social hypotheses (e.g., "Is Zoe an extrovert?"), they are inclined to seek out evidence that is consistent rather than inconsistent with their preexisting expectations. For example, when people are asked to find out whether someone like Zoe is an extrovert, most people ask a preponderance of questions that are designed to elicit extroverted responses. For example, people are more likely to ask Zoe what she would do to liven things up at a dull party than they are to ask her when she is most likely to be interested in spending time alone. Almost anything Zoe says about livening up a dull party is likely to make her sound pretty extroverted—regardless of whether she really is the life of the party.

One well-documented social psychological analogue of the positive test bias is **behavioral confirmation**, the tendency for social perceivers to elicit behaviors from a person that are consistent with their initial expectancies of the person (Snyder & Swann, 1978). One of the best-known examples of research on behavioral confirmation is a study by Snyder, Tanke, and Berscheid (1977). These researchers gave some men the hunch that women they were getting to know over a laboratory "telephone" were either sociable or shy (by giving the men fake photos depicting either extremely attractive or unattractive women). The men who *thought* they were talking to highly attractive women later reported that they had expected the women to be highly sociable and entertaining. Moreover, in the course of their conversations with the presumably attractive woman, the men *made these expectations come true*. The men were more animated and entertaining themselves when they thought they were talking with an attractive woman. The most interesting aspect of this study, however, is that the women on the other end of the phone (who knew nothing about the misleading photographs) *confirmed* the men's originally false expectations by behaving in a highly sociable fashion themselves (as confirmed by raters who did not see the photos and only listened to what the women were saying).

Large bodies of research on self-fulfilling prophecies, experimenter bias, and stereotyping tell a very similar story (see Allport, 1954; Darley & Gross, 1983; Hamilton & Sherman, 1994; Rosenthal & Jacobson, 1966). Once we get an idea in our heads, most of us tend to engage in hypothesis-confirming behaviors that may falsely convince us that the idea is correct. Of course, an important consequence of confirmatory judgment biases is that people often believe that they have confirmed hypotheses that are not true. Moreover, once we have been exposed to some tentative evidence in support of our theories or ideas, we also become very reluctant to give them up—even in the face of strong disconfirming evidence that comes along later (e.g., see Ross, Lepper, & Hubbard, 1975; Swann, 1987, 1992). In fact, Dan Gilbert and his colleagues have gathered evidence suggesting that it may be impossible for human beings to *comprehend* a statement without initially encoding the statement as true (see Gilbert, 1991).

If you are one of those people who fell prey to the positive test bias, and if you are still feeling a little foolish, why not try a different version of the E, K, 4, 7 problem? We strongly suspect that if we had originally given you this alternate version of the problem, you would have performed brilliantly. Imagine that you are the manager of Blanton's Bar & Grille. Your job is to test the following hypothesis: *if a person has been served an alcoholic beverage, then that person must be at least 21 years of age.* Now look at the four cards (representing four different people) depicted in Figure 2.2. On one side, each card tells you whether a person is at least 21 years of age. On the other, each card tells you whether that person was served an alcoholic beverage. As you can see, Person E was served an alcoholic beverage, and Person K was not. Further, Person 4 is over 21 years of age, and Person 7 is not. Which cards would you need to turn over to evaluate this hypothesis?

As you can see, this situation is logically identical to the E, K, 4, 7 situation. Being a vowel has the same logical status as drinking a beer, being an even number has the same logical status as being over 21, and so forth. When Cox and Griggs (1982) gave this kind of familiar, concrete problem to a large group of participants, they found that very few people fell prey to the

Figure 2.2

A set of cards involving a concrete, familiar version of Wason's problem (adapted from Cox & Griggs, 1982)

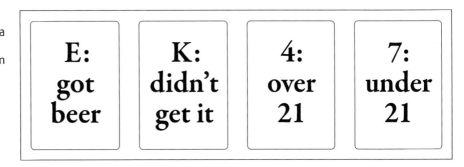

positive test bias. Most people correctly went right for the equivalent of the E (the person who was drinking a beer) and the 7 (the 17-year-old who got caught trying to use his older brother's expired Arizona driver's license). And most people, exactly like you, were quite correct.

What does all of this have to do with the ways in which scientists typically evaluate hypotheses? The main connection is that psychologists (and other scientists) sometimes show the same bias as laypeople who are evaluating unfamiliar hypotheses. They may spend a great deal of time and energy trying to validate their hypotheses and spend little or no time and energy trying to prove these same hypotheses wrong. On the other hand, like laypeople, scientists do not *always* engage in confirmatory approaches to hypothesis testing. Instead, they usually fall into one of three different camps. The three general approaches that scientists seem to adopt when testing hypothesis include validation, falsification, and qualification. We now review each of these three basic approaches to hypothesis testing.

Validation   The most common approach to hypothesis testing among scientists is probably validation, and psychologists are no exception to this rule. **Validation** is an approach to hypothesis testing in which researchers attempt to gather evidence that supports or confirms a theory or hypothesis. It is the rough scientific equivalent of the positive test bias. When researchers adopt this approach, they make implicit choices about what kind of data to examine, and they may even engineer laboratory situations that are highly conducive to supporting their theory or hypothesis. Is this fair? Popper would certainly be critical of this approach, and it'd be hard to blame him. On the other hand, this problem is serious only if scientists pretend that their tests of their hypotheses are free of any bias. For example, researchers who are testing a novel theory sometimes want to know if the theory is true under *any* circumstances. In such a case, any conscious or unconscious biases toward selecting just the right sample or just the right situation might be forgivable. After all, if a phenomenon proves to be interesting, future researchers will almost always try to identify the limitations (i.e., the boundary conditions) of the theory.

To illustrate, consider Festinger's (1957) theory of *cognitive dissonance*. Cognitive dissonance theory states that when a person simultaneously holds two beliefs that are dissonant (i.e., logically inconsistent), the person will experience an aversive state of arousal. The theory further states that the person will be highly motivated to *reduce* this aversive arousal (i.e., this dissonance) by making the two beliefs more compatible. Many hypotheses can be derived from this theory, and some of them are probably wrong. However, in the early days of dissonance theory, researchers wanted to know if the theory had any merit whatsoever. Thus, they began by creating contrived laboratory situations in which they expected people to do some pretty interesting things to reduce their cognitive dissonance. In so doing they were actively trying to confirm the new theory. In one famous study (Festinger & Carlsmith, 1959) participants spent an hour engaging in an extremely boring peg-turning task. The experimenter then convinced participants that they would be doing him a big favor if they would tell an unsuspecting person (who was waiting to begin the same task) that the wearisome task was extremely interesting. Although the experimenter made people feel that he really needed their help, he did not absolutely insist on the favor. Instead, he made people feel personally responsible for their behavior by letting them know that, as much as he needed their help, participants had the choice not to help him. In a sense, participants didn't *really* have a choice about helping the experimenter. Virtually every one of the thousands of participants who have been placed in situations like this one have agreed to help the experimenter—and harm the person waiting to begin the study—by agreeing to tell the lie. In other words, the experimental situation is carefully engineered to give participants the illusion that they freely chose to lie about the task when the experimenter was actually in full control of participants' behavior.

The experimenter was also in control of whether people had an *excuse* for the glaring contradiction between their direct experiences of boredom and their direct reports of fascination because the experimenter offered people different amounts of reward for "helping him out." In one condition, the experimenter offered people the paltry reward of $1 to lie to the potential peg-turners. In a second condition, he offered people a $20 reward to tell the same lie. Presumably, $20 was enough to prevent people from experiencing a great deal of dissonance about telling the lie. However, $1 was not. How could the $1 participants reduce this dissonance? One way would be to decide that the task was quite a bit more enjoyable than they had originally thought. This is exactly what the poorly paid participants did. They justified their deceptive behavior by *changing their attitudes* to be more consistent with their behavior. In comparison with the well-paid participants (or an additional group of participants who were not induced to lie at all), the $1 participants reported that they felt the experimental task was quite interesting. The results of this study are summarized in Figure 2.3.

Figure 2.3

Dissonance reduction: participants' ratings of how much they enjoyed a boring task as a function of whether they were induced to lie about the task and how much money they were offered to do so (from Festinger & Carlsmith, 1959)

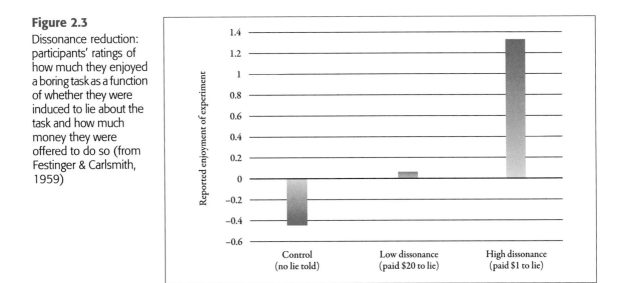

Notice that Festinger and Carlsmith didn't try to dream up a situation in which people's dissonance would have no psychological consequences, nor did they try to dream up a situation that *should* lead to dissonance according to Festinger's theory but *wouldn't* do so in practice. Instead of looking for evidence that could invalidate dissonance theory, they looked for evidence that could confirm it. As you will soon see, this didn't prove to be a serious problem because many generations of future researchers worked hard to identify the precise boundary conditions of this interesting theory. Nonetheless, in light of what you learned about the positive test bias and about the inductive problem, you may be a little concerned that researchers often adopt the approach of validation. If you are of this opinion, you might be happy to learn that psychologists sometimes adopt a very different approach to hypothesis testing. Sometimes, psychologists take Popper's advice to heart and engage in the strategy of falsification rather than validation.

Falsification   Falsification is an approach to hypothesis testing in which researchers attempt to gather evidence that invalidates or disconfirms a theory or hypothesis. If you are still wondering why anyone would actively strive to disprove something, remember Popper's philosophy of logical positivism and the lesson of the positive test bias. Theories or hypotheses that survive careful attempts at falsification are all the better for it. And theories that do not, according to Popper, should be discarded (hopefully, in favor of better theories).

In truth, it is hard to find examples of theorists who have tried hard to falsify their *own* theories. Trying hard to falsify your own theory is a little like trying hard to find out if your 14-year-old daughter has taken up smoking. Researchers know they *should* actively look for evidence that their theories are wrong, just as concerned parents know they should actively look for evidence that their children have taken up smoking. Instead of asking Jennie an innocuous question such as "You're not a smoker, are you?" it might be better to ask Jennie to take a saliva test that would reveal if she has smoked lately. But just as most parents really want to believe that their kids are truthful, most psychologists really want to believe that their theories are truthful.

Fortunately, science is different from parenting in at least two important ways. First, some aspects of falsification are simply an inherent part of scientific investigation. Because scientists have to justify and carefully describe their methods to other scientists, they can't usually get away with biased approaches to hypothesis testing. Along similar lines, any study that involves careful, objective data collection can yield results that are the opposite of what a researcher might have hoped for or predicted. Some aspects of the scientific method promote falsification whether a researcher likes it or not. To put it a little differently, you must be trained to follow a minimal set of rules if you wish to be a scientist. Unfortunately, no training of any kind is required if you wish to be a parent. A second way in which being a scientist is different from being a parent is that although children are rarely interrogated by anyone other than their parents, theories are often scrutinized by a great number of scientists, including those whose biases run contrary to those of a theory's proponents. Whereas Dr. Jordan is unlikely to try to falsify his own theory of memory, Dr. Ericson (who proposed a competing theory of memory) may be quite happy to falsify Jordan's theory. Like most other sciences, psychology has a healthy tradition of adversarial theory development. Accordingly, researchers from different "camps" often try to validate their own theories while trying to falsify the theories from opposing camps.

Research on cognitive dissonance theory provides some good examples of exactly this kind of process. Researchers often tried to disconfirm or falsify cognitive dissonance theory as a way of advancing compelling alternative theories. One researcher who became extremely well known for trying to falsify dissonance theory was Daryl Bem (1967, 1972). Bem was skeptical of some of the underlying assumptions of cognitive dissonance theory, and he conducted a series of very clever studies designed to cast doubt on this famous, heavily studied theory. Bem's criticism of dissonance theory was based on the fact that he wasn't a big fan of motivational processes. He developed a theory that accounted for the results of previous studies of cognitive dissonance without making any assumptions about the aversive motivational state that Festinger called cognitive dissonance.

In one classic study Bem asked participants to judge the attitudes of another person (a college sophomore named Bob Downing) who had ostensibly taken part in a study identical to the Festinger and Carlsmith $1 and $20 study. In other words, Bem repeated all the crucial manipulations and procedures of the Festinger and Carlsmith study but had people judge the attitudes of *someone else* who was turning tedious pegs and spinning dubious tales at the request of an experimenter. Bem's participants judged Bob Downing exactly the same way the real Bob Downings had judged themselves in the original study. When Bob told the white lie for $20, or wasn't asked to tell a lie at all, Bem's participants inferred that Bob probably thought the peg-turning task was quite boring. However, when they learned (as Bob presumably had in the actual study) that Bob had described the apparently boring task as interesting for only $1, they concluded that Bob must have felt that the task was pretty interesting.

Because these findings bear such a striking resemblance to the findings of Festinger and Carlsmith, you may be wondering why such findings would cast doubt upon dissonance theory. The reason is that one of the core assumptions of dissonance theory is the assumption that aversive arousal is a crucial component of cognitive dissonance. Presumably, it is this aversive arousal that fuels dissonance reduction (including dissonance-based attitude change). But Bem demonstrated attitude change (differences in the attitudes people attributed to another person) in a situation in which his participants should have been extremely unlikely to experience any kind of aversive arousal. Telling people *yourself* that a boring task was interesting might make you experience some discomfort, but watching a stranger do so shouldn't cause you any personal discomfort at all.

So why did Bem's participants conclude that Bob Downing was a big fan of peg-turning when he said so for only $1? Because people are pretty good at drawing reasonable inferences about a person by observing that person's behavior in context. Even if Bob hated the task, he would probably say it was interesting for $20 (recall that in the 1950s $20 was a lot of money). But if Bob said that the task was interesting for only $1, he must have actually thought it was pretty interesting. In social psychological terms, Bem adopted an *attributional* perspective on how people understand the behavior of other people. He referred to his particular attributional perspective as *self-perception theory*, and he argued that attribution theories such as self-perception theory could account not only for his findings but also for the large body of findings that researchers had previously explained in terms of cognitive dissonance theory. In the case of the original dissonance studies, Bem argued that people made use of exactly the same attributional principles they use to understand *others* to understand *themselves*. Just as an outside observer might calmly conclude that Bob must like the task if he said it is interesting for only $1, Bob, too, might calmly conclude that he must like the task if he said it is interesting for only $1. Bem's insight was that when we are trying to figure out our own attitudes, we might use the same rules we use to figure out other people's attitudes. For a better understanding of the difference between cognitive dissonance theory and self-perception theory and the way each theory explains Festinger and Carlsmith's findings, refer to Table 2.1.

At the risk of sounding a little repetitious, the main difference between these two accounts is that only dissonance theory assumes that the experience of discomfort (i.e., "aversive arousal") is the driving force behind attitude change. Self-perception is not a highly motivational theory; it just assumes that people want to figure out the world (themselves included). Notice that if

Table 2.1 A tale of two theories: Cognitive dissonance or self-perception?

I. How **cognitive dissonance theory** explains Festinger and Carlsmith's findings:
  A. In the $1 condition:
    1. "I just told someone that this peg-turning task is interesting."
    2. "That *really* bothers me! Why would I have said that when I don't believe it?"
    3. "I certainly wouldn't have done it for a dollar. I still feel bad."
    4. "But wait, maybe it's not so boring after all. Yeah, that's it. I actually *liked* it."
  B. In the $20 condition:
    1. "I just told someone that this peg-turning task is interesting."
    2. "That *really* bothers me! Why would I have said that when I don't believe it?"
    3. "For $20, that's why! I'd say just about anything for $20!"
    4. "Yep, the task is pretty boring. I just said it was interesting to get the money."

II. How **self-perception theory** explains the same findings:
  A. In the $1 condition:
    1. "I just told someone that this peg-turning task is interesting."
    2. "Hmm … that's interesting. I wonder why I said that?"
    3. "Let's see; I don't think I would have done it for a mere dollar."
    4. "The only logical conclusion is that I must have liked it more than I thought."
  B. In the $20 condition:
    1. "I just told someone that this peg-turning task is interesting."
    2. "Hmm … that's interesting. I wonder why I said that?"
    3. "Well, the experimenter did pay me $20 to say it. That's certainly a good reason."
    4. "Yep, the task is pretty boring. I said it was interesting to get money."

you make Bob the actor in the top half of Table 2.1, the description no longer makes sense. Why should it make *you* feel guilty, uncomfortable, or nervous to see that some stranger (Bob) told a white lie? Cognitive dissonance theory cannot readily explain our judgments about other people's attitudes. In contrast, the self-perception account (in the lower half of Table 2.1) still makes perfect sense if you make Bob the actor. You wonder why Bob did it (without feeling guilty or uncomfortable), and you draw a logical conclusion based on whether Bob was paid a lot of money to do so. Self-perception theory explains the original Festinger and Carlsmith study, and it also explains Bem's replication involving people's judgments of Bob Downing.

Although Bem's findings did not guarantee that there is no such thing as cognitive dissonance, they cast doubt on the idea that dissonance reduction processes are the driving force behind the kinds of attitude change observed in experimental tests of dissonance theory. Although dissonance reduction processes *could* be the reason Festinger and Carlsmith's $1 participants decided they liked peg-turning, self-perception theory has a leg up on dissonance theory because it is more parsimonious. First, unlike dissonance theory, self-perception theory does not require any elaborate assumptions about aversive states of arousal. Second, if we extend the principle of parsimony to the understanding of research traditions (rather than single studies), it seems more parsimonious to endorse a single theory that can explain two different research traditions than it does to endorse both of the theories. Now that you realize that Bem was only trying to falsify cognitive dissonance theory because he was trying to validate a theory of his own, you may wonder if Popper would have approved of Bem's approach to hypothesis testing. We suspect that Popper would have been pretty pleased. After all, Popper didn't have anything against theories. He simply wanted people to put theories, anyone's theories, to the kinds of critical tests that could lead to at least one theory's rejection.

Qualification   If you are the open-minded person you have always prided yourself on being, you may still be wondering if there isn't enough room in a big field like psychology for *both* cognitive dissonance theory and self-perception theory. As it turns out, there is. Moreover, one of the main reasons that we know this involves a third basic approach to hypothesis testing. This third approach, which we will refer to as **qualification**, has become increasingly popular with psychologists over the past couple of decades. Qualification is an approach to hypothesis testing in which researchers try to identify the boundary conditions under which a theory or hypothesis is and is not true. In many cases, this strategy can lead to the integration of two apparently contradictory theories by specifying the conditions under which *each* of the theories is correct. During the numerous debates between advocates of dissonance and self-perception theory, some researchers began to speculate that each of the two theories was correct under different conditions.

One of the best-known efforts to integrate or qualify each of the two theories was a paper by Fazio, Zanna, and Cooper (1977). These researchers argued that a crucial determinant of when people engage in dissonance reduction versus self-perception has to do with the precise degree to which people's behavior is inconsistent with their attitudes. According to Fazio et al., when people engage in behaviors that are only *slightly to moderately* inconsistent with their own attitudes (inconsistent behaviors that still fall within people's "latitudes of acceptance"), they will experience little or no aversive arousal and will engage in self-perception processes. In contrast, when people engage in behaviors that are *highly* inconsistent with their own attitudes (inconsistent behaviors that fall in people's "latitudes of rejection"), people will be likely to experience a great deal of aversive arousal and will engage in dissonance reduction.

Fazio et al. tested their ideas by using a variation of an established technique for inducing dissonance-based attitude change. In particular, they induced people to write attitude-inconsistent essays and were careful to make some participants feel that they had freely chosen to write the essays. Importantly, for some of these high-choice participants, the attitude-discrepant essays they were asked to write differed greatly from their original attitudes (and should have aroused dissonance). In contrast, for other participants, the essays fell within a range that participants had identified as discrepant but still acceptable (meaning that writing the essays should have aroused little dissonance). If Fazio et al. expected to see attitude change in both conditions, how could they know that the two kinds of attitude change were the results of different psychological processes? They found out by making use of an experimental manipulation that they expected to influence dissonance reduction but *not* self-perception. Specifically, they gave some participants the impression that the small booths in which they were taking part in the laboratory study would make most people feel nervous and uncomfortable. For people who were experiencing aversive arousal (a.k.a. cognitive dissonance), this would give them the opportunity to mistakenly attribute their arousal to the unnerving booths rather than to their decision to write the unnerving essays. Thus, Fazio et al. expected that this unusual manipulation would eliminate dissonance-related attitude change (in the high discrepancy condition) but would have no influence on self-perception processes (in the low to moderate discrepancy condition).

This is exactly what they found. The suggestion that the booth could make people uncomfortable completely eliminated attitude change for the participants who had written the extremely discrepant essays. However, this dissonance-erasing manipulation had no effect whatsoever on attitude change for people who had written the discrepant but not completely disagreeable essays. These participants showed plenty of behavior-consistent attitude change regardless of whether they were given an excuse to ignore any potential feelings of dissonance. (For further evidence of the limiting conditions of dissonance-based attitude change, see Collins & Hoyt, 1972.)

If you noticed that Fazio et al.'s experiment is a bit more complex than some of the experiments mentioned earlier, you are correct. One drawback to qualification as an approach to hypothesis testing is that it is inherently complicated. It requires researchers to have some sophisticated ideas about the world, and it requires more complicated experiments and more complicated statistical analyses than do simpler approaches to hypothesis testing.

A theory will usually have to reach a pretty advanced state of development before researchers can begin to offer reasonable speculations about the boundary conditions under which the theory is most and least likely to be correct. Despite this fact, however, a huge advantage of qualification is that it combines the desirable features of both validation and falsification. Moreover, because of the inherent complexity of human social behavior, research based on qualification will typically represent a closer approximation to reality than simpler approaches based solely on either validation or falsification. Qualification is probably the best road to uncovering laws.

Although qualification has become an increasingly popular approach to hypothesis testing in psychology, it could be argued that some of the confirmatory biases that are an inherent part of validation can easily become an inherent part of qualification. For example, researchers who are interested in falsification or qualification are typically just as interested in producing a specific pattern of research findings as are researchers interested in validation. It is simply the case that the specific pattern of results they are interested in confirming is a little bit more complex than the pattern of results that might be expected by a researcher who is interested in validating a simpler, less well-developed hypothesis. In other words, it could be argued that the distinctions made here have a lot more to do with the stage of development of a particular research question than they do with the basic approach that psychologists adopt to test their hypotheses. From this perspective, researchers are almost always trying to validate some theoretical perspective. The nature and complexity of the theoretical perspective changes, not necessarily the nature of how researchers test their theories. Regardless of which particular perspective you personally come to adopt on hypothesis testing, it is important to keep in mind that scientists are probably prone to some of the same hypothesis-confirming biases that characterize human judgment in general.

To add a limitation to this limitation, our discussion of hypothesis testing may give you the false impression that it is extremely easy to gather support for a scientific theory or hypothesis. After all, if most researchers spend a disproportionate amount of time trying to validate their theories, then most researchers must generate misleadingly large amounts of evidence in favor of their theories. As we noted earlier, however, there are at least two important checks on this problem. The first is that there are so many different theories (and scientists) out there. As illustrated by our abbreviated history of cognitive dissonance theory, this means that many common theories of human social behavior are opposed by *competing* theories from opposing camps. While some dedicated researchers are busy trying to show that "birds of a feather flock together," other equally dedicated researchers are just as busy trying to show that "opposites attract." If both camps advocate theories that are true in some circumstances, then both camps will benefit from having worthy adversaries. The opposing camp that does not kill your own theory only makes your theory stronger. To relate all this more directly to qualification, researchers who appreciate the merits of more than one theory (i.e., qualificationists) sometimes bridge the gap between validation and falsification by trying to figure out exactly *when* each of a given set of competing theories is correct. You might think of these researchers as the scientific equivalent of U. N. peacekeepers. They go around and ask "Can't we all get along?" With any luck, these peacekeepers will be able to identify research boundaries that both sides can agree upon.

As we noted earlier, a second reason that validation does not get completely out of hand has to do with the difference between scientific approaches to discovery and the scientific method. Even when researchers carefully, actively, even shamelessly, seek out evidence in support of their ideas (including their ideas about how to integrate two opposing theories), they are held to certain scientific standards of "proof." Another way of putting this is that scientists cannot expect to convince others to accept any evidence in support of their theories unless this evidence passes some very strict standards. But what are these standards? What are the basic rules of the game of psychology? In a sense, the rest of this book is designed to answer this question. However, because the primary goal of this chapter is to acquaint you with the logic of scientific discovery, this chapter would be incomplete without a brief summary of the basic research paradigm that has become the gold standard of psychological research: an ideal set of research procedures that serves as the model for almost all psychological research. We refer to this paradigm as the **experimental paradigm** because it is grounded in the assumption that experimentation is the most useful tool for figuring out the true causes of human behavior. However, this paradigm is much broader than experimentation. As you will see, it provides some basic rules and guidelines for almost any kind of systematic research.

THE ART OF SCIENTIFIC DISCOVERY

Up to this point, we have focused your attention on the logic of scientific discovery. Now we turn to what might be called the art of scientific discovery. This transition is an admission on our part that science does not create itself. Science advances only when creative scientists come up with new ideas that change the way we think about the world. True, these new ideas need to survive the scrutiny of the scientific method, but the process of scientific discovery always begins with some kind of creative spark or inspiration. Furthermore, unless a person with a new idea can convince other people that the new idea is worth pursuing, it is unlikely that the idea will ever change the way other scientists think. In this regard, it is informative to consider scientific works that have influenced how scientists think and compare them with those that have not. Consider the highly influential researcher, Charles Darwin. During his distinguished scientific career, Darwin published some extremely influential books on some very important topics. These include such famous books as *On the Origin of Species by Means of Natural Selection*, first published in 1859, and *The Expression of the Emotions in Man and Animals*, published in 1872. In 1881, the year before he died, Darwin capped off his career by publishing a book that, frankly speaking, didn't exactly bowl a lot of people over. The title of this book is *The Formation of Vegetable Mould, Through the Action of Worms: With Observations on*

Their Habits. Although we have not read this book, our suspicion is that Darwin exercised the same care and attention to detail in this book that he had exercised in his earlier works. Although we do not want to make light of the scientific contribution of Darwin's final book, this book clearly did not have the same scientific impact as his earlier works. Why not? Of course, there are many answers to this rhetorical question, but if we are willing to ignore a bit of folk wisdom and judge a book by its cover, the most obvious answer is that questions about the nature and formation of mold simply aren't as provocative as questions about the nature and origins of human beings. There was only so much that even Charles Darwin could do to pique people's curiosity about mold and worms. This point is related to one of the major themes of this chapter: the theme of how to generate research ideas. Being methodologically sophisticated is an important key to becoming a good scientist, but it is even more important to have an interesting topic to study in the first place.

McGuire (1973) made a similar point long ago. He wrote:

> It is my guess that at least 90% of the time in our current courses in methodology is devoted to presenting ways of testing hypotheses and that little time is spent on the prior and more important process of how one creates these hypotheses in the first place.

McGuire's estimate that 90 percent of all methodology courses are devoted to hypothesis testing (rather than hypothesis generation) is probably pretty generous. In fact, very few research methods texts make any mention of hypothesis generation at all. Fortunately, however, McGuire (1973, 1989) tackled this problem head-on by identifying some fruitful rules of thumb for generating specific research hypotheses (as well as general programs of research). In fact, McGuire has done such an excellent job of mapping out strategies for hypothesis generation that we have found it difficult to add much to what he has already said. Thus, this section is based almost exclusively on McGuire's previous analysis. Although we have organized McGuire's principles into two general categories and must take credit for a couple of omissions, most of what follows here is simply our attempt to recapitulate what McGuire (1973) had to say about this topic in the early 1970s.

Philosophers, logicians, and psychologists generally agree that people reason (i.e., develop hypotheses) about the world in two basic ways. The first way of thinking, induction, refers to reasoning from the specific to the general. (Remember Hume's analysis of the inductive problem?) The second way, deduction, refers to reasoning from the general to the specific. To emphasize the fact that different kinds of reasoning are data driven or theory driven, respectively, cognitive psychologists use the terms "bottom-up" and "top-down" processing to make a very similar distinction. As it turns out, McGuire's rules for generating research hypotheses may be organized around these two basic themes.

Inductive Techniques for Developing Ideas

The inductive techniques McGuire identified are all based loosely on some kind of specific observation. One very useful source of observations that can be used either to test or to generate hypotheses is **case studies**, that is, carefully documented observations of a specific group or person. (Case studies are discussed in more detail in Chapter 6.) McGuire notes that great thinkers such as Freud and Piaget formulated many of their theories and hypotheses on the basis of formal or informal case studies. Freud carefully observed his patients' mental disorders, and Piaget carefully observed his children's cognitive development. As a social psychological example, Cialdini (1993) states that he became interested in the topic of social influence techniques early in his career precisely because he was always falling for the social influence techniques of real-world persuasion artists such as panhandlers and automobile salespersons. In fact, Cialdini reports that he discovered at least one social influence technique, the lowball technique, by simply observing automobile salespersons in action.[4] After discovering how effectively the technique worked on him, Cialdini used it, for example, to get people to do crazy things like sign up as participants in psychology experiments that begin at 7 A.M. (see Cialdini, Cacioppo, Bassett, & Miller, 1978). We suspect that all researchers base at least some of their research hypotheses on life experiences that they themselves have found puzzling or intriguing. For example, what psychology courses have you found most intriguing, or what would you like to study if you could do research on any topic you wish? We suspect that you could identify some personal reasons why you are interested in certain issues and that some of your important experiences might give you special insights into these issues. There may be some truth to the idea that "research is me-search."

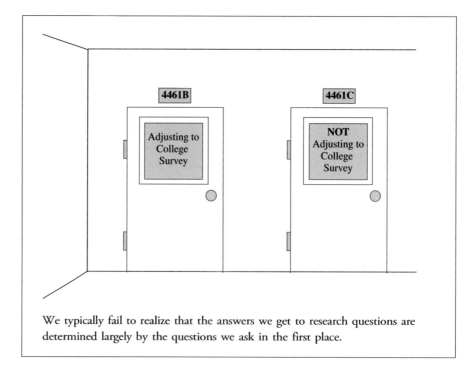

We typically fail to realize that the answers we get to research questions are determined largely by the questions we ask in the first place.

A second inductive approach to generating research hypotheses is what McGuire refers to as trying to account for **paradoxical incidents** (i.e., puzzling or nonsensical observations). He cites a case in which the rumors that circulated after an earthquake were almost always disturbing rather than gratifying. This observation presumably played a role in Festinger's formulation of a revolutionary theory about how people try to make sense of their worlds by minimizing inconsistencies in their belief systems. Cognitive dissonance theory may have arisen, in part, from the rubble of an earthquake in Bihar, India. Asking why so many people gamble when doing so is clearly a long-term losing proposition, why some people remain in abusive romantic relationships, why John F. Kennedy's popularity increased after he publicly took the blame for the Bay of Pigs invasion, or why being the home team sometimes seems to be a disadvantage in the World Series are other examples of how unusual events can prompt researchers to develop theories and hypotheses to account for unusual or paradoxical events.

A third inductive technique is what McGuire calls **analyzing the practitioner's rule of thumb**, i.e., analyzing things that experts in a particular area do to achieve certain outcomes. Cialdini's examples of techniques used by automobile salespersons could have also been placed in this category. Observing the favored strategies of athletes or chess champions, asking waiters and waitresses how they remember which dish to serve to each customer, or asking successful coaches how they motivate their players to perform well are additional examples of how we can identify psychological principles by observing people who have picked up special knowledge or skills in the real world. McGuire also reminds us that we can often learn as much from failure as we can from success. Asking novice chess players or losing coaches the same questions that we put to their more skillful counterparts may also yield useful information about what works, what doesn't work, and why.

As we already mentioned, one of the great fans of the inductive method was B. F. Skinner. Although Skinner might quibble with McGuire's assumptions about the usefulness of people's self-reports about their behavior, he would probably approve of McGuire's inductive principles. In fact, he might insist on adding a fourth important inductive technique to McGuire's list. Skinner was fond of noting that **serendipity** (luck or good fortune) played an important role in most of his big discoveries. For example, one of B.F. Skinner's most important discoveries about learning was the *partial reinforcement effect*—the tendency for responses to be more resistant to extinction when they are reinforced inconsistently rather than uniformly. In addition to having enormous practical applications, this finding flew in the face of certain traditional conceptions of the nature of reinforcement. For example, it was inconsistent with the assumptions of early learning theorists that rewards "stamp in" responses. If they do, why does a little bit of sporadic stamping make a stronger impression than a lot of consistent stamping? Skinner reported that he discovered this principle completely by accident when he ran low on food pellets while running a simple conditioning experiment (see Schultz, 1981). Of course, to benefit from serendipity, a researcher has to be willing and able to put two and two together. But according to researchers like Skinner, the very nature of the experimental method (e.g., the isolation of variables) often sets the stage for fortuitous observations.

Deductive Techniques for Developing Ideas

McGuire also identifies a series of techniques for generating research hypotheses that we consider primarily deductive. One of the foremost of these is **reasoning by analogy**. McGuire himself has made excellent use of this technique in his own research on *attitude inoculation* and persuasion. Specifically, McGuire drew an analogy between biological resistance to disease and psychological resistance to persuasion. One of the basic forms of inoculation against disease consists of exposing people to a weakened version of a virus or antigen, a version that the person's immune system easily resists. In the process of dealing with the weakened version of the biological threat, the immune system becomes better able to defend itself against a full-blown version of the same virus or antigen. McGuire demonstrated a psychological analogue of this effect by giving people practice defending themselves against weakened versions of persuasive arguments. When people are later exposed to full-blown attacks on their belief systems, those who have been psychologically inoculated are much more resistant to persuasion (McGuire, 1961). This technique has proven to be an especially useful means of preventing adolescents from taking up smoking. Interestingly enough, biologists also explain the basic activity of the immune system by relying on analogies. Antigens (substances that attack the immune system) and antibodies (part of the body's defense system) are said to be analogous to locks and keys, respectively. Only antibodies ("keys") with specific physical and chemical properties can attach themselves to specific antigens ("locks"). And of course, if you noticed our use of words like "attack" and "defense" to describe the operation of the immune system, you can probably appreciate just how much we rely on analogy to understand—and test hypotheses about—all kinds of difficult concepts.

Carver and Scheier's (1990) reliance on the thermostat as a metaphor for understanding self-regulation, Dennett's (1991) reliance on the computer monitor as a metaphor for understanding consciousness, and Bowlby's (1977) reliance on observations of attachment behavior in primates as a metaphor for adult romantic attachment also represent profitable lines of research that have been enriched (and constrained) by the metaphors and analogies that have been used to derive many of the basic predictions and implications of these models.

A second deductive heuristic for generating research ideas is what McGuire calls **applying a functional or adaptive analysis** to a particular research question. Researchers who adopt this strategy ask themselves basic questions about what organisms have to do to successfully master their environments. For example, McGuire notes that Hull (1943) built up much of his theory of drive states and learning by asking questions about the minimum structural and procedural requirements of a behavioral system that can learn from experience (without abandoning old rules the first time they fail to work and without failing to detect changes in what does work). What, exactly, does any system have to do to be able to learn (and relearn) things about the environment? More recently, Gilbert (1991) developed a model of how mental systems represent incoming information whose truth or falsity is unknown. He appears to have done so, at least in part, by considering the functional or adaptive significance of different kinds of representational systems. Haselton and Gildersleeve's (2011) work on human ovulation detection (summarized in Chapter 12) and Shubin's (2008) analysis of continuity in the fossil records of fish and people serve as additional examples of how an adaptive analysis can yield novel, counterintuitive hypotheses.

A third deductive technique for generating research ideas is the **hypothetico-deductive method**. This approach was popularized by Hull (1943), who believed that a good way to go about research is to begin with a set of a basic assumptions (or observations) and to derive one or more logical consequences from these basic principles. Swann's (1992) work on self-verification theory is an excellent example of this approach to research. A great deal of Swann's research builds on two intuitively appealing ideas. The first idea is that organisms prefer environments that are stable, predictable, and controllable. The second idea is that people's relationships and social interactions play an important role in regulating their beliefs about themselves. However, by building upon each of these intuitive assumptions, Swann has generated a wide range of counterintuitive hypotheses about how people take active steps to confirm their existing self-views (e.g., by seeking out information about one's weaknesses in areas in which one possesses negative self-views).

Tesser (1986) adopted a very similar approach in his research on self-evaluation maintenance. He began with three basic variables that presumably play a role in people's general self-evaluations: (1) people's feelings of closeness to a partner in a social interaction, (2) social comparison information about how people are performing relative to this partner, and (3) the personal relevance of a given self-concept dimension (or area of performance). By making a couple of simple assumptions about how these three variables work together to influence self-evaluation (e.g., if Eric is a math major, his best friend's perfect score on a calculus midterm will be more threatening to Eric's self-concept than it would be if Eric were an art major), Tesser developed an entire research program to investigate the ways in which people orchestrate their performances, their relationships, and the relevance of their self-views in ways that maximize overall self-evaluation.

To provide a few more examples of the hypothetico-deductive approach, Petty and Cacioppo's (1986) elaboration likelihood model of persuasion; Chaiken, Liberman, and Eagly's (1989) heuristic-systematic model of social inference; Taylor and Brown's (1988) work on optimistic illusions; Wegner's (1994) research on ironic thought processes; and Higgins's (1989) research on self-discrepancies all build on this approach. These researchers all begin with a few guiding principles and derive specific hypotheses by combining the principles together in novel ways. The result of these derivations is typically a set of research hypotheses that researchers would have been unlikely to generate in the absence of a coherent theoretical framework.

A fourth deductive strategy for generating research hypotheses is **accounting for conflicting results**. McGuire notes that primacy and recency in learning are principles that make opposite predictions about what people will learn best. Self-verification and self-enhancement theories also make opposite predictions about people's behavior under at least some conditions. When do people strive to maintain a positive overall self-evaluation (as predicted by Tesser's self-evaluation maintenance model), and when do people strive to confirm their negative self-views (as predicted by Swann's self-verification theory)? When do people engage in perceptual assimilation (over-emphasizing the similarity between two stimuli), and when do they engage in perceptual contrast (exaggerating or enhancing the differences between two stimuli)? According to Johnson and Stapel (2011), for example, a person's current mood provides one answer. People in a good mood often interpret and use social comparison information in whatever ways will allow them to maintain that good mood. By struggling to fit contradictory theories together into a more comprehensive theory, researchers often generate research ideas that would not have been generated by either theory alone.

A fifth deductive approach to hypothesis generation is **accounting for exceptions** to well-established psychological principles. Much of McGuire's approach to research is based on a contextualist theory of knowledge that assumes that almost everything is true under some circumstances. Social behavior is, in fact, a very complex can of worms, and thus many tried and true principles of behavior have their limitations and exceptions. From this perspective, the goal of psychological research is not to determine what is true; instead it is to determine when (or for whom) a given psychological principle is true (see also Schaller, Crandall, Stangor, & Neuberg, 1995). McGuire cites Hovland's classic research on the "sleeper effect" as an example of this principle. Persuasive messages are generally thought to have their greatest impact shortly after people have digested them, but in some cases the impact of a persuasive message actually increases over time (see Hovland & Weiss, 1951). Trying to figure out the situations under which a sleeper effect was most likely to occur apparently prompted Hovland to consider a number of important ideas about when and why delayed psychological responses to stimuli occur. Similarly, research on taste aversion and one-trial learning contradicted the accepted wisdom of the day that learning is a slow and gradual process. Usually it *is*, but researchers who dared to ask whether this rule is truly ironclad prompted a very interesting and influential area of research.

A more contemporary example of this approach can be found in Krull's (1993) research on the correspondence bias. In the wake of a large body of research suggesting that people tend to focus too much on dispositional explanations for people's behavior, Krull showed that when people's goals are to figure out *situations* rather than people, this otherwise robust inferential bias can be eliminated or even reversed (see also Fein, Hilton, & Miller, 1990; Krull & Erickson, 1995). Research on the "pratfall effect" (the tendency to like a talented person more when you discover that person has made a blunder; see Aronson, Willerman, & Floyd, 1966), research on the positive consequences of depressive symptoms (Pelham, 1991b), and research on overjustification (the tendency for rewards to diminish people's interest in an activity; see Lepper, Greene, & Nisbett, 1973) represent additional examples of the principle of finding exceptions to general rules.

THE ETHICS OF SCIENTIFIC DISCOVERY

To this point, we have discussed the logic and the art of knowledge acquisition, but we would be remiss if we did not explore the *ethics* of knowledge acquisition. The truth is that not all interesting ideas can be tested in the most informative or the most creative manner. For instance, if you have a theory that genocide is most likely to occur when an autocratic ruler takes control of an economically challenged country with a history of ethnic strife, you obviously cannot create these conditions in your research laboratory to see if you are right, and it would not be ethical to try. This example might seem obvious, but even more mundane theories than this can pose serious ethical challenges.

One particularly tricky thing about doing experimental research in psychology is the fact that it is often necessary to distract or deceive people to get them to behave naturally. In the specific case of social psychology, another tricky thing is the fact that psychologists are interested in some of the most sensitive topics anyone could ever wish to study. Such delicate topics as aggression, confession, depression, drug possession, and romantic obsession are all of great interest to social psychologists. In fact, some of the most famous and important studies in the history of social psychology have also proven to be some of the most ethically controversial. In the specific cases of developmental psychology and clinical psychology, researchers often must consider the ethics of studying special groups that may not be competent to give informed consent to participate in studies (e.g., young children, people with schizophrenia). In the case of behavioral neuroscience, researchers must consider equally difficult questions about when and whether it is appropriate to cause animals physical pain to study important questions (including questions about pain). In the remainder of this chapter, we provide a couple of historical examples of studies that have raised important ethical questions among social psychologists, psychologists, and researchers in general. We then summarize how the American Psychological Association (APA) has responded to controversial or unethical studies such as these by summarizing the current ethical guidelines of the APA regarding research with human participants. It goes beyond the scope of this chapter to discuss all of the ethical hurdles one must clear to conduct research. Our goal here is more modest: to clarify the most basic responsibilities researchers must consider. To learn more about ethical guidelines for research with human subjects, references to Websites run by the U.S. Department of Health and Human Services (DHHS) as well as an online tutorial sponsored by the National Institutes of Health (NIH) are included at the end of this chapter. Each of these major government agencies also provides detailed guidelines for the ethical treatment of research participants.

The Evolution of Ethical Guidelines

During the early days of research with human participants, no real guidelines existed concerning either the rights of human participants or the responsibilities of researchers to their participants. Most researchers simply put their faith in the good judgment of their fellow researchers and assumed that no one would ever allow anything bad to happen to his or her participants.

This faith in the good judgment (and good will) of all researchers turned out to be somewhat misguided. For example, in an infamous medical study begun in 1932, the researchers wanted to learn about the effects of untreated syphilis (untreated syphilis eventually leads to insanity and death). In the early days of the study, there was no known cure for syphilis, and thus the study didn't violate any ethical rules. However, in 1943, researchers discovered that penicillin cures syphilis. Instead of seeking out their patients and treating them, the researchers specifically ordered doctors *not* to treat their patients. When some of the men were drafted during World War II, the researchers even broke state and federal laws to prevent the men from receiving the treatment that otherwise would have been given to them after their medical examination for the draft. It is probably no coincidence that the patients in the study were about 600 rural Black men living in Alabama (whereas the researchers—though not all of those involved in the project—were White).

Although this study was conducted by medical researchers rather than psychologists, this study and others like it prompted enough attention to ethics in research with human participants that the APA eventually came up with a set of ethical standards for psychological research with human participants. The first set of standards was published in 1958, but psychologists didn't pay much attention to these standards until much later—in the wake of controversial studies that *were* conducted by psychologists. One of the controversial studies that rekindled people's interest in ethical issues was Milgram's famous study of obedience to authority. As you may recall, Milgram (1963) demonstrated that about 65 percent of a sample of normal, healthy men were willing to deliver what they thought were extremely painful and potentially life-threatening shocks to a learner.

Critics of Milgram's famous study (e.g., Baumrind, 1964) argued that his study was probably unethical. They pointed out, for example, that his research procedure was inherently coercive. Milgram responded that he was studying the important social problem of coercion. Critics noted that Milgram lied to his participants. He retorted that he conducted extensive debriefing sessions with his participants. During these sessions, his participants were given a great deal of information about the true purpose of the study, were told why it was necessary to use deception, and were told that the study was yielding information that could have widespread positive social consequences. Critics noted that the experiences Milgram put his participants through could cause them serious psychological harm. Milgram replied that most of his participants reported feeling that they had learned something extremely important about themselves by taking part in the study.

Although debates over the ethics of the Milgram study continue to this day, most contemporary researchers would probably consider the study unethical. Regardless of one's opinion on the ethicality of these studies, almost all researchers agree that one positive consequence is that they prompted serious action on the part of the APA. When the APA came out with a revision of its ethical principles in 1972, many more people took note. These principles were elaborated and revised again in 1992 and in 2002. Due in large part to federal regulations, all universities whose students and professors conduct research with human participants have created committees whose job it is to review this research. The point of these reviews is to make certain that the research is conducted in ways that are consistent with the principles of professional governing bodies such as the APA, the ASA (the American Sociological Association), and the AMA (the American Medical Association). The ethical guidelines of the APA are pretty extensive. They deal with a wide range of issues ranging from how practitioners should present themselves to the public to how collaborators should determine authorship on research papers. In the next section, we provide a brief primer on modern views of ethics in research.

Modern Internal Review Boards and Risk-Benefit Analyses

All psychological research involves ethical issues. Psychologists typically take it for granted that they have a right to conduct research, but this entire enterprise of doing research is based on a *means-end assumption*. That is, research is built on the assumption that it is permissible to use other people as a means to reach a desired end. (In the case of psychological research, the desired end is to learn something about psychology, and the means to accomplish this is to have other people participate in studies that test psychological theories.) As someone taking psychology courses, you might feel comfortable with a means-end analysis as a justification for psychological research. However, there are many cases in life when most people question means-end thinking. For instance, if you and your friend Justin Bieber were in the same methods course, and Justin decided to quit attending class because he would rather sleep in, you probably would resent him borrowing your class notes so that he can do well on the tests. (Your resentment would probably grow even greater if Justin ended up getting a better grade than you did.) Even if Justin only asked to borrow your notes when you were not using them, you might still feel used. You might question the ethics of Justin's behavior. This same type of moral dynamic occurs with psychologists. In a very real way, psychologists are like your friend Justin in that they satisfy their own desires by taking something from other people.

With these considerations in mind, the ethics of all psychological studies are examined under an umbrella principle that is referred to as a **risk-benefit analysis**. The idea here is that some greater good must come from psychologists' use of human subjects in their studies. At the least, this means that subjects should get something back for participating. For example, although you may not benefit in any way from lending Justin your notes, you should benefit in some way from being in Dr. Hessling's psychology study. If you are a student taking a psychology course, then the act of being in studies can be informative and useful to you. You will see how research is done, and perhaps this will help you improve your own studies when you are an experimenter. Because researchers owe their participants something in return, most debriefings include detailed information about the theory being tested and a description of why this question is important. Of course, it is too much to expect that every single research participant will learn something useful from every single study in which he or she participates. Because some participants may have no real interest in learning about psychology, most risk-benefit analyses consider not only the benefits to individual research participants but also to society more generally. For example, suppose that Justin suffered through a mildly boring perceptual study that strongly suggested that painting fire trucks neon green would cut down on accident rates. If follow-up studies with real fire trucks confirmed this finding on the street, and if red fire trucks were slowly replaced by the neon green variety (which are, in fact, safer), then Justin himself would be as likely to benefit from this finding as anyone else. Of course, a focus on the societal benefits of research cannot be carried to its logical extremes. Even the prospect of extremely large benefits to society would not justify running over Justin with a red versus a neon green fire truck.

Although a risk-benefit analysis provides some useful guidance for evaluating research, a risk-benefit analysis conducted by a researcher on his or her own work can create many challenging moral dilemmas—and there are no formal rules to guide a person through them all. For this reason, psychologists draw heavily on *consensus information*. As we noted above, federal regulations now require all universities and other research institutes to maintain an internal ethical review board that reviews and evaluates studies that use human participants. Although **internal review boards** (often known as **IRB**s) differ somewhat in their concerns from university to university, they all have the same purpose. They perform risk-benefit analyses to ensure that all studies meet consensual community standards of ethical behavior. To this end, these committees are typically made up of (1) a group of instructors and researchers employed at the university, (2) one or more university staff members with special expertise in the area of research protocol, and (3) one or more laypeople from the local community (e.g., a minister or businessperson who is active in community service). If a researcher wants to conduct research on human participants, he or she must submit a formal proposal to the IRB at the university with which he or she is affiliated. Such proposals typically include (1) a careful but nontechnical summary of the practical and theoretical goals of the research project and (2) a detailed description of the procedures to be followed in the research.

The description of the research procedures includes information about how participants will be selected for inclusion in the study, the setting in which the research will be conducted (e.g., a classroom, a laboratory), and copies of all the materials that participants will be given during the study (e.g., the informed consent form, copies of survey questions or experimental stimuli, debriefing sheets, etc.). It also includes a description of any procedures the researcher will use to minimize risks to his or her participants (e.g., a description of how participants' responses will be kept anonymous). When a study (1) does not make use of deception and (2) does not pose any meaningful risks to research participants, some universities provide a route through which the study may be "exempted" from a full review by the IRB. When a researcher requests such an exemption from full review, one or two of the experienced members of the committee (usually the committee chair) will read the proposal and make a decision regarding its suitability for exemption. If it is very clear that the study poses no reasonable ethical risks, it may be exempted from a full review (and approved directly by the chair or acting committee members). On the other hand, if the reviewer disagrees with the researcher's conclusion that the study poses no ethical risks of any kind, the researcher may be asked to make changes to the study or to resubmit the study for review by the full committee. In either case, the researcher must await some kind of approval from the IRB. Although the exact review procedures vary slightly from university to university, the days in which researchers could decide for themselves whether their research is ethically defensible are in the past.

In short, if you wish to conduct research on students who are enrolled at a specific American university, you will need to get approval from your own specific university's IRB. In fact, if you are a student or professor at a specific university but plan to collect data from participants who have nothing to do with your university (e.g., the adult shoppers at a local supermarket), you still need to get permission from your university's IRB to conduct your research. In this case, the working assumption is that you are acting as a representative of your home university when you present your research findings, and so your university's IRB should review your research to be sure that it meets their consensual ethical standards. Incidentally, the rule that your university has to approve your research only applies if you are behaving as a researcher. If you ask your friend Lincoln what his favorite color is simply because you are curious, you obviously do not need permission from your IRB to do so. However, if you ask him this question as part of a systematic research study, whose results you might wish to publish in a scientific journal, you have now entered the territory that is carefully regulated by your local IRB.

In short, your IRB should be involved any time you engage in a systematic investigation that might contribute to the scientific literature. Not only would you be violating consensual standards of professional scientific ethics by operating independently, you would be prevented from publishing your findings in scientific journals if you did try to fly solo. Just like research institutions, scientific journals have policies about ethics, and they will not publish your findings if you do not have the blessing of an institutional review panel.

A Brief Primer in Ethical Guidelines

Given the logic of the risk-benefit ratio we mentioned previously, IRBs must consider two main issues. As you might guess, one of these issues has to do with risks, and the other has to do with benefits.

Let's begin with the easier issue—benefits. No matter how personally interesting you might consider a topic to be, you must always document that the research holds the possibility of some kind of reasonable benefit. In other words, if the benefits of a study are zero, this value of zero cannot outweigh even a very low cost (to those who participate in the research). Thus, if you wanted to hand out questionnaires in your biomechanics class just because you are curious to see what students might say about their lives, you are not likely to receive the approval of your local IRB. Typically, IRBs are hesitant to evaluate the scientific or societal benefits of such studies because the questions are highly subjective and probabilistic. For example, to some people a questionnaire assessing people's stereotypes about the intelligence of different breeds of dogs might sound ludicrous. To others, it might seem obvious that if we could better understand why people stereotype dogs we might better understand why we stereotype each other. And if we could better understand why people stereotype each other, we might someday be able to reduce ethnic stereotyping or even ethnic cleansing. Who is right in this case? Fortunately, most IRBs realize that it is very hard to predict which research studies will change the world and which will not, and thus most IRBs are willing to assume that the ultimate benefits of a research study may not be known for years or even decades. Thus, even if it seems like a tremendous long shot that your study of dog stereotypes will ever help to eliminate ethnic cleansing, most IRB members will probably give you the benefit of the doubt, so long as you can also document that you are making every effort to protect your research participants. It is our guess that, apart from a little boredom, the greatest risk associated with answering an anonymous questionnaire about breeds of dogs is the ever-present risk of a paper cut. Most IRBs are willing to live with minor risks such as boredom or paper cuts because these risks are also present, to a greater or lesser degree, when someone is reading *Vogue* magazine or the book of Exodus.

Having said this, we should note that the issue of risks is quite a bit trickier than we have made it sound so far. This is because many research projects involve activities that pose more substantial risks than answering a few harmless questions about dogs. IRBs focus most of their attention on the issue of risks. The job of each board is to see to it that participants do not incur mental or physical costs that are unusual or extreme. Of course, the most important task for these boards is to ensure that no physical or psychological harm will come to study participants. *Researchers are not allowed to knowingly place their participants in any kind of unusually risky or dangerous situation.* All reasonable precautions and safeguards to minimize risks of physical or psychological harm must be followed during all phases of a study. In the case of a questionnaire, keeping people's responses anonymous (and telling people so) is a useful way to protect people while also increasing the likelihood that participants will respond honestly. In the case of a lab experiment in which people are asked to think about a highly sensitive topic such as suicide, it might be necessary to screen potential participants for depression and to eliminate depressed people from the study. By requiring researchers to apply these minimal standards, IRBs strive to protect participants from any kind of psychological or physical harm. However, IRBs also hold researchers to much higher standards, standards that not only protect research participants but also promote the positive well-being and education of most research participants. Some of the most important rules that IRBs enforce as a precondition for approving a research proposal are described below.

Informed Consent   Before participants agree to take part in research, they must be informed about any potential risks of the research, however remote or slight (e.g., they must be told about any aspect of the research experience that may be embarrassing or stressful). This does not mean that researchers have to compromise the integrity of their investigations by telling their participants their hypotheses in advance. Instead, it means that if a study poses any foreseeable risk of anxiety, discomfort, or embarrassment, participants should be informed of this fact prior to agreeing to take part in the study, so that they can make an enlightened decision about whether to participate.

Freedom From Coercion   No undue pressure should be placed on participants to take part in a study. This means that researchers cannot place people under any kind of psychological pressure to take part in or remain involved in a study. Researchers are not only forbidden to order people, threaten people, or make them feel guilty in an effort to secure participation, but they are also forbidden to offer people exorbitant payments or rewards for taking risks that they might not otherwise take. It is also important that the researcher not be in a position of authority or control over participants. It is not appropriate, for instance, for a researcher to ask his or her employees to "volunteer" to be in a study. Employees may not feel that they can decline such a wonderful offer. Similarly, professors should not require their students to participate in their studies because students might worry that their grades will suffer if they refuse. But, wait a minute. Don't instructors require research participation in introductory psychology all the time? Although many courses do have a research requirement, instructors are supposed to provide students with an alternate way of satisfying this requirement. Professors should provide students in their classes an opportunity to write a paper, take an additional exam, or attend additional lectures if they do not want to participate in psychology studies. These alternative requirements should be as easily available as research studies, and they should be no more onerous.

Confidentiality   Experimenters often ask participants to reveal embarrassing or personal information, but participants have the right to confidentiality for even the most mundane answers. Many IRBs require experimenters to assign all participants a confidential experimental identification number. This number is used to label all responses from the participant. Thus, if the data were to be misplaced or fall into someone else's hands, they might know that participant #1089 recently went through a difficult breakup, but they do not know that this person was Jennifer Rene Preston who lives at 2020 East Main Street. For experimental identification numbers to be of any use, it is also important that the questionnaire not ask any information that could identify the participant. It is fine to ask age, race, ethnicity, and other questions that provide details about a person, but it is not permissible to ask participants to list current and past street addresses or other information that is reasonably unique to them. If this information were given on the question-naire, then a research assistant entering the raw data from a recent study might be able to infer that respondent #1089 is Jennifer Rene Preston, the roommate who shared an apartment with her at 2020 East Main Street. In some rare cases, it is necessary for experimenters to keep a list of the names of respondents and their identification numbers so that different sources of data can be matched together. As an example, when participants are tracked over long periods of time, it is not reasonable to expect them to remember their identification number. In these cases, experimenters keep a file that matches names and identification numbers in a locked cabinet that is not in the same location as the other locked cabinet that holds all of the partici-pants' data. As soon as the study is completed, however, this list of names is destroyed so that no one can come through later and link names to identifica-tion numbers.

Debriefing If any deception takes place during a study, the researcher must inform the participant of the deception and the reason for it as soon as possible. In addition, because of the risk-benefit rule, researchers should share information about their research hypotheses with their participants whenever they can. Finally, whenever possible, participants should leave the study in a psychological state that is at least as positive as the state they were in when they showed up for the study. For example, if you put some participants in a negative mood in a study of mood and memory, then you should probably do something to put them in a positive mood before they leave the experiment. For this same reason, experimenters are not supposed to give any feedback that will cause participants to draw inferences about themselves. Unless parti-cipants have explicitly signed up to receive psychological diagnoses as part of a research study, they should not be told how to interpret their answers to study questions. Thus, if Dr. Boggs was studying "unconscious racism" (because he thinks that some people are prejudiced but don't know it), it is ethically questionable for him to tell Jennifer Rene Preston that her test score indicates that she is much higher in unconscious racism than is the average person. (This would be especially true if the test Dr. Boggs gave her were new or if it were still undergoing psychometric refinements to improve its validity.) On the other hand, it would be fine for him to tell Jennifer that his past research suggests that the large majority of college students he has tested so far possess automatic negative associations to certain ethnic group names, and to discuss with her the wide variety of ways in which different psychologists might interpret this finding. The key idea here is that Jennifer should leave the study feeling educated or enlightened rather than distressed or inadequate.

Although this review of the ethical principles of the APA should give you a good feel for the major issues that researchers need to consider when plan-ning and conducting ethical research on human participants, you might wish to familiarize yourself with some of the details of these principles. The most recent version of the ethical principles of the APA can be found at http://www.apa.org/ethics/. The National Institutes of Health (NIH) also has a detailed set of ethical guidelines one must conform to in order to get government funding for research through their agency. They provide a useful tutorial on their ethics procedures, which you can find at http://www.nihtraining.com/ohsrsite/faq.html. Finally, the NIH also provides an excellent summary of the history behind the famous Belmont Report, which summarized the ethical conclusions of a national commission of ethical experts and led to the passage of the National Research Act in 1974. For an excellent summary of this landmark report see the Website http://ohsr.od.nih.gov/guidelines/belmont.html.

SUMMARY

This chapter focused attention on the logic, art, and ethics of discovery, beginning with the logic of discovery. The purpose of science is to uncover fundamental laws of human behavior. Skeptics may believe that psychology cannot uncover laws because it is usually impossible to predict how any given person will act at any given time. However, laws of human behavior do exist, even if we lack the ability to identify all of the causal factors that influence a specific person in a specific situation. Nevertheless, psychologists typically focus less on uncovering universal laws than on developing theories. Theories are general statements about how the world works, but they only make predictions under well-specified conditions. Good theories can be used to help generate a wide range of testable hypotheses that apply across a wide range of different situations. Hypotheses are specific predictions that are derived from theories. Hume's problem of induction and Popper's response tell us that more can be gained when researchers try to generate hypotheses that will falsify theories, than can be gained by generating hypotheses that might validate theories. An alternative to both falsifying and validating is to seek theoretical qualifications. This approach to hypothesis testing can help identify the conditions under which a theory makes accurate predictions and the conditions under which it does not. The art of discovery includes a series of inductive and deductive techniques that can help researchers generate interesting and testable ideas that might change the way we think. The *ethics of discovery are critical in psychology*. Internal review boards apply a risk-benefit analysis to ensure that research studies meet both professional and community ethical standards.

STUDY QUESTIONS

1. The goal of science is to uncover laws (universal statements of the nature of things). In contrast, psychology is a specific field of study that seeks to understand and predict how people think, feel, and behave. Unfortunately, it is difficult, if not impossible, to uncover laws that dictate how any one specific person will think, feel, or behave within any given situation. Given this fact, how can psychology be considered a scientific discipline?

2. What is the method of induction? What limitation to this method did David Hume identify? How was this limitation addressed by Karl Popper's analysis of the method of deduction?

3. In what way is validation (and related processes such as the positive test bias) a threat to science? How is this threat addressed when researchers seek either to falsify or qualify their own psychological theories?

4. The ethics of a study are evaluated, in part, by applying a risk-benefit analysis. At colleges and universities in the United States, who determines what risks and what benefits apply for any given study? What formal procedures are added to most psychology studies to minimize the risks and maximize the benefits?

5. Turn back to question 4 at the end of Chapter 1. Answer this question again, but this time consider the role of deductive theory testing and how it helps researchers make more definitive tests of theories.

NOTES

1. If you love card games, empirical research suggests that you'll love PRIME. To ask for a free deck, simply email the first author at brettpel@yahoo.com using the subject line "SEND ME PRIME!" and your preferred shipping address. If you are one of the first 100 readers to make this request, you'll get a free deck.

2. Occasionally, hypotheses may also be generated on the basis of a researcher's intuitions (in the absence of any formal theory). However, we suspect that very few hypotheses are generated in a true theoretical vacuum. In most cases, researchers who generate hypotheses intuitively base them either on tacit or implicit (i.e., unconscious) theories or on folk wisdom. Folk wisdom has roughly the same logical status as a theory. For example, the opposing ideas that "opposites attract" or that "birds of a feather flock together" can each be converted into formal theories.

3. There is actually some controversy regarding whether people in Eastern cultures commit the fundamental attribution error. Regardless of one's position on this specific controversy, our basic point remains. Scientists often draw reasonable conclusions based on the scientific method only to learn later that these conclusions were wrong.

4. When social influence agents use this tactic, they get people to agree to a "good deal" (or a prosocial request) that becomes less desirable (or more costly) once people have committed themselves. Once they become committed, people are reluctant to back out even if the deal is one they never would have agreed to up front. Salespeople often take advantage of this technique by offering potential customers a seemingly great deal on a product (such as a new car) and later informing the potential customer that they can't quite honor the original promise. ("Oh Larry, I hate to tell you this, but my boss just told me that the free air conditioner only applies to last year's model. You know what, though? I think I can still get you a discount on it.")

Moving from Fact to Truth: Validity, Reliability, and Measurement

People who say, "Lightning never strikes twice" oughtta go out and get a better lightning rod.
—William Stacy Pelham

Fact is stranger than truth.
—Junior Samples *(from the TV show* Hee Haw)

In this chapter, we discuss validity, reliability, and measurement scales as they apply to psychological research. There are many ways to think about and assess validity and reliability, and maximizing both is crucial to all forms of psychological research. As we explain later, however, it is not possible to maximize all types of validity and reliability simultaneously. This is true, for instance, because specific research methods that increase one kind of validity often have the drawback of decreasing some other kind of validity. For this reason, we suggest ways of trying to capitalize on the advantages of a given method while minimizing its disadvantages. Finally, we conclude the chapter by discussing the important question of scaling and measurement in psychological research, with an emphasis on how scaling and measurement relate to validity and reliability.

THREE STRANGE STORIES

One of us has a friend who says that everyone he has ever met is interested in at least two of the five most boring things on earth: weather, politics, train trips, golf, and aerobic exercise. We're sure that this person is wrong. We say this because we happen to know of some interesting stories or events that have to do with at least three of these five topics.

Let's start with weather. Did you know that on January 9, 1934, in Boulder, Colorado, the high temperature reached 77°? Exactly two years earlier, on January 9, 1932, the high temperature in Paris Water Works, Illinois, reached a balmy 80°.

Now in case you don't get too excited about weather, here's a story about a train trip (adapted from Plous, 1993). Not too long ago, one George D. Bryson took the train from St. Louis to New York City. Along the way, Mr. Bryson decided to stop over for a couple of days in Louisville, Kentucky, a city he had never before visited. Mr. Bryson got off in Louisville and asked a clerk at the station to recommend a local hotel. Mr. Bryson took the advice of the clerk and proceeded to the Brown Hotel, where he was given room 307. After checking in (just for fun) Mr. Bryson asked if he had any mail. The desk clerk obligingly handed him a letter addressed to "Mr. George D. Bryson, Room 307." Of course, if Rod Serling (from the *Twilight Zone*) had been telling this story, the man would have learned that there was an identical George D. Bryson who was living his life in another time dimension, exactly two days ahead of him. The real story is a little less bizarre. The last person to have occupied room 307 just happened to have been a *different* George D. Bryson, and the first Mr. Bryson had failed to pick up his last piece of mail.

Of course, this story could have been even stranger. For example, if the same thing had happened to either Jerry Derryberry, Jr. (who is a cousin of the first author) or Bubba Skaggs (who is an old friend of the first author), it'd be a little more impressive. For every guy in the world named Jerry Derryberry, Jr. or Bubba Skaggs, there must be at least 20 or 30 guys named George D. Bryson.

Speaking of Bubba Skaggs takes us to our third strange story. During the late 1970s and early 1980s, Bubba was a student at a small liberal arts college near Rome, Georgia. Bubba swears that, prior to taking a college course in beginning golf, he had never touched a golf club in his life. (On the basis of both his name and his reputation for honesty, we are strongly inclined to believe him.) On the first day of Bubba's beginning golf class, the instructor pointed across an open field to a large tree that stood about 100 yards away. An old tire was hanging from the tree and swaying gently in the warm Georgia breeze. The instructor announced that if anyone could drive a golf ball through the tire on his or her first attempt, this person would receive an A in the course and be excused from attendance. Like all the students this instructor had taught over the years, the other students in Bubba's class failed miserably in their shots at the tire. Then came Bubba. Although Bubba probably provided a textbook example of horrible form, he dropped the first golf shot of his life right in front of his target and watched gleefully as it bounced right through the middle of the tire. (The not-so-honest instructor made him take the rest of the course anyway.)

By now you may be wondering what hot winter days, George D. Brysons, and lucky golf shots have to do with research methods. The main answer has to do with your likely reaction to each of these stories. In particular, your reaction should reflect something important about your intuitive appreciation of reliability and validity. For example, we suspect that you're not planning to pack up your swimsuit this coming January and head off to Paris Water Works, Illinois, for a balmy vacation. Furthermore, despite Bubba's impressive debut as a golfer, we suspect that you're not wondering why you never saw him on the leader board at the Masters Golf Tournament. This is because you have a clear intuitive appreciation of the fact that almost all measurements include components of error or noise (i.e., good or bad luck). In simpler terms, the main thing you probably appreciate is the fact that Junior Samples was right. In a very important sense, fact is stranger than truth. The *fact* is, it was quite warm in Paris Water Works on January 9, 1932. The *truth* is, winters in Paris Water Works are typically colder than a pair of brass underwear. The *fact* is, Bubba hit a great golf shot his first time up to the tee. The *truth* is Bubba was a raw beginner who never became a highly skilled golfer. Because our only glimpses at psychological truths are based on particular facts (particular manipulations and measurements), we need to know as much as we can about the validity and reliability of our psychological manipulations and measurements. This is because the validity and reliability of our manipulations and measurements in any investigation are important determinants of the degree to which our research findings (our facts) are likely to be good approximations of the truth.

VALIDITY

Let's begin with a discussion of **validity**. The validity of a psychological statement refers to the relative accuracy or correctness of the statement. Sometimes the term is used narrowly—to describe individual propositions or research claims. At other times it is used much more broadly—to describe a particular investigation or even an entire research program. Like many other broad concepts, validity takes a variety of forms and has a range of different meanings. These forms and meanings include statistical conclusion validity, divergent and convergent validity, discriminant validity, predictive validity, and so forth (see Campbell & Fiske, 1959; Cook & Campbell, 1979; Shadish, Cook, & Campbell, 2002). In this chapter, however, we focus on the four forms of validity that provide the basic foundation you need to understand the key challenges facing empirical psychologists. These four types are internal, external, construct, and conceptual validity.

Internal Validity

Internal validity refers to the extent to which a set of research findings provides compelling information about *causality*. When a study is high in internal validity, we can confidently conclude that variations in the independent variable caused any observed changes in the dependent variable. Of course, because we can never conclude anything with absolute confidence, issues of validity are always relative rather than absolute. Given this caveat, however, laboratory experiments tend to be very high in internal validity. This is true because laboratory experiments do two very important things. First, they control for individual differences. Second, they allow researchers to isolate their independent variables from potential sources of contamination.

As an example, suppose you are a methodologically sophisticated but biologically naive researcher who wants to know if water causes plants to grow. Let's say that you purchase 20 healthy bean plants and randomly assign each plant to an experimental or a control group. You then place all the plants in a hothouse for a month and water the experimental plants twice a day, leaving the poor control plants to wither away from thirst. Finally, at the end of the month, you measure the heights or weights of the plants. Because the first author has unintentionally placed dozens of innocent houseplants in the control condition of this hypothetical experiment throughout his adult life, he knows that your control plants would be much smaller and much less healthy than your experimental plants. We hope you realize that if you perform this simple experiment carefully and sensibly, your findings would be likely to reveal an important truth about the causal role of a regular water supply in plant growth. In other words, your study would be very high in internal validity.

Internal validity is crucial to testing theories because theories are all about causality. As we noted in Chapters 1 and 2, a theory is a general statement about the *causal* relation between two or more variables. If a study does not say much about causality, then it makes a limited theoretical contribution. This point is simple enough. However, the problem is that it is surprisingly difficult to demonstrate that one variable is the cause of another. Most researchers who wish to understand causality rely heavily on the framework proposed by the 19th-century philosopher John Stuart Mill. Mill argued that three requirements must be met to establish firmly that one thing causes another. The first condition, **covariation**, is probably the easiest. For one variable to cause another, Mill argued, changes in one variable must correspond with changes in the other. As an example, high levels of frustration often go hand in hand with high levels of aggression. This suggests that frustration *might* cause aggression, but it does not guarantee it. We need to know more. For one thing, we'd want to see if aggression is causing frustration rather than the reverse. Simple covariation is consistent with both possibilities.

This leads us to Mill's second requirement, **temporal sequence**. To argue that changes in one variable cause changes in a second, the changes in the first variable must precede the changes in the second. This is not always easy to know. For instance, researchers commonly measure a wide range of variables at the same time to see if different variables covary with one another in ways that are consistent with a particular theory. With this kind of research design, it is impossible to establish temporal sequence, and thus it is impossible to know what caused what. In light of this problem, researchers sometimes measure variables over time (in prospective or longitudinal studies) to see if changes in one variable do, in fact, precede changes in a second.

Although this is a big improvement over a cross-sectional design, a researcher can never be certain that the potential cause that he or she selected was the *only* potential cause whose changes preceded changes in the other variable. For instance, if our longitudinal study of adolescent development showed that increases in kids' heights predicted their increased interest in sex, it would be unwise to conclude that height causes interest in sex. Other variables that are likely to have covaried with an increase in height (e.g., puberty) seem like much better causal candidates than height.

This leads us to Mill's third and final requirement for establishing causality, **eliminating confounds**. Unfortunately, unless a researcher can conduct a true experiment on his or her topic of interest, eliminating confounds can be extremely difficult. Let's consider a slightly trickier confound than the example of height and puberty. Specifically, consider the finding that as the national levels of ice cream sales increase, national homicide rates also increase. Do ice cream sales cause murders? Should we outlaw the production and distribution of ice cream as a means of lowering homicide rates? Probably not. In this case, it seems extremely likely that both ice cream sales and homicide rates are influenced by a third variable, namely seasonal variation in the weather. When it's hot out, people buy more ice cream. In addition, when it's hot out, people become more easily frustrated, and so they become more prone toward violence. This relation is a clear example of a type of confound that is also known as the **third-variable problem**. Because heat is causing changes in both variables, the two variables will covary with one another and give the false appearance of a causal relation. So far, so good. We figured out—and logically eliminated—the confound involving heat and ice cream. Now we know that frustration, specifically the frustration of being overheated, is the true cause of homicide. Or do we? Unfortunately, it is possible that frustration, heat, and ice cream sales are all confounded with something *else* that is the true cause of homicide. Worse yet, this true cause may be a lot less interesting than frustration. Perhaps people simply (1) drink more alcohol, (2) socialize more, (3) get out of doors more, or (4) travel more when it is hot out. All these variables are probably confounded with the weather. Furthermore, any or all of these variables could conceivably contribute to homicides. For instance, if homicides are more likely to occur when people are drinking, or when people are socializing, we have a serious problem with our explanation based on frustration.

As we explain in more detail in Chapter 7, the research design that is best suited to establishing causality (i.e., internal validity) is the laboratory experiment. The fact that laboratory experiments allow researchers to assess covariation, to establish the temporal sequence of events, and to eliminate a great number of confounds (by means of random assignment and the manipulation of variables) means that they are the ideal research tools for establishing internal validity. Nonetheless, laboratory experiments have drawbacks as well as advantages, and one of these drawbacks is that they are not always very high in a second very important kind of validity—namely, external validity.

External Validity

External validity refers to the extent to which a set of research findings provides an accurate description of what typically happens in the real world. When a study is high in external validity, or *generalizability*, we can confidently conclude that the findings of the study will apply to other people, other physical or social environments, and perhaps even other cultures. As it turns out, life is complex enough that even the most basic research findings fail to generalize to every imaginable sample or situation in which we might hope to apply them. For instance, even in the case of our simple experiment on water and plant growth, the truth behind our finding has some clear limits. If a group of researchers tried to repeat our study using cacti rather than bean plants, it is unlikely that they would observe the same results (daily watering kills most cacti). Even if we stick with bean plants, our experiment certainly does not tell us everything there is to know about plant growth. If we had kept all our plants in a dark closet rather than a hothouse or restricted their access to soil or carbon dioxide, we might have failed to realize that water plays a role in plant growth only when certain other preconditions are met. Another way to put this is that external validity is closely associated with the important concept of boundary conditions. When the boundary conditions of a specific research finding are very narrow, this finding is low in external validity.

It should go without saying that people are at least as complex as plants. For example, suppose we were interested in empathy and helping. If we manipulated empathy in the laboratory and found that it makes male college students more likely than usual to help a female student who appears to be in distress, we could be pretty certain that it was our manipulation of empathy and not something else that caused our participants to behave this way in the lab. However, we couldn't be quite so certain that a different manipulation of empathy would have the same effect on the members of a Gaelic knitting group who are asked to donate money to charity.

If you are wondering how anyone could ever keep track of all the hundreds of ways in which a research finding should be generalizable, you might be happy to learn that most of the concerns researchers have about external validity can be mapped onto only two forms of generalizability. First, researchers are often concerned about *generalizability with respect to people*. In these instances, researchers want to know that the results they observed in a given sample would occur in other samples (i.e., for other kinds of people). Researchers become particularly concerned about this issue when their samples are composed exclusively of people who are all members of the same social group (e.g., people over the age of 65, White men, firefighters, new mothers). For instance, in social and cognitive psychology, studies are often conducted on large groups of mostly White college students. This situation has led many to question whether the results of such studies generalize to more diverse groups of people (Sears, 1986). Similarly, some have criticized the entire field of psychology because the bulk of psychological research has been conducted in the United States and Western Europe (Henrich, Heine, & Norenzayan, 2010; Markus & Kitayama, 1991). If we truly wish to understand human nature, we should study a broad range of human beings.

A second concern regarding generalizability (and thus a second form of external validity) is *generalizability with respect to situations*. This second form of external validity has to do with the degree to which a set of research findings applies to different real-world settings or contexts. Researchers may become particularly worried about this issue when a research setting bears little resemblance to any real-life situations. Suppose, for instance, that a laboratory researcher frustrates some of her participants by having them work on a fascinating intellectual task that they are never allowed to complete. She finds that her frustrated participants (as compared with nonfrustrated participants) are later more likely to insult a mildly annoying **confederate** (trained research assistant) who bumps into them in the hallway. Is it safe to assume that these findings would generalize to predict real-world incidents of "road rage"? It is not at all clear. Findings in the hallway do not always travel well to the highway.

Do *any* studies tend to be high in external validity? Yes. Passive observational studies, especially when they are conducted on diverse groups of people in real-world situations, tend to be high in external validity. If you showed that incidents of road rage in a large and ethnically diverse city such as Los Angeles are more likely to occur on days when traffic (a.k.a. frustration) is heavier than usual, you would have some pretty good evidence for the external validity of your finding. On the other hand, a drawback of this approach is that you couldn't be sure that it was frustration *per se* (rather than variations in the time of day or the day of the week) that was the true cause of road rage. This is the dilemma that almost all researchers face in psychology. Laboratory studies tend to be high in internal validity but low in external validity. Passive observational studies tend to be high in external validity but low in internal validity. This concept of trade-offs between internal and external validity is sufficiently important that we expand on it in great detail in Chapters 7 and 12. For now, remember that few studies can be extremely high in both internal and external validity. As a culinary metaphor, being really high in both internal and external validity is like being really nutritious and really delicious. Both of these things are highly desirable properties of food, but they do not usually go hand in hand.

Construct Validity

A third important form of validity is **construct validity**. Construct validity refers to the extent to which the independent and dependent variables in a study truly represent the abstract, hypothetical variables of interest to the researcher. That is, it has to do with whether the manipulated and/or measured variables in a specific study accurately reflect the variables the researcher hoped to manipulate or measure. Yet another way of putting this is that construct validity is a direct reflection of the quality of a researcher's operational definitions. To the degree that a researcher's operational definitions do a good job of converting the abstract to the observable, construct validity is high.

Fortunately, some important hypothetical constructs are easy to convert to measurable events. For instance, hours of food deprivation is probably a very good proxy for the theoretical construct "hunger." Conversely, operationalizations that are less than ideal will sometimes stick out like an extra thumb. The amount of time participants in an experimental waiting room spend reading a *Zagat Restaurant Guide* is a questionable proxy for hunger because it is likely to reflect many things other than hunger (e.g., socioeconomic status, interest in fine dining). Whether a person wears eyeglasses is an even poorer index of hunger because it is difficult to dream up any possible connection between this event and hunger. We don't want to offend any hunger researchers by trivializing the richness and complexity of hunger, but one nice thing about hunger is that it's pretty easy to come up with good operational definitions of it.

On the other hand, many important hypothetical constructs are more difficult to convert to measurable events. One of the biggest challenges facing researchers who study highly unobservable cognitive or emotional constructs is maximizing the construct validity of their independent and dependent variables. Sometimes it is hard to know how to measure a variable because the theoretical construct itself is poorly understood, complex, or multifaceted. As an example, imagine that you want to know if self-esteem is associated with satisfaction in close, long-term romantic relationships. Are people who are usually happy with themselves usually happier than usual with their romantic partners? To figure this out, we need to decide what we mean by constructs such as self-esteem and romantic satisfaction. One popular view of self-esteem is that it is merely the sum of people's positive and negative attitudes about themselves (Marsh, 1993). A second view emphasizes the idea that self-esteem contains components of both competence ("Am I good at stuff?") and likability ("Do people like me?"; see Tafarodi & Swann, 1995). A third view is that self-esteem consists of both what you *think* about yourself (your cognitions) and how you *feel* about yourself (your affect; Pelham & Swann, 1989). Furthermore, whereas some people view self-esteem as a stable personality trait, others might argue that it is better understood as a state than as a trait (Heatherton & Polivy, 1991). Finally, the two authors of this textbook disagree about how likely it is that implicit (i.e., unconscious) self-esteem exists, and if so how it ought to be measured (cf., DeHart, Pelham, & Tennen, 2006, with Buhrmester, Blanton, & Swann, 2011). And if you think self-esteem is hard to get a handle on, remember that we still haven't decided how to assess romantic satisfaction. We don't want to overstate this problem. There is actually pretty good consensus regarding the best ways to measure constructs such as self-esteem and romantic satisfaction. Nonetheless, part of the challenge, and fun, of research is coming up with good measures of what you wish to study. When researchers begin to disagree with one another about the best way to measure something, things often get interesting. It then becomes the challenge of researchers in a field to determine whether different operationalizations of the same underlying construct have different consequences for different aspects of human thought, feeling, and behavior.

Conceptual Validity

The final form of validity we wish to emphasize is **conceptual validity**. Conceptual validity refers to how well a specific research hypothesis maps onto the broader theory that it was designed to test. Recall from Chapter 2 that the deductive method asks you to develop hypotheses from general theories, which are then tested against observations. For these tests to be informative, however, the hypotheses must first be appropriate to the theory. As a specific example, recall from Chapter 2 that Festinger and Carlsmith (1959) hypothesized that people would be more likely to change their attitudes to be consistent with a lie if they were paid $1 as opposed to $20 for telling the lie. This specific hypothesis was derived from a much more general theory. The theory, cognitive dissonance theory, states that people have a need to resolve inconsistencies in their thoughts and/or actions. Most people can readily see that this specific hypothesis follows logically from cognitive dissonance theory. For the sake of comparison, let's imagine that Festinger and Carlsmith (1959) had decided to test cognitive dissonance theory by testing the specific hypothesis that people prefer $100 to being poked in the eye with a sharp stick. After all, with a little creative stretching, an interesting theory like cognitive dissonance theory *could* conceivably be used to generate this incredibly uninteresting prediction. If most people possess the belief that they love being paid and hate being poked, then shouldn't it arouse cognitive dissonance to choose a poke in the eye over $100? So shouldn't people minimize their dissonance by gravitating toward the money?

It seems like a safe bet that if Festinger and Carlsmith had run this alternative study, they would have observed very strong support for their predictions. In fact, unless their participants were downright crazy, it seems likely that *no one* would have chosen a stick in the eye over $100. After dozens of successful replications of this finding, perhaps dissonance theory would have been elevated to the exalted status of a psychological law! Perhaps not. The problem here is twofold. First of all, this kind of prediction is not really one of the first things to come to mind when one gives some serious thought to cognitive dissonance theory. In other words, the prediction does not follow all that logically from cognitive dissonance theory. Second, it is very easy to generate this prediction in the complete absence of cognitive dissonance theory. Worse yet, most of the theories that do readily suggest this specific prediction are extremely obvious, extremely well-established, or both.

Most psychologists would probably agree that the basic hypothesis in Festinger and Carlsmith's $1 and $20 study did follow quite logically from cognitive dissonance theory. Furthermore, at the time, very few other theories existed that would generate the same predictions. (Remember that self-perception theory didn't come around until much later.) When there is clear consensus regarding the kind of hypotheses that follow logically from a theory, it is easy for researchers from different theoretical camps to agree about the best way to test the theory. At times, however, researchers disagree, and these disagreements often reveal differences in people's preexisting assumptions about human nature.

As a more contemporary example of a research finding that is high in conceptual validity, consider a provocative study of close relationships conducted by Murray, Holmes, and Griffin (1996). Murray et al. developed a theory regarding positive illusions in close relationships. Positive illusions are unrealistically favorable views of one's relationship partner. As an example, if Sondra is in love with **Diederik**, she might believe that Diederik is as handsome as Brad Pitt and as funny as Woody Allen. In reality, Diederik might be about as funny as Brad Pitt and about as handsome as Woody Allen. Some theories of clinical and social psychology suggest that these unrealistic beliefs would wreak havoc in Sondra and Diederik's relationship. After all, there's a word for people who are out of touch with reality, and this word is "crazy." However, Murray et al. assumed that for a relationship to survive the day-to-day threats and crises that always come along (e.g., a minor argument, a slightly flirtatious phone call from Brad Pitt), most people need to believe that they have latched onto someone who is truly special, someone who approaches their ideal partner. In a sense, then, illusions about one's partner are a healthy defense against the sometimes harsh realities of close relationships.

But how could you ever *measure* illusions? How could you know whether Sondra's view of Diederik is unrealistically favorable? A simple way that Murray et al. developed was to compare what people thought about their partners with what *these partners* thought about themselves. If Sondra's general evaluations of Diederik are much more favorable than Diederik's own self-evaluations, it seems pretty likely that she has developed an overly generous view of Diederik. Of course, without subjecting Diederik to dozens of objective tests of his true level of wonderfulness, we can never know with absolute certainty whether Sondra has overestimated Diederik's wonderfulness (e.g., the degree to which he is kind, patient, understanding, a good poker player, etc.). But if we make some reasonable assumptions, we can be pretty darn sure—just as we can be pretty darn sure that people who are paid $20 to tell a white lie won't sit around wondering why they told the lie.

So far, so good. Murray et al. found a simple way to assess something that, at first blush, would seem very difficult to measure. But where to go next? Recall that their theory suggested that optimistic illusions in close relationships are *good* for people. The next step, then, was to decide what "good" is and to measure it. This turned out to be a lot easier than measuring illusions. For example, one way to measure whether or not a relationship is "good" is to ask people how satisfied they are with their relationships. Murray et al. assessed relationship satisfaction using a simple, reliable, and valid measure, and they then tested to see whether people whose partners viewed them in unrealistically favorable ways were, in fact, more satisfied with their relationships. They were. That is, the more people's partners idealized them (relative to how they viewed themselves), the more satisfied people reported being with their relationships. People who were idealized by their partners also reported experiencing less conflict in their relationships, suggesting that the benefits of being idealized were pretty general. Finally, Murray et al. observed this same pattern of results in both dating and married couples—suggesting that their model applies to at least two different kinds of important relationships.

To appreciate why Murray et al.'s study was high in conceptual validity, you should also know that a few other theories in social psychology make predictions opposite to those made by Murray et al.'s theory. For example, an interpersonal variation on cognitive dissonance theory would suggest that it would make people feel uncomfortable to know that someone they loved held views of them that were radically inconsistent with (i.e., dissonant with) their own self-views (see also Swann, 1987). Murray et al.'s study was high in conceptual validity largely because the theory of positive illusions makes unique predictions. Finally, notice that Murray et al. did *not* ask participants who were idealized by their partners if they preferred being idealized to receiving a sharp stick in the eye. Murray et al.'s theory of positive illusions *could* be used to generate this prediction, but a study testing this prediction wouldn't be very high in conceptual validity.

If you think that conceptual validity sounds a lot like construct validity, you are correct. In addition to the fact that both forms of validity start with the same three letters, both construct and conceptual validity have to do with how well what a researcher did maps onto what the researcher meant, said, or should have done. However, there is an important difference between these two forms of validity. Whereas construct validity has to do with how well a specific manipulation or measure maps onto the specific hypothetical construct in which a researcher is interested (i.e., is spitting on someone a good measure of aggression?), conceptual validity is much broader. It has more to do with whether the researcher should have been interested in that specific hypothetical construct in the first place (e.g., does dissonance theory *really* lead to this novel hypothesis about aggression, or does the prediction come out of left field?). In short, construct validity has more to do with specific manipulations and measures in specific studies, and conceptual validity has more to do with research hypotheses and, in some cases, entire research programs.

RELIABILITY

In addition to validity, another crucial aspect of almost all research is **reliability**, which refers to the consistency or repeatability of a measure or observation. For instance, suppose we have a theory that there are two types of people in the world: (1) people who are "partiers" and love meeting new people, being in loud social gatherings, and staying out all night and (2) people who are "wallflowers" and prefer being by themselves, staying in quiet settings, and going to bed early. If our study has a reliable measure of this psychological construct, then the group of people categorized as "partiers" on one week should be included in this same group a week later. If we do not have a reliable measure, then these people will fall into different categories from week to week simply due to random factors that alter their test scores from week to week. Notice that by this definition, a reliable measure need not be valid. Suppose, for instance, that we decide to categorize people as "partiers" if they wear belts and as "wallflowers" if they wear suspenders. It turns out that the preference for belts versus suspenders has nothing to do with how people act in social situations. The belt-suspender measure thus is not a valid indicator of the partier-wallflower dimension. But, this measure could be reliable. If the same people wear belts day after day, week after week, then our measure would reliably categorize people into two different distinct categories. Our measure would do this, even though it does not validly categorize people. Of course, reliability is of greatest use if a measure is also valid. Let's suppose that a researcher develops a 10-item questionnaire that assesses self-esteem. If this measure is valid (i.e., it does measure self-esteem) and it is reliable (i.e., it gives a consistent picture of people's self-esteem), then it will provide a powerful tool for testing theories about self-esteem. Researchers who use this scale will know that they are likely to get the same (valid) information about a person's true self-esteem every time they use this measure.

How do you assess the reliability of a measure? If you believe that your measure assesses a stable individual difference, the most sensible way is to assess **test-retest reliability** by measuring (or testing) a group of individuals at one time and then having them come back a second time to take the test again. If people who scored high, medium, and low at "time 1" are still scoring high, medium, and low (respectively) at "time 2," then you have pretty good evidence that the measure is reliable. Not surprisingly, researchers typically are most impressed with test-retest reliability after a long period of time has passed. It would not be particularly impressive if you test a group of participants at 1:00 in the afternoon and then test them again four minutes later—only to find out that people give similar answers at 1:04. In contrast, if you give this measure to fourth graders and find that scores in the fourth grade strongly predict scores at age 40, then this would be impressive indeed.

Although longer time periods generally are more impressive than shorter time periods, there is an upper limit to what one can ask of a measure. This is because people do change. Suppose, for instance, that you ask a group of 14-year-olds if they think the legal age for driving an automobile should be dropped from age 16 to age 14. Many would say yes because they feel able to drive at their age and think such a law would be reasonable. If you return two years later, many who said yes might now say no. Is this evidence that this measure of "driving age attitudes" is not reliable? Probably not. Over this two-year period, attitudes on this issue probably changed. In particular, attitudes probably changed for many respondents on the day of their 16th birthday. ("If I waited until I turned 16 to drive and it didn't kill me, then I see no reason why others can't wait this long!") Clearly, it can be impressive when responses on a measure are reliable over a long period, but the longer the time period, the more people actually do change. Thus, the less one should expect to observe test-retest reliability if a measure truly is valid. Because people may change between testing sessions, most assessments of test-retest reliability use long enough time periods so that most respondents may have changed their frame of mind, but not so long that they will have changed their way of life. This typically translates into roughly a two- to four-week gap between test sessions, but the time frame can vary quite a bit depending on the topic being studied.

Interestingly, many assessments of reliability use the shortest time period possible and assess reliability during a single testing session. Participants come to the laboratory once, and the researcher uses their responses at this single session to estimate the measure's reliability. You may be wondering how this is possible. If Dr. Swinkels only gives the measure one time, how can he use people's responses on this measure to estimate whether they will be consistent over test sessions? Although this seems bizarre at first glance, you can estimate test-test reliability in a very simple way with a single test session. Suppose you have a 10-item measure assessing self-esteem. You give this measure just once to a sample of 200 people, and now you want to estimate whether people will remain consistent in their self-esteem ratings over time. Again, you gave this test just once, right? Or, did you? In a sense, you actually gave this measure *ten times*. If each question is viewed as a separate test session, then you have a basis for determining whether people remained consistent over the "ten times" they took your measure.

This approach to assessing validity is termed **internal consistency**, and Table 3.1 shows bogus data for two hypothetical measures of self-esteem. Both measures assess self-esteem by having five participants (Brett, Jeb, Uri, Steve, and Hart) rate the degree to which various positive traits apply to them using a scale that ranges from 1 = "not at all" to 7 = "extremely." Test X uses the traits "proud," "confident," "capable," "secure," and "competent." Test Z uses the

Table 3.1 Responses to two hypothetical self-esteem scales. Participants rate how much each trait applies to them (on a scale from 1 = "not at all" to 7 = "extremely"). One test has high internal consistency, and the other test has low internal consistency.

Test X	Person	Proud	Confident	Capable	Secure	Competent	Test Score
	Brett	6	6	4	4	3	23
	Jeb	5	5	3	3	3	19
	Uri	4	4	3	2	3	16
	Steve	3	3	2	2	1	11
	Hart	2	3	2	1	1	9
	Item total	20	21	14	12	11	

Test Z	Person	Proud	Happy	Lucky	Strong	Funny	Test Score
	Brett	6	4	2	1	3	16
	Jeb	5	5	3	3	1	17
	Uri	4	6	3	2	3	18
	Steve	3	3	4	2	1	13
	Hart	2	3	2	4	3	14
	Item total	20	21	14	12	11	

traits "proud," "happy," "lucky," "strong," and "funny." Table 3.1 gives the ratings that these fictitious people gave to each of the traits on these two hypothetical scales. If you look at the ratings of the individual participants in Table 3.1, you'll see that one scale has high internal reliability whereas the other does not. Before continuing, take a close look at the table and see if you can figure out which scale has high internal consistency and which one does not. Are you done?

We hope you can see that the test with a high degree of internal consistency is Test X. If you are not sure why, look at the responses to "proud" in Test X and Test Z. On both tests, Brett gave himself the highest rating (6), Jeb gave himself the second-highest rating (5), and so on. This same rank order is preserved for every item in Test X (allowing for some ties), but it is not preserved for every item in Test Z. People who reported feeling proudest on Test X also reported feeling the most confident, capable, secure, and competent. In this sense, five separate attempts to measure self-esteem give much the same picture: Brett and Hart are at the extremes, and Jeb, Uri, and Steve are in the middle. A much different picture emerges with Test Z. The person who reported being the proudest did not report being the happiest. This is not surprising because even proud people such as Brett can have unhappy days. Maybe he just found out that the used minivan he bought three days ago is going to need a new engine. Along the same lines, Brett reported being much prouder than Hart, but Hart reported being much stronger than Brett. Perhaps Hart's lack of pride is why he feels a need to compensate by bragging about his physical prowess. In short, the four items in Test Z do not give a consistent picture of who has high self-esteem and who has low self-esteem. The items in Test Z do not all appear to be measuring the same thing.

Table 3.1 also reveals a very important consequence of using tests with high internal reliability. Examine the totals for these five different people on the two different tests. Notice that Test X yields a wide range of scores (from 9 to 23). In contrast, the range of scores on Test Z is much narrower (from 13 to 18). The greater variability in scores for Test X make it a better measure for testing most psychological theories because we often test theories by determining whether one or more variables covary (i.e., correlate) with one another in a way that is predicted by a theory. (We elaborate on this point further in Chapter 6.) The more that individual scores on a test or questionnaire vary, the more potential there is for these individual scores to covary with other scores. Thus, for example, if someone believes that people with high self-esteem should report higher life satisfaction, Test X will easily make it possible to see if this is true, whereas Test Z will not. After all, how well can scores on Test Z covary with scores on life satisfaction if the scores on Test Z never vary to begin with?

Before leaving the topic of reliability, we consider a third way that reliability is sometimes assessed. This third form of reliability applies when human judges make some kind of psychological ratings, and it is known as **interobserver agreement**. Also known as **interrater reliability**, it refers to the degree to which different judges independently agree upon an observation or judgment. When you ask your roommate or romantic partner whether your maroon sweatshirt clashes with your green pants, you are demonstrating an implicit understanding of one aspect of this important form of reliability. If you are the only one who thinks your maroon sweatshirt looks good with the green pants but you both agree that it goes well with the black pants, you would be wise to go with the black ones. For the black pair, your informal measure of interobserver agreement is relatively high. Many important real-world judgments involve interobserver agreement. For example, performances in figure skating, gymnastics, and diving typically are evaluated by a group of several highly trained judges. Each judge carefully and independently observes each performance and provides a single numerical rating of the performance. These ratings are then averaged together to yield a summary judgment of the quality of a performance. Moreover, the judges of many of these athletic competitions appear to have some appreciation of the fact that the individual ratings should be consistent with one another. In an effort to make their ratings more consistent, judges sometimes discard the highest and lowest ratings before determining the final score (e.g., for a floor routine that received ratings of 9.5, 9.8, 9.8, 9.8, 9.8, 9.9, and 10.0, the 9.5 and 10.0 would be discarded prior to averaging).

It is important to note that the ratings of multiple judges are useful only if they are made by trained and independent judges. Depending on the complexity of what is being coded, raters may need to spend several minutes, several hours, or even several months learning a coding scheme before they are ready to serve as judges. For example, if you want to determine whether the participants in your research project are clinically depressed, your raters will all need to undergo extensive training in some kind of structured clinical interview technique. Most such techniques require a minimum of a couple of weeks of training, even for a person who is already trained in many facets of clinical psychology. On the other hand, if you merely need to decide how frequently your participants smile during a 4-minute videotaped interaction with a confederate, you might be able to develop your own coding scheme and train yourself and your two experienced research assistants to make reliable ratings of these smiles in a couple of hours. Regardless of the complexity of a coding task, judges are free to discuss their ratings with one another in detail during the training phases of this aspect of research. However, once they actually begin making their ratings for a given research project, they should not discuss their ratings with other judges. The main reason for this rule is that violating the principle of independence of ratings can falsely increase the reliability of a set of ratings without necessarily increasing their validity. If you ask your sister what she thinks of your maroon sweatshirt, and she checks with your mom before answering, you don't really have the opinions of two separate raters. And if your mom happens to be a big fan of green pants, you might not make a valid decision about your wardrobe.

Although the use of multiple judges is important for establishing interobserver agreement, it is also important to note that the ultimate goal of measurement in research is to achieve a high level of reliability rather than a high number of judges. When interobserver agreement is high, researchers often have two or three raters judge a subset of all their observations, measure the level of interrater reliability, and then fall back on the ratings of one or two raters once it has been shown that the behavior in question can be judged with a very high degree of reliability by the raters in question. In other cases, when it is harder to get a reliable set of ratings about a behavior, researchers may make use of a team of multiple raters for all their observations.

When are the ratings of a group of judges most likely to serve as a key variable of interest to a researcher? This typically occurs when the researcher is studying a construct that cannot be measured using self-ratings or when a behavior that cannot be assessed in a simple physical way (such as the number of times that a participant presses a shock button or whether a participant gives money to someone who asks for it). Behavioral ratings from multiple raters are particularly likely to be useful when participants themselves do not have the ability or the motivation to introspect on their experiences and report what is happening. For example, if we want to determine how nervous people appear to be during an interaction with an attractive confederate, it would probably be unwise to ask people questions about their own nonverbal behavior. However, it should be no problem to train a group of research assistants to make these kinds of ratings objectively and reliably.

RELIABILITY, VALIDITY, AND THE "MORE IS BETTER" RULE

Although reliability can be broken down into at least three different categories, one idea is common to all three forms of reliability—the idea that the reliability of most measures is likely to increase as we increase the number of observers, observations, or occasions that go into the measure. All else being equal, ten raters usually produce more reliable ratings than five raters; 20-item self-esteem scales are usually more reliable than 10-item scales; and an assessment of people's attitudes that was based on observations made at four different times is typically more reliable than an assessment collected at a single session. If it is not intuitively obvious to you why this is the case, consider the following thought question. Imagine that you are told that you will be paid $1,000,000 if you can beat NBA superstar LeBron James in a game of one-on-one basketball. LeBron generously offers to let you start with the ball, and he tells you that he will allow you to decide how many points will constitute a game. Taking it as a given that your chances of winning would be extremely slim, would you prefer to play a game to 20 baskets or a game to one basket? If you have good intuitions about reliability, you should greatly prefer the 1-basket game. In a 1-basket game, you have a slim chance to get off a quick shot before LeBron decides to take you seriously. And of course, if your shot happens to fall, you would win the game. In a game to 20 baskets, however, the likelihood that you could string together 20 such lucky shots would be much, much lower. The principle behind this is that a small number of observations is more likely than a large number of observations to reflect the operation of chance or error.

This thought exercise should also make it clear that reliability and validity are not completely separate concepts. After all, if a 20-basket game gives

LeBron James a much better chance of beating you, then the 20-basket game must be higher in validity than the 1-basket game (unless you happen to be Derrick Rose or Lincoln Polan). This is generally true; more reliable measures are usually more valid measures. One good way to think about this is that reliability is a *necessary* but not a *sufficient* condition for validity. As a physical example of this, imagine that you are given an oversized ruler that has been mislabeled with 1-inch marks made at 4-inch intervals. The ruler would probably yield highly reliable or consistent measurements, but the measurements obviously would not be valid. Now imagine that you are asked to make some extremely precise measurements and are given a metal yardstick whose length is perfectly accurate only at a temperature of 70°. At lower temperatures the yardstick would shrink a little, and at higher temperatures it would expand a little. Although this yardstick would yield measurements that aren't perfectly reliable, the validity of these measurements would still be very high. And the *more* measurements we take of something using this yardstick (under a variety of different temperatures), the more closely we would approximate the object's true length—because the underestimates and the overestimates would begin to average out.

The ancient measuring unit known as a cubit illustrates this point in a slightly different way. The ancient definition of a cubit is that it is the length of a man's arm from the elbow to the fingertips. For most men today, this is somewhere around 18 inches. If we modernize this male-centered measure to include the 51 percent of the human population that happens to be female, the value would change a little, but the concept is obviously the same. A "true" cubit, by definition, is the average value of a cubit for everyone on the planet. However, if we ask people to report the length of a specific object in cubits, we would get different answers from different people. Whereas a typical NBA center might correctly report that a DVD is only a fifth of a cubit wide (because his arms are so long), a typical jockey might correctly report that a DVD is about a third of a cubit wide. There would still be some agreement (some reliability) in a large set of such measures as long as we have people measure objects of greatly differing sizes (the measurements of both the center and the jockey would clearly show, for example, that SUVs are much wider than DVDs). When averaged across a reasonable number of judges, the reliability of this method for assessing length would be high, but it certainly wouldn't be perfect. However, if we average the length estimates (in cubits) for a variety of standard objects provided by *every person on earth*, the average length estimate for each object—by definition—would be perfectly valid. For example, if a cubit proved to be 16.81 inches (because that's exactly how long the average human arm is from elbow to fingertip), we could rest assured that the average length estimate we'd receive for an object that is exactly 16.81 inches long would be exactly 1 cubit (assuming, of course, that people are properly trained to measure things in cubits). In other words, adding a large number of measures together not only increases reliability, but it usually increases validity as well.

One final point to consider where reliability is concerned is that all three common forms of reliability can be readily quantified using some relatively simple statistics. For example, a common statistical indicator of internal consistency is *Cronbach's alpha* (α). Alpha values strongly resemble correlations, and they are closely tied to the average correlation that exists between multiple indicators of a single construct. Similarly, to assess temporal stability, researchers can simply take a measurement on two different occasions and correlate people's scores at time 1 with their scores at time 2. In this case, the statistical indicator of reliability in question doesn't resemble a correlation; it *is* a correlation. Appropriately enough, it is referred to as a test-retest correlation. In contrast, no statistics easily compute the degree of internal, external, construct, or conceptual validity possessed by a given study. Most forms of reliability can be assessed statistically; most forms of validity require not only statistical tests but also a healthy dose of logic and intuition.

MEASUREMENT SCALES

In our discussions of validity and reliability, we have thus far ignored an important set of distinctions among different kinds of measures. Most psychologists and statisticians identify four distinct kinds of variables or measurement scales, and these distinctions correspond roughly to the mathematical complexity or sensitivity of the different scales. As one might think, more sensitive scales can provide more information, but they also require stronger measurement assumptions. We now review the four types of scales and discuss their relevance to validity.

Nominal Scales

The simplest kind of measurement scale (or the "lowest level") is a **nominal, or categorical, scale.** As the word "nominal" implies, nominal scales involve meaningful but potentially arbitrary and nonnumerical names or categories. A person's sex is a good example of a nominal variable. For most practical purposes, it takes on only two mutually exclusive and exhaustive values, and these values have nothing to do with counting or quantity. If we want to keep track of sex in a survey study, we could code men as 1 and women as 2. However, we could just as meaningfully code women as 1 and men as 2 (or code men as 1492 and code women as 1776). This is because numbers in nominal scales work simply as tags or labels (names) for different categories. Product identification numbers, license plate numbers, social security numbers, months or days of birth, and telephone numbers are good examples of nominally scaled variables. Many clinical diagnostic categories and health outcomes also constitute nominal variables. A bone is either broken or intact. A woman is either pregnant or not. A patient might or might not qualify as schizophrenic, autistic, or clinically depressed. A golf shot either falls into a cup or it doesn't. There is no in-between, and there are no numerical properties that are inherently a part of these arbitrarily assigned numerical categories.

Ordinal Scales

The first step toward scales that do have clear numerical properties is **ordinal scales**. As the name implies, ordinal scales are scales that involve order or ranking. A person's birth-order or ranking in a dessert-eating contest is an example of an ordinal variable. Like categorical scales, ordinal scales involve a set of mutually exclusive and exhaustive labels. In the case of ordinal scales, however, there is a clear ordering or hierarchy to the labels. Just as a ranking of first always precedes a ranking of second, a ranking of 145th always precedes a ranking of 146th. Although ordinal scales provide some information about the relative value or position of different people or things (e.g., the *L.A. Times* is the largest newspaper in the city; Shira finished third in the state bench-press championships), they are not at all sensitive to the absolute differences between these things. Knowing that you finished second in a three-person footrace against both the champion sprinter Usain Bolt and the aging rapper Heavy D doesn't tell us much about your precise running speed.

Of course, unscrupulous researchers, advertisers, and reporters may sometimes take advantage of the imperfect or relative properties of ordinal scales by selectively reporting rankings that portray an observation in the best possible light. For example, there is a story that back in the early days of the Cold War, President John F. Kennedy ran a two-person, long-distance footrace against Soviet Premier Nikita Khrushchev. It is said that *Pravda* gave a technically correct but misleading report of the outcome of this race. Specifically, the newspaper reported that both men ran in a grueling long-distance footrace (without revealing that they were the only ones in the race). *Pravda* further reported that whereas Khrushchev finished in second place, Kennedy finished next to last.

Interval Scales

Whereas ordinal scales do not provide any information about absolute differences between stimuli, interval scales do. **Interval scales** are measurement scales that make use of real numbers designating amounts to reflect relative differences in magnitude. Unlike ordinal scales, interval scales can sometimes take on negative values ($-12°F$ is a value on an interval scale of temperature). Most importantly, the unit in an interval scale corresponds to a specific amount of the construct being measured. Consider adult body weight. If we measure weight in pounds, then each measurement unit (one pound) is equivalent regardless of a person's weight. Thus, the difference between 125 and 135 is the same as the difference between 200 and 210. Although this is perfectly obvious, such properties often do not occur with measures of psychological constructs. Imagine that you have a depression inventory that gives all respondents a score between 0 and 50. Although the difference between 10 and 15 is still *numerically* the same as the difference between 40 and 45, the difference in the *level of depression* implied by these two sets of scores will not necessarily be identical. It may be that people with scores of 10 and 15 would appear to have very similar levels of depression by any assessment. In contrast, the gap between 40 and 45 might be the difference between a high suicide risk and little or no suicide risk. If so, a greater difference in depression is implied by five units at the high end of the scale than five units at the low end of the scale. Though many physical measures have interval (or even ratio) properties, it's hard to establish true interval properties of psychological measures (e.g., love, fear). Nonetheless, many such measures come close enough to being interval scales that this is how they're usually classified.

Ratio Scales

Ratio scales are very much like interval scales except that they have an important additional property. Unlike the lower-level scales, ratio scales always have a true zero point—at which none of the quantity under consideration is present. (This means that ratio scales can never take on values less than zero.) For instance, someone who has smoked 0 cigarettes in the past has a complete absence of past cigarette smoking. One practical consequence of the nature of ratio scales is that they allow us to speak meaningfully about ratios of values. For example, it is correct to say that a 90-year-old is twice as old as a 45-year-old, that a 50-pound bag of potatoes is five times as heavy as a 10-pound bag, or that participants in an experimental condition were given ten times the monetary reward given to participants in a control condition. However, it would not be correct to say that a person with an IQ of 140 is twice as smart as a person with an IQ of 70 (which is why the first author didn't feel much like he was being flattered when his older brother used to tell him that he had "the IQ of two morons"). Similarly, it would also be incorrect to say that the participants in the experimental condition who received ten times as much money as those in the control condition were ten times as happy as those who received the smaller rewards.

The Validity of Measurement Assumptions

Before leaving our discussion of measurement scales, it is important to stress a point we've alluded to twice now: One cannot determine the properties of a measurement scale simply by looking at the numbering system on the response scale. By this, we mean that it is not possible to create a ratio scale merely by constructing a measure whose possible values start at 0 and that moves in seemingly equal increments up to some maximum value. For example, if you want to know how much people like Pepsi and you construct a liking scale that ranges from 0 to 7, it would *not* be safe to assume that a person who reports that her liking for Pepsi is a 6 likes Pepsi exactly twice as much as someone who reports that her liking for Pepsi is a 3. Likewise, it would be virtually impossible to know whether a score of 0 on this scale truly reflects an absolute absence of any liking for Pepsi. Even scales that might appear to have interval or ratio properties on the surface lose these properties when we are assessing psychological rather than physical constructs. For example, as we noted previously, physical distance can be assessed using a ratio scale. If you live exactly 1.3 miles from St. Edward's University, you live exactly half as far from St. Ed's as someone who lives exactly 2.6 miles from St. Ed's. On the other hand, if you sit exactly 1.3 feet from an attractive confederate, it is *not* safe to assume that you *like* this confederate exactly twice as much as someone who sits 2.6 feet away. This does not mean that it is unwise to measure attraction by assessing seating distance (e.g., see Algeier & Byrne, 1973). Instead, it simply means that researchers need to be careful about the kind of conclusions they draw when they assess psychological constructs using scales that might sometimes qualify as interval or ratio scales when used to measure physical constructs (see Blanton & Jaccard, 2006, for a more complete discussion).

SUMMARY

The four forms of validity are internal, external, construct, and conceptual. Although the distinctions between these four forms of validity are important, the primary point to remember is that each of the four forms of validity has to do with a different form of psychological accuracy or "truth." Am I correct in inferring causality from a correlation (internal validity)? Am I correct when I try to generalize my laboratory findings to the real world (external validity)? Am I correct when I argue that my manipulation makes people angry rather than afraid (construct validity)? Am I correct in concluding that my series of three field studies validated one theory rather than another (conceptual validity)? In a similar fashion, the three forms of reliability—test-retest, internal consistency, interrater—are different from one another, but each focuses on an issue related to consistency. Is my test sorting people in a consistent manner over time (test-retest reliability)? Are the individual items of my test contributing to a consistent image of people (internal consistency)? Are different judges consistently making similar judgments of identical stimuli (interrater reliability)? A clear understanding of

levels of measurement (i.e., measurement scales) is important. Higher level measurements, such as ratio scales, typically yield more information about participants, but it can be tricky to decide whether a psychological scale truly qualifies as an interval or ratio scale.

In case we haven't quite driven home the point that validity and reliability are extremely important aspects of psychological research, we repeat this familiar theme. As a matter of fact, you could think of this entire textbook as a detailed recipe for maximizing the validity and reliability in psychological research. If you'd like your methodological world simplified even further, consider that *everything* really boils down to validity. As important as reliability is, it is only of value insofar as it is paired with validity. Thus, the major goal of this book is to outline things researchers can do to maximize the validity of their theories, their methods, and their conclusions. Before we can do this, we first have to discuss some basic tools you'll need to run valid research. The next chapter begins this process by addressing a very simple question: how do you ask a question?

STUDY QUESTIONS

1. What is the difference between external and internal validity? Which of these two forms of validity is maximized by the use of
    (a) random assignment to conditions,
    (b) random selection, and (c) the elimination of confounds?

2. Reliability does not generally guarantee validity. Consider the specific case of external validity. What is the difference between external validity and reliability? Can an experimental finding be both reliable and externally invalid?

3. Explain the logic of inferring whether or not a test will have high test-retest reliability by examining the internal consistency of the test. Why are measures with higher internal consistency better suited for testing psychological theories regarding covariation?

4. The subtitle of this book alludes to a story in which Sir Walter Raleigh placed a wager that he could measure something elusive, namely the weight of smoke. Both construct validity and conceptual validity refer to things more elusive than the weight of smoke, because both try to link real observations to hypothetical constructs or abstract theories. What are these two forms of validity, and how do they differ from one another? How might you determine if a given study, or program of research, is high in these two forms of validity?

5. Suppose you are interested in measuring people's weight. Provide an example of a nominal, ordinal, interval, and ratio scale that would accomplish this. If you are assessing a psychological construct (e.g., self-esteem) with an externally valid scale that ranges from 0 ("low self-esteem") to 7 ("high self-esteem"), which levels of measurement are likely satisfied and which are questionable?

Moving from Notions to Numbers: Psychological Measurement

In early November of 2000, while your authors were working diligently (so they say) on a previous edition of this research methods textbook, a faulty research method may have been changing modern American history. Specifically, voters in Palm Beach County, Florida, were voting for the U.S. President using the new "butterfly ballots" that had been designed to improve the voting process. Unlike the old ballots that preceded them, the new butterfly ballots put all of the candidates for U.S. President on a single page. Although this seemed like a good idea in principle, it turned out that the butterfly ballot created many more problems than it solved.

As shown in Figure 4.1, voters were supposed to punch a hole next to the name of their preferred presidential candidate, but the order of the holes and the order of the candidates did not match up in an ideal way. The Democratic party candidate (Al Gore) was the second choice in the left-hand column of the ballot, but the Reform party candidate (Pat Buchanan) was the second choice in the center column, where people actually punched their votes. Many people have argued that this confusing ballot cost Al Gore the presidency. Despite the fact that Palm Beach County was a stronghold of the Democratic party, a large number of voters punched the hole that corresponded to Pat Buchanan. On most issues, Buchanan's platform was considerably more conservative than George W. Bush's platform. Furthermore, Palm Beach County was not only a Democratic party stronghold, but it was also populated heavily by Jewish retirees—a group that had never been known for supporting Pat Buchanan. Statisticians who analyzed this situation estimated that this imperfect ballot cost Al Gore about 6,600 votes, more than ten times the number of votes he needed to overtake George W. Bush and win the 2000 presidential election. Thus, this poorly designed "questionnaire" may have changed modern U.S. history.

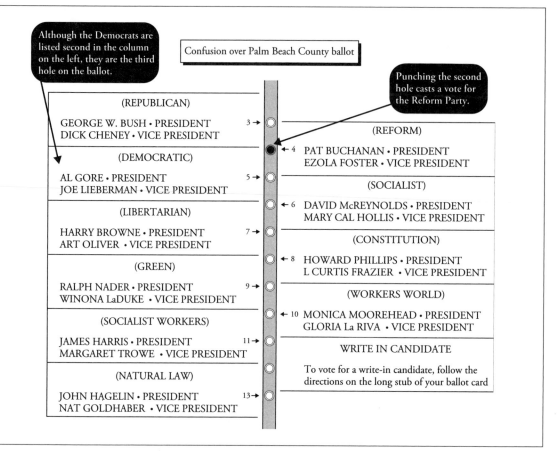

Figure 4.1
History suggests that this was a hard question to answer. Some political analysts have argued that this ballot really isn't quite as confusing as Gore's supporters cracked it up to be. With a little patience and common sense, it would seem that most anyone could use it to vote correctly. Without delving too deeply into this controversy, we simply point out that perhaps this ballot was less than ideal for the senior citizens of Palm Beach County, Florida. Unless you need reading glasses or have recently re-entered college after working for 40 years, this ballot probably seems easier to you than it was for the people who had to use it to vote. The point is not that the butterfly ballot was the worst imaginable nightmare in the history of voting; it is that the ballot was imperfect.

This highly publicized story about the butterfly ballot illustrates one of the central problems facing researchers who wish to assess people's beliefs, desires, moods, intentions, personality traits, and, yes, voting preferences. How do you translate the unobservable internal states of human beings into things that can be tallied, averaged, or correlated with some other meaningful value? If we couldn't translate psychological states or properties into numbers or values, psychology would not be a science. One of the primary points of this chapter is that the process of converting psychological notions (e.g., feelings of self-esteem) into numbers (e.g., a numerical score on a self-report self-esteem scale) is one of the most important, and poorly appreciated, parts of the research process. Our goal in this chapter is to provide a logical framework that you can use to develop measures for a wide variety of psychological constructs. However, in light of the enormous diversity of topics studied by psychologists, it is important to note that this chapter focuses almost exclusively on the subset of psychological measurements that rely on people's ability to report verbally on their experiences. Thus, if you are a budding behavioral neuroscientist who wishes to understand the role of the neurotransmitter dopamine in the subjective experience of pain, this chapter will not help you assess the density of dopaminergic receptors in the nucleus accumbens, but it should help you develop a good self-report measure of pain.

CONVERTING NOTIONS TO NUMBERS: THE TWO MAJOR CHALLENGES

Any researcher who ever asks a research participant any kind of self-report question faces two very tall hurdles. To make matters worse, these two tall hurdles often remain invisible until a researcher learns after the fact (as public officials learned in Palm Beach County) that one of the hurdles got in the way of the research process. The first hurdle has to do with making sure that people are considering the right question—that is, *ensuring that research participants are thinking about the same question that the researcher was thinking about.* The second hurdle has to do with making sure that once participants have considered the right question, they are able to convert their reaction to the question into a meaningful answer—that is, *ensuring that participants are able to translate their internal psychological state into some kind of value on a response scale.* To put this in more formal language, experts in questionnaire methods have argued that no matter what sample a researcher is studying and no matter what topic the researcher is investigating, all respondents go through the same two mental steps any time they answer a survey question. Participants first go through a **judgment phase,** and then they go through a **response translation phase** (Blanton & Jaccard, 2006; Schwarz, 1999; Tourangeau, Rips & Rasinski, 2000).

In the first part of this chapter, we focus on the judgment phase, with a special emphasis on how researchers can ensure that most, if not all, participants who respond to a specific self-report question are answering the specific question that the researcher hopes they are answering. In the second part of the chapter, we focus on the response translation phase, and we provide some advice about how to help people translate their subjective judgments into categories or numbers. Finally, after spending a great deal of time summarizing one particular way of assessing people's thoughts, feelings, dispositions, or motivational states (what we call **structured self-report questions**), we describe a few alternate ways of assessing these things, pointing out the advantages and disadvantages of the various approaches. The common theme that unites all the material in this chapter is that the business of getting people to report what they are thinking is surprisingly tricky. The butterfly ballot disaster is not an isolated event in the history of failed efforts to measure people's attitudes or desires. Perhaps you are wondering why anything as simple as getting people to tell you what they are thinking would warrant a detailed discussion in a textbook as delightful and provocative as this one. If you are wondering how hard it can really be to do something this simple, remember the advice that golf pros often give to beginning golfers. "Golf is the simplest game in the world. All you have to do is hit a small white ball with a club and get it into a well-marked hole—in as few strokes as possible." Many beginning golfers often reply excitedly that this sounds very easy, whereupon the golf pros correct them by saying, "I said golf was *simple*; I didn't say it was *easy*." Writing excellent self-report questions is simple enough, but it's rarely easy.

The Judgment Phase

During the judgment phase of answering a self-report question, participants determine what question is being asked, and they form some initial response to the question. Suppose you are asked the following question:

How much do you like your roommate?

To answer this question, you must perform mental operations to come up with an answer. You might form a mental picture of Jessica and make a judgment of how good or bad you feel when you are around her. Alternately, you might ponder the last two or three interactions you had with Jessica and estimate whether these interactions were mostly pleasant or mostly unpleasant. Finally, if you are particularly thorough, you might think back to your first meeting with Jessica and mentally walk forward through a series of typical interactions with her, including your most recent conversation about who deserved to get voted off the island. As this example shows, you could conceivably perform a large number of mental operations to try to answer this question. Good question askers begin by deciding what question they want answered (e.g., should I ask a specific question about liking or a more global question about relationship satisfaction?), but they also ask what kind of judgment process they want research participants to go through as they try to answer that question. Then they develop a specific question that is designed to send most people down the same mental road.

In a sense, then, researchers are like expert travel guides who would like to give good directions to travelers, and who themselves would like to travel on the path that will get them quickly and easily to a specific destination. But even when both the traveler and the friendly travel guide have the same goals, many things can go wrong when people are receiving and interpreting directions. In our opinion, one of the things that goes wrong most frequently has to do with the fact that researchers who write questions often have a difficult time taking the perspective of the research participants who are asked to answer them. Because it is so important for researchers to be able to do this, we first discuss how researchers can write questions that will make sense from the perspective of their research participants. We then discuss specific rules that researchers can follow to refine the actual wording of their survey questions.

Walking a Mile in Someone Else's Moccasins:
Perspective Taking

Very few researchers have much difficulty deciding what questions they would like to ask. And yet, even highly skilled researchers often have a great deal of difficulty knowing how to ask their questions in ways that will make the most sense to their research participants. To stay close to home, consider the problems faced by us, the authors of this textbook. Like most other psychologists, we conduct most of our laboratory research on college students, whose average age is about half our own. Of course, it should go without saying that we are incredibly cool for middle-aged college professors, but this is a lot like saying that the first author's 2002 Mazda MPV minivan is incredibly cool for a minivan. Because of our age, we often have trouble knowing if the self-report questions we design will make sense to college students—or if, instead, these questions will have that certain ring that comes from people who are total squares. (Young people still call older people "squares," don't they?) Of course, the two of us are not simply older than most of the participants in our studies. We also happen to be research psychologists who are accustomed to speaking the technical language of social cognition (a highly specialized subfield of the highly specialized field of social psychology). Thus, we are sometimes tempted to ask our research participants about the extent to which they "have a prevention-focused mind-set when they enter a social contract with familiar conspecifics." You, on the other hand, might find this question a bit opaque. (Young people still call confusing, unclear questions "opaque," don't they?)

If you recall our discussion of operational definitions from Chapter 1, you may have realized that this tricky situation involving opaqueness and **conspecifics** is merely one specific example of the pervasive problem of accurately translating a hypothetical construct (e.g., extraversion, hunger) into something that is observable and thus measurable (e.g., a circled response on a 7-point scale). In the case of creating a typical self-report question, a key to translating a hypothetical construct well is to write questions that clearly direct people to the specific psychological state or experience that you wish to measure. First and foremost, researchers who wish to do this should ask questions using familiar language that participants will easily understand. But how exactly do you go about using familiar, understandable language when it may not be at all familiar to you? One solution is to read the research literature to find out how other researchers may have solved this problem for you. But what happens when you are developing your own measure of a *new* construct for a sample of participants who have not been studied before? How do you decide how to word your new questions for a sample of people that you may not understand very well? Arguably, the best approach is to consult a panel of experts who know a great deal about these people. For example, one group who knows a great deal about how college students think, feel, and behave is *college students*. Along the same lines, a group who knows a lot about the language used most comfortably by Jewish senior citizens from Palm Beach, Florida, is Jewish senior citizens from Palm Beach, Florida. In other words, one of the best ways to decide how to ask people self-report questions about something is to get a group of these people together and ask them how they think about something. This approach may take any of several specific forms, but each form qualifies as a form of **pilot testing**.

Pilot testing is a very broad methodological term, but this term is used most frequently to refer to the use of practice studies that are designed to help researchers refine the measures or manipulations they wish to use in the full-blown version of a real study. You will learn more about pilot testing in Chapter 7. For now, suffice it to say that several kinds of pilot tests may be used to help researchers develop and refine structured self-report measures. For example, scientists who wish to ask people questions effectively can borrow an idea from marketing researchers who wish to sell products effectively. Marketing researchers often make use of relatively informal discussion sessions with **focus groups**. In a well-conducted focus group, a small but representative sample of participants from the group a researcher wishes to understand meet together to discuss their experiences. These semi-structured discussions are typically led by the researcher, whose goal is to make sure that the focus group stays, well, focused. For instance, after helping people feel comfortable speaking in the group, the researcher might ask each of them to answer some **open-ended questions** about the proposed research topic. For example, if the researcher worked for Procter and Gamble, she might ask focus group members to report what they each liked most and least about a specific brand of laundry detergent. On the other hand, if the researcher were a health psychologist interested in the psychology of bereavement, she might recruit a group of people who have recently lost a loved one and ask each one to describe his or her feelings of loss. In either case, the open-ended questions would allow people to respond in any way that they liked, using their own spoken or written words, rather than using some kind of structured rating scale. Notice that this approach differs from the structured self-report questions that researchers use much more frequently in questionnaire or survey research. Whereas open-ended questions allow people to respond however they see fit, structured self-report questions force people to use a specific response scale (e.g., by circling a single number on a 7-point scale, by indicating agreement or disagreement with a specific statement).

In a pilot study, such as a focus group session, a careful researcher might give people a structured self-report question *and* an open-ended question, each of which was designed to assess exactly the same thing. Comparisons between the two kinds of questions can often be very informative. Specifically, people's responses to open-ended questions can often be used to refine or improve structured self-report questions. This is because people's responses to open-ended questions are, almost by definition, worded in ways that make sense to people. Moreover, people's responses to open-ended questions sometimes illustrate that a structured question may not be doing its job. As an example, imagine that Dr. Rothman asked both a 55-year-old business executive and a 58-year-old foundry worker to report "how much negative affect you experienced in the month after you lost your spouse." Suppose both men reported a "3" on a 9-point scale that ranged from 0 ("none at all") to 8 ("the most I have ever felt"). Suppose further that in response to an open-ended question, the executive reported:

> I know this sounds terrible, but I didn't really feel so bad the first month after the funeral. There was a lot going on in my professional life, and I sort

of buried myself in my work. I know it probably wasn't very healthy, but as long as I stayed busy, I didn't feel all that bad. The truth is that I was never all that close to my wife, and at first I coped with her death by withdrawing to my work—the same way I had done when she was living.

Contrast this report with the foundry worker's response to the same open-ended question:

Sometimes I was real sad, but most of the time I didn't feel nothing. It was like I was walking around in somebody else's skin. I remember once I woke up early of a morning, and I went to the kitchen thinking Dottie'd have me some eggs on the table, like she always used to before I went to work. I'd done set down at the table before I knew they wasn't no eggs. And it was only then I remembered they wasn't no Dottie. I crawled back into bed, hoping maybe if I could go to sleep and wake back up, I'd get back that little minute at the kitchen table—when I thought she was still alive. But I never could get back to sleep. I just laid there thinking about how cold her side of the bed was and wishin' I could get back that minute at the kitchen table. That was when I really knew she was gone. It was when I knew I couldn't even get that minute back.

Dr. Rothman would not need to conduct any kind of statistical analysis of these responses to know that the structured question about negative affect was working just fine for the business executive but wasn't working nearly as well for the foundry worker. Perhaps the foundry worker was unfamiliar with the word "affect." Or perhaps he understood the word perfectly but somehow felt that his feelings of numbness and emptiness were best described as a *lack* of affect. Needless to say, Dr. Rothman would need to develop a structured question about negative emotions that would work equally well for each of these two men.

Incidentally, this example also highlights the fact that open-ended questions may be used in two very different ways. First, as we have suggested here, open-ended questions often generate unpredictable responses that allow researchers to refine structured ratings scales (e.g., by revising the wording of a question, by adding questions that tap aspects of an experience that researchers may not have previously considered). Second, some qualitative researchers use open-ended questions as their primary source of data and completely steer away from structured questions that require participants to use rating scales. If some researchers use open-ended questions exclusively, it raises an obvious question. Why doesn't everyone just stick to open-ended questions? That is, why use structured rating scales at all? After all, some critics argue that structured self-report questions turn interesting people into uninteresting numbers. In light of this criticism, consider the following question, which might be asked by a psychologist interested in relationship satisfaction:

On the whole, how satisfied are you with your relationship? (Circle one number.)

0	1	2	3	4	5
not at all					extremely satisfied

In light of the responses of the two widowers discussed above, it is easy to imagine that two people who each responded to the above question with a 3 might have very different perceptions of their relationships. Let's compare the structured and the open-ended question again:

Caryl

Question: On the whole, how satisfied are you with your relationship?

Answer: Like I said, I guess I'm a 3. My boyfriend is always there for me, and I feel like I can trust him. Trust is very important to me, and at times I think this should be enough. But I suppose I might need more, and that's why I didn't say 4 or 5. Although Jimbo's loyal and attentive, sometimes I feel that something is missing. We're very close, but I wish we had more passion.

Penny

Question: On the whole, how satisfied are you with your relationship?

Answer: Like I said, I'm a 3. Sophocles can be a real jerk and he's not the kind of person I see myself settling with over the long-run. I mean, he wore shorts to my best friends' wedding! But, we were hot for each the first time we hooked up, and our relationship is just as hot now as it ever was. We get on each others' nerves but we can't keep our hands off each other.

Do these two 3s look the same to you? We hope not. For Caryl, a 3 conveyed strong feelings of companionship that occurred despite a relative lack of passion. For Penny, the same 3 conveyed a less emotionally satisfying relationship that was nonetheless full of passion (and some typos). All this detail would have been lost if these two participants had simply been assigned the same number on a satisfaction scale. We agree that this illustrates a potential limitation of structured rating scales. However, a thoughtful researcher could bypass this problem by paying attention to the fact that there appear to be at least two distinct *routes* to relationship satisfaction. For instance, in response to these open-ended questions, a careful researcher could supplement her question about relationship satisfaction with some additional questions about what Hatfield (1978) referred to as passionate (i.e., "steamy") versus companionate (i.e., "trustworthy") love. The moral of this story is that researchers do not necessarily lose information by using rating scales. It is true that relying on a single rating scale will not always tell us everything we would like to know about people. However, the same rich picture of people that can emerge from an analysis of people's responses to open-ended questions can be generated directly from an analysis of multiple structured self-report questions. Moreover, structured self-report questions readily provide researchers with something that open-ended questions do not—meaningful numbers.

Some fans of open-ended questions might be quick to point out that open-ended questions can be coded, after the fact, in a nearly endless number of ways, allowing researchers to visit and revisit the same data as they refine their theories. Although this is true, it is worth noting that open-ended questions can only be used as data once the answers to these questions are coded, often painstakingly, by teams of highly trained raters, into the same kind of numbers that participants themselves are more than willing to provide (if researchers only have the forethought to ask them to do so). Ironically enough, then, open-ended questions can only yield data once we convert them into closed-ended numerical ratings. Furthermore, anyone who has ever collected people's responses to open-ended questions knows that they have another major drawback. For most open-ended questions, there will almost always be participants whose answers provide little or no information about a particular construct. For example, what if Penny had answered the open-ended question about relationship satisfaction by failing to mention *anything* about how emotionally connected she felt to Sophocles? This would make it impossible for even the most careful rater to extract any information about her feelings of emotional connectedness to her partner.

Even so, we are not saying that open-ended questions are useless in psychological research. First, sometimes researchers know so little about a new research question that they may need to begin by asking open-ended questions about the phenomenon. Second, as we hope we have illustrated, open-ended questions can be useful tools for developing and refining more structured questions, typically by using them in pilot studies. Needless to say, however, there are good reasons why most researchers make heavy use of structured self-report questions and use open-ended questions less frequently.

Comparing open-ended and structured self-report questions is only one of many things researchers can do in pilot studies. Moreover, a focus group represents only one kind of pilot study. A much more common kind of pilot study is simply a preliminary version of the full-blown study that a researcher eventually hopes to conduct. In this kind of pilot study, Dr. Visser may not ask her participants to talk about their experiences at all. Instead she might simply take a close look at people's responses to the structured self-report questions she hopes to develop further to be sure that the questions have desirable methodological properties. For example, if all participants respond at the same high or low level to a specific question (e.g., if everyone strongly agrees, if everyone strongly disagrees), Dr. Visser would want to revise that question to be sure that it elicits meaningful variation in people's answers. As we already noted, we discuss pilot studies in greater detail in our discussion of experimental research in Chapter 7. For now, suffice it to say that pilot studies have many uses, and one of these uses is to help researchers develop new self-report questions that truly measure what they are supposed to measure. One key to doing this is to be sure that these self-report questions make sense to the specific population the researcher has chosen to study.

Taking the perspective of one's research participants is probably the biggest single piece of advice that researchers have to consider when creating self-report questions. As it turns out, however, many small pieces of advice can also help researchers develop better self-report questions, and most of them are general enough to be applicable (with minor adjustments) to any kind of audience. In other words, some things will influence the way almost anyone interprets or decodes a question, and our discussion of the judgment phase of answering questions would be incomplete if we did not summarize some of the tips for helping almost any participant understand a self-report question. Although most of these tips have to do with the ways in which researchers word specific research questions, the broader context in which a specific question appears may also influence how people interpret the question. With this in mind, here are some tips for writing self-report questions that are likely to be as clear as possible.

Wording Questions Well for Everyone: Being Clear and Simple

To illustrate how important it is to word questions well, let's begin by examining a *badly* worded question. This question has a nice response scale, and it focuses on a very nice topic (our favorite textbook), but that's about all we can say for it:

> To what extent do you *not* like *Measuring the Weight of Smoke* when you enumerate it to the other methods books and supplements you have read and/or heard? In answering, consider only perennial publications that have a chapter on asking questions, and focus mainly on your sentiments rather than your cogitations. (Circle one number.)
>
> | 1 | 2 | 3 | 4 | 5 | 6 | 7 |
> |-----|-----|-----|-----|-----|-----|-----|
> | not at all | | | | | | extremely |

We hope you'll agree that this is a poorly worded question, but it might be useful to elaborate why. We do this by reviewing some important "rules" for writing good questions.

Keep It Simple   This rule is first because it is the most important. The question above is too complex. It uses a couple of words that are probably unfamiliar to most people, it uses at least one of these words incorrectly, and it forces people to try to hold a lot of thoughts in their heads. It also forces people to flip one of these thoughts around backwards, because of the unnecessary modifier "not." Compared with this question, the infamous butterfly ballot doesn't seem that bad after all. A much better version of the question might simply read, "How much do you like the textbook *Measuring the Weight of Smoke?*"

Use Informal Language   A related piece of advice has to do with the kind of language you use. Unless your respondents are unusually sophisticated, it's best to use proper terms and to be grammatically correct, but it's also important to use relatively informal language. It's equally important to avoid using psychological jargon or catchphrases. For instance, for the same reason that you shouldn't ask people about their "cogitations," you shouldn't ask people if they have ever suffered from "auditory hallucinations." Instead, ask people if they have ever heard any voices or sounds that may not have been real. Instead of asking people if they are "bulimic" or "anorexic," ask them simple and specific questions about eating, body image, and concerns about weight. Instead of asking respondents about their "yearnings" and "aspirations in life," ask them about their wishes and dreams. If your 14-year-old cousin has difficulty understanding your survey questions, you should simplify them. And, if you are studying 14-year-olds or people who are not highly educated, you should simplify your questions even further. A good rule of thumb is that survey questions should make comfortable reading for people several grade levels lower than your intended audience. In case this sounds really easy, remember that a second rule of thumb is not to overdo this. If you phrase your questions at *such* a low level that you sound patronizing, all of your participants will probably understand you, but some of them will find you annoying. Because finding the perfect balance can be tricky, pilot testing is very useful in this area.

Avoid Negations   Do you usually fail to not dislike questions that do not fail to omit the word *not*? We hope not. Actually, after a careful second reading, we *think* we hope so. As the opening sentence to this section illustrates, questions that contain negations such as "not" often lead to confusion. Research in cognitive psychology has shown that people process affirmations ("Hart is writing this chapter to be informative") more quickly and efficiently than negations ("Hart is not writing this chapter to be uninformative"). In fact, research has shown that when people process negative statements, they sometimes misinterpret them. Reading the newspaper headline "Chris Federico Not Linked to Mafia" is unlikely to give you the impression that Chris Federico is an especially upstanding citizen (Wegner, Wenzlaff, Kerker, & Beattie, 1981; see also Gilbert, 1991). Even worse than using negatively worded questions is using *double negatives*. Ignoring possible concerns about social desirability, an item such as "It's OK to run a stop sign every now and then" is better than "No one should be ticketed for not stopping at stop signs." Similarly, "I am always delighted to watch re-runs of *Glee*" is better than "There are no times when I am not delighted to watch re-runs of *Glee*." Of course, at times you will have to ask about things that negate something else. In such situations, you should try to use words that express negation in a familiar and transparent way. For example, the words "naked" and "nude" mean the same thing as "not clothed," but "naked" and "nude" are slightly easier to process. Along similar lines, words or phrases that directly express the absence or opposite of something (e.g., lonely, empty, tired) are generally better than negations expressing the same concept (e.g., without friends, no longer full, not energetic).

Avoid Double-Barreled Questions   Suppose we were to ask you, "How much do you like vacations and ear infections?" We suspect you would have trouble responding because you love vacations but hate ear infections. This is an example of a **double-barreled question**, a question that asks you to evaluate two different things using a single response. You should avoid asking double-barreled questions. It may seem obvious to you that you should ask one thing at a time, but it is easy to write a double-barreled question without realizing it. In an effort to be thorough or efficient, for example, researchers sometimes slip into asking more than one thing at a time. Consider the following item designed to assess self-esteem:

I am a lovable and capable person. (Circle one number.)

$$-6 \quad -5 \quad -4 \quad -3 \quad -2 \quad -1 \quad 0 \quad 1 \quad 2 \quad 3 \quad 4 \quad 5 \quad 6$$

extremely   extremely
disagree   agree

Now consider an item designed to assess graduate students' feelings of being overworked:

> I am in favor of cutting back to a six-day workweek and letting people take regular lunch and restroom breaks.
>
> (Circle one option.) true   false

Each of these questions is problematic. If Jonathan feels lovable but not capable, or capable but not lovable, how is he supposed to respond to the first question? Similarly, if Alyse is opposed to cutting back to a six-day workweek, undecided about regular lunch breaks, and in favor of regular restroom breaks, how is she supposed to respond? The simple solution to double- (or triple-) barreled questions is to break them up into two (or three) separate questions. Changing the first item to "I am lovable" and adding the separate item "I am capable" would be a big improvement.

Avoid Forced-Choice Items   The same logic that suggests avoiding double-barreled questions also suggests a subtler lesson. It is wise to avoid **forced-choice questions**, which are questions that ask participants to select one of two or more options. As examples, we might ask:

> Do you prefer apples or oranges?
>
> If you were getting a pet, would you rather have a cat or a dog?
>
> Which do you hate more, food poisoning or *Measuring the Weight of Smoke?*

Although these questions do allow people to indicate a preference, they do not yield the kind of information researchers usually like to have about people. Consider the first question. Rick and Rhonda might both indicate that they prefer apples rather than oranges. Do they have the same attitudes? Perhaps not. Rick might truly adore oranges, but he might adore apples even more. In contrast, Rhonda might find both of these fruits disgusting, but she might find apples slightly less repulsive than oranges. As is the case with double-barreled questions, it usually is best to break forced-choice items into two or more questions about single items so that you can get independent ratings of each item. In this case, asking both "How much do you like apples?" and "How much do you like oranges?" would be more informative than asking the original, forced-choice question.

Avoid Questions That Do Not Yield Any Variance   Some questions will be answered by almost everyone in the same way. Suppose someone were to ask you (a) whether you think puppies are cute and (b) whether you think it is a good idea to prejudge people on the basis of their skin color. We strongly suspect that you'd agree with the vast majority of your peers who are avidly pro-puppy and anti-racism. As we mentioned briefly in our discussion of pilot testing, researchers only get useful information from participants when participants differ from one another on the questions asked. If you get no variability in your responses, then you cannot use these responses to predict variability in other responses. If *everyone* gets a perfect score on your new physical fitness test, then you cannot use scores on this new test to pre-dict people's running times in a 5K race.

Sometimes it is hard to know when everyone will give the same answer to a question. When you conduct a study on a new topic, it is especially impor-tant to get a feel for what questions generate variability. If you are concerned that very few people in your sample will say "It's OK to drive past the posted speed limit," you might replace this item with something like "I think traffic laws are more severe than they need to be." If you are studying budding friendships, an item such as "My love for my friend is immeasurable" might not be very useful because very few people in your sample might endorse it (and if anyone does, you might be studying romantic relationships instead of friendships). Conversely, items such as "I like my friend" or "I feel close to my friend" might have the opposite problem. A more technical way of put-ting this is that it is important to avoid both **floor effects** and **ceiling effects** in self-report questions. Floor effects occur when almost everyone in a sample responds at the same low level on a question or dependent measure (e.g., when everyone circles a 0 on a Likert scale that goes from 0 to 6). Ceiling effects are just the opposite, but they are equally problematic. They occur when almost everyone in a sample responds at the same high level on a question or dependent measure. Floor and ceiling effects are both examples of the problem of **restriction of range**, which occurs anytime people's scores on a measure have little or no variation.

When there is restriction of range on a measure, it is difficult, if not impos-sible, to find anything that will predict people's scores on that measure. Inciden-tally, restriction of range has at least as much to do with the specific sample you are studying as it does with the specific measures you are using. For instance, if you correlate graduate students' GRE scores and their grade-point averages in graduate school, you will usually see only a modest correlation—not because GRE scores don't predict performance, but because only students with pretty high GRE scores make it into graduate school in the first place. When you are writing questions, the main thing you can do to avoid restriction of range is to know your sample and to adjust your questions, and sometimes your response scales, accordingly. When necessary, you should consider pilot testing. As an example, suppose you conducted a pilot study in which you ask dating couples the following question:

I am in love with my partner. (Circle one number.)

0	1	2	3	4	5	6
not at all		slightly		quite a bit		very much

If everyone in your pilot study circles a 5 or 6 on this scale, you can do several things. First, you might check to see how long the people in your pilot sample have been dating. If they are all in well-established relationships, you might consider sampling people who haven't been dating so long. On the other hand, if it's crucial that you study well-established relationships, you might try changing "in love" to "deeply in love." You might also consider expanding your 7-point scale to a 9-point scale and adding a more extreme endpoint (e.g., "completely"). If these options don't work, you may have to resort to hyperbole, as DeHart, Murray, Pelham, and Rose (2003) did when they asked mothers to report how much they loved their sons or daughters. The positive endpoint of their 9-point scale assessing mothers' love for their children was "as much as is humanly possible." A mother's love can force researchers to do unusual things.

Avoid Loaded Questions   One notorious problem that plagues many self-report questions is based on the fact that when people answer self-report questions, they are usually reporting about themselves. As the social psychologist Louis Penner often says, "Nobody likes to look like a schmuck." This means that people will not always be completely truthful when answering sensitive, loaded, or socially desirable questions. You can minimize this problem by writing questions in ways that do not indicate which response the researcher considers most desirable. Suppose, for instance, that you are interested in measuring people's level of trust in police officers. People certainly vary in the trust they place in the police; however, we hope you can see that the following question might fail to capture this variability:

To what extent do you trust the police who protect and serve our city's residents? (Circle one number.)

0	1	2	3	4	5	6
not at all						extremely

The use of the phrase "who protect and serve our city's residents" strongly suggests that most reasonable, moral, and peace-loving people should place quite a bit of trust in the police. In a sense, the person asking the question has tipped his or her hand and has *communicated* information rather than merely extracting it. What's the solution? Ask the question in plain and simple language, free of any evaluative baggage. For example, a less loaded question might read:

To what extent do you trust the police? (Circle one number.)

0	1	2	3	4	5	6
not at all						extremely

Although the flaw in this original question seems obvious, subtler biases can easily make their way into self-report questions. Moreover, because some topics (e.g., sex, politics, drug use) are inherently loaded, it may be difficult or impossible to come up with questions that are truly neutral. In such cases, researchers may occasionally wish to *use* loaded questions to get people to admit what they might otherwise deny. A classic example of this appeared in Kinsey's famous work on the sexual behavior of American men (Kinsey et al., 1948). Kinsey wanted to find out about the sexual histories of men, but he knew that many men would be reluctant to admit that they had violated social taboos. Thus, he used loaded questions to imply that people commonly engage in some very, very naughty behaviors. For instance, when he asked about masturbation, he asked men, "How old were you the first time you masturbated?" Notice how this question implies that *everyone* has masturbated. In this case, Kinsey used a technique that most researchers would agree is methodologically naughty to get most men to admit their own naughtiness. We cannot know for sure what consequence this question had, but it seems likely that it encouraged more honest responding.

Make Sure Your Questions Are Relevant to Everyone in Your Study   It is important that your questions make sense to everyone in your sample. For example, if you are studying close relationships, you should not take it for granted that everyone in your sample is heterosexual. If you are studying family dynamics, you should not take it for granted that everyone in your study has a meaningful relationship with both of their biological parents. Similarly, you should work hard to write questions that are gender neutral and culturally unbiased. This is not simply a matter of courtesy; it is also about construct validity. If the perspective of your self-report questions ignores the thoughts and feelings of a significant portion of your sample, that portion is unlikely to provide useful data. Thus, whenever possible, word your questions so that they are relevant to everyone. For example, you can do this by referring to participants' "romantic partners" rather than their "spouses" (unless you are only sampling married couples). Along the same lines, if you are asking adults to think about the family environment in which they grew up, you should probably ask people about their "principal caregiver(s)" rather than their mothers. The cost of doing this, of course, is that it is probably necessary to define "principal caregiver" in your instructions. This point is very similar to our earlier point about perspective taking. The subtle difference here is that you do not merely need to get a sense for the *typical* member of your sample. You also need to consider the fact that there is often a great deal of diversity within a specific sample.

Write Multiple Questions to Assess the Same Construct   Sometimes, you only need to ask one question to find out what you want to know about people. Consider sex. In most research applications, it is sufficient to ask people about their sex with a single question, which might read something like this:

What is your sex? (Please circle one.) Male Female

In the case of other psychological constructs, however, it is often desirable to ask people numerous questions to capture fully the construct of interest. Consider the two questions below, each of which is adapted from the popular Rosenberg (1965) self-esteem scale:

I feel that I have a number of good qualities. (Circle one number.)

| 0 | 1 | 2 | 3 | 4 | 5 | 6 | 7 |
| not at all | | | | | | | extremely |

I feel that I am a person of worth, at least on an equal basis with others. (Circle one number.)

| 0 | 1 | 2 | 3 | 4 | 5 | 6 | 7 |
| not at all | | | | | | | extremely |

Researchers who use the Rosenberg scale ask participants to respond to these questions, along with eight others. They then average the ten items together to create a single self-esteem score. Why is it useful to ask people ten different questions to assess one single thing (self-esteem)? As you may recall from our discussion of the "more is better" rule of reliability, using more than one question to assess a single construct increases the reliability of that measured construct. This happens, for example, because all of the idiosyncratic things that might make some people respond to any one specific item in a scale tend to average out as we add more and more items to the scale. Consider the first question, which asks you if you have a "number of good qualities." A small subset of people with high self-esteem might not endorse this item very strongly because they believe they possess a small number of incredibly great qualities. Thus, this would make this a bad self-esteem item for this particular subset of people. Another subset of people with high self-esteem might strongly endorse the first item while failing to strongly endorse the second item. Perhaps this second group feels that the phrase "person of worth" is offensive because they feel that *everyone* is a person of worth, and they worry that endorsing the second item would suggest otherwise. However, as we add more and more items to a scale, we hope you can see that the idiosyncratic sources of noise associated with each single question will get watered down if not cancelled out by the sources of noise associated with all of the other items.

Mix It Up Although multiple-item scales tend to be more reliable than single-item scales, this is only the case if the various items in a multiple-item scale are idiosyncratic in their own unique ways. This will not happen if you ask questions that are merely subtle variations on one another. The reason for this should be obvious when you consider this set of four separate self-esteem items:

1. I feel that I am a person of worth, at least on an equal basis with others.
2. I feel that I am a person of worth, at least on an equal plane with others.
3. I feel that I am a person of worth, when measured against most others.
4. Relative to others, I feel that I am a person of worth.

These four questions all conceptualize having self-esteem as being a "person of worth," and so they will all be influenced by the same idiosyncratic response tendencies. To benefit from the inclusion of multiple items, a self-report scale must include multiple items that get at the same basic construct in somewhat different ways. For this reason researchers sometimes try to make use of both *positively worded* and *negatively worded* questions. Positively worded items are designed to be endorsed more strongly by people who are high on a construct. In contrast, negatively worded questions are designed to be endorsed more strongly by people who are low on a construct. It is often a good idea to use both kinds of questions because some people differ (idiosyncratically) in their overall tendency to agree or disagree with questions in general. When researchers only use positively worded questions, this form of *response bias* can sometimes taint people's responses.

For example, if Barry strongly endorses both of the two positively worded self-esteem items just discussed, it *might* mean that Barry feels that he has a lot of good qualities and that he is a person of worth. On the other hand, it might also mean that Barry is simply a "yea-sayer," that is, a person who tends to say yes to everything. And of course, if Barry is a "naysayer," the opposite form of response bias would create the opposite problem. For this reason, the Rosenberg (1965) scale includes five positively worded items (two of which you recently saw) and five negatively worded items—items such as "I certainly feel useless at times," and "I wish I could have more respect for myself." These negatively worded items are *reverse coded* before they are summed with the positively worded items. In this way, researchers can create a single self-esteem score, for which higher numbers correspond to higher self-esteem levels. The fact that the negatively worded items are reverse coded (i.e., recoded so that a 0 becomes a 7, a 1 becomes a 6, etc.) means that individual differences in people's tendency to endorse any old question that you put in front of them averages out across the positively and negatively worded items. In this way, negative response bias (in its simplest form) does not influence people's self-reported self-esteem scores.

Although negatively worded items can be useful solutions to certain kinds of response bias, we should point out that writing negatively worded items can be a tricky business. You will notice, for example, that Rosenberg's negatively worded items are more than simply negations of his positively worded items. Instead, they ask people questions such as whether they ever feel useless or wish they could have more self-respect. One of the main tricks to writing good negatively worded items, then, is to do so without using negations that only substitute one problem for another. Of course, if you are developing a new scale and you are not sure if your own negatively worded items are doing their job, you can always address this question in a pilot test. Do the (recoded) negatively worded items correlate well with your positively worded items? Does your new scale correlate more strongly with behavior when you include the negatively worded items in the scale? If these things are true, then you have probably done your job well. If they are not true, then you probably need to go back to the drawing board.

Establish a Judgmental Context Perhaps one of the most frequently overlooked facts that influences the judgment phase of answering structured self-report questions is the fact that most judgments are relative. To be more specific, people almost always evaluate things *relative to other things*. As an example, suppose you are asked "On a scale from 1 to 10, how much do you like warm, sunny days?" The best answer to this question is probably, "Compared with what?" In comparison with cold, dreary days, your answer might be a 10. But if you are asked to evaluate a long list of things that most people consider wonderful (e.g., winning the lottery, going out on a date with the love of your life), your view of a warm, sunny day might be a little less sunny. Although it is difficult to do justice to this complex topic, researchers can do at least two things to ensure that participants evaluate statements in the right kind of judgmental context. First and foremost, researchers can include instructions that establish the appropriate context. For example, a researcher who wants participants to compare our textbook with other text-books could begin with a set of instructions explaining that we are interested in their attitudes about different research methods textbooks. Alternatively, if the researcher is more interested in how people respond to different kinds of reading materials (e.g., newspapers, textbooks, works of fiction), he or she could write a set of instructions to clarify this broader sort of comparison. Second, to be sure that participants who have not read their instructions care-fully still have a good sense of the appropriate judgmental context, research-ers can sometimes include warm-up or practice items at the beginning of a survey. Such practice questions can establish the judgmental context implicitly rather than explicitly. For example, suppose you are asked:

1. How much do you like *Measuring the Antiweight of Antimatter* by Einstein and Oppenhemier?

2. How much do you like *Research Methods for Psychopaths* by Klutz and Dumbas?

3. How much do you like *Measuring the Weight of Smoke* by Pelham and Blanton?

The two warm-up questions that precede the crucial question about this text would obviously create a different frame of reference than two warm-up questions that focused, say, on Ernest Hemingway's *The Old Man and the Sea* or Jane Austen's *Pride and Prejudice*. Which of these two contexts is cor-rect depends on your research goal, but it is best to keep that goal firmly in mind as you create your instructions and make decisions about the use of warm-up questions. If these examples seem a bit contrived, consider a real example from questionnaire research by Schwarz, Strack, and Mai (1991). Schwarz et al. asked married adults two simple questions: (1) how satisfied they were with their marriages and (2) how satisfied they were with their lives. In the absence of any instructions about the judgmental context, peo-ple's responses to the two questions were not very strongly related ($r = .18$). Presumably, people looked at the second question and thought something like, "Well, I just said that I have a good *marriage*, so now I guess I should try to separate that out from the other aspects of my life." In a second condi-tion, however, Schwarz et al. included some brief instructions that encour-aged a different way of framing the two questions. Specifically, they added, "We now have two questions about your life. The first pertains to your mari-tal satisfaction and the second to your general life satisfaction." When the instructions placed the two questions in the broader context of people's entire lives, people's answers to the two questions were strongly related ($r = .61$).

As this example shows, instructions can have a dramatic influence on how participants interpret the meaning of a question. It should go without saying that no one set of instructions will be right for every research occasion. However, by paying careful attention to the fact that people answer most questions in a particular judgmental context, you can try to establish the most appropriate context for your own research. Remember that in many situations, you will want to supplement your instructions with a few warm-up or practice questions to focus participants on the correct judgmental context. However, even if you are absolutely certain that your instructions give participants the right feel for what you are studying, warm-up questions can also be used to your benefit for a very different purpose, namely to get people to open up about sensitive topics.

Ease Into Socially Sensitive Questions

Research psychologists often have to ask people personal questions. When this is the case, it is usually a good idea to move gradually to socially sensitive questions. As a concrete example of the kind of thing we're talking about, consider the following story about a soldier who gets a brief letter from an old friend. The letter cuts right to the chase:

> Dear Pete:
>
> I'm sorry to say that your favorite cat Fluffy keeled over dead yesterday.
>
> Sincerely,
>
> Ben

The soldier is crushed, not only by the sad news about Fluffy, but also by his friend's insensitivity in communicating the news so bluntly. He writes a letter back to his friend, trying to give some constructive advice about breaking bad news to people:

> Dear Ben:
>
> I can't believe your last letter. Here I am trying to cope with a war, and I get this letter from you just telling me that Fluffy keeled over dead. You just don't do that kind of thing to a guy, Ben. You need to break that kind of news to a guy slowly. You might start off with a letter telling a guy that his cat is on the roof. In your next letter, you might add that the cat won't come down and that you're starting to get a little worried. In the third or fourth letter, you might let a guy know that you had to call the fire department to get the cat down, that they finally retrieved her, and that she is in intensive care at the veterinary hospital. In your fifth letter, you might let a guy know that his cat's chances of pulling through don't look very good. And in a sixth letter, you might finally tell the guy that they did everything they could for her but that Fluffy just didn't pull through. Finally, in the seventh letter, you tell the guy about the wonderful memorial service everyone had for Fluffy and remind him of what an inspiration she was to you. I hope you will be a little more careful in dealing with matters like this in the future.
>
> Sincerely,
>
> Pete

About a week later, Pete gets another very brief letter from Ben:

> Dear Pete:
>
> Your wife is on the roof.
>
> Sincerely,
>
> Ben

One premise that helps to make this story amusing is the idea that people deal better with tragedy when it is broken to them slowly. We're not really sure if this is true, but we do know that people deal better with sensitive survey questions if such questions are broken to them slowly. In light of this fact, one of the first things to consider when you are creating questionnaire items (including a set of dependent measures) is *what* to ask people *when*. If you have to ask sensitive questions, it's usually best to warm your respondents up with easy or innocuous questions first and to ask the sensitive questions once they are feeling pretty comfortable. If questions about masturbation or sexual positions appear on the first page of a survey, the researcher has probably cut to the chase too quickly. A little methodological foreplay can go a long way to enhance the honesty of participants' answers to sensitive research questions.

Ask Sensitive Questions Sensitively It is not enough simply to ease into sensitive questions. You also need to tread lightly when you ask them. When asking questions on such topics as stereotypes, sexual behavior, or illicit drug use, remember that people are not always dying to tell you about their deepest secrets. Therefore, carefully worded questions can diminish the likelihood that people will hold back the truth. For example, if you want to know whether people have ever used marijuana, and you simply ask "Have you ever used marijuana?" many people would be reluctant to admit having done so. After all, using marijuana is still illegal in some U.S. states. However, if you list a wide range of legal and illegal drugs (e.g., caffeine, alcohol, heroin, crack cocaine, marijuana), and ask people to place a check mark next to all the drugs they had ever used, many people would feel less inhibited about checking off a drug like marijuana (especially if the list includes what most people consider to be more serious drugs). When you ask people about sensitive topics, it is even more important than usual to be clear about what you mean and to phrase questions in ways that are not pejorative or judgmental. Giving people a clear idea of what you mean by "sexual partner" and then asking people how many sexual partners they have had would probably yield more useful and accurate information than asking people if they are "sexually promiscuous."

Guarantee Participants' Anonymity A final piece of advice for encouraging participants to respond honestly (i.e., truthfully, accurately) is to tell them honestly (i.e., truthfully, accurately) that you have gone to great lengths to preserve the anonymity of their responses. For example, if you are administering a pencil and paper survey, both your verbal and written instructions should remind participants that you are not interested in the responses of any single person, that they should not include any personally identifying information on their questionnaires, and that their responses will only be seen by the researchers who are entering and coding the data. Better yet, researchers who have access to sophisticated optical scanning equipment can tell participants truthfully that their computer answer sheets will be scanned and scored by a computer, so that no one will ever see their individual responses. If you administer surveys in a large auditorium or classroom setting you can take additional precautions—such as giving participants a colorful cover sheet and instructing them to use it to cover their answers as they work. Finally, if you are lucky enough to collect your data on a computer (whether in your lab or via the Web), you can remind participants that their responses are being recorded and organized by a computer software program, and that your electronic approach to data collection is specifically designed to protect participants' privacy. Taking such steps to guarantee privacy to participants is a good scientific idea, and, as you learned in Chapter 2, it is a good ethical idea as well.

By now, we hope that you have a good sense of the many things researchers have to do to start participants on the path toward answering self-report questions accurately. So far, however, we have only discussed the first half of the process. You may recall that answering self-report questions involves both an initial judgment phase, which we have now discussed in some detail, and a subsequent response translation phase, which we have addressed only in passing. How does this response translation phase work? That is, how can researchers get participants to do a good job of converting their thoughts, feelings, or self-reported behavior into responses on a categorical or numerical rating scale (e.g., "not at all–1–2–3–4–5–very much")? We cannot overstate the importance of this response translation process. In fact, we believe that researchers ignore this critical aspect of research all too often. This is unfortunate because a carefully developed rating scale can be the difference between a scientific breakthrough and a promising study that fails.

To understand the importance of the response translation phase, reconsider the metaphor that we suggested at the beginning of this chapter. The challenge of making good psychological measurements is very much like the challenge of giving good directions to a traveler who wants to get to a specific destination. From the perspective of this metaphor, all that we have discussed so far is how to make sure that travelers know exactly where they have been told to go (and that they are willing to try to go there). But how exactly do they get there? Without taking this metaphor too seriously, the response translation phase of answering questions can benefit enormously from the same kind of attention to detail that is beneficial to travelers who want to get to Kansas City. Instead of telling travelers, "Go a little way until you get to a gas station," people who give good driving directions are more likely to say, "Go about six blocks until you see a BP station on your left and a Texaco station on your right." Mapquest and Google Maps aren't quite this specific (yet) about gas stations, but they are extremely specific about distances and street names. Along similar lines, researchers who write good structured self-report questions take great pains to help participants know exactly where to stop along a categorical or numerical response scale. Here, then, are some keys to creating good response scales.

THE RESPONSE TRANSLATION PHASE

When designing a numerical rating scale, there are essentially three issues to consider. First, you need to consider how many numbers to use. Second, you need to decide what anchors to build into your numeric scale. Third, you need to decide on the best numbering system. Let's begin at the beginning, with the number of items to use.

The Number of Scale Points

Consider these two ratings scales:

How satisfied are you with your life right now? (Circle one number.)

1	2
not at all	extremely

How satisfied are you with your life right now? (Circle one number.)

1 2 3 4 5 6 7 8 9 10 11 12 13 14 15 16 17 18 19 20 21 22 23 24 25 26 27 28
not at all   extremely

In all likelihood, you would not be very comfortable using either scale. The first scale asks you to make a judgment that is too crude, whereas the second asks you to make a judgment that is too refined. The first scale does not allow you to give any detail about your life satisfaction. The second scale asks you to split judgmental hairs. The second scale might be an improvement over the first because it allows someone who is moderately satisfied to express this view, but a moderately satisfied person who is given the second scale might not know whether to circle 11, 19, or some number between these two.

These two scales illustrate the delicate balancing act that researchers must go through when creating response scales. On the one hand, a good response scale allows participants to express a wide range of opinions. On the other hand, a scale that provides too many response options may create confusion or even resentment. Because different questions often invite different numbers of responses (consider biological sex versus degree of self-perceived femininity), there is no single answer to the question of how many response options are contained in an ideal rating scale. Fortunately, researchers have looked at this issue in great detail, and the view among most *psychometricians* (experts in scale construction and psychological measurement) is that rating scales for most psychological constructs should have an intermediate level of responses. Typically, this converts to somewhere between three and ten response options (see Boote, 1981; Givon & Shapira, 1984; Komorita & Graham, 1965; Matell & Jacoby, 1971; McKelvie, 1978; Orth & Wegener, 1983). As suggested by the example of sex versus femininity, there are exceptions to this general rule. If you ask someone to report whether they voted in the last election, if they've ever smoked before, or if they've ever had the chicken pox, you can and should use a rating scale that only has two responses ("yes" and "no"). But, when measuring psychological constructs such as political ideology, attitudes toward smoking, or feelings of vulnerability, you'll want to use rating scales that permit some optimal middle range of responses. In fact, even if you are asking yes/no questions it is usually extremely useful to have a "don't know" option. This way, participants who are not sure where they stand on an issue or who have never heard of the person, place, or thing you want them to evaluate have a valid way of letting you know this (instead of merely leaving the question blank, which could indicate inattentiveness rather than ignorance or indecision).

The Importance of Anchors

The question of exactly how many response options to provide on a psychological rating scale turns out to be loosely tied to the seemingly independent question of what kind of **anchors** one uses on a scale. Anchors are simply adjectives that lend meaning to the numbers on a scale. Consider these two questions:

How satisfied are you with your life right now? (Circle one number.)

    1   2   3   4   5   6

How satisfied are you with your life right now? (Circle one number.)

    1   2   3   4   5   6
not at all   extremely

If you're like most people, you find the second scale easier to use than the first. The anchors provided on this second scale give people something meaningful to associate with the numbers 1 and 6. Otherwise, Billie Sue might assume that the number 1 corresponds to, "my life is a living hell" whereas Mary Ailas might assume that a 1 corresponds to, "my life isn't quite as peachy keen as it used to be." Just as a boat floats around aimlessly without an anchor, participants' responses to a 7-point scale can float around aimlessly if you do not tell them what meanings to associate with different points on the scale. It is important, then, that researchers choose their anchors carefully because changing the anchors on a scale can have a big effect on people's answers. Notice how the last question can change when a different anchor is used:

How satisfied are you with your life right now? (Circle one number.)

    1   2   3   4   5   6
not very much   completely

Most people feel that the word "completely" conveys a higher level of satisfaction than the word "extremely." Furthermore, almost everyone agrees that "not very much" is more than "not at all." Thus, if we were to give people this second scale it would be surprising if we didn't observe a lower mean response to this second scale. We discuss some rules of thumb to apply when choosing anchors a bit later. For now, we simply note that the meaning of any given number will change depending on the anchors used. Thus, it is important to choose your anchors wisely. Let's reconsider the second version of the scale having to do with life satisfaction:

How satisfied are you with your life right now? (Circle one number.)

    1   2   3   4   5   6
not very much   completely

Although the use of *endpoint anchors* is very useful, this scale still leaves something to be desired. In particular, how are people supposed to decide between numbers such as 3 and 4, or 4 and 5? Although this scale is not nearly as annoying as the 28-point scale we used earlier, it would be easier to use if it contained *middle anchors*. Like endpoint anchors, middle anchors lend meaning to the numerical values of a scale, making it easier for respondents to translate their subjective judgments into a numerical response.

Here are two examples of a scale with middle anchors. Notice how the meaning of the scale changes depending on the anchors:

How satisfied are you with your life right now? (Circle one number.)

1	2	3	4	5	6
not at all			very		extremely

How satisfied are you with your life right now? (Circle one number.)

1	2	3	4	5	6
not at all	slightly	quite	mostly	very	extremely

The first scale gives you a strong sense of how to interpret 4 and lets you know that 5 is meant to convey a value halfway between "very" and "extremely," but it still leaves you in the dark a bit when it comes to a response of 2 or 3. Some people might also debate whether it is wise to make 4 correspond to very, when 4 is just barely above the scale midpoint. In contrast to the first scale, the second scale provides participants with a useful anchor for every point on the scale. The only grounds on which we might critique the second scale have to do with whether it could be made a little more sensitive and whether the label chosen by the researcher for each number offers a good fit with that number. This raises a subtle but important question. How do researchers make sure that the numbers and anchors they use in their response scales fit together appropriately?

Choosing Anchors to Create Equal Appearing Intervals
Look again at the last scale we presented. By using this specific 6-point scale (with this specific set of anchors), the questioner is implying that the same amount of psychological difference in satisfaction exists when one moves, say, from 2 to 3 or from 4 to 5. But, suppose that most people believe that the jump from "slightly" to "quite" is a lot bigger than the jump from "mostly" to "very." This points to a key consideration in scale construction. In the case of any numerical scale, it is important to use anchors that are meaningfully related to the numbers used. In particular, it is important to use anchors that create scales with **equal appearing intervals**. A scale has equal appearing intervals whenever the psychological distance implied by a single-unit difference on the rating scale remains constant across the entire range of the scale. Ideally, the difference in satisfaction implied by a rating of 1 versus 3 should be the same as the difference in satisfaction implied by a rating of 4 versus 6. It might seem impossible to know how to create psychological rating scales with equal appearing intervals. If we define equal appearing intervals very strictly, it may actually *be* impossible, but researchers have done a lot of

work to find the best ways to approximate equal appearing intervals in response scales.

The best guide comes from research on the *measurement of meaning* (Osgood, 1952; Osgood, Suci, & Tannenbaum, 1957). To understand the goals of this research, imagine that you and a friend are in a rainstorm and that you hear a loud clap of thunder. You say to your friend, "That was a very loud thunder clap." Later, you hear another thunder clap, and you say, "That was an *extremely* loud thunder clap." Researchers who study the measurement of meaning are interested in figuring out what psychological quantities are implied by the use of words such as "very" versus "extremely." In this research area, participants are often asked to put words in rank order based on the amount or magnitude implied by the word. Alternately, participants are sometimes asked to evaluate words along different dimensions. Using such data, psychometricians can determine how the meaning of almost any concept changes as a function of its description by using different modifiers. Although we could discuss these methods in greater detail, the most important finding from this line of work is that (in most instances) adverb modifiers such as "very" or "extremely" convey the same information whether they are used to describe the loudness of thunder, the deliciousness of cantaloupe, or the messiness of your roommate's desk (Osgood, 1952; Osgood, Suci, & Tannenbaum, 1957). The best estimates we know of for the *amounts* conveyed by different scale modifiers were revealed in a study by Cliff (1959). His estimates are shown in Figure 4.2. As you can see, when a speaker modifies a concept with the word "slightly," he or she is saying that about 0.56 as much of that concept is there as would be there if the concept were not modified at all. Thus, based on the way most people use the word "slightly," a "slightly messy" desk should be about 0.56 times as messy as a "messy" desk, and someone who is "extremely in love" with Linda Jean is about 1.55 times as in love as someone who is just "in love" with Linda Jean. Of course, there are exceptions to these general rules, but in the absence of any other guidelines for choosing anchors for rating scales, it is hard to imagine a better way to go about the business of choosing middle anchors.

Consider the words "not," "slightly," "quite," and "extremely." If you study these words and their ratings carefully, you'll see that they appear at intervals that are roughly 0.5 units from one another (0, 0.56, 1.11, 1.55).

Figure 4.2

Scale anchors
(from Cliff, 1959)

Not	0.00
Slightly	0.56
Somewhat	0.72
Rather	0.89
Pretty	0.96
Unmodified	1.00
Quite	1.11
Decidedly	1.23
Unusually	1.32
Very	1.32
Extremely	1.55

The fit is not perfect, of course, but it's pretty darned close. Research by others generally supports the view that these four anchors fall on equal appearing intervals (Osgood, Suci, & Tannenbaum, 1957; Howe, 1962, 1966a, 1966b). Related research also suggests that the use of middle anchors can improve the reliability of rating scales (Weng, 2004; Dobson & Mothersill, 1974). Taken together, this all suggests that you can place these four adverbs at equal intervals in the middle of your rating scales with a high degree of confidence that you are improving your measure. To illustrate, let's return to the life-satisfaction question. Putting together everything we have discussed so far in this chapter, consider the following structured self-report question:

How satisfied are you with your life right now? (Circle one number.)

0	1	2	3	4	5	6
not at all satisfied		slightly satisfied		quite satisfied		extremely satisfied

This question has some very desirable qualities. First and foremost, we can feel pretty sure that the scale anchors imply roughly the same psychological gap between ratings of 0 and 2, 2 and 4, and 4 and 6. Second, notice that the word "satisfied" is incorporated into both the question itself and the scale anchors. It is not always possible to do this kind of thing, but it's a good practice whenever you can do so because it helps keep respondents focused on what question they are answering. Third, notice that this new scale begins at 0 rather than 1. For most people the connection between "not at all" and 0 is more intuitive than the connection between "not at all" and 1. This is simply another way to increase the psychological fit between the numbers in a scale and people's subjective experiences. Finally, notice how this scale has a single number between each of the anchors. This feature allows participants to "split the difference" between two responses when they are unable to decide between two equally self-descriptive anchors. Someone who is more than "quite" satisfied but less than "extremely" satisfied can always choose 5. In fact, we think it's extremely likely (i.e., about 1.55 times more likely than "likely") that such a person would do so.

This kind of scale incorporates a lot of research on scale numbering systems and scale anchors, and it can be adapted to measure a wide range of thoughts and feelings. Consider, for example, how you might use this kind of scale to assess three very different things (our apologies in advance for a double-barreled question about guns):

How much do you enjoy your research methods class? (Circle one number.)

0	1	2	3	4	5	6
not at all		slightly		quite a bit		extremely

How much fear do you have of snakes? (Circle one number.)

0	1	2	3	4	5	6
no fear		a slight fear		quite a fear		an extreme fear

How much do you agree with the statement, "Guns don't kill people; bullets do."? (Circle one number.)

0	1	2	3	4	5	6
I do not agree at all.		I agree slightly.		I agree quite a bit.		I agree extremely.

Although this simple 7-point scale can be adapted for use with almost any psychological construct, some researchers would raise good questions about whether this scale can truly serve as an all-purpose scale. This is because some psychological constructs are best captured with **bipolar scales** rather than **unipolar scales**.

Unipolar Versus Bipolar Rating Scales

Almost all of the rating scales we have presented thus far have been unipolar scales. That is, almost all of these scales ask respondents to make ratings on dimensions that begin at some very low value (often zero) and move upward to a subjective maximum point on the dimension of interest. But what if we want our life-satisfaction scale to be more sensitive to the possibility of extreme dissatisfaction? Wouldn't a really miserable person like to express something more distressing than a mere lack of satisfaction? The ultimate answer to this question goes beyond the scope of this book (e.g., see Cacioppo, Gardner & Berntson, 1997), but it is worth noting that many times researchers might prefer to use bipolar scales rather than unipolar scales. Bipolar scales ask respondents to rate a quantity that deviates in both directions from a zero point. For example, here is a bipolar life-satisfaction scale that has a well-chosen zero point and uses meaningful anchors:

How satisfied are you with your life right now? (Circle one number.)

−6	−5	−4	−3	−2	−1	0	1	2	3	4	5	6
extremely dissatisfied		quite dissatisfied		slightly dissatisfied		neither satisfied nor dissatisfied		slightly satisfied		quite satisfied		extremely satisfied

This scale encourages a judgmental focus on bad as well as good life events. It also uses empirically justifiable anchors. However, you might notice that the new scale violates one of our suggestions. Recall that we argued for scales that have between three and ten response options. This bipolar scale has 13! Although we do believe that having three to ten response options is generally a good idea, this rule is modified in the case of bipolar scales. With these response scales, it appears that most participants break the response process into two steps. First, participants decide where they fall in relation to the midpoint. Then, they use only the side of the scale that is appropriate for their rating. Thus, if you use the scale above to rate your own life satisfaction, you would probably first decide whether you are more "satisfied" or more "dissatisfied." Then, if you are the satisfied type, you would use only the six options that are available on the right-hand side of the scale. Of course, if you are dissatisfied, the same logic would apply to the left-hand portion of the scale. And if you are neither satisfied nor dissatisfied, we hope you would circle the 0.

Putting It All Together: The EGWA Scale

To summarize our discussions of scale numbering and anchoring systems, we advocate the use of a very simple rating scale that can be used in many different research situations. We refer to this scale as the EGWA scale because it is an Empirically Grounded, Well-Anchored response scale. Here is how one might adapt the EGWA to find out how much someone likes this textbook:

To what extent do you like the textbook *Measuring the Weight of Smoke?* (Circle one number.)

0	1	2	3	4	5	6
not at all		slightly		quite a bit		extremely

On the other hand, if a researcher feels strongly that positive and negative evaluations should be considered separately, he or she could use the bipolar (i.e., two dimension) version of the EGWA to see how much someone likes this textbook:

How favorable or unfavorable is your evaluation of *Measuring the Weight of Smoke?* (Circle one number.)

−6	−5	−4	−3	−2	−1	0	1	2	3	4	5	6
extremely negative		quite negative		slightly negative		neutral		slightly positive		quite positive		extremely positive

Of course, we are not arguing that the EGWA represents the only route to good measurement, but it is one very simple and direct route that is based on an exhaustive body of careful research. We think you can adapt this logic to most if not all of the specific topics you would like to study.

Unfortunately, we have to note that the care we gave to creating these EGWA scales appears to be the exception rather than the rule. That is, in our experience, very few researchers use scales that resemble the EGWA scales we have just presented. Thus, we are in the awkward position of sounding like nagging parents who dutifully prescribe rules that very few children (or parents) actually follow. However, one difference between the advice we offer and the advice many parents offer is that we developed this advice based on the careful work of real experts. And we both follow this advice in our own work. With this in mind, we suggest that if you understand and apply our logic to the development of your own scales, you will have a head start on other researchers who rely on response scales with anchors that are based solely on their own intuitions. As Sir Isaac Newton said, "If I have seen further than others, it is only because I have stood on the shoulders of giants." If you want to see further than other researchers, you need only to stand on the shoulders of the giants who studied the measurement of meaning and facilitated the development of good rating scales.

Special Cases Require Special Scales

Needless to say, there are exceptions to every rule. This means that at times you will want to depart from the expert advice we have so generously offered. For instance, if you are a developmental psychologist working with pre-adolescent children, you may want to limit yourself to scales that use as few as three or four response options. You thus might ask 11-year-old kids questions in this format:

How much do you like green eggs?

_____ I do not like them.

_____ I like them a little bit.

_____ I like them.

_____ I love them.

If pilot testing reveals that kids had trouble using all four options, you might cut your question further:

How much do you like green eggs?

_____ I do not like them.

_____ I like them OK.

_____ I love them.

Of course, if researchers studying the measurement of meaning had spent their careers studying the ways in which *children* use adverbs, you might be able to capitalize on their wisdom in designing EGWA scales that you can give to children. But, with few exceptions (see Bashaw & Anderson, 1968) this group has only studied adults. Thus, all you can do is apply some common sense to determine the number of options and the type of anchors that will be best for a given age group. It is our guess that gifted pre-adolescents who are avid readers would probably have little trouble with the two EGWA scales we designed for adults. But if you are not so sure, and if you do not have a developmental psychologist on hand to give you expert guidance, you can always conduct a pilot study.

It may also be useful to simplify scales in certain testing environments. As an example, survey researchers often call people on the phone to ask their opinions. However, it is extremely difficult to get telephone respondents to use a 7-point scale without a visual aid. Thus, those who conduct telephone surveys often break up their scales so that respondents only need to consider one part of a scale at a time. For example, an interview might go as follows:

Interviewer: Do you like *Measuring the Weight of Smoke*? Please answer "yes," "no," or "indifferent."

Sam: Yes. Yes I do. I do like this book.

Interviewer: OK. Do you like *Measuring the Weight of Smoke* "slightly," "quite a bit," or "extremely"?

Of course, if Sam does not like the book, the questioner would ask him if he dislikes it "slightly," "quite a bit," or "extremely." If Sam chooses the option "indifferent," then the interviewer would simply record this response and move on to the next question. By using this two-stage format, the survey researcher avoids giving interviewees more options than most people can handle. Nonetheless, the end result is that answers are converted into a 7-point scale that ranges from −3 ("extreme dislike") to +3 ("extreme like") with a midpoint of 0 ("indifferent").

As we noted in our original discussion of pilot testing, researchers sometimes modify their response scales because of concerns about restriction of range. As you know, restriction of range means that most, if not all, participants give the same answer to a question. The second author encountered this problem once while working with an army officer who was studying trust in leaders. The participants in this study were soldiers who had been asked to identify their "most trusted leader" prior to and during the second war in Iraq. Soldiers were then asked to rate how much they trusted this particular leader. In the pilot study, the officer used this question:

To what extent do you trust your most trusted leader? (Circle one number.)

0	1	2	3	4	5	6
not at all		slightly		quite a bit		extremely

Can you guess the problem? Almost every soldier circled the number 6. This is because (duh!) the person most soldiers chose as their "most trusted leader" was usually someone in whom they placed a lot of trust! To increase variability on the scale, the second author and his colleague modified the scale slightly so that more options were offered at the top end of the scale. The scale that resulted was as follows:

To what extent do you trust your most trusted leader? (Circle one number.)

0	1	2	3	4	5	6	7	8	9	10	11	12
not at all			slightly			quite a bit			extremely			completely

By adding the upper anchor, "completely," and by giving more choices between the anchors, the researchers were able to get a wider range of responses (and they were also able to discover some useful things about trust during war). Of course, this scale seems to violate a rule because it has 13 response options. However, pilot testing showed that soldiers would only use the upper end of the scale anyway. Essentially, this scale became a 5-point scale that ranged from 8 to 12 instead of a 13-point scale. (If you don't think this is a good thing to do, you're just going to have to trust us on this one. After all, we are probably two of your most trusted leaders.)

FROM WRITING QUESTIONS TO CREATING SCALES

At this point, we have given you a great deal of advice on how to write specific items in a questionnaire. However, we have not yet addressed the important question of how to generate and refine enough specific items to develop a full-blown, multiple-item questionnaire. After all, your beautiful EGWA scale is not of much use to anyone if you can't come up with a list of questions to attach to it. Remember that researchers who are developing new measures usually want to come up with a set of multiple items that all assess the same thing in slightly different ways. For example, you might want to develop a short (5-item) childhood version of a popular 20-item adult self-esteem scale—so that your nine-year-old participants don't get too bored or distracted while filling it out. How exactly do you go about picking five good questions that can be combined to create a single kiddie self-esteem score?

Three Steps to Designing Questionnaires

Some of the most important decisions researchers make have to do with this kind of process, that is, the process of item generation and selection. Although the process of thinking up good questionnaire items may seem more like an art than a science, most seasoned researchers follow some simple scientific rules when they are developing new measures. Perhaps the most important rule is that, after you have generated a bunch of questions to presumably measure that new thing you were hoping to measure, you must begin to rely on data to select and refine those questions. Questions that seemed excellent to you and your colleagues when you were dreaming them up might prove to be terrible, and questions that seemed like long shots may emerge as the best items in your scale. For this reason, careful researchers almost always evaluate the items in a new scale empirically before they rely on the items to test their theories. The process of evaluating the quality of questionnaire items follows these three steps.

Step 1: Step Back and Think First and foremost, be sure to ask yourself exactly what it is you want to measure. Suppose, for instance, that you want to measure individual differences in how much people trust the police. You might begin by considering whether this is really any different than the more general tendency to trust authorities (e.g., ministers, professors, judges). You might discuss this notion with a friend who suggests that your ideas about trusting the police and authorities is related to people's more general belief that the world is a fair and just place. Specifically, your friend notes that there is an established scale that measures the strength of people's "belief in a just world" (Lerner, 1980). We won't belabor this potentially lengthy point, but the general idea is that by kicking your idea around and discussing related ideas with other people, you would eventually settle on the exact concept you wish to measure. Along the way, you'd also be likely to come across some established measures that are possibly related to, but not identical to, your new measure. Of course, by including these established scales in your pilot research, you'd be on the road to figuring out what's new and different about your own measure. But remember, you don't really have a new measure yet. How do you generate the items that you will eventually include in your measure?

Step 2: Write Lots and Lots of Questions If you hope to create a good 8- or 10-item measure, you might be surprised to know that you'll probably want to start with a list of something more like 40 or 50 items (with roughly equal numbers of positively and negatively worded items). You'll need all these items at first because you'll eventually abandon many of them. Even if you could generate all of these items yourself, you probably shouldn't. Instead, you should probably generate ten or 20 items and then conduct the kind of focus group we discussed earlier in this chapter. Your pilot participants can then help you generate new items (by means of their comments and open-ended answers to your interview questions).

Step 3: Analyze Your Scale and Derive the Best Items   After all the work you do to generate an initial pool of items, you will then need to do even more work by giving all of these items to a large sample of people just like the people you eventually hope to study. Assuming you really can get a pretty large sample (e.g., 200–1,000 people), you might consider conducting a *factor analysis* to determine whether the items in your scale really do tend to be correlated with one another. It is possible, for example, that most of the items don't tend to correlate with one another very well. It is also possible that various subsets of the items tend to cluster together. For example, a factor analysis might tell you that the various items in your scale are really measuring two separate things—when you had hoped to be measuring only one. This would mean that you have a big decision to make. Do you keep only the items that seem to be measuring what you had originally hoped to measure? Or do you decide that, to appreciate how much people trust the police, you need to create two different scales? There is no way to answer this question in the abstract, but we hope it is clear that, whichever route you take, you will want to be sure that the items in any given scale are reliable. Recall from the last chapter that this question can be answered by determining which items within a given scale have high inter-item reliability. Just as importantly, you'd also want to perform analyses that assess your scale's validity by seeing if it correlates in predictable ways with other established scales or with behaviors or demographic characteristics that are theoretically connected to trust in the police. For instance, if your scale truly measures trust in the police, you should probably expect to find that it correlates positively with personal income. All else being equal, wealthy people probably tend to place more trust in the police than poor people do.

If you're getting tired thinking about all this work, we have to tell you that it's rarely this simple or this easy. In fact, researchers often move back and forth between the three steps we have described here, and it is sometimes necessary to generate and regenerate items several times and to collect pilot data many times before determining that a new measure is both reliable and valid. On the other hand, once this initial work is done, things usually start to get interesting. Once you have a pretty good measure of something, the list of ways in which you can use it is limited only by your imagination. For example, should we expect ethnic differences in people's trust for the police? Do these ethnic differences still exist once we control statistically for the likely effects of poverty? Does priming people with positive images of heroic police officers temporarily increase people's trust in the police? Does showing people a short movie clip about a corrupt, abusive police officer temporarily reduce it?

Regardless of where you decide to take your scale, you should be sure that you construct it properly. If you do so, you will not only be in a better position to know what your scale predicts, but you will also be in a better position to know what it does not predict. When a poorly constructed scale does not predict anything, we cannot know whether this finding is informative or whether it merely means that the scale doesn't measure what it is supposed to measure. In contrast, when a well-constructed scale predicts some things but not others, we are in a much better position to draw some reasonable conclusions about the construct the scale was designed to measure.

Alternate Measures

So far in this chapter, we have spent a lot of time focusing on only one of many basic ways of measuring psychological constructs, namely the development of the multiple-item scale that consists of the sum or average of a set of specific items. Before we conclude, however, we want to remind you that (a) it's not always this complex, but (b) it's not always this simple. To start with why it's not always this complex, remember that many physical, psychological, and demographic variables (e.g., height, age, gender, ethnicity) can be measured with one or two items that have obvious face validity. Along similar lines, some important behaviors can be assessed directly by means of absolute scales. When participants answer questions using **absolute scales,** they report magnitude (i.e., amount, frequency, probability) in a direct and obvious way. For instance, clinical, social, and health psychologists who study smoking or drinking might ask participants to report how many cigarettes they typically smoke per day or how many alcoholic beverages they consumed last week. The use of absolute scales raises important questions about how well people can remember their own behavior, but it does not usually require researchers to go through all the machinations we have described in this chapter.

So that's the good news. Things aren't always so complex. Of course, things aren't always so simple either. Over the years, researchers have developed a wide variety of highly sophisticated (but less popular) methods for assessing how people evaluate things. We believe you will be best served in most instances if you stick to questionnaires that rely on EGWA scales, but we would be shortchanging you if we failed to mention at least a couple of these alternative methods.

The Semantic Differential   This scale has an interesting history, and our coverage of it begins with a researcher who was interested in the measurement of meaning. The most influential thinker in this area was a psychologist named Charles Osgood. He was interested in knowing how we mentally represent concepts and how these representations then get translated into everyday language. To address this issue, Osgood took on an enormous project. He and his students pored laboriously over an unabridged dictionary—in the days before they could get much help from a computer—and pulled out *every adjective in the English language.* In a systematic series of studies, Osgood and his students gave adjectives from their enormous list to thousands of participants who were asked to organize them, sort them, make different ratings of them, and so on. From these heroic efforts, they began to discern a predictable structure to the way in which concepts are described, and they found that the same general structure held when they moved their research to other languages and other cultures. Osgood and his colleagues found that virtually all concepts could be evaluated on a small set of core dimensions that were anchored by paired adjectives. For instance, every culture they studied had ways of describing objects along a dimension anchored by the equivalent of the English adjectives "*good*" versus "*bad*." According to Osgood, a few universal adjective pairs form endpoints of dimensions that make sense to people all over the world, whether you are describing Timbuktu to your roommate Tim or describing your roommate Tim to a stranger in Timbuktu.

To be more specific, Osgood found that the majority of adjectives in language fall neatly into one of three different categories that can be used to evaluate almost any object in almost any culture. These categories are *adjectives of evaluations* (good–bad, nice–awful, easy–difficult), *adjectives of potency* (strong–weak, dominant–submissive, powerful–powerless) and *adjectives of activity* (fast–slow, sedentary–mobile, alive–dead). Osgood capitalized on this cross-cultural constancy to create a straightforward way to ask questions. He designed questionnaires that identified individual target items, and he then had people rate these specific items using a list of paired adjectives that placed concepts on the three dimensions of interest. In Figure 4.3, we show how this strategy might be used to measure your evaluation of this textbook. (Notice that our version of this scale not only uses Osgood's three dimensions, but it also incorporates the equal-appearing anchors that we took from Cliff, 1959, and includes a bipolar numbering system that is meaningful in this context.)

Although measures such as this can yield rich information about how people evaluate objects, this approach is not without its complexities. First, although people typically evaluate objects along all three dimensions, some dimensions simply do not make sense for some objects. For instance, you probably have a pretty strong sense of our book in terms of its evaluation, but you have probably given much less thought to its potency or its activity. Second, although Osgood did find that there was a meaningful structure underlying adjective pairs, he at times noticed minor deviations in this structure when he went from one object to another. For instance, the adjective pair "hard–soft" was found to correspond to the dimension of evaluation when used to describe people, but it was found to correspond to the dimension of potency when used to describe a war. For this reason, you should not use Osgood's rating system without conducting a factor analysis to ensure that the scale has a meaningful structure. If it is not possible to conduct a factor analysis, you should avoid this evaluation system.

Thurstone and Guttman Scales

In all of the examples you've seen so far, researchers have designed scales to yield a single number, or *scale total*. This value is computed by taking either the sum or the average of all the

How Do You Rate *Measuring the Weight of Smoke,* 4th Edition?

Evaluation

Bad	□	□	□	□	□	□	□	Good
	−3	−2	−1	0	1	2	3	
	extremely	quite	slightly	neutral	slightly	quite	extremely	

Awful	□	□	□	□	□	□	□	Nice
	−3	−2	−1	0	1	2	3	
	extremely	quite	slightly	neutral	slightly	quite	extremely	

Unhelpful	□	□	□	□	□	□	□	Helpful
	−3	−2	−1	0	1	2	3	
	extremely	quite	slightly	neutral	slightly	quite	extremely	

Difficult	□	□	□	□	□	□	□	Easy
	−3	−2	−1	0	1	2	3	
	extremely	quite	slightly	neutral	slightly	quite	extremely	

Potency

Weak	□	□	□	□	□	□	□	Strong
	−3	−2	−1	0	1	2	3	
	extremely	quite	slightly	neutral	slightly	quite	extremely	

Powerless	□	□	□	□	□	□	□	Powerful
	−3	−2	−1	0	1	2	3	
	extremely	quite	slightly	neutral	slightly	quite	extremely	

Submissive	□	□	□	□	□	□	□	Dominant
	−3	−2	−1	0	1	2	3	
	extremely	quite	slightly	neutral	slightly	quite	extremely	

Shallow	□	□	□	□	□	□	□	Deep
	−3	−2	−1	0	1	2	3	
	extremely	quite	slightly	neutral	slightly	quite	extremely	

Activity

Slow	□	□	□	□	□	□	□	Fast
	−3	−2	−1	0	1	2	3	
	extremely	quite	slightly	neutral	slightly	quite	extremely	

Dead	□	□	□	□	□	□	□	Alive
	−3	−2	−1	0	1	2	3	
	extremely	quite	slightly	neutral	slightly	quite	extremely	

Inactive	□	□	□	□	□	□	□	Active
	−3	−2	−1	0	1	2	3	
	extremely	quite	slightly	neutral	slightly	quite	extremely	

Sedentary	□	□	□	□	□	□	□	Mobile
	−3	−2	−1	0	1	2	3	
	extremely	quite	slightly	neutral	slightly	quite	extremely	

Figure 4.3
Semantic differential

items on the scale (after some items possibly have been reverse coded). This single score is then used to represent a person's standing on the psychological construct of interest. Importantly, however, not all scales are scored in this manner.

One example of a scale that uses a different coding method is shown in Figure 4.4. This scale was designed in the 1930s by a famous psychometrician named L. L. Thurstone to measure attitudes towards war. Although some of

Attitude Towards War

Statement	Scale Value
Every last one of us should refuse to take part in any way in any war.	0
There is no conceivable justification for war.	0.2
War should be avoided at any cost.	0.4
War is simply murder sanctioned by governments.	0.7
War is a futile struggle resulting in self-destruction.	1.4
War in the modern world is as needless as it is terrible.	1.6
War destroys the finest of the nation's manhood.	2.1
The soldier suffers terribly and gains nothing.	2.2
War is an unnecessary waste of human life.	2.4
There will be no more wars when people become really civilized.	3.0
The benefits of war are not worth its misery and suffering.	3.2
A host of young men returned from the war disillusioned and cynical.	3.3
International disputes should be settled without war.	3.7
War is hardly necessary in the modern world.	4.2
We want no more war if it can be avoided without dishonor.	4.6
War brings out both good and bad qualities in men.	5.4
It is hard to decide whether wars do more harm than good.	5.5
War has some benefits; but it's a big price to pay for them.	6.0
Peace and war are both essential to progress.	6.3
There are some arguments in favor of war.	6.6
Another war would be terrible but it might be worth the price.	7.0
Under some conditions, war is necessary to maintain justice.	7.5
War is sometimes necessary because right is more important than peace.	7.8
The desirable results of war have not received the attention they deserve.	8.3
War is a satisfactory way to solve international difficulties.	8.5
Every man should enlist as soon as war is declared.	8.8
War develops the moral strength of men.	9.2
High idealism is born in war.	9.5
War stimulates men to their noblest efforts.	9.8
There can be no progress without war.	10.1
The highest duty of man is to fight for the power and glory of his nation.	10.8
War is glorious.	11.0

Figure 4.4

Thurstone Scale (adapted from Thurstone, 1931)

the items are now dated, we think you will see that people differ in terms of which items they rate the most highly. If you are strongly opposed to war, you probably find yourself most strongly endorsing the items that fall at the low end of the scale (e.g., "Every last one of us should refuse to take part in any way in any war"). If you are strongly in favor of war, you probably find yourself most strongly endorsing the items that fall at the high end of the scale (e.g., "War is glorious"). If you are a moderate when it comes to war, you probably find yourself most strongly endorsing the items that appear in the middle of the scale (e.g., "Under some conditions, war is necessary to maintain justice"). Moreover, if you are a moderate, you probably find your-self rejecting items at both the high end and the low end of the scale. Thus, to score "war attitudes" with this scale, a researcher should not average together a respondent's answers to all of the items. Instead, a researcher should deter-mine which items a respondent endorsed most strongly. This is the logic of *Thurstone Scales.* Researchers design these scales so that different items imply different levels of evaluation. They then compute scores that reveal whether a rater most strongly endorses the items that conveyed low evalua-tions, the items that conveyed medium evaluations, or the items that conveyed high evaluations.

A similar type of measure was designed by the psychometrician Jon Gutt-man. A typical *Guttman Scale* is shown in Figure 4.5. This scale was designed to measure attitudes towards abortion. Take a second to see how you would answer each of the four questions on this scale. In all likelihood, if you responded "no" to the first item ("Do you think abortion should be available to a woman after rape?"), then you answered "no" to all of the items that follow it. And in all likelihood, if you responded "yes" to the fourth item ("Do you think that abortion should be available on demand?"), then you responded "yes" to all of the items that precede it. This is how Guttman scales work. As with Thurstone scales, Guttman scales are designed so that items imply stronger and stronger evaluations as they move up the scale. Unlike Thurstone scales, however, Guttman scales are built on the assump-tion that people have some "threshold level," at which they move from

---

Attitude Toward Abortion

1. Do you think that abortion should be available to a woman after rape? Yes   No

2. Do you think that abortion should be available when there is threat to the physical health of the woman? Yes   No

3. Do you think that abortion should be available when there is a threat to the woman's emotional well-being? Yes   No

4. Do you think that abortion should be available on demand? Yes   No

Figure 4.5
Guttman scale (adapted from Mooney & Lee, 1995)

endorsing all items to rejecting all items. In other words, once you say "no" to an item, you're expected to continue to say "no" to all of the items that follow it. To compute someone's score using a Guttman scale, researchers therefore identify the highest item a person will endorse.

Both Thurstone and Guttman scales are similar in that researchers do not compute a scale total. Instead, they use scoring procedures that reveal which items are being endorsed and which items are not. Researchers can thus learn more about people than they would learn if they only focused on computing a scale total. They not only learn whether respondents have relatively positive or negative evaluations about wars and abortions, but they also learn why people feel the ways they do. As desirable as this feature might be, the downsides to these scales are obvious. First, both Thurstone and Guttman scales are extremely difficult to design. They are so difficult, in fact, that we cannot elaborate on the procedures involved in designing these types of scales in the space we have here (but see Eagley & Chaiken, 1993, for a nice introduction). Second, both types of scales can produce some complex scoring issues. What do you do, for instance, if a respondent embraces the high and low items on these scales but not the middle? Neither scale allows an easy interpretation of such a response pattern, but it does emerge sometimes. Psychometricians have responded to this issue by creating complex scoring algorithms that get around undesirable responses. Nevertheless, if you understand the basic logic behind these scales, you will be in a good position to understand the interesting ways in which these scales are used in psychological research, as well as the controversies their use can spark.

SUMMARY

One of the most important (and most frequently overlooked) aspects of research has to do with the tricky process of how researchers convert hypothetical, abstract constructs (e.g., altruism, fear, love) into things that are observable and thus open to psychological investigation. Very often this boils down to converting people's subjective thoughts or feelings into responses that people can report on by using some kind of simple response scale. This basic process can be broken down into a judgment phase (How do you make sure people are thinking about what you want them to think about?) and a response translation phase (How do you make sure that people convert their thoughts or feelings reliably into meaningful numbers or categories?). In this chapter, we reviewed some basic rules of thumb that researchers should follow if they wish to help their participants through this interesting

but sometimes complex process. Recall that the researcher is like a person giving directions to a traveler who needs to know exactly where he or she is supposed to go and exactly how to get there. When researchers take the perspective of their research participants by conducting careful pilot work, they set the stage for good research. However, like travel guides who need to provide travelers with specific directions by using familiar landmarks and precise mile markers, researchers also must pay attention to the details of psychological measurement, including the details of how to best anchor their response scales. Finally, researchers need to remember that just as there are different modes of travel, there are also different modes of measurement. The popular structured self-report response scales that work so effectively for most researchers most of the time may occasionally prove to be inferior to less popular methods. Choosing the specific measurement method that is best for your participants will depend not only on who your participants are but also on the psychological destination you have in mind for them.

STUDY QUESTIONS

1. The judgment phase and the response translation phase highlight different challenges that psychologists must consider when writing good research questions. What are these challenges?

2. Consider the following (open-ended) survey question:

   > To what extent do you not venerate psychology generally or research methods more specifically because you think it is of great consequence? Rate your response from 1 ("yes, very much") to 4 ("no, not at all").

   List five or more problems with the way this question is worded.

3. What problems do floor and ceiling effects create for researchers who wish to test theories of covariation? What can be done to minimize the likelihood of these problems?

4. You are interested in knowing more about the factors that cause some men to batter their spouses. You therefore plan to study a group of highly violent men who have been incarcerated for violence against women. You hope that your study will yield important insights that might help researchers reduce this crime, and you want to start developing the questions you will ask. So, where do you start? What steps would you follow to increase the likelihood that your questionnaire can yield insights into this social problem?

5. Research can usually let participants answer specific research questions using either continuous (e.g., 7-point) or dichotomous (e.g., "yes" vs. "no") response scales. What are the advantages of using continuous scales? What guidelines for choosing the number of responses and number of anchors are suggested in this chapter's discussion of the EGWA scale? What is the difference between the bipolar and unipolar EGWA scale, and why do these two forms exist?

6. This chapter presents a Thurstone scale for measuring attitudes towards war and a Guttman scale for measuring attitudes towards abortion. What is the difference between these two types of scales? What would a Guttman scale measuring attitudes towards war look like? What would a semantic differential measure assessing attitudes toward abortion look like? What are the specific challenges that make it difficult to construct Thurstone, Guttman, and semantic differential scales?

How Do We Misinterpret? Common Threats to Validity

This was a creature, more troublesom to be drawn, then any of the rest, for I could not, for a good while, think of a way to make it suffer its body to ly quietly, in a natural posture; but whil'st it was alive, if its feet were fetter'd in Wax or Glew, it would so twist and wind its body, that I could not any wayes get a good view of it; and if I killed it, its body was so little, that I did often spoile the shape of it, before I could thoroughly view it: for this is the nature of these minute Bodies, that as soon, almost, as ever their life is destroy'd, their parts immediately shrivel, and lose their beauty. So it is ... with ... Animal substances; the dead body of an Ant, or such little creature, does almost instantly shrivel and dry, and your object shall become quite another thing, before you can half delieneate it....

—Robert Hooke *(Micrographia, 1665) on the difficulty of rendering drawings of ants from microscopic observations*

For if we wish to form a picture of the nature of these elementary particles, we can no longer ignore the physical processes through which we obtain our knowledge of them.... In the case of the smallest building particles of matter, every process of observation produces a large disturbance. We can no longer speak of the behaviour of the particle independently of the process of observation.

—Werner Heisenberg *(1955) on the impossibility of precisely assessing certain properties of subatomic particles*

ONE STRANGE AND LUCRATIVE STORY

When Brett Pelham (the first author of this text) was in the third grade, he did a very unscrupulous thing. He had gotten into the habit of selling and swapping candy, toys, and magnets with the other kids in his third-grade class, and on this particular day he really needed a quarter. Unfortunately, all he had to work with was a lead fishing weight. The lead weight couldn't be made into any kind of toy, and it didn't do anything fun or exciting. In fact, being made of lead, it wouldn't even stick to a magnet. In a moment of inspiration (or perhaps desperation) Brett decided that the fishing weight was actually a lucky charm, and he further decided to try to pawn it off on his good friend David Hare. David had traded with Brett before, and when Brett claimed to possess a lucky charm that he was willing to sell for only a quarter, David was justifiably skeptical. Brett proposed a simple test of the efficacy of the charm. He told David to put the charm in his pocket and ask Jill Long to give him a dime so that he could buy an ice cream. (At Happy Valley Elementary School, ice cream was always available right after recess, and the price was only a dime.) Brett wasn't sure if he really expected the scam to work, but he figured that if it didn't, he would be none the worse for it. Of course, if it *did* somehow work, Brett would have his desperately needed 25 cents (or 2½ ice creams, to put it in perspective). After putting the charm to the test, David came back to Brett beaming with joy and announced (1) that Jill Long had given him the dime and (2) that he would be delighted to purchase the charm.

One of us would like to believe that Brett was smart enough to pull the wool over David's eyes, but in all honesty, Brett was almost as persuaded about the efficacy of the "charm" as David was. Brett vividly remembers being *extremely* reluctant to sell the charm once he learned how well it had worked. His ultimate decision to sell probably says a lot more about his inability to delay gratification than it does about his intellectual precocity. Of course, we all know now that the test Brett proposed to David had some very serious flaws. In retrospect it's pretty clear that David's profitable exchange with Jill Long had a lot more to do with David's ability to be charming (and Jill's generosity) than it did with the charming powers of a lead fishing weight.

This story is a fitting introduction to the topic of threats to validity because the crucial test described in the story has some intuitive appeal but suffers from many of the problems that characterize research studies that are low in validity. In the case of the test of the fishing weight, Brett had asked David to do several problematic things: to make a single observation, to gather data from a biased sample of "participants" (himself and Jill), and to fail to include the equivalent of a control group (i.e., some observations in which he asked people like Jill for money *without* the charm). These kinds of issues are the topic of this chapter: issues that determine the validity of a set of research findings. Many of the specific threats discussed here have been discussed in detail by Cook and Campbell (1979). Thus, much of this chapter (and much of what we know about psychological research methods) is a tribute to their insights.

This chapter focuses on four general categories of threat to the validity of a set of research findings. We divide each of these four general categories of threat into two or three more specific categories, and in the case of each specific threat, we discuss exactly what kind of validity it threatens (e.g., internal or external validity). Finally, we also make some suggestions for how to reduce or eliminate each threat to validity. To begin with the broad categories first, we argue that almost any threat to the validity of a research finding can be placed under one of three broad categories. These categories include the ideas that (1) people are different, (2) people change, and (3) the process of studying people changes people. Let's begin with the idea that people are different.

PEOPLE ARE DIFFERENT

Individual Differences and "Third Variables"

Your mother loves stir-fried vegetables and classical music. Your father cares little for either. *You* are wondering intensely how we knew about your parents' taste in food and music. Another reader whose parents have precisely the same taste is far less curious. These are simple examples of the fact that people are different. Although everyone seems to know that people are different, not everyone appreciates the implications of this simple fact for research methodology. (In other words, people differ in how much they appreciate the implications of being different.) As it turns out, one of the most common and pervasive category of threats to validity is based on this obvious fact about people.

The type of research claim that is most susceptible to this threat is probably best thought of as a **pseudo-experiment** or false experiment. However, because people often treat pseudo-experiments as if they were true experiments, it is worth beginning our list of threats to validity with a discussion of how individual differences could cloud the interpretation of this intuitively appealing but analytically appalling approach to research. As the term is used here, a pseudo-experiment is a research design in which someone tests a claim about a variable (e.g., a product, a charm, a clinical treatment) by exposing people to the variable of interest and noting that these people feel, think, or behave as expected. Examples of claims based on pseudo-experiments include things like "Melanie wore her lucky bowling shoes and bowled a 247," "LJ took the Ivy Review LSAT Course and aced her LSATs," and "David carried a fishing weight in his pocket and got a dime from Jill Long." Although there are other problems with claims such as these, the most serious problem is that some particular people happen to be good at bowling, taking exams, and getting dimes. In the absence of some kind of comparison with a **control group**, we have no idea what would have happened if the same person had engaged in the same behavior *without* being exposed to the variable of interest. Individual differences provide a very good alternate explanation for the findings observed in pseudo-experiments, especially those involving a small number of research participants.

We discuss the ways in which researchers try to create control conditions to address individual differences in Chapter 7 (Experimental Research Designs) and Chapter 8 (Quasi-Experimental Research Designs). For now, we simply note that individual differences do not merely undermine pseudo-experiments, but they can also undermine careful, systematic, scientific observation. Consider a hypothetical correlational study. Imagine we told you that we have obtained strong evidence that tattoos are a leading cause of death. We did so by conducting a ten-year longitudinal study of 12,000 middle-aged men living in small rural towns in the southern United States. In this hypothetical study, we simply measured the number of tattoos that each man had and examined death rates over the ten-year period for men with different numbers of tattoos. Figure 5.1 illustrates the findings from this hypothetical study. The findings clearly show that the more tattoos men had, the more likely they were to die during the ten-year period. In a sample this large, these findings would undoubtedly be highly significant. Does this mean that tattoos are a public health menace? Obviously not. Quite a few variables are confounded with the number of tattoos that middle-aged people have, and they provide a much more reasonable account of these findings. Because we both grew up in rural southern towns, and because one of us has quite a few tattooed relatives, we hesitate to contribute to stereotypes of middle-aged people with tattoos. Nonetheless, restricting our analysis to what the first author has directly observed in his own tattooed relatives, we are willing to suggest that, in this specific age group, men who have a lot of tattoos might be more likely than their untattooed peers to (1) use tobacco products, (2) drive motorcycles, (3) eat high-fat, low-fiber diets, (4) consume large quantities of alcohol, (5) fail to wear their seat belts when driving, (6) get into bar fights, (7) fail to get adequate medical treatment for their high blood pressure or diabetes, and (8) insult other tattooed people who are known to carry handguns. Because any one of these eight competing individual differences might be enough to explain the observed findings regarding tattoos and death rates, few people would be tempted to conclude that tattoos play a direct role in causing death.

Figure 5.1

Probability of death from all causes as a function of number of tattoos processed (data are hypothetical)

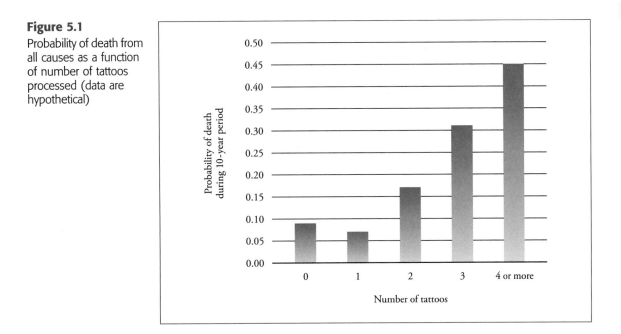

Selection Bias and Nonresponse Bias

The examples above indicate that individual differences create a potential threat to the internal validity of many research studies. Individual differences can also be a threat to the external validity of many research studies. If people are different and if a sampling technique somehow favors one particular kind of person, we might draw general conclusions about people (in either experimental or nonexperimental studies) that apply only to the particular people, or kinds of people, that we have sampled. Sampling people from an unrepresentative sample (by using imperfect sampling techniques) is referred to as **selection bias**. A famous example of selection bias that led to a failed prediction about a U.S. presidential election occurred back in 1936 when researchers were still struggling to develop valid sampling techniques. A group of researchers from the prestigious *Literary Digest* mailed postcards to 10 million Americans and asked them who they planned to vote for in the upcoming presidential election. Well over 2 million people returned the postcards, and the results of the poll suggested strongly that the Republican candidate, Alf Landon, was the people's choice. Of course, the results of this gigantic poll were wrong. Otherwise, you'd probably see a tiny profile of Alf Landon every time you looked at a dime. The Democratic candidate, Franklin D. Roosevelt, won the election in a landslide.

Why were the *Literary Digest* pollsters wrong? Because they made use of biased sampling techniques. In particular, they sampled their pool of potential voters by selecting names from places like telephone directories and automobile registration records. Not surprisingly, the kinds of people who owned cars and telephones back in the Depression-riddled 1930s were pretty rich. As it turns out, the 1930s represented a turning point in American voting patterns. This just happens to have been the time in American history when people began voting with their purses. Thus, in 1936, wealthy people were much more likely to vote Republican. Although this is not always mentioned in discussions of the *Literary Digest* error, not everyone expected Alf Landon to win. In particular, researchers from the recently formed Gallup organization conducted a much smaller poll of about 50,000 people. (That's a sample about 1/48th the size of the *Literary Digest* sample!) In their poll, the Gallup group used methods that much more closely approximated true random sampling. These procedures appear to have been much less biased than those of the *Digest*. In contrast to the predictions of the *Digest*, the Gallup group predicted that Roosevelt would get about 56 percent of the vote. In actuality, he got 62 percent. The Gallup pollsters were less than perfect, but they correctly predicted that Roosevelt would win.

Another important form of bias that is likely to have played a role in the *Literary Digest* error is **nonresponse bias**. Nonresponse bias is closely related to selection bias except that in the case of nonresponse bias, the respondents themselves are the source of the bias. Because people who choose to answer surveys are systematically different from people who choose *not* to do so, surveys that have low response rates may yield information that is highly misleading. In the case of the *Literary Digest* error, only about 24 percent of those who were mailed postcards asking them about the election bothered to return the cards. Although this still yielded a very large sample, the size of this sample was meaningless. More than 2 million badly sampled voters are still badly sampled. The most likely result of nonresponse bias in this particular case is that the people in this sample who were on the fence about the election may have been less likely to send in the postcard. Given the general sampling bias that favored Alf Landon, nonresponse bias is likely to have exaggerated an already serious problem. Modern survey researchers have developed a wide range of solutions to the problem of nonresponse bias. For example, most modern pollsters now conduct most of their interviews over the phone rather than by mail-in surveys (see Freedman, Pisani, Purves, & Adhikari, 1991). Furthermore, when choosing who to sample, modern pollsters take into account the constantly increasing percentage of Americans who no longer have landline telephones at all but rely completely on their cell phones.

On the other hand, because response rates to telephone surveys have gotten lower and lower over the past couple of decades, the researchers who conduct the General Social Survey (GSS) every two years have chosen to recruit a representative sample of Americans by going door to door and doing face to face surveys. The GSS survey is extremely expensive compared with telephone surveys, but it typically yields a very high response rate (about 70 percent). Nonetheless, even a 70 percent response rate can sometimes be a problem. Thus, modern survey researchers have developed sophisticated ways of minimizing and adjusting for nonresponse bias. For example, one approach to reducing nonresponse bias is to weight individual respondents based on known population values. If you happened to sample more men than women, for example, you could weight women's responses more heavily than men's – to minimize the biases that would likely result from this imperfect sampling outcome.

One might assume that *all* modern pollsters and survey researchers would have learned their lesson from the *Literary Digest* error, but the results of poorly conducted polls can still garner a great deal of public attention. Back in the early 1990s, *TV Guide* reported the results of a poll of people's attitudes about television. In particular, they asked people if they would be willing to forgo *ever* watching television again for an absurdly huge amount of money (something like a million dollars). A ridiculously high proportion of those polled reported that the rough psychological equivalent of being given a dump truck full of money would not be enough to convince them to abandon TV forever! As much as Americans (the current authors included) rely on TV for daily doses of enlightenment, we were shocked to learn about the results of this poll. When we later learned that *TV Guide* had sampled people who (1) just happened to subscribe to their weekly TV magazine and (2) had bothered to return their questionnaire, we were less a lot less shocked.

To bring the issue of selection bias a little closer to home, Sears (1986) argued that the common practice of relying heavily on samples of convenience (i.e., on college students) in research may represent a serious shortcoming of much psychological research. In fact, Sears argued that some of our most important conclusions about human nature may be somewhat wide of the mark. For example, he argued that research on attitudes may underestimate the stability and potency of people's attitudes. Because college students are still forming many of their important attitudes, their attitudes may be less likely to predict behavior than the attitudes of a typical sample of older adults. Similarly, Sears argued that college students may be more obedient to authority than are older adults. Although it is possible to take issue with some of his assertions (e.g., that college students are highly deferent to authorities), it is hard to argue with his general point. As we noted in Chapter 3, Henrich, Heine, and Norenzayan (2010) have taken Sears's point one step further by noting that even if we sampled a highly representative group of Americans or Western Europeans, we would still fail to describe the psychology of the billions of people worldwide who live in cultures that are radically different from modern Western cultures (see also Hofstede, 2003; Markus & Kitayama, 1991; Triandis, 1989; but cf. Becker, 2009, or Hetts, Sakuma, & Pelham, 1999).

Although selection bias clearly threatens the external validity of descriptive findings, it does not necessarily threaten the internal validity of an experimental finding. For instance, suppose a researcher uses random assignment and demonstrates that college students are more persuaded by logical arguments than by emotional appeals. The use of random assignment to condition offers some reassurance that some types of arguments are more likely than others to produce (i.e., cause) attitude change. However, there is no guarantee that this same causal relation would hold up in a sample of truck drivers or dairy farmers. And even if it did, this additional finding is no guarantee that it would hold up in Burundi or Malaysia. In short, knowing that a cause and effect relation is present for a given sample (internal validity) does not offer assurances that it generalizes to other samples drawn from different populations (external validity). At the same time, evidence that an effect does not generalize to different populations does not mean that the original effect was not present.

Finally, it is important to note that the efficacy or utility of a sampling technique depends as much on the group of people about whom we would like to generalize, or the specific point we wish to make, as it does on the group of people we have sampled. If we are interested in the attitudes of truck drivers, college students, or fashion models, it would obviously be highly inappropriate to collect data from a random sample of American voters. There are also some times when a highly unrepresentative sample might be more useful and impressive than a truly random sample. For example, if you wished to document that human beings sometimes fail to behave logically or rationally, it would probably be particularly impressive to document that a group of philosophy professors or statisticians did so.

PEOPLE CHANGE

Another category of threats to validity is based on the idea that people differ not only from one another but also from *themselves*. That is, people sometimes change. You are not exactly the same person you were four years ago.

You also are not the same person when you are with your best friend that you are when you are with your mom (unless your mom happens to be your best friend). Just as differences between people can sometimes masquerade as meaningful research findings, differences in the *same person* across time and situations can sometimes do the same. This can be true even when researchers make use of both a pretest and a posttest to assess changes in people's behavior. If people change for reasons that have nothing to do with a researcher's treatment, then these changes can lead to some very inappropriate conclusions about the treatment. We break these changes down into two broad categories. One category is history and maturation. The other category is regression toward the mean.

History and Maturation

History and maturation each represent common threats to internal validity. These threats are most likely to pose a problem when a researcher conducts a pretest-posttest study in which all participants receive the treatment of interest (i.e., in a repeated measures study in which there is no control group). As the name implies, **history** refers to changes that occur more or less across the board in a very large group of people such as a nation or culture. In contrast, **maturation** refers to the specific developmental or experiential changes that occur in a particular person, or a particular age cohort, over time. During times of famine in a particular culture or region, most people lose weight. During adolescence, most people grow and gain weight. Like individual differences, history and maturation represent a serious threat to validity only when a researcher does not conduct a true experiment. However, unlike individual differences, history and maturation still pose serious problems even when a researcher attempts to control for individual differences by assessing the responses of the same person before and after a treatment.

For example, imagine that a researcher is interested in improving people's dancing ability by using mental imagery. Assume that the researcher convinces a group of 20 adolescent ballet dancers to take part in a 12-week mental imagery study in which the dancers spend five minutes per day vividly imagining graceful dance moves. Suppose further that the researcher measures people's performance during a dance recital both before and after the 12-week treatment and finds that the average participant increased the quality of his or her dances by about one point on a well-validated 14-point scale of dance performance. Although the researcher might wish to conclude that mental imagery can improve people's dancing ability, it would probably be much more reasonable to conclude that 12 weeks of dance classes, or perhaps 12 weeks of simple physical maturation, led to the average increase.

How could the researcher correct this problem? One way is to conduct a true experiment in which he or she randomly assigns dancers to either a mental imagery condition or a control condition (a condition that does *not* include any mental imagery training). If the study is conducted with an appropriate level of care, and if the gains posted by the experimental group are significantly larger than those posted by the control group, it would be reasonable to attribute the difference in improvement between the two groups to the experimental imagery treatment. Learning and maturation would almost certainly happen, but they should happen *equally* to dancers randomly assigned to each of the two conditions.

Where threats to validity are concerned, the problems of history and maturation can also refer to relatively short-term changes in a person's physical or psychological state—changes that may occur over a couple of weeks, or even a few minutes, rather than a few months. One of our favorite examples of relatively short-term "maturation" comes from an episode of the 1960s TV show *The Beverly Hillbillies*. In this episode, Granny claims to have developed a cure for the common cold. When queried about her remedy, Granny dictates that people afflicted with severe cold or flu symptoms should (1) drink her special, home-brewed elixir once a day, (2) consume plenty of other fluids, and (3) rest in bed for about two weeks. Less entertaining examples of this logic appear frequently in TV commercials for pain relievers. Such commercials often include testimonials from people who, for example, had a throbbing headache, took a dose of a pain reliever, and felt better a little while later. Anyone who has ever had to endure a headache when no pain reliever was handy knows that throbbing headaches eventually stop throbbing. Sound evidence of the relative superiority of a particular pain reliever would require evidence from a true experiment in which a control group received a brand of pain reliever other than the one being advertised.

Regression Toward the Mean

A phenomenon that is closely related to maturation also represents a threat to internal validity, and it is important enough to deserve a discussion of its own. This threat to validity is **regression toward the mean**: the tendency for people who receive high or low scores on a particular measure to score closer to the mean on a subsequent testing. This movement of means can sometimes cause researchers to misinterpret their data. For instance, suppose a researcher develops an experimental treatment in order to raise the test performance of a group of high school students. Consistent with predictions, students who receive the treatment do show an increase in performance. It would be a mistake, however, to conclude that this change was a "treatment effect" if it occurred because of regression toward the mean. Changes in human performance due to regression toward the mean are most frequently attributed to a treatment when researchers conduct the kind of pretest-posttest designs that are also susceptible to threats like history and maturation. However, in the pure case of regression toward the mean, changes that are mistaken for experimental treatments occur when research participants do not experience any true changes (such as maturation) but nonetheless score differently than they did originally when they take a retest of a particular measure of personality or performance.

If this sounds a little puzzling, consider a concrete example. Suppose you are shooting a few baskets with your friend Brook, who used to play high school basketball and is rumored to be a very good free-throw shooter.

When you press her to tell you *exactly* how good she is, she replies that she hasn't played much in the past six months but adds that her free-throw shooting percentage in high school was 80 percent. Being the skeptical type, suppose you hand her the ball and ask her to shoot 20 free throws to document her prowess. Now suppose she makes an impressive 19 of 20 shots. That's 95 percent, which is quite a bit better than what she claimed. Would you call your friend a liar and insist that her free-throw percentage in high school must have been 95 percent? We're guessing you wouldn't. And you shouldn't. Simple things like luck (a couple of good rolls on shots that normally don't fall) or having a "good day" (e.g., having had a good night's sleep) are likely to have made a contribution to her stellar performance at the stripe. Finally, suppose you are asked to predict how many free throws (out of 20) Brook will make *tomorrow*. You probably shouldn't predict 19. If Brook was truly an 80 percent free-throw shooter in high school, and if she hasn't changed much lately, you would probably predict better if you guessed that her performance would match her "true score," which appears to be about 80 percent (or 16 out of 20).

The only problem with this analysis is that people often fail to appreciate just how pervasive and predictable regression toward the mean really is. For example, many parents, coaches, and trainers of fighter pilots appear to believe that punishment is a more effective training tool than is reinforcement. Kahneman and Tversky (1973) noted that experienced trainers of fighter pilots expressed a great deal of confidence in this belief about the effects of rewards and punishments on performance in the cockpit. They defended the belief by noting that reinforcing pilots for excellent performance was typically followed by a drop in performance. In contrast, they noted, punishing pilots for poor performance was typically followed by an improvement in performance! In both cases, of course, the changes in the pilots' behavior can be readily explained by regression toward the mean.

Table 5.1   Regression toward the mean in professional sports

---

1. **2009 NFL Regular Season Rushing Leaders (Rankings):**
   Chris Johnson, #1,   Steven Jackson, #2,   Thomas Jones, #3

   2010 NFL Rushing Rankings for Same Three Players:
   Chris Johnson, #4,   Steven Jackson, #8,   Thomas Jones, #20

2. **2009–2010 NBA Regular Season Free-Throw Percentage Leaders:**
   Steve Nash, #1 (93.8%),   Dirk Nowitzki, #2 (91.5%),   Ray Allen, #3 (91.3%)

   2010–2011 Rankings (and Free-Throw Percentages) for Same Three Players:
   Steve Nash, #4 (91.2%),   Dirk Nowitzki #7 (89.2%),   Ray Allen, #9 (88.1%)

3. **2009 WTA End of Season Singles Rankings**
   Serena Williams, #1,   Dinara Safina, #2,   Svetlana Kuznetsova, #3

   2010 WTA Rankings for Same Three Players
   Serena Williams, #4,   Dinara Safina, #62,   Svetlana Kuznetsova, #27

4. **2009 PGA Tour Official World Golf Rankings:**
   Tiger Woods, #1   Phil Mickelson, #2   Steve Stricker, #3

   2010 Rankings of Same Three Players:
   Tiger Woods, #2   Phil Mickelson, #4   Steve Stricker, #7

People who believe that award-winning rookie athletes experience a "sopho-more slump" (because they get lazy or arrogant) or that making it to the cover of *Sports Illustrated* spells doom for a college football team may also fail to appreciate the potency and ubiquity of regression toward the mean. Some additional observations that are consistent with regression toward the mean in sports appear in Table 5.1. In fact, in a wide range of areas in which people must use less-than-perfect indicators to make inferences about a person's traits or abilities, human judges often fail to appreciate regression toward the mean. For instance, when a top-selling CD wins a major award or breaks a sales record, people often express disappointment that the sub-sequent CD didn't do as well as the one that preceded it. Moreover, fans and critics alike often struggle to understand what caused the artist to lose his or her touch in the subsequent album. A good example of this kind of analysis came after Hootie and the Blowfish's *Cracked Rear View* CD sold millions of copies in 1994 and 1995. Their next album, *Fairweather John-son*, was reasonably successful, but it sold considerably less well than the blockbuster CD that preceded it. In his unofficial Web page, one of the oth-erwise admiring fans of this group lamented the mistake that he felt could cost Hootie and the Blowfish their careers:

> Can you recall an 80s band named "Men at Work"? Well, they too had great success with their first album like Hootie. Here's where the similarities get ugly; Men at Work's second album did OK but not as good as the first album ... same with Hootie. Then Men at Work took a year off, again just like Hootie is planning to do. Finally when Men at Work came back and put out their 3rd album (Two Hearts) it BOMBED big-time! Sooo, let's hope this time off is good for Hootie and that they don't end up ... like Men at Work....

How can things like free throws, album sales, or IQ scores reflect regres-sion toward the mean even when there is no real change in a person's talents or traits in a given area? The key to answering this question centers around the distinction between a *performance* or *observed score* (e.g., scoring 132 on an IQ test, making 19 of 20 free throws, producing a CD that sells over 10 million copies) and a *true score*: an underlying ability or trait that the observed score presumably reflects (being smart, being a good free-throw shooter, being musically gifted). Almost by definition, true scores are much more stable than observed scores. They reflect the stable characteristics of the person in an idealized setting in which things like good or bad luck are held constant. In contrast, performances or observed scores are influenced not only by true scores (real attributes of the person in question) but also by *error* (chance factors that influence performance). These sources of error are things that are unsystematic and difficult or impossible to predict. They include both fluctuating personal variables like physical health, fatigue level, or brief lapses in attention, and fluctuating environmental variables like room temperature, court conditions, or whims in the public's musical taste.

Regression toward the mean is such an important concept that we have included a special activity on this methodological concept in Appendix 1 (Hands-On Activity 2). Until you have completed that exercise, the best way to think of regression toward the mean is that it exists because performance is always a joint product of skill and luck. Unusually good or bad performances are typically composed of a combination of relatively low or high ability, *plus* unusually bad or good luck. The ability factor doesn't usually change at a second testing, but luck typically does. Our best guess about luck is that it is likely to be average anytime we assess it, and this means, for example, that really good luck is usually followed by luck that isn't quite so good. This, of course, leads to scores or performances that aren't quite so good.

As mentioned earlier, the kinds of studies that are most likely to be influenced by regression toward the mean are pretest-posttest studies that do not involve a control group. For instance, imagine that you identify a group of people in a physical education course who all score below the mean on a measure of free-throw shooting. After recording each person's score, you might give all these people some coaching in free-throw shooting. If you test them again and find that the average person shows large gains in free-throw shooting percentage, there would be two good explanations for the observed changes. One possibility is that the coaching was successful. The other is that the group showed regression toward the mean. This should be the case because, *as a group*, your free-throw shooters are likely to have had below-average luck at the free-throw line during the pretest. On the whole, their luck during the posttest should be neither bad nor good, and thus the average score for the group as a whole should increase.

How can you separate regression toward the mean from an experimental treatment? The easiest way would be to divide your group of poor shooters in half (at random) and to give half of the group no coaching. If the group that received coaching showed a larger increase than did the control group, it would be reasonable to conclude that your coaching techniques had been effective. The same situation would apply if you identify a group of people who score high on a self-report measure of depression and give half of them two weeks of intensive psychotherapy. Unless you have a control group that does *not* receive therapy, you won't know if the observed improvements in the well-being of your treatment group reflect (1) the effectiveness of your therapy or (2) regression toward the mean. In fact, in the extreme case, you could give people therapy that actually makes them worse and still see improvements in your treatment group! If your control group shows significantly *more* improvement than your treatment group, this would be very bad news indeed for the usefulness of your treatment. In other words, if people who are left to their own devices improve more than people who are treated, it would be better to leave people to their own devices!

THE PROCESS OF STUDYING PEOPLE CHANGES PEOPLE

As suggested by the quotation that begins this chapter, Robert Hooke (1665) experienced great difficulty performing early microscopic studies of ants and other small insects. The primary difficulty that plagued Hooke is the fact that ants, like people, do not always welcome being studied. Hooke's eventual solution was to put his uncooperative subjects to sleep by placing them "into a drop of very well rectified spirit of Wine." When the spirits evaporated, the ants were preserved intact, ready for careful microscopic examination. Two hundred and ninety years later, Werner Heisenberg (1955) wrote of a similar but even greater problem, the impossibility of observing certain properties of subatomic particles without changing the nature of the particles. Heisenberg's uncertainty principle dictates, among other things, that there is no way to know simultaneously both the position and the momentum of subatomic particles such as protons or electrons. Translating loosely, one aspect of the Heisenberg uncertainty principle is that subatomic particles do not like to be observed. Although the amount of error or unpredictability introduced by the uncertainty principle is very small, its theoretical implications have been large enough to turn modern physics on its head.

At about the same time that physics was being reinvented by people like Heisenberg and Einstein, researchers at the Hawthorne Plant of the Western Electric Company (in Chicago, Illinois) were learning that studying people can be just as tricky as studying ants or electrons. Researchers at the Hawthorne Plant were interested in the effects of environmental factors such as lighting on worker productivity. According to traditional interpretations of the Hawthorne studies, the workers at the Hawthorne plant responded to almost *any* changes in working conditions by working harder than usual. For example, both increases and decreases in lighting levels appeared to make people work harder. Over the past 70 years or so, researchers have dubbed this effect (the increases in productivity that occur when workers know they are being studied) the **Hawthorne effect**. According to some contemporary researchers (see Dooley, 1995), however, the Hawthorne effect actually has a somewhat shaky empirical foundation. At least some of the quasi-experimental manipulations performed in the Hawthorne studies may have been confounded with other factors such as personnel changes.

On the other hand, even if the Hawthorne effect is a bit of a misnomer, a large body of research in psychology suggests that the act of studying people can dramatically change the way that people behave. One of the most dramatic instances we know of is called the *mere measurement effect*. This effect refers to the tendency for participants to change their behavior simply because they have been asked how they will act in the future. Suppose, for instance, that we ask you if you intend to exercise after class today. You tell us that you do intend to do this. If we check back with you tomorrow, perhaps we will learn that that you did indeed exercise after class. But, would you have exercised if we had not asked you what you intended to do? Research suggests pretty clearly that your chances of exercising in this situation would be higher than usual, simply because we asked you if you intended to exercise. In one particularly dramatic instance of this phenomenon, Morwitz, Johnson, and Schmittlein (1993) found that simply asking a group if they intended to buy a car increased their chances of buying an automobile in the next six months by 35 percent! (Also, see Morwitz & Fitzsimons, 2004; Williams, Fitzsimons, & Block, 2004.) Because many, many research studies ask participants to answer questions about their behavior (see Chapter 4), it is entirely possible that many studies have the unintended consequence of changing research participants' behavior in some small way. The mere measurement effect thus speaks to the external validity of research. If a study documents an effect on behavior, it is possible that the documented result would not generalize to people who have not been in a research study that asked them about their behavior. Researchers who have documented the mere measurement effect and other ways in which studying people can change them might thus argue that Hooke and Heisenberg had it easy. At least ants and subatomic particles don't have to fill out questionnaires.

Testing Effects

Another way in which studying people changes them is similar to the mere measurement effect but actually poses more of a threat to internal than to external validity. This threat to internal validity, called **testing effects**, is a problem in pretest-posttest designs that have no control group. Testing effects refer to the tendency for most participants to perform better on a test or personality measure the second time they take it. This improvement typically occurs even on clinical and IQ tests, and it often occurs even when people are given an alternate form of the test at the second testing.

There are many potential explanations for testing effects. To a great extent, testing effects probably reflect learning on the part of the test taker. In the case of an IQ test, for example, test takers may belatedly come up with a good strategy for approaching a certain kind of test question. Similarly, highly motivated takers of IQ tests might even go to the trouble to look up the answers to some of the questions that they were unable to answer. In the case of tests of knowledge or physical skills, the simple act of taking the test provides practice at retrieving information or doing the task, respectively (e.g., see Karpicke & Blunt, 2011). In the case of attitude, personality, or self-concept measures, on the other hand, what people may learn is what the test measures or what kinds of responses are socially desirable. In the case of many psychological tests, yet another way of thinking about testing effects is that they may represent a form of *attitude polarization*. Research on attitude polarization has shown that simply allowing people to give a little thought to their attitudes often leads them to become more extreme in these attitudes. Because most people's scores on most socially desirable psychological measures tend to be positive in the first place, we might expect that the simple opportunity to think about or express these positive attitudes (by filling out a psychological measure) will lead to a strengthening or polarization of these attitudes (Tesser & Valenti, 1981).

Regardless of exactly why testing effects occur, they may masquerade as treatment effects anytime a researcher tests a group of participants twice without including a pretested control group. Testing effects can even occur for people who score at or above the mean on a psychological measure. Because testing effects are in opposition to regression toward the mean for people who initially obtain high scores on a particular measure, you may be

Figure 5.2

Simultaneous regression toward the mean and testing effects for novice bocci ball players

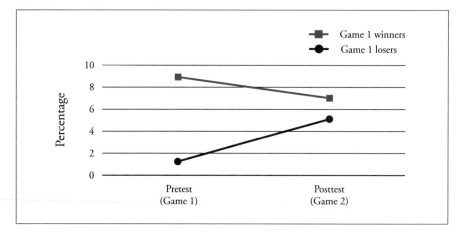

wondering how testing effects and regression toward the mean can both be true. In fact, they can both occur even in the same study or performance situation. Figure 5.2 illustrates a hypothetical data set in which regression toward the mean and testing effects occur simultaneously. For this hypothetical group of beginning bocce players, the score of the average participant increased by exactly a point (from 5.0 to 6.0) from the first to the second game. At the same time, the group of low scorers (those who had lost their first game) scored better in game 2, and the group of high scorers (those who had won their first game) scored worse in game 2. The reason there could still be a testing (or practice) effect is that the four-point gains of the initial losers more than made up for the two-point losses of the initial winners.

There are several ways to correct the problem of testing effects. As suggested above, one simple way is to conduct a true experiment with a pretested control group. This will not eliminate testing effects, but it will allow you to separate them from your experimental treatment. On the other hand, if you are strongly interested in obtaining a posttreatment score that is not in any way influenced by a pretest, you can conduct a true experiment in which you simply eliminate the pretest. Although this approach may not be quite as sensitive or statistically powerful as the approach that makes use of a pretest, notice that this simplified design still allows you to draw firm conclusions about your treatment. For example, if you identify a large group of children who are at risk for developing low self-esteem, you could randomly determine that half of them would receive an experimental intervention—without ever measuring anyone's self-esteem prior to the intervention. As long as you randomly assign the children to two groups, you could safely assume that the initial self-esteem levels of the two groups are identical. Barring a failure of random assignment, any meaningful differences that exist between the two groups *after* the intervention would thus have to be a consequence of the experimental intervention. Finally, if you have no other choice (e.g., if ethical or practical concerns make it impossible to have a control group), you could minimize the possibility of testing effects by waiting as long as possible to administer your posttest (and perhaps by using an alternate version of the test). Presumably, if you wait long enough, your participants might forget most of what they learned by taking the initial test.

Experimental Mortality (Attrition)

It would be nice if the worst thing that ever happened to people when they took part in psychological research was to learn the lowdown on a particular psychological test. Unfortunately for researchers as well as for participants, another thing that some participants learn about some investigations is that they wish to withdraw from them. The failure of some of the participants in an experiment to complete the study is known as **experimental mortality**, or **attrition**. Depending on exactly what form it takes, this problem can represent a threat to internal validity, a threat to external validity, or a threat to both.

One troublesome form of experimental mortality happens in experiments or longitudinal studies that take a very long time to complete. In the case of lengthy experiments, people may get tired or bored and fail to respond at certain crucial points in the study. In the case of longitudinal survey studies, people may move away to Chicago or Kamchatka. As a more detailed example, consider a lengthy experiment on *implicit learning* (learning without awareness). Implicit learning is a very interesting topic. It has to do with how people can be taught to behave as if they know things (such as rules for categorizing stimuli) without being able to report consciously the basis of their knowledge (see Reber & Kotovsky, 1997, for an example). However, from the perspective of research participants, studies of implicit learning can be extremely boring because they require people to process seemingly meaningless stimuli for very long periods (for hours or occasionally even days at a time).

Suppose a researcher wants to find out if people can implicitly learn some of the important grammatical rules of an artificial language. To find out, imagine that she exposes her participants to an experimentally generated language for a total of 12 hours (over a period of four days). Suppose further that the researcher manipulates limitations on people's working memory to test her prediction that people will show implicit learning only when they are able to devote their full attention to the experimental task. Finally, suppose that a lot of people get sick of reading a meaningless artificial language for 12 precious hours of their lives. That is, assume that the researcher's study is plagued by a high rate of experimental mortality. To be more specific, imagine that she starts out with 40 participants divided evenly between her two conditions but loses exactly six people in each of the two conditions of her study. Finally, assume that the remaining 28 participants confirm her predictions perfectly. Only the participants in the low-load (high-attention) condition show evidence of implicit learning.

Can the researcher confidently conclude that her manipulation had its intended effect? In other words, is her study high in internal validity? Probably so. Although the 12 people who dropped out of her study are almost certainly different from the 28 who stayed in, it is noteworthy that the proportion of people who dropped out of the study (the attrition rate) is *exactly the same* in the two different conditions. Studies in which there is an equal level of attrition across all of the experimental conditions suffer from simple or **homogeneous attrition**. Any individual differences associated with attrition should thus be constant in the two different conditions. This does not mean that the study is perfect. Instead it means that the high attrition rate observed in the study is predominantly a threat to *external* rather than internal validity. There is a good chance that these findings apply only to the kind of highly motivated, tolerant, or easygoing person who can endure 12 hours of exposure to artificial language. Whether the results would generalize to the kinds of people who dropped out of the study is open to debate.

A second form of mortality does represent a serious threat to internal validity. This more troublesome form of mortality is known as differential or **heterogeneous attrition**. Heterogeneous attrition occurs when the attrition rates in two or more conditions of an experiment are noticeably different. Suppose, for example, that in an even more tedious version of the hypothetical study described above, the cognitive load manipulation turns out to be just enough to make the study interesting for the participants who receive this load. If this is true, we might expect participants in the super boring control condition to drop out of the study at a much higher rate than participants in the mildly boring cognitive load condition. For the sake of simplicity, imagine that no one drops out of the mildly boring load condition while fully half of the participants in the wearisome control (i.e., no-load) condition drop out. Now suppose that the ten abnormally persistent people who endure the tedious control condition learn their grammar better than do the 20 normal people who have an additional task to keep them occupied. This would be a highly ambiguous finding. We wouldn't know if the experimentally manipulated surplus of mental capacity or the naturally occurring surplus of mental tenacity led to the superior performance of the ten unique people in the control condition. Another way of putting this is that differential mortality rates erase all the normal benefits of random assignment. After heterogeneous attrition, the people in one condition of the study are systematically different from the people in some other condition of the study.

What can be done to reduce or eliminate the problems associated with mortality or attrition? The first thing is to do anything within reason to keep people from dropping out of your study. Communicating the personal or scientific importance of the study to participants and presenting the study to people with authority and enthusiasm are good starting points. When done carefully, warning people that the study may not be all that exciting can also be helpful. Whenever it is possible to do so, scheduling breaks or rest periods for participants is yet another helpful strategy. Finally, offering people significant academic or financial rewards for completing the study is sometimes an additional option.

When all this is not enough, researchers might consider one additional thing if they are concerned about differential attrition, especially in studies that are not very time consuming. If some particular aspect of the study is aversive, and if the participants in one condition of the study aren't supposed to be exposed to this aspect of the study, put them in this condition *after* they've completed the part of the study they were originally expected to complete. Presumably, some of them will drop out of the study. This is good because it will allow you to delete these participants from the condition that normally would have had very few experimental casualties. That is, it will allow you to *equalize* attrition in the two conditions of your experiment. Moreover, it will also allow you to compare those who eventually dropped out with those who didn't to determine if attrition was really a serious threat in the first place. Of course, like the other solutions to attrition, this solution raises serious pragmatic and ethical issues. For example, is it ethical to offer people large amounts of money to endure painful electric shocks so that very few people will drop out of your study? Is it ethical to expose so many people to painful shocks? In principle, solutions to the problem of attrition can mean the difference between a methodologically sound study and a study that is very low in both internal and external validity. In practice, researchers must consider the ethical implications of any strategies designed to equalize attrition across experimental conditions.

Participant Reaction Bias

In addition to testing effects and experimental mortality, a third way in which the process of studying people can threaten validity occurs almost anytime people realize that they are being studied. The broad term for this specific category of threats is **participant reaction bias**: the bias that occurs when people realize they are being studied and behave in ways that they normally wouldn't. Because people are complicated, they may respond to the realization that they are being studied in a wide variety of ways. However, most forms of participant reaction bias can be boiled down to about three basic varieties. First, people may try to do what they think the researcher *expects*. Second, people may try to do the *opposite* of what they think the researcher expects. Third, people may try to do whatever will make them *look good*. More briefly put, people may be too cooperative, too stubborn, or too egotistical. These incidental motivations all represent a threat to internal validity because any of them may mask or mimic the potential effects of the independent variables under investigation.

The first, and probably the most problematic, form of participant reaction bias is **participant expectancies**. Participant expectancies occur when participants, consciously or unconsciously, try to behave in ways they believe to be consistent with the experimenter's hypothesis. Participants might do this for several different reasons: in an effort to please the experimenter, in an effort to feel normal, or as part of a desire to fill an implicit social contract with the experimenter (see Grice, 1975). Of course, participants can try to do as expected only when the expectations are somehow revealed to them (when experimenters tip their hands, so to speak). Characteristics of an experiment itself that subtly suggest how people are expected to behave are referred to as **demand characteristics,** and demand characteristics often play a role in the operation of participant expectancies.

A great deal of research on human aggression has been criticized due to participant expectancies or demand characteristics. In numerous laboratory and field studies of the *weapons effect,* Berkowitz and his colleagues (e.g., Berkowitz & Lepage, 1967) have shown that the mere presence of a gun can act as a cue that triggers aggressive responses. More specifically, Berkowitz and Lepage (1967) gave male participants the opportunity to shock a confederate who the participants believed had previously chosen to shock them. The participants delivered more shock than usual in retaliation when a rifle and a revolver (as opposed to a couple of badminton racquets) happened to be sitting near the shock key. On the basis of studies such as these, Berkowitz has argued that cues that are associated with aggression can eventually come to elicit aggressive responses on their own.

Critics have argued that demonstrations of the weapons effect are likely to reflect the operation of participant expectancies or demand characteristics. From this perspective, instead of stimulating aggressive thoughts because of classical conditioning, the guns that happen to be lying around in experiments on the weapons effect are stimulating participants' thoughts about how the experimenter expects them to behave. Although there is still some debate over this issue, Berkowitz and colleagues have presented at least some evidence suggesting that demand characteristics or participant expectancies are unlikely to account for the weapons effect. For instance, Turner, Simons, Berkowitz, and Frodi (1977) reported that either making participants more suspicious than usual or increasing participants' awareness of the experimental hypothesis tended to *decrease* participants' levels of aggressiveness in the presence of weapons.

In the case of the weapons effect, the tendency of well-informed participants to be experimentally uncooperative was pretty good news for Berkowitz. In many other cases, however, the tendency of research participants to rebel against an experimental manipulation isn't so reassuring. In fact, the tendency of participants to try to disconfirm an experimenter's hypothesis represents a second form of participant reaction bias, namely **participant reactance.** Although there could be other reasons, the main reason that participants might work hard to *disconfirm* an experimental hypothesis is probably grounded in people's basic desire for autonomy or independence (see Brehm, 1966). No one likes to feel like a puppet, and if people get the feeling that the experimenter is pulling their strings, they may pull back by doing the opposite of what they think the experimenter expects. To see how this could be a problem, imagine that Berkowitz had incorrectly hypothesized that guns serve to make people fearful and thus *reduce* aggressive behavior. Assume further that he cranked up the volume on his manipulations by making people highly aware of the presence of the guns. If people responded with reactance to their natural inclinations and failed to shock other people in the presence of the guns (even though they otherwise would have wanted to do so), it might appear that the guns had made people fearful when they had actually made people uncooperative! This would clearly represent a threat to internal validity. On the other hand, assuming that participant reactance normally works in opposition to an experimenter's predictions, it can still be a problem. In particular, reactance could easily mask the operation of a true effect, leading researchers to falsely reject a valid hypothesis.

A third form of participant reaction bias could also threaten internal validity by working either for or against an experimental prediction. This third form of bias is referred to as **evaluation apprehension**. Evaluation apprehension refers to people's concerns about being judged favorably or unfavorably by another person (Rosenberg, 1965). It can easily threaten the validity of a research study by causing people to do whatever they expect will portray them in a favorable light (i.e., by trying to look good in front of the experimenter). To stick with studies of aggressiveness, people who might privately wish to shock the beans out of an annoying confederate might refrain from doing so during an experiment because they realize that their shocks are being counted up as an index of aggression. If the presence of a weapon somehow clued people in to this possibility, the weapon might decrease aggressive behavior in the laboratory when the most common effect of weapons in the real world is to make people more aggressive. Alternately, if an experimenter somehow communicated to participants that aggressiveness was a highly desirable trait, the presence of guns could artificially promote aggressive behavior in the laboratory even if guns truly had no such effect under normal circumstances. Similarly, as suggested by traditional interpretations of the Hawthorne effect, either increases or decreases in illumination levels could falsely appear to increase worker productivity. An increase in productivity might happen if improved lighting and the presence of psychologists measuring productivity levels caused workers to behave as if someone was constantly looking over their shoulders.

Fortunately, researchers can do several things to reduce or eliminate most forms of participant reaction bias. First, researchers can take steps to guarantee the anonymity or privacy of their research participants. In the case of survey research on attitudes or the self-concept, this safeguard is especially important. Self-concept researchers who are concerned about evaluation apprehension almost always instruct participants not to put any identifying information on their surveys. Researchers may also ask participants to seal their surveys in plain, unmarked envelopes before they turn them in. As described in Chapter 4, if participants are taking the surveys in a relatively public setting such as a classroom, researchers may even give them brightly colored cover pages so that they can cover up their responses as they fill out the surveys (the bright colors help the experimenter see to it that everyone is using the cover pages).

In purely experimental research, when there is some chance that people will guess the experimental hypothesis, it is sometimes possible to gain control over expectancies by giving participants in the experimental and the control group exactly the same expectancy. Typically, this would be one that has little or nothing to do with the real predictions of the experiment. This false expectancy is often part of a **cover story**, a false and often elaborate story about the nature and purpose of the study. In

Milgram's classic study of obedience, the cover story was that participants were playing the role of teacher to teach word pairs to a learner. In Asch's study of conformity, the cover story was that participants were helping the experimenter learn about visual perception and judgment. In studies such as these, the researchers go to great lengths to convince their participants that they are studying something that has little or nothing to do with the real purpose of the study. Although the use of deception to reduce participant reaction bias can be extremely effective, its utility must be weighed against the ethical implications of telling people elaborate lies.

A less actively deceptive approach to some forms of participant reaction bias involves keeping participants in the dark in various ways. For instance, in some studies researchers can simply keep people blind to the experimental conditions to which they have been assigned. In more naturalistic studies with behavioral-dependent measures, researchers can also make use of surreptitious (secret) or **unobtrusive observations**. In the case of studies making use of unobtrusive measurements, research participants do not realize that they are being studied at all. Even in laboratory experiments in which people do know that they are being studied, the use of unobtrusive measures may prevent people from realizing *which aspect* of their behavior is being studied. For example, if we want a direct measure of how much someone likes a similar versus a dissimilar experimental confederate, we could simply ask participants how much they like the confederate on a typical EGWA scale. However, as discussed briefly in Chapter 4, if we are concerned that participants might not be willing to report their true feelings about the confederate, we might unobtrusively measure how much physical distance participants maintain between themselves and the confederate during a staged interaction (e.g., by seeing how far participants sit from the confederate when they are working together at a large table).

Yet another approach to reducing the effects of evaluation apprehension requires researchers to convince their participants that researchers can read people's minds. This may sound a bit far-fetched, but Jones and Sigall (1971) developed a technique based on exactly this idea. More specifically, Jones and Sigall brought people to their laboratory and hooked them up to a phony lie detector. Because Jones and Sigall had previously gone to the trouble of measuring their participants' attitudes in a pretest, they were able to convince their participants that the machine could read people's minds (by detecting minute changes in the way participants held onto an "attitude wheel" that resembled a steering wheel). Jones and Sigall found that when people were hooked up to this *bogus pipeline*, they were more willing to admit having negative feelings about stereotyped group members such as Blacks and the physically handicapped. In their review of research using the bogus pipeline, Roese and Jamieson (1993) reported that the bogus pipeline has turned out to be an extremely useful technique for getting people to report how they really feel about things.

Another approach to minimizing almost any kind of participant reaction bias (especially evaluation apprehension) is to make use of indirect measures of people's attitudes and opinions. As an example of indirect measures, consider a clever study of attitudes and behavior conducted by Vargas, von Hippel, and Petty (1998). These researchers were interested in people's attitudes about cheating. Among other things, they wanted to know if people who have relatively favorable attitudes about cheating might be more likely to cheat than people who have more traditional (i.e., unfavorable) attitudes. The problem with trying to study this important question is that very few people are willing to admit being thumbs-up on cheating. Vargas et al. solved this problem by developing an *indirect measure* of attitudes about cheating. They asked participants to make some judgments about the appropriateness of *another person's* decision to obtain a copy of a highly desirable and presumably expensive library book—by claiming to have lost the book and paying the library a modest replacement fee. Not surprisingly, some participants reported that they considered this morally questionable act morally bankrupt. In contrast, other participants (like the CEOs of some large energy companies) reported that they considered the act to be little more than a matter of creative bookkeeping. Vargas et al. assumed that their participants' true attitudes about cheating would play an important role in how they evaluated the morally ambiguous book buyer. Specifically, they assumed that people who had relatively lax attitudes about cheating would be less likely to view the book buyer as dishonest. In other words, these researchers used people's judgments of the morally ambiguous target as an indirect measure of their attitudes about cheating. This indirect measure proved to be directly related to cheating behavior. Specifically, the indirect measure was a good predictor of their participants' actual tendencies to cheat on a test involving extremely difficult anagrams.

The key to the success of indirect measures of attitudes is that they constitute a pencil-and-paper version of unobtrusive measures. That is, when participants fill out questionnaires containing indirect measures of attitudes, they don't realize what is actually being measured. Another way researchers can measure attitudes without having to worry about participants catching on to what is being measured is to measure attitudes that participants do not realize they possess. After all, if participants do not realize that they possess a specific attitude, it will be pretty hard for them to hide this attitude from an experimenter. Of course, if participants are unaware of their attitudes, you may be wondering how an experimenter could ever measure them. Researchers have recently addressed this problem by developing implicit (i.e., nonconscious) measures of people's attitudes. For example, Greenwald, McGhee, and Schwartz (1998) used the Implicit Association Test (IAT) to assess people's unconscious associations about objects as varied as insects, flowers, and ethnic groups. Many versions of this test have been created, but the basic idea behind the test is always the same—to see how easily (i.e., how quickly) people can associate different things. For example, if a person finds it easy to pair photos of Black faces with negative words such a "death" but finds it easy to pair photos of White faces with positive words such as "peace," Greenwald and colleagues would consider this an indicator that the person possesses negative implicit (i.e., unconscious) attitudes about Blacks. Many other researchers have expressed serious concerns about these conclusions (Blanton & Jaccard, in press; Karpinski & Hilton, 2001; Fazio & Olson, 2003; Rothermund & Wentura, 2001) and some argue that the IAT has a number of undesirable psychometric properties that stand in the way of its validity (Blanton, Jaccard, Gonzales, & Christi, 2006). Nevertheless, the IAT is an influential example of a recent implicit measure, and research using the IAT has stimulated a great deal of provocative new theory regarding human motivations.

Researchers have also developed a wide variety of measures to assess people's unconscious attitudes about *themselves*. Hetts and colleagues refer to people's unconscious attitudes about themselves as *implicit self-regard* or *implicit self-esteem*. To measure implicit self-esteem, Hetts, Sakuma, and Pelham (1999) activated people's thoughts about themselves and then examined how these activated thoughts influenced the ways in which people subsequently processed information. One measure that Hetts et al. used was an adaptation of a very useful priming technique pioneered by Fazio and colleagues (Fazio, Jackson, Dunton, & Williams, 1995; Fazio, Sanbonmatsu, Powell, & Kardes, 1986). This procedure required people to make some rapid judgments about words that appeared on a computer screen. Participants were quickly exposed to a priming word such as "me" or "I." Shortly after a priming word disappeared, participants were asked to identify a favorable or unfavorable word (e.g., "good" or "bad") that was flashed in the same spot on the computer screen. If the presentation of self-relevant primes (e.g., "me") makes it easier than usual for a person to identify favorable words (and has the opposite effect for unfavorable words), researchers using this technique assume that this person is *high* in implicit self-regard. That is, this person appears to possess mostly positive associations about the self. On the other hand, if getting a person to think about the self makes it easier than usual for him or her to process negative words (and harder to process positive words), researchers assume that the person is relatively *low* in implicit self-regard. Hetts et al. have found that implicit self-regard is not correlated with traditional (explicit) measures of self-esteem. Nonetheless, implicit self-regard is correlated with a number of important behaviors and judgments (e.g., the kind of culture in which a person was reared, Hetts, Sakuma, & Pelham, 1999; people's mothers' reports of how nurturing the mothers were when people were growing up; DeHart, Pelham, & Tennen, 2006; and see Greenwald & Banaji, 1995; Wilson, Lindsey, & Schooler, 2000, for extensive discussions of unconscious aspects of social attitudes).

To summarize work on indirect and implicit attitudes, this work appears to provide some promising solutions to the problem of participant reaction bias. In the past two decades, research using implicit measures has mushroomed, and it appears that this interest in implicit social judgments will only increase in the years to come (for a description of an additional measure of implicit self-esteem, see Kitayama & Karasawa, 1997; Koole, Smeets, van Knippenberg, & Dijksterhuis, 1999; Fazio & Olson, 2003). Having said all this, it is worth adding that some significant barriers to the measurement of implicit attitudes exist. For example, the test-retest reliability of most implicit measures is much lower than the test-retest reliability of explicit measures of the same construct. In light of this problem, DeHart et al. (2006) advised researchers who wish to assess implicit self-esteem to measure it on several occasions (and average all the scores together). It is a lot of work to measure an implicit attitude on three or four different occasions, but failing to do this extra work means running the risk of working with a measure of implicit attitudes that simply is not reliable. Although the first author is much more optimistic than the second author that implicit measures of attitudes sometimes predict real-world behavior, the first author does agree with the second that critical tests of the validity of implicit attitudes will require much more careful attention to psychometric issues in the future.

Experimenter Bias

One of the most obvious ways laboratory studies differ from passive observational studies (e.g., studies that make use of unobtrusive observations) is that participants in laboratory studies interact with experimenters. This rather mundane observation leads us to one of the more subtle threats to validity. This threat can happen when experimenters' expectations about their studies bias their experimental observations. Appropriately enough, this unintentional bias on the part of experimenters is referred to as **experimenter bias**, and it may take either of two distinct forms. The first form occurs when researchers make biased observations in an experiment. Because experimenters are only human, they sometimes see what they expect to see and observe support for their hypothesis when an unbiased observer might not see any. A second form of experimenter bias occurs when experimenters actually treat their participants differently according to their expectations about how their participants should perform. In the case of this second bias, even a perfectly objective observer might observe differences in the behavior of people in different experimental conditions. However, these differences would have more to do with subtle differences in the way the experimenter treated the participants than they would with the true manipulations of interest.

In one of the first studies to call attention to experimenter bias, Rosenthal and Fode (1963) observed each of these two forms of experimenter bias. They trained a group of highly motivated experimenters and asked them to test the performance of groups of carefully bred "maze-bright" and "maze-dull" rats in a laboratory maze. As Rosenthal and Fode expected, the maze-bright rats learned their way around the mazes more quickly than did the maze-dull rats. This seemingly trivial finding may seem a little less trivial when you consider the fact that the two groups of rats were actually identical. Rosenthal and Fode simply got a bunch of run-of-the-mill, maze-mediocre rats and randomly split them into the two different groups. The important thing is that Rosenthal and Fode's bright and highly motivated experimenters *thought* that some of the rats were brighter (and perhaps more highly motivated) than the others. Why did the rats that were labeled more favorably perform more favorably? Because the experimenters unwittingly *treated*

"'Maze-dull,' 'a little slow,' 'maze-impaired.'
It all starts to get to a guy after a while."

them more favorably. The experimenters not only petted the presumably bright rats more and handled them with greater care, but they also encouraged the rats more when the rats were running in the mazes. Rosenthal and Fode also observed evidence of experimenter bias when they looked carefully for coding errors committed by the experimenters. The coding errors favored the presumably maze-bright rats quite a bit more frequently than they favored the less highly regarded maze-dull rats.

It is important to realize that Rosenthal and Fode's experimenters were not consciously engaging in any form of scientific dishonesty. They were simply letting their expectations get the better of them—in much the same way that hypothesis testers who are asked to solve the E, K, 4, 7 problem (from Chapter 2) often let their hypotheses about vowels and even numbers get the better of them. It is very hard to look for what you do not expect to see. As an anonymous social critic once put it, "I'll see it when I believe it." Rosenthal and colleagues might add that if we believe something strongly enough, we may do more than simply see it; we may also unknowingly work to make it happen (see Snyder, Tanke, & Berscheid, 1977).

You may have noticed that there is a very fine line between experimenter bias (also known as experimenter expectancies) and the participant expectancies discussed in the last section. At some point, experimenter expectancies can get translated into participant expectancies, and the research participants can thus become unwitting participants in the experimenter's self-fulfilling prophecies. However, these two forms of bias do have some differences. In addition to the obvious difference about who does the expecting, there is a difference in how these biases relate to experimental manipulations. In its prototypical form, experimenter bias refers to things that alter the experimental manipulation (unintentionally giving some rats a few extra pets, unknowingly smiling more at the teacher's pet, offering subtle encouragement to the participants who are expected to persist longer at unscrambling anagrams). In contrast, participant expectancies can occur even when a study is perfectly executed by the experimenter. The only trouble with participant expectancies is that participants are sometimes smarter than experimenters give them credit for being. Nothing extraneous that the experimenter is doing is different in the two conditions. The participants simply figure out the manipulation.

As subtle and potentially injurious as experimenter bias is, it is relatively easy to fix. Researchers who wish to avoid experimenter bias simply need to keep themselves *blind* to (i.e., unaware of) their participants' treatment conditions. This can be done, for example, by having one researcher interact with participants while a separate researcher keeps track of participants' experimental conditions using arbitrary code numbers. When this is not possible, it is often possible to standardize most aspects of the instructions that participants receive (e.g., by presenting the instructions in recorded form). The only portion of the recorded instructions that changes is the portion that is essential to the experimental manipulation. Finally, whenever possible, researchers concerned about the biasing influences of any kind of expectancies often make use of a **double-blind procedure** in which both the experimenter and the research participants are kept unaware of the participants' treatment conditions.

When approaches such as these cannot easily be adopted, researchers have occasionally resorted to deceiving their experimenters! In a study of the "door-in-the-face" technique for increasing compliance, Cialdini and Ascani (1976) did exactly this. In particular, Cialdini and Ascani trained experimenters to ask college students to perform a painful but socially desirable favor—giving blood. In a control condition, the experimenters simply asked participants to give blood (tomorrow). In the door-in-the-face condition, the experimenters preceded this same request (to give blood tomorrow) with an additional, gigantic and unreasonable request that everyone refused—agreeing to give blood every six weeks for the next two years. Because the experimenters in this study approached students on a college campus and hit them up with their requests, it was impossible to keep the experimenters blind to participants' conditions. Cialdini and Ascani informed their experimenters that they should expect to see lower rates of compliance with the target request among those in the door-in-the-face (ridiculous request first) condition. Moreover, they did this knowing full well that they could be setting the stage for experimenter bias. However, because they actually expected their door-in-the-face condition to elicit *higher* than usual levels of compliance, they were stacking the deck *against* their hypothesis. As everyone but the experimenters expected, Cialdini and Ascani found that participants who received the door-in-the-face manipulation were much more likely to agree to give blood the next day. Moreover, after the door-in-the-face participants had actually given blood, they were also about twice as likely as participants in the control condition to agree to give blood again in the future. The results of Cialdini and Ascani's experiment are summarized in Figure 5.3. Experimenter bias cannot provide a very good explanation for these findings.

MOVING FROM THREE THREATS TO TWO: CONFOUNDS AND ARTIFACTS

Instead of simply providing a laundry list of threats to validity in this chapter, we have organized them around three broad themes that we hope provide a good way of thinking about threats to validity. We now simplify this scheme even further by making a second pass on the common threats to validity. This time, we use just two categories rather than three. This second pass offers an opportunity to develop a greater appreciation for the material we've already

Figure 5.3

Giving blood and agreeing to give blood again as a function of compliance technique used during recruitment (from Cialdini & Ascani, 1976)

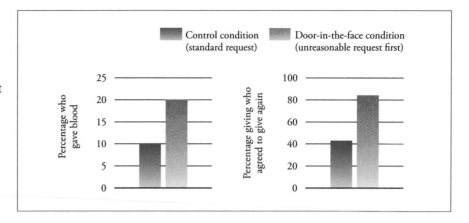

covered. In our two-category scheme, the threats to validity can be viewed as either **confounds** or **artifacts**.

Confounds

A confound (sometimes referred to as a nuisance variable) is a broad term used to identify any situation in which some additional variable (a) varies systematically with the independent variable and (b) also varies systematically with the dependent variable. Confounds are variables that a researcher hadn't thought about or couldn't control, but ones that could be leading to a spurious (or false) association between an independent and dependent variable. Confounds are thus a threat to internal rather than external validity.

A clear example of a confound can be found in the tattoo example summarized by the hypothetical tattoo data in Figure 5.1. There, we focused our attention on a passive observational (i.e., "correlational") study because this kind of study is particularly susceptible to "third variables," another name for confounds. It is important to note, however, that even the best-laid plans of the most careful experimenters sometimes prove to be susceptible to confounds. In fact, in principle, *any* study is open to potential confounds. Given the specific threats discussed in this chapter (e.g., individual differences, history, testing effects, expectancy effects, experimenter effects), it is clear that in many of these cases, the problem was that something the researcher hadn't taken into account was accompanying the researcher's independent variable and thus could be having a spurious effect on the dependent variable. Although the researcher who is plagued by a confound has usually tried to isolate the cause of some outcome of interest, this cause has turned out not to have been isolated after all. Things like preexisting differences between people, differences in how much an experimenter smiled at someone, or differences in people's familiarity with a test from pretest to posttest were always *confounded* with whatever independent variable the researcher really cared about. The presence of this confound then led the unsuspecting researcher to draw faulty conclusions about the influence of the independent variable on the dependent variable.

Although confounds are pervasive, they are not always as easy to identify as our tattoo example might have suggested. Even carefully designed laboratory experiments suffer from potential confounds, and this can be true even when researchers take great pains to design procedures that seem on the surface to be confound-free. Consider some carefully designed experimental studies of mood and helping. Theory and common sense suggest that under at least some circumstances, people who are in a good mood might be especially likely to offer help to those who need it. Early experiments designed to test this hypothesis involved giving some people positive feedback about their personalities to see if the increase in positive mood would lead to increases in helping. Although studies such as this supported the idea that happiness leads to helpfulness, it is possible that giving people positive feedback might do more than simply elevate their mood. Positive feedback also increases people's beliefs about their competence, and people who think they are competent appear to be more likely to help others, even when their feelings of competence do not necessarily put them in a good mood. For example, people who are told that they have a knack for handling rats are more likely to help people who feel threatened by rats than are people who are told that they shouldn't quit their day jobs to become rat handlers.

Two researchers, Isen and Levin (1972), were aware of this potential confound between mood and self-perceived competence, and so they developed a manipulation of mood that was not confounded with people's beliefs about their competence. Specifically, they gave cookies to some men who were sitting in a library to see if those who had been given the cookies would be more likely to help a fellow student. The men who had just been given cookies were indeed more likely to help. However, this alternate manipulation of mood appears to be confounded with a *different* variable. Specifically, those participants who received something nice from a stranger (a cookie) had just been exposed to a *prosocial model*, and exposure to prosocial models is known to increase helping behavior (Bandura, 1977). As a result, both a good mood and a prosocial model varied across experimental conditions. To correct for this and other problems, Isen and colleagues eventually developed the "found dime" paradigm for manipulating mood. Researchers who make use of this mood manipulation simply arrange for some participants to "find" a dime (or some other amount of money) in a place such as a public telephone booth. It seems safe to assume that it takes very little skill to pick up a found dime, and so people probably weren't feeling more competent than usual if they were in the condition that allowed them to reach down and grab a dime. In addition, the only thing modeled by the unknown person who presumably left a dime behind is forgetfulness. Nonetheless, Isen and her colleagues found that this new manipulation of mood reliably increased a wide variety of helping behaviors in the same way that the previous manipulations did (see Isen, 1987).

Because the concept of confounds is so important, we discuss confounds (and Isen and Levin's experiments) in much more detail in Chapters 6 through 8. For now, we emphasize that this example of carefully conducted research on mood and helping illustrates just how pervasive confounds can be—even when a researcher is conducting a true experiment. The mood and helping study also points to three ways to try to eliminate confounds. First, *be careful.* It is clear in reading Isen and Levin's research that they gave a great deal of thought to their experimental manipulation and that they knew it would be tricky to develop a pure, unconfounded manipulation of mood. Reading as much as possible about what has already been studied on your topic and giving a great deal of thought to the design of your experiment can greatly reduce the likelihood that you will either (1) repeat the mistakes of previous researchers or (2) generate novel mistakes of your own. A second way to eliminate confounds is to *replicate.* Notice that Isen and Levin were not just careful. They also covered their flanks by replicating their findings. When researchers establish a basic effect and then replicate this effect using different experimental procedures (e.g., manipulating mood by moving from delightful feedback, to delicious cookies, and then to detected dimes), it becomes much harder than it would be otherwise to argue that any one specific confound led to the same conceptual pattern of results in each study. A third and final solution to the problem of confounds was not pursued by Isen and Levin, but it is also a useful approach (especially in correlational studies such as the hypothetical tattoo study). This third solution is to *measure and control for confounds.* Any variables that are likely to be confounded with the variable or variables in which you are interested can be measured and then statistically controlled. Statistical techniques such as the analysis of covariance (ANCOVA), partial correlation, and multiple regression are specifically designed to allow researchers to see if their independent variables are still associated with a dependent variable, once the effects of a potential confound have been statistically removed. For instance, Isen and Levin could have given their participants who received positive versus neutral feedback a questionnaire to see how competent they felt after receiving the feedback. Then they could have statistically removed any potential effects of self-perceived competence on helping behavior. If the feedback manipulation still exerted an influence on helping after any effects of competence were statistically controlled, then this would make a much stronger case that the feedback manipulation was exerting its effect as a result of mood.[1] Researchers use many sophisticated statistical techniques to control for confounds, and Methodology Exercise 1 on partial correlation (see Appendix 2) should give you some additional basic insights into this statistical control process.

In summary, confounds present a very broad threat to an experiment, and they mainly threaten internal validity. When an unknown or unmeasured variable covaries with the independent variable and might influence the dependent variable, a researcher could unwittingly draw faulty inferences about the relation between an independent and a dependent variable. Approaches to eliminating confounds include using clean and well-established manipulations, conducting replication studies in which you use decidedly different manipulations of the same basic construct, and measuring and controlling for confounds using sophisticated statistical techniques.

Artifacts

In contrast to a confound, which varies accidentally along with an independent variable, an artifact is a broad term for important but overlooked variables that are held constant in a given study or set of studies. Like confounds, however, artifacts are also serious threats to the validity of a set of research findings. Because artifacts refer to variables that are held constant, you might wonder why they are problematic. After all, if it is hot in the experimental *and* the control condition of your experiment, you have no need to worry about how heat could masquerade as your independent variable. This is true enough. Artifacts do not threaten internal validity. However, artifacts do threaten *external* validity. When an artifact is at work in a study, it means that the independent variable is only associated with the dependent variable under the specific (and perhaps unusual) set of conditions under which you chose to conduct your study. This leads to the concern that the effects you observed would not occur if the artifact (e.g., a high temperature, a sample of all male participants) were allowed to vary— or if it were held at a different constant level. A good example of this is selection bias. Suppose you have a theory that perceiving the self as unique causes a person to have higher self-esteem. You run a questionnaire study and find evidence of this effect. You find that people who feel more unique do, in fact, have higher self-esteem. However, being savvy to the problem of confounds and the need to replicate findings, you realize that you should test your hypotheses again using different methods. You then run a laboratory study and randomly assign half of your participants to receive feedback suggesting that they are "highly unique," while telling the other half that they are "very common." Consistent with your first study, you find that those who are induced to feel unique show increases in self-esteem, whereas those who are induced to feel common show decreases in self-esteem. Being careful, you then replicate this effect using several other manipulations and measures of uniqueness, and you continue to find support for the effect. You thus feel very confident that your effect is probably "real," and you therefore conclude that increases in the perception of uniqueness cause increases in self-esteem. However, there is potentially a big problem with your research.

When you discuss your results with a friend who studies culture, she says that your results probably would not hold up in Eastern cultures. As luck would have it, you are planning to take a summer vacation in Beijing. So you ask one of your friends who grew up in China to translate one of your questionnaires into Mandarin, and you set off to do a little cross-cultural research. (Of course you are careful to get approval from your school's internal review board before you leave.) When you run this questionnaire study in Beijing, you find that greater feelings of uniqueness are associated with *lower* levels of self-esteem. You now realize that your studies lacked external validity. Although you probably did demonstrate a "real" causal effect in the Western samples you studied (i.e., your internal validity was high), your findings did not *generalize* to Eastern samples (i.e., your external validity was low). You didn't know this at the time, but culture was an artifact in your original work.

If it is a challenge to eliminate potential confounds, it is a far greater challenge to eliminate potential artifacts. Just think of the many variables that might be held constant in a given program of research. Perhaps most, if not all, of the English-speaking college students you studied are female, young, and relatively wealthy—at least by the standards of most third world countries. Even if you work hard to find new samples that vary on all of these dimensions, members of these new samples would probably all have been born in the 20th century (unless you are studying very young children) and eaten at least one meal the day before (unless you are studying victims of famine). Many, many variables are held constant in most research studies, and it is entirely possible that many seemingly well-established research findings would not generalize if any of the unknown artifacts that have always been present were allowed to vary.

Because it is impossible to list all the factors that are held constant when you write up a study (e.g., "All participants were between the ages 18 and 23, were in college, breathed air, had at one time or another been served pasta at a restaurant, wore clothes, had skin...."), researchers typically only worry about artifacts that (a) might vary in the settings or samples in which a researcher most likely wishes to generalize his or her results and (b) have some kind of theoretical connection to a particular research finding. Consider research on language acquisition (i.e., how people learn to understand and speak a language). It is hard to imagine that people who have never eaten tomatoes would acquire language in a different way than people who have. However, it is much easier to imagine that the rules of language acquisition might differ somewhat for people exposed to tonal and non-tonal languages or for languages that do or do not conjugate verbs to represent time. So, although a history of tomato eating could technically be considered an artifact in research on language acquisition, researchers who study language acquisition would be wise to worry more about artifacts that have to do with major properties of language.

Are there any systematic rules for identifying the potential artifacts in a particular study or program of research? This is hard to say, but as a rule of thumb, you might consider the common threats to validity that we have already discussed in this chapter. If you go back over these threats to validity, you will see that some of them speak directly to factors that are likely to be held constant in most programs of research. As our hypothetical study of uniqueness suggests, selection bias is a very common artifact. If all of the participants in your study have similar background or demographic characteristics and you wish to generalize your findings to other groups, then you should think about artifacts. At least some effects of history can also be thought of as artifacts. If Dr. Pyszczynksi studied predictors of attitudes towards war in the U.S.

during the 1990s, it is quite possible that his findings would no longer hold up after September 11th, 2001. Perhaps the most profound and far-reaching examples of artifacts are related to subtle effects such as the mere measurement effect, participant reaction bias, and experimenter bias. These threats all occur, in slightly different ways, because the mere process of studying people changes people. To the degree that studying people changes them, it is very difficult to know when a specific research finding will travel to the "real world" of mostly unstudied people.

In summary, artifacts represent a very broad threat to external validity. When an unknown or unmeasured variable is held at one constant level in a study, researchers might observe effects they would never have observed if this variable had been set at a different constant level or allowed to vary. In principle, it is easy to address the problem of artifacts by systematically varying potential artifacts in follow-up studies. However, artifacts are often hard to detect precisely because they are so pervasive. Just as it never dawned on Don Quixote that he had spent most his life speaking prose, and just as it would probably never dawn on sentient fish that they had spent their lives living in water, researchers sometimes fail to realize that they have investigated a phenomenon for years without stepping outside the cultural or contextual box of past research.

Table 5.2 Confounds and artifacts

Construct	Definition	Threat	Examples
Confound	A variable that: (a) varies systematically with the independent variable and that (b) could exert an effect on the dependent variable	Internal validity	A study of weight loss finds a significant effect of an experimental treatment, but half of the respondents in the experimental condition quit the study early, whereas all of the no-treatment control participants remained through the duration of the study. (*heterogeneous attrition*)
			An experimenter expects a set of educational materials to help boys (in the treatment condition) more than the girls. (*experimenter bias or demand effect*)
			The tattoo example in Figure 5.1 (*individual differences*)
Artifact	A variable that: (a) is held constant in a study or series of studies and that (b) might represent a restricted context under which the effect will observed	External validity	A longitudinal study shows that most college students engage in risky drinking behavior. However, the questions in the study caused students to think that heavy drinking is common, and this caused them to drink more. (*mere measurement effect*)
			A researcher finds that "economic concerns" are the most important attitudinal predictor of voting patterns, but he fails to realize that this effect only occurs because his study occurred during a difficult economic cycle. (*history effect*)
			The faulty survey that led the *Lit-erary Digest* to conclude that Alf Landon would beat Franklin D. Roosevelt in the 1936 U.S. presidential election. (*selection bias and nonresponse bias*)

Confounds Versus Artifacts

The difference between confounds and artifacts might seem subtle, but these two threats to validity are essentially polar opposites. A confound is a variable that should have been held constant within a specific study but that was accidentally allowed to vary (and covary with the independent variable). Confounds thus threaten *internal* validity. In contrast, an artifact is a variable that should have been systematically varied, either within or across studies, but that was accidentally held constant. Artifacts thus threaten *external* validity. To help you understand the difference between artifacts and confounds, these differences are highlighted in Table 5.2.

 SUMMARY

Common threats to validity can be organized around three broad themes. Specifically, (1) people are different, (2) people change, and (3) the process of studying people changes people. This simple organizational scheme helps clarify that only a few general things can go wrong in psychological research. An alternative way of organizing the threats is by exploring confounds versus artifacts. Because confounds can crop up in research in a great number of ways, many chapters later in this text elaborate on the concept of confounds—describing specific types of confounds, the specific threats they pose to validity, and the fact that some specific research methods tend to raise concerns about confounds whereas others tend to raise concerns about artifacts. Fortunately, just as there are many unique kinds of confounds and artifacts, there are also many unique things researchers can do to correct these problems. A primary goal of this book from this point forward is to help you learn how to identify and eliminate confounds and artifacts (i.e., threats to validity), so that they do not undermine your own ability to interpret and conduct psychological research.

STUDY QUESTIONS

1. What are the differences between artifacts and confounds? How do these terms relate to (a) internal versus external validity and (b) random selection versus random assignment?

2. People are different, and this fact leads to two threats to validity: the third-variable problem and selection bias. How do these two threats relate to the concept of artifacts versus confounds? Which is a threat to internal validity and which to external validity?

3. In the summer of 2004, a rural county in Texas had three separate instances of high school drivers causing serious automobile accidents. In the ten years prior to this summer, there had been only three such accidents involving teen drivers. The local superintendent of schools responded by requiring all high school students of driving age to take both beginner and advanced driver's education courses. There were no such accidents the following summer. Why might you be cautious about concluding that the new driver's education classes prevented automobile accidents?

4. The text discusses both heterogeneous and homogeneous attrition. What are these concepts, and how do they relate to internal versus external validity? How do they relate to artifacts versus confounds?

5. The act of studying people may change them. List three safeguards researchers can take to prevent these effects from introducing confounds or artifacts into psychological research.

NOTE

1. The researcher might also collect a separate measure of mood. In this case, mood would not be viewed as a "confound," but it would be viewed as a "mediator." The idea here is that the effect of the feedback manipulation on helping was "mediated by" mood. Mediation would be established if the statistical analyses revealed that (a) the feedback manipulation increased helping, (b) the feedback manipulation increased mood, and (c) the feedback manipulation had no effect on helping after mood was statistically controlled (Baron & Kenny, 1986). This set of analyses would suggest that any of the effect of feedback on helping was "mediated by" or "flowed through" mood.

Nonexperimental Research Designs

You can observe a lot just by watching.
—Yogi Berra

In the American educational system children are reprimanded by two separate, but equally important groups: the teachers who threaten them and the principals who actually punish them. These are their stories. Actually, to be more accurate, this is just one of their stories, told to the first author's brother by a fellow elementary school principal (whose name we have changed to JH in the rich history of case studies).

One of the first things JH noticed when she became an elementary school principal was that children were constantly tattling to her about the misdeeds of their classmates. This had virtually never happened when JH was a mere teacher rather than an authority figure, and sometimes it took an interesting twist. For example, 6-year-old Ray Ann once approached JH on the playground and said, "Principal, PJ called me the B-word." JH was at first stunned that PJ (who she knew was only a first grader) may have used such coarse and sexist language. But then she reminded herself that Ray Ann might not mean the same thing by "the B-word" that an adult might. She was hoping for "butt-head" or "booger-nose." So, somewhat reluctantly, she asked: "Ray Ann, I know that's a bad word, but can you tell me exactly what B-word it was, so that I can talk to PJ about what he did?" She replied "Yeah, but I have to whisper it; it was asshole." If you will forgive us for using such coarse language, we hope you can find a methodological point in this colorful story. You can observe a lot just by watching but you can sometimes learn even more by doing careful *interviews*. As a case in point, JH's next question was, "By the way, who is your teacher?" She needed to know this, of course, because she was much more distressed to learn that a six-year-old didn't know the difference between the letter A and the letter B, than she was to learn that PJ was a potty mouth. When conducted and interpreted wisely, passive observational studies can sometimes yield diagnostic information that even experiments might not reveal. That is the theme of this chapter.

By focusing on the details of nonexperimental research designs, this chapter provides our first detailed look at the nuts and bolts of psychological research methods. Specifically, it provides descriptions of some of the most commonly used nonexperimental research designs. We begin with a description of case studies or single-participant designs. We follow this with a description of single-variable studies whose purpose is to describe the state of the world. After discussing single-variable research (e.g., epidemiological research, public opinion surveys), we discuss four kinds of multiple-variable or *correlational* research (e.g., archival research, survey and interview research). In the case of each design, we show how measurement in naturalistic settings provides opportunities to maximize external validity. However, this opportunity often comes at the cost of increased concerns about internal validity. Addressing these concerns about internal validity represents much of the challenge, and the excitement, of correlational research.

DESCRIBING THE WORLD OF A SINGLE PARTICIPANT: CASE STUDIES

One of the most interesting ways in which researchers study human behavior is by conducting case studies, that is, by making careful analyses of the experiences of a particular person or group. Case studies are most likely to capture our attention when they focus on people whose extraordinary experiences would be difficult or impossible to re-create in the laboratory. Moreover, case studies often involve remarkable people with conditions so rare that it would be very difficult to identify and study them in large numbers (either in the laboratory or in the real world). When people develop amnesia, survive massive head injuries, compose symphonies as children, or become old as children (by prematurely aging), inquiring minds want to know about it. Inquiring scientific minds also want to know about it. However, unlike casual analyses of people's behavior, scientific case studies are usually aimed at uncovering general psychological principles. Like any other approach to research, case studies are usually designed to generate, delineate, corroborate, or invalidate theories. Pretty often, case studies are carried out when little if any systematic research has been conducted on a topic. In such cases, the careful, detailed observations that make up good case studies can provide researchers with the insights they need to develop new theories, theories that are eventually tested out on large groups of people.

The psychologists who make the most frequent use of case studies are clinical psychologists and behavioral neuroscientists. That much being said, we suspect that theory development in other areas of psychology could be greatly enriched by the use of case studies. In fact, most researchers who would never consider conducting case studies themselves would probably have to agree that we have learned a great deal from case studies. In fact, one of the most famous and influential studies in the history of psychology is a case study that was documented more than 150 years ago. For both historical and theoretical reasons, the story behind this particular case study still fascinates many researchers. The story in question is that of Phineas Gage.

Please Don't Try This at Home: The Case of Phineas Gage

Phineas Gage was a likable, energetic, and industrious foreman who had an excellent but hazardous job. In the summer of 1848, he was supervising a large group of workers who were laying down railroad tracks near the town of Cavendish, Vermont. Gage was a hands-on supervisor who personally performed some of the most dangerous tasks required to construct a railway. On the day that Gage became famous, he was blasting away some rocks when a freak accident cost him a substantial portion of his brain. During the accident, Gage was holding onto a tamping iron, a 43-inch-long, 13¼-pound iron rod about as thick as a broomstick. When Gage unwittingly tapped the tool into a large charge of explosives, the rod was suddenly transformed into a high-speed projectile. It blasted through Gage's face in a split second, entering below his left eye and exiting the top of his head. The bar landed over 100 feet away and took with it a large chunk of Gage's brain. Phineas Gage's life wasn't over, but it was forever changed.

In addition to a lot of luck, Gage's youth and strength somehow allowed him to survive both this incredible accident and the infections that followed in its wake. Within two months, Gage was considered cured and was back on his feet again. He was now blind in his left eye, and he must have had a very nasty scar on the left side of his face. Otherwise, however, he seemed to have experienced very few physical repercussions from the accident. Gage could speak normally and had lost none of his senses or physical abilities. Even his higher-order mental capacities, such as his memory and attention, seemed to have been spared any meaningful damage. However, there was one pretty dramatic consequence of Gage's accident. As Damasio et al. (1994) put it, "Gage was no longer Gage." Despite his normal-to-superior cognitive capacities, this previously likable and disciplined man had been turned into nothing short of a social and emotional disaster. Both his language and his behavior became abusive and socially irresponsible. He made such an art of cursing that people often tried to keep women and children away from him. He could no longer hold down a regular job, and he had little or no ability to manage his money or his emotional life. Gage appears to have been robbed completely of the ability to make important decisions, and he alienated almost everyone who had ever cared about him.

Gage's case is interesting for many reasons. For instance, after some of the scientific dust settled over the case, it eventually convinced most scientists that damage to specific brain areas is in fact associated with specific kinds of psychological deficits. Almost 150 years after Gage's life-altering accident, researchers were still analyzing his injury and publishing scientific papers on its apparent consequences. For example, Damasio et al. (1994) used state-

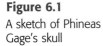

Figure 6.1

A sketch of Phineas Gage's skull

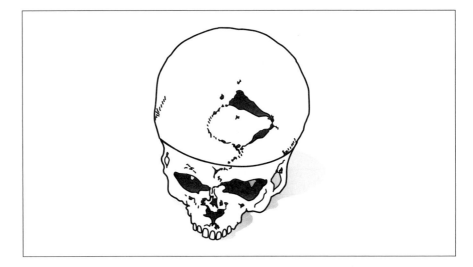

of-the-art neuroimaging techniques (magnetic resonance imaging) to analyze Gage's skull and make inferences about the precise brain regions that were likely to have been damaged during his accident. These sophisticated studies suggested that damage to the prefrontal cortex was primarily responsible for the social and emotional deficits that plagued Gage after his accident. Studies with modern-day Phineas Gages, people who have sustained other forms of injury to the prefrontal cortex, have confirmed the same predictable constellation of social and emotional problems. A sketch of Gage's skull, suggesting the approximate location of the damage to his brain, appears in Figure 6.1.

My Life as a Dog: The Case of Stephen D.

Sometimes case studies give us a glimpse into how different the world would be if our normal experiences were cranked up or down a couple of notches. By providing information about the extremes of human experience, such studies often provide clues to the adaptive significance of ordinary experiences that most people take for granted. When such extremely unusual experiences can be attributed to some physical or chemical change in a person's brain or body, they may also yield important insights about the biological underpinnings of many ordinary human experiences (as was the case with studies of Phineas Gage). Many such case studies have been documented by the neurologist Oliver Sacks. In Sacks's clinical experience, he has come across an enormous number of patients whose unusual experiences cast ordinary experience in a whole new light. One such patient was Stephen D.

Stephen D. was an otherwise ordinary medical student with an unfortunate addiction to amphetamines. One night he had an intensely vivid dream that he was a dog. When he awoke the next day, he found that pieces of his dream had become reality. The main sense in which this was true was olfactory. Stephen awoke with an appreciation of smells that practically hijacked his entire way of being. Quoting liberally from Stephen D. himself, Sacks (1985) provides a colorful description of Stephen's transformation:

"Hey, isn't that ol' Rex Conley over there? Why… I haven't smelled him in years!"

'I had never had much of a nose for smells before, but now I distinguished each one instantly—and I found each one unique, evocative, a whole world.' He found he could distinguish all his friends—and patients—by smell: 'I went into the clinic, I sniffed like a dog, and in that sniff recognised, before seeing them, the twenty patients who were there. Each had his own olfactory physiognomy, a smell-face, far more vivid and evocative, more redolent, than any sight face.' He could smell their emotions—fear, contentment, sexuality—like a dog. He could recognise every street, every shop, by smell—he could find his way around New York, infallibly, by smell.

Stephen's incredible world of smell evaporated after about three weeks and never returned. Ultimately, Stephen's loss of his extreme sensitivity to smell was probably a blessing. While possessed of his incredible sense of smell, Stephen reported having great difficulty thinking and reasoning. The richness and potency of his immediate sensory experiences simply did not allow him the luxury of sitting back and analyzing the world in an intellectual fashion. Dogs would apparently make poor philosophers or rocket scientists, even if we gave them big neocortexes. Sacks concludes that Stephen's experience was probably an amphetamine-induced dopaminergic excitation. In other words, a neurotransmitter that plays an important role in smell was artificially kicked into overdrive and briefly gave Stephen a dog's perspective on the world.

Really, Really Late Night with Peter Tripp

Whereas Phineas Gage and Stephen D. never asked to become objects of intense psychological scrutiny, a few people have become the objects of intensive scrutiny by choice. About 40 years ago, Peter Tripp was a successful New York disc jockey who decided to stage a 200-hour "wakeathon." What would happen to a person who went without sleep for eight consecutive days? The first thing, as you might guess, is that the person would get very, very sleepy. If your study habits are as poor as the first author's were when he was in college, you may have some idea of what it was like for Tripp to stay awake for 40–50 hours. He not only experienced an enormous desire to sleep but also started to have difficulty thinking and performing routine activities. However, these problems paled by comparison with what followed after 100 hours of sleep deprivation. At this point, Tripp began to have active and intense hallucinations. Shoes grew cobwebs, clocks grew human faces, clothing turned into worms, and many things burst into flames in his presence. Three days later, after about 170 hours of wakefulness, Tripp was barely able to maintain contact with reality and often questioned who he was. By the end of the horrific experience, Tripp had become nothing short of a raging lunatic, and he had to be restrained by the scientists who were monitoring his excruciating personal experiment (see Suter & Lindgren, 1989, for a more detailed summary).

As Suter and Lindgren (1989) noted, Tripp's experiences seem to suggest that extreme levels of sleep deprivation are virtually intolerable. However, Suter and Lindgren also noted that at least one other high-profile case of prolonged sleeplessness yielded findings that were much less dramatic. In 1965, a student named Randy Gardner apparently stayed awake for a full 11 days as part of a high-school science project. Gardner appeared on national television at the end of his 11-day ordeal, and he exhibited very few of the problems that had plagued Tripp. Anyone who observed a weary but essentially normal Gardner would have wondered if Tripp might have had a couple of loose screws well before his wakeathon. The consequences of extreme sleep deprivation are apparently less predictable than those of having an iron bar blasted through one's prefrontal cortex.

The Life and Very Hard Times of Sarah

Although Peter Tripp's self-inflicted nightmare seems bad, it pales by comparison with the extended nightmare that many abusive parents chronically inflict on their children. Understanding the consequences of exposure to physical and sexual abuse is an important social problem. The way victims respond to such abuse also provides psychologists with some important raw material for forming or evaluating theories of stress, coping, and the self-concept. For example, many self-concept researchers would like to know exactly how victims of chronic abuse deal with the trauma. If such victims are able to do so at all, how do they manage to develop a positive sense of self? In the book *Sarah: A Sexual Biography*, Abramson (1984) provides some clues to questions such as this by analyzing the life of a young woman he calls Sarah.

Sarah was the product of a broken home: an irresponsible-to-abusive biological father, an abusive-to-reprehensible stepfather, and a passive mother who did little or nothing to protect Sarah from the sexual assaults, physical abuse, and insults that she received at the hands of her stepfather. As a result of this abuse, Sarah became sexually active at a very early age, entered numerous abusive and neglectful relationships (sexual and otherwise), worked for a few months as a high-paid prostitute, and wandered all over the United States and Europe trying to figure out who she was and what she wanted out of life. (She could afford to travel, by the way, because some members of her family happened to be extremely wealthy.)

Although Sarah's candid reports of her life and times revealed dozens of seemingly self-destructive decisions, she ultimately appeared to resolve many of her conflicts. By the end of Sarah's story, she had adopted a very traditional, and seemingly healthy, lifestyle. She had a loving husband and had become a devoted mother and homemaker. According to Abramson, Sarah's transformation from victim to victor provides evidence of the presumably universal motives to feel good about ourselves and to make sense of our worlds. Of course, just as people differ enormously in their responses to sleep deprivation, they differ enormously in their responses to a childhood full of assault and battery. Many people (including Sarah's sister) respond to the kind of abuse that Sarah experienced by becoming severely depressed or even psychotic. Although Sarah's story provides us with a successful example of how a particular person was able to fulfill her basic needs for coherence and self-worth, it can provide us with only preliminary clues about how something as complex as the self-concept takes shape in adulthood.

The Man Who Forgot His Wife and His Hat

Although no case study can definitively answer basic research questions, case studies *can* sometimes be used to test specific research hypotheses. As an example of just this kind of case study, consider a study of memory and the self-concept presented by Tulving (1993). During the mid- to late 1980s, researchers interested in memory and the self-concept began to collect evidence suggesting that *trait information* (e.g., "I'm introverted," "I'm a great cook") and *autobiographical information* ("I went to the library instead of the party on Friday," "The curried chicken I cooked up last week was delicious") are represented separately in memory. This means, for instance, that once people have developed an abstract representation of their level of introversion or culinary prowess, they should be able to tell you exactly how introverted they are, or exactly what caliber of chef, without having to retrieve any specific memories of difficult conversations or delectable collations (see Klein, Sherman, & Loftus, 1996).

Klein et al. tested this hypothesis experimentally, and they came up with some good evidence for it. For instance, in some studies Klein et al. manipulated whether people had or had not recently retrieved biographical memories that were relevant to a specific trait. They then asked people to make a trait judgment about themselves on the same dimension that had just been activated during the autobiographical memory task. To the degree that people's trait judgments (i.e., people's self-views) are intimately connected to their autobiographical memories, doing the autobiographical memory task first should make it easier for people to judge the self-descriptiveness of the traits. However, to the degree that autobiographical information and trait information are functionally independent in memory, remembering a specific behavior first shouldn't really have any effect on the second judgment. Klein et al. found that unless people knew very little about themselves in a specific area (i.e., unless people hadn't yet formed a coherent self-view), autobiographical retrieval did little or nothing to facilitate trait judgments in a given area.

The strong form of Klein et al.'s hypothesis is pretty radical. It suggests that people who can't recall a single introverted or extroverted thing they have ever done might still be able to tell you precisely how introverted or extroverted they are. This should sound at least a little outlandish. How can people know that they are good cooks if they can't recall a single time when they ever did any cooking? And even if they do decide that they're great cooks, would anyone else be able to validate such claims by independently agreeing with the judgments? Tulving was intrigued enough with this version of Klein et al.'s hypothesis that he decided to put it to a direct test. Enter K. C.

K. C. was born to an upper-middle-class Canadian family in 1951. He was a good son and a pretty successful student. His life was relatively uneventful until, at age 30, he was nearly killed in a high-speed motorcycle accident. Like Phineas Gage, K. C. experienced a severe head injury. Also like Phineas Gage, K. C. was a survivor. Nonetheless, after more than seven months of hospitalization and rehabilitation, it was clear that K. C. would no longer be able to care for himself. Despite having a normal to above-average IQ, K. C. was forced to live under the direct care of his parents. The reason for K. C.'s dependence on others is the fact that he developed one of the most profound cases of amnesia ever known. His amnesia was particularly pronounced when it came to *episodic* memory, that is, memory for autobiographical events. As Tulving (1993) put it, K. C. became "incapable of recollecting any events or happenings from any period of his life once they receded beyond the reach of short-term memory … a time span measured in a few minutes." K. C. lives forever in the present.

Although K. C. couldn't tell you what he had for breakfast this morning or what he was doing ten minutes ago, he isn't completely devoid of abstract knowledge about his physical and social world. For instance, he has no difficulty using language, he can somehow remember the difference between stalagmites and stalactites, and he can identify the location of his family's summer cottage on a map. However, the most amazing thing about K. C. is that, despite having no memory of anything he has ever done, he can tell you exactly what kind of person he is. In other words, K. C. still has a self-concept. In fact, like most people without any kind of memory problem, K. C. appears to possess a self-concept that is (1) relatively stable over time and (2) highly consistent with what his mom thinks about him. To examine this second idea, Tulving asked both K. C. and K. C.'s mother to rate K. C.'s personality using the kind of standard trait terms that self-concept and personality researchers use all of the time. K. C. and his mother agreed very well about what traits K. C. did and did not possess. In fact, even when forced to make "either-or" judgments about trait terms that K. C. had originally found impossible to distinguish (e.g., when asked to report whether K. C. is more "artistic" or more "musical," or to report whether he is more "quarrelsome" or "selfish"), K. C. and his mother agreed on 73% of the traits. Finally, because K. C. underwent some dramatic personality changes after his accident, it was possible to see how much of K. C.'s self-concept reflected the "new" versus the "old" K. C. When K. C.'s mom was asked to make separate ratings of the old and the new K. C., only her ratings of the *new* K. C. agreed closely with K. C.'s self-ratings. In combination with the experimental findings of Klein et al., K. C.'s case study strongly suggests that people's abstract self-views are quite distinct from their episodic or autobiographical memories.

By the way, the fact that case studies often focus on highly unusual people does *not* mean that it's impossible to study such people using other research designs. It's simply that really unusual people are hard to gather up in large numbers (imagine trying to run an entire experiment using only participants named Jerry Derryberry, Jr.). Nonetheless, researchers who put their minds to it can sometimes overcome this practical barrier. As a case in point, Lieberman, Ochsner, Gilbert, and Schacter (2001) wanted to know whether amnesiacs (people like K. C.) would reduce their cognitive dissonance surrounding events that they had completely forgotten. (Recall that dissonance occurs when people become aware that they possess two contradictory beliefs.) Lieberman et al.'s research strongly suggests that amnesiacs reduce their cognitive dissonance in much the same way that people with intact memories do. This is interesting because it suggests that at least some aspects of the dissonance reduction process are probably unconscious. Even if amnesiacs consciously reduce their dissonance while they still remember what caused it, for example, it looks like dissonance reduction persists even when people can no longer remember the *source* of their dissonance. Have you ever known that you *really* like something without having any idea why? That kind of thing must happen to K. C. all the time.

What Makes a Case Study Scientific?

As illustrated by the diversity of the case studies summarized here, case studies are almost always a rich source of ideas for theory building, and they can also be used to test the plausibility of existing theories. This raises the question of what makes a case study scientific. Laypeople describe the quirks and eccentricities of their friends all the time. Supermarket tabloids provide extensive accounts of the deeds and misdeeds of the rich and famous. Do such analyses qualify as case studies? Scientifically speaking, the answer is no. Unless the goal of these accounts is the development or refinement of theories of human behavior, they should not be considered case studies. An important difference between scientific and informal analyses is that scientific analyses of extraordinary events often demystify them by explaining them in terms of established scientific principles—principles that presumably apply to everyone, given the right circumstances. As a brief example of the difference between case studies and less reputable news stories, consider the fictional case of Mr. Zelick, a modern-day "Elephant Man." Instead of speculating, as a tabloid author might, that Mr. Zelick was bitten by a radioactive elephant and may have fathered the love-child of an aging soap opera vixen, a scientific analysis would be more likely to provide a deterministic, empirically grounded, parsimonious, and testable explanation for Mr. Zelick's strange behavior:

> Yes, it's fascinating that Mr. Z. thought he was an elephant, ate only peanuts and acacia bark, and (according to his medical records) gained over 80 pounds during the three weeks that he suffered from this delusion. Given Mr. Z.'s chronic problems with nasal congestion, it is even more impressive

that he developed the ability to hold nearly a pint of water in his nose and showered naked in public by spraying the water on his back. Although his condition is highly unusual, careful radioimaging of Mr. Z.'s brain suggests a straightforward account for this transformation.... It now seems likely that *anyone* who suffers a lesion in this specific area of the ventromedial hypothalamus will develop the same syndrome of physical and behavioral symptoms.

Needless to say, only this second hypothetical account would qualify as a scientific case study. By providing detailed records of rare events, case studies try to explain unusual events by relying on established scientific principles.

To provide a complementary perspective on what makes a case study scientific, it is necessary to consider the attitude of the authors of case studies toward how audiences should respond to them. Abramson (1992) argued that the crucial determinant of whether a case study is scientific is the same standard Popper set for what makes *anything* scientific. We use case studies to develop and sometimes test theories that are open to falsification. As discussed in Chapters 1 and 2, scientific statements and analyses are those that are open to disconfirmation. Science is all about openness to criticism and revision. According to this definition, *any* approach to increasing knowledge, be it history, particle physics, or musicology, qualifies as scientific as long as its proponents are willing to change their minds in the face of information that raises doubts about their original positions. Although the specific facts behind case studies are rarely refuted, the conclusions drawn from these facts are often the subject of serious scientific debate. For instance, no one seriously questions whether Phineas Gage was the victim of an unusual and unfortunate accident. However, early interpretations of Gage's behavior raised some interesting, and testable, questions about the degree to which different mental and emotional functions were tied to specific brain areas (e.g., see Damasio, 1994). The story of Phineas Gage didn't teach behavioral neuroscientists everything there is to know about the prefrontal cortex, but it did inspire them to begin asking the right questions.

Of course, case studies, like all other approaches to research, have their drawbacks. For example, case studies do not always lend themselves well to the use of operational definitions or statistical analyses. In addition to these rational critiques, we suspect that the lack of respect for case studies sometimes observed in some scientific circles has at least a little to do with the legacy of Sigmund Freud. Because Freud was an ardent fan of case studies, and because he is much better known for his creativity and imagination than for the scientific rigor of his analyses, case studies may have gotten something of a bad rap among many researchers. This is unfortunate because, like more contemporary research designs, case studies can yield some extremely important information about the nature of human experience. (It is also unfortunate because Freud, though wrong about a lot of details, was pretty darned insightful.)

DESCRIBING THE STATE OF THE WORLD AT LARGE: SINGLE-VARIABLE RESEARCH

Although case studies typically focus on a single person or group, they can be a rich source of information about people in general. Nonetheless, one of the biggest drawbacks of case studies is the fact that we do not usually know how well the results of a case study apply to people in general. The fact that most case studies focus on highly unusual people sometimes adds to this concern. This is a theoretical as well as a practical problem. Sometimes nothing could be more important than knowing exactly how well a specific observation describes people in general. *Single-variable* studies are designed with precisely this goal in mind: to describe some specific property of a large group of people. As examples, single-variable studies might address questions about the popularity of gun control below the Mason-Dixon Line, the prevalence of clinical depression in Canadian high schools, or the proportion of eligible voters in Barcelona who plan to vote for an incumbent in a mayoral election. If these questions seem largely descriptive rather than theoretical, it is because they are. Because single-variable research focuses on a single question or type of question, it cannot usually be used to answer questions about causes.

Although there are a couple of exceptions to this general rule, the exceptions exist only when there is a strong reason to expect a large group of people to do something other than what they turn out to do. For instance, if a representative survey of American women reveals that 89 percent of them are dissatisfied with their bodies, this would lend some support to the claims of many clinical and social psychologists that women are socialized to adopt unrealistic, and potentially unhealthy, body images. A search for the causes of this phenomenon would be the next logical step. For now, however, let's stick with the first step. What kind of single-variable studies are performed by researchers who simply want to provide accurate descriptions of the world?

Population Surveys

Two of the most important types of single-variable research are the **census** and the **survey**. The goal of each of these techniques is to produce a clear picture of a specific group of people, that is, a population. Of course, a census has one important goal that doesn't really apply to surveys. This is the goal of simply counting the number of people in a population. To illustrate each of these two techniques, imagine that a researcher wants to determine how satisfied students enrolled in Canadian colleges and universities are with their education. How could this be done? One obvious way would be to identify *all* the students enrolled in Canadian institutes of higher learning in a given year. Every single student could then be given an inventory assessing educational satisfaction. Needless to say, this would not be easy to do. First, it would be extremely difficult for anyone to obtain such an exhaustive list of students in the first place. Second, even if anyone could, it would be even more difficult, expensive, and time consuming to contact everyone on such a huge list. This example reveals the difficulty of conducting a census. A **census** is a body of data collected from every (or virtually every) member of a population of interest. In the United States, for example, government officials conduct a census every ten years. This is an enormous and expensive undertaking, which is part of the reason that the U.S. government does it only every ten years.

Because it is incredibly difficult to conduct a true census, researchers more typically estimate the characteristics of populations by using surveys. Surveys identify a subset of people in the population (or a *sample*) who are then studied. The responses of this subset are then used to estimate the responses of the entire population. Let's return to our example of Canadian college students. Rather than asking each and every Canadian student about his or her educational satisfaction (a census), we could ask a smaller sample of students how they feel (a survey). The assumption here is that the attitudes of this subset would probably represent the attitudes of the entire population. Of course, this might not be the case. Suppose that the large majority of sampled students attend college in Montreal. Suppose further that students in the Montreal area not only speak French better than most other Canadians but also have unusually favorable attitudes about college. This would obviously lead to biased estimates of the attitudes of Canadian students on the whole.

As another example, suppose researchers sample mostly college seniors, who might have a more jaded view of college than their younger classmates do. This, too, would lead to a biased estimate of the attitudes of the population. As you may recall from our discussion of selection bias in Chapter 5, survey researchers always have to worry that the people they have sampled may be different from the population of people about whom they want to know. For this reason, survey researchers often employ a special type of survey called a **population survey**. A population survey uses *random sampling* (to be defined formally in Chapter 7) to identify a sample of people to be surveyed. If you find it confusing that this approach is referred to as a population survey, just remember that the goal of a population survey is to describe the population by carefully selecting just the right sample. We could thus conduct a population survey by first getting a *population list* of all of the Canadians who are currently enrolled in college and assigning each person a number. We could then use a *random numbers table* or a computer program with a *random number generator* to pull numbers at random from this large population of numbers. In essence, we would be conducting a lottery to see which lucky students win the "prize" of receiving our survey about educational satisfaction. Because there is good reason to believe that a randomly selected group of students have attitudes that are highly similar to the attitudes of the population as a whole, we could feel reasonably confident that our sample would give us a sense of the attitudes of Canadian students in general.

The main advantage of conducting a population survey is that it is usually much easier to do this than to conduct a census. That said, population surveys aren't exactly a piece of cake. First, it is often very hard to find a population list. How would you ever get a complete list of every Canadian student? You might have to conduct a census to get that kind of information! And, even if one had such a list and identified a sample of these students, think of how hard it would be to test everyone who might be selected for the study. If you want to sample 1,000 Canadian students, a random number generator might send researchers to 1,000 different places, ranging from Salmon Arm, British Columbia, to Moose Jaw, Saskatchewan.

Survey researchers typically get around this problem by using more pragmatic sampling methods. One such method is **cluster sampling.** A survey that uses a cluster sampling method is still a population survey, but it uses a modified version of random selection. Researchers who use cluster sampling begin by creating a manageable list of all the possible locations in which they can find members of the population in which they are interested. To study Canadian college students, researchers would thus create a list of every college and university in Canada. That'd be a pretty long list, but it'd seem like nothing compared with the original list of individual student names. The next step would be to select a reasonable number of schools from the larger list. Suppose researchers randomly sample 20. Working from this list, they could contact the registrars of the 20 schools and ask each registrar for an official student body list. Then researchers might randomly sample 50 students from each school to produce a total sample of 1,000 students. Assuming they could persuade most of these students to respond to their population survey, this limited number of students would provide the information they could use to estimate the attitudes of the total population.

With the benefit of cluster sampling, researchers can make some very good guesses about the attitudes of extremely large groups of people while avoiding the enormous headaches they might encounter with a census or with a survey that uses true random selection. However, it should go without saying that the characteristics of our sample will rarely be *exactly* like the characteristics of our population. Let's say, for instance, that exactly 80 percent of the college students in our survey of 1,000 Canadians say they are satisfied with their educational experience. We know that a little bit of good or bad luck with sampling may have influenced this careful, scientific estimate. It's unlikely that *precisely* 80.00 percent of *all* Canadian college students are satisfied with their educations. But just how far off could our estimate be? Could the correct answer be 20 percent? Fortunately, there is a way to answer this kind of question using statistics. By performing statistical calculations, survey researchers estimate how much error is likely to exist in any specific set of population survey findings. The error that may have gone into the estimate is called **sampling error.** Sampling error reflects the likely discrepancy between the results one obtains in a specific sample and the results one would have been likely to have obtained from the entire population. This value is also called the *margin of error.* Using conventional probability values, a 3 percent margin of error in our study would mean that we could be 95 percent sure that the actual proportion of students in the population who are satisfied with their educations is 80 percent, *plus or minus* this 3 percent error value. To put it a little more simply, this would mean that the actual proportion of Canadian college students who are satisfied with their educations is very likely (95 percent likely) to be somewhere between 77 percent and 83 percent. That's not a perfect estimate, but most people would probably be pretty satisfied with it.

One of the interesting things about carefully conducted surveys is that very precise estimates of population characteristics can usually be obtained using samples that are much, much smaller than the population of interest. As an example, assume there are roughly a million students enrolled in colleges and universities in Canada. If we used a careful sampling technique such as cluster sampling to estimate the percentage of students who are satisfied with their educations, we'd obtain a sampling error of about 3 percent in a sample of only 1,000 students. Granted, 1,000 people is a lot, but it is certainly a lot less than a million. We'd cut down our work (i.e., our data collection) by a factor of a *thousand* and get nearly the same gain in information. If we had some way of using true random sampling, by the way, our estimate would become even more accurate. And if we used cluster sampling to estimate the attitudes of an extremely large group of people (e.g., the residents of China, whose population is well over a *billion* people), we'd be about as accurate as we are in this estimate of the attitudes of only a million Canadian college students. Because the population survey is such a powerful research tool, it has been used in a wide variety of applied domains in which researchers need to know about the characteristics of a particular population. Two of the more important applications of population surveys are in the areas of **epidemiological research** and research on **public opinion**.

Epidemiological Research

As it is defined by scientists in general, **epidemiology** refers to the scientific study of the causes of disease. But when clinical psychologists speak of epidemiological research, they are typically referring to descriptive studies that focus primarily on the prevalence of different psychological disorders within meaningful, well-defined populations. Clinical epidemiologists who wish to estimate the proportion of people in a population who suffer from specific disorders such as depression, schizophrenia, obsessive compulsive disorder, or substance abuse face a particularly daunting task. To attain the ideals of population surveys, they would like to randomly sample a population of interest and conduct clinical diagnostic interviews with each person in their sample to determine the precise percentage of people who meet strict clinical criteria for a disorder. An example of research that approximated this ideal state of affairs is the Epidemiological Catchment Area (ECA) project conducted in the United States in the early 1980s (see Regier & Burke, 1987). In the ECA studies, interviewers sampled large groups of people using a variation on the cluster sampling procedure just described. One variation from a strict cluster sampling procedure was that, to avoid undersampling mentally ill people who weren't living at home, the researchers supplemented their large community samples at each of five sampling sites with smaller samples of people who were institutionalized in or near each site (in places like hospitals, prisons, and nursing homes).[1]

Needless to say, this enormous study posed some enormous practical and technical problems. For example, how could the researchers minimize non-response bias (the bias that occurs when some people refuse to take part in a study)? This is particularly problematic in research of this sort because people who suffer from mental illness are precisely the kind of people who might be most unwilling or unable to respond to a request to be interviewed. When all was said and done, the researchers found creative ways around this and other practical problems, and thus they were able to come up with some good estimates of the frequency and distribution of different mental illnesses. For example, in comparison with previous estimates of illness rates that were estimated indirectly from the use of mental health services, the results of the ECA studies suggested that anxiety disorders, especially phobias, are much more common than researchers had previously believed. Although the ECA studies were largely descriptive, many of the findings that have emerged from these studies appear to have important practical and theoretical implications for the understanding and treatment of mental illness.

Although the ECA studies should primarily be considered single-variable studies, it is important to note that studies that focus exclusively on a single variable are extremely rare. After all, the only thing researchers need to do to turn a single-variable study into a multiple-variable study is to measure a second or third variable. Most of the theoretically interesting findings from the ECA studies involved two or more variables rather than one. As an example, the ECA studies revealed some interesting things about gender and the prevalence of different mental disorders. First of all, in contrast to the findings of many existing studies, the results of the ECA studies suggested that there is little or no *overall* difference between women and men in rates of mental illness. However, on an illness-by-illness basis, there were some notable differences. For instance, relative to men, women were about twice as likely to be diagnosed as clinically depressed but more than five times *less* likely to be diagnosed with either antisocial personality disorder or disorders involving the abuse of alcohol (Regier & Burke, 1987). Both clinical psychologists interested in the causes of mental illness and social psychologists interested in gender and socialization are likely to be intrigued by these differences.

Research on Public Opinion

Another important form of single-variable research that typically requires the use of population surveys is research on public opinion—research designed to determine the attitudes and preferences of specific populations, such as voters or consumers. As we are using the phrase here, public opinion research also includes **marketing research**, that is, research designed to assess consumers' attitudes about and preferences for different products and services. You may wonder why political groups, government agencies, and manufacturers are willing to go to so much effort to find out people's attitudes about everyday things like guns and butter. One simple answer is purely pragmatic. It makes good economic and political sense to know the attitudes of one's consumers

Table 6.1 Estimating public opinion (from Pelham, 1998)

In a survey, what percentage of UCLA students reported that:

1. they typically carry $1.50 or more in coins in their pocket or purse? _____%

2. they have ever been camping? _____%

3. they had worn blue jeans at least once in the week prior to the survey? _____%

4. they preferred ice cream over apple pie as a dessert? _____%

5. they had ever visited Disneyland? _____%

6. they would choose a $40,000 Mercedes Benz over $30,000 in cash? _____%

Note: The proportions of students answering each question in the affirmative are as follows: (1) 47%, (2) 87%, (3) 94%, (4) 51%, (5) 99%, (6) 16%.

and constituents before trying to sell them either a new brand of soft drink or a new brand of foreign policy.

For the sake of argument, however, assume that someone interested in public opinion decides to save some research money by estimating public opinion intuitively instead of using a population survey. Although the intuitive approach does have some obvious advantages when it comes to time and money, it also comes with certain serious risks. To get a feel for how the intuitive estimation of public opinion works, try your hand at estimating the results of a survey study conducted on a group of UCLA students (Pelham, 1998). Six of the 28 questions these students answered can be found in Table 6.1. For the purposes of this activity, let's generously assume that the sample was fairly representative of UCLA students.

To make this exercise work, take out a sheet of paper and record your best guess for each of the six questions. Please do so before you read any further! If your judgments follow some of the basic principles of cognitive and social psychology, we're betting that these judgments, while generally pretty accurate, reflect a couple of interesting biases. First of all, we're guessing that your judgments probably reflect some degree of conservatism, or what we might call *regression toward the midpoint*. As a potential example, compare your estimate for question 2 with the 87 percent of UCLA students who actually reported that they had been camping. We're guessing that your estimate was at least a little lower than this pretty high value.

Before we discuss your estimates for any of the other questions, let's take a slightly different approach to these questions. Imagine that you had been a participant in the original study. Stop to consider how *you* would have answered question 1. That is, do you typically carry more than $1.50 in coins in your pocket or purse? If you do, we're guessing that your estimate on this question was higher than the correct answer of about 47 percent. On the other hand, if you do *not* typically carry around large quantities of change, we're guessing that your estimate was lower than the correct answer of 47 percent. Why should your own coin carrying habits have anything to do with your guess about how other people would answer this question? From a purely rational standpoint, they shouldn't. But the point is that they probably do. Research on the *false consensus effect* (Ross, Greene, & House, 1977) has shown that most people overestimate the proportion of other people whose attitudes and behaviors are similar to their own. Among the UCLA students who answered the questions sampled in Table 6.1, false consensus effects occurred on 25 of 28 questions. For example, people who reported carrying around a lot of change estimated that 75 percent of the students in their class also carried around a lot of change. Those who did *not* report being heavy change carriers disagreed. As a group, they estimated that only 25 percent of their fellow students typically carried around a lot of change.

The finding that human judges frequently fall prey to biases such as regression and false consensus suggests that people who need to make decisions based on public opinion could run into trouble if they rely too heavily on their intuitions. Because social judgments are both statistically regressive and egocentric, people who are members of small minorities may be especially prone to overestimate the proportion of people who share their opinions. In the UCLA study, for example, the 13 percent of the students who reported that they had never been camping estimated that 50 percent of their UCLA peers had never been camping. To translate this into practical terms, if you are a marketing researcher who wants to know about the size of the market for camping equipment, the last person you should ask (if you're only going to ask one person, that is) is someone who has never been camping. Similarly, if you want to know what most people think about a radical change in public education policies, you would probably do well to ignore the opinions of the three specific people who personally formulated the radical new policy.

Incidentally, problems in judgment, such as egocentric biases and regression toward the midpoint, are sometimes made worse by the fact that people who make erroneous judgments often place undue confidence in them (see Fischhoff, 1982). Because of this tendency toward overconfidence, novice marketers and politicians might often place undue confidence in their intuitions regarding other people's attitudes and opinions. Thus, they might forgo conducting systematic surveys to gather important descriptive data about the people they wish to influence or understand. If you really want to know what a particular population thinks about something, you should locate a random sample that is drawn from this population and ask them what they think. You can use the responses you get from this small sample to obtain fairly accurate estimates of the views of the larger population.

Limitations and Drawbacks of Population Surveys

Population surveys are a highly cost-effective way to learn a lot about a population of interest. For this reason, they are usually much better than surveying everyone (taking a census of people's attitudes) or sampling no one (performing an intuitive assessment of people's attitudes). This being said, there are some serious limitations to the use of population surveys. First and foremost, population survey research requires a very careful consideration of a wide variety of potentially complex sampling issues. Although we do not wish to overstate this problem, most people who wish to conduct population surveys should consult a trained expert in survey research. As the popular commercial warning says, "Please don't try this at home." Consider, for instance, the numerous sampling issues researchers must have had to address in the ECA studies. In addition to developing an effective sampling scheme and dealing with nonresponse bias, the directors of this nationwide project had to train a great number of interviewers to conduct valid and reliable clinical interviews. Furthermore, if a potential respondent did not speak English, it raised a host of issues regarding translations and minority representation. Although population surveys are much easier and cheaper than censuses, the complex problems that must be solved in population surveys sometimes make these surveys more expensive and labor intensive than one might think.

Over the past decade or so, a growing problem for researchers who conduct almost all kinds of population surveys is that the American public has become increasingly skeptical of unsolicited surveys, regardless of their content. Ironically, then, the growing popularity of survey research, especially the popularity of telephone and mail surveys, has made it increasingly difficult to conduct this kind of research (because many people have grown weary of responding to surveys). Telemarketers and salespeople who disguise their pitches as research surveys further compound this important problem. In a world where people are bombarded with offers to purchase timeshares in Puerto Vallarta or change their cable and/or Internet service provider, well-intentioned researchers who wish to assess people's political attitudes or find out how Americans approve of specific health care reforms are facing an uphill battle that seems to grow a little steeper every year.

Finally, the fact that population surveys so effectively achieve their goal of being highly representative creates an additional problem for population survey researchers. Unlike experimenters who study college students, epidemiologists, market researchers, and public opinion pollsters have to be prepared to deal with a very wide range of research participants. This means that survey and interview questions have to be written so that people of varying ages, educational levels, language skills, and cultural backgrounds can readily understand all the questions. Given this constraint, researchers usually keep their population surveys short and to the point. Doing so necessarily limits the total amount of information researchers can gather from each individual participant. A closely related problem has to do with the diversity of the population survey research setting (most often, participants' homes). Unlike participants who have settled into the quiet confines of the laboratory, participants who pick up the phone and agree to respond to a public opinion poll may continue to watch *Wheel of Fortune*, pedal on an exercise bike, or both, while responding to the survey. This loss of control relative to the laboratory is not always this extreme, but it is an inherent part of many population surveys. The diversity of survey respondents and the noisy nature of many survey settings create problems for survey researchers that laboratory researchers rarely have to face.

Single-Variable Convenience Samples

Before we move on from single-variable to multiple-variable research, we should point out that for a couple of forms of single-variable research, researchers justifiably show very little concern for whether the people they sample are representative of some larger group of people. Sometimes, it is possible for a clever researcher to create a demonstration of human judgment or behavior that is so interesting, or disturbing, that it is surprising to see it occur in *any* sample. If the responses of normal, healthy people from any walk of life challenge researchers' well-established assumptions about human nature, these findings are likely to generate quite a bit of scientific interest. For instance, as you may recall, Milgram's (1963) original obedience study caused quite a stir even though he did not make use of random sampling (and did not include any kind of explicit control group). By showing that 65 percent of normal adults were willing to deliver potentially life-threatening shocks to a stranger merely because an authority figure told them to do so, Milgram documented a behavior so disturbing and surprising that he did not need a randomly sampled experimental and control group.

More recently, a great deal of research on **judgment and decision making** has challenged a different but equally cherished assumption about human nature. One spin on the Milgram obedience studies is that Milgram showed that human beings are not quite as principled as we might hope. There is also a great deal of single-variable research in judgment and decision making showing that human beings are not quite as good at using principles as we might hope. Moreover, much of this research is also based on convenience samples (usually college students). Because it is usually possible to specify exactly how a rational, logical decision maker would make certain kinds of judgments, and because systematic errors in people's judgments often reveal something about the decision rules people use to arrive at these judgments, it is often useful simply to know how good people are at making basic cognitive or social judgments. In other words, it is often highly informative to know the proportion of people who make a specific judgment or decision correctly. As an example, consider the following story about Linda.

> Linda is 31 years old, single, outspoken, and very bright. As a college student, she majored in philosophy and was deeply concerned with issues of discrimination and social justice. She also participated actively in antinuclear demonstrations. Please choose the most likely alternative:
>
> 1. Linda is a bank teller.
> 2. Linda is a bank teller and is active in the feminist movement.

When Tversky and Kahneman (1983) gave this problem to a large group of college students, they found that 85 percent of their participants indicated that the second option was more likely than the first. Presumably, almost everyone who reads the brief vignette about Linda develops an image of her that is much more consistent with the second description. Linda doesn't sound much like a bank teller at all, but most people seem to conclude that she's more likely to be a *feminist* bank teller than she is to be a bank teller. This highly intuitive conclusion turns out to be highly illogical. One of the fundamental laws of probability theory is the idea that a conjunctive or compound event (both A and B) can never be more likely than one of its component parts (either A alone or B alone). Thus, it *cannot* be the case that Linda is more likely to be a feminist bank teller than she is to be a bank teller because the category of bank teller includes *all* bank tellers, both feminist and nonfeminist alike. When a person violates this basic principle of probability theory by judging a compound event to be more likely than one of its component events, that person has committed what Tversky and Kahneman call the *conjunction fallacy*.

Many studies of judgment and decision-making use single-variable designs. Likewise, most of the same studies use convenience samples (college students) rather than random samples to make their points. Knowing that 85 percent of people will readily violate a basic principle of logic is inherently informative. This is true in much the same way that it is inherently informative to know that about 65 percent of people will sometimes violate a basic principle of social responsibility (e.g., by delivering intense shocks to a hapless victim). Of course, just as epidemiologists, pollsters, and marketing researchers often build on their single-variable population surveys by trying to identify the predictors of depression or preferences for Alf Landon, researchers interested in judgment and decision making often try to identify when people are more or less likely to make suboptimal judgments (see Fischhoff, 1982; Gilbert, 1989; Pelham & Neter, 1995; Tetlock, 1985). However, for studies about when and why people stray from ideal standards of judgment, a common starting point is to conduct single-variable studies that simply document that people often go astray.

DESCRIBING ASSOCIATIONS: MULTIPLE-VARIABLE RESEARCH

Correlational Methods

Once researchers have developed a descriptive account of the variables in which they are interested, they typically become interested in understanding the causes of these variables. That is, they become interested in identifying the variables that are responsible for their observations. Of course, this represents a quest for internal validity, and no method surpasses the experimental method for its potential to identify causes. For reasons we describe in detail later in this book, however, many important research topics do not lend themselves well to experimentation. When this is the case, researchers sometimes test their theories and hypotheses by looking at the associations of variables in natural settings. These studies use **correlational methods**.

The basic idea behind correlational research is to generate a fixed set of observations about a group of people and to test hypotheses about the associations between different variables. Do men and women differ in their attitudes about capital punishment? Are the typical residents of China, Japan, or India really more modest than the typical residents of the United States? Do cities with warmer climates have higher crime rates? Although it is not usually all that difficult to answer these interesting questions, it is usually extremely difficult to know what theoretical conclusions we can draw from them. Recall that theories are causal statements about the relations between two or more variables. This means that correlational research can be used in theory testing only to the degree that this research allows us to draw some reasonable conclusions about causality.

For example, suppose you want to argue that depression influences people's specific self-views. That is, you want to argue that when people become depressed, they start to see the world through the filter of their unhappiness and so they rate themselves more negatively than they ordinarily would (see Bargh & Tota, 1988; Pelham, 1991b). If you measure depression by means of a careful clinical interview and then assess the favorability of people's specific self-views using a pencil-and-paper survey (e.g., "I am attractive," "I am a good leader"), correlational analyses could be carried out to document that people who are more depressed do in fact possess more negative self-views. However, even if this connection between depression and self-evaluation could be established, a critic could make at least two good arguments against the idea that depression causes people to view themselves negatively. First, there could be a third variable that is actually responsible for the observed association between depression and self-evaluation. Second, the problem of *reverse causality* could be at work. Let's use this example as an opportunity to discuss each of these problems in detail.

First of all, the critic could argue that some third variable is actually responsible for the association between depression and people's specific self-views. For instance, it could be that anxiety or low self-esteem (which are both strongly correlated with depression; see, for example, Dobson, 1985) represents the real reason why depressed people tend to view themselves negatively. To be a little more specific, the critic might argue that anxiety causes people to feel depressed and also causes people to develop negative views of their attractiveness or leadership abilities. To the degree that this is true, a successful intervention designed to lower depression will *not* cause people to develop more favorable self-views (unless the intervention also happens to lead to decreases in anxiety).

As we hope you recognized, the potential problem discussed here is the familiar problem of confounds (see Table 5.2). As we suggested in Chapter 5 with our fictitious tattoo study (see Figure 5.1), nonexperimental approaches to research are almost always susceptible to confounds. The careful researcher must therefore take steps to consider any and all plausible confounds (i.e., third-variable explanations) before making any claims about causality. In this section, we elaborate on the specific kinds of confounds that can undermine correlational research. We describe three distinct kinds of confounds.

Person Confounds

The first confound is the classic case. It's what we call a **person confound**. This occurs when a variable (such as depression) seems to cause something because people who are high or low on this variable also happen to be high or low on some *individual difference* variable (i.e., some personality variable or demographic characteristic) that is associated with the outcome variable of interest. This sort of confound was just illustrated. People who are depressed usually tend to suffer from a lot of anxiety as well. As a result, a finding that seems to show that depression influences people's self-views may actually reflect the influence of anxiety on people's self-views. The only way to address this ambiguity with correlational data is to measure the confounding variable of interest and make some kind of statistical adjustment. (In case you are wondering how this statistical adjustment works, you have the opportunity to see it at work firsthand in Methodology Exercise 1 on partial correlation in Appendix 2.) For example, in an effort to determine whether depression or anxiety is causing changes in self-views, you could pit these two competing predictors against one another in a regression analysis designed to predict self-views. If you find that depression is associated with people's self-views only because it happens to be correlated with anxiety, the original correlation between depression and self-views would not provide any support for your original theory of depression.

Environmental Confounds

A second important kind of confound is the **environmental confound**. Environmental confounds are very much like person confounds except that they refer to environmental (i.e., situational) rather than personological nuisance variables. As an example, stressful life events might cause people to become more depressed while simultaneously lowering people's self-views. If this happens, it might appear that depression is influencing self-views when it is not. Life events are influencing depression, and the *same* life events are also influencing self-views. Environmental confounds and person confounds are obviously similar in that they both represent clear threats to the internal validity of a research finding. They are obviously different in that they refer to events that exist outside versus inside the person. In the case of both person confounds and environmental confounds, a third variable clouds the picture of whether one variable truly causes another. Does depression really cause people to adopt negative self-views, or is it the anxiety that so often goes hand in hand with depression? Or is it the negative life events that often cause depression in the first place? It is important to realize that in each of these instances, there was a meaningful association between depression and the person confound or environmental confound that created interpretation problems. Like height and weight, depression and anxiety really are correlated. The same is true for depression and negative life events. Something like anxiety or negative life events can only be a confound when it is correlated (in the worrisome direction) with both your original independent variable (e.g., depression) and your original dependent variable (e.g., self-views).

Operational Confounds

Operational confounds are closely tied to the notion of operational definitions. They occur when a measure designed to assess a specific construct such as depression, memory, or foot size inadvertently measures *something else* as well. Operational confounds are easiest to distinguish from person or environmental confounds when this something else that is inadvertently measured (1) has nothing to do with the predictor variable that the researcher really wished to measure but (2) has a lot to do with whatever outcome the researcher wished to predict (see Table 5.2).

As an example, suppose that Dr. Young developed a pencil-and-paper measure of depression. Furthermore, for some very good reasons, Dr. Young wanted to measure depression without really tipping participants off to what he was measuring. Thus, he might want to steer away from normally useful survey items such as "I feel so miserable that I can't stand it," or "I have recently contemplated suicide." Instead, he might decide to focus disproportionately on the physical or somatic symptoms of depression. The typical items in his survey might thus include "I've had trouble concentrating lately," "I have trouble getting out of bed in the morning," "I've lost some of my interest in food," and "I don't sleep as well as I used to." Nice job. This measure might allow Dr. Young to assess some of the symptoms of depression without really cluing people in to the nature of his interests.[2] Furthermore, imagine that Dr. Young randomly sampled 500 Americans and found that those with higher scores on his measure reported having more negative beliefs about themselves. This included people's assessments of their physical and cognitive skills as well as their assessments of their physical attractiveness. People scoring high on his new measure were even more likely to report, for example, that "My life feels like it is out of my control." Can Dr. Young conclude that depression causes people to view themselves and their social worlds more negatively than usual? Unfortunately not. Despite all the sophisticated advice that you offered Dr. Young when he hired you as a high-paid methodological consultant, Dr. Young unintentionally allowed a construct that has nothing to do with depression to sneak into his measure.

This construct is called age. If you look back over the questions in Dr. Young's measure, you can see that senior citizens, especially those whose bodies have begun to give out on them a little, would probably be more likely than their younger counterparts to endorse the questions in Dr. Young's "depression" measure. Dr. Young had *hoped* that people who said they had trouble getting out of bed would always be reporting a common symptom of depression. Instead, however, the older people in his sample might simply be reporting that it was physically hard to get out of bed in the morning! To add insult to injury, it would come as no surprise to learn that most old people do not feel quite as able-bodied or attractive as they did back when Grover Cleveland was president. Furthermore, if the ravages of time have confined some older people to wheelchairs or extended-care facilities, you can see why they might feel that they no longer have complete control over their lives. In short, an operational confound might be at work. Age is not really correlated with depression, but age seeped into Dr. Young's *measure* of depression, and age is also correlated with Dr. Young's outcome measure (specific self-evaluations of ability, attractiveness, and control).

Notice that this criticism of Dr. Young's research questions the validity of the causal interpretations in the study (i.e., it questions internal validity). But, in this case, the assumption is that *something* about Dr. Young's new measure really *does* cause people to report negative self-views. So the claim made here is not that the observed relationship is completely spurious (as we argued in the case of the particular person and environmental confounds we chose). In this particular case, what Dr. Young measured might (all by itself) be causing a change in negative self-views. It just happens that he not only measured depression, he also measured a confounding third variable that is a lot less interesting, and this factor is causing his "depressed" participants to feel out of control.

There are several ways to fix an operational confound. First, you can discard or revise your measure to remove the confound that you unknowingly built into it. In other words, you can go back to the drawing board. A second approach is to do the same thing you would have done if you were worried about a person confound or an environmental confound. You could measure the nuisance variable that you think is really accounting for the action (in this case, age) and perform statistical tests that are designed to tell you which of two competing variables is really responsible for an outcome. Finally, a third approach is probably a little more intuitive. Run a replication study in which you focus exclusively on participants who are roughly the same age. For instance, if Dr. Young had conducted his study on students enrolled in an introductory psychology course, he would have little to worry about when it came to this specific operational confound (because there would probably be few, if any, senior citizens in this sample). As you can see, just as there are multiple ways to get into trouble in correlational research, there are usually multiple ways to try to get out of it.

A Reminder about Reverse Causality

The three confounds we reviewed here all have the unfortunate effect of causing the researcher to draw faulty inferences about the meaning of a connection between two or more variables. As serious as all these confounds are, they are only part of the story. As you may recall, researchers who rely on correlational methods must worry not only about confounds or third variables. In addition, they have to be concerned with reverse causality. In our running example involving depression and negative self-views, a researcher who has controlled for every conceivable person, environmental, and operational confound might be tempted to conclude that depression does indeed cause people to evaluate themselves negatively. However, it is always possible that negative self-evaluations lead to depression rather than the reverse. Believing that one is incompetent might cause a person to become depressed.

To address the problem of reverse causality, researchers often follow people over time and make repeated assessments of the variables in which they are interested. **Longitudinal designs** such as this can go a long way toward suggesting causal connections between variables. (Recall that one of John Stuart Mills's time-honored requirements for establishing causality is showing that changes in one variable precede changes in the other.) However, longitudinal analyses are not a foolproof guarantee against reverse causality. Imagine that we conduct a longitudinal study in which we measure children's school performance at ages eight, nine, and ten. Furthermore, imagine that increases in children's school performance during the first year of the study predict increases in parents' income during the second year of the study. It would be pretty wacky to conclude that children's grades cause parents' incomes to increase. A more likely interpretation of the findings is that as parents' incomes increase over the long haul (beginning when children are born, perhaps), children do better in school (e.g., because of improvements in children's health, diet, or access to computers in the home). To definitively establish that changes in one variable lead to changes in another, it is usually necessary to conduct an experiment.

As this review reveals, correlational research is always susceptible to the third-variable problem (i.e., confounds) as well as the bidirectionality problem, both of which are summarized in Figure 6.2. This might make you wonder why researchers interested in testing theories would ever bother to conduct correlational research. There are many answers to this question, but for now we will focus on only two. First, for reasons that we discussed in much more detail in Chapter 2, many things simply cannot be studied ethically or efficiently in the laboratory. Second, precisely because researchers know about the threats imposed by confounds and reverse causality, they try to design correlational studies in ways that will help minimize these threats. Although correlations are rarely taken as proof for a specific causal argument, carefully conducted correlational studies that rule out a large number of confounds and deal honestly with questions regarding reverse causality

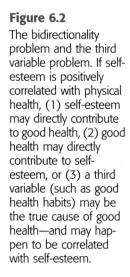

Figure 6.2

The bidirectionality problem and the third variable problem. If self-esteem is positively correlated with physical health, (1) self-esteem may directly contribute to good health, (2) good health may directly contribute to self-esteem, or (3) a third variable (such as good health habits) may be the true cause of good health—and may happen to be correlated with self-esteem.

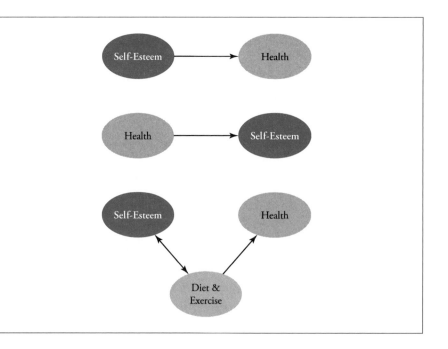

can do a great deal to advance our knowledge. Another way to put this is that the gain in external validity that is often provided in correlational studies sometimes compensates for any losses in internal validity, especially if you can minimize these losses. Finally, as you are about to learn, there are a wide variety of correlational research methods. Some of these methods are relatively immune to some specific types of confounds, and others are sometimes immune to reverse causality. Thus, by learning to make use of multiple research methods (a topic we discuss further in Chapter 13), researchers can sometimes maximize both the internal and external validity of their correlational research. With this idea in mind, let's take a look at three different examples of correlational research methods, each of which has something unique to offer us. We begin with a discussion of archival studies, move on to observational studies, and conclude with a discussion of field studies.

ARCHIVAL RESEARCH

When a topic is ethically sensitive, when a variable is difficult or impossible to manipulate, or when a researcher is especially motivated to conduct a study that is high in external validity, researchers may make use of **archival research** designs. Archival research refers to research in which investigators examine naturally existing public records to test a theory or hypothesis. There is almost no limit to the kinds of data sources that can be used in archival studies. To provide only a few examples, police reports, records of jury decisions, hospital records, weather reports, outcomes of sporting events, marriage licenses, speeches made by politicians, divorce records, newspaper circulation rates, census data, Tweets, and telephone directories have all provided the database for archival research designs.

An excellent example of an archival research design is provided by Peterson and Seligman (1987), who were interested in self-evaluation and physical well-being. These researchers collected old newspaper records of interviews conducted with famous baseball players who had all been inducted into the Baseball Hall of Fame. The researchers were particularly interested in how the players explained positive and negative things that happened to them on the baseball diamond. More specifically, the researchers wanted to know if there are any long-term consequences of making self-serving or self-protective attributions for one's successes and failures in life (e.g., "I won the big game today because nobody could hit my new curveball," "I lost the big game today because I got a lot of bad calls on my new curveball"). To see if egoistic attributions had positive consequences, they asked a group of blind judges to rate all their interviews for the degree to which the players made self-serving and self-protective attributions for their athletic performances. They then correlated these ratings with a very simple and important health outcome: how long the players lived. For these men, making self-serving attributions appeared to have lifesaving consequences. The players who made more self-enhancing and self-protective attributions lived noticeably longer than players who were less self-serving!

Phillips's research on emulative suicide ("copycat suicide") also provides an excellent example of archival research. Phillips and colleagues made use of public records of suicides along with information about the media coverage received by different suicides. In several studies of this type, Phillips documented national or statewide increases in suicide rates following highly publicized suicides. He also found that when more television networks covered a particular suicide, subsequent increases in suicide rates were greater than when a suicide was less well-publicized. These findings were especially prevalent for teenagers, who are known to be more suggestible than adults. More troubling still, Phillips found that media discussions of suicide in the form of public-service programs had much the same effect as the sometimes reckless suicide stories that appear in the news (e.g., see Phillips & Carstensen, 1986).

A third example of archival research is relevant to many different areas of psychology. To be more specific, researchers interested in attitudes, person perception, prejudice, stereotyping, and political psychology have conducted numerous archival studies of ethnicity and capital punishment. Quite a few large-scale studies, mostly conducted in the southeastern United States, have examined the rates at which prosecuting attorneys ask for the death penalty for Black versus White defendants who are being tried for murder. For example, Paternoster (1983) examined the decisions of prosecuting attorneys to request the death penalty in 1,805 South Carolina homicide cases. Because records of criminal proceedings provide quite a bit of information about the characteristics of alleged murderers and their victims, it is possible to relate different characteristics of defendants and victims to the harshness of various penalties meted out by the legal system. Paternoster's analysis suggested that when it comes to requests for the death penalty, justice is far from blind. When a Black defendant had allegedly murdered a White as opposed to a Black victim, prosecutors were *40 times* more likely to request the death penalty when presenting the case to the court. Moreover, research that has controlled for variables that could conceivably be confounded with ethnicity (e.g., socioeconomic differences between Black versus White defenders, severity of the crime committed, number of victims) has found that ethnicity is still strongly associated with requests for capital punishment when these confounds are statistically controlled.

Other archival studies of this type have revealed that Black defendants are also more likely to *receive* the death penalty once convicted. In fact, archival studies that have adopted a historical perspective on capital punishment have even revealed that there are differences in the *kind* of capital punishment that has been meted out to White versus Black offenders. In particular, Sidanius and Pratto (2000) analyzed records of more than 7,000 executions performed in the United States over a 383-year period (between 1608 and 1991). They broke down the executions into three categories based on how gruesome or brutal the executions were. At one end of this category, they included relatively humane (i.e., less gruesome) forms of execution (namely, asphyxiation in the gas chamber, being shot, or receiving a lethal injection). At the other extreme, they included only the most brutal or gruesome forms

Figure 6.3

Ethnicity of person executed and brutality of capital punishment, 1608–1991 (from Sidanius & Pratto, 2000)

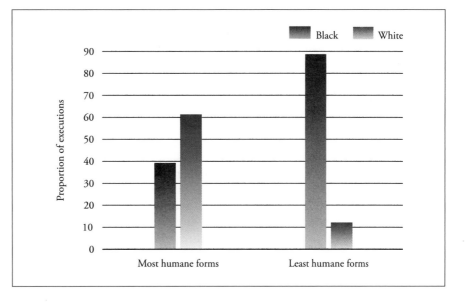

("pressing, breaking on the wheel, burning, hanging in chains, bludgeoning, and gibbeting"). Their findings were simple—and sobering. Among those executed using relatively humane methods, 61% were White and 39% were Black. In contrast, among those executed using the most heinous methods, only 11.6% were White and 88.4% were Black. A summary of these findings appears in Figure 6.3.

The great advantage of archival research is its potential for high levels of external validity. Although it is obviously possible to conduct a highly contrived archival study that has little to do with real-world behavior, studies such as those reviewed here generally get high marks for external validity. If you are interested in studying suicide, and you want to find a dependent measure that translates well into real suicides, you would be hard-pressed to find a better measure than records of real suicides. Archival research can also maximize external validity by eliminating any worries about whether a set of research findings occurred because the people being studied are trying to manage a positive impression with an experimenter. (This is a pretty common concern in certain kinds of lab experiments.) For instance, unlike laboratory participants who are asked to rate the aggressiveness of a Black or White target person, prosecutors who have to decide whether to request the death penalty for a particular Black or White defendant probably do not stop to consider whether their request will someday be analyzed by a social scientist.

Although external validity is often high in archival research, researchers usually have to work very hard to maximize the internal validity of such research. For instance, if you want to be absolutely positive that fluctuations in national suicide rates were caused by fluctuations in media coverage of suicides, you would want to consider a wide range of potential confounds, such as a slumping economy, disturbing historical events, or the possibility that grief over the death of a well-loved celebrity rather than copycat suicide was responsible for Phillips's findings. For these reasons, Phillips examined a very wide range of third variables that could have spuriously produced his findings. To provide only one example, he showed that media attention to the suicides of people who were almost universally disliked (e.g., a leader of the KKK) produced increases in suicide rates. In contrast, media attention to the nonsuicidal deaths of extremely beloved people (e.g., President Kennedy) did not yield increases in suicide rates. Grief apparently has little to do with Phillips's findings.

Of course, ruling out confounds does little or nothing to address the important issue of reverse causality, and Phillips was aware of this problem. In the case of his findings regarding suicide, it is conceivable that increases in suicide rates increase the amount of coverage that newspapers decide to devote to stories of suicides. To address this concern, Phillips carried out painstaking analyses using many data sets, and he showed time and again that the news stories regarding suicides always *preceded* increases in suicide rates. Fortunately, some archival researchers do not have to worry about reverse causality the way Phillips did. That is, in some archival research reverse causality simply is not a serious worry. Because some events simply cannot cause others, archival researchers can sometimes capitalize on this fact. It seems pretty unlikely, for instance, that being executed in a cruel versus a more humane way ever changes a person's ethnicity. Along similar lines, consider the finding that people are more likely to commit aggressive crimes on days when it is particularly hot (Anderson, 1987; 1989). As we noted in Chapter 3, heat may be confounded with other sources of aggressive behavior. However, it is extremely unlikely that aggressive behavior is a cause of warm temperatures. Although archival research must always be interpreted with some degree of caution, there comes a point at which the most parsimonious account for a carefully studied real-world phenomenon is the idea that one variable caused another.

Despite the enormous advantages that archival research can have when it comes to external validity, one potentially frustrating aspect of archival research is the fact that people who generate public records of real-world events often do so for reasons that have nothing to do with research. Psychologists might fantasize about a world in which people who create public records are always thinking first and foremost about research opportunities. ("OK, Jimmy, I know you're new at this, but I don't want you writing any more stories about aggressive crimes that don't include official records of temperatures on the day of the crime!") However, the reality is that people who create public records have their own goals and agendas. When observations can't be carefully planned in advance, researchers have little choice but to wait around (or look around) for observations that happen to be relevant to the research question in which they are interested. By doing this, they relinquish some control over the quality of their data. In the case of emulative suicide, for instance, it could be a problem if coroners are sometimes reluctant to label probable suicides as suicides. After all, coroners are people, and people might stretch the truth around the edges a little to avoid stigmatizing a deceased person and thus causing increased suffering for the person's family.

If this happens sometimes, the differences in suicide rates following media exposure might have *nothing* to do with actual suicide rates! Instead, they might have more to do with what coroners are willing to label a suicide. This would happen, by the way, if high-profile stories about suicides cause coroners to feel more comfortable reporting the truth when they detect a suicide.

Phillips examined this alternative hypothesis in a very simple and compelling way. In follow-up studies, he showed that high-profile suicides led to increases in "hidden suicides." For instance, following suicide stories, there are significant increases in single-auto accidents in which people seemed to lose control of their car for no reason and die. Moreover, these automobile accidents happen more often to people who more strongly resemble the person who committed suicide. Thus, young people are disproportionately more likely to crash their cars when a young rather than an old person has committed suicide. Phillips suggested that these car accidents reflect the known tendency for people to commit suicide in private, by manufacturing auto accidents that will cause their untimely death.

In case you're still not convinced, Phillips also showed that the *kind* of motor vehicle accidents that increase following well-publicized suicides are the kind that are more likely to reflect suicides. When a person is trying to commit suicide by crashing his or her vehicle (e.g., by pressing the gas rather than the brake when heading toward an embankment), the person should be more likely to die quickly following the crash. Sure enough, Phillips showed that accidents involving rapid deaths increased at a higher rate following suicides than did accidents involving slow deaths. Still not convinced? Phillips also tackled the coroner coding problem directly rather than indirectly. If coroners change their coding tactics after front-page suicides, rates of all other kinds of deaths should go down to about the same degree that rates of suicides go up after front-page suicides. They don't. Suicide rates go up while deaths from all other causes remain constant. All this being said, Phillips's research shows just how far archival researchers often must go to address potential biases in their data sets. Another way around this problem is to avoid analyzing data that someone else has collected. In this spirit, some researchers tackle their questions head-on by collecting their own data.

OBSERVATIONAL RESEARCH

Research in which investigators record the real behavior of people in their natural environments is often referred to as **observational research**. Notice that observational research is very similar to archival research. The behaviors that researchers examine in observational research are always real, and the researchers do not manipulate anything. The difference between observational and archival research is the fact that, in observational research, the people making the observations are the researchers themselves. This not only gives researchers some control over exactly *what* they observe but also gives them some control over *how* they observe it. From a methodological perspective, the best kind of observational research is usually **unobtrusive observations,** meaning (1) that researchers do not interfere in any way with people's natural behavior and (2) that people do not realize that they are being studied. An excellent example of unobtrusive observational research was conducted by Colette and Marsh (1981). Colette and Marsh were interested in gender differences in mundane social behavior. To examine the specific gender differences in which they were interested, they placed a video recorder on the seventh floor of a building overlooking a busy walkway. However, they were less interested in walking than they were in squeezing. Specifically, they focused their observations on instances in which people had to squeeze past one another to get where they were going. Under these conditions, they found that 75 percent of the men in their study faced their fellow pedestrians as they squeezed by them. In contrast, only 17 percent of the women faced others as they squeezed by them.

Of course, Colette and Marsh couldn't say exactly *why* men and women use different techniques to slip past strangers. One possible theory is that men are inherently more sociable than women. As a case in point, the two of us would like to confess that we often get together over coffee or tea and do nothing but sit around and talk for hours with our closest male friends. In contrast, most of the women we know get together with other women only when they want to play some kind of competitive sport or watch TV. Our casual observations of women under such circumstances have also revealed that many women who get together under such conditions hardly talk to one another at all—at least not until they've had a few beers to help break the awkwardness. Colette and Marsh realized that there could be more than one way to explain their findings, and so they took a second look at their observations. They found that in the rare instances in which women *did* slip past other people in a facing direction, they often engaged in a very telling behavior: they covered their breasts by folding their arms across their chests. So much for our theory!

Another example of an unobtrusive observational study also involves getting from one place to another, and it also involves gender. However, this study has to do with zipping through instead of squeezing past. McKelvie and Schamer (1988) made unobtrusive observations of whether drivers obeyed posted stop signs. Specifically, they made 600 unobtrusive observations at stop signs, coding for whether people (1) stopped completely, (2) performed a "slow stop," or (3) failed to stop at all. They also coded for driver gender and whether each driver was carrying any passengers. Finally, they made observations both during the day and at night to determine whether people's behavior might differ as a function of whether it was dark. It did. When a driver was alone in the car and there was no oncoming traffic, rates of both *complete* stops and *non*stops increased at night. That is, at night there were increases in both the number of people who obeyed the letter of the law and the number of people who disregarded the law completely. However, these transformations at night depended very much on gender. As summarized in Figure 6.4, solo male drivers who approached intersections at night were just as likely to disregard the stop sign (36 percent) as they were to

Figure 6.4

Gender behavior at stop signs at night (from McElvie & Schamer, 1988)

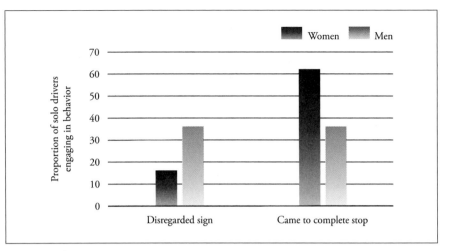

stop completely (also 36 percent). On the other hand, solo female drivers who approached the same intersections at night were much more likely to do the right thing (62 percent stopped completely and only 16 percent disregarded the sign). McKelvie and Schamer couldn't check to see if the women who failed to stop were busy folding their arms across their chests, but these findings certainly suggest that women were exercising a certain kind of caution. The shroud of night seemed to make women more concerned about safety. It seemed to make men less concerned about getting caught for blowing a stop sign.

Unobtrusive measures are not limited to studies of locomotion. They can also be used to see how long people stay in one place. Because the "hatching chicks" exhibit was the most popular exhibit at Chicago's Museum of Science and Industry for many years, this meant that museum officials were required to replace the floor tiles around this exhibit about every six weeks. Floor tiles around the other exhibits typically lasted for years. This unobtrusive measure thus provided a nice index of popularity that museum officials could use to determine patrons' attitudes (see Webb, Campbell, Schwartz, & Sechrest, 1966). In a similar way, mechanics who examine the rear shocks on a car to estimate the car's true mileage are also using wear and tear as an unobtrusive measure. Horse traders who examine a horse's teeth for signs of excessive wear (i.e., signs of excessive age) are also relying on unobtrusive measures. Incidentally, just to keep you up to date on all of your horse aphorisms, people are referring to exactly this kind of critical inspection when they say "Don't look a gift horse in the mouth." Unobtrusive measures may occasionally be misleading (e.g., a young horse may have had a bad dentist), but unlike people, they never lie on purpose.

Measures of wear and tear are not the only common form of unobtrusive measure. People's accents may tell you something about where they grew up. Their clothing may tell you something about their bank accounts. If you want to get a relative estimate of auto theft rates in different U.S. cities, you might sample a few grocery store parking lots and tally the percentage of cars that have Clubs™ or other lock-on devices attached to their steering wheels. Both marketers and private detectives who want to know what someone smokes, drinks, or eats sometimes resort to rummaging through the person's trash to determine his or her brand loyalties (a practice known affectionately as *garbology*). Both Sherlock Holmes and Shawn Spencer (of *Psych* fame) would have rarely needed to stoop to garbology to figure out people's personal habits and preferences. If you have ever read Sir Arthur Conan Doyle, or watched any re-runs of *Psych*, you know that some highly astute people can observe a lot about a person just by watching.

When it comes to external and internal validity, observational studies are in much the same boat as archival studies. Their tremendous potential for external validity is grounded in features of the research that sometimes get in the way of internal validity. Nonetheless, by being creative in their choice of measures and thorough in their efforts to control for confounds, researchers who conduct observational studies may reveal important facts about people that would be difficult to uncover any other way.

CONFOUNDS CAN BE MEASURED TOO!

One of the main themes of this chapter is that the results of nonexperimental studies often contain confounds. Although this problem applies to all nonexperimental studies, researchers don't have to sit on their hands and let confounds run amuck. Instead, they can try to take control of confounds. Recall from Chapter 5 that one way to fight confounds is to measure known confounds and then statistically remove their influences. If Dr. Pepper still observes a clear association between two variables after all known confounds have been removed, then she can feel much more comfortable than she might otherwise feel that her results do not reflect the operation of confounds. (As we mentioned in Chapter 5, it goes beyond this book to explain exactly how researchers statistically remove the influence of confounds. We presume you will cover this in your favorite statistics courses, but see Methodology Exercise 1 in Appendix 2 to get some understanding of this process.)

An example of research that followed this strategy can be found in a study by Jaccard, Blanton, and Dodge (2005). They were interested in seeing if close friends influence one another during adolescence. In particular, they wanted to know if adolescents in grades 7–11 would be more likely to have sex a year later if they had a best friend who had already had sex at the time the study began. Past research had suggested that best friends might exert very strong influences on one another in this way. Thus, if Bruce and Alex are best friends in eighth grade and Bruce has already had sex, past research suggested that Alex would be much more likely to have sex in ninth grade than he would have been otherwise. (By the way, insight into this kind of effect is one reason why most parents try very hard to influence their kids' choice of friends!) The problem with this type of finding, however, is that we have very little idea *why* it is true. On the one hand, maybe kids like Bruce directly encourage kids like Alex to have sex by convincing them that having sex is "cool" or "fun." (As an aside, sex is neither fun nor cool until age 43.) On the other hand, it is possible to dream up less interesting accounts for this finding—based on both person confounds and environmental confounds. As an example of a person confound, perhaps the kind of kids who are disproportionately interested in sex tend to hang out with other kids who share this interest. That is, perhaps Alex's friendship with a kid like Bruce was simply a reflection of his personal opinions and desires about sex, or simply his level of sexual maturity. As an example of an environmental confound, perhaps kids whose parents are highly permissive are not only more likely to hang out with kids like Bruce but also more likely to get into all kinds of trouble (sexual or otherwise).

Because of the wide range of person and environmental confounds that could be operating in this situation, Jaccard, Blanton, and Dodge (2005) measured as many of these confounds as they possibly could. Because they went to the trouble to measure all of these confounds, they were able to conduct a statistical analysis in which they controlled for all of these potential confounds to see if a "best friend effect" still remained once they had made use of their statistical controls. It did. Jaccard et al. controlled statistically for a wide range of confounds, including (a) parenting style, (b) quality of parent-child relationships, (c) parental attitudes towards sex, (d) parental education, (e) students' level of physical development, (f) students' academic standing, (g) student dating status, and (h–j) student gender, age, and ethnicity. After all of these confounds were considered and statistically removed, a "best friend effect" remained in the data. Of course, no matter how many confounds you measure and remove in a nonexperimental study such as this one, you can never be positive that you got them all. (This is similar to the problem of induction discussed in Chapter 2.) Nonetheless, by measuring and removing confounds, researchers can greatly improve upon the quality of nonexperimental research. Although Jaccard, Blanton, and Dodge did not prove that best friends influenced one another, they made a strong case that past evidence of peer influence was not solely driven by the most obvious of confounds.

SUMMARY

The nonexperimental designs discussed in this chapter all have an important place in the toolbox of the versatile methodologist. Moreover, like the tools in a real toolbox, each of these methodological tools has its own specialized purpose—and its own limitations. Case studies provide us with detailed portraits of the experiences of an individual person or group, but whether the findings of a specific case study can be safely generalized to people or groups not sampled is often open to debate. Less debatable is

the fact that case studies can almost always be used to inspire or generate new research hypotheses. In some ways, single-variable studies such as epidemiological studies, studies of people's attitudes, or studies of judgment under uncertainty represent the polar opposite of case studies. They focus on a single variable rather than many variables, and they make use of many participants rather than a single participant. Such studies often do a great job of describing the state of the world at large, but they do not necessarily tell us very much about exactly why it is that way. Finally, multiple-variable, correlational research designs, such as archival studies, unobtrusive observational studies, and questionnaires share many of the strengths of case studies and descriptive studies. In particular, they usually involve observations or recollections of the experiences of people in their natural environment. These studies take us a step closer to understanding the causes of a phenomenon because they assess the relation between two or more variables. Despite this fact, such studies are typically open to criticisms based on potential confounds. For this reason, researchers measure and statistically control for confounds, but no correlational study can ever control for every conceivable confound. The limitations of nonexperimental approaches to research often inspire researchers to venture into the world of the experimental laboratory where confounds can be brought under tighter control. We explore this world in detail in the next chapter.

STUDY QUESTIONS

1. What specific steps should you take to ensure that case studies are scientific?

2. What is the difference between a census and a survey? How does this distinction relate to the issue of external validity? What sampling procedures have been developed to make it easier to conduct valid surveys?

3. Distinguish between person confounds, environmental confounds, and operational confounds. Provide a specific example of each kind of confound, and point out how it could threaten the validity of a research study.

4. Consider the kind of archival studies conducted by Phillips and colleagues (who studied emulative suicide). Relative to a typical cross-sectional survey study, were Phillips's archival studies usually higher or lower in internal validity? What about external validity? Phillips conducted many additional analyses to convince skeptics that his effects were truly there. Was he trying to assure these individuals that his study was high in internal or external validity?

5. Nemo conducted a self-report study in a small sample of college students in which he assessed both self-esteem and aggression. Nemo found that students with higher self-esteem (i.e., those reporting more pride in past accomplishments) also reported being more aggressive (e.g., they reported more instances of arguing loudly with friends and roommates). Nemo concluded that high self-esteem causes aggression. List at least one potential person confound, one potential environmental confound, and one potential operational confound that might threaten Nemo's conclusions. Describe procedures that could be pursued to reduce or evaluate these threats. What could be done to increase the external validity of this study? What could be done to reduce concerns regarding reverse causality?

NOTES

1. When a sample size is chosen to yield the specific level of sampling error that researchers are willing to accept (e.g., 2 percent versus 5 percent), this sample size is based on the population as a whole rather than subgroups within the sample. Thus, a sample that will yield a 3 percent sampling error for estimates of disease prevalence for a specific population of 10 million people will always yield a somewhat larger sampling error for estimates of disease prevalence in small subsamples within the

population (e.g., for African Americans). Researchers deal with this problem by oversampling subgroups they want to study so that these subgroups have sampling errors that are not excessively large.

2. We hasten to add that to assess depression in ways that would satisfy an expert (i.e., a clinical psychologist) one would need to conduct a clinical interview for depression. It is possible to measure depressive vulnerabilities or depressive symptoms in a wide variety of ways, but you cannot diagnose people for depression without an appropriate clinical interview such as the SCID (Structured Clinical Interview for DSM Disorders). Interviews are necessary, for example, because there is no one single defining feature of depression and because part of the definition of depression is that problems such as suicidal ideation, difficulty concentrating, and a failure to enjoy activities that are normally pleasurable must occur for at least two consecutive weeks.

Experience Carefully Planned: Experimental Research Designs

Regard no practice as immutable. Change and be ready to change again. Accept no eternal verity. Experiment.
—B. F. Skinner

This chapter focuses on experiments, including both laboratory and field experiments. We begin the chapter by briefly reviewing the history of experimentation, with an emphasis on how R. A. Fisher integrated the two crucial ingredients of experimentation as applied to human research participants. These two ingredients are the manipulation of variables and random assignment. We follow this with a discussion of the advantages and disadvantages of experiments, with an emphasis on how to maximize the advantages and minimize the disadvantages. Finally, we conclude the chapter with a discussion of the trade-offs between internal and external validity.

A WONDERFUL METHOD

In the classic Frank Capra film *It's a Wonderful Life*, the protagonist, George Bailey, gets the opportunity to see what the world would have been like if one and only one thing had been different—if he had never been born. As you well know, if you are familiar with the movie, this experience profoundly changes George's view of his life. He sees exactly how important he proved to be to his friends, his family, and his community, and he thus comes to appreciate how wonderful his seemingly difficult life really is. This touching film often brings a tear to our eye because it so beautifully illustrates the value of laboratory experiments. OK, we're kidding, but not entirely. This film really does illustrate what is wonderful about laboratory experiments. Lab experiments show us exactly how the world changes when you change *one and only one thing*. In so doing, they give us information about causality that is otherwise extremely difficult to obtain.

In the real world, after all, it is incredibly rare for one and only one thing to change in a person's life, and this is why, in the real world, it can be very difficult to pinpoint the exact causes of a person's behavior. If Ren becomes a happier person after receiving a big promotion, is it because his level of occupational prestige increased, because he began making more money, because he was given more flexible work hours, or because he always looks forward to summer and just happened to receive his promotion, and his new motorcycle, in late May? It's very hard to know. Whoever coined the Latin phrase *ceteris paribus* ("all else being equal") must have appreciated this problem. If you want to know whether one thing alone affects something else, you must hold *everything else* but that one thing constant. Everything else is an awful lot, and the beauty of experiments is that they provide researchers with an elegant way of doing just this—*ceteris paribus*, manipulating one and only one thing.

By now, you know that another way of describing the wonderful thing about experiments is that they tend to be very high in internal validity. Recall that a study is high in internal validity only to the degree that the researcher can confidently assert a causal relation between the independent and dependent variables. Internal validity is crucial to theory testing because all theories are statements about the causal relations between variables. When a researcher can't be sure about causes (when internal validity is low), the researcher can't claim to have gathered good support for his or her theory. It is largely for this reason that researchers often conduct experiments. By now, you also have a pretty good idea of what an experiment is. But so far, we haven't really fleshed out the details of what experiments are, exactly how they are conducted, and what they can and cannot do for us. This is the primary goal of this chapter.

A BRIEF HISTORY OF TRUE EXPERIMENTS

So let's begin at the beginning, starting with the simplest possible kind of experiment. To be considered an experiment, first and foremost, a study must make use of a **manipulation**. A manipulation occurs when an experimenter systematically alters the levels of a variable (i.e., the independent variable). The goal in so doing is to see if changes in the independent variable lead to corresponding changes in some outcome variable (i.e., the dependent variable). If a manipulation does, in fact, lead to changes in the dependent variable, an experimenter can feel fairly certain that the independent variable caused this change. If these effects are predicted from a known psychological theory, this theory moves up in the world of science. If these effects either contradict or fail to support a known psychological theory, this theory moves down in the world of science. Perhaps the theory is falsified and thus rejected. However, it is much more likely that researchers will modify the theory in light of this new information about the theory's limitations. We have referred to this process elsewhere as identifying the boundary conditions of a theory. Identifying the boundary conditions of a theory is a very important part of the scientific process, and a great deal of psychological research is all about this process. In science, as in life, it is sometimes just as important to know what someone or something cannot do as it is to know what that someone or something can do. In short, experiments can tell you exactly what a manipulation can and can't do.

It is difficult to say who invented manipulation, for much the same reason that it is difficult to say who invented cooking, the wheel, or agriculture. This is because manipulation has been around for so long that the origins of this "invention" have long been lost to the passage of time. When prehistoric people made crude tools and weapons by chipping away the edges of flint stones, they were manipulating natural objects to achieve certain desired results. In so doing, they were learning important lessons about the world (e.g., flint makes better blades than granite). Similarly, when prehistoric people learned that exposing meat to fire increases its shelf life, they were learning from direct manipulation. Nonetheless, it took ancient philosophers and scientists a long time to settle on manipulation as the preferred tool for figuring out the world. Aristotle made some very important contributions to science, but manipulation wasn't really one of them; he preferred argumentation to experimentation. In our opinion, the person who probably deserves the most credit for bringing manipulation to center stage in science was Galileo Galilei, who popularized the idea of manipulation by performing some of the first systematic experiments in science. Remember his experiments rolling balls down inclined planes (in Chapter 1)? With a little help from people like Sir Isaac Newton (the famous physicist and mathematician) and John Locke (one of history's biggest fans of empiricism), the idea of manipulation eventually took hold in the social as well as the physical sciences.

But manipulation is only half the story. Once we enter the realm of social science, manipulation alone does not make true experiments. True experiments also require the use of **random assignment**. It is impossible to overstate the importance of random assignment to experimental research in psychology. Because random assignment is an essential ingredient to modern experimentation, you should probably know something about how this essential research technique was cooked up. A long time ago researchers woke up at the crack of dawn, walked to their labs in the wind and snow, and, if you can believe it, weren't lucky enough to live in a world with random assignment. In the early history of psychology, that is, random assignment simply hadn't been invented yet. In these early days, researchers were still uncertain of their methods. From their knowledge of the physical sciences, psychologists knew that manipulation was a crucial tool for learning about causes. However, psychologists faced a huge problem rarely faced by physical scientists. We might think of it as the problem of ceteris *non* paribus. When a physicist or chemist manipulates some aspect of the physical world, it is very easy to do so using objects or substances that are known to be identical. Take two identical objects, expose only one to radiation, heat, or dihydrogen oxide (i.e., water), and you can easily observe the consequences of your manipulation. It's not hard at all to create two or more identical physical objects (samples of pure sodium, 50-gram ball bearings) that become the objects of your scientific manipulations. Now, try doing this with people. (It's called cloning, it's potentially unethical, it takes a long time, and it didn't exist a hundred years ago.)

The history of the true experiment in the biological and social sciences is essentially the history of how researchers got around this thorny problem. It's the problem of individual differences we brought up in Chapter 5. Early experimenters realized that individual differences were a huge barrier to experimentation, but they didn't quite know how to overcome them. A common approach adopted in the old days was **matching**. By matching each participant in an experimental condition with a very similar participant in a control condition, researchers hoped to guarantee that their experimental and control groups would be "equal" prior to their experimental manipulations. As it turned out, however, matching wasn't all that it was cracked up to be. The two biggest problems were (1) that it was really hard to do and (2) that it didn't really work. The researcher who managed to match experimental and control groups on one dimension (such as intelligence) often found that these groups differed on many other dimensions (such as age or sex, for example). Some researchers tried matching their participants on several dimensions at the same time, but this often proved to be very difficult. Where do you find an exact match for a 6′ 3″ tall, 308-pound, 25-year-old plumber with an IQ of 124, a low need for achievement, a moderately active sexual history, and seven siblings? And, even if you could find this guy's twin brother, Zeke, how would you get him here from Alabama to participate in your experiment?

Even more to the point, even if two or more groups of participants were matched on a large number of different dimensions, one would never know for sure that the groups were equivalent on *all* of the dimensions that might influence the results of an experiment. Imagine, for example, that you are a political and cognitive psychologist who is a little ahead of your time in 1896. You want to study the effects of classical conditioning on people's attitudes toward the current U.S. president, Grover Cleveland (see Staats & Staats, 1958, for some useful details about how you could do this). Specifically, you want to see if pairing pleasant versus unpleasant words (e.g., "happiness," "vomit") with President Cleveland's last name would eventually influence how much people said they *liked* President Cleveland. Let's further assume that you use matching to create two very similar groups of participants, one of whom always sees Cleveland's surname associated with pleasant words during a judgment task and one of whom always sees his surname associated with unpleasant words during the very same task. After working very, very hard at it, you matched the two experimental groups pretty well on five presumably important variables: age, income, gender, ethnicity, and political party affiliation. Hopefully, you can see that any of these variables could influence how much people would like President Cleveland. So far, so good.

Now suppose that the people who see the name "Cleveland" paired with words like "love" and "chocolate" do, in fact, report liking this name more than the people who see the same name paired with words like "disease" and "slime." Can you be sure that the conditioning manipulation, and nothing else, led to this group difference? Maybe. After all, the two groups are very similar on five different variables that might predict how much people like Cleveland. Or maybe not. What if you learn that four of the ten people in the positive word condition (and none of the people in the other condition) happen to be from Cleveland, Ohio? Or what if most of the people in the positive word condition happen to be highly optimistic people who view the world (including U.S. presidents) through rose-colored lenses? Or what if more members of the negative word group have recently been laid off from their jobs? Isn't a president usually one of the first people to get the blame for economic woes? The list could go on and on. Your imperfect experiment wouldn't be useless, but it certainly wouldn't be airtight. The impossibility of establishing a "perfect match" is similar to the inductive problem discussed in Chapter 2. A researcher simply cannot know with certainty that two matched groups have been equated on all the relevant dimensions that could influence the dependent variable. Even if two groups are matched on many, many variables, they may still differ from one another on some important variable that was not considered by the researcher.

The solution to this tricky problem was laid out most clearly by a scientist named R. A. Fisher. In the 1920s and 1930s, Fisher wrote two landmark books that dramatically shaped the way psychologists (and many other scientists) think about research. Collectively, these two books, *Statistical Methods for Research Workers* (1925) and *The Design of Experiments* (1935), probably represent the biggest analytical breakthrough in the history of psychology. Fisher was a scientific genius who spent much of his time obsessing about issues such as buttercups and horse manure. That is, as an agricultural biologist, Fisher wanted to answer practical questions having to do with things like the amounts or compositions of manures that would maximize crop yields. Fortunately for psychologists, plants are a lot like people. Every plant is different, and this makes it difficult to know with any certainty whether a given plant grew large because it was fertilized, because it was otherwise well-tended, or because it was blessed with good genes. This meant that if Fisher wanted to study the influence of fertilizer on plant growth, he had to figure out how to make two or more groups of plants equivalent. He was just as interested in figuring out exactly what fertilizers make beets grow large as psychologists are in figuring out exactly which moods cause people to engage in altruistic acts, which drugs cause people to experience hallucinations, and which childhood traumas cause normal children to grow up and become fanatically interested in beets.

We said that it is fortunate for experimental psychologists that plants are a lot like people. In fact, plants are so much like people that Fisher's solutions to his inferential problems turned out to be just as applicable to people as they are to sugar beets and buttercups. Fisher solved the problem of creating two groups of identical plants (or people—who could then be experimented upon) by popularizing the use of **random assignment**. Random assignment is the closest thing to magic that researchers have ever discovered. It is a strange blend of precision and chaos—almost the opposite of matching. Whereas matching involves placing people in conditions on a very systematic basis, random assignment involves placing people in conditions on a totally arbitrary basis. In studies that use experimental manipulations, this means that every participant has an equal chance of being assigned to any specific condition of an experiment.[1] For example, an experimenter might assign people to conditions in a study either by flipping a fair coin or by using a random number generator. The fact that Lucinda has been assigned to the "good mood" condition and thus gets a cookie does not have any influence on Belinda's chances of being assigned to the same condition. She has the same chance of getting a cookie as Lucinda did, but she's also a coin toss away from being assigned to the "bad mood" condition, which means that she'll get a painful electric shock. (Sorry, Belinda.) Whenever laypeople "draw straws" or flip a coin to give two or more people an equal chance of experiencing something (the chance to receive a kickoff, the mission of crossing an enemy minefield), they are expressing an intuitive appreciation of the logic of random assignment. And random assignment, like coin flips, is fair and logical. In addition to being a lot easier and quicker than matching, random assignment does what matching cannot do. It equalizes two or more groups on practically every dimension imaginable.

Notice that we said that randomization equalizes *groups*. This was Fisher's great insight. He realized that he could not make two specific seeds grow at exactly the same rate, but he could make two *groups* of seeds grow at the same rate *on average*. This same principle applies in psychological research. Two groups of people can be virtually identical as groups, even though each group is made up of completely different people. To see that random assignment really does this, we encourage you to try your hand at the random assignment exercise in Appendix 2 (Methodology Exercise 2). For now, just remember that random assignment assigns people in an arbitrary fashion to different groups. Thus, there is no reason to expect the groups to differ from one another before the experimental manipulation is performed. Of course, random assignment isn't perfect. Occasionally you will end up with a lot of particularly helpful, psychotic, or agriculturally inclined people in one group, just like you will occasionally get a lot of salt on one particular French fry, receive five cards of the same suit in one specific poker hand, or hit a bull's eye twice in a row out of blind luck. On the whole, however, random assignment does a surprisingly effective job of equating two or more experimental groups. Better yet, random assignment doesn't just equate groups on the two, three, or 15 dimensions that one particular experimenter might care about. It essentially equates groups on *every* dimension imaginable (especially when you average across many different experiments or use a very large sample).

Before we move on to discuss the role that random assignment plays in experimental research, we feel it is important to compare it with random sampling (also known as random selection), which we covered in the last chapter. Because random sampling and random assignment are often confused, textbooks on research methods typically emphasize the fact that random sampling and random assignment are very *different* things. It is true that they are different. Random sampling is used in population surveys to help you increase the likelihood that the small sample in your study generalizes to a larger population of interest. In contrast, random assignment is used in experiments to help equate different experimental conditions before manipulations are applied. Random selection has to do with external validity, and random assignment has to do with internal validity. Yet beginning students often confuse the two techniques. Of course, to us, these two techniques seem *totally* different, almost as different as mauve and lavender, or Monet and Renoir. Although it is obviously important to keep these two methodological terms straight, it does make sense that people often confuse them. The truth is that these two distinct forms of randomization are not quite as different as some methodologists might like you to believe. In fact, in one very real sense, these two procedures do exactly the same thing. *Both of these forms of randomization maximize the likelihood that two separate groups of people will be as similar as possible.* The only difference has to do with which groups of people you are most worried about. If you want to be sure that the people in your study are exactly like the people in the real world, pull people at random from the real world to be in your study (make use of random sampling). On the other hand, if you want to be sure that the people in one of your experimental groups are exactly like the people in another group, randomly assign them to a condition (make use of random assignment). So these two strategies are quite different, and yet they are quite the same.

Another way in which random assignment is similar to random sampling is that it does not always work perfectly. That is, it will rarely be the case prior to your experimental manipulation that your experimental and your control group each have IQs of exactly 100 and are each exactly 55 percent female. However, this is why researchers conduct statistical tests on their data—to see if any differences that they observe between conditions are "real." In the context of experiments, statistical testing helps researchers determine whether any observed differences between experimental conditions (after the manipulations) are greater than the differences that one would expect on the basis of luck alone. It is precisely because researchers know that random assignment isn't absolutely perfect that they have developed some simple statistical tests to help them determine when to believe a set of results and when to doubt them. If a pattern of experimental findings could easily reflect minor imbalances in random assignment, researchers have to conclude that their manipulations probably didn't have any effect. Conversely, researchers conclude that their manipulation had its predicted effects only when the two treatment groups in an experiment differ in predictable ways that greatly exceed the kind of differences one would expect based on chance alone. If a researcher is still worried that a result may be simply a fluke, it would be good to try to replicate the finding in a new study that *also* uses random assignment. If an effect is observed time and time again across a series of experiments, it is extremely unlikely that random assignment failed time and time again (and in exactly the same way). Instead, it is much more reasonable to assume that the experimental manipulation influenced people's responses on the dependent variable (and that random assignment, in fact, created two or more groups of people who were very similar prior to the experimental manipulation).

In summary, true experiments capitalize on two procedures that distinguish them from other forms of investigation: manipulation and random assignment to condition. Needless to say, we wouldn't devote an entire chapter to true experiments if we didn't feel that they represent an extremely useful research technique. In the following section, we describe some of the most important advantages of true experiments relative to other research designs. As you will see, the most important advantages are that experiments do the two things they were designed to do. They solve the problem of individual differences, and they help to minimize confounds. These are also the two main reasons why true experiments are usually very high in internal validity. However, experiments have several other important advantages, some of which have more to do with other forms of validity.

STRENGTHS OF TRUE EXPERIMENTS

True Experiments Eliminate Individual Differences

To illustrate how true experiments solve the problem of individual differences, let's take a close look at both (1) the classic study of mood and helping we discussed in Chapter 5 (Isen & Levin, 1972) and (2) an ingenious study of behavioral priming (Bargh, Chen, & Burrows, 1996). Recall that Isen and Levin wanted to see if positive mood contributes to helping. Specifically, they proposed that people who feel happy are more likely than usual to help those who need help because helping allows people to maintain a good mood. To test this theory, they developed a simple and clever mood manipulation that involved (1) giving some people free cookies and (2) observing whether these people were more likely than usual to help a stranger. The participants were men who were sitting in a campus library, and the opportunity to help someone else came when an unfortunate fellow student (a trained research assistant who was in cahoots with the experimenters) dropped his books. Isen and Levin found that the men who received a cookie were more likely to help the student than were a comparable group of men who did not receive a cookie. They concluded that the cookie caused an increase in helping. If this conclusion were correct, then the results would support their theory of mood and helping. But was it correct? Was this study high in internal validity? Does being in a good mood really make people helpful?

Isn't it possible that the men who got cookies were simply different in some important ways from those who did not get cookies? Compared with the men in the control condition, maybe a lot of these cookie recipients were from Cleveland, Ohio (where people are reputed to be unusually helpful). Or maybe they simply had more time on their hands. The differences in helping behavior across conditions might have occurred for reasons that had little or nothing to do with the independent variable. That is, the real explanation for Isen and Levin's findings might be individual differences. Right? Wrong. Although anything is possible, it's highly unlikely that these two groups of men were highly different prior to receiving their level of the experimental manipulation. The reason is that Isen and Levin used random assignment to place the men in different conditions. Whenever Isen and Levin selected a man in the library as an unwitting participant, they consulted a random number table to determine the man's treatment condition. For the sake of simplicity, assume that the table simply contained a long string of 0s and 1s. If the first number consulted happened to be a 1, the first participant identified would be assigned to the experimental condition and would thus receive a cookie. If the next number consulted happened to be a 0, the next participant would be assigned to the control condition and would *not* receive a cookie. If the experimenter followed this procedure carefully (e.g., without peeking to see the first number before seeing the first participant), then it is highly unlikely that the men in the experimental and control conditions differed in any important ways. Random assignment solves the problem of individual differences.

Now let's consider a more completely different example. Bargh, Chen, and Burrows (1996) conducted a lab experiment in which they primed their participants to think about stereotypes of old people versus a control topic. Participants thought they were taking part in a study of language proficiency. The language proficiency task required participants to unscramble 30 sets of words to form 30 sentences. In reality, the scrambled sentences were a priming manipulation. For half of the participants, the scrambled sentences almost always referred to old people. They thus contained key stereotypic words such as "Florida," "gray," "wrinkle," "retired," "old," "forgetful," and "bingo." Other participants unscrambled 30 sentences that had nothing to do with old people. The key words were words such as "thirsty," "clean," and "private." Bargh et al. assumed that activating people's associations about old people might cause people to behave in ways that they stereotypically associate with the members of this social group. The idea is that if you have recently been thinking about grandmothers, you might actually *behave* in a slightly more grandmotherly fashion than usual. Short of inviting their participants to bake cookies and pinch the cheeks of small children, how could Bargh et al. test this idea in the lab? They did it by telling participants that they were done with the study of language proficiency, thanking participants, giving them their research credit, and then *secretly timing them* to see how quickly they walked down the hall as they left the study! Their logic, of course, is based on the stereotype that old people walk slowly.

They accomplished this last, crucial task with the aid of a research assistant who appeared to be casually hanging out in the hallway. This assistant (who had no idea which set of sentences participants had unscrambled) timed each participant as he or she walked down the hallway toward an elevator. Those who had been thinking about old people walked quite a bit more slowly than those in the control condition. By now, you probably realize that individual differences (e.g., differences in walking speed, differences in whether people were in a hurry) do *not* provide a plausible alternate explanation for this finding. In case you're still a little skeptical, we should add that, to remove any lingering doubts about whether their results were a fluke, Bargh et al. ran this walking study twice from start to finish, and they got the same results in both studies. They also observed very similar findings in two other studies in which they used different specific priming manipulations. For example, by priming rudeness versus politeness in one study, they were able to get students to behave rudely versus politely to an experimenter who appeared to be ignoring them. We haven't done the math, but the likelihood that the results of all four of Bargh et al.'s priming studies are due to four separate failures of random assignment is roughly equal to the likelihood that Democrat Grover Cleveland will be elected the next U.S. president (by carrying a Republican county in Florida that used a butterfly ballot designed by Michelle Obama). Clearly, random assignment, when combined with thoughtful replication, provides a powerful response to the problem of individual differences.

True Experiments Eliminate Other Kinds of Confounds

As you may recall from Chapter 5, the individual difference problem we just discussed may be thought of as a confound. A confound is a nuisance variable that (1) varies systematically with the independent variable and (2) might be causally related to the dependent variable. If Bargh et al. *had* somehow confounded walking speed with their experimental priming manipulation, this confound would completely undermine their claim about how priming affects behavior. Although random assignment solves the problem of individual differences, it does not guarantee that an experiment is completely free of confounds.

The reason for this is that random assignment, in and of itself, fixes only one specific kind of confound: person confounds. You first learned about person confounds in Chapter 6, when we discussed them in the context of correlational research. To translate person confounds into the language of true experiments rather than correlational studies, person confounds exist when individual differences covary with an experimental treatment condition and are related to the dependent variable. As we hope you just saw, random assignment renders person confounds much less problematic in true experiments than they are in other kinds of research.

However, person confounds are not the only category of confounds. A second category of confounds is **procedural confounds**. In experimental research, procedural confounds are the logical equivalent of the environmental confounds we discussed in the context of nonexperimental research. We use the term "procedural" here to reflect the fact that experiments consist of planned procedures rather than naturally occurring events. Procedural confounds occur when an experimenter unwittingly manipulates two or more things at once. They happen when something the experimenter did not intend (a seemingly innocuous or tangential aspect of a procedure) is allowed to covary with the independent variable. For example, suppose that an experimenter interested in stereotyping wants to manipulate the ethnicity of a person who asks strangers for a favor. He happens to have three excellent research assistants who are eager to work on the project: John (a White man), Stacey (a Black woman), and Mauricio (a Latino man). The researcher decides to do the study in a busy shopping mall. He begins by carefully training the three confederates to make exactly the same polite request for help to many different male shoppers. ("Excuse me, sir, I lost my cell phone. Could you possibly lend me 35 cents to make a phone call?") The three confederates find a way to sample shoppers at random, and the dependent measure is the proportion of shoppers who give a confederate money. As predicted, shoppers are more likely to help the White as opposed to the Latino confederate. However, the Black confederate receives the most help of all. The results of the study seem to suggest that people's attitudes toward Blacks are much more favorable than the researcher assumed. However, a pretty serious procedural confound is at work here, and we hope you spotted it. The confederate who gets the most help not only happens to be the only confederate who is Black but also happens to be the only confederate who is female. In short, race and gender are perfectly confounded with one another, and so it is not clear whether the Black woman is helped more because of her race or because of her gender (not to mention her charming personality).

Does this mean that true experiments don't provide much protection against procedural confounds? Absolutely not. It just means that experimenters must sometimes take careful precautions to be sure they are not accidentally building procedural confounds into their manipulations. Consider a study by Stewart and Payne (2008), who were interested in seeing if people automatically associate Black men with weapons. To test this idea, Stewart and Payne used a simple and elegant priming manipulation. This meant that on a particular trial of their experiment, participants saw one stimulus (a prime) flashed briefly in the middle of a computer screen. Shortly thereafter, they saw a different stimulus (a target) in the same location. To the degree that primes and targets are conceptually or evaluatively similar, primes usually facilitate recognition of targets. Stewart and Payne's participants were primed with a Black or a White face (like the ones in the left-hand portion of Figure 7.1) for just 200 ms (1/5 of

Figure 7.1

Two of the faces (primes), the mask, and four of the objects (targets) used by Stewart and Payne (2008). A prime, the mask, and a target always appeared in the center of the screen (in that order, trial after trial).

Courtesy of Keith Payne

a second). After a specific face disappeared, a mask appeared briefly (in the same spot on the screen) to ready people for the next image. Then the crucial target image appeared. Participants simply had to report quickly, by pressing a specific key on their computer keyboards, whether the target image was a gun or a tool (like the ones in the right-hand portion of Figure 7.1).

Stewart and Payne found that people were quicker to identify (a) tools when they had been primed by White as compared with Black faces and (b) guns when they had been primed by Black as compared with White faces. It is worth noting that Stewart and Payne were worried enough about procedural confounds that they did not simply use the two faces you see in Figure 7.1 Instead, they carefully pretested photos of many Black and White male faces and chose 12 Black and 12 White faces that were judged to be (a) prototypical of their ethnic group and (b) equal in perceived physical attractiveness. We should also add that Stewart and Payne's decision to use only young, male Black and White faces controlled for any procedural confounds involving age or gender. In the absence of careful pretesting, we might be worried, for example, that if the 12 Black faces were less attractive than the 12 White faces, we would not know whether perceived attractiveness or ethnicity was behind any observed priming effects.

Of course when dealing with naturally existing stimuli such as photos of people, one can never know for sure whether the photo sets differ *only* in the precise way the experimenter had in mind. For example, if you check out the complete set of faces shown in Figure 7.2, you will notice that Black men

Figure 7.2

The complete set of 24 Black and White faces (primes) used by Stewart and Payne (2008). (These are grayscale versions of their original color stimuli.)

Courtesy of Keith Payne

are more likely than the White men to have facial hair. People who adhere to the strictest possible definition of a procedural confound would probably say that this is a procedural confound. However, what if, in the real world, Black men in this age group are simply more likely to sport facial hair than are White men? Is this *still* a procedural confound? To take this tricky question a step further, what if Stewart and Payne had been studying gender rather than ethnicity? Would it be a procedural confound to include several men (but no women) with facial hair?

We are not trying to muddy the waters of procedural confounds. Suffice it to say that in the case of this specific study, it was not Stewart and Payne's goal to identify and manipulate the one necessary and sufficient cue to ethnicity that could be responsible for their predicted priming effects. Instead, they just wanted to show that under predictable conditions, people automatically associate Black men with weapons. We believe they did that. Furthermore, suppose you happen to believe that facial hair is the most important and understudied variable in all of psychology. That is, suppose you are convinced that facial hair is the real reason behind Stewart and Payne's observed priming effects. The beauty of using multiple stimuli in an experiment is that you could address this concern empirically. That is, by keeping track of participants' responses trial by trial, you could see if facial hair made any differences in participants' responses to the faces. And if it did, you could correct for this, for example, by focusing your statistical analyses only on the Black and White faces that don't have any facial hair (see also Payne, 2001, who used a different set of Black and White faces that had no facial hair at all and observed the same priming effect).

So to a greater degree than any other research technique, true experiments allow researchers to manipulate one and only one variable at a time. Researchers simply have to make sure that they don't miss out on this wonderful opportunity by making procedural errors. Good experimenters take many steps to ensure that the *only* aspects of their procedures that vary across conditions are the ones that they intended. For instance, in their study of mood and helping, Isen and Levin used a male book dropper in both experimental conditions. They also made sure that the book dropper stood roughly the same distance from the participants in the two mood conditions, and they even trained him to drop the same number of books in both conditions. Furthermore, they made sure that the book dropper was always blind to whether a participant had been given a cookie. This assured that the confederate wouldn't change his behavior across conditions in subtle ways he himself might fail to realize. True experiments conducted carefully minimize the chances of procedural confounds.

Nonetheless, even when researchers take every conceivable step to eliminate person and procedure confounds, a third type of confound can still occur. We've seen this type of confound before, and it is an operational confound. As we noted when discussing confounds in nonexperimental designs, our use of the word "operational" reflects the fact that this boils down to making a mistake in one's operational definition of a construct. As with nonexperimental designs, the question at hand is not whether there is a causal relation but whether the observed causal relation was interpreted correctly.

When an experimental manipulation suffers from an operational confound, we still know that the independent variable (and nothing but the independent variable) caused the observed changes in the dependent variable. However, we become worried that the independent variable might not represent the construct that the experimenter originally had in mind. Thus, a causal relation is established but the preferred causal interpretation is at risk.

When an operational confound occurs, a manipulation influences more than one psychological construct, each of which may influence the dependent variable. As a result, what we had hoped was a very clean, simple manipulation proves to be dirtier and more complex than we had intended. We thus don't know for certain why our experimental and control groups behaved differently. To illustrate, let's return again to the study by Isen and Levin (1972). Recall that Isen and Levin gave their participants a cookie because they believed that it would put participants in a good mood. They were correct. Free cookies do, in fact, put most people in a good mood. However, recall also that a free cookie may have influenced helping in this study for reasons that had little or nothing to do with mood. An alternative reason that receiving a cookie may have led to helping behavior is that people who received the cookie from a stranger were exposed to a prosocial model (Bandura, 1977). Modeling refers to copying the behavior of other people, and it is an extremely well-documented phenomenon. It is thus possible that by using cookies to create good moods, Isen and Levin caused two factors to covary with condition: (a) mood and (b) a prosocial model—and either one of these factors might have caused the effect on helping.

After reading all this, you may be a little disappointed to learn that being in a positive mood may not necessarily lead to helping after all. Cheer up, have a cookie; it looks like positive mood *does* contribute to helping. The reason we know this is that Isen and colleagues eventually developed a way of manipulating mood that eliminated the operational confound related to prosocial modeling. As we noted briefly in Chapter 5, Isen and colleagues developed the "found dime" procedure. This procedure does not appear to suffer from this confound (because people only find a dime rather than being given one). This alternate manipulation of mood reliably increased a wide variety of helping behaviors (Isen, 1987), suggesting that at least part of the reason cookies make people more helpful is that cookies (like dimes) put people in good moods. And so, as Sesame Street's Cookie Monster might put it, "If it's good enough for found dimes, it's good enough for me!"

True Experiments Pull Researchers into the Laboratory

Finally, it is worth noting that although all true experiments fix the problem of individual differences (via random assignment), some specific kinds of true experiments help minimize other types of confounds more readily than others. In particular, true experiments that are conducted in the laboratory make it a little easier to eliminate confounds than do true experiments conducted in the field (i.e., in the real world). The reason for this is that in the laboratory, researchers can "play God" by creating exactly the kind of psychological situation they want to create. For example, it is slightly easier to get people to eat cookies or find dimes in the laboratory than it is in the real world (where distractions sometimes interfere with such manipulations). More important, the freedom experimenters have to create highly unusual situations in the lab can help researchers separate variables that are typically confounded in the real world. For instance, in the real world people are typically exposed to things that they like more often than they are exposed to things that they dislike. So the frequency with which people are exposed to things is naturally confounded with the favorability of these same things. In the lab, however, it is very easy to expose people to some things more frequently than to others, independent of their favorability. The laboratory, then, is a place where natural confounds can often be eliminated. As an example from physics, consider Galileo's theory that bodies of differing weights fall at the same rate. This is a difficult theory to test outside the laboratory because an object's weight (and especially its density) is strongly confounded with the degree to which it is affected by wind resistance. Feathers and soap bubbles are easily carried away by the wind. When cannonballs and taxicabs are carried away by the wind, it's time to look for an underground shelter. In the laboratory we can minimize this potent natural confound. Under the highly artificial but scientifically informative context of a vacuum, a feather drops like a stone. In a very similar way, when psychologists bring participants into the psychological vacuum of the laboratory, they can easily conduct experiments that minimize confounds.

As we have suggested thus far, researchers can avoid virtually any kind of confound in their research if they follow three simple steps: (1) randomly assign participants to conditions, (2) develop manipulations that are free of obvious procedural and operational confounds, and (3) move studies to the laboratory where greater control can be exerted. However, experiments, especially laboratory experiments, also have a few other important advantages, and our description of experiments would be incomplete if we did not mention some of these additional advantages.

True Experiments Allow Researchers to Observe the Invisible

A third major advantage of experiments, especially laboratory experiments, is that they allow researchers to observe things that they could not observe any other way. Just as microscopes and telescopes allow biologist and astronomers to see what they could never see with the naked eye, sophisticated psychological measurement techniques allow psychologists to do the same. The list of experimental techniques that allow psychologists to observe things that would be unobservable outside the lab is growing on an almost daily basis. For example, researchers who study attitudes and persuasion can determine whether people like or dislike things by measuring very low levels of electrical activity in the specific facial muscles that play a role in smiling or frowning (see Tassinary & Cacioppo, 1992). Computerized response latency measures, functional magnetic resonance imaging (better known as fMRI), and implicit memory measures (remember the "ele _____"?) are just a few of the hundreds of possible ways to measure the otherwise unmeasurable in the laboratory.

A more elaborate example is Patricia Devine's (1989) influential study of the the cognitive bases of prejudice and stereotyping. Devine hypothesized that prejudiced beliefs might exist at two distinct levels of mental representation. Specifically, she suspected that people possess both automatic (overlearned, nonconscious) and controlled (carefully considered, consciously reportable) stereotypic beliefs. This general idea that belief systems have automatic, non-conscious components was pretty well accepted by cognitive and social psychologists by the time that Devine applied it to stereotyping. For example, it is well established that proficient readers are not consciously aware of what they are doing when they convert letters on a page into meaningful words and ideas. After years of practice, much of your "knowledge" about reading has become so automatic that you are no longer consciously aware of it. The same thing is true of many other beliefs and behaviors (e.g., beliefs about how to drive a car). As a potential example of how automatic reading is for you, check out the first sentence of this paragraph. As you were reading it, did you notice the repetition "the the"? Most people don't. The reason most people don't is that part of being a proficient reader is learning to ignore certain kinds of redundant information when reading. To get back to the point: Devine wanted to extend established research on automatic and controlled information processing to the important topic of prejudice. She felt that even highly nonprejudiced people might possess overlearned, automatic associations about ethnic minority groups. Furthermore, she tested this idea not by waiting to observe evidence of this in a naturalistic setting, but by conducting a controlled laboratory experiment.

In her experiment, Devine subliminally exposed people to a long list of words and then examined their judgments about an ambiguously aggressive, race-unspecified target person named Donald.[2] For some people, the word list to which they were subliminally exposed before judging Donald consisted mostly of words that are stereotypically associated with African Americans (e.g., "ghetto," "basketball," "Negroes"). For others, the subliminal word list consisted mostly of words that were stereotype-irrelevant (e.g., "thought," "water," "people"). In other words, Devine manipulated the accessibility of people's automatic associations about African Americans. She expected that doing so would influence people's subsequent judgments of Donald's aggressiveness (because aggression is part of the stereotype of African Americans). It did. People who, without knowing it, had been exposed to the stereotype-relevant primes judged Donald to be more aggressive than did people exposed to the relatively neutral primes. Thus, Devine demonstrated that beliefs that occur outside a person's conscious awareness can influence that person's social judgments. More important, Devine also demonstrated that this automatic priming effect occurred even for participants who had extremely egalitarian attitudes about African Americans. Just as being less racist than average didn't provide people with any immunity from this priming effect, being more racist than average didn't make people especially susceptible to it. Needless to say, demonstrating that people's conscious and nonconscious belief systems operate differently would have been extremely difficult to do without the benefits of experimentation (and the precise experimental techniques, such as priming, that have been developed and refined as part of the experimental paradigm).[3]

True Experiments Provide Information about Statistical Interactions

The first three advantages of experimentation are all connected to the idea that experimentation allows researchers to carefully isolate the independent and dependent variables that they wish to investigate. A fourth advantage of experimentation is that experiments are well suited not only to the isolation of variables but also to the careful, systematic blending of variables. To be more precise, experiments provide especially clear and useful information about how multiple variables work together to determine behavior. To put this more methodologically, experiments are typically better than are naturalistic designs at providing information about *interactions* between two or more independent variables. This is a statistical term indicating that the effect of one independent variable on a dependent variable is different at different levels of the *other* independent variable. By giving researchers complete control over their independent variables, experiments make it easier than usual to disentangle two or more variables for the purpose of detecting interactions. This is true in great part because lab experiments often allow researchers to separate two or more variables that may be highly correlated in the real world.

For instance, suppose a researcher wants to know how highly popular versus unpopular children respond to acceptance versus rejection from peers. This would be hard to study in a natural situation such as the classroom for two closely related reasons. First, almost by definition, highly popular students rarely experience rejection. Second, highly unpopular children rarely experience acceptance. In the laboratory, this would be very easy to fix: Identify the two groups of children you want to study, create two forms of false but convincing experimental feedback, and use random assignment to decide which kind of feedback (acceptance or rejection) each kid gets. In this way, plenty of popular kids would experience rejection, and plenty of unpopular kids would experience acceptance. You could then see, for example, whether popular versus unpopular kids respond differently to exactly the same positive versus negative experimental feedback. (Of course, you know from Chapter 2 that a study such as this involves some tricky ethical issues. When done correctly, studies should be just as ethically sensitive as informative.)[4]

In short, experiments help researchers figure out when the combined influence of two or more independent variables is different from the sum of their individual influences. When this happens, when two or more independent variables work together in unexpected ways, we have observed a statistical interaction. It may seem a little ironic that we need to separate two or more variables to appreciate how they work together. We will say more about interactions later on, but for now a couple of culinary analogies might help to clarify this point. Imagine that cocoa, sugar, and butter *always* come together as a package. That is, assume that neither chefs nor scientists have any way of ever separating these three ingredients. If this were the case, you would have no possible way of knowing that the combination of these three ingredients is much more delicious than any one ingredient in isolation. We know of no shops devoted exclusively to sugar, to butter, or to cocoa, but we can think of many devoted to that curious and addictive combination best known as chocolate. The same thing is true, by the way, for good ingredients that become worse rather than better when you put them together. If you are trying to invent a new dessert, and you suspect that two delicious ingredients taste even more delicious together, you'd need to isolate the two ingredients. Then you'd want to blend them (and only them) together before adding them to your recipe. If the two individually delectable ingredients (say, for example, peppermint and orange) taste horrible together (as they do when you have some orange juice after having just brushed your teeth), you would probably keep experimenting instead of throwing them both into your novel recipe for key lime pie.

Interactions are very important because they identify the limiting conditions of a specific theory. Recall that all theories have their boundaries: conditions under which they do and do not apply. No theory is correct under all possible circumstances. Many times, researchers thus conduct experiments with the specific intention of determining when a specific theory is and is not true. As discussed in Chapter 2, this approach to hypothesis testing is known as qualification, and it requires the analysis of interactions. To illustrate qualification as it might apply to a specific research finding, consider the boundary conditions of a typical **semantic priming** effect. Semantic priming refers to the finding that people recognize most words more quickly than usual when they have just been exposed to words that have a similar meaning (Neely, 1977). For instance, you should be able to identify the word "money" more quickly than usual if you have just been exposed to the word "bank." Interestingly enough, this priming effect occurs even when a prime (the word that comes first) is flashed up so briefly that people don't realize they were exposed to it. Is this priming effect really based on the semantic overlap (i.e., the overlap in meaning) between different words? To find out, you might use the word "bank" as a prime for the word "money" under neutral control conditions, and hope to replicate the usual priming effect (people should recognize the word "money" more quickly than usual). However, to test the limiting conditions of this effect, you might use exactly the same prime for participants who had just read a story about the *banks* of the Mississippi River. Under this set of conditions (when the meaning of the word "bank" has been temporarily altered), the usual priming effect would probably disappear. This interaction between (1) the presence versus absence of a prime and (2) the temporary meaning of the prime would be easy to detect in an experiment. Furthermore, it could tell you something important about the nature and limits of semantic priming.

True Experiments Minimize Noise

In addition to all the other strengths we have mentioned, a final strength of experimentation applies to a much greater extent to *laboratory* experiments than to experiments in general. Nonetheless, this advantage is worth mentioning, not only because the large majority of experiments happen to be conducted in the laboratory, but also because this advantage is so important in its own right. In contrast to most other research settings, laboratory settings provide researchers with a unique ability to minimize **noise**. Students often confuse noise with confounds, but the two concepts are quite different. As you know very well by now, experimental confounds are nuisance variables that covary systematically across levels of the independent variable, raising the question of whether a large difference between an experimental and a control group really means anything after all. In contrast, noise refers to extraneous variables that influence the dependent variable but are evenly distributed across experimental conditions. Nonetheless, noise can create so much variability in the dependent variable that it makes it hard to see the true effects of any independent variables.

To appreciate the problem of noise, consider some of the many variables that are likely to influence how long it takes a person to recognize words that appear in the middle of a computer monitor (this is an extremely useful measure of information processing). To begin with some features of words themselves, both the frequency of a word in the English language (e.g., "good" versus "goop") and word length ("cat" versus "catastrophe") have a big influence on how quickly people recognize words. A wide variety of contextual factors ranging from the size of the computer screen to the brightness of the testing room might also influence how quickly people respond in such a task. Finally, many individual differences (e.g., fluency in English, level of achievement motivation, visual acuity) influence people's responses. Suppose we decide to test the hypothesis that an experimenter's ethnicity influences participants' ability to recognize words related to ethnicity. (Don't worry; this time we got rid of procedural confounds.) If we allow all these other factors to vary randomly, it would be *extremely* difficult to detect a real effect of the treatment in the midst of all this noise. However, if we take advantage of the control we have in the laboratory by holding all these sources of noise constant (e.g., by selecting only fluent speakers of English, controlling screen size and illumination levels, keeping word length more or less constant, etc.), we'd have a much better chance of detecting a true effect of the experimenter's ethnicity.

Concerns about reducing noise sometimes motivate psychologists to use highly homogenous samples of research participants, that is, participants who do not differ very much from one another (e.g., college students, children of the same age and/or gender). By studying groups who are similar in some important way, researchers often hope to eliminate much of the noise that occurs as a result of individual differences. As discussed below, however, the use of noise-free laboratories and homogenous samples has caused many people to ask whether the results of laboratory studies generalize to the real world, where noise and individual differences abound. For the present purposes, suffice it to say that this is a reasonable question, but it is certainly no reason to abandon the precision and control over independent and dependent variables that is so readily afforded by the laboratory.

A Summary of Experimentation

A simple way to summarize almost everything we have said about experimentation thus far is to say that experiments provide researchers with clear and compelling information about causality. An even simpler way to put it is that experiments are especially high in internal validity. This is especially important because the whole goal of science is to understand causes. True experiments that use random assignment to eliminate person confounds, that take steps to eliminate procedural and operational confounds, and that police noise yield a lot of information about causes that would usually elude researchers using most any other method. Experiments thus allow researchers to determine whether the independent variable, the whole independent variable, and nothing but the independent variable has an impact on some outcome of interest. As R. A. Fisher (1935) put it, virtually every new thing human beings have come to know throughout history is based on "learning by experience." In this regard he added, "Experimental observations are only experience carefully planned in advance." Experimentation is about making careful observations under the best possible viewing conditions.

ARE TRUE EXPERIMENTS REALISTIC?

Although experimentation may be the cat's meow, anyone who has been around a meowing cat for very long knows that meowing cats have some drawbacks. In this next section, we discuss the most serious potential disadvantage of experimentation, the fact that experiments may be unrealistic. We then devote a great deal of attention to the question of what can be done to address this potential problem. We expand on the potential list of disadvantages of experiments in Chapter 8, by the way, when we discuss quasi-experiments, close cousins of true experiments that represent a different answer to the question of how to make the results of laboratory experiments more realistic.

The Problem: Artificiality

Perhaps the most common criticism of experiments is that they are "artificial" and thus may not reflect what happens in the real world. Consider the Isen and Levin (1972) study described near the beginning of this chapter. These authors showed that receiving a cookie made people more helpful than usual. But how often do people receive a cookie prior to witnessing someone else's need for help? This must rarely happen, and so it is worth asking whether more realistic mood manipulations (e.g., watching a happy movie, winning money at a casino) would have exactly the same effect on people's likelihood of helping a stranger whose car has broken down on the New Jersey Turnpike. If realism is a mild problem for Isen and Levin's study of helping, it might appear to be a total disaster for Festinger and Carlsmith's (1959) study of cognitive dissonance. Recall that they asked people to lie to another student for $1 or $20 by saying that a boring peg-turning task was enjoyable. Have *you* ever been asked to perform a boring peg-turning task? Did the person who asked you to do so then offer you $1 or $20 to tell a stranger that the boring task was actually quite interesting? If so, we suspect that this happened while you were a participant in a psychological experiment. So can this famous study tell us anything about how a hit man would reduce his dissonance when he realized that he had accidentally killed the wrong person? What about an 11-year-old girl who smokes a cigarette to impress a friend and then reduces her dissonance by convincing herself that she likes smoking?

The lack of realism in psychology experiments points to a potential artifact in all laboratory studies. Recall that artifacts are variables that are held constant in studies and that may nonetheless influence a set of research findings. A particularly critical critic could argue that the process of studying people in the laboratory might be an artifact. After all, by definition, everyone in a laboratory study is in the laboratory. Perhaps the effects observed in most lab studies would not occur outside the lab. What's more, many laboratory studies increase worries about artifacts by trying to reduce noise. By ensuring that their samples are relatively homogenous (e.g., composed of only female college freshmen), researchers eliminate noise, but in so doing, they increase the possibility of artifacts. Over the years, this concern has received a great deal of critical attention. In the late 1960s and early 1970s, the field of social psychology experienced a sort of crisis in confidence regarding this issue. Because experimental laboratories are artificial situations and because they often use convenience samples of college students, a growing contingent of psychologists became concerned about the ability of laboratory research to say anything meaningful about the real world. In its most extreme form, this criticism holds that laboratory research can tell us only how a particular group of people will respond to particular manipulations while they are in the laboratory—and nothing about how anyone else responds to anything else while they are anyplace else. Can laboratory research tell us anything about broad principles of human nature? As you know, this concern has to do with the external validity of laboratory research. External validity refers to the extent to which a set of research findings provides an accurate description of what typically happens in the real world. An externally valid laboratory finding applies to lots of different people in lots of different natural situations.

The Solution: Two Forms of Realism

In a climate where many people were questioning the value of laboratory experiments, some researchers decided to take a stand in favor of experimentation. One pair of influential researchers who took such a stand was Aronson and Carlsmith (1968). In the spirit of Fisher's original claim that experimentation is merely experience carefully planned, Aronson and Carlsmith argued that there is no inherent reason that lab experiments have to be low in external validity. Furthermore, they made some concrete, practical suggestions about what researchers can do to maximize the external validity of psychological experiments. According to Aronson and Carlsmith, concerns about the artificiality of laboratory experiments, though well intended, missed the most important point behind these experiments. The point is not so much to emulate reality as to reveal what lies beneath the surface of reality. Nonetheless, Aronson and Carlsmith noted that one simple way to make laboratory experiments more realistic would be to make them more physically similar to the real world. To use their terminology, studies that physically resemble the real world are high in **mundane realism.** To increase mundane realism, simply make a study as similar as possible to the real-world setting you care about. If you are interested in studying gambling behavior, for example, you might consider setting up a real roulette wheel, hiring a research assistant to deliver free beers to your participants, and giving them a real stake of casino chips that they could gamble with under different experimental conditions (say, for example, after having had three regular or three alcohol-free beers). The setting of this study would strongly resemble the setting of a real casino, and thus it might reassure some people that the study's findings would travel well to real casinos. Although there is some merit to this approach, Aronson and Carlsmith argued that laboratory experimenters can best increase the external validity of their research findings by means of a radically different approach. They argued that rather than pursuing mundane realism, laboratory experimenters would usually be better off pursuing **experimental realism.**

Experimental realism refers to the degree to which a research study is psychologically meaningful to research participants. We might also call it *psychological realism.* If a study is high in mundane realism when it *looks* just like the real world, a study is high in experimental realism when it *feels* just like the real world. The issue behind experimental realism is that research participants should truly experience the psychological states in which the experimenters are interested and thus behave naturally and spontaneously rather than artificially or self-consciously. A good example of a research program that appears to have been very high in experimental realism is Asch's (1955, 1956) research on conformity. Conformity was particularly interesting to psychologists in Asch's day because many psychologists had been personally affected by the events of World War II. Researchers hoped that gaining a better understanding of conformity could give them a better understanding of some of the horrible events of this war. At a much more mundane level, just about everyone knows what it is like to want to be like others. Asch knew this very well. If he had been strongly concerned about mundane realism, Asch could have asked teenagers to come into the laboratory to see how individual teenagers would respond to subtle group pressures to try a cigarette. Alternatively, Asch could have asked a group of upper-level managers to try to reach a difficult financial decision, to see if those who held a minority viewpoint would conform to the opinions of the majority. Instead of doing either of these things, Asch created a completely novel situation that bore very little physical resemblance to the schoolyard or the boardroom.

Asch did this by bringing participants to his laboratory for what appeared to be a boring study of visual perception. From the perspective of

Asch's participants, their job was very simple: to make a series of judgments about the lengths of some lines. After taking a seat at a table with six other people who appeared to be co-participants, the real participants patiently waited their turns to announce which of three lines printed on a card was equal in length to a standard line. An example of one of the stimulus sets used by Asch appears in Figure 7.3. The first couple of trials of this experiment passed uneventfully as the real participants watched their peers announce the obvious answers to Asch's perceptual questions. However, in several crucial trials, most participants found themselves rubbing their eyes in disbelief. One by one, each of the first five participants calmly and confidently provided patently incorrect answers to the questions. In some trials, for instance, these trained research assistants announced that line A was identical to the standard.

This placed the real research participants in a big dilemma. Would they shoot straight from the hip and deviate from the unanimous judgments of the other group members? Or would they ignore what their eyes were telling them and cave in to the subtle but potent pressure of the group? Most participants (75 percent) caved in and conformed on at least some of the crucial trials. If the facial expressions of Asch's participants were any indication of their state of mind during the experiment, this study was *very* high in experimental realism. In some of the surviving photos of participants in these studies, participants appeared to be dumbfounded by the misguided judgments of their peers, and yet they often parroted these incorrect judgments to the experimenter as if they were their own. This is exactly the sort of conformity process that researchers wanted to understand. Asch's methodology proved to be an excellent tool to study conformity not only because it maximized experimental realism but also because it readily permitted the use of experimental manipulations. In a careful set of studies using this line-judging procedure, Asch systematically manipulated a variety of variables that proved to have a potent effect on conformity rates. For instance, when Asch planted a single

Figure 7.3

One of the stimulus sets used in the Asch (1955) study of conformity

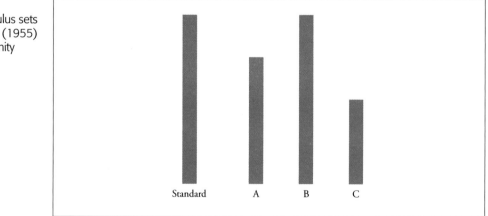

Standard   A   B   C

Reproduced with permission. Copyright © 1955 Scientific American, Inc. All rights reserved.

Figure 7.4

Do you think the guy in the middle was taking Asch's contrived situation seriously—or not?

dissenter in the otherwise unanimous majority, conformity was reduced to about 20 percent of the original levels. This finding suggests that adolescents would be in a much better position to avoid smoking if they could locate a single ally who was willing to march to the beat of a healthier drummer. Although the unique and contrived setting that Asch created bore little resemblance to most real-world settings, the psychological experiences of Asch's participants appear to have been very genuine and meaningful. His participants truly were confused, they truly did not want to risk the rejection of others, and they truly reported judgments that flew in the face of reality.

Another classic example of an experiment that appears to have been high in experimental realism is Triplett's (1898) study of competition and performance. From his own experience as a bicyclist, Triplett noticed that trained athletes appeared to perform better when competing head to head with other athletes than when performing alone. For example, Triplett's careful observations of highly trained cyclists revealed that they produced better times when racing against one another than when racing against the clock (typically in an effort to break a record). If you think about how enormously important fast times are to highly trained cyclists, you might assume that these highly motivated and conditioned athletes would always push themselves to the limits of their abilities every time they raced—whether they were racing against the rapidly turning hands of a stopwatch or the rapidly churning legs of another rider. But Triplett noticed that the presence of a competitor seemed to improve people's performances. To put his observations to an experimental test, Triplett brought 40 children to his laboratory and had them play a game in which they tried to pull a small flag as quickly as possible around a 4-meter racecourse. They did so by reeling in a long silk string that was attached to a fishing reel. Triplett observed the same thing among kids trying to reel in flags that he had observed in the real world of athletes trying to reel in trophies. The presence of competitors facilitated performance.

Was Triplett's study high in experimental realism? Ironically, some of the best clues come from some of the rare participants in his experiment who did *not* confirm Triplett's predictions regarding social facilitation. Although Triplett found that competition usually facilitated performance, he also noted that competition sometimes caused people, especially young children, to become "overstimulated," leading to decreases in performance. In the interest of fairness, Triplett described the participants who disconfirmed his expectations just as carefully as he described those who confirmed them. He noted that whereas virtually everyone in his experiment tried harder to do well when competing against another person, some people's efforts did not pay off. After providing a statistical summary of the behavior of the ten participants who fell apart under the pressure of competition, Triplett provided a verbal description that suggests that his experiment was indeed high in experimental realism:

> This [reduction in performance] seems to be brought about in large measure by the mental attitude of the subject. An intense desire to win, for instance, often resulting in over-stimulation. Accompanying the phenomena were labored breathing, flushed faces and a stiffening or contraction of the muscles of the arm. A number of young children of from 5 to 9 years, not included in our group of 40, exhibited the phenomena most strikingly, the rigidity of the arm preventing free movement and in some cases resulting in an almost total inhibition of movement. The effort to continue turning in these cases was by a swaying of the whole body.

Triplett studied adults as well as children in his experiment, and his descriptions of the adults also make it clear that his participants cared deeply about his experimental task. Incidentally, we want to remind you that Triplett was forthright enough to describe the behavior of participants whose behavior was disrupted rather than facilitated by the presence of other people. Interestingly, Triplett's observations of the participants who fell apart under social pressure are consistent with contemporary research showing that the presence of other people can either facilitate or disrupt performance. Whether the presence of other people facilitates or disrupts performance depends on the degree to which the behavior being performed is easy or well learned. The presence of other people contributes positively to our performance only when the behavior in question is easy or well practiced (Zajonc, 1965).

A more contemporary example of a study high in experimental realism can be found in Judith Edney's (1979) research on the *commons dilemma*. In her research on this social trap, Edney introduces a group of real participants to an experimental game in which they are allowed to remove desirable resources (such as nuts, candies, or game tokens)

It was just Lenny's luck to draw a first-round match against last year's champion.

from a common pool that is replenished after each round of play (after each time that all participants have individually had an opportunity to withdraw as many units as they wish from the pool). Edney's participants learn at the outset of the game that the experimenter will double all the remaining units of the resource at the end of each round (for a limited number of rounds or until the pool of resources is exhausted, whichever comes first). So if her participants played it smart, they would all withdraw nothing from the pool until the final round, at which time an equal split of the resources would give everyone more than any one participant could have possibly gained by taking everything on the first round. Experimental gaming studies such as these have consistently yielded an interesting and distressing finding: people rarely cooperate. Very few groups make it past the first round without exhausting the pool of resources. In fact, during the first round of the game, participants usually begin a mad dash to grab the resources. Some groups of participants have even knocked bowls of nuts to the floor as they scrambled to claim the lion's share of the initial pool of resources. As contrived as this situation might be, it appears to contain the essential psychological ingredients of many real-world commons dilemmas (e.g., the bulldozing of tropical rain forests or the over-fishing of lakes and rivers). This artificial situation strongly piques people's interest in a limited resource, and it produces meaningful levels of greed based on mutual distrust.

To get a better feel for the lengths to which psychologists will sometimes go to create an ideal experimental environment, consider the following passage in which MacDonald, Zanna, and Fong (1995) describe the use of deception in a study of how alcohol influences judgment. To address concerns that some of their previous experimental findings might be attributable to placebo effects (i.e., to people's expectancies about how alcohol influences judgment), MacDonald et al. conducted a simple study in which they tried to convince all their participants (even those who were not intoxicated) that they had consumed quite a bit of alcohol:

> Nevertheless, to ensure that our results were not due to expectancy effects, we ran a placebo experiment, comparing the responses of people who received alcohol ($n = 27$) with those in a placebo condition ($n = 23$). Participants in the placebo condition were led to believe that they were consuming alcohol and Wink [a brand of soda] through smell, sight, and taste cues, but they were really receiving only a minute amount of alcohol. From our reading of alcohol studies that include a placebo condition ... we took a number of steps to ensure that our manipulation was convincing to participants. While participants were completing a measure in another room, we sprayed the room where they would be consuming their drinks with a mixture of water and alcohol to provide smell cues. Participants also saw us pour their drinks: We had put flattened tonic water into an alcohol bottle so that participants in the placebo condition could see us pouring a clear liquid from an alcohol bottle into their drinks. Finally, we put a very small amount of alcohol (1 teaspoon) disguised as lime juice on top of their drinks so that the first taste of their drinks was mostly alcohol. Our manipulation did indeed convince placebo participants that they had consumed alcohol: Despite the fact that their actual breathalyzer readings

were .000% or .001% in all cases, the average BAL [blood alcohol level] estimate for the placebo group was .072%, which was comparable to the actual BAL of participants in the intoxicated condition ($M = .067\%$). None of our placebo participants expressed any suspicion during the debriefing—in fact, a number of them reacted with surprise and disbelief that they were not actually intoxicated.

MacDonald et al. follow this description with a footnote that adds a colorful and concrete picture of the effectiveness of their placebo strategy:

One participant in the placebo condition actually refused to believe that he was not intoxicated. After the experimenter showed him the breathalyzer reading of .000, he argued that the breathalyzer must be "rigged," and he insisted on remaining in the laboratory until he felt sober enough to leave.

MacDonald et al. then demonstrated that there were important differences between the behavioral intentions of the participants in the placebo condition and the intentions of those in the intoxication condition. Relative to those who thought they were intoxicated but were actually sober, those who actually were intoxicated were less negatively disposed toward the idea of drinking and driving. MacDonald et al. appear to have captured a sobering psychological truth about drinking and driving. The fact that careful laboratory experiments often require the use of deception raises some difficult ethical issues. These important issues are discussed in detail in Chapter 2.

IS THERE A RECIPE FOR EXPERIMENTAL REALISM?

At this point, you may have noticed that we identified a serious criticism of experimentation and then quickly countered this criticism with a discussion of how experimental realism can save the day. Having said this much, we hasten to add that, just as nonexperimental researchers need to think long and hard about internal validity, laboratory experimenters need to think long and hard about external validity. Experimental realism only comes to the rescue when we know how to dial the right number. That is, experimental realism increases our confidence in the external validity of experimental research findings only when we can be certain that the participants in an experiment do, in fact, experience the psychological states the experimenter hopes to create. This can be difficult to establish. It essentially boils down to deciding whether a measure or manipulation is high in construct validity.

Construct validity provides us with a good way of thinking about experimental realism. For example, it highlights the fact that assessing any kind of validity often boils down to thinking carefully about whether a researcher did things the way he or she should have. Was Festinger and Carlsmith's famous experiment high in construct validity? As a big point in their favor, the whole reason that this study became so famous is that it struck most people that these experimenters had found an excellent way of creating dissonance in the laboratory. On the other hand, creative researchers who were not huge fans of cognitive dissonance theory were able to come up with a variety of alternate perspectives on what happens in the hearts and minds of participants who take part in studies of cognitive dissonance. Bem (1967), as you may recall, raised some excellent questions about whether Festinger and Carlsmith's participants were truly experiencing cognitive dissonance. (Remember the Bob Downing study?) In the end, however, critical analyses of cognitive dissonance theory only made the theory stronger by identifying its boundary conditions.

So how, exactly, do we know when a study is high in experimental realism? Unfortunately, it is hard to say. In fact, creating experimental realism is probably as much an art as it is a science. If there is a crucial ingredient, it is probably the same kind of thing that goes into activities like acting, stage direction, and puppeteering. It is the ability to identify the gist of a psychological experience and translate it into the precise but limited language of the lab without losing anything important. To paraphrase a famous definition of pornography, most psychologists would probably say that even though they cannot provide a simple formula for guaranteeing experimental realism, they can always recognize it when they see it. Fortunately, there are also empirical answers to questions about experimental realism. If you're not so sure that you've latched onto a manipulation that is high in experimental realism, you can always ask your research participants themselves what they think. Specifically, researchers can include **manipulation checks** in their experiments. The basic concept of a manipulation check is pretty simple. A manipulation check is a measure designed to see if a manipulation truly puts people in the psychological state that the experimenter wishes to create. For instance, if you are trying to manipulate the physical attractiveness of a confederate who asks participants for a favor, you could ask participants to report how physically attractive they find the confederate with whom they interact. Alternately, if you are worried that questions about the confederate's attractiveness will make participants suspicious, you could show photos of the confederates to a group of people who aren't actually taking part in the study and have them make some ratings. In either event, you could address the psychological realism of your manipulation empirically.

If one defines "ingredients" loosely, it may be possible to identify an additional ingredient of experimental realism. Unfortunately, high levels of experimental realism usually require the use of at least some minimal level of deception. Pretty frequently, the quest for experimental realism requires researchers to convince their participants that they are taking part in one kind of study when they are actually taking part in a completely different kind of study. At a bare minimum, experimental realism almost always requires a more passive sort of lie in which experimenters fail to inform participants up front about the precise reasons the study is being conducted. In other words, experimental realism is about creating convincing illusions that cause people to experience the precise situations you care about as a researcher. Just as Festinger and Carlsmith weren't really studying peg-turning, Asch wasn't really interested in visual perception. Even Edney, whose study involved no elaborate lies or cover-ups, was interested in much more than a simple game involving nuts.

The use of deception appears to be on the wane in psychology, and we personally see this as a favorable development. Although at times it is very difficult to study phenomena at all without using deception, the routine use of deception can erode people's trust in the science of psychology. We discussed this issue in Chapter 2. Here, we simply note that a shift away from using deception in laboratory experiments reflects a changing sensibility among psychologists. To some degree, this change may reflect a tendency for researchers to forgo the experimental realism of the laboratory in pursuit of the mundane realism in the world around them. For better or worse, researchers who tell their participants that they are interested in visual perception or peg-turning are not studying topics such as conformity or cognitive dissonance. Increasingly, they are studying topics such as visual perception or peg-turning.

TRADE-OFFS BETWEEN INTERNAL AND EXTERNAL VALIDITY

It has been suggested many times that there are strong trade-offs between external and internal validity, as if researchers often need to choose one form of validity over the other. However, as suggested by our discussion of experimental realism, the methodological trade-off between internal and external validity isn't quite as hard and fast as one might think. After all, we just saw that cleverly designed laboratory studies that mimic the psychological states occurring in everyday life can sometimes prove to be very high in external validity. By the same token, carefully designed naturalistic studies that do not use experimental manipulations and that do not take place in the laboratory sometimes prove to be very high in internal validity. This is important to remember because experimental and nonexperimental results sometimes contradict one another, and people most often jump to the conclusion that the laboratory study must be more internally valid than the field study. A potential case in point comes from social psychological research on depression. In the late 1970s, laboratory researchers carefully documented what became known as the "sadder but wiser" effect. In a highly influential laboratory study, Alloy and Abramson (1979) found that depressed and nondepressed students possessed very different opinions of their level of control over a series of lights in a laboratory contingency task. You might expect the pessimistically biased, depressed students to underestimate their degree of control over the lights. After all, most of us tend to assume that depressed people view the world in negatively biased ways. However, this is not what Alloy and Abramson observed. Instead, the depressed students reported highly *accurate* views of their degree of control over the experimental task. The biased ones were the nondepressed students, who greatly overestimated their degree of control. This study, along with many subsequent laboratory studies, led most researchers to conclude that depressed rather than nondepressed people see the world as it really is.

However, in the early 1990s, Dunning and Story (1991) pointed out that the laboratory judgment task used by Alloy and Abramson might not be telling the whole story about depression. They suggested that a more reasonable index of the accuracy of people's judgments could be obtained by asking people to make predictions about real, personally meaningful life events that could conceivably befall them in the future (e.g., getting placed on academic probation, getting dumped by a relationship partner, getting fired or demoted at work). When Dunning and Story compared people's predictions about the events (e.g., "I think that five of the ten bad things you asked me about will happen to me this semester") with the actual occurrence of the events over the course of the semester (e.g., "three of the ten bad things on your list actually happened to me this semester"), they observed results that were strikingly different from those of Alloy and Abramson. They found that it was actually the depressed people who were more optimistic! As Alloy and Abramson might have expected, the depressed people did make somewhat gloomy predictions about their futures. However, the actual futures of the depressed people were noticeably gloomier than the depressed people had predicted. In contrast, the futures of the nondepressed students were typically about as rosy as they had predicted.

Despite the rigorous nature of Alloy and Abramson's laboratory task, they may have drawn an inaccurate conclusion about the true relation between depression and judgment. Depression may actually foster optimism rather than accuracy or pessimism (see Pelham, 1991b, for additional evidence that depression is occasionally associated with optimism). Of course, Dunning and Story do not argue that depression is good for you. Depression is a leading cause of suicide and has many other negative consequences. Their point was that laboratory studies may have yielded a misleading answer to the specific question of how depression biases judgments and predictions. On the other hand, even if we assume that Dunning and Story's story about depression and judgment is the bottom line, it does not mean that Alloy and Abramson's research was uninformative. First, probably some real-world judgments bear a greater resemblance to Alloy and Abramson's contingency task than they do to Dunning and Story's prediction task. For these kinds of judgments, Alloy and Abramson may still be correct. Second, if we assume that one of the goals of research is to move toward greater and greater approximations of the truth, Alloy and Abramson's work played an extremely important role in revealing truths about depression by prompting a tremendous amount of research (including the research of Dunning and Story) on this important topic.

A similar example of an internally valid naturalistic study that convinced some people to rethink findings from the laboratory can be found in the research on temperature and aggression. The results of laboratory experiments involving direct manipulations of temperature have been surprisingly complex and somewhat inconsistent. For example, some experiments have revealed that increases in temperature lead to increases in aggression only when research participants have received positive rather than negative evaluations from the potential target of their aggressive behavior (Baron & Bell, 1976). Other experiments have revealed that increases in temperature increase aggression only to a point. (They suggest that the relation between temperature and aggression is curvilinear.)

In contrast to the mixed bag of findings that have been observed in the laboratory, field studies have consistently yielded much clearer and simpler findings. Specifically, most passive observational studies have revealed simple, linear relations between temperature and aggression. For example, among drivers in frequently sweltering Phoenix, Arizona, rates of aggressive horn honking at a stopped car increased as a direct function of temperature. Moreover, the increases were most pronounced among drivers who had their windows rolled down on hot days (and presumably didn't have the relief provided by air conditioning; Kenrick & MacFarlane, 1986). Similarly, in a large archival study of violent and nonviolent crime, Anderson (1987) observed that rates of hostile crimes such as murder, rape, and assault were higher in hotter cities than in cooler cities and were higher than usual during hotter quarters and hotter years within a given city. Moreover, rates of less violent crimes showed little or no increase as temperatures climbed. Similar findings have been observed in other natural settings. For example, in an archival analysis of over 800 major-league baseball games, Reifman, Larrick, and Fein (1991) found that pitchers were more likely to hit batters during games played on hot days. This tendency for hotter days to produce more "beanballs" appears to be linear: the hotter the day, the more likely pitchers are to throw at batters rather than at strike zones.

It is noteworthy that the participants who have been studied in naturalistic investigations such as these have never known that their aggressive behavior was the subject of psychological scrutiny. In lab experiments, however, it seems much more likely that some participants may have been able to guess that their aggressive behavior was the subject of psychological investigation (see Anderson, 1989). As we noted earlier, another reason that field experiments may yield better than usual information about causality is that they often can rule out third-variable concerns. In the case of research on temperature and aggression, for instance, we noted that we can confidently assume that aggression does *not* cause heat. In many other areas of research, bidirectionality is possible. For example, do high levels of self-esteem cause people to seek out favorable social feedback, or does favorable social feedback lead people to develop high self-esteem? Either causal account is plausible. Moreover, because temperature is a simple, objectively measurable environmental variable, it is probably a little easier than usual to disentangle the effects of temperature from the effects of naturally occurring confounds (such as unemployment rates or seasonal variations in testosterone levels) that might also account for the observed connection between temperature and aggression. For reasons such as these, we suspect that in comparison with lab experiments, carefully conducted naturalistic studies of temperature and aggression may be just as high in internal validity. That is, they may provide equally accurate information about the causal role of heat in aggression, even though they disagree with the results in the laboratory. In short, inconsistencies between experimental and correlational results do not mean that one result or the other needs to be discarded. These inconsistencies often reveal a more interesting story than one would learn from a reliance on one method or the other.

When causal claims seem reasonable in field research, the boost in external validity that comes from field settings makes for some very compelling research statements. Nonetheless, we want to make it clear that laboratory experiments still hold certain clear advantages over correlational or passive observational studies. First, recall that despite some interesting exceptions, laboratory experiments usually yield superior information about causality. Second, even when it comes to sensitive topics such as aggression, laboratory experiments may yield important insights into the psychological mechanisms that are responsible for a research finding documented in the field. For example, Rule, Taylor, and Dobbs (1987) conducted an experiment in which they asked people to complete ambiguously aggressive story stems under cool or hot working conditions. They found that, relative to cool and comfortable participants, their overheated participants generated story completions containing significantly more negative emotions, more themes of frustration, and more themes of aggression. These findings suggest that one specific route through which temperature leads to aggression is by making aggressive thoughts more *cognitively accessible* than usual. Needless to say, it would be hard to document this kind of thing in a passive observational study. To paraphrase Fisher, observations such as these have to be carefully planned in advance. As this example should also suggest, the most compelling way to make a solid case for a theory (e.g., a theory of heat and aggression) would be to make use of a wide variety of different methods and hope that they all converge on the same conclusion. Laboratory findings such as those of Rule et al. have helped researchers figure out the precise reasons why so many other researchers have found correlational evidence that heat fosters aggressive behavior. Thus, field research told researchers what they should try to understand, and the laboratory research helped them do exactly that.

As a final comparison between laboratory and naturalistic studies, we want to emphasize the fact that good, careful naturalistic studies are not good and careful just because they happen to be conducted outside the laboratory. Simply going to "the field" is no guarantee of *any* kind of validity, external or otherwise. Although it is often assumed that conducting a study in the field guarantees that the study will be high in external validity, this is not always the case. In principle, field settings can be just as narrow and delimiting as lab settings. The real world, after all, isn't simply one gigantic, homogeneous field (see Banaji & Crowder, 1989). As a case in point, consider a very creative field experiment on self-awareness and socially undesirable behavior. A good deal of theory and research suggests that self-awareness (the awareness of our personal identities as well as our internal ideals and standards) reduces the likelihood that people will engage in socially undesirable behaviors such as lying or cheating. Beaman, Klentz, Diener, and Svanum (1979) decided to test this idea by conducting a field experiment focusing on trick-or-treaters who had the opportunity to steal pieces of candy. As the Halloweeners were entering a home, Beaman et al. manipulated the kids' levels of self-awareness in two distinct ways—by asking some of the kids their names and by sometimes placing a mirror in front of the bowl of candy. Regardless of the kids' level of manipulated self-awareness, the adult who interacted with the kids always directed them to the bowl of candy, asked them to take only a *single* piece, and walked away. As illustrated in

Figure 7.5

Proportion of trick-or-treaters stealing candy as a function of anonymity and presence of mirror (from Beamen et al, 1979)

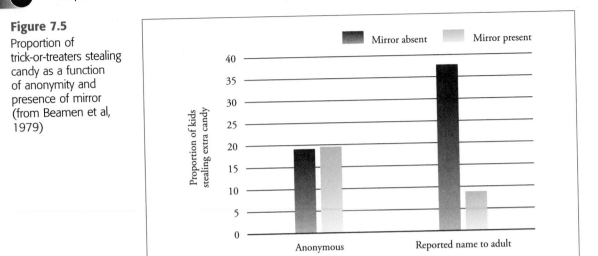

Figure 7.5, the kids who were least likely to take extra candy were those who were most likely to have been made highly self-aware. Specifically, among the kids who had been asked their names and who were also exposed to the mirror, only about 9 percent took extra candy. In contrast, among those who had been asked their names but who were not exposed to the mirror, almost 38 percent took extra candy. Among those who had not been asked their names, the presence of the mirror made no difference.

Although this clever study involved the real behavior of real kids in the real world, this does not guarantee that these results would generalize to the hundreds of different real situations in which self-awareness might be expected to influence behavior. This study simply shows that self-awareness *can* influence behavior in some instances. If you think about it, you'll realize that this is exactly what a laboratory study always shows you. It shows that certain variables can influence certain outcomes in certain situations, but this only begs the question of how often these variables do influence these outcomes and in how many different situations. From this perspective, assessing the generalizability of a research finding should be done by seeing just how well the finding really does generalize across people and situations, and this question can never be answered by a single study, regardless of its methodology. No matter where a set of findings occurs, the question of external validity has to do with the degree to which the findings can be obtained in a wide variety of different settings using a wide variety of sensible manipulations and measures. In the case of self-awareness, by the way, there is good evidence that self-awareness plays an important role in reducing the likelihood that people will behave dishonestly. In a wide variety of settings, self-awareness manipulations have had a potent effect on people's tendencies to behave dishonestly (e.g., see Diener & Wallbom, 1976). This is just one example of how a little study can advance a big idea.

Some other examples of how field studies can sometimes be more impressive than lab studies that make the same theoretical point include (a) Miyake et al.'s (2011) field experiment showing that a simple self-concept manipulation can substantially increase women's performance in college physics class, (b) Burger et al.'s (2005) field experiment showing that people are more likely than usual to help a stranger who appears to share their first name, and (c) Medvec and Gilovich's (2001) study of "counterfactuals" showing that Olympic bronze medalists appear to be much happier about their outcomes in an important sports competition than Olympic silver medalists.

THE "HOW-TO"S OF LABORATORY STUDIES

At this point, we hope that you have a clear sense of the methodological strengths and weaknesses of laboratory experiments. As you now know, laboratory experiments can yield information that is impossible to obtain using any other research method. Although we hope that you now have a keen appreciation of what laboratory experiments can do, we suspect that you have a lot less information about how laboratory experiments are done. That is, we have not yet discussed the nuts and bolts of how laboratory experiments are conducted. Some researchers have argued that whereas running a good laboratory study is a skill, running a *great* laboratory study is both a skill and an art. With this idea in mind, here are some of the skills you will need if you ever hope to create your own experimental masterpiece.

Setting the Stage

Many of the mistakes made by human beings are based on some combination of the optimistic bias and the planning fallacy. The optimistic bias refers to the fact that most people think that they will have better outcomes in life than is usually the case. For example, most college students think that they will contract fewer major illnesses in the future than will most other college students (Weinstein, 1980). Along similar lines, the planning fallacy is based loosely on the idea that most people think that most things they do will go more swimmingly than they actually do. Thus, most people underestimate the amount of time it will take them to complete a major task (e.g., writing a term paper, planning a wedding, digging a subway; Kahneman & Tversky, 1979). In the case of both the optimistic bias and the planning fallacy, planners often seem to assume that most aspects of a planned task will go exactly as they imagine in an ideal world. It should come as no surprise to you, then, that most people who are planning an experiment often fall prey to these two powerful biases. That is, most novice experimenters plan their experiments assuming that all of their procedures and measures will work in exactly the way they intended. This rarely happens! Instead, laboratory studies are a lot like complex theatrical productions. The experimenter has written a complex screenplay, designed a set, possibly hired a crew of actors (confederates), and then invited a group of, get this, *strangers* (who've never seen the script) to walk in and play the lead part. It would be ambitious to assume that everything will go off without a hitch during the first "showing" of an experiment.

For this reason, seasoned experimenters usually conduct one or more brief pilot tests before conducting a full-blown experiment. We discussed pilot tests in Chapter 4 in the context of writing questions. We noted that it is often good to give your survey questions to a small sample of participants to see if these participants interpret your measures as you intended. Pilot testing is of even greater use with complex laboratory experiments. It can allow you to identify potential holes in your cover story, find out that people are falling asleep in the middle of your computerized response latency task, or learn whether your primary manipulation is truly having the psychological consequences you intended. In short, pilot tests can help you identify almost anything that is wrong (or right) with your experiment.

As we mentioned previously, one way to maximize the chances that you benefit from a pilot test is to include a manipulation check. For example, if you are pilot testing an experiment to see if anxiety facilitates certain kinds of problem solving, you might wait until your participants have completed their assigned problem-solving task and then ask them how anxious they felt while they were performing the task. If your manipulation of anxiety is successful, you should find that, relative to the participants in the low-anxiety condition, those in the high-anxiety condition report having felt much more anxious. If they don't, you will need to look for either a more effective manipulation of anxiety or a more effective manipulation check.

Even if you do not run any pilot tests, it is always a good idea to include a manipulation check in your actual experiment. A failed study is more informative when it includes a manipulation check. For example, if your manipulation check for anxiety suggests that your manipulation was extremely effective but you observed no effects of your anxiety manipulation on problem solving, it would be safer than usual to conclude that anxiety has no effect on this particular form of problem solving. Nonetheless, despite their enormous advantages, one tricky aspect of manipulation checks is that they aren't always easy to perform. One of the biggest hurdles when conducting manipulation checks is the fact that participants may be either unwilling or unable to report on some of their experiences during an experiment (see Nisbett & Wilson, 1977). When this is the case, you might need to look for indirect ways of documenting that your manipulation created the psychological state that you intended (e.g., having blind judges decide how anxious participants appear to be, measuring anxiety by measuring people's galvanic skin response, etc.).

Alternately, if giving participants a manipulation check would get in the way of your experimental task, you might want to run a pilot test with the sole purpose of documenting the effectiveness of your manipulation. For instance, if you want to document that participants who are rehearsing an 8-digit number are more cognitively taxed than those who are not, you might conduct a pilot test in which you enact this manipulation while people attempt to perform a cognitively demanding signal-detection task. If the cognitively taxed participants have longer reaction times or make more errors than the participants in the control group, you will have independent evidence of the effectiveness of your manipulation of cognitive load. If they do not, it is probably time to go back to the drawing board and develop a new and improved manipulation.

Regardless of whether you include manipulation checks in any pilot tests you run, such preliminary studies can go a long way toward increasing the likelihood that your revised experiment will reveal something informative. Pilot tests are never as fun to conduct as the real thing. After all, they usually end up telling you more about what you were doing wrong than about what you were doing right. However, more than any other aspect of research preparation, pilot research can turn ordinary researchers into apparent geniuses. If you want to look like an experimental genius, remember the advice of Thomas Edison. Edison argued that "genius is 1% inspiration and 99% perspiration."

Rehearsing and Playing the Part

In addition to conducting pilot tests, there is usually one more thing you will need to do before you start running participants in your actual experiment. The main thing is to rehearse all your instructions and directions until you can run participants through your study like a true expert. Practicing the entire experiment a few times on a friend, a graduate student collaborator, or your academic adviser will help you identify and correct any weaknesses in your delivery. Because one of us often forgets to tell his students—especially his best students—that experimentation is a complex skill that must be practiced and mastered, he recently devised a list of do's and don'ts that he shares with any beginning student who comes to work in his lab. Here, then, is our adaptation of these six commandments of being a good experimenter:

Commandment 1: Be Suave   Dress and behave professionally. The only cues that your participants have about your expertise are the ones that you give them during the course of your 5- to 50-minute interaction. Your participants do not know that you have a master's degree in engineering or that you were on the dean's list for 23 consecutive quarters, and so you must let them know that you are a professional by speaking and, most of all, *dressing* professionally. In graduate school, one of us dressed very informally. He wore t-shirts and blue jeans to his graduate classes, to professional conferences, and even to his cousin's wedding. But after experimenting with his dress as an experimenter, he quickly realized that, unlike his colleagues, his participants took him seriously only when he looked serious on the outside. Thus, after a few of his participants treated him like a kid, he began to dress like a grown-up. He quickly found that dressing more professionally made most participants take him much more seriously. When you dress the part, your data won't magically begin to confirm all of your predictions and reveal great psychological truths, but your participants will definitely be more likely to take you seriously.[5]

Commandment 2: Be Nice   It is important to be professional, but it's also important to be polite and friendly. Even if a participant is rude, you should try to maintain a pleasant demeanor throughout the experiment (while keeping careful notes about the participant's rudeness). Does this mean you should let rude participants bully you into doing the experiment their way? Absolutely not. Be polite, but keep the experiment running the way it was designed to be run. If an obstinate participant absolutely refuses to comply, then you may either (1) continue the experiment and make a note of the fact that the participant failed to follow instructions or (2) stop the experiment and give the participant full credit for taking part in the study. Even if people aren't very likable, they have the right to refuse to participate in a study.

Commandment 3: Be Educated   Know your experiment well. It's hard to run a good experiment if you don't know what you are predicting or why you are predicting it. If you are going to pick up on the subtle things that may be going wrong in a study, you must know how things should look if the experiment is going right. If you don't know your experiment, do some homework or talk with someone who knows more about it (e.g., your advisor) to get a better understanding of what should be happening in the study.

Commandment 4: Be Honest   One of the dangers of knowing your study is that knowing exactly how your participant *should* respond opens the door to the Pandora's box of experimenter bias (see Chapter 5). Nothing is worse than an experiment that works for the wrong reasons, and if you know your hypothesis well, it is possible that you may let your participant know in subtle ways how you would like him or her to respond. For example, if you give verbal instructions or clues about how the experiment works, it is always possible that you may give better instructions or clues to the experimental group than to the control group. You do not always have to be blind to the condition of your participants to avoid experimenter bias, but you should be aware of the subtle ways in which you can bias a participant's responses so that you can work hard to treat all participants exactly the same way (except, of course, for the delivery of your manipulation). The easiest way to do this is to have a script that you stick to very closely during the experiment. After you have run 20 or 30 lab experiments, you may find that you no longer need a script to be suave, nice, smart, and honest, but during your first few years of experimentation, a script is a good idea.

Commandment 5: Be a Good Liar   If you are running a deception study, remember that you can never blow your cover until the experiment is over. Use mechanical props to help aid you in your deception if necessary (in some studies, one of us has played tape-recorded conversations between himself and a fictitious participant in the next room to be sure that the real participant believed the fictitious person was actually present). In addition, if a participant expresses suspicion about your cover story, try to think on your feet and answer his or her concern without stepping out of the imaginary world that you have tried to create. For example, "Well, it is a little strange that your partner has exactly the same birthday as you, but it's probably not as unusual as it seems because we usually try to pair people up who are as close as possible in age. In this case, it looks like your ages happen to be identical."

Commandment 6: Be Attentive   If you really care about your experiment, you will watch your participants the way you watch a person you care about deeply. If your participant appears apathetic or confused, you will try to find out why, and you will make a written record of this. If your participant shows up drunk and smothered in mayonnaise—or stone sober and wearing a chicken suit—you may want to make a polite excuse to end the experiment early. This, too, is the kind of unusual thing you should carefully document. In short, you should pay close attention to your participant, and you should try to put yourself in his or her shoes so that if something is going seriously wrong, you can fix it before your next participant arrives. Of course, this also includes keeping careful notes on the behavior of any participant who does not appear to be behaving normally. That is, just as you would want to make a note about the behavior of an unusually rude participant, you'd also want to make careful notes about the behavior of a highly suspicious, mildly inebriated, or downright confused participant. Later on, you and your adviser or colleagues might want to make a careful decision about whether to use the data from people who have not followed your directions. A key point here is that you should make any such decisions *before* you peek at a participants' data. Kicking a *slightly* rude person out of your experiment after the fact because her data were not friendly to your hypothesis is a serious potential form of experimenter bias, and you must guard against this.

When the Study Is Done: Replicate as Needed

We have mentioned that studies are always more convincing if you replicate your findings, but we would be remiss if we did not repeat this point. We might even be slightly more remiss if we did not repeat it again. Studies are always more convincing if you replicate your findings. In truth, once you have gone to all the trouble to find just the right manipulation, just the right dependent measure, just the right delivery in your experiment, and just the result you expected, you might feel a strong desire to stop—but this is the last thing you should do. There is always a good chance that all your "just right" procedures are "completely wrong." It is always possible that you have happened upon the one particular set of circumstances under which your hypothesis is true. If you recall our discussion of artifacts, you know that you can only find out whether artifacts are at work in your research by trying to replicate your findings using different samples or procedures. In keeping with his contextual approach to research, McGuire (1973) expressed a very similar sentiment about experimental research in social psychology. After noting that almost all research hypotheses are both correct and incorrect (under different conditions), McGuire wrote:

> If the experiment does not come out "right," then the researcher does not say that the hypothesis is wrong but rather that something was wrong with the experiment, and he corrects and revises it, perhaps by using more appropriate subjects, by strengthening the independent variable manipulation, by blocking off extraneous response possibilities, or by setting up a more appropriate context, etc. Sometimes he may have such continuous bad luck that he finally gives up the demonstration because the phenomenon proves to be so elusive as to be beyond his ability to demonstrate. The more persistent of us typically manage at last to get control of the experimental situation so that

we can reliably demonstrate the hypothesized relationship. But note that what the experiment tests is not whether the hypothesis is true but rather whether the experimenter is a sufficiently ingenious stage manager to produce in the laboratory conditions which demonstrate that an obviously true hypothesis is correct. In our graduate programs in social psychology, we try to train people who are good enough stage managers so that they can create in the laboratory simulations of realities in which the obvious correctness of our hypothesis can be demonstrated.

McGuire's point was not that research is a bankrupt enterprise or that experiments do not reveal any truths. Instead, he was mainly making the point that the simplistic and pristine image that we get of research in journal articles is often a far cry from what actually happens in the lab. In fairness to both McGuire and experimental social psychology, we think that to some extent researchers have finally begun to take his advice about research. Researchers still work hard to confirm their hypotheses, and they are still more likely to interpret failed experiments as failures of technique rather than failures of their hypotheses. However, social psychology (like many other areas of psychology) has become much more of a contextual enterprise over the past few decades. Instead of simply predicting that two variables are related, contemporary psychologists are much more likely to try to identify the conditions under which an effect *does* and *does not* turn out to be true. In statistical terms, many of the hypotheses that psychologists test these days are hypotheses about interactions.

Another trend that appears to have taken place over the past couple of decades is that major journals that publish research papers that rely on experimental methods rarely publish papers unless these papers contain two or more experiments that demonstrate consistent support for a hypothesis. We touched on this point when we discussed a series of behavioral priming studies published by Bargh, Chen, and Burrows (1996). Bargh et al. conducted four different laboratory studies showing that primes can have an unconscious influence on mundane behavior. Of course, there are different ways to be a good at replicating. Papers often make the most convincing case for a phenomenon when they include data from both experimental and nonexperimental studies. For instance, a tightly controlled laboratory study might be used to establish the causal nature of an effect that might then be replicated in a survey study or field study. By taking advantage of "multiple methods" to test a single hypothesis, researchers address the question of artifacts head on.

As a good example of this second approach, consider a pair of studies on the allure of secret relationships. If you have ever had the feeling that there is something exciting, almost erotic, about keeping a secret, you are not alone. Research on the paradoxical effects of thought suppression suggests that trying to suppress secret or forbidden thoughts can actually increase our obsession with these thoughts. The harder we try not to think about a scrumptious but forbidden bowl of chocolate ice cream, the more preoccupied we may become with it. Wegner, Lane, and Dimitri (1994) felt that this might be true of secret passions for other people as well as secret passions for things like ice cream. To test this idea, they first conducted a couple of correlational studies in which they asked people about the degree to which various past romantic relationships had been secret. In addition, they asked people about the degree to which they were still obsessively preoccupied with those past relationships. The more their participants reported that a past relationship had been a secret one, the more these participants reported that they were still preoccupied with the relationship. Of course, nonexperimental findings such as this are consistent with the idea that secrecy intensifies preoccupation, but they are also consistent with the idea that preoccupation somehow intensifies people's memories of the secrecy of a past relationship—or that some third variable (e.g., whether one's parents disapproved of the relationship) is associated with both secrecy and preoccupation.

Wegner et al. were aware of such criticisms, and thus they replicated their correlational findings in a laboratory experiment. Specifically, they brought college students to their laboratory in groups of four people (two women and two men), and they paired each participant with an opposite-sex teammate in a card game. Before the game began, the members of one of the two mixed-sex teams were always instructed to play the game using a form of "natural nonverbal communication." More specifically, the members of one couple were always told to maintain foot-to-foot contact during the game in an effort to transmit useful information to each other. The members of the other couple were given no such instructions. (In fact, they were seated far enough apart—at a rectangular table—that they couldn't have maintained any foot-to-foot contact even if they had spontaneously decided to.)

Importantly, the couples who were randomly assigned to the footsie condition were further divided into (1) those who were instructed to keep their footplay a secret from the other team and (2) those who were told that it was fine if the other team knew what they were doing. After the couples had been allowed to play the game for about ten minutes, the male and female participants were separated, and all the participants were asked to report, among other things, their level of romantic attraction (1) to their opposite-sex partner and (2) to their opposite-sex opponent. Figure 7.6 contains a summary of some of the major findings of the experiment. As you can see, those who secretly

Figure 7.6

Reported attraction to a partner and to an opponent after playing secret or nonsecret footsie with partner (from Wegner, Lane, & Dimitri, 1994)

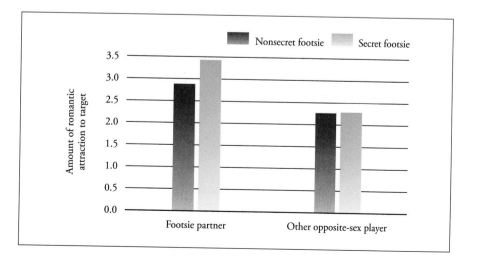

played footsie with their partner reported being more attracted to their partner than did those who openly played footsie with their partner. Moreover, this increase in attraction was directed specifically toward their footsie partner. Participants' reported level of attraction to their opposite-sex opponents was not influenced by the secrecy manipulation. Together with the findings from their two nonexperimental studies, this experimental replication suggests that Wegner et al. have probably latched onto an important truth underlying secret versus open romantic relationships.

SUMMARY

Laboratory studies are among the most powerful methods available to research psychologists, because they help pin down causal relations (i.e., they are high in internal validity). True experiments make use of both (1) experimental manipulation and (2) random assignment to conditions. In combination, these two techniques help to eliminate person confounds. In addition, the tight control provided by laboratory environments also helps to eliminate procedural confounds and to reduce noise. Just as important, laboratory experiments provide a window on events that few, if any, other approaches to research can provide. The main drawback of laboratory experiments is that they often lack realism. Many of the procedures and measures used regularly in laboratory experiments are highly contrived and simply do not exist in the real world. Nevertheless, by designing studies that are high in experimental realism, experimenters can often minimize concerns about the artificiality of lab experiments. Finally, experiments can only be high in experimental realism when they are conducted carefully. We closed this chapter by reviewing some of the practical issues one must consider when conducting laboratory studies. We also noted the value of conducting research that uses multiple methods, because this approach can address the concerns of artificiality in laboratory studies by demonstrating that one's laboratory results travel well to the real world.

STUDY QUESTIONS

1. In your own words, define and distinguish between the three confounds that are most applicable to laboratory experiments (person confounds, procedural confounds, and operational confounds). What can be done to reduce each of these types of confounds? Which of these confounds is typically eliminated by the use of random assignment? What can be done to address the other confounds?

2. Define and distinguish between confounds, artifacts, and noise. Which of these three problems is typically reduced or eliminated by (a) choosing a homogeneous rather than a heterogeneous sample, (b) using random assignment, (c) using random selection, (d) creating experimental conditions that differ along only one meaningful dimension, and (e) maximizing experimental realism in a study? How do these three concepts relate to internal and external validity?

3. A health psychologist is interested in how peer pressure influences risky health behaviors (e.g., becoming a smoker, having unprotected sex). She hopes to design a lab experiment on this topic. Explain why it would probably be difficult and/or unethical to design a lab experiment on this topic that is high in mundane realism. Now explain why it might be a lot easier to design experiments on

this topic that are high in experimental realism.

4. It is often said that there is a conflict or trade-off between internal and external validity.

Why is this said? What strategies can be pursued to minimize such conflicts?

NOTES

1. Although this simple definition is very popular, it is not technically correct to equate "randomness" with "equal chances." One could assign men to one condition and women to another condition. Because everyone has a roughly "equal chance" of being a male or a female, this could be construed as fitting our definition of random. Alternately, one might assign participants to conditions based on whether their performance on a psychology mid-term put them in the top or the bottom half of the grade distribution. Thus, a person in this study would have an "equal chance" of being in one condition or the other. Although both of these methods of assignment give respondents an equal chance of being in the different conditions, neither qualify as random. To be truly random, the assignment must be made independently of any known feature of the respondents. Thus, one should not assign participants to conditions "at random," based on their gender, their grades, their height, their IQ, or any other known attributes. The best way to accomplish this is to use a device such as a fair coin or a table of random numbers. Because coins and random number tables do not know anything about your participants, they are very good devices for assigning people randomly (i.e., *arbitrarily*) to conditions.

2. By subliminal priming, we mean presenting words (or other stimuli) to people very, very briefly and following the briefly presented words immediately with some kind of mask. In Devine's case this meant presenting words for 80 milliseconds (a little less than 1/12th of a second) and following the words immediately with a series of random letters. The important thing about subliminal priming is

that people are unaware of having seen the priming words (and cannot tell you what the words were). Nonetheless, the priming words often influence people's judgments in subsequent tasks.

3. Also, technically speaking, this is not a true experiment. This is because one of the independent variables was measured rather than manipulated. However, the basic point remains. It's much easier to combine multiple independent variables in experiments than in other research designs.

4. As we will discuss in Chapter 8, a factorial study that crossed randomly assigned feedback with measured popularity would be a *person by treatment quasi-experiment* rather than a true experiment. This is because popularity would have to be measured and only feedback could be determined by using random assignment.

5. There is at least one interesting exception to the general rule that experimenters should dress professionally. In a study of terror management (a defensive process that people engage in after having been asked to think about their own mortality), Simon et al. (1997) directly manipulated whether their experimenter dressed (and acted) in a highly formal or informal fashion. Simon et al. found that participants who had been asked to contemplate their own mortality made defensive judgments (e.g., derogating a person who expressed negative opinions of the United States) only when the experimenter dressed informally. Apparently, highly formal experimenters induce a deliberative, rational form of information processing that short-circuits certain kinds of primitive defensive mechanisms.

Experience Carefully Exploited: Quasi-Experimental Research Designs

But Daniel resolved not to defile himself with the royal food and wine, and he asked the chief official for permission not to defile himself in this way ... but the official told Daniel, "I am afraid of my lord the king, who has assigned your food and drink. Why should he see you looking worse than the other young men your age? The king would then have my head because of you." Daniel then said ... "Please test your servants for ten days: Give us nothing but vegetables to eat and water to drink. Then compare our appearance with that of the young men who eat the royal food and treat us in accordance with what you see." So he agreed to this and tested them for ten days.

—Daniel 1:8–14

ONE VERY OLD STORY

Unless you are well versed in both the ancient book of Daniel and the modern logic of quasi-experiments, you may not be in the best position to appreciate the important methodological lesson behind Daniel's proposal to this chief official of the Babylonian King, Nebuchadnezzar. In the interest of learning as much as possible from the Israelites he had conquered, King Nebuchadnezzar brought a group of scholarly young Jews into his palace for some intellectual discussions. The king rolled out the red carpet by providing these young men from the enemy camp with the same royal food and wine that he provided to his own royal servants. It seems safe to assume that Nebuchadnezzar would have been annoyed to learn that these young men refused to eat his royal food (because it wasn't kosher). This put the king's chief official in a difficult position. He really liked these young men, and he personally didn't mind it if they wanted to pass up on all these royal delicacies. However, if he allowed these young men to eat nothing but the rough equivalent of bread and water, he figured they would soon become unhealthy. At this point, the king would demand to know what was going on, heads would roll, and the chief official's head might roll first. Daniel proposed a simple quasi-experiment designed to address the chief official's worries about their highly restricted diet, and you now know why.

So Daniel was apparently a pretty smart cookie (despite the fact that his diet never included any). But would Daniel's proposal have differed if he had known about the beauty and power of the experimental method? Could he have proposed a more sophisticated design? Perhaps he should have proposed the following test instead:

> Please test your servants for ten days: *randomly assign half of them to receive vegetables to eat and water to drink, and assign half of them to receive royal food to eat and wine to drink*. Then have trained judges who know not of the experimental manipulation compare the appearances of the servants in the vegetable-and-water lot with those in the royal-food-and-wine lot. Let conventional statistical tests be used to determine if these two groups differ from each other, and, verily I say unto thee, treat us in accordance with the results of these analyses.

Although this design may *sound* more sophisticated than Daniel's design, it is actually what we sometimes like to call an ill-conceived, or *Dumas*, design. (It's pronounced Dew-*moss*, but if you add the letters "b" and "s" in certain strategic locations, you'll see what we mean.) This design would be useless as a test of Daniel's position because his position was tightly linked to his deeply held religious beliefs about diet. Daniel wasn't arguing that vegetables and water build better bodies than royal food and wine. Instead, he was proposing that God would keep him and his friends healthy *even if* they ate only vegetables and water. This story thus illustrates one of the most important reasons why people don't always conduct true experiments to test important ideas. They often don't because they often can't.

Before we discuss exactly why researchers can't always conduct true experiments, let's pause to appreciate the research design that Daniel actually proposed. His proposed design is a pretty good example of a **quasi-experiment**. Quasi-experiments are research designs in which researchers have only partial control over their independent variables. Strictly speaking, this means that participants are assigned to one or more conditions in a study by some means other than random assignment. This is what makes a study a quasi-experiment, and quasi-experiments are what this chapter is all about. After reviewing some of the considerations that lead researchers to conduct quasi-experiments, we will explain the logic of conducting and interpreting quasi-experiments. As we will show, the use of quasi-experimental designs can sometimes pose problems for a study's internal validity. However, these problems can often be addressed by identifying meaningful control groups that test for the influence of possible confounds. When threats to internal validity are carefully addressed, quasi-experiments become extremely useful research tools because, relative to true experiments, quasi-experiments typically provoke fewer concerns about external validity.

WHY QUASI-EXPERIMENTS?

As Cook and Campbell (1979) put it, quasi-experiments are "experiments that have treatments, outcome measures, and experimental units, but do not use random assignment to create the comparisons from which the treatment-caused change is inferred." As an example of one common kind of quasi-experiment, consider a hypothetical study of instructor teaching styles and student performance. Suppose that at the end of a ten-week statistics course, a researcher gives a standardized quiz to the students of two different statistics professors, Professor Simone and Professor Hardine. If Professor Simone's students outperform Professor Hardine's students, it might be because Professor Simone has an exceptional teaching style. However, it could also be because Professor Simone has a reputation for being exceptionally difficult. Only the brightest and most motivated students may have the gumption to sign up for his course in the first place. As this example illustrates, quasi-experiments often raise concerns about internal validity because person confounds might be causing the appearance of effects that would disappear if random assignment were used. Nevertheless, as we hope to demonstrate in this chapter, quasi-experiments can be quite effective at identifying causes and effects when researchers pay careful attention to potential confounds.

For now, we simply point out that quasi-experiments are often the method of choice among researchers who wish to maximize both internal and external validity. One of the primary reasons for this is that true experiments are often impossible to conduct. In other words, all else being equal, possible studies are to be preferred over impossible ones. To illustrate, it simply is not possible to randomly assign people to be male or female, but we know that sex and gender play tremendously important roles in human social behavior. Thus, we often study gender even though we cannot manipulate it. Similarly, it is not possible to manipulate natural disasters, the presence or absence of motorcycle helmet laws, or the attitudinal similarity of romantic partners. Nevertheless, these variables have some extremely important consequences, and so we don't allow our inability to study them using random assignment to stand in the way of studying them at all. On a closely related note, some topics that *can* be studied experimentally are still very difficult to study experimentally. Experimentation sometimes requires equipment and resources that many researchers cannot afford (such as computers, fMRI magnets, particle accelerators, and royal food and wine). Sometimes we are forced to abandon "experience carefully planned" in favor of the observations that are provided by nature.

On top of all this, even when random assignment could be done, in many instances, it *shouldn't* be done. For ethical reasons, many potentially informative manipulations that could be performed in principle will be avoided in practice. For example, if we really wanted to know more about the causes of AIDS, lung cancer, or heart disease, we could probably make some pretty rapid progress by choosing a group of research participants and exposing a randomly assigned half of them to HIV, asbestos, or diets extremely high in saturated fats. Clearly, there are ethical limitations on what researchers can study using the experimental method. This is true for studies of psychological as well as physical outcomes. If researchers manipulated psychological variables that are thought to influence physical well-being (e.g., social support during bereavement, psychological stress during pregnancy), they could be randomly assigning some people to conditions that lead to serious health problems. Careful, longitudinal studies of pregnancy, for example, have shown that women who experience high levels of stress during pregnancy are more likely than usual to give birth to premature or low birth weight babies (e.g., see Lobel, Dunkel-Schetter, & Scrimshaw, 1992; and see Taylor, Repetti, & Seeman, 1994, for a general review). When it comes to important life outcomes involving physical health, Mother Nature's cruelest manipulations are best left to Mother Nature. Ethical concerns also come into play in the study of sensitive, socially relevant topics such as stereotyping, prejudice, intergroup relations, and aggression. Consider, for example, trying to manipulate the degree to which White people hold intolerant versus egalitarian attitudes about ethnic minorities. Even if such a thing were experimentally feasible, it certainly would be unethical. Few experimental psychologists would feel comfortable creating a group of racists.

KINDS OF QUASI-EXPERIMENTS

To summarize thus far, quasi-experiments are often the design of choice over true experiments for the simple reason that quasi-experiments can often be conducted when true experiments cannot. The fact that people often conduct quasi-experiments when it is impossible or unethical to conduct true experiments might tempt you to think of the quasi-experiment as the cubic zirconium of the methodological world, but nothing could be further from the truth.[1] Quasi-experiments are better thought of as hybrid designs that combine many of the desirable features of both experimental and nonexperimental research designs. Sometimes quasi-experiments do this by bringing measured rather than manipulated variables to the laboratory, and at other times they do so by allowing researchers to investigate a naturally occurring event that approximates an experimental manipulation. Another way to say this is that there are different kinds of quasi-experiments. In this chapter we focus predominantly on the two most commonly used quasi-experimental designs. We refer to these as **person-by-treatment quasi-experiments** and **natural experiments**.

Person-by-Treatment Quasi-Experiments

In social, personality, and clinical psychology, the most common kind of quasi-experiment is probably the person-by-treatment quasi-experiment. Person-by-treatment quasi-experiments are designs in which the researcher *measures* at least one independent variable and *manipulates* at least one other independent variable. Thus, person-by-treatment quasi-experiments almost always take place in the laboratory, and researchers who use this design always use random assignment to get experimental control over at least one of the independent variables. The only catch is that they also measure at least one other independent variable (e.g., self-esteem, extraversion, depression). For example, a clinical researcher who is interested in depression might identify patients at a clinic who are interested in taking part in laboratory research. Participants qualify for the study only if they clearly do or do not meet the diagnostic criteria for a major depressive episode. Depression is thus a measured independent variable. However, once depressed and nondepressed people arrive at the laboratory, they might be asked to perform an experimental task designed to put them in either a positive or a negative mood. Importantly, participants are randomly assigned to this experimental condition, independent of their level of depression. The dependent measure might be the kind of explanation people offer for negative life events (e.g., being fired from a job, being rejected or ignored by a friend). If the results of this hypothetical study resemble the results of real quasi-experimental studies of depression, we might find that depressed and nondepressed participants explain negative events differently (i.e., depressed people blame themselves more than nondepressed people do) *only* when participants are in an experimentally induced negative mood.

A real example of a person-by-treatment quasi-experiment is a study by Johnson, Richeson, and Finkel (2011). Johnson et al. were interested in a rarely studied form of stigma, namely being a poor or even middle class student enrolled in an elite university (Northwestern) where the majority of students come from high income families. Johnson et al. did not believe that students from poor or middle class families walked around every moment of their college lives feeling out of place at Northwestern. Instead they hypothesized that less wealthy students' feelings of inferiority or not "fitting in" would arise mainly when the students were focused on academic issues. Finally, they didn't think students would have an easy time articulating their feelings of unease, so they relied on indirect measures of "ego depletion" as their dependent variables. In one study, their indirect measure was how much trouble people had resisting candy (M&Ms and Twizzlers) during an ostensible taste test. In the study on which we'll focus here, the indirect measure was how long it took people to complete a computer-administered Stroop interference task (much like the one discussed in Appendix 3). The logic of using this task is that if people become ego-depleted by wrestling with subtle feelings of inferiority, they might have more trouble than usual inhibiting the automatic, overlearned tendencies that produce interference in the Stroop task. So Johnson et al. *measured* income and *manipulated* the topic (academic or non-academic) about which their participants had to make a recorded speech. As expected, Johnson et al. observed income differences on the Stroop interference task (such that poorer students showed larger interference effects) only after students had just been talking about an academic topic. In the control condition, the two income groups did not differ at all.

In social and personality psychology, researchers often do this kind of thing by **prescreening** people on an individual-difference measure prior to running their laboratory study. At universities, this initial prescreening session often happens in introductory psychology classes. The advantage of measuring the individual-difference variable in a pretest (during which people respond to many different measures) is that by the time people make it to the lab for the quasi-experiment, they are unlikely to have any guesses about which individual-difference measure this particular quasi-experimenter is studying. Researchers who go to the trouble to pretest often use these pretest scores to identify two or more **extreme groups**. Extreme groups are groups of people taken from the upper and lower ends of the distribution of an individual-difference measure. The idea behind creating extreme groups is to create categories of research participants who closely resemble the other members of their own groups on the dimension of interest but who differ greatly from the members of the *other* group. For instance, a researcher might use pretest data on a well-validated self-esteem measure to identify groups of people who score in the top or bottom 25 percent of a distribution of self-esteem scores. In this way, the researcher creates two groups that can be considered qualitatively different from each other. Notice that this would not be true if the researcher created groups by identifying people in the top or bottom half (i.e., top or bottom 50 percent) of the total distribution of scores. This second procedure, known as a **median split**, was once a popular technique. Researchers who used this technique simply labeled those above the median as "high" and those below the median as "low." They then treated this categorical variable like a manipulated independent variable in their statistical analyses. For instance, a researcher who used a median split might compare people who scored high versus low in extraversion to see if the group who scored high on the measure of extraversion sat closer to a confederate, wore flashier clothes, or spoke up more often in a group discussion. This is a very easy way to see if an individual difference variable predicts behavior, but it is methodologically crude. The problem with the median split approach is that the people who fall very near the cutoff score for the two groups (e.g., those who fall either barely below or barely above the median score) are much more similar to one another than they are to the extreme members of their own groups (e.g., those with extraversion scores at the tenth and 90th percentiles). Thus, a lot of information is lost when researchers create categories using a median split. (Incidentally, this problem is highly similar to a problem we discussed in Chapter 4. When it comes to measuring most psychological traits, continuous scales are generally superior to dichotomous scales.) For this reason, among others, contemporary researchers usually steer away from the use of median splits in favor of the extreme groups approach.

Having said all this, we should note that there are times when researchers are forced to resort to some variation on a median split approach. For example, in the Johnson et al. (2011) studies just discussed, income data were highly skewed. In this case, this meant that about half of the Northwestern University students they pretested fell into the top category on their five-category income measure (based on the U.S. Census measure). For this reason, Johnson et al. simply created two income groups for most of their analyses: a wealthy group (the top income group) and a "not wealthy" group (all four of the other income groups). In this particular case, it is important to note that the researchers had no *a priori* reason to expect middle class students to differ meaningfully from poor students. If they had, this approach could have substantially reduced statistical power relative to a continuous (or extreme groups) approach to defining income. In fact, doing a median split probably *did* reduce statistical power in this specific study, but sometimes reducing power is preferable to (a) drawing inferences based on very small numbers of people or (b) allowing one or two people with really extreme scores to play a disproportionate role in your findings (as can sometimes happen with highly skewed data).

When researchers are able to make use of extreme groups in person-by-treatment quasi-experiments (with a substantial sample size in both extreme groups), you might worry that they will not learn anything about people in the middle of the distribution. It is certainly true that you do not learn much about people that you do not study. However, in most instances, it is pretty safe to assume that people who possess a medium amount of an attitude or personality trait will respond to treatments in "medium amounts" when compared with people who score at the extremes. The advantage of using only extreme groups in quasi-experiments has to do with *test sensitivity* or the statistical power to detect real effects if they exist. Most researchers feel that if any effects are to be found, they will usually find them using the extreme groups method. On the other hand, if researchers do not find any effects using extreme groups, it is usually unlikely that effects will be found at the center of the distribution. This rationale allows researchers to conduct quasi-experiments using a smaller number of people (pulled from the extremes) than they would need if they were to study people across the full range of their individual-difference measure. This is particularly important if a laboratory manipulation is difficult, expensive, or time consuming. Thus, there are usually some simple, pragmatic reasons to use extreme groups in quasi-experiments. Incidentally, choosing extreme groups is the rough equivalent of what true experimenters almost always do when they manipulate variables in the lab. For instance, if you were manipulating temperature to see if people behave more aggressively than usual when it is hot, it would *not* usually be wise to create ten or 12 different temperature conditions. Instead, you'd probably just settle on a single comfortable and a single uncomfortable temperature. If a critic had good theoretical reason to believe that medium levels of a variable (like temperature or self-esteem) would yield effects that you had not originally anticipated, then nothing would be holding him or her back from replicating your quasi-experiment and adding a middle group to the mix.

To illustrate a person-by-treatment study that used extreme groups, consider a laboratory study of attitude change by Swann, Pelham, and Chidester (1988; Study 1). These researchers wanted to change the attitudes of people who were highly certain of their opinions. Previous research suggested that this would be a very tall order. Unlike people who aren't so sure of what they think, people who are highly certain of their opinions typically resist other people's efforts to change their opinions. These researchers suspected that it might be possible to turn this resistance to an advantage in some persuasion settings. This particular laboratory study focused on female students at the University of Texas. *All* the women in the study were selected because they possessed relatively traditional sex-role attitudes. However, some were highly certain of their conservative attitudes, and some were much less certain. Notice that women were *not* randomly assigned to have different levels of self-certainty. Although it might be possible, in principle, to manipulate self-certainty, this study treated self-certainty as an individual-difference variable. Thus, self-certainty was measured in a pretest, and participants were categorized as high or low in self-certainty before being brought to the laboratory for an experimental manipulation.

In one experimental condition, these "old-fashioned" women were exposed to a common persuasion technique. Namely, they were asked a series of leading questions that subtly encouraged them to make relatively liberal statements (e.g., "Why do you think women make better bosses than men?" "What do you like best about men who are sensitive to others?"). Because these women were asked to adopt a view that was different from their own, Swann et al. expected them to adopt more liberal attitudes—*but only when they originally weren't very sure of their attitudes*. In the other experimental condition, participants were exposed to a paradoxical persuasion technique. Specifically, they were asked a series of extremely conservative leading questions (e.g., "Why do you think men always make better bosses than women?" "Why do you sympathize with the feelings of some men that women are better kept barefoot and pregnant?"). Because these questions implied an *extremely* conservative position, Swann et al. felt that participants who knew exactly where they stood would actively resist the premises of the questions (e.g., "Well, I'm not exactly a radical feminist, but it makes me mad when men treat women like they were put here on earth to make babies!"). Thus, by working hard to make it clear that they disagreed with the radically conservative positions implied in these extreme questions, these highly self-certain participants would have to take a stand in a slightly liberal direction. Having done so, they should decide that they were a little more liberal than they had once thought (see Bem, 1967; Festinger & Carlsmith, 1959).

This study supported Swann et al.'s predictions, and Figure 8.1 summarizes the main findings. As you can see, the effects of the two different

Figure 8.1

Effects of self-certainty and persuasion technique on attitude change (from Swann, Pelham, & Chidester, 1988)

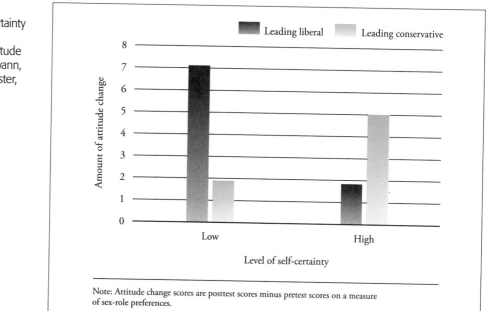

Note: Attitude change scores are posttest scores minus pretest scores on a measure of sex-role preferences.

persuasion techniques depended on who was being persuaded. Among the women who were uncertain of their opinions, those exposed to the conventional (leading liberal) persuasion technique became more liberal, and those exposed to the paradoxical (leading conservative) technique showed little change. On the other hand, among the women who were highly certain of their opinions, the opposite pattern was observed. Those who were asked leading liberal questions showed little attitude change, and those who were asked leading conservative questions became more liberal.

Many attitude and self-concept studies make use of designs very much like this one. Researchers who conduct these studies expect different *persons* (i.e., people with different attitudes, personalities, or self-conceptions) to respond differently to different *treatments* (i.e., different experimental manipulations)—thus the name "person-by-treatment" quasi-experiment. As another example of this kind of quasi-experiment, consider a hypothetical study of how people's self-concepts influence their choice of social interaction partners. Suppose you arrange for your participants to help you with some "marketing research" by playing a game of skill and hand-eye coordination with a stranger (actually a confederate). Furthermore, suppose that you make certain that your real participants always overhear a conversation between the confederate and the experimenter during a break in the action. Specifically, suppose you randomly assign your participants either to hear the confederate evaluate them positively ("Wow, she seemed really athletic; I guess this study was right up her alley") or negatively ("I guess this study wasn't much fun for her; she doesn't seem very athletic"). Which type of feedback would your participants prefer? At first blush, it seems obvious. It seems that participants would prefer the positive feedback because we all like to hear people say nice things about us. Wouldn't you rather hang out with someone who thinks you're athletic than with someone who thinks you're athletically challenged?

According to *self-verification theory*, it depends. A person's preference for positive or negative feedback should depend not only on the favorability of the feedback but also upon the self-concept of the person receiving the feedback. In the case of this hypothetical quasi-experiment, it should depend on the favorability of the athletic self-views of the people who overhear the comment. Self-verification theory is a self-consistency theory (in the same family as cognitive dissonance theory). One of the interesting predictions of self-verification theory is that people should prefer to associate with other people who view them the same way they view themselves. This seems pretty straightforward, but self-verification theory takes an extreme view and argues that people with negative self-views will actually choose to hear negative rather than positive feedback when it is consistent with their own self-views. Thus, self-verification theory predicts that people who perceive themselves as unathletic will express more interest in interacting with the confederate when this person evaluates them negatively rather than positively. Of course, the opposite should be true for people who believe that they are highly athletic. They should express more interest in interacting with the confederate when this person evaluates them positively rather than negatively. In studies very much like this one, Swann and his colleagues have found this to be the case (e.g., see Swann, Pelham, & Krull, 1989). People with negative self-views prefer to interact with people who hold negative impressions of them, but people with positive self-views prefer to interact with people who hold positive impressions of them.

Person-by-treatment quasi-experiments such as the one by Swann et al. offer an excellent way to examine the role of people's self-views in their interpersonal preferences. However, because researchers do not have experimental control over the variables that they have measured, they can never know for certain that their measured variables are truly responsible for their findings. In the study by Swann, Pelham, and Chidester (1988), for example, it is possible that some other individual-difference variable (such as reactance or stubbornness) rather than self-certainty was the true determinant of how people responded to the two different kinds of leading questions. This is the problem of person confounds discussed in Chapters 6 and 7. The experimenter is only measuring (and not manipulating) the individual-difference variable, and if that variable is important, it might be associated with many other variables. If you were to run a study that looks at people who are high versus low in self-esteem, just think of how many variables would probably correlate with that individual difference. Variables shown to correlate with self-esteem include gender, socioeconomic status (SES), depression, anxiety, professional success, physical health, and life satisfaction. Any one of these variables might offer a competing (third variable) account for any observed effects of self-esteem. As a result, researchers need to consider these confounds and test to see if they are leading to the observed effects. In a similar way, researchers who conduct person-by-treatment quasi-experiments must consider operational confounds. As already mentioned, it is possible that a measure of self-esteem might accidentally measure another variable, such as age. If so, this too should be considered in analyses. We discuss strategies a researcher might use to deal with confounds in the next section. For now, the important point is that the *problem of induction* simply won't go away! It is always possible that researchers will correct for a dozen important confounds but fail to consider a thirteenth confound that is the true cause of a commonly observed effect.

Natural Experiments

In person-by-treatment quasi-experiments, the researcher maintains partial control over the world by measuring individual differences and then manipulating other variables of interest. Thus, the researcher still has experimental control over at least one of his or her independent variables. In a second type of quasi-experiment, the experimenter does not use true random assignment at all and thus relinquishes experimental control completely. Control is "released to the wild," and all the variables of interest are measured. Quasi-experiments such as this one are often referred to as natural experiments because they involve naturally occurring "manipulations." It might seem odd to think that nature ever plays the role of experimenter, but this is true plenty of times. Think of a time in your life when you were blindsided by some random life event that was caused by factors that had nothing to do with you or with any other aspect of your life. In essence, you were chosen at random by fate to experience some event. Perhaps you happened to be standing near a tree at the very moment that a branch snapped and caused you some serious injury. Or perhaps fate brought you good luck rather than bad. Perhaps you just happened to win a raffle conducted at the local Home Depot™ store and won a lifetime supply of duct tape. Attorneys and insurance agents often refer to events such as snapping tree branches as "acts of God"— random events that people themselves do not choose. Winning a lottery or a raffle is very similar in the sense that doing so happens as a result of a person's selection at random.

Of course, it would be hard to convert the extremely rare hypothetical events we described here into a quasi-experiment. That is, it's hard to imagine a quasi-experiment investigating "the stress-buffering effects of winning duct-tape lotteries after succumbing to tree-branch injuries." However, many random events occur frequently enough that they can be studied with large samples. Consider natural disasters. In any given year, many people who live in the Great Plains or Southeastern U.S. will have their homes damaged or destroyed by tornadoes while their neighbors somehow escape the same fate. Tornadoes have been known to destroy one home completely and do practically no damage to a very similar home only 50 feet away. Although people living in the Great Plains or Southeast certainly differ from people living in other parts of the United States, it seems unlikely that tornadoes seek out one particular type of Great Plains or Southeastern resident over another. Thus, within these tornado-prone regions, tornadoes reach out to touch a mostly random group of people. It would thus be reasonable for a researcher to see if people who have their homes struck by tornadoes experience higher rates of anxiety, depression, or post-traumatic stress disorder than their neighbors who have somehow been spared. In this way, a researcher could treat tornado exposure as a naturally occurring independent variable while treating outcomes such as anxiety or depression as dependent variables.

If natural manipulations always met the strict definition of absolute randomness, then it would be reasonable to think of natural experiments as true experiments. Most often, however, natural experiments focus on events that are more or less arbitrary but, strictly speaking, do not occur *completely* at random. In the case of tornadoes, for example, certain regions of a state or county (e.g., wide open spaces where people are likely to be farmers) might be more susceptible to tornadoes than others. A quasi-experimenter studying tornado victims and nonvictims who live in the same very small geographic area wouldn't have to worry very much about this potential confound. In contrast, however, a researcher comparing victims in Dorothy County with nonvictims in Glinda County would have a little more to worry about.

As another example, consider a researcher who wants to determine if seat-belt laws influence traffic fatality rates. The researcher might compare states that have such laws with those that don't. Evidence that traffic deaths are lower in states that require the use of seat belts might show that seat-belt laws save lives. In truth, however, third variables might be at work. For instance, seat-belt laws might be passed in states that also impose stricter than usual speed limits or in states that make greater efforts to crack down on drunk driving. In these cases, researchers often treat these natural events *as if* they were experimental manipulations, but they usually have to work hard to establish the comparability of their two different treatment groups. In the case of states with different seat-belt laws, for example, researchers might try to demonstrate that states that did and did not pass seat-belt laws had comparable traffic fatality rates just prior to the time that they adopted new seat-belt laws. This would help a lot, but the researchers would still need to be sure that nothing else changed at the same time the seat-belt laws changed.

Another way of gaining control over an independent variable in a quasi-experiment is to measure any differences that do exist between people exposed to two different levels of a natural manipulation—that is, to measure any existing confounds. Researchers could then gain statistical control over such confounds by conducting special analyses that statistically equate two otherwise different groups. As a simplified example, suppose that a state that passed strict seat-belt laws in 1990 had a higher proportion of licensed female drivers than a similar state that did not pass such laws that same year. This is a problem because, on average, female drivers are safer than male drivers. If researchers knew this, however, they could simply compare fatality rates in the two states controlling for gender. One of the numerous ways this could be done would be to compare fatality rates (or better yet, changes in fatality rates) within each gender across the two states.

As examples such as this one suggest, the distinction between natural experiments and nonexperimental correlational designs is not always as clear as one might like. However, to the degree that the levels of a naturally occurring variable truly are determined arbitrarily, we are on safe ground labeling a naturalistic study a quasi-experiment. A potential point of debate might have to do with studies of naturally occurring events that can be defined categorically (so that we have the appearance of treatment conditions) but that do not happen all that arbitrarily. For example, it wouldn't make sense to most researchers to consider a person's status as a prisoner or a nonprisoner a natural manipulation. However, what about convicted offenders who have committed exactly the same crime just before or just after their eighteenth birthdays? Unless one believes that something dramatic happens to people between the ages of 17.9 and 18.0 years, the important variable of whether offenders are tried as juveniles or adults would seem to be largely arbitrary in this specific case. Thus, it would seem appropriate to conceive of this situation as a natural experiment looking at the long-term consequences of being placed in the adult versus the juvenile justice system. The tricky part of deciding whether a study is a natural experiment centers around the question of exactly *how* arbitrary natural manipulations must be to count as arbitrary. This is further complicated by the fact that researchers can sometimes equate groups statistically that do not start off as equivalent.

To muddy the waters a little further, many *archival studies* also qualify as natural experiments (recall our discussion of archival research in Chapter 6). After all, records of tornadoes, traffic fatalities, and crimes can often be found in archival sources. As an example of an archival study that also qualifies as a quasi-experiment, consider a study of professional baseball players conducted by Baumeister and Steinhilber (1984). They tested the hypothesis that baseball teams sometimes choke under the pressure of trying to claim a "desired identity" (a World Series pennant) in front of a home audience. Baumeister and Steinhilber expected that the familiar "home-field advantage" observed in baseball games would be an advantage only during the first few games of a seven-game World Series. They argued that when a team played a decisive seventh game at home, playing in front of a home-field audience might actually become a disadvantage (because people feel more pressure to please those they care about than to please a bunch of strangers). It is worth noting that, during the historical era reviewed by Baumeister and Steinhilber, the National League champions and the American League champions were awarded home field advantage arbitrarily, by simply alternating, from year to year, which league was awarded home field status. (That procedure is no longer in place.) Thus, for example, the scheduling of World Series games was *not* based on the win-loss records of the two teams. As a result, inferior teams (e.g., the New York Yankees) were awarded the "home-team advantage" just as often as superior teams (e.g., the Boston Red Sox). Thus, we hope you can see that it was highly appropriate to consider the home-field advantage in the World Series to be a natural manipulation.

Baumeister and Steinhilber analyzed the outcomes of World Series games played from 1924 to 1982. They conducted many different analyses, but one of the simplest and most informative involved a comparison of the number of games won by home and visiting teams in games 1 and 2 versus game 7. The results of this analysis are summarized in Figure 8.2. As you can see, the home team won about 60 percent of the early games in a series (59 out of 98 games). When it came to a decisive game 7, however, the home team won less than 40 percent of the games (ten out of 26). Is it reasonable to conclude that this finding reflected "choking" on the part of the home team? To find out, Baumeister and Steinhilber supplemented their analysis of wins and losses with an analysis of the number of fielding errors committed by the home and visiting teams (in the same games they analyzed for wins and losses). These results appear in Figure 8.3. As you can see, the average number of fielding errors committed by

Figure 8.2
The home-field disadvantage in crucial World Series baseball games, 1924–1982 (from Baumeister & Steinhilber, 1984)

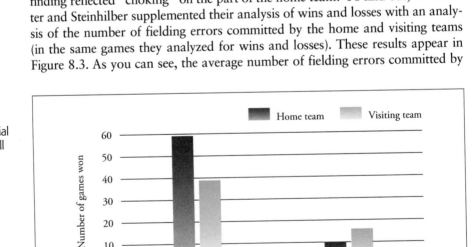

Note: Same pattern held for last games other than game 7.

Figure 8.3

Average number of fielding errors committed in World Series baseball games (from Baumeister & Steinhilber, 1984)

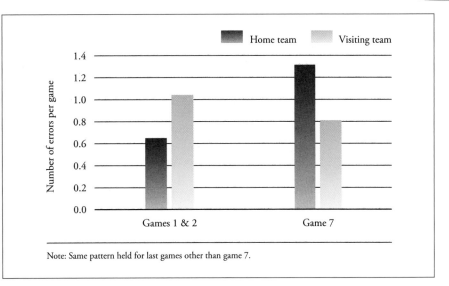

Note: Same pattern held for last games other than game 7.

the home team was twice as high in game 7 as it was in games 1 and 2. Error rates for the visiting team actually dropped slightly from games 1 and 2 to game 7. However, a statistical test showed that this drop was not significant. This effect is consistent with Baumeister and Steinhilber's hypothesis, and it thus offers nice support for their theory of choking under pressure. When the stakes get as high as they can possibly get, it looks like the familiar home-field advantage in baseball may become a home-field disadvantage.

Nature and Treatment Designs

The two kinds of quasi-experiments we have reviewed here do *not* cover the universe of all possible kinds of quasi-experiments. By jointly considering exactly how people come to be assigned to different groups, what kinds of treatments people receive, and where people receive their treatments, it is possible to generate many other kinds of quasi-experimental designs. As it turns out, none of these other designs is as popular as person-by-treatment quasi-experiments or natural experiments. Nonetheless, to give you a better feel for quasi-experimental designs, we provide you with a couple of brief examples of these alternative designs.

One kind of quasi-experimental design that is probably more useful in applied settings than in basic research settings is roughly the opposite of the person-by-treatment quasi-experiment. Specifically, researchers sometimes want to study people who have already sorted themselves into natural groups that cannot be pulled apart. Furthermore, sometimes these groups of people are highly similar rather than highly different. Finally, rather than exposing each group to both levels of an experimental manipulation, a researcher might expose each group to a *different* level of a single manipulation. We refer to this design as a *natural groups with experimental treatment* design because it involves taking two naturally occurring groups of people and treating them differently in a very precise way. This design yields useful data only if we can safely assume that the two groups (1) were extremely similar in some important way(s) to begin with but (2) were subsequently exposed to different levels of an experimental treatment, without otherwise being treated differently. This design is the rough equivalent of a simple two-groups experimental design, except that these two similar groups are not created using random assignment. The two groups already exist, and for legal, ethical, or pragmatic reasons, they cannot be reconfigured.

An excellent example of this design is the quasi-experiment that Daniel proposed to the king's chief official. Presumably, the two groups of men who ate very different diets were highly similar in physical size and strength prior to the manipulation. If they became different after the manipulation, it would seem pretty safe to attribute this emerging difference to the manipulation. When a company changes the health insurance plan for one group of employees without changing the plan for a very similar group, this might set the stage for a quasi-experimental study of the effects of the new plan on preventive medicine. If a city imposes stricter physical requirements for its firefighters' exam but does not make the same change for police officers, then the stage is set for a very different quasi-experiment. In cases such as these, we obviously could not reassign people to occupations to take advantage of random assignment. However, if we carefully assessed changes in people's health or physical prowess before and after the imposed changes, we could probably get a good feel for the consequences of the new policies.

It might also seem possible to generate novel quasi-experimental designs by combining natural manipulations with laboratory manipulations, or by assessing individual differences among people and then waiting for them to experience truly arbitrary natural events. These things are indeed possible, but in reality, these kinds of designs are extremely rare. For instance, it is very rare for researchers to be able to identify people who are likely candidates for a natural manipulation prior to the time that people actually experience the natural manipulation. If we knew that the residents of Ozburg, Kansas, were going to be hit by a tornado next month, we'd know the unknowable. Moreover, we'd also have a pretty big ethical obligation to warn people about the upcoming disaster. On the other hand, some natural manipulations are easier to predict and control than others, and creative researchers have occasionally created what might be termed *nature-by-treatment* studies. For instance, Pyszczynski, Greenberg, and Solomon (1997) conducted such a study to see how people psychologically defend themselves against thoughts of death. They did so by approaching research participants who did or did not happen to be standing within view of a funeral home (this was the natural manipulation). They then asked these participants to evaluate a person who either praised or criticized the American way of life (this was the experimental manipulation). As predicted, Pyszczynski et al. found that people were much more critical of a person who disagreed with the basic values of their culture when people were faced with a subtle reminder of their own mortality. When reminded of our own fragility, we rise to the defense of the core beliefs and values that we share with the other members of our social worlds.

As you can see, then, quasi-experiments come in many shapes and sizes. However, some theoretical and pragmatic constraints limit our ability to conduct quasi-experiments. The biggest of these constraints is probably that good quasi-experiments must solve the tricky problem of comparability.

COMPARABILITY

To appreciate the role of *comparability* in quasi-experiments, let's return to the Baumeister and Steinhilber study of home-field status in baseball playoff games. We suggested that home-field status constitutes a good natural manipulation because teams are assigned to this condition independently of their win-loss records. It is just as important, however, that the home-team status variable can be studied by creating *comparable and non-overlapping groups*. These groups can easily be compared with one another to determine the effects of home versus visiting team status. In many instances, however, random events occur, but researchers who want to study them are left guessing about what kinds of comparisons they should make to do so. As an example, consider how a researcher might study a freak natural disaster. Suppose a meteor were to strike a rural farming community in the Midwest. Suppose further that the meteor happens to wipe out a large grain-collection facility at the outskirts of town, dealing a devastating blow to the local economy. You'd have to agree that this event is about as random as it possibly could be. The meteor could have hit anywhere on the earth's surface, and the people in this community did nothing to bring this event about. As honky-tonk singer Delbert McClinton would say, these folks are "victims of life's circumstances." Given this fact, it would be entirely appropriate to view the meteor strike as a natural manipulation. However, suppose a group of psychologists came along in the ensuing months to see if the meteor had caused increased levels of post-traumatic stress disorder (PTSD) in this community. The psychologists would run into a big problem: they would need to find a reasonable comparison group.

As you know from Chapter 7, experiments require comparison groups because raw numbers are rarely informative on their own. To know what a number means, a researcher must compare it with some other number to show that it is bigger or smaller than would be expected. To illustrate, imagine that researchers observe that 2.9 percent of the residents in this farming community experience PTSD three months after the meteor strike. Should they conclude that the meteor led to an *increase* in PTSD? Is a 2.9 percent rate of PTSD higher or lower than the national average? What about the national average for rural farming communities? What about the average for rural midwestern farming communities? Does it matter how big the communities are? Or what crops they grow? Clearly, to assess whether the meteor had any effect, one must identify some sort of group against which the group of interest can be compared.

The identification of a control group can be a very difficult task. Imagine, for instance, that researchers decide that they should compare PTSD levels in the meteor county with levels in the county just to the west. A consultant points out, however, that people in this county might be too close to the meteor strike because they also use the grain-collection facility that was destroyed by the meteor. Thus, there could be carryover effects, raising the PTSD levels in that county as well. When the researchers move another county to the west, they hit a community that has a large Amish population. The meteor struck a county that did *not* have a large Amish population, and so this new county would not make a useful comparison. When the researchers move one county further to the west, however, they cross the state line and thereby encounter numerous social, economic, and political changes (not to mention different state laws regarding health care, which could influence rates of PTSD). For this reason, the researchers decide to look two counties to the *east* of the county where the meteor fell (skipping over the county just to the east because of concerns about carryover effects). When they do this, they come to a large, mostly urban county that includes the state capital, and they thereby encounter a whole host of new problems. It may seem that these poor researchers are almost as unlucky as the poor people who happen to be the victims of the meteor, but we hope you see the point. It is often difficult to find an ideal control group when you are unable to make use of random assignment.

In short, even when events occur to some people more or less at random, it is not always clear where to find a group of people who are in all other ways exactly like these people. This problem is just as pronounced when a researcher identifies an unusual group of people that he or she wishes to study in the laboratory rather than in the field. Suppose, for instance, that a researcher wants to study the laboratory responses of people with clinical levels of a specific phobia (e.g., extreme fear of heights). People who possess phobias probably differ from the majority of people in a population in a wide variety of ways, and thus a comparison with a group of adults who do not suffer from any form of clinical disorder whatsoever might not be ideal. A better control group, for example, might be people who have an equally serious but qualitatively different clinical disorder (e.g., a minor form of depression, a different kind of phobia). The fact that it is so difficult to identify the ideal comparison group in many quasi-experiments is one of the primary reasons researchers developed the notion of **patching**.

PATCHED-UP DESIGNS

Recall the extremely useful phrase *ceteris paribus* ("all else being equal") from Chapter 7. This phrase reminds us of the core principle behind true experiments: if you want to show that an independent variable is influencing a dependent variable, you must hold *everything else* but the independent variable constant across experimental conditions. As you know, this requires both random assignment (to deal with person confounds) and procedural control (to deal with operational confounds). This very high level of control is not possible with quasi-experiments. By using nonrandom assignment to conditions and moving to the real world, researchers increase the risk of confounds. In the world of quasi-experiments, that is, all else is not *exactly* equal.

Extraneous personality and environmental factors might cause the appearance of a treatment effect when no treatment effect actually exists.

Because it is not possible to hold all possible extraneous variables constant across quasi-experimental conditions, researchers must often decode the meaning of observed treatment effects by using a different method. This method is called **patching**. Patching occurs when a researcher adds new conditions to a study to help establish the size of a quasi-experimental effect, to test for the influence of conceivable confounds, or both. The end result is often what Campbell and Stanley (1966) referred to as a **patched-up design**. Patched-up designs thus occur when researchers continually add control groups to a quasi-experimental design. In the end, a carefully patched-up study will often resemble a patchwork quilt, with many different conditions sewn in to the original design, each to deal with different specific concerns. When using this approach, it is the researcher's responsibility to think of all the possible control groups that should be included to help clarify the exact meaning of any effects that are found. In a sense, then, quasi-experiments require researchers to focus their attention not only on the groups or conditions that are of interest but also on the groups or conditions that are *not* of interest.

This is a good idea. To illustrate its use, we ask you to consider a hypothetical example in which a researcher tests a simple, applied idea about teaching methods. With this example, we attempt to demonstrate how careful attempts to establish the validity and magnitude of an effect will result in a systematic increase in control groups. After this detailed example, we walk you more briefly through a series of real quasi-experiments that used archival methods to document the potency of a laboratory research finding in the real world.

Example 1: Evaluating a Teaching Tool

It should come as no surprise that the two of us have both taught many courses in research methods. Relying on our individual experiences as instructors, we have occasionally debated the merits of posting study guides on our course Web pages. In this vein, imagine that one of us thinks that study guides help students make the most of a course because motivated students can study ahead and come to class a bit more prepared than they otherwise would. Imagine, however, that the other one of us thinks that study guides encourage an overreliance on the guides and underreliance on lectures. (This is a polite way of saying that he thinks study guides may encourage students to skip class.) To resolve this debate, we could run a study to examine the impact of study guides on class grades. Let's imagine that the one of us who believes in the benefits of study guides—we'll call him Dr. Pelton—decides to run a study-guide efficacy study. As you will see, the simplest kind of study one might be tempted to run will require a great deal of patching to become convincing.

Imagine that Pelton posts study guides for the course on his course Web page, so that students can easily download the guides well in advance of the midterm and the final exam. After doing this, Pelton determines that the class average on the final exam is 90 out of 100. This finding is illustrated in Figure 8.4. We've seen this sort of design before in the tornado study, and we now call it a

Figure 8.4
One-group design

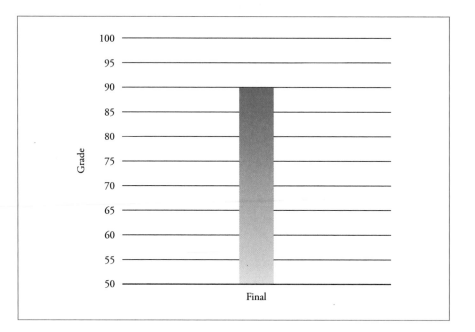

one-group design. All our participants are in one group, the group that received the quasi-experimental treatment. As you may recall from Chapter 5, this design without a control group is also an example of a pseudo-experiment. (It is a bit atypical, however, because pseudo-experiments usually focus on a single person whereas we looked at an entire group.) As we hope you'll agree, the results of studies such as this are uninformative, because they do not provide meaningful comparisons. We do not know if a 90 is typical for students in the class—if it is high for them or if it is low.

To see whether the study guides influenced class grades, we need to have some sort of comparison to show that the grades are different than they would have been in the *absence* of the study guides. To get at this, we might patch in a new condition. For this purpose, Pelton could create a comparison by introducing the study guides for the final exam but not for the midterm. It would then become possible to compare grades on the midterm, taken before the study guides were provided, with grades on the final, taken after the guides were posted. This design is referred to as a **one-group, pretest-posttest design** (Campbell & Stanley, 1966). Using this design, Pelton could see if grades improved after the study guides were posted. Assume that when Pelton does this, he observes a significant increase in grades, from 82 to 90. The results of this patched-up study are shown in Figure 8.5. This design is an improvement over a one-group design, but it is still open to many alternative explanations. It is possible, for instance, that grades increased over the semester as students adapted to Dr. Pelton's awkward lecture style, or learned to decipher his strangely worded tests (a form of testing effects). It is also conceivable that Dr. Pelton simply developed a final exam that was easier than the midterm. Finally, experimenter bias could be at work because Dr. Pelton was aware of administering the study guide manipulation. Thus, he might

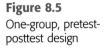

Figure 8.5
One-group, pretest-posttest design

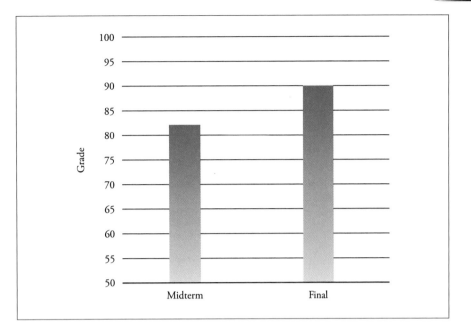

have unknowingly treated the students differently in other ways after the manipulation. If so, this 8-point increase from the midterm to the final might have been observed even if the study guides had not been posted. It is conceivable that the study guides actually made things worse! Without them, perhaps the class average would have increased even more.

Instead of trying to look for change in this specific class, Dr. Pelton could try a different kind of patch by comparing the final grades in this class with the final grades in a highly similar class that did not receive any study guides. For instance, he could compare the final exam grades for this class with the final exam grades from the same class when he taught it a year earlier. It just so happens that Dr. Pelton teaches exactly the same class every spring semester. Furthermore, because Pelton is so lazy, he uses *exactly* the same exams every year, withtou even correctgin the newmerous typso that drive students crazy. Thus, there is no obvious reason to expect final exam grades to be different in the two classes in the absence of the study guide manipulation. This new design is referred to as a **posttest-only design with nonequivalent groups** (Campbell & Stanley, 1966). When this comparison is carried out, Pelton sees that the class receiving the study guides averaged a 90 on the final, whereas the previous class averaged a 79. The results of this further patched-up design are shown in Figure 8.6. This is a large difference in grades, and it certainly suggests that the study guides may be beneficial. However, upon further reflection, Dr. Pelton realizes that last year's class was taught in the afternoon, whereas this year's class was taught early in the morning. This could be a *treatment confound* because students who are willing to sign up for a 6 A.M. class might be more serious than students who sign up for the same class offered at 3 P.M. To deal with this problem, Pelton should test to see if the two classes were roughly the same at the beginning of the two courses,

Figure 8.6

Posttest-only design
with nonequivalent
groups

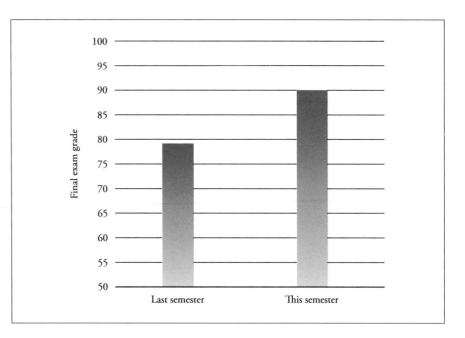

prior to the time that he posted the study guides in the second course. This is an example of matching. We criticized matching before, but that was because we had the option of using random assignment. Now that random assignment is no longer possible, and now that nature has done the matching for us, matching doesn't look so bad after all. To see if these two groups are well matched, Pelton compares both the midterm and the final grades for the two classes. His prediction is that the two groups should get similar grades on the midterm (because this test was given before the treatment), but they should get different grades on the final (because this exam was given after the treatment). This design is referred to as a **pretest-posttest design with nonequivalent groups** (Campbell & Stanley, 1966). When Pelton uses this design, he observes the findings depicted in Figure 8.7. The two classes only began to look different after the point at which class 2 received the study guides.

At this point, Pelton would have pretty good reason to believe that the study guides are beneficial. However, his confidence in this assertion would hinge on (1) the assumption that experimenter bias is not very likely to have occurred in this situation and (2) that the small between-groups difference observed on the midterm is not meaningful. In short, Pelton has to convince himself (and his critics) that these minor differences halfway through the semester cannot somehow produce the major differences observed on the final exam. These small differences at pretest (or midterm) might show that the treatment group is slightly more prepared at the start than the control group. As a result, they might have been in a better position to improve after the midterm. In light of this, Pelton might want some harder evidence that the two groups were roughly equivalent before the treatment. This is a common dilemma for researchers using quasi-experimental designs. They often want to compare two groups, and they often want to state that the two groups would be equivalent—if not for the influence

Figure 8.7

Pretest-posttest design with nonequivalent groups

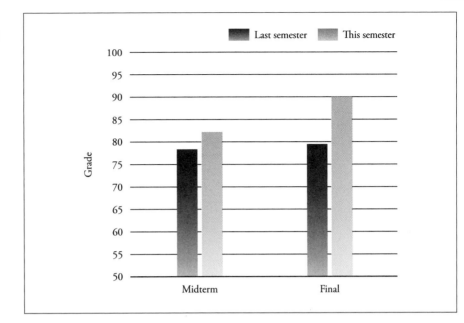

of some independent variable being studied. However, one or two comparisons are not usually enough for someone who wishes to be extremely confident of the equivalence of two groups prior to a manipulation.

For this reason, researchers often use **time-series designs**. With time-series designs, researchers look at long runs of data to show equivalence prior to a quasi-manipulation. The professor might not have time-series data for the two classes for major exams because he gives only a midterm and a final. However, he could look at performance on weekly quizzes. By looking at quiz performance in the first six weeks of the semester, which happened before the posting, and in the second six weeks of the semester, which happened after the posting, he can get a strong sense of the comparability of the two groups. If the addition of the study guide is beneficial, the two classes should show very similar quiz performance in the first six weeks, but the experimental group should start to pull away from the control group at the point at which the study guides were first provided. A pattern of data like this is shown in Figure 8.8. With the increased information gained from having multiple pretest and posttest scores, Pelton now feels pretty confident that study guides are useful teaching tools. The two classes were doing about the same over an extended period, but at the precise point when the study guides were introduced in the second class, the second class began to do better. It now seems very likely that the study guides had an effect. It is always *possible* that some confounding factor caused this shift, but many confounds that would have been serious cause for alarm using less sophisticated designs are no longer a problem.

Even if Pelton is pretty confident of his account for these findings, however, a critic might attack Pelton's interpretation. Remember, Pelton believes that study guides improve grades because the guides help students study more effectively than usual. Perhaps study guides do improve grades, but for

Figure 8.8
Time-series design

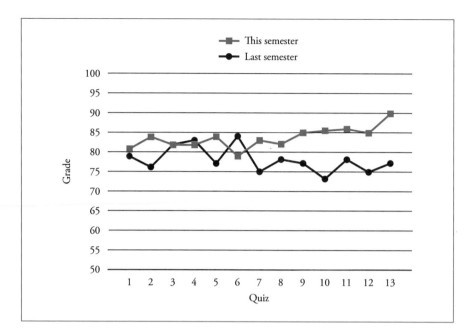

reasons that have more to do with student spirits than with student study habits. More specifically, students might do better in classes when study guides are provided because they interpret the study guides as a sign that the professor cares about their well-being. By showing that he cared, Pelton may have encouraged students to ask more questions during lectures, to come to office hours more regularly, or to feel more optimistic about the course. These things might all lead students to perform better in the course, but they involve an entirely different psychological process than the one Pelton assumes. How might we resolve this issue?

When psychologists want to pinpoint the precise mechanism behind a finding, they often patch by making use of some kind of **internal analysis**. When conducting internal analyses, psychologists break one or more groups into additional subgroups to test for subgroup differences that are consistent with the focal theory or with competing theories. To illustrate, Pelton assumes that if study guides improve grades, they do so by helping students study more effectively. The alternative theory was that study guides have no actual influence on the way students organize and internalize the material. Instead, they just serve as a morale booster. If this latter account is true, it shouldn't really matter whether students actually view the guides on the Web or not. All that matters is that they know that Pelton cared enough to provide the study guides. These two theories lead to different predictions based on a specific kind of internal analysis. Unlike the alternative theory, the original theory suggests that students should improve their grades only to the degree that they actually *used* the study guides. This suggests an internal comparison between the students in the second class who did versus did not use the study guides. If these two groups were pulled out of the time-series design in the last figure, it might lead to the pattern of data shown in Figure 8.9. This pattern,

Figure 8.9

Time-series with internal analysis

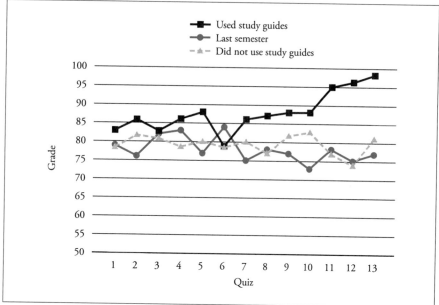

if obtained, would strengthen the interpretation that study guides truly *guide studying* rather than merely boost morale.

Can we be absolutely positive that this is the case? Unfortunately, the answer is still no. If we study Figure 8.9 carefully, we can still dream up some other reasonable explanations for this pattern of findings. For instance, students who report that they actually used the study guides could simply be more motivated and diligent than students who report that they did not. Pelton might counterargue that if this were the case, these highly diligent students should have done better on the *first* exam, too, which they did not. We might counter this counterargument by pointing out that we believe motivation ebbs and flows from week to week rather than operating as a permanent aspect of students' personalities. If this doesn't prompt Pelton to call us nasty names, it might prompt him to come up with yet another patch based on a different kind of internal analysis. Although we might never settle the issue once and for all, we hope you can see that the more times a study survives a new patching process, the more confident you should become that a researcher's preferred explanation was at the root of his or her findings. A theory that survives a great deal of patching will gain a lot of scientific credibility. The canon of parsimony dictates that we should usually prefer a simple theory that can explain an entire patchwork quilt of research findings rather than relying on three or four alternative explanations.

Example 2: Would a Rose by Any Other Name Move to Rosemont?

The last example used fictitious data to illustrate the general concept of patching. In the world of real quasi-experiments, however, it is almost never possible to perform all the many forms of patching that one might ideally like to perform. Sometimes pretest data simply do not exist. At other times, a researcher might be unable to identify a group of people who serve as an ideal control group for the people who were subjected to a natural manipulation. The real world does not sit around trying to dream up ways of making things easy for quasi-experimenters. Nonetheless, researchers who work hard at it can usually come up with patches that will address the most serious criticisms of their quasi-experimental findings. In the next section, we provide you with some examples of real research findings that address the question of whether human beings are truly in control of their major life decisions. In this case, the researchers in question used patching to try to make the point that people make important life decisions (where to live, what to do for a living) for unusual reasons that most people would probably find slightly embarrassing.

Before we discuss this research, however, please take a minute to list your six favorite and your six least favorite letters of the English alphabet. Work as quickly as possible, based on your gut impressions. When you are done, be sure to give each list of six letters a label such as "favorites" and "least favorites." Please do not continue until you have done this! When you are done, you should then circle all the letters (from each list) that happen to occur in either your first or your last name. Most people who do this activity find that the letters in their first and last names frequently make it to the list of strongly liked letters but rarely make it to the list of strongly disliked letters. This is usually true even for people whose names contain relatively rare and typically disliked letters of the alphabet such as J, K, or Z.[2] This is an example of a very well-documented laboratory finding called the **name-letter effect**. The name-letter effect refers to the finding that people like letters that occur in their own names quite a bit more than they like letters that do not. This effect occurs for all the letters in people's names, but it is particularly pronounced for people's first and last initials. This preference for one's own name letters was first documented by Josef Nuttin (1985, 1987), and it has subsequently been observed in at least 15 countries (e.g., Greece, Japan, Singapore, Spain, and the United States).

Presumably, the reason that most people prefer the letters in their own names is that most people feel very good about themselves. Ultimately people's good feelings about the self seem to rub off onto their feelings about anything that becomes *associated* with the self. Thus, in much the same way that people or animals come to like arbitrary things (e.g., musical tones, symbols) that are associated with food, praise, or other rewards, people seem to like anything that becomes associated with the self. Nuttin was so convinced that name-letter preferences reflect people's good feeling about the self that he referred to the name-letter effect as a form of unconscious narcissism. Like the mythical Narcissus, who fell in love with his own reflection, most people seem to fall in love with things (like names or possessions) that have come to symbolize who they are. OK, so people are a little stuck on themselves. Justin and Jordan probably think that J is totally phat, whereas Amber and Alyse probably think that A is completely sweet. But what do name-letter preferences have to do with major life decisions?

Pelham, Mirenberg, and Jones (2002) reasoned that if people really do have strong preferences for the letters in their names, then people's real-life decisions should reflect these preferences. As hypothetical examples, just as Dennis Smiler might find dentistry to be an especially appealing profession, Kelly Hildebrandt might feel a profound attraction to another person who happens to share both her first and last name. Pelham et al. referred to this general idea as *implicit egotism*: If people prefer things (e.g., the letters in their own names, their birthday numbers) that they associate with the self, then by extension people should prefer people, places, and occupations whose names or titles resemble their own first or last names (or their birthday numbers).

Pelham et al. first tested this idea by systematically generating a couple of European American male and female first names that closely resemble large American city names. They then narrowed down this list to two male and two female first names that were most likely to come from the same age group (e.g., Which would be a better age match for the name Virginia? Dorothy or Jessica?). The male name pairs they chose in this way were Jack and Philip, which happen to closely resemble the city names Jacksonville and Philadelphia. Finally, these researchers consulted U.S. death records to see exactly how many men named Jack and Philip (regardless of their last names) had died while living in Jacksonville, Florida and Philadelphia, Pennsylvania. The results of this study are shown in Table 8.1. As you can see, just as Jacksonville seems to have been disproportionately inhabited by Jacks, Philadelphia seems to have been disproportionately inhabited by Philips. This effect replicated, by the way, for the female first names Virginia (Virginia Beach) and Mildred (Milwaukee). So there you have it. If you think of people's first names as arbitrary variables, you have ironclad quasi-experimental evidence that people make major life decisions (where to live) on the basis of the associations they have to their own first names. Or do you? Can you think of any alternative explanations for these initial findings?

One very plausible alternative explanation is an interesting form of reverse causality. Do people's names cause them to live in certain cities, or does living in certain cities cause parents to give their children certain kinds of names? One way to patch up this design would be to perform an unusual variation on a pretest-posttest design by seeing how many of these men and

Table 8.1 Likelihood of living in a city as a function of one's first name (adapted from Pelham et al., 2002)

| City | First Name | | Row Totals |
	Jack	Philip	
Jacksonville	436 (288)	111 (259)	547
Philadelphia	968 (1,116)	1,153 (1,005)	2,121
Column Totals:	1,404	1,264	2,668

Note: Numbers in parentheses indicate expected values, that is, the number of men with each name one would expect to live in each city if people's first names were unrelated to where they lived.

women had *moved to* the cities where they died. For example, if Jack Florian's "pretest" score for place of birth was any place *other* than Jacksonville, and his "posttest" score for his last known residence was Jacksonville, this would be much stronger evidence for the idea that name-letter preferences were actually at work. Unfortunately, it was usually impossible to tell exactly where people were born from the archival records used to generate the data for this study. Thus, most of the time this patch was simply unavailable.

However, in a series of follow-up studies, Pelham et al. performed a different kind of patch to address the same concern. Although it's possible that people living in Jacksonville are especially likely to name their children Jack, it's *not* very plausible that people ever change their *surnames* because they happen to live in a specific city. On the basis of this idea, Pelham et al. conducted a number of very large replication studies in which they tested to see if people were disproportionately likely to live in cities or states whose names began with the first few letters of their surnames. People were. For example, just as people whose surnames began with "Cal" were disproportionately likely to live in California, people whose surnames began with "Tex" were disproportionately likely to live in Texas. Furthermore, because these two states have very similar proportions of White and Latino residents, it's pretty unlikely that this finding reflects some kind of ethnic confound. In additional patches, Pelham et al. controlled for people's age and ethnicity in other ways (e.g., by focusing solely on people born in the same year), and they still observed strong support for their predictions. People still gravitated toward places that resembled their own first or last names. In one very large study, Pelham et al. were also able to identify a large subgroup of people who moved from one state to another during their adult lives. Just as women named Georgia were disproportionately likely to move to Georgia, women named Virginia were disproportionately likely to move to Virginia. Women named Florence and Louise showed the same effect, as did men with names such as George, Kenneth, and Louis.

These results notwithstanding, we could still quibble about whether these studies truly constitute natural experiments. Exactly how arbitrary is a person's first or last name? Although our names clearly chose us rather than the reverse, we have already listed quite a few variables that are confounded with people's names. These include gender, age, and ethnicity, all three of which are pretty serious potential confounds. So try as we might to rule out all possible confounds, there is always a nagging concern that some unknown confound might be lurking beneath the surface. Sometimes researchers can minimize concerns about internal validity by moving from one specific kind of dependent measure (that is prone to a specific kind of confound) to a different kind of dependent measure, which is not prone to the same confound. In the case of research on implicit egotism, Pelham et al. showed that people's preferences for their name letters appear to predict people's choices of what to do for a living as well as people's choices of where to live. For example, they showed that people with names such as Dennis, Denis, Denny, Denver, Denise, Dena, Denice, and Denna are overrepresented among dentists. Studies of this sort rule out reverse causality because almost everyone is given a name well before the time that the person chooses an occupation. The likelihood of ethnic confounds can be minimized by adding direct comparisons with traditionally European American names whose objective frequency is identical to that of target names such as Dennis or Denise. By making repeated use of patching and studying more than one major life decision, Pelham et al. argued that their findings are pretty likely to reflect true name-letter preferences (see also Jones, Pelham, Mirenberg, & Hetts, 2001; Pelham, Jones, Mirenberg, & Carvallo, 2002). Finally, several of Pelham et al.'s studies allowed them to make use of the specific form of patching that we referred to as internal analysis. For example, they found that behavioral name-letter preferences were larger than usual for people who had highly uncommon rather than common first or last names. If people's behavioral preferences really are based on their preferences for their names, it stands to reason that people might show stronger name-letter preferences (behavioral or otherwise) when their names do a good job of distinguishing them from other people. Whereas relatively rare names such as Hart, Brett, or Nebuchadnezzar do an excellent job of discriminating their owners from most other people, more common names such as Tom, Dick, or Harry probably do a lot less to discriminate people from every other Tom, Dick, or Harry in the world. This internal analysis involving name frequency thus lends some support for a name-letter interpretation of Pelham et al.'s findings.

As a second example of an internal analysis, laboratory research has also shown that relative to men, women usually show stronger preferences for the letters in their first names (because their first name is the only name that many women know they will keep forever; see Kitayama & Karasawa, 1997). Pelham et al.'s archival studies revealed a similar pattern. Preferences based on people's first names were usually stronger for women than for men.

Finally, sometimes researchers can blend archival methods with other research methods to conduct very precise internal analyses. Along these lines, Pelham and Carvallo (2011) conducted a hybrid "archival-plus-survey" study of living men named Cal and Tex who resided in either California or Texas. The archival portion of this study (which consisted of simple counts of where all the men lived) replicated what they had seen using a large set of archival death records. These men were clearly overrepresented in the states that resembled their names. Because Pelham and Carvallo patched on a brief email survey to this archival study, they were also able to show, for example, that the tendency for men named Tex to be overrepresented in Texas still held up for men who reported that they had *moved* to Texas. Finally, because Pelham and Carvallo assessed how much these men liked their first initials, they were even able to show, for example, that men named Tex who lived in Texas liked the letter T more than men named Tex who lived in California (and more than men named Cal who lived in Texas). Although one of your authors is admittedly a little biased toward the hypothesis of implicit egotism, this kind of internal analysis strengthens our confidence in a finding that is otherwise very difficult for some people to believe (see Simonsohn, 2011, for example, who is not very convinced by the bulk of these archival studies).

So as was the case with our hypothetical example involving study guides, internal analyses are always open to criticism. However, they can go a long way toward increasing our confidence in a specific interpretation of an effect. So remember that if you really, really like this textbook and your name is Harbrett Pelton, the book may not be quite as good as it seems. Even more important, of course, remember that patching and internal analyses are two of the best ways to minimize the drawbacks of quasi-experiments.

WHEN TRUE EXPERIMENTS AND QUASI-EXPERIMENTS COLLIDE

Now that we have discussed most of the basic features of quasi-experiments, we are in a good position to address an important issue that was raised earlier—validity. It should be clear by now that true experiments, especially laboratory experiments, are superior to quasi-experiments when it comes to identifying causes. For this reason, good quasi-experimental researchers are often their own harshest critics. They are constantly looking at their own work and trying to think of potential confounds, so that they can address them as carefully as possible. On the other hand, perhaps good quasi-experimenters are their own biggest fans. If they truly believe in an effect, then they do not give up easily when critics launch attacks on their findings. By paying careful attention to potential confounds and identifying patches that help to address these confounds, quasi-experimental researchers can sometimes silence critics who are reluctant to believe in their findings. Of course, this will happen only if the results of a patched-up study actually turn out to support a researcher's favored theory.

Unfortunately, confounds actually do prove to be the true reasons behind some otherwise interesting research findings. For example, for many years, experimenters felt they had identified a simple and potent way of demonstrating gender bias in people's evaluations of other people's work. Specifically, in experiments in which judges were asked to evaluate an essay that had presumably been written by either "John" or "Joan," lots of studies showed that Joan's essay was rated more negatively than John's (Goldberg, 1968). This simple, potent experimental manipulation of gender appeared to reveal a large bias in the scales of social justice. As it turns out, however, there was a big problem with virtually all the studies that made use of this simple, clever manipulation. Most of these studies confounded the gender of names such as John or Joan with other important variables such as apparent age, likability, or apparent intelligence. Instead of showing a preference for men over women, these studies may have shown only that people strongly prefer certain specific names over others. If one selects equally youthful, equally smart sounding, and equally likable male and female names in studies of the John-Joan variety, the same essay that is purportedly written by either Christine or David usually gets identical marks (Kasof, 1993).

Incidentally, does this mean that there is no gender bias in work evaluation? No, not at all. It just means that we have no good evidence of gender bias using this particular method. We still know that real women in the real world are paid a lot less than real men for performing the same kind of real work. For researchers who wish to understand social injustices regarding gender and labor, the challenge is to identify valid ways of studying social injustice in the laboratory. One solution to this problem, by the way, is to get women and men to work on some kind of engaging and meaningful task and then to ask people how much they should be paid for their own work. Studies making use of this self-pay paradigm are free of any concerns regarding name confounds. Interestingly, they also reveal a clear bias for women to pay themselves less than men pay themselves for exactly the same work (Jost, 1997; Major, 1994). On the basis of this research, we have learned that gender bias may be even more profound than it might have seemed from the John-Joan studies. That is, it is pretty clear that when it comes to gender discrimination, many women are so strongly socialized to believe in the fairness of the status quo that they may unknowingly play a hand in perpetuating biases in pay. An important social implication of this finding is that the members of underprivileged groups must sometimes resocialize themselves (as well as the rest of the world) if they wish to change the status quo.

To get back to our major theme, when concerns regarding internal validity can be carefully addressed, quasi-experiments have some methodological advantages over their true-experimental cousins. First and foremost, quasi-experiments can determine whether effects observed in the laboratory generalize to the real world. As we discussed before, researchers often want to know that the basic theories they test in the laboratory generalize to important applied problems. Quasi-experiments can do this because they often focus on real-world outcomes.

Quasi-experiments are also useful for testing basic theories. Moreover, quasi-experiments can test theoretically derived hypotheses that simply cannot be studied in the lab. For both practical and ethical reasons, we cannot conduct true experiments in which we manipulate people's biological sex, whether people are struck by a tornado, or whether people are bullied as children. As these examples show, there are times when only quasi-experiments allow researchers to test the most important hypotheses that can be derived from their theories. In these instances, laboratory studies might be conducted to gain important information about some pieces of a theoretical puzzle (e.g., exactly what aspects of immune system functioning are compromised by stress), but they cannot close the circle completely and allow a full test of a large-scale theory. Theories of longevity, for example, cannot easily be tested in a one-hour lab study.

Having said this, of course, we hasten to add that true experiments and quasi-experiments are often carried out at roughly the same level of analysis, with the intent of making roughly the same point about roughly the same theory. In these instances, the benefits of quasi-experiments are that they provide us with the opportunity to see if laboratory findings that get right to the heart of a theory will travel well outside the lab. When they do, we have usually learned something important. When they do not, things often get really interesting. It now becomes a challenge to understand why two different windows on the world reveal different pictures.

As an example of this kind of phenomenon, consider experimental versus quasi-experimental research on self-esteem. True experimenters have often tried to get a handle on self-esteem in the laboratory by using random assignment to manipulate people's self-esteem levels on a temporary basis. A researcher who adopts this approach might attempt to create groups of participants who are high versus low in self-esteem by randomly assigning participants to receive either positive (esteem-enhancing) or negative (esteem-diminishing) feedback. The researcher could then study the judgments or behavior of the two groups to examine the consequences of experimentally engineered self-esteem levels. For instance, suppose that an experimenter manipulates self-esteem by telling people that they have scored really well or really poorly on a test of social percep-tiveness. After this manipulation, all participants are asked to take a recently developed test of creativity, presumably to help the experimenter decide if the new test is valid or not. All participants learn that they performed poorly on the test. The dependent measure in this experiment might be the degree to which people make excuses for their poor performance (e.g., by reporting that they got very little sleep last night, by reporting that the test was probably biased) ver-sus deciding that they simply aren't all that creative.

In such a study, we strongly suspect that the participants in the manipu-lated high self-esteem condition would make fewer excuses for their failure at the second task. The reason for this is that a great deal of research shows that people respond to positive feedback by becoming *less* defensive than they would otherwise be (Blanton, Cooper, Skurnik, & Aronson, 1997; Blanton, Pelham, DeHart, & Carvallo, 2001; Steele & Liu, 1987). Thus, true experi-ments on the judgmental consequences of self-esteem could lead us to the rea-sonable conclusion that being low in self-esteem causes people to be self-serving (e.g., by making self-protective excuses), whereas high self-esteem causes people to steer away from self-protective explanations. However, this reasonable conclusion would be erroneous. Quasi-experimental research that has *measured* the trait of self-esteem rather than manipulating it has consis-tently shown that people who are high rather than low in self-esteem make more self-serving and self-protective judgments (e.g., see Campbell, 1986; Taylor & Brown, 1988). In short, true experimental research using manipula-tions of self-esteem has consistently shown that high levels of self-esteem lead to *less* defensive judgments. In contrast, quasi-experimental research using measures of self-esteem has consistently shown that high levels of self-esteem lead to *more* defensive judgments. This would seem to be a problem.

Although we do not claim to have the definitive solution to this puzzle, we think a road trip to a Nazi concentration camp (i.e., a case study) could reveal some answers. In his classic case study of Jews who were imprisoned by Nazis in World War II, Bettleheim (1947) made a number of very interest-ing observations. Almost without exception, prisoners initially resisted the insults and psychological abuses of their captors. That is, they worked very hard to maintain a sense of self-worth in the face of horrific feedback about who they were. After a while, however, many of the prisoners were worn down by all the physical and psychological abuse they received at the hands of the guards. Many of them eventually adopted patently anti-Semitic beliefs, siding with the guards. Bettleheim referred to this as "identification with the aggres-sor," and he believed that it was much more than a simple act designed to gain the approval of the guards. Sadly, many of the prisoners seemed to internalize a profound sense of their own inferiority while simultaneously admiring and respecting their captors. Some prisoners even collected scraps of clothing and patches from the guards as souvenirs of the people they admired. Bettleheim's analysis suggests that the way people respond to an initial self-concept threat (e.g., laboratory feedback suggesting that one is socially unskilled) is very different from the way they respond to a long series of threats (e.g., growing up in poverty and being told by your teachers that you are a bad kid).

Research on self-esteem and social development is consistent with Bettleheim's analysis. That is, it seems likely that self-esteem manipulations do influence self-evaluation, but they do not do so by creating a low level of self-esteem. Because most people have a clear, and positive, sense of who they are, and because people do not like to change their identities from moment to moment, most people seem to respond to recent self-relevant experiences by working to *restore* their self-esteem to its naturally existing level (see Swann, 1987, 1992). In the short run, that is, self-esteem regulation may operate much like a thermostat that is set at a specific level. For most people, this level is pretty high, and thus most people respond to suggestions that they aren't so wonderful by thinking up ways in which they actually *are* wonderful (just as they have always known).

In other words, a high self-esteem person who has just been told by an experimenter that she is a loser is likely to behave very differently than a person who has received no experimental feedback but whose parents have been telling her that she is a loser ever since she was a child. Presumably, developing a true and stable sense that one is not worthwhile is what causes people who are chronically low in self-esteem to make self-disserving judgments relative to their high self-esteem counterparts. To dramatize this point, imagine that researchers interested in gender conclude that we can understand gender differences only by ignoring participants' preexisting conceptions of their gender and by randomly assigning people to be treated like men or women during an experiment. ("OK, Candice, since your previously sealed medical records indicate that you are genetically male, I'm sure you won't mind if we all call you Buster during today's group activity....") Although a highly creative experimenter might be able to figure out a way to manipulate some specific aspects of gender, it is hard to imagine that an experimenter could reverse 20 or 30 years of sex-role socialization during a brief experimental manipulation. Assuming that our explanation holds up to more careful scrutiny, does this mean that quasi-experiments involving self-esteem yield more valid information than true experiments? In this specific case, yes, as long as we agree that self-esteem per se is difficult if not impossible to manipulate in the lab. However, the laboratory experiments we mentioned presumably *have* yielded valid information about how people respond to different kinds of feedback. To a great degree, resolutions of debates such as this one boil down to questions about construct validity and conceptual validity. At any rate, we hope that you can see that it is possible to learn something from contradictory results.

On a more positive note, the results of true experiments and quasi-experiments prove to be very similar plenty of times. As an example, one of the authors once tested a theory about *image appeals* using both true experimental and quasi-experimental methods (Blanton, Stuart, & VandenEijnden, 2001). An image appeal is a persuasion technique designed to change a person's attitudes or beliefs by capitalizing on people's desire to adopt positive images and avoid negative images. If you grew up in a highly industrialized country, you have undoubtedly been the target of thousands of image appeals in your life. Marketers constantly try to get you to buy particular brand names by linking them to "cool" or desirable images. Tommy Hilfiger took this method to new heights when he worked hard to get people to associate his name with coolness and then got dozens of different clothing companies to sell him items of clothing to which he merely attached his name. (To our knowledge, Tommy Hilfiger has never designed or manufactured any of the popular items of clothing that bear his name.)[3] Of course, image appeals can be used for the public good as well as for the good of Tommy Hilfiger. For example, health psychologists often try to persuade people to live healthier lifestyles by linking safe sex practices with images of responsibility or by linking drunk driving with images of irresponsibility.

As it turns out, image appeals can be a complex as well as a profitable business. For instance, are image appeals that capitalize on negative images as effective as those that capitalize on positive images? Blanton et al. addressed this question by using image appeals to try to influence people's intentions to use condoms (Blanton, Stuart, & VandenEijnden, 2001). They focused on whether one should try to promote condom use by using positively framed appeals (e.g., "*Be responsible.* Use condoms every time you have sex.") versus negatively framed appeals (e.g., "*Don't be irresponsible.* Use condoms every time you have sex."). Blanton et al. felt that effects of framing would depend heavily on the perceived social norms surrounding condom use. Specifically, they thought that a positive frame would be most effective when people thought that most other people were behaving badly (by practicing unsafe sex). This prediction was based on the assumption that image appeals are most effective when they tell people the social consequences of being *different.* When people think that others are *not* using condoms, a positive frame says it is different to be responsible. By the same logic, it should be more effective to use a negative frame when people think that most people behave well (by consistently using condoms). When people think that most people use condoms, a negative frame says it is different to be irresponsible, and people do *not* like to be different when it means being something bad.

These predictions were tested in two different studies. In one study, these researchers manipulated norm perceptions by randomly assigning participants to read one of two studies: one study suggested that most sexually active students use condoms, and the other study suggested that most sexually active students do *not.* In a quasi-experimental follow-up study, Blanton et al. measured norm perception by simply asking participants to rate the prevalence of condom use among sexually active students. Whether norm perception was measured or manipulated, the results were the same. Image appeals were most effective when they focused on what it took to feel different in a desirable way. Thus, positive frames worked best when people believed that most of their peers were *not* using condoms, and negative frames worked best when people believed that most of their peers *were* using condoms. The consistency of results across methods suggests that norm perception is an important determinant of message framing across many social contexts.

SUMMARY

In this chapter, we hope you have learned at least two important things. First, there are many different kinds of quasi-experiments, and each unique quasi-experimental design has its own unique strengths and weaknesses. Second, quasi-experiments solve a great number of practical and theoretical research problems. They do so by allowing researchers to study phenomena that otherwise could not be studied, by providing information about the external validity of findings from laboratory experiments, and, occasionally, by revealing that the lessons that are revealed in laboratory experiments are in need of revision. The ideal research strategy involving quasi-experiments is often the same as the ideal research strategy involving any other research design: it is to make use of different designs that complement one another in an ideal way. In

short, quasi-experimental designs are an important tool that can help psychologists better understand human nature. However, simply using quasi-experiments, alone or in conjunction with other techniques, is no guarantee of being a successful researcher. Successful researchers must not only be familiar with a wide variety of research designs, but they must also know how to use each specific design effectively. This second key to being a good researcher might be referred to as effective tool use. It is the difference between knowing what a hammer can do for you and knowing how to hammer. This second topic, effective tool use, is the focus of Chapter 9. Thus, in Chapter 9 you will learn how to choose and implement a specific research design—that is, how to design an actual study.

STUDY QUESTIONS

1. What is "patching"? Why is patching relevant to quasi-experiments more than true experiments? Does the effective use of patching usually increase internal validity, external validity, or both? (*Hint*: is patching typically aimed at reducing confounds, artifacts, or noise?) What are the potential advantages of conducting multi-study research that makes use of both quasi-experiments and true experiments?

2. What are the potential benefits of (a) employing time-series designs, (b) conducting internal analyses, (c) studying extreme groups, and (d) assessing key dependent variables both at both pre-treatment and post-treatment?

3. Explain why a pretest-posttest design with nonequivalent groups is likely to be higher in internal validity than either (a) a one-group pretest-posttest design or (b) a posttest-only design with nonequivalent groups.

NOTES

1. Cubic zirconium is an artificial stone that strongly resembles a real diamond but is not very valuable.
2. We used this simple measure of preferences only because it is much easier to score (and to explain) than more sensitive and methodologically rigorous measures. For instance, a more sophisticated measure of name-letter preferences would require people to report how much they like each of the 26 letters of the alphabet using a variation on the EGWA scale

discussed in Chapter 4. Using this measure, it is possible to calculate how much a person likes each individual letter in his or her name relative to how much other people like that same letter (when their names do *not* include this same letter). Scoring this measure, however, is a bit of a pain in the butt. If you want to see exactly how it's done, see Koole, Smeets, Dijksterhuis, and van Knippenberg (1999).
3. We thank Shira Gabriel for this example.

Choosing the Right Research Design

ONE OBSCURE MOVIE

The independent film *El Norte* offers a sobering view of the difficult lives of two illegal immigrants to the United States, Enrique and his sister Rosa. After narrowly escaping death at the hands of guerillas in their rural village in Guatemala, Enrique and Rosa eventually make their way to the United States, where they take on any work they can find. Because Rosa speaks no English, she encounters some serious problems in her first day at work as a housekeeper. These problems are compounded by the fact that Rosa's only exposure to modern appliances in Guatemala came from her indirect exposure to the magazine *Buen Hogar* (*Good Housekeeping*). After struggling unsuccessfully for a long time with the modern washer and dryer she has been charged to use, Rosa eventually resorts to doing her first day's wash by hand in the kitchen sink, and laying it on the lawn to dry in the sun. Needless to say, Rosa did not win many points with her employer in her first day on the job.

The problem had nothing to do with Rosa's general knowledge of washers and dryers. She understood exactly what these appliances are designed to do. The problem was that Rosa didn't know how to *operate* a washer or dryer. Rosa fully appreciated the magic of these modern conveniences, but she didn't know the words to any good spells. That is, she simply didn't know which buttons to push. At this point, we suspect that you are in a position that is very similar to Rosa's. Of course, you have a lot more general information about research methods than Rosa had about washing machines, but your position is similar to hers in the sense that you have been given almost no instructions about how to put your general knowledge of research methods to work. This is the basic goal of the remainder of this book: to provide you with the missing details that you will need if you plan to conduct and interpret your own research. Learning these additional details will also put you in a much better position to evaluate research conducted by others. Thus, even if you are not planning a career as a researcher, the remaining chapters in this book provide some specific knowledge that will make you a better consumer of research.

In keeping with this general goal, this chapter introduces you to two of the most important categories of information about research design. We begin by discussing two basic kinds of designs, those that have only a single independent variable (one-way designs) and those that have two or more independent variables (**factorial designs**). We follow this with a discussion of two basic approaches to design, designs that use between-subjects manipulations and those that use within-subjects manipulations. Although we will focus heavily on the design of experiments in this chapter, almost all the basic ideas we introduce apply to nonexperimental as well as experimental research. For example, when planning both experimental and nonexperimental research, researchers usually begin by deciding exactly how many independent variables they should include. Counting begins at one, and thus we begin with a discussion of designs that include only a single independent variable.

ONE-WAY DESIGNS

The simplest possible experimental design is a **one-way design**, in which there is one and only one independent variable. Furthermore, the simplest possible kind of one-way design is the aptly named **two-groups design**. In experiments employing a two-groups design, there is only one independent variable (i.e., only one experimental manipulation), and this variable has only *two levels*. A two-groups design often consists of an experimental group (a group that receives a treatment) and a control group (a group that does not). Strictly speaking, however, many two-groups studies do not really fit this scheme. For instance, a researcher interested in figuring out the ideal dosages for a new pain reliever might give people either 50 or 100 mg of the new drug, wait for the drug to kick in, and check to see whether the 50-mg group or the 100-mg group reported less discomfort while performing a cold-pressor task (i.e., while submerging one hand as long as possible in a bucket of ice water). In cases such as this, the important thing is whether the two groups differ from each other on the dependent variable. It is not always necessary to include a group that receives no treatment.

Dooling and Lachman (1971) made use of a two-groups design to investigate some simple properties of memory. Put yourself in the place of the participants in their control group. These participants were asked to read the following cryptic passage:

> With hocked gems financing him, our hero bravely defied all scornful laughter that tried to prevent his scheme. Your eyes deceive, he had said. An egg, not a table, correctly typifies this unexplored planet. Now three sturdy sisters sought proof. Forging along sometimes through calm vastness, yet more often over turbulent peaks and valleys, days became weeks. As many doubters spread fearful rumors about the edge, at last, from nowhere, welcome winged creatures appeared signifying momentous success.

When the control group participants were asked to remember this story after a delay, they had great difficulty doing so. Participants in the experimental group read exactly the same story. However, prior to doing so, they were provided with a telling title for the story: "Christopher Columbus Discovering America." In comparison with the control group, those who were told the title remembered the story quite well. If you read the story again with this title in mind, you'll see why this was so. The title allowed people to make sense of the story by using a well-learned knowledge structure (a schema). When people can make sense of things, they are much more likely to remember them. (Please try to remember that!)

Some intriguing examples of two-groups designs can be found in the literature on person perception and stereotyping. Figure 9.1 provides a crude picture of some potential stimuli that might be used in a very simple two-groups study of person perception. Take a look at the character on the left-hand side of Figure 9.1. How would you size him up intellectually? Now look at the character on the right. Does he look any smarter? How about any less sociable, or athletic? If we used the two characters depicted in Figure 9.1 as stimulus persons in a two-groups experiment, we would want to show each of our two groups of participants one and only one of these two drawings and ask them to rate the character on whatever traits we expected to be influenced by the manipulation involving eyeglasses. And we'd expect our simple manipulation to have a pretty dramatic effect. Most people usually judge characters wearing eyeglasses to be more intelligent than their eagle-eyed counterparts. Person perception studies in which participants have been presented with photos of real people instead of cartoon characters have yielded exactly this result. When you are going out on a first date, it may be safe to leave your glasses at home. However, when you are going out on your first job interview, you would be well advised to wear them.

As psychological research has become more sophisticated over the past century or so (especially the past few decades), the two-groups design has become a less popular research design. On the other hand, when an idea is really simple, really novel, or both, it is often easiest to convince people that

Figure 9.1

Potential stimuli for a simple two-groups study of person perception

the idea has merit by documenting it in the simplest way possible. A more cynical way to put this is that if you'd like to use a simple two-groups research design, you'd better have a pretty interesting effect to demonstrate. For example, Valdesolo and Desteno (2011) used a two-groups design to show that people were more likely to engage in a costly behavior to help a suffering stranger when they had recently spent a few minutes tapping a song to the same beat as the stranger (rather than tapping to a different beat at the same time, with the same stranger). Thus, a simple manipulation of behavioral "synchrony" (which people knew to be arbitrarily assigned by the experimenter) increased people's willingness to do a costly favor for the stranger. We suspect that more complex follow-up experiments will document the boundary conditions of this intriguing effect. Because this finding is pretty counterintuitive, however, it was probably a wise decision to keep the initial demonstration experiment as simple as possible.

In addition to two-groups designs, experimenters often make use of one other kind of one-way design, namely, the **one-way, multiple-groups design**. This is another design in which there is only a single independent variable. In this case, however, the independent variable takes on three or more levels. A one-way, multiple-groups design would be very appropriate for a more sophisticated version of the hypothetical drug-dosing study described earlier. To get a more precise estimate of the ideal dosage for the new drug, an experimenter might give one group of participants a **placebo** (a pill with no active ingredients) and give four other groups of participants increasingly large doses of the drug. For example, participants might receive 0, 25, 50, 75, or 100 mg of the new drug.

One-way, multiple-groups designs also come in handy in studies of person perception. For instance, a researcher interested in whether people "judge a book by its cover" might present three different groups of participants with identical written descriptions of a target person's personality while systematically varying the target person's level of physical attractiveness. Past research of this type has identified the existence of a *physical attractiveness stereotype*. Most people assume that physically attractive people possess a specific set of personality characteristics, most of which are favorable. Specifically, relative to their less attractive peers, physically attractive people are judged to be happier, better adjusted, and much more sociable (see Eagly, Ashmore, Makhijani, & Longo, 1991, for a review). By including multiple levels of an independent variable in this kind of experiment, researchers sometimes discover things that would go undetected in a two-groups design. For example, if both physically attractive and physically unattractive people are judged to be less intelligent than *moderately* attractive people, researchers could learn this only by conducting studies that include at least three levels of physical attractiveness. Of course, the additional information that can be gained from multiple-groups designs comes at a cost. It almost always takes more time, more resources, and more research participants to conduct experiments that have more than two conditions.

As you may recall from our discussion of quasi-experiments, both experimenters and quasi-experimenters often begin a new research program by studying only high and low levels of an independent variable. Only after documenting an effect by looking at two groups (e.g., people very low versus very high in self-esteem, a very comfortable versus an uncomfortably hot room) do researchers typically begin to test hypotheses involving multiple levels of a variable (e.g., low, medium, or high levels of self-esteem). This initial bias toward simpler designs often saves time and energy. Moreover, in the absence of a theory suggesting that something interesting is going on at the middle levels of an independent variable, this approach is often justified. However, as research accumulates, it often becomes useful to ask more precise questions about, for example, the dosing of an independent variable. Thus, it often becomes worthwhile to invest some time and energy into examining multiple levels of an independent variable.

FACTORIAL DESIGNS

Although one-way designs have been the workhorses of psychological research for many years, even a workhorse can do only so much work. The major limitation of one-way designs is the fact that they allow researchers to look at only one independent variable at a time. A great deal of human behavior is the product of multiple variables acting *together*. With this idea in mind, R. A. Fisher popularized the use of **factorial designs**. Factorial designs are designs that contain two or more independent variables that are completely crossed—meaning that every level of every independent variable appears in combination with every level of every other independent variable. That's a lot of "everys," but it's not quite as complex as it sounds. It just means that you create every possible combination of all the levels of all your independent variables.

Ins and Outs of Factorial Designs

Factorial designs come in many shapes and sizes, and so researchers have developed precise conventions for describing specific factorial designs. The label a researcher gives a factorial design specifies both (1) how many independent variables exist in the design and (2) how many levels of each independent variable exist in the design. Thus, a 2 × 3 factorial design (stated "two by three") has two independent variables (because there are two numbers in the description), the first of which has two levels and the second of which has three. The two numbers in the design are separated by a multiplication sign (meaning "by"), which is a reminder that the two variables are completely crossed. Using this coding scheme, a 2 × 2 has two independent variables (because there are two numbers), both of which have two levels. The description of a factorial design also tells researchers exactly how many "cells" (i.e., how many unique conditions) are in a study. You can easily figure this out in a factorial design by simply multiplying the numbers that identify the design. Thus, a 2 × 2 factorial design always has four cells. A 2 × 3 design always has six cells, and a 2 × 2 × 3 (three different independent variables, two with two levels and one with three) has 12 cells.

This system also serves as a reminder of the kind of *statistical analysis* that should be conducted to analyze the data from a factorial experiment. If you conduct an experiment with a 2 × 2 factorial design, you would need to conduct a two-way analysis of variance (abbreviated ANOVA) to analyze your data. If your experiment has a more complex 2 × 2 × 2 design, you would conduct a three-way ANOVA, and so forth. In this system, the word "way" simply indicates the number of independent variables in the experiment. If you are wacky, and hardworking, enough to conduct a 2 × 2 × 2 × 2 × 2 × 2 design, you would need to conduct a (count 'em) *six-way* ANOVA to analyze the data from the 64 unique conditions in your experiment. Incidentally, if you've been wondering why we refer to designs with only one independent variable as "one-way" designs, you now have your answer. Because they have only one independent variable, these simple designs are typically analyzed using a one-way ANOVA.

If little white stars are beginning to spin around your head as you ponder the potential complexity of factorial designs, we have some very good news. One of the most commonly used experimental designs in psychology is the 2 × 2 factorial, which is the simplest possible factorial design. The 2 × 3 factorial design is also pretty common, but many seasoned experimenters devote themselves almost exclusively to 2 × 2 designs. As a result, if you can understand a basic 2 × 2 factorial design, you are well on your way to understanding most of the experimental designs you are likely to encounter in psychological research.

Because the basic idea behind factorial designs is to yield a more complete picture of the world than we can gain from one-way designs, it might seem that researchers should just conduct the study to end all studies by running something like a 2 × 2 × 3 × 3 × 4 × 4 × 5 × 5 factorial study. In this way, they could identify *all* the known causes of a phenomenon and examine all these independent variables at once, in a single, huge factorial study. Although this might seem reasonable at a glance, this is not a good idea for many reasons. The simplest reason is purely pragmatic: this huge study would simply be *too* huge. Remember that the more variables you have, and the more levels you have of each variable, the more cells (i.e., unique conditions) you always have in your design. Conducting research is a resource-limited enterprise, and thus you have to think very carefully about whether you really *need* to know all about a particular variable before you incorporate it into your design.

The hypothetical eight-way factorial design we just mentioned has 14,400 unique conditions! At 20 participants per cell, this study would require 288,000 research participants! Assuming that most of the adult population of Wyoming is willing to serve as your participant pool for this study, and assuming it takes about an hour to run each participant, it would take a small army of ten full-time experimenters about 15 years to complete this study! By this time, your multibillion-dollar research grant would be exhausted, your list of likely causes would be 15 years out of date, and no one anywhere would be able to understand findings as complex as those you'd be likely to observe. Worse yet, we'd worry that if you had used a slightly different manipulation of a couple of your independent variables, you would have observed very different results. A simpler way to put this is that increasingly complex factorial designs do not become more enlightening at the same rate as they become more exhausting.

Even when studies are quick and easy to run, researchers still turn to the 2 × 2 design more often than any other factorial design. A second reason why researchers usually stick to simple rather than complex factorial designs is that many researchers refine theories by engaging in qualification (as discussed in Chapter 2). When they do this, they attempt to show that a theory is true under some conditions but not under others. The easiest way to do this is to show that the effect of an independent variable on a dependent variable depends on the level of a second independent variable. When the effect of one independent variable differs depending on the level of a second independent variable, these two variables are said to *interact*. McGuire (1989) endorsed qualification as an approach to theory testing when he said that researchers pursue interactions to clarify the "circumstances under which a hypothesis is true and those under which it is false" (p. 7). We discuss interactions in more detail in the next section. For now, we simply wish to emphasize that the concept of qualification in scientific hypothesis testing is tightly linked to the concept of interactions. Furthermore, it is possible to test for interactions by making use of factorial designs. Finally, because it is usually hard for people to keep track of more than one qualification of an effect at a time, 2 × 2 factorial designs usually provide researchers with the most efficient way of specifying when an effect is and is not observed.

A slightly different way of understanding why researchers typically lean toward simple as opposed to complex factorial designs has to do with the fact that the goal of most research is usually to test predictions derived from one or two theories at a time. Most theories consist of one or two core principles, and thus they usually generate predictions that usually involve one or two variables. Even in the interesting case when two theories make opposing predictions about a phenomenon, this is true precisely because each theory suggests that the *same* manipulation will have different effects on some important outcome. Thus, it is often possible to conduct a simple factorial study whose findings will be relevant to more than one theory. Finally, most theories exist in some kind of logical "If A, then B" form. Cognitive dissonance theory states that if people realize that their behavior is inconsistent with their attitudes, they will try to resolve this inconsistency. Frustration aggression theory states that if frustrated, people will behave aggressively. These simple causal accounts of a phenomenon usually map onto only one independent variable. Thus, it usually takes only one manipulation (e.g., a high versus a low level of frustration) to provide initial support for a theory, and it usually takes only one more manipulation (e.g., whether the person who frustrated you did so on purpose or by accident) to *qualify* the first manipulation. Additional manipulations (e.g., whether the person who frustrated you can see you) often represent interesting but unnecessary detours into the domain of a totally different theory. If theories were typically more complex ("If A *and* B *and* C, then D"), higher-order factorial designs might be a lot more popular. Thankfully, most theories are simple, and thus most factorial designs are simple as well.

Main Effects

Given that factorial designs are so popular, it is important to know exactly what's so special about them. What can we learn from factorial designs that we cannot learn from one-way designs? To answer this question fully, let's begin at the beginning. First, because experiments with factorial designs always have at least two independent variables, such experiments can answer questions that cannot be addressed by studies that have only a single independent variable. One obvious sense in which this is true has to do with the fact that factorial designs allow researchers to answer questions about more *than one independent variable at the same time.* The simple, straightforward effects of independent variables in factorial studies are referred to as **main effects.** Main effects are the factorial equivalent of the only kind of effect that you can detect in one-way designs. A main effect in a factorial design refers to the overall effect of an independent variable, averaging across all levels of the other independent variable(s). For instance, if you conduct a quasi-experiment involving the effects of gender and frustration on aggression, you might observe a main effect of gender. All else being equal (ignoring the frustration manipulation), men might engage in higher levels of aggression than women. In your study of gender, frustration, and aggression, you might also observe a main effect of frustration. Averaging across men and women, people who are experimentally frustrated might generally be more aggressive. Main effects are simple. They only have to do with one variable. Thus, to determine whether your factorial study yielded a main effect of a specific variable, you collapse across all the levels of all other independent variables in a factorial design.

Another example of a main effect in a 2 × 2 factorial study is summarized in Figure 9.2. Greenwald, Spangenberg, Pratkanis, and Eskenazi (1991) conducted a clever 2 × 2 study to assess the effects of expectancies on memory.

Figure 9.2

Perceived memory improvement as a function of subliminal tape content and (label-based) expectancies for memory improvement (Greenwald et al., 1991)

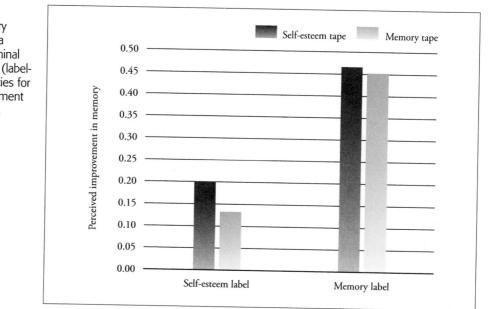

Participants in their study listened to one of two different subliminal self-help tapes for five weeks. Some of the tapes contained hidden messages designed to improve self-esteem, and some included hidden messages designed to improve memory. This was one of Greenwald et al.'s manipulations: the true subliminal content of the tapes. The other manipulation was how the tapes were labeled, regardless of what was actually on the tapes. This second variable was manipulated by simply switching the labels on half of the tapes. Thus, regardless of what subliminal messages participants were *actually* listening to, half of them *thought* they were listening to messages that would boost their memory, and the other half thought they were listening to messages that would boost their self-esteem. When Greenwald et al. looked at perceived memory improvement over the course of the study, they observed only one finding: a large main effect of the tape labels. They found no main effect due to the actual tape content, meaning that the content of the tapes had no significant effect on whether people reported improved memories. Consistent with other research on participant expectancies, people's *expectations* about the tapes had a dramatic effect on the degree of perceived improvement in their memories.

In this study, one advantage to using a 2 × 2 design was that these researchers were able to demonstrate expectancy effects in exactly the same sample of participants and in exactly the same context in which they observed no evidence at all for the effectiveness of this popular form of subliminal message. This increases our confidence that this was a fair test of the effects of each of these two independent manipulations because any idiosyncrasies associated, for example, with this specific sample were common to both manipulations. If Greenwald et al. had run a one-way design in which they had *only* manipulated the true content of the messages, they presumably would have observed a *null effect* (a lack of an effect) of tape content. This wouldn't be all that informative. We might worry, for instance, that this particular group of research participants just wasn't paying any attention at all to anything about the tapes. The 2 × 2 factorial design makes this worry unlikely. If these people simply weren't paying attention, then why did the tape labels have such a large effect? A second advantage of using a 2 × 2 design, by the way, is that Greenwald et al. were able to show that they observed an expectancy effect *regardless* of whether their participants were in a situation that might have justified this expectation. This suggests that expectancy effects truly are independent of message content effects (at least when it comes to this particular kind of subliminal content). It also suggests that expectancy effects occur in at least two different contexts (when people get one kind of subliminal message, and when they get another). We return to this final point later in this chapter.

Interactions

In addition to yielding information about main effects, studies making use of factorial designs can yield a second, very important kind of information—a kind of information that can never be gained from studies making use of one-way designs. As we noted earlier, factorial designs allow researchers to detect the presence of statistical interactions. Recall that interactions always mean "it depends." Interactions exist when the effect of one independent variable on a dependent variable depends on the level of a *second* independent variable. To explore the concept of interactions in more detail, let's take a close look at a couple of 2 × 2 factorial experiments in which researchers observed interactions. Let's begin with one of the first author's favorite examples of a 2 × 2 factorial design: a study of causal attribution conducted by Gilbert, Pelham, and Krull (1988, Study 1).

Most theories of causal attribution share the basic assumption that people come to understand other people's attitudes and personalities by considering the behavior of other people in its social context. Gilbert et al. were interested in the question of when people are most likely to take the social context into consideration when they are judging other people's personalities. To put this more concretely, imagine that you see a woman who is behaving very anxiously (e.g., shifting around nervously in her seat, averting her eyes from her conversation partner). Furthermore, imagine that you can't hear anything the woman is saying but learn that she is involved in a getting-acquainted conversation with a stranger. Your first inclination might be to conclude that the woman is the kind of nervous person who is always uncomfortable in social situations. However, that's where the idea of the social context comes into play. Imagine that you learn that the woman is being asked to talk about anxiety-provoking topics such as whether she has ever been publicly humiliated, what her sexual fantasies are, and what she considers her most significant personal failures. Does this change your impression of her disposition? It should! If you give the issue a little thought, you should realize that almost *anyone* would feel uncomfortable talking about these sensitive topics with a stranger. With this in mind, you should not necessarily conclude that the woman is a highly anxious person.

Now imagine that you observe the same woman engaging in exactly the same nervous behavior, but under very different conditions. In this case, suppose you learn that the woman is being asked to discuss pleasant topics such as foreign films, ideal vacations, and her favorite hobbies. Knowing this should also change your impression of the woman. People who give this second piece of contextual information a little thought might conclude that the woman is a real basket case (i.e., that she is an *extremely* anxious person). After all, if she gets this anxious when she is talking about relaxing topics like these, there is no telling how anxious she would be in a more stressful situation.

Notice that we could conduct a simple two-groups study to see if people engage in this kind of carefully reasoned logical analysis. In such a study, we could manipulate the social context under which the woman's behavior presumably took place by showing two groups of participants the same videotape of the same woman behaving anxiously while manipulating their beliefs about the discussion topics. Relative to participants who thought the woman was discussing relaxing topics, those who thought she was discussing anxiety-provoking topics should judge her to be a less anxious person. Gilbert et al. made use of exactly this manipulation of social context in their study of person perception. However, they also manipulated a second variable, making

Figure 9.3
The design of Gilbert et al.'s study of automatic and controlled attributions: Because this was a factorial design, every combination of every level of every variable was present in the design.

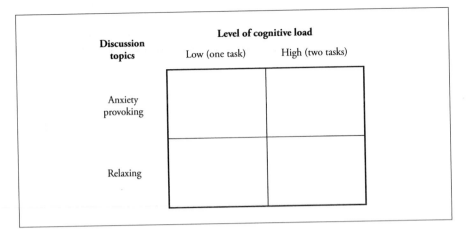

their study a 2 × 2 factorial. The second independent variable in this study was the level of *cognitive load* participants experienced as they tried to figure out the woman's personality. Half of the participants in this study simply tried to figure out the woman's personality. The other half tried to figure out her personality while they *also* performed a cognitively taxing secondary task (in this case, a memory task). A summary of the design of Gilbert et al.'s 2 × 2 factorial study appears in Figure 9.3. Notice that the two independent variables were completely crossed. The study included every combination of every level of the two independent variables.

Gilbert et al. found that when people were not cognitively loaded, they did an excellent job of taking the situation into account when they judged the woman's personality. As you can see in Figure 9.4, participants who thought that the woman had been placed between a rock and a hard place decided that she was probably hardier than she appeared. Relative to people who thought she was talking about pleasant, innocuous topics, they concluded that she probably *wasn't* such an anxious person. However, Gilbert et al. found that when

Figure 9.4
Judged trait of anxiety of target as a function of cognitive load and situational constraint information (from Gilbert et al., 1988)

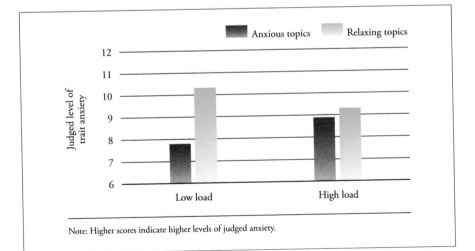

people had two things to do at once, they were unable to make any corrections in their judgments. The manipulation involving the anxiety-provoking versus pleasant discussion topics no longer had any effect on participants' judgments. Instead, they simply concluded that the woman was an anxious person, period. This pattern of findings means that Gilbert et al. observed an interaction between the information provided about the discussion topics and the cognitive load variable. Recall that interactions occur when the effects of one independent variable depend on the level of some other independent variable. In this case, the effect of the information about discussion topics on people's judgments of the woman's anxiety level depended on people's level of cognitive load.

On the basis of findings such as these, Gilbert (1989) concluded that person perception is a multistep process. During the early stages of this process, anyone who sees a person behaving a certain way (e.g., anxiously, aggressively, sadly) automatically jumps to the conclusion that the person is a certain *kind* of person (in this case, an anxious person). Whether people are able to correct their initial conclusions about a person in light of information about the situation depends on the degree to which people have full access to their higher-order cognitive resources at the time they render their judgments. Many other studies of social judgment—including studies of attitude change, stereotyping, and judgment under uncertainty—have yielded results highly similar to these (see Petty & Cacioppo, 1986). When people's cognitive resources are taxed, they are much more likely to rely on simplistic judgments ("The people in that commercial look so happy; maybe *I'd* be that happy if I bought that car") and much less likely to engage in more sophisticated forms of reasoning ("On second thought, that car has a very poor reputation for reliability. How fun would it be to get pulled around in that car by a tow truck?"). Studies such as these are almost always factorial studies because they make the point that judgment is a joint product of more than one variable: some aspects of the information people are given to make their judgments and some aspects of people's willingness or ability to use this information.

Notice that interactions are very different from main effects. For example, if there had simply been a main effect of cognitive load in the Gilbert et al. experiment, we might have seen that the cognitively loaded participants—as a group, independent of the manipulation about the discussion topics—judged the woman to be more anxious than did the cognitively unloaded participants. We *didn't* see this, of course, but we *could* have. Similarly, if we had only observed a main effect of discussion topic (no main effect of cognitive load and no interaction), we would have simply observed that, averaging across the two levels of cognitive load, the discussion topics influenced people's judgments. If we had *not* observed an interaction, the effects of the discussion topics would have been roughly equal in the load and no-load conditions. The effect of the discussion topics would *not* have depended on the cognitive load manipulation. Our findings would have resembled Greenwald et al.'s findings on the effects of subliminal tape labels.

To get a better feel for the difference between main effects and interactions in factorial studies, let's consider a hypothetical factorial study that might have been conducted by R. A. Fisher. Suppose we are interested in how the growth

Figure 9.5

Design of a hypothetical study of plant growth

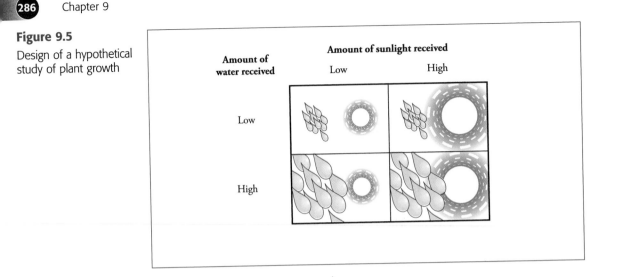

rate of bean plants is influenced by (1) the amount of sunlight to which the plants are exposed and (2) the amount of water the plants are given. If we want to conduct a 2 × 2 factorial study to address this question, we might take a group of 40 healthy bean sprouts and randomly assign the plants to the four treatment conditions summarized in Figure 9.5. Let's begin with the plants in the low sunlight condition. For the duration of the study (say 30 days), some of these plants would get only a little sunlight along with very little water, and some would get only a little sunlight along with a lot of water. Now consider the plants in the high sunlight condition. Like those in the low sunlight condition, some of these plants would get very little water and some would get a lot. In other words, the two independent variables would be completely crossed.

The results of this hypothetical study are summarized in Table 9.1. If we analyze the data from this hypothetical study using a traditional two-way (ANOVA), we would probably observe three findings. As suggested by the means in Table 9.1, this study appears to have yielded (1) a main effect of sunlight, (2) no main effect of water, and (3) a Sunlight × Water interaction. The main effect of sunlight is indicated by the fact that the plants that received high levels of sunlight grew to be about twice as tall (31.4 versus 16.6 inches) as those that received low levels of sunlight. Similarly, the absence of a main effect for water reflects the fact that the plants that got a lot of water and the plants that got very little water grew to exactly the same average height. However, the

Table 9.1 Results of a hypothetical study of plant growth

| Amount of Water Received | AMOUNT OF SUNLIGHT RECEIVED | | |
	Low	High	Row Means
Low	22.4	25.6	24
High	10.8	37.2	24
Column means	16.6	31.4	

presence of an interaction indicates that the main effects do not tell the whole story about sunlight, water, and plant growth. As it turns out, the effect of water on plant growth depended heavily on how much sun the plants received. Plants that got very little sun actually did better when they got only a little water. Plants that got a lot of sun did much better when they got a lot of water.

Notice that if we had looked only at main effects in this study, we would have come away with a very misleading picture of the role of water and sunlight in plant growth. First of all, we would have concluded that water plays no role in plant growth! Second, we would have come away with an imprecise understanding of the role of sunlight. Whereas the main effect of sunlight (i.e., the average effect of sunlight, averaged across watering levels) was pretty large, the true size of this effect depended heavily on watering levels. When plants received very little water, high levels of sunlight made only a tiny contribution to growth. However, when plants received a lot of water, the effects of sunlight were enormous. This second point reveals another important characteristic of interactions. Interactions are *always* about two (or more) variables. In this case it is not only true that the effects of water depended on the levels of sunlight; it is also true that the effects of sunlight depended on the levels of water. In the case of two-way interactions, it is always possible, at least in principle, to look at the same interaction from two different vantage points.

Another important thing to know about interactions is that they can be reflected by a wide range of data patterns.[1] Even in the case of two-way interactions, researchers often distinguish between two distinct data patterns, each of which reflects an interaction. One common pattern of data that qualifies as a two-way interaction occurs when an independent variable has an effect under some conditions but has less of an effect (or no effect at all) under other conditions. When an effect exists at one level of a second independent variable but is weaker or nonexistent at a different level of the second independent variable, the observed pattern is often referred to as an **ordinal** or **spreading interaction**. An example of a spreading interaction appears in Figure 9.6. This figure is

Figure 9.6

Size of tuition increase students were willing to accept as a function of head nodding and topic of persuasive argument (from Wells & Petty, 1980)

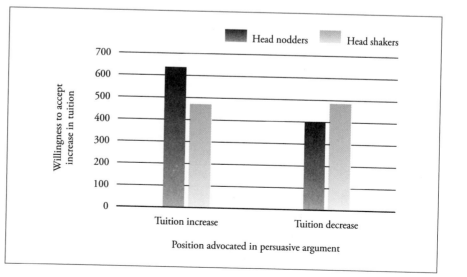

based loosely on the results of an experiment on attitude change conducted by Wells and Petty (1980). Wells and Petty believed that people sometimes infer their attitudes from their own physical responses to a persuasive argument. To test this idea, they asked participants to help them evaluate some stereo headphones that presumably had been designed for use during exercise. While listening to one of two different persuasive arguments about tuition over the headphones, some participants were asked to shake their heads from side to side, and others were asked to nod their heads up and down (presumably to simulate the head motions of different forms of exercise). As you can see in the left half of Figure 9.6, head nodding facilitated attitude change, but *only* when participants listened to a counterattitudinal argument (in favor of increases in tuition). Another way of looking at this same interaction is that the counterattitudinal argument (in favor of tuition increases as opposed to decreases) led to attitude change only when people were nodding their heads up and down.

A second pattern of data that reflects a two-way interaction is depicted in Figure 9.7. This figure is based loosely on the results of a series of experiments on person perception conducted by Martin, Seta, and Crelia (1990). Martin et al. made use of some well-established priming manipulations to get people into the mind-set of thinking about either negative (e.g., "stubborn") or positive (e.g., "persistent") personality traits. They also examined the effects of variables (such as cognitive load or personal accountability) that they expected to influence how carefully people would think about a judgment. Thus, all their experiments were 2 × 2 factorials. Each of their factorial experiments yielded an interaction. The particular kind of data pattern they observed is often called a **disordinal** or **crossover interaction**. A disordinal or crossover interaction occurs (1) when there are no main effects of

Figure 9.7

Favorability of judgments of a target as a function of priming and amount of thought devoted to judgment (data approximate overall findings of Martin, Seta, & Crelia, 1990)

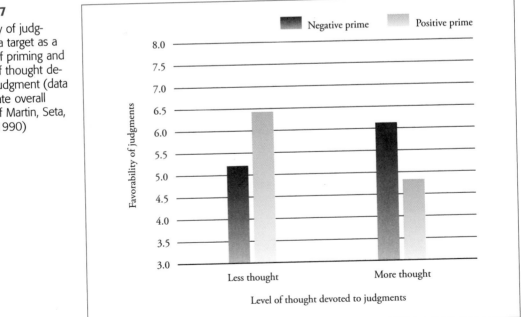

either independent variable and (2) when the effects of each independent variable are opposite at different levels of the other independent variable. In the case of Martin et al.'s studies, the effects of the primed concepts were opposite for people who gave a little versus a lot of thought to the person-perception task. Those who devoted very little thought to their judgments judged the target person more favorably when they had been primed to think about the favorable as opposed to unfavorable concepts. In contrast, those who devoted a great deal of thought to their judgments judged the target person less favorably when they had been primed to think about the favorable as opposed to unfavorable concepts. Another way to put this is that Martin et al. observed *assimilation* toward the primed categories when their participants weren't thinking hard about their judgments but observed *contrast* when their participants were thinking hard about their judgments.

When the results of a factorial study are represented in line graphs, an interaction will always show up in the form of **nonparallel lines**. (This lack of parallel lines is a direct reflection of the meaning of an interaction: the effects of one variable are *different* at different levels of some other variable.) In the case of a crossover interaction, these nonparallel lines actually cross over one another at or very near the middle of the two lines, hence the term "crossover interaction." If you would like to see another approximation of a crossover interaction, take a look back at Figure 8.1. If you converted this bar graph to a line graph, you would see that the two lines are not only nonparallel, but also cross over one another pretty near the middle. There were no main effects of Swann et al.'s persuasion techniques, and these techniques had roughly (though not perfectly) opposite effects for people who differed in terms of their level of self-certainty.

Whether the data pattern in a 2 × 2 design fits the form of a spreading interaction or a crossover interaction can sometimes be a tricky issue. For example, take a look at the two graphs in Figure 9.8. *Each* of these two graphs summarizes the results of the same experiment, namely the Gilbert et al.

Figure 9.8

Two different ways of graphing the results of Gilbert et al.'s (1988) anxious woman study

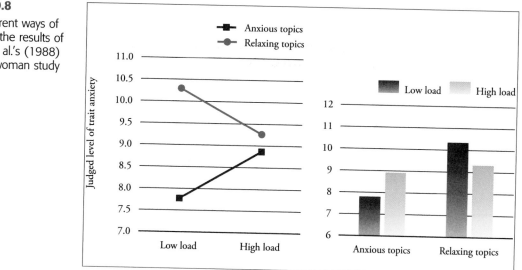

experiment. According to the way that some methods texts define spreading and crossover interactions, the graph on the left appears to depict a spreading or ordinal interaction. Specifically, the line graph shows that the discussion topics had no effect when people were cognitively loaded but had a substantial effect when people were not. However, according to the way that some texts define spreading and crossover interactions, the graph on the right appears to depict a crossover or disordinal interaction. This graph shows that the cognitive load manipulation had *opposite effects* for the two different kinds of discussion topics. When the topics were anxiety provoking, being cognitively loaded caused participants to judge the woman as *more* anxious. When the topics were relaxing, however, being cognitively loaded caused participants to judge the woman as *less* anxious (the bar graph, incidentally, is merely a rearrangement of Figure 9.4).

Which kind of data pattern did Gilbert et al. observe? As we have defined the terms here, they observed a spreading interaction. The main reason for this is that they observed a main effect (a main effect of their discussion topics). This means that even though their cognitive load manipulation did have opposite effects for different kinds of topics, the two lines that represent their findings do not cross at all (much less cross in the middle). When a researcher observes a true crossover interaction in a two-way factorial study, the effects of *both* independent variables are opposite (and roughly equal) at the different levels of the other independent variable. In the first of Martin et al.'s (1990) two studies of person perception, it was not merely the case that the effects of the priming manipulation were opposite at different levels of load. It was *also* the case that the effects of load were opposite at different levels of the priming manipulation. This symmetrical situation can be the case only when researchers observe an interaction in the absence of any main effects.

Because experimenters like to know exactly what kind of patterns they have observed in their research studies, and because a visual inspection of a set of means can sometimes be misleading, researchers usually conduct a set of very specific statistical tests after they have observed a statistically significant interaction in a two-way factorial design. In particular, they usually conduct **simple effects tests**, also known as **simple main effects tests**, to see which specific mean comparisons are significant in their factorial study. Simple effects tests are typically very simple statistical tests. In fact, most often they are simply t-tests.[2] In the case of the first Martin et al. study, for example, one simple effects test would be conducted to determine whether the positive effect of the priming manipulation observed for cognitively loaded participants was significant. That is, did the loaded participants who received the positive prime judge the target person significantly more favorably than did the loaded participants who received the negative prime? The other simple effects test would be exactly the same specific comparison, except that it would be conducted for the participants who were *not* cognitively loaded. This statistical test would tell us whether the nonloaded participants who received the positive prime judged the target significantly less favorably than did the nonloaded participants who received the negative prime. If we are dealing with a cut-and-dried case of a crossover interaction, each of these simple effects tests will be significant. If either one of these two simple effects tests is not quite significant, there will be some question as to whether we have observed a true crossover interaction.

Putting together everything that we've seen so far about factorial designs, let's consider what Fisher had to say about the advantages of factorial designs over simpler, one-way designs. Fisher noted that two of the major selling points of factorial designs are that they are both more efficient and more comprehensive than one-way designs. Factorial designs are efficient in the sense that they allow us to look for more than one main effect at a time in a single study. They are comprehensive in the sense that, unlike one-way designs, they tell us more of the whole story behind a specific phenomenon—by allowing us to see how different variables work together to influence the phenomenon. In addition to these two advantages of factorial designs, Fisher also noted that there is a third, less commonly appreciated, advantage of factorial designs. Although the term hadn't yet been coined in Fisher's day, modern methodologists would say that this third advantage has to do with external validity. As Fisher (1935) put it:

> There is a third advantage ... which, while less obvious than the former two ... has an important bearing on the utility of the experimental results in their practical application. This is that any conclusion, such as that it is advantageous to increase the quantity of a given ingredient, has a wider inductive basis when inferred from an experiment in which the quantities of other ingredients have been varied, than it would have from any amount of experimentation, in which these had been kept strictly constant. The exact standardisation of experimental conditions, which is often thoughtlessly advocated as a panacea, always carries with it the real disadvantage that a highly standardised experiment supplies direct information only in respect of the narrow range of conditions achieved by standardisation. Standardisation, therefore, weakens rather than strengthens our ground for inferring a like result, when, as is invariably the case in practice, these conditions are somewhat varied.

In other words, a researcher who observes main effects in a factorial study can be reasonably sure that any observed main effects will generalize across whatever levels of the other independent variables exist in the study. If these other variables were held at a single, constant value, as is necessarily the case in a one-way design, it would always be possible that the researcher had identified the one and only one set of conditions under which the observed effect usually occurs. Of course, main effects are often qualified by interactions, but as we have noted repeatedly, learning about the existence of interactions is also something that we can do only by using factorial designs. The topic of interactions is sufficiently important that we have created a special methodology exercise on interactions. This exercise, Methodology Exercise 3, is included in Appendix 2, and it should help you review and apply your knowledge of interactions. In other words, if you are still feeling a little unclear about the nature of main effects and interactions, this exercise should help you sharpen your knowledge of these important concepts.

WITHIN-SUBJECTS DESIGNS

Earlier in this chapter, we said we were going to discuss two basic kinds of experimental designs and two basic approaches to experimental design. As you now know, the two basic kinds of experimental designs we were talking about are one-way designs and factorial designs. The two basic approaches to research design include **between-subjects designs**—the only approach to experimental design that we've discussed thus far—and **within-subjects designs**, which are the final topic of this chapter. Between-subjects designs are designs in which each participant serves in one and only one condition of an experiment. If you think back to all the studies we discussed in the first part of this chapter, it should be clear that participants in these studies experienced only one level of each manipulation they received. In contrast, within-subjects or **repeated measures designs** are those in which each participant serves in more than one (perhaps all) of the conditions of a study.

Most of the design issues that apply to between-subjects designs also apply to within-subjects designs. Most notably, within-subjects designs include both one-way designs (that have only a single independent variable) and factorial designs (that range from simple 2 × 2 factorials to designs with three or more independent variables). Like between-subjects designs, within-subjects designs are also analyzed using ANOVA. Of course, differences in the exact calculations underlie between-subjects and within-subjects ANOVA. In this regard, the main difference between a between-subjects and a within-subjects ANOVA is the fact that the within-subjects ANOVA takes into account that the observations in the different cells of a within-subjects design are not statistically independent (because they are no longer coming from separate people). However, the precise calculations that reflect this fact are very complex (and they are typically handled by powerful computer software programs such as SAS, R, or SPSS).

A simple example of a within-subjects design appears in the left half of Figure 9.9. One way in which you could demonstrate the famous checker-shadow illusion would be to ask people who are not familiar with this illusion to estimate (say, on a 10-point scale) (a) how dark rhombus A is as well as (b) how dark rhombus B is. Of course, you would take great pains to explain to your participants that you are not asking them to judge how dark shape A or shape B would be if this were a *real* checkerboard. Instead you were asking them to judge the darkness of the ink used to print these two rhombuses. If you are familiar with this visual illusion, you know that shapes A and B are exactly the same shade of grey, and thus you know that if you included some additional within-subjects conditions in this study (by connecting rhombus A and rhombus B with lines that are uniformly grey, as we did in the right half of Figure 9.9), you'd see that people had no trouble seeing that the two shapes are equally dark. In this within-subjects study, you wouldn't have to worry about whether a person confound or a failure of random assignment made some people say that rhombus A was darker than rhombus B because the very same people would serve as the judges of both rhombuses. In fact, most visual illusions

Figure 9.9

Squares A and B in the left-hand image are exactly the same shade of grey. The right-hand image shows this by connecting "squares" A and B with two grey lines of uniform color.

are interesting, in part, because you can essentially serve as a participant in a within-subjects study whose effect is so robust that virtually everyone can serve in two different within-subjects conditions—and see or feel the difference between the two conditions. In the case of the checker-shadow illusion you can see that "squares" A and B look very different when they are part of the checkerboard image. But you can also see that they are identical (as suggested by the uniformly grey lines that connect the two squares in the right half of Figure 9.9).

To appreciate the power of within-subjects designs, imagine what might happen if you used a traditional between-subjects design to study this powerful visual illusion. More specifically, suppose you asked five participants to rate the darkness of square A and asked five *different* participants to rate the darkness of square B (using a 10-point scale). Because you randomly assigned participants to conditions, this would be a true experiment. We hope you can imagine that it would be possible (even if somewhat unlikely) to observe the following results by experimental condition, ranked in ascending order in each condition, to facilitate a comparison:

Participant	Square A	Participant	Square B
Alvin	5	Bob	4
Alisa	5	Brian	5
Alex	6	Bill	5
Andy	9	Billy	7
A-Train	9	Billie	8

If you were to conduct a statistical test on these data (a simple *t*-test), you'd find that the 1.0 point difference between the two experimental conditions, though in the predicted direction, does not even approach statistical significance ($p > .40$). However, we hope you can see that if we had asked each of these same participants to rate the darkness of both squares, making this a within-subjects study, there probably wouldn't have been anyone who didn't rate square A as substantially darker than square B. If this were the case, a within-subjects statistical test would clearly yield a significant result ($p < .0001$).

Participant	Square A	Square B	Difference
Alvin	5	4	+1
Alisa	5	3	+2
Alex	6	2	+4
Andy	9	7	+2
A-Train	9	5	+4
Bob	7	4	+3
Brian	8	5	+3
Bill	7	5	+2
Billy	9	7	+2
Billie	10	8	+2

Notice that none of our hypothetical participants changed their original between-subjects ratings. Alvin, for example, still gave a rating of 5 to square A whereas Bob still gave a rating of 4 to square B. However, the within-subjects nature of the new design removed a huge source of error, which seems to have been individual differences in how people used this 10-point scale. The advantages of within-subjects designs won't always be this dramatic, but we hope you can see how useful within-subjects designs can be.

Advantages of Within-Subjects Designs

Within-subjects designs have some enormous advantages over between-subjects designs. The most straightforward is the fact that within-subjects designs require fewer participants than between-subjects designs—especially when it comes to complex factorial designs that have many different conditions. As an example, consider a study in which a researcher working for a national testing service wants to investigate the joint effects of three different variables on intellectual performance. Specifically, imagine that she has designed a factorial study in which she wants to examine the joint effects of task difficulty, time pressure, and type of task on the quality of people's performance. If she designs a 3 (task difficulty: low, medium, or high) × 3 (task type: verbal, mathematical, or analytical) × 2 (time pressure: low versus high) between-subjects factorial study to address her research question, her design would have 18 (3 × 3 × 2) unique conditions! If she needs to randomly assign 50 people to each condition to get a stable estimate of what's going on in each condition of the study, she would need to run 900 participants! On the other hand, if this researcher runs a completely within-subjects study, and exposes each participant to all 18 cells of her study, she would need to run only 50 participants to have 50 in each cell. That's a good deal! But wait, there's more! The second advantage is that, in all likelihood, if the researcher in this study used a within-subjects design, she would be able to get away with running far fewer than 50 participants (perhaps 25 or 30) to have the same ability to detect effects for which she would have needed 50 per cell to detect effects in a between-subjects design. This is because the factors in a within-subjects design do not have to "fight" all the noise occurring between conditions due to individual differences.

This leads to the second advantage of within-subjects designs: they eliminate person confounds. Recall that researchers usually eliminate person confounds by randomly assigning different participants to different conditions in between-subjects experiments. When researchers use within-subjects manipulations, however, they eliminate person confounds in a much more direct fashion. They ask the very same people to serve in the different experimental conditions in which they happen to be interested. In a sense, then, within-subjects designs take advantage of the only perfect form of matching. In so doing, they totally eliminate person confounds. If the very same people serve in both your experimental condition and your control condition, you don't have to worry very much about whether the people in these two conditions are different from one another. If Alfredo is a highly intelligent, extroverted cello player when he serves in your experimental condition, then we can rest assured that he is still a highly intelligent, extroverted cello player when he serves in your control condition. Needless to say, this is a very nice feature of within-subjects designs.

With this in mind, you may be wondering why anyone would ever bother to run more than a single person in a within-subjects experiment. After all, a single person could participate in all the conditions in a within-subjects study, and we wouldn't have to worry at all about person confounds. Within-subjects studies require multiple participants for several reasons, but one of the most important reasons has to do with the fact that we would like to be sure that the results we observe in an experiment apply to people in general, rather than to one particular person. In other words, running only one person in a within-subjects study would raise serious concerns about external validity. We'd have no way of knowing whether the findings of a single-participant study would apply to anyone else. This concern about external validity gets translated into a statistical concern as well. Recall that statistical analyses essentially tell us whether we can safely draw conclusions about some general population of people from whom our sample of participants was drawn. When we have sampled only one participant, we cannot draw any safe statistical inferences about populations. (This concept makes its way into statistical analyses in the sense that you can't even conduct most standard statistical tests unless you have a minimum of five to ten participants per condition in an experiment.) On the other hand, within-subjects studies are generally more powerful than between-subjects studies. Thus, when researchers are fairly certain that their within-subjects studies are high in psychological realism (see Chapter 7), they can often make pretty safe inferences about people in general by sampling surprisingly small numbers of research participants. Within-subjects designs represent a very powerful research technique.

Disadvantages of Within-Subjects Designs

In light of how well within-subjects designs control for person confounds, and in light of how powerful and efficient they are, you may
now be wondering why anyone would ever waste his or her time by running a between-subjects study! However, despite all the advantages of
within-subjects designs, they also have some disadvantages. That is,
studies that use within-subject designs sometimes introduce biases that
are unlikely to emerge in between-subjects designs. Although it is possible to reduce or eliminate *most* of these potential biases, some of them
are potent enough that they sometimes force researchers to stick with
between-subjects designs.

Three primary, and closely related, biases are applicable to within-
subjects designs. The first bias has to do with the fact that people's psychological states change as they spend time working on one or more
tasks. More specifically, **sequence effects** can pose serious problems for
within-subjects designs. Sequence effects occur when the simple passage
of time begins to take its toll on people's responses (e.g., when people get
bored or tired). In the hypothetical within-subjects study of intellectual
abilities described above, you can probably see how anyone would start
to get a little tired by the time he or she reached the set of ten problems
that constituted the 18th unique condition of the study. Of course,
researchers could compensate for this problem to some degree by giving
people breaks or making their experimental tasks as brief as possible.
However, this would not completely eliminate this serious problem. Most
people will simply be in a different frame of mind when they are about to
finish a task than they were when they started it. In other words, within-
subjects studies run the risk of confounding a specific condition or manipulation with a specific level of boredom, fatigue, or excitement that a task
is almost over.

A second, closely related, drawback of within-subjects designs has to
do with **carryover effects**. Carryover effects occur when people's responses
to one stimulus in a study directly influence their responses to a second
stimulus. As an example, consider a study by Stapel and Schwarz (1998).
They asked participants to report their attitudes about the Republican
party after answering a simple question about either General Colin
Powell or Senator Bob Dole. Both Colin Powell and Bob Dole are Repub-
licans. However, at the time of Stapel and Schwarz's study, Powell was
very popular, but Dole was not. As a result, participants who first
reported their attitudes toward Powell rated the Republican party more
favorably than those who first reported their attitudes toward Dole. We
can imagine that many of the participants in the Colin Powell condition
thought something like "Colin Powell is a Republican, and I really like
him. So I guess the Republican party can't be all that bad." For similar
reasons, participants in the Bob Dole condition may have allowed their
negative feelings about Bob Dole to spill over into their feelings about
the Republican party. Their thoughts might have even resembled the
thoughts of the misinformed political activists who once boycotted Dole

pineapples because of their distaste for Bob Dole (who has nothing to do with the Doles who sell pineapples).

This particular kind of carryover effect is known as an **order effect**. Order effects occur when a question takes on a different meaning when it follows one question than when it follows another. As a second example of order effects, Strack, Martin, and Schwarz (1988) asked college students to report both their general life satisfaction and their dating frequency. When the general life satisfaction question came first, the two items had practically nothing to do with one another ($r = -.12$). However, when the dating frequency question came first, the two items were very strongly correlated ($r = .66$). The more people said they dated, the happier they said they were with their lives. Apparently, students who answer life satisfaction questions do not usually give much thought to their dating frequency, *unless they have just been asked to think about dating*. Thus, a single question that drew attention to dating frequency caused students to interpret life satisfaction from the idiosyncratic vantage point of dating frequency. Carryover effects such as question order effects can create serious problems for within-subjects studies.

Another kind of carryover effect can occur when participants knowingly or unknowingly learn something by performing an experimental task. When participants' experience with one task makes it easier for them to perform a different task that comes along later, they have benefited from **practice effects**. As you might guess, this is a problem because researchers cannot tell if people's superior performance on the second task happened because of an experimental manipulation or because of simple practice. Practice effects are closely related to testing effects, which we discussed in Chapter 5. Recall that testing effects occur when people perform better on a test the second time they take it. The primary difference between testing effects and practice effects is that practice effects occur even when the second test measures something very different than the first. (In the case of testing effects, the second test is designed to measure exactly the same thing as the first test, and the two tests are very similar if not often identical.) For instance, a person who benefits from practice effects might respond more accurately to multiple choice questions during the latter part of an experiment merely because he or she was becoming familiar with a multiple-choice question format. The specific topic of the questions wouldn't necessarily matter.

Of course, people's experience doing one thing does not *always* make it easier for them to do something else. In fact, the reverse is sometimes the case, especially when two tasks follow one another in close succession. When performing one task disrupts people's performance on a second task, this is referred to as an **interference effect**. Interference effects constitute a third kind of carryover effect. To see what we mean by an interference effect, please provide a brief, *one-word answer* to each of the following questions. It is important that you answer each question as quickly as possible!

What's a three-letter word for police officer?

Name something rabbits do to get around.

What do you usually do with an ax?

What's the opposite of bottom?

What do you do at a green light?

If you were tempted to say that you "stop" at the green light, you experienced a subtle form of interference effect. Interference effects are the opposite of practice effects, but they are equally problematic in within-subjects designs. If a person's performance in the second of two conditions in a within-subjects study deteriorates, we always have to worry that an interference effect, rather than an experimental manipulation, could have been at work.

Even if sequence or carryover effects are not a problem in within-subjects studies, a third drawback of within-subjects designs is that they increase the likelihood that participants will be able to figure out an experimenter's hypothesis. Consider, for instance, a study of gender stereotypes in which participants view a videotape of a man aggressing against a woman. After making some trait ratings of both the man and the woman, the same participants watch a very similar videotape. In fact, *everything* is the same except that the woman is now aggressing against the man. Most participants in a within-subjects study such as this one would quickly realize that the study has something to do with how we judge men and women who perform exactly the same behavior. Participants might not be able to spell out the experimenter's exact hypothesis, but they certainly wouldn't offer the kinds of natural responses to the second videotape that they might have offered to the first. We suspect that most participants would probably assume that the experimenter is *hoping* to see evidence that men are seen as more aggressive than women. If participants are sufficiently motivated to please the experimenter, they might fall prey to demand characteristics (see Chapter 5). If they do so, they might try to act in ways that are consistent with the experimenter's hypothesis. That is, they might try to be "good subjects" and thus might report what they think the experimenter wants to hear (Orne, 1962). Most likely, this would mean rating the man as more aggressive than the woman. Alternatively, it is possible that participants will succumb to evaluation apprehension (also reviewed in Chapter 5). If they do so, they will report whatever they think portrays them in the most favorable light possible (Tedeschi, Schlenker, & Bonoma, 1971). Given that stereotyping people on the basis of gender is generally frowned upon, participants might report that the man and the woman seemed equally aggressive, even if they secretly feel that the man seemed more aggressive than the woman. In short, lots of things can conceivably go wrong when a researcher makes use of a within-subjects manipulation. In light of all these things that can go wrong, you may be wondering why anyone would ever waste his or her time by running a within-subjects study. Thankfully enough, the answer is that many of the potential problems that apply to within-subjects studies are pretty easy to fix.

Solutions

Although within-subjects designs have serious drawbacks, many of these problems can be reduced or eliminated using some specially designed control techniques. We begin by recalling the two general categories of problems that we reviewed first: sequence effects and carryover effects. A very useful control technique for reducing or eliminating both sequence and carryover effects is **counterbalancing**. This is a method of control whereby the researcher varies the order in which participants experience the different conditions of a within-subjects study. Because there are many different kinds of within-subjects studies, there are many different kinds of counterbalancing. The most comprehensive form of counterbalancing is appropriately referred to as **complete counterbalancing**. Researchers who use complete counterbalancing present every possible order of all their experimental treatment conditions. This means, of course, that different participants receive different orders (by virtue of their random assignment to these different orders). Complete counterbalancing works best when a within-subjects study has only two or three conditions. You can compute all the possible orders needed to perform complete counterbalancing by taking the factorial of the number of unique conditions that you have in your study. If you have only two within-subjects conditions, you have only 2! (two factorial = 2×1) or two possible orders. These orders are often written in a shorthand in which a different letter is used to represent each unique condition of the study. These letters are then written in the order in which they are presented to participants. In a simple one-way, within-subjects experiment with only two levels of the independent variable, the two orders would be summarized AB and BA. Some people get condition A followed by condition B. Others get condition B followed by condition A. It's that simple.

Once you graduate to within-subjects studies that have three or more unique conditions, you begin to find a lot of possible orders of presentation of your experimental conditions. When you have three different conditions in a one-way within-subjects study, there are 3! ($3 \times 2 \times 1$) or six possible orders of presentation, and when you have just four conditions, there are 4! or 24 possible orders. Jump up to a 2×3 factorial (with six unique conditions), and you have 720 possible orders (that's 6! = $6 \times 5 \times 4 \times 3 \times 2 \times 1$). The 18-cell study of intellectual performance mentioned earlier would include a cumbersome 18! possible orders. That's $6.402373706 \times 10^{15}$ or about 6 quadrillion, 402 trillion, 373 billion, 706 million possible orders. Even if we only ran one participant in each order, we'd run out of people on earth at about the time that we finished a *millionth* of all these possible orders. From this perspective, the between-subjects study that requires 900 participants probably doesn't sound so bad after all!

When it is impractical to use complete counterbalancing, researchers typically make use of one of two kinds of **incomplete counterbalancing**. The simplest kind of incomplete counterbalancing is **reverse counterbalancing**. Researchers who use this technique simply generate a single order (either a meaningful order or a random order), and then they reverse it. This not only produces two different orders, but it also guarantees that the average serial position of any given condition in a study (e.g., whether this condition came first, second, third, and so forth) is exactly the same for all the unique conditions. Notice, for example, that if a researcher simply used the orders ABCDE and EDCBA, then each of the five unique conditions would occur, on the average, in the *third* of the five possible positions. Take condition B, for example. For half of the people this condition came second, and for half it came fourth. The average of second and fourth is third. It's that simple.

However, reverse counterbalancing has a fairly serious drawback. Although it does control for average serial position, it doesn't control for how frequently all possible conditions occur first or last. For example, in the case of reverse counterbalancing just provided, condition C always occurs smack in the middle of the experiment. It's never first, and it's never last. Most forms of **partial counterbalancing** (a second general category of incomplete counterbalancing) take care of this problem. A commonly used form of partial counterbalancing involves choosing a limited number of orders (say ten or 12) at random from the pool of all possible orders. In this way, the experimenter is using random selection and choosing a sample of orders from the entire population of possible orders. One conceivable problem is that it is always possible for the random selection process to produce orders that share many similar features. For instance, it is possible that condition A will always appear in the first half of the study. By choosing many different random orders, a researcher can minimize the likelihood of this problem. However, he or she will have to go to the trouble of choosing, creating, and keeping track of dozens of different orders.

As an alternative to choosing orders at random, a researcher who wants to control as completely as possible for order might also make use of a **Latin square** procedure to generate a fixed number of orders. In the case of four within-subjects experimental conditions, a Latin square could be used to generate four orders such that each of the four unique conditions appeared (1) exactly once in each possible serial position (first through fourth) and (2) exactly twice *before* and exactly twice *after* each of the other three unique conditions. Such an ideal Latin square for four orders is summarized in Table 9.2. Unfortunately, this ideal Latin square is impossible to achieve for many other designs. For example, if you have an odd number of unique orders, it will never be possible to achieve this second criterion. However, the one thing you can *always* do in any kind of Latin square is to arrange things so that each condition appears exactly once in each possible serial position. A Latin square for five conditions that fulfills this requirement also appears in Table 9.2. Finally, because there are some drawbacks to this specific approach to a Latin square (e.g., condition B usually occurs immediately after condition A), researchers sometimes choose several different Latin squares at random and make use of more than one Latin square in a single

Table 9.2 An ideal Latin square for four within-subjects conditions and a popular Latin square for five within-subjects conditions

ABCD	ABCDE
BADC	BCDEA
CDAB	CDEAB
DCBA	DEABC
	EABCD

study. A detailed treatment of Latin squares is beyond the scope of this text. If you run into a particularly complex problem involving Latin squares, you can find advice in most advanced statistical texts. For most purposes, however, one of the basic forms of counterbalancing we have reviewed here will suffice. The basic point we wish to emphasize is that counterbalancing goes a very long way toward resolving problems such as sequence and carryover effects. The specific form of counterbalancing you use to resolve these problems will depend on the complexity of your within-subjects design.

Incidentally, we should make it clear that counterbalancing does *not* erase sequence or carryover effects. These effects exist sometimes, and there is usually little we can do to make them go away. Instead of erasing these effects, counterbalancing simply unconfounds them with particular treatment conditions. If all your treatment conditions occur with equal frequency in the early and late portions of an experimental session, then you have controlled for problems such as order and contamination effects. This doesn't mean that people don't get tired, or that they don't get better or worse at experimental tasks as they work their way through a study. These effects still exist, but they have been balanced (you might even say *counter*balanced) equally across all your treatment conditions. Moreover, if you go to the trouble to randomly assign your participants to the different orders of your within-subjects studies, you can check to see if order has any effects on your findings by treating order as an independent variable in an ANOVA and analyzing for it. When you do so, you will usually hope that you *don't* find any effects of order. However, in case there are any order effects, you will know that you have controlled for them. Moreover, you will be able to take a close look at them to see if they tell you anything interesting about what you have been studying.

So counterbalancing can help solve two of the three big problems that sometimes affect within-subjects designs. But what about the problem that participants in within-subjects studies are especially likely to figure out a researcher's hypothesis? Counterbalancing can also make a small contribution to dealing with this problem. Recall that researchers randomly assign people to different orders in a within-subjects design. This means that researchers who are worried that their use of a within-subjects manipulation has clued participants in to what they are studying can simply look at people's judgments in the *first* condition to which participants were exposed (before they could have easily figured out what was being manipulated). This boils down to conducting a between-subjects analysis on a limited portion (the very first portion) of a within-subjects study. If the between-subjects analyses strongly resemble the within-subjects analyses, it suggests that the within-subjects manipulation may not have created the problem of cluing participants in to what is being studied.

On the other hand, maybe things are even worse than the researcher had feared. Perhaps the manipulation is so transparent that many participants figured out what was being studied before they ever got to the second experimental condition! This is to say that an analysis of participants' responses on a dependent measure cannot completely reassure us that participants haven't figured out what was being manipulated in a study (regardless of whether the study involves a within-subjects or a between-subjects manipulation). When researchers really wish to know what people were thinking while they took part in a within-subjects study, they need to find good ways to ask them. With this idea in mind, researchers who use repeated measures designs often rely on some kind of **structured debriefing**. This is an interview conducted with participants immediately after they have completed a study to determine exactly what they thought the researcher expected to find. Because it makes participants seem smart to have figured out what a researcher was studying, it is often possible to simply come right out and ask people what they think the researcher's hypothesis was or what they think he or she expected to find. At other times, it might be necessary to provide participants with some options to see if they can guess the hypothesis at an above-chance level. If they can, this usually a pretty serious problem. However, all may not be lost. For example, the researcher could reanalyze his or her data, focusing only on the participants who did not figure out (or guess) the hypothesis. This isn't as ideal as running a study in which no one realizes what you expect to find, but it's a step in the right direction. Because of the complexity of solving the "transparency problem" in within-subjects designs, researchers often avoid using within-subjects designs when doing so would make it clear what they are studying.

In some cases, that is, the only real solution to worries about transparency is to use a between-subjects design. Returning to the last example, a participant who sees *either* a film of a man aggressing against a woman *or* a film of a woman aggressing against a man will usually have no idea that the experimenter has created multiple versions of the same video. As a result, participants in this between-subjects study will probably rate the aggressors just as they see them, without realizing that stereotypes may have influenced their judgments.

In short, one reason experimenters sometimes rely on between-subjects designs is that some experiments are difficult to pull off using within-subjects designs. In addition to this, an even more serious problem is that some experiments are absolutely impossible to pull off using within-subjects designs. Within-subjects designs are feasible only to the degree that you can readily alter a state once you have created it. It's very easy to show participants a big circle and later show them a little circle to see if the size of the circle affects how much they like it. However, it is much trickier to put participants in a good mood and expect that you can put them in a bad mood a few seconds (or even a few minutes) later. And in some cases, what's done can never be undone at all, no matter how hard you try. For instance, neuroscientists or other biologically-oriented psychologists who give their non-human participants brain lesions or injections of growth hormones cannot usually return their participants to their original state to see how they would behave under a different set of experimental conditions. Similarly, natural manipulations such as gender, ethnicity, and a person's name are essentially irreversible. You can't study something on a within-subjects basis if you can't push it back and forth on a within-subjects basis.

MIXED-MODEL DESIGNS

As we just noted, one solution to the problem of participant expectancies in within-subjects designs is to forget about using within-subjects designs anytime it could be easy for a participant to figure out your experimental

Figure 9.10

Stimuli from one of the between-subjects conditions of Pelham et al. (1994). Using the square as a 1.0 unit frame of reference, (1) estimate the area of the single circle above the square (e.g., 1.2 units, 3.8 units) and (2) estimate the total area of the eight triangles below the square.

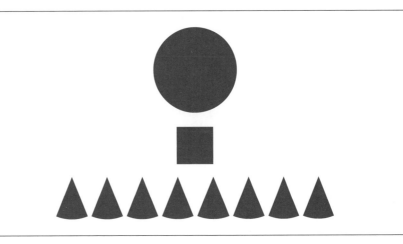

hypothesis. However, a better solution is probably to utilize the advantages of both within-subjects and between-subjects designs by conducting studies with **mixed** or **mixed-model designs**. Mixed-model designs are designs in which (1) at least one independent variable is manipulated on a between-subjects basis and (2) at least one other independent variable is manipulated on a within-subjects basis.

You probably won't be too surprised to learn that one of the first author's favorite examples of this kind of design is a study conducted by Pelham and colleagues. Pelham, Sumarta, and Myaskovsky (1994) were interested in a judgmental heuristic they referred to as the *numerosity heuristic*: the tendency to estimate quantity or magnitude by basing one's judgments disproportionately on the number of units into which a stimulus is divided—without fully adjusting for other important variables (like the size of the units). In one very simple study, Pelham et al. (1994, Study 1) presented people with two different stimuli: (1) an intact circle similar to the one at the top of Figure 9.10 and (2) a lot of little triangles similar to those at the bottom of Figure 9.10. Because people judged the total area of *each* of these two stimulus sets,* the study contained a within-subjects manipulation (whether a stimulus was divided into a lot of pieces or not). Pelham et al.'s participants judged the total area of the triangles to be quite a bit greater than the area of the single, intact circle.

However, if you look at Figure 9.11 on p. 305, you will see that it is possible to help people overcome this judgmental bias based on numerosity. When Pelham et al. made it easy for a second group of participants to see how the triangles could be pushed together to form a circle—by showing them a set of stimuli similar to those that appear in Figure 9.11—these participants were much less likely to base their judgments on numerosity. This second manipulation, the difficulty of reassembling the little triangles into a single circle, was manipulated on a purely between-subjects basis. If we had

---

*Using the square in the middle as a standard, 1-unit comparison.

tried to manipulate this variable on a within-subjects basis, a counterbalancing procedure would have been pretty useless. In particular, the participants who got the easy version of the problem first would almost certainly approach the difficult version of the problem differently than would naive participants. Just as quasi-experiments sometimes allow researchers to take advantage of the best aspects of experimental and nonexperimental research, mixed-models designs (whether they involve purely experimental manipulations or quasi-experimental manipulations) sometimes allow researchers to take advantage of the desirable qualities of between- and within-subjects designs.

SUMMARY

This chapter describes some basic designs that researchers often employ in experimental and quasi-experimental research. Simple between-subjects designs, one-way designs and multiple groups designs, are used when one is only interested in examining the influence of one independent variable. Some between-subjects designs are more complex. Factorial designs look at the main effects of, and interactions between, two or more independent variables. Among other things, these highly efficient designs allow researchers to identify the situations under which a specific main effect does and does not generalize. A second general category of research design is within-subjects designs. Although within-subjects designs represent a creative solution to the problem of individual differences, unless they are conducted very carefully, within-subjects designs have some serious potential drawbacks. In particular, participants who have been exposed to

one experimental condition might respond differently to a subsequent experimental condition than they otherwise would have. Problems such as order effects, practice effects, and interference effects can all wreak havoc on the internal validity of within-subjects designs. For this reason, researchers often use a variety of counterbalancing procedures or employ mixed-model designs. When these solutions are not feasible, researchers most typically return to between-subjects designs (factorial or otherwise). Choosing the right design for a given study (within-subjects or between-subjects) depends on issues such as how easy it is to undo a manipulation and how easy it is to disguise the fact that a within-subjects manipulation is at work. Regardless, each of these basic approaches to research is a versatile tool in the toolbox of a good methodologist.

STUDY QUESTIONS

1. What is a factorial design? How do factorial designs differ from one-way, multiple-groups designs? What are the potential benefits of employing factorial designs in research? If a researcher conducts a study that is a "2 × 5 × 6 factorial," what does this mean? Why might it be preferable to design a series of studies that use 2 × 2 factorials, rather than a single study that uses a 2 × 5 × 6 factorial?

2. What is the maximum number of main effects that can be found in a 2 × 2 × 2 factorial design? What is the difference between a statistical main effect, an interaction effect, and a simple main effect? Is it possible to test for an interaction effect when using a one-way design? Is it possible with a factorial design? What is the difference between a crossover versus a spreading interaction pattern?

3. What are the main advantages to using within-subjects designs? Given these advantages, why is it often preferable to use between-subjects designs? Which of the potential disadvantages to within-subjects designs can be addressed by the use of a Latin Square procedure?

4. Define mixed-model designs. If a hypothetical study uses six within-subjects manipulations and only one between-subjects manipulation, would it still be classified as a mixed-model design? Discuss how using mixed-model designs can sometimes allow researchers to enjoy the benefits of within-subjects designs while avoiding some of their most serious drawbacks.

NOTES

1. In a statistical sense, all of the interactions we cover in this book result from the same interaction pattern. The statistical test in a 2 × 2 ANOVA tests for the presence of a crossover interaction. The other interaction patterns we show in Figures 9.4, 9.5, 9.6, and 9.8 all occur when a statistical crossover interaction is combined with one or more statistical main effects. However, to get an initial grasp on the concept of interactions, many students find it useful to consider the difference that we have described in the language of spreading versus crossover interactions. For additional reading on this issue, check out Rosnow and Rosenthal (1991).

2. Ideally, the *t*-tests that should be performed to conduct simple main effect tests are conceptually identical to, but statistically more complex than, the simple *t*-tests that one conducts in a basic two-sample design. The added complexity arises from the fact that a typical 2 × 2 factorial design usually involves more participants (i.e., a larger *N*) than a typical two-groups design. There are useful ways to capitalize on this fact and base each simple effects test on the entire sample size rather than merely the sample size of the two specific cells that one might wish to compare.

Figure 9.11
Stimuli from the other between-subjects condition of Pelham et al. (1994)

A Brief Course in Statistics

Figures can't lie, but liars sure can figure.
—American folk saying

Although few students are so disenchanted with **statistics** as to adopt this folk saying as a personal credo, many students who take methodology courses are thumbs-down on statistics. In fact, many students report that some of the most frustrating aspects of research methods are the parts having to do with statistics. It's true that a really good methodologist must have at least a working knowledge of statistics. However, it's also true that it's easy to be a really good methodologist *without* being a statistical genius. The statistical skills it takes to be a good methodologist are mainly conceptual rather than computational. If you can understand the logic of **inferential statistics** and familiarize yourself with a few relatively simple statistical tests, you will have the working knowledge of statistics it takes to be a superb methodologist. The purpose of this chapter is to give you that working knowledge. Because inferential statistics are grounded partly in **descriptive statistics**, we cover descriptive statistics first before moving on to inferential statistics.

Before we jump into a detailed discussion of either descriptive or inferential statistics, however, we'd like to remind you that (a) statistics is a branch of mathematics and (b) statistics is its own very precise language. This is very fitting because we can trace numbers, and ultimately statistics, back to the beginning of human language and thus to the beginning of written history. To appreciate fully the power and elegance of statistics we need to take a quick detour to the ancient Middle East.

HOW NUMBERS AND LANGUAGE REVOLUTIONIZED HUMAN HISTORY

About 5,000 years ago, once human beings had began to master agriculture, live in large city-states, and make deals with one another, an unknown Sumerian trader or traders invented the *cuneiform* writing system to keep track of economic transactions. Because we live in a world surrounded by numbers and written language, it is difficult for us to appreciate how ingenious it was for someone to realize that writing things down solves a myriad of social and economic problems. When Basam and Gabor got into their semi-monthly fistfight about whether Gabor owed Basam *five* more or *six* more geese to pay for a newly weaned goat, our pet theory is that it was an exasperated neighbor who finally got sick of all the fighting and thus proposed the cuneiform writing system. The cuneiform system involved making marks with a stylus in wet clay that was then dried and fired as a permanent record of economic transactions. This system initially focused almost exclusively on who had traded exactly what with whom – and most importantly in what quantity. Thus, some Sumerian traders made the impressive leap of impressing important things in clay. This early cuneiform writing system was about as sophisticated as the scribbles of your four-year-old niece, but it quickly caught on because it was *way* better than relying on spoken language alone.

Figure 10.1
Image of Kirkor Minassian tablet. Cuneiform script circa 2040 B.C. (after about 1,000 years of evolution and refinement).

© U.S. Library of Congress

For example, it apparently wasn't too long before the great, great, great grandchild of that original irate neighbor got a fantastically brilliant idea. Instead of drawing a stylized duck, duck, duck, duck to represent four ducks, this person realized that *four-ness* itself (like two-ness and thirty seven-ness) was a concept. He or she thus created abstract characters for numbers that saved ancient Sumerians a *lot* of clay. We won't insult you by belaboring how much easier it is to write and verify the cuneiform version of "17 goats" than to write "goat, goat, goat, goat, goat, goat, goat, goat, goat, goat, goat, goat, goat, goat, goat, goat …" oh yeah "… goat," but we can summarize a few thousand years of human technological and scientific development by reminding you that incredibly useful concepts such as zero, fractions, π (pi), and logarithms, which make possible great things such as penicillin, the Sistine Chapel, and iPhones would have never come about were it not for the development of abstract numbers and language.

It is probably a bit more fascinating to textbook authors than to textbook readers to recount in great detail what happened over the course of the next 5,000 years, but suffice it to say that written language, numbers, and mathematics revolutionized—and sometimes limited—human scientific and technological development. For example, one of the biggest ruts that brilliant human beings ever got stuck into has to do with numbers. If you have ever given much thought to Roman numerals, it may have dawned on you that they are an inefficient pain in the butt. Who thought it was a great idea to represent 1,000 as M while representing 18 as XVIII? And why the big emphasis on five (V, that is) in a base-10 number system? The short answer to these questions is that whoever formalized Roman numbers got a little too obsessed with counting on his or her fingers and never fully got over it. For example, we hope it's obvious that the Roman numerals I and II are standins for human fingers. It is probably less obvious that the Roman V ("5") is a stand-in for the "V" that is made by your thumb and first finger when you hold up a single hand and tilt it outward a bit (sort of the way you would to give someone a "high five".) If you do this with both of your hands and move your thumbs together until they cross in front of you, you'll see that the X in Roman numerals is essentially, V+V. Once you're done making shadow puppets we'd like to tell you that, as it turns out, there are some major drawbacks to Roman numbers because the Roman system does not perfectly preserve place (the way we write numbers in the 1s column, the tens column, the hundreds column, and so on).

If you try to do subtraction, long division, or any other procedure that requires "carrying" in Roman numerals, you quickly run into serious problems, problems that, according to at least some scholars, sharply limited the development of mathematics and perhaps technology in ancient Rome. We can certainly say with great confidence that, labels for Popes and Superbowls notwithstanding, there is a good reason why Roman numerals have fallen by the wayside in favor of the nearly universal use of the familiar Arabic base-10 numbers. In our familiar system of representing numbers, a five-digit number can never be smaller than a one-digit number because a numeral's position is even more important than its shape. A bank in New Zealand (NZ) got a painful reminder of this fact in May of 2009 when they accidentally deposited $10,000,000.00 (yes, ten *million*) NZ dollars rather than $10,000.00 (ten *thousand*) NZ dollars in the account of a couple who had applied for an overdraft. The couple quickly fled the country with the money (all three extra zeros of it).[1] To everyone but the unscrupulous couple this mistake may seem tragic, but we can assure you that bank errors of this kind would be way more common, rather than less common, if we still had to rely on Roman numerals.

If you are wondering how we got from ancient Sumer to modern New Zealand—or why—the main point of this foray into numbers is that life as we know and love it depends heavily on numbers, mathematics, and even statistics. In fact, we would argue that to an ever increasing degree in the modern world, sophisticated thinking requires us to be able to understand statistics. If you have ever read the influential book *Freakonomics*, you know that the authors of this book created quite a stir by using statistical analysis (often multiple regression) to make some very interesting points about human behavior. (Do real estate agents work as hard for you as they claim? Do Sumo wrestlers always try to win? Does cracking down on crime in conventional ways reduce it? The respective answers appear to be no, no, and no, by the way.) So statistics are important. It is impossible to be a sophisticated, knowledgeable modern person without having at least a passing knowledge of modern statistical methods. Barack Obama appears to have appreciated this fact prior to his election in 2008 when he assembled a dream team of behavioral economists to help him get elected—and then to tackle the economic meltdown. This dream team relied not on classical economic models of what people *ought* to do, but on empirical studies of what people actually do under different conditions. For example, based heavily on the work of psychologist Robert Cialdini, the team knew that one of the best ways to get people to vote on election day is to remind them that many, many *other* people plan to vote (Can you say "baaa"?).[2]

So if you want a cushy job advising some future president, or a more secure retirement, you would be wise to increase your knowledge of statistics. As it turns out, however, there are two distinct branches of statistics, and people usually learn about the first branch before they learn about the second. The first branch is descriptive statistics, and the second branch is inferential statistics.

DESCRIPTIVE STATISTICS

Statistics are a set of mathematical procedures for summarizing and interpreting observations. These observations are typically numerical or categorical facts about specific people or things, and they are usually referred to as **data**. The most fundamental branch of statistics is descriptive statistics, that is, statistics used to summarize or describe a set of observations.

The branch of statistics used to interpret or draw inferences about a set of observations is fittingly referred to as inferential statistics, which are discussed in the second part of this chapter. Another way of distinguishing descriptive and inferential statistics is that descriptive statistics are the *easy* ones. Almost all the members of modern, industrialized societies are familiar with at least some descriptive statistics. They include things such as means, medians, modes, and percentages, and they are everywhere. You can scarcely pick up a newspaper or listen to a newscast without being exposed to heavy doses of descriptive statistics. You might hear that LeBron James made 78 percent of his free throws in 2008–2009 or that the Atlanta Braves have won 95 percent of their games this season when they were leading after the eighth inning (and 100 percent of their games when they outscored their opponents). Alternately, you might hear the results of a shocking new medical study showing that, as people age, women's brains shrink 67 percent less than men's brains do, or you might hear a meteorologist report that the average high temperature for the past seven days has been over 100°. The reason that descriptive statistics are so widely used is that they are so useful. They take what could be an extremely large and cumbersome set of observations and boil them down to one or two highly representative numbers.

In fact, we're convinced that if we had to live in a world without descriptive statistics, much of our existence would be reduced to a hellish nightmare. Imagine a sportscaster trying to tell us exactly how well LeBron James has been scoring this season without using any descriptive statistics. Instead of simply telling us that James is averaging 30 points per game, the sportscaster might begin by saying, "Well, he made his first shot of the season but missed his next two. He then made the next shot, the next, and the next, while missing the one after that." That's about as efficient as "goat, goat, goat, goat...." By the time the announcer had documented all of the shots James took this season (without even mentioning *last* season), the game we hoped to watch would be over, and we would never have even heard the score. Worse yet, we probably wouldn't have a very good idea of how well James is scoring this season. A sea of specific numbers just doesn't tell people very much. A simple mean (or percentage) puts a sea of numbers in a nutshell.

Central Tendency and Dispersion

Although descriptive statistics are everywhere, the descriptive statistics used by laypeople are typically incomplete in a very important respect. Laypeople make frequent use of descriptive statistics that summarize the **central tendency** (loosely speaking, the average) of a set of observations ("But my old friend Michael Jordan once averaged 32 points in a season"; "A follow-up study revealed that women also happen to be exactly 67 percent less likely than men to spend their weekends watching football and drinking beer"). However, most laypeople are relatively unaware of an equally useful and important category of descriptive statistics. This second category of descriptive statistics consists of statistics that summarize the **dispersion**, or **variability**, of a set of scores. Measures of dispersion are not only important in their own (descriptive) right, but as you will see later, they are also important because they play a very important role in inferential statistics.

One common, and relatively familiar, measure of dispersion is the **range** of a set of scores. The range of a set of scores is simply the difference between the highest and the lowest value in the entire set of scores. ("The follow-up study also revealed that virtually *all* men showed the same amount of shrinkage. The smallest amount of shrinkage observed in all the male brains studied was 10.0 cc, and the largest amount observed was 11.3 cc. That's a range of only 1.3 cc. In contrast, many of the women in the study showed no shrinkage whatsoever, and the largest amount of shrinkage observed was 7.2 cc. That's a range of 7.2 cc.") Another very common, but less intuitive, descriptive measure of dispersion is the **standard deviation**. It's a special kind of average itself— namely, an average measure of how much each of the scores in the sample *differs* from the sample mean. More specifically, it's the square root of the average squared deviation of each score from the sample mean, or:

$$S = \sqrt{\frac{\sum(x-m)^2}{n}}$$

Σ (sigma) is a summation sign, a symbol that tells us to perform the functions that follow it for all the scores in a sample and then to add them all together. That is, this symbol tells us to take each individual score in our sample (represented by x), to subtract the mean (m) from it, and to square this difference. Once we have done this for all our scores, sigma tells us to add all these squared difference scores together. We then divide these summed scores by the number of observations in our sample and take the square root of this final value.

For example, suppose we had a small sample of only four scores: 2, 2, 4, and 4. Using the formula above, the standard deviation turns out to be:

$$\sqrt{\frac{(2-3)^2 + (2-3)^2 + (4-3)^2 + (4-3)^2}{4}}$$

which is simply:

$$\sqrt{\frac{1+1+1+1}{4}}$$

which is exactly 1.

That's it. The standard deviation in this sample of scores is exactly 1. If you look back at the scores, you'll see that this is pretty intuitive. The mean of the set of scores is 3.0, and every single score deviates from this mean by exactly one point. There is a computational form of this formula that is much easier to deal with than the definitional form shown here (especially if you have a lot of numbers in your sample). However, we included the definitional formula so that you could get a sense of what the standard deviation means. Loosely speaking, it's the average ("standard") amount by which all the scores in a distribution differ (deviate) from the mean of that same set of scores. Finally, we should add that the specific formula we presented here requires an adjustment if you hope to use a sample of scores to estimate the standard deviation in the population of scores from which these sample scores were drawn. It is this adjusted standard deviation that researchers are most likely to use in actual research (e.g., to make inferences about the population standard deviation). Conceptually, however, the adjusted formula (which requires you to divide by n − 1 rather than n) does *exactly* what the unadjusted formula does: it gives you an idea of how much a set of scores varies around a mean.

Why are measures of dispersion so useful? Like measures of central tendency, measures of dispersion summarize a very important property of a set of scores. For example, consider the two groups of four men whose heights are listed below:

	Group 1	Group 2
Tallest Guy	6'2"	6'9"
Tall Guy	6'1"	6'5"
Short Guy	5'11"	5'10"
Shortest Guy	5'10"	5'0"

A couple of quick calculations will reveal that the mean height of the men in both groups is exactly six feet. Now suppose you were a heterosexual woman of average height, and you needed to choose a blind date by drawing names from one of two hats. One hat contains the names of the four men in group 1, and the other hat contains the names of the four men in group 2. From which hat would you prefer to choose your date? If you followed social conventions regarding dating and height, you would probably prefer to choose your date from group 1. Now suppose you were choosing four teammates for an intramural basketball team, and you had to choose one of the two *groups* (in its entirety). In this case, we assume that you would choose group 2 (and try to get the ball to the big guy when he posts up under the basket). Your preferences reveal that dispersion is a very important statistical property because the only way in which the two groups of men differ is in the dispersion (i.e., the variability) of their heights. In group 1 the standard deviation is 1.58 inches. In group 2 it's 7.97 inches.[3]

Another example of the utility of measures of dispersion comes from a 1997 study of parking meters in Berkeley, California. The study's author, Ellie Lamm, strongly suspected that some of the meters in her hometown had been shortchanging people. To put her suspicions to the test, she conducted an elegantly simple study in which she randomly sampled 50 parking meters, inserted two nickels in each (enough to pay for 8 minutes), and timed with a stopwatch the actual amount of time each meter delivered. Lamm's study showed that, on average, the amount of time delivered was indeed very close to eight minutes. The central tendency of the 50 meters was to give people what they were paying for.

However, a shocking 94 percent of the meters (47 out of 50) were off one way or the other by at least 20 seconds. In fact, the range of delivered time was about 12 minutes! The low value was just under two minutes, and the high was about 14 minutes. Needless to say a substantial percentage of the meters were giving people way less time than they paid for. It didn't matter much that other meters were giving people *too much* time. There's an obvious asymmetry in the way tickets work. When multiplied across the city's then 3,600 parking meters, this undoubtedly created a lot of undeserved parking tickets.

Lamm's study got so much attention that she appeared to discuss it on the David Letterman Show. Further, the city of Berkeley responded to the study by replacing their old, inaccurate mechanical parking meters with much more accurate electronic meters. Many thousands of people who had once gotten undeserved tickets were presumably spared tickets after the intervention, and vandalism against parking meters in Berkeley was sharply reduced. So this goes to prove that dispersion is sometimes more important than central tendency. Of course, it also goes to prove that research doesn't have to be expensive or complicated to yield important societal benefits. Lamm's study presumably cost her only $5 in nickels and a little bit of money for travel. That's good because Lamm conducted this study as part of her science fair project—when she was 11 years old.[4] We certainly hope she won a blue ribbon.

A more formal way of thinking about dispersion is that measures of dispersion complement measures of central tendency by telling you something about how *well* a measure of central tendency represents all the scores in a distribution. When the dispersion or variability in a set of scores is low, the mean of a set of scores does a great job of describing most of the scores in the sample. When the dispersion or variability in a set of scores is high, however, the mean of a set of scores does *not* do such a great job of describing most of the scores in the sample (the mean is still the best available summary of the set of scores, but there will be a lot of people in the sample whose scores lie far away from the mean). When you are dealing with descriptions of people, measures of central tendency—such as the mean—tell you what the *typical* person is like. Measures of dispersion—such as the standard deviation—tell you how much you can expect specific people to differ from this typical person.

The Shape of Distributions

A third statistical property of a set of observations is a little more difficult to quantify than measures of central tendency or dispersion. This third statistical property is the *shape* of a distribution of scores. One useful way to get a feel for a set of scores is to arrange them in order from the lowest to the highest and to graph them pictorially so that taller parts of the graph represent more frequently occurring scores (or, in the case of a theoretical or ideal distribution, more probable scores). Figure 10.2 depicts three different kinds of distributions: a **rectangular distribution**, a bimodal distribution, and a **normal distribution**. All of the scores in a rectangular distribution are about equally frequent or probable. An example of a rectangular distribution is the theoretical distribution representing the six possible scores that can be obtained by rolling a single six-sided die. In the case of a bimodal distribution, two distinct ranges of scores are more common than any other. A likely example of a bimodal distribution would be the heights of athletes attending the annual sports banquet for a very large high school that only has two sports teams: women's gymnastics and men's basketball. If this example seems a little contrived, it should. Bimodal distributions are relatively rare, and they usually reflect the fact that a sample comprises only two meaningful subsamples. The third distribution depicted in Figure 10.2 is the most important. It is a normal distribution: a symmetrical, bell-shaped distribution in which most scores cluster near the mean and in which scores become increasingly rare as they become increasingly divergent from this mean. Many things that can be quantified are normally distributed. Distributions of height, weight, extraversion, self-esteem, and the age at which infants begin to walk are all examples of approximately normal distributions.

The nice thing about the normal distribution is that if you know that a set of observations is normally distributed, it further improves your ability to

Figure 10.2

A rectangular distribution, a bimodal distribution, and a normal distribution.

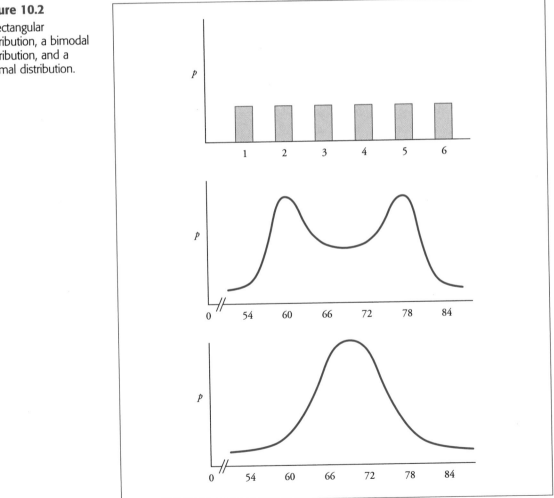

describe the entire set of scores in the sample. More specifically, you can make some very good guesses about the exact proportion of scores that fall within any given number of standard deviations (or fractions of a standard deviation) from the mean. As illustrated in Figure 10.3, about 68 percent of a set of normally distributed scores will fall within one standard deviation of the mean. About 95 percent of a set of normally distributed scores will fall within two standard deviations of the mean, and more than 99 percent of a set of normally distributed scores will fall within three standard deviations of the mean. For example, scores on modern intelligence tests (such as the Wechsler Adult Intelligence Scale) are normally distributed, have a mean of 100, and have a standard deviation of 15. This means that about 68 percent of all people have IQs that fall between 85 and 115. Similarly, more than 99 percent of all people have IQs that fall between 55 and 145.

This kind of analysis can also be used to put a particular score or observation into perspective—a first step toward making *inferences* from particular observations. For instance, if you know that a set of 400 scores on an astronomy midterm (a) approximates a normal distribution, (b) has a mean of 70, and (c) has a standard deviation of exactly 6, you should have a very good picture of this entire set of scores. Also, you should know exactly how impressed to be when you learn that your friend Amanda earned an 84 on the exam. She scored 2.33 standard deviations above the mean, which means that she probably scored in the top 1 percent of the class. How could you tell this? By consulting a detailed table based on the normal distribution. Such a table will tell you that only about 2 percent of a set of scores are 2.33 standard deviations or more from the mean. And because the normal distribution is symmetrical, half of the scores that are 2.33 standard deviations or more from the mean will be 2.33 standard deviations or more *below* the mean. Amanda's score was in the half of that 2 percent that was well above the mean. Translation: Amanda kicked butt on the exam.

Figure 10.3

Approximate proportion of scores falling within one, two, and three standard deviations from the mean of a normal distribution.

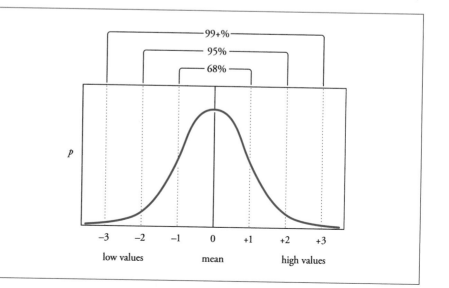

As you know, if you have had any formal training in statistics, there is much, much more to descriptive statistics than we have covered here. For instance, we skipped many of the specific measures of central tendency and dispersion, and we didn't describe all the possible kinds of distributions of scores. However, this overview should make it clear that descriptive statistics provide researchers with an enormously powerful tool for organizing and simplifying data. At the same time, descriptive statistics are only half of the picture. In addition to simplifying and organizing the data they collect, researchers also need to draw conclusions about populations from their sample data. That is, they need to move beyond the data themselves in the hope of drawing general inferences about people. To do this, researchers rely on inferential statistics.

INFERENTIAL STATISTICS

The basic idea behind inferential statistical testing is that decisions about what to conclude from a set of research findings need to be made in a logical, unbiased fashion. One of the most highly developed forms of logic is mathematics, and statistical testing involves the use of objective, mathematical decision rules to determine whether an observed set of research findings is "real." The logic of statistical testing is largely a reflection of the skepticism and empiricism that are crucial to the scientific method. When conducting a statistical test to aid in the interpretation of a set of experimental findings, researchers begin by assuming that the **null hypothesis** is true. That is, they begin by assuming that their own predictions are *wrong*. In a simple, two-groups experiment, this would mean assuming that the experimental group and the control group are not really different after the manipulation—and that any apparent difference between the two groups is simply due to luck (i.e., a failure of random assignment). After all, random assignment is good, but it is rarely perfect. It is always *possible* that any difference an experimenter observes between the behavior of participants in the experimental and control groups is simply due to chance. In the context of an experiment, the main thing statistical hypothesis testing tells us is exactly *how* possible it is (i.e., how likely it is) that someone would get results as impressive as, or more impressive than, those actually observed in an experiment if chance alone (and not an effective manipulation) were at work in the experiment.

The same logic applies, by the way, to the findings of *all* kinds of research (e.g., survey or interview research). If a researcher correlates a person's height with that person's level of education and observes a modest positive correlation (such that taller people tend to be better educated), it is always possible (out of dumb luck) that the tall people in this specific sample just happen to have been more educated than the short people. Statistical testing tells researchers exactly how likely it is that a given research finding would occur on the basis of luck alone (if nothing interesting is really going on). Researchers conclude that there is a true association between the variables they have manipulated or measured only if the observed association would rarely have occurred on the basis of chance.

Because people are not in the habit of conducting tests of **statistical significance** to decide whether they should believe what a salesperson is telling them about a new line of athletic shoes, whether there is intelligent life on other planets, or whether their friend's taste in movies is "significantly different" from their own, the concept of statistical testing is pretty foreign to many budding methodologists. However, anyone who has given much thought to how American courtrooms work should be extremely familiar with the logic of statistical testing. This is because the logic of statistical testing is almost identical to the logic of what happens in an ideal courtroom. With this in mind, our discussion of statistical testing focuses around the simile of what happens in the courtroom. If you understand courtrooms, you should have little difficulty understanding statistical testing.

As mentioned above, researchers performing statistical tests begin by assuming that the null hypothesis is correct—that is, that the researcher's findings reflect chance variation and are not real. The opposite of the null hypothesis is the **alternative hypothesis**. This is the hypothesis that any observed differences between the experimental and the control group *are* real. The null hypothesis is very much like the presumption of innocence in the courtroom. Jurors in a courtroom are instructed to assume that they are in court because an innocent person had the bad luck of being falsely accused of a crime. That is, they are instructed to be extremely skeptical of the prosecuting attorney's claim that the defendant is guilty. Just as defendants are considered "innocent until proven guilty," researchers' claims about the relation between the variables they have examined are considered incorrect unless the results of the study strongly suggest otherwise. ("Null until proven alternative," you might say.) After beginning with the presumption of innocence, jurors are instructed to examine all the evidence presented in a completely rational, unbiased fashion. The methodological equivalent of this is to examine all the evidence collected in a study on a purely objective, mathematical basis. After examining the evidence against the defendant in a careful, unbiased fashion, jurors are further instructed to reject the presumption of innocence (to vote guilty) only if the evidence suggests *beyond a reasonable doubt* that the defendant committed the crime in question. The statistical equivalent of the principle of reasonable doubt is the **alpha level** agreed upon by most statisticians as the reasonable standard for rejecting the null hypothesis. In most cases, the accepted probability value for alpha is set at .05. That is, researchers may reject the null hypothesis and conclude that their hypothesis is correct only when findings as extreme as those observed in the study (or more extreme) would have occurred by chance alone less than 5 percent of the time.

If prosecuting attorneys were statisticians, we could imagine them asking the statistical equivalent of the same kinds of questions they often ask in the courtroom: "Now, I'll ask you, the jury, to assume, as the defense claims, that temperature has no effect on aggression. If this is so, doesn't it seem like an *incredible coincidence* that in a random sample of 40 college students, the 20 students who just happened to be randomly assigned to the experimental group—that is, the 20 people who just happened to be placed in the uncomfortably hot room instead of the nice, comfortable, cool room—would give the stooge almost *three times* the amount of shock that was given by the people in the control group? Remember, Mr. Heat would have you believe that in comparison with the 20 participants in the control group, participants number 1, 4, 7, 9, 10, 11, 15, 17, 18, 21, 22, 24, 25, 26, 29, 33, 35, 36, 38, and 40, as a group, just *happened* to be the kind of people who are inherently predisposed to deliver extremely high levels of shock. Well, in case you're tempted to *believe* this load of bullsh ..." "I object, your Honor! The question is highly inflammatory," the defense attorney interrupts. "Objection overruled," the judge retorts. "As I was saying, in case any one of you on the jury is tempted to take this claim seriously, I will remind you that we asked Dr. R. A. Fisher, an eminent mathematician and manurist, to calculate the *exact probability* that something this unusual could happen due to a simple failure of random assignment. His careful calculations show that if we ran this experiment thousands of times without varying the way the experimental and control groups were treated, we would expect to observe results as unusual as these less than *one time in a thousand!* Don't you think the defense is asking you to accept a pretty incredible coincidence?"

A final parallel between the courtroom and the psychological laboratory is particularly appropriate in a theoretical field like psychology. In most court cases, especially serious cases such as murder trials, successful prosecuting attorneys usually need to do one more thing in addition to presenting a body of logical arguments and evidence pointing to the defendant. They need to identify a plausible motive, a good reason why the defendant might have wanted to commit the crime. It is difficult to convict people solely on the basis of circumstantial evidence. A similar state of affairs exists in psychology. No matter how "statistically significant" a set of research findings is, most psychologists place very little stock in it unless the researcher can come up with a plausible reason for why one might expect to observe those findings. In psychology, these plausible reasons are called theories. It is quite difficult to publish a set of significant empirical findings unless you can generate a plausible theoretical explanation for them.

Having made this "friendly pass" through a highly technical subject, we will now try to enrich your understanding by using inferential statistics to solve a couple of problems. In an effort to keep formulas and calculations as simple as possible, we have chosen some very simple problems. Analyzing and interpreting the data from most real experiments actually requires more extensive calculations than those you will see here, but, fortunately, these labor-intensive calculations are usually carried out by computers rather than by people. Regardless of how extensive the calculations are, however, the basic logic underlying inferential statistical tests is almost always the same—no matter which specific inferential test is being conducted.

Probability Theory

As suggested in the thought experiment with American courtrooms, all inferential statistics are grounded firmly in the logic of probability theory. Probability theory deals with the mathematical rules and procedures used to predict and understand chance events. For example, the principle of regression toward the mean (from Chapter 5) can easily be derived from probability theory. Similarly, the odds in casinos and predictions about the weather can be derived from straightforward considerations of probabilities. What is a probability? From the classical perspective, the **probability** of an event is a very simple thing: it is (a) the number of all specific outcomes that qualify as the event in question divided by (b) the total number of all possible outcomes. The probability of rolling a three on a single roll with a standard six-sided die is 1/6, or .167 because there is (a) one and only one roll that qualifies as a three, and (b) exactly six (equally likely) possible outcomes. For the same reason, the probability of rolling an odd number on the same die is ½, or .50—because three of the six possible outcomes qualify as odd numbers. It is important to remember that the probability of *any* event (or complex set of events, such as the observed results of an experiment) is the number of ways to observe that event divided by the total number of possible events.

With this in mind, suppose the Great Hartini tells you that he has telekinetic powers that allow him to influence the outcome of otherwise fair coin tosses. How could you test his claim? One way would be to ask him to predict some coin tosses and to check the accuracy of his predictions. Imagine that you pull out a coin, toss it in the air, and ask Hartini to call it before it lands. He calls heads. Heads it is! Do you believe in Hartini's self-proclaimed telekinetic abilities? Of course not. You realize that this event could easily have occurred by chance. How easily? Fully half the time we perform the test. With this concern in mind, suppose Hartini agrees to predict exactly ten coin tosses. Let's consider a number of possible outcomes of this hypothetical coin-tossing test. To simplify things, we'll assume that Hartini predicts heads on every toss.

One pretty unremarkable outcome might be that he'd make five out of ten correct predictions. Should you conclude that he does, indeed, have telekinetic abilities? Or that he is *half* telekinetic (perhaps on his mother's side)? Of course not. Making five of ten correct predictions is no better than chance. To phrase this in terms of the results of the test, the number of heads we observed was no different than the *expected frequency* (the average, over the long run) of a random series of ten coin tosses. In this case, the expected frequency is the probability of a head on a single toss (.50) multiplied by the total number of tosses (ten). But what if Hartini makes six or seven correct predictions instead of only five? Our guess is that you still wouldn't be very impressed and would still conclude that Hartini does not have telekinetic abilities (in statistical terms, you would fail to reject the null hypothesis). OK, so what if he makes a slightly more impressive eight correct predictions? What about nine? You should bear in mind that Hartini never said his telekinetic powers were absolutely flawless. Hartini can't *always* carry a glass of water across a room without spilling it, but his friends usually allow him to carry glasses of water unassisted. Despite your firmly entrenched (and justifiable) skepticism concerning psychic phenomena, we hope you can see that as our observations (i.e., the results of our coin-tossing test) depart further and further from chance expectations, you would start to become more and more convinced that something unusual is going on. At a certain point, you'd practically be forced to agree that Hartini is doing something to influence the outcome of the coin tosses.

The problem is that it's hard to know exactly *where* that certain point is. Some people might be easygoing enough to say they'd accept eight or more heads as compelling evidence of Hartini's telekinetic abilities. Other people might ask to see a perfect score of ten (and still insist that they're not convinced). After all, extraordinary claims require extraordinary evidence. That's where inferential statistics come in. By using (a) some basic concepts in probability theory, along with (b) our knowledge of what a distribution of scores should look like when nothing funny is going on (e.g., merely flipping a coin ten times at random, simply randomly assigning 20 people to an experimental or control condition), inferential statistics allows us to figure out exactly how likely it is that a given set of usual or not-so-usual observations would have been observed by chance. Unless it is pretty darn *un*likely that a set of findings would have been observed by chance, the logic of statistical hypothesis testing requires us to conclude that the set of findings represents a chance outcome.

To return to our coin-tossing demonstration, just how likely *is* it that a person would toss nine or more heads by chance alone? One way to figure this out is to use our definition of probability and to figure out (a) all the specific ways there are to observe nine or more heads in a string of ten coin tosses and (b) all the specific outcomes (of any kind) that are possible for a string of ten coin tosses. If we divide (a) by (b), we should have our answer. Let's begin with the number of ways there are to toss nine or more heads. At the risk of sounding like the announcer who was describing Lebron James's scoring history without using inferential statistics, notice that one way to do it would be to toss a tail on the first trial, followed by nine straight heads. A second way to do it would be to toss a head on the first trial and a tail on the second trial, followed by eight straight heads. If you follow this approach to its logical conclusion, you should see that there are exactly ten specific ways to observe exactly nine heads in a string of ten coin tosses. And in case you actually want to see the ten ways right in front of you, they appear in Table 10.1—along with

Table 10.1   All the possible ways to toss nine or more heads in ten tosses of a fair coin: a single tail can come on any of the ten trials, or it can never come at all

1. THHHHHHHHH
2. HTHHHHHHHH
3. HHTHHHHHHH
4. HHHTHHHHHH
5. HHHHTHHHHH
6. HHHHHTHHHH
7. HHHHHHTHHH
8. HHHHHHHTHH
9. HHHHHHHHTH
10. HHHHHHHHHT
11. HHHHHHHHHH

all of the unique ways there are to observe *exactly* ten heads. As you already knew, there is only one of them. However, it's important to include this one in our list because we are interested in all of the specific ways to observe nine *or more* heads in a series of ten coin tosses.[5] So there are 11 ways.

But how many total unique outcomes are there for a series of ten coin tosses? To count all of these would be quite a headache. So we'll resort to a less painful headache and figure it out logically. How many possible ways are there for one toss to come out? Two: heads or tails—which turns out to be 2^1 (2 to the first power). How about two tosses? Now we can observe 2^2 (2 × 2) or four possible ways, namely:

HH, HT, TH, or TT

What about three tosses? Now we have 2^3 (2 × 2 × 2), or eight possible ways.

HHH, HHT, HTH, THH, HTT, THT, TTH, or TTT.

Notice that our answers always turn out to be two (the number of unique outcomes for an individual toss) raised to some power. The power to which two is raised turns out to be the number of trials or specific observations we are making. So the answer is 2^{10} (2 × 2 × 2 × 2× 2 ×2 × 2 × 2 × 2 × 2) or 1,024 possible unique outcomes for a series of ten coin tosses. This value of 1,024 includes every possible number of heads (from zero to ten) and every possible order or position (first through tenth) for all of these possible numbers of heads. So now we have our probability. The probability of observing nine or more heads in a series of ten truly random coin tosses is thus 11/1024, or .011. So for every 100 times we conduct our coin-tossing study, you'd expect to see nine or more heads only about once. That's only 1 percent of the time, and it's pretty impressive. (In fact, it's exactly as impressive as Amanda's score on the astronomy midterm, and we, for what it's worth, were very impressed with Amanda.) So if we treat this study like a real experiment, if we set alpha at .05, and if we observe nine heads, we would have to conclude that Hartini does, in fact, possess the ability to influence the outcomes of otherwise fair coin tosses.

Now perhaps you're the literal type who is saying, "Wait a minute. I still wouldn't believe Hartini has telekinetic abilities, and I certainly don't think most scientists would, either." You are correct, of course, because the theory that you have been asked to accept flies in the face of everything you know about psychology and physics. A much more reasonable explanation for the observed findings is that Hartini has engaged in some form of trickery, such as using a biased coin. However, this simply means that, like any scientific practice, the practice of conducting statistical tests must be carried out using a little common sense. If someone is making a truly extraordinary claim, we might want to set alpha at .001, or even .0001, instead of .05. Of course, setting alpha at a very low value might require us to design a test with a much greater number of coin tosses (after all, ten out of ten tosses, the *best* anyone could possibly do, has a probability higher than .0001—it's 1/1024, which is closer to .001), but the point is that we could easily do this. The exact design of our study is up to us (and, to some extent, to our critics). If people are sufficiently skeptical of a claim, they might also want to see a *replication* (i.e., a repeat) of a questionable or counterintuitive finding. If Hartini replicated his demonstration several times by correctly predicting nine or more heads, and if we enacted some careful control procedures to prevent him from cheating (e.g., we let a group of skeptics choose and handle the coins), even the most ardent anti-telekinetician should eventually be persuaded. And if he or she weren't, we would argue that this person wasn't being very scientific.

The logic of the coin-tossing experiment is exactly the same as the logic underlying virtually all inferential statistical tests. First, a researcher makes a set of observations. Second, these observations are compared with what we would expect to observe if nothing unusual were happening in the experiment (i.e., if the researcher's hypothesis were incorrect). This comparison is ultimately converted into a probability, namely, the probability that the researcher would have observed a set of results at least this consistent with his or her hypothesis if the hypothesis were incorrect. Finally, if this probability is sufficiently low, we conclude that the researcher's hypothesis was probably correct. Because inferential statistics are a very important part of the research process, let's look at another highly contrived but informative question that could be answered only with the use of inferential statistics.

A Study of Cheating

Suppose we offer a group of exactly 50 students the chance to win a very attractive prize (say, a large amount of cash, or an autographed copy of this textbook) by randomly drawing a lucky orange Ping-Pong ball out of a large paper bag. Assume that each student gets to draw only one ball from the bag, that students return the drawn balls to the bag after each drawing, and that the bag contains exactly ten balls, only one of which is orange. Because our university is trying to teach students the values of honesty and integrity, university regulations require us to administer the drawing on an honor system. Specifically, the bag of Ping-Pong balls is kept behind a black curtain, and students walk behind the curtain (one at a time, in complete privacy) to draw their balls at random from the bag. After drawing a ball, each student holds it up above the curtain for everyone else to see. Anyone who holds up an orange ball is a winner.

Suppose that we're the curious types who want to find out if a significant amount of cheating (peeking) took place during the drawing. At first blush, it would seem like there's nothing we could do. Unless we engage in a little cheating ourselves (e.g., by secretly videotaping the drawings), how can we figure out whether people were peeking as they selected their balls? We're at a complete loss to observe the unobservable—unless we rely on inferential statistics. By using inferential statistics, we could simply calculate the number of winners we'd expect to observe if *no one* was cheating. By making a comparison between this expected frequency and the number of winners we actually observed in our drawing, we could calculate the exact probability (based on chance alone) of obtaining a result as extreme as, or more extreme than, the result of our actual drawing. If the probability of having so many winners were sufficiently low, we might reluctantly reject the null hypothesis (our initial assumption that the students were all innocent until proven guilty) and conclude that a significant amount of cheating was happening during the drawing.

Let's find out. To begin with, we need to assume that our suspicions about cheating are completely unfounded and that no one peeked (as usual, we begin by assuming the null hypothesis). Assuming that no one peeked, what's your best guess about how many students should have selected a winning ball? If you are a little fuzzy on your probability theory, remember that you can figure out the expected frequency of an event by multiplying (a) the probability of the event on a single trial by (b) the total number of trials in the series of events. This is how we knew that five was the expected number of observed heads in a series of ten coin tosses. It was .50 × 10. The answer here is also five (it's .10 × 50). Now imagine that we had six winners. Or nine winners, or 15—or 50. Hopefully, you can see, as you did in the coin-tossing study, that as our observed frequencies depart further and further from the frequency we'd expect through the normal operation of chance, we become more and more strongly convinced that our observed frequencies are *not* the product of normal chance processes.

To actually see some inferential statistics in action, let's assume that we had exactly ten winners in our drawing. Because our outcome was a categorical outcome ("success" or "failure" at the draw), and because we had a pretty large sample, we'd probably want to conduct a χ^2 (chi-square) test on these data. The formula for this test appears below:

$$\chi^2 = \sum \frac{(f_o - f_e)^2}{f_e}$$

Recall that Σ (sigma) is a *summation sign* that tells you to add together all the appropriate examples of the basic calculation.

f_o refers to the *observed frequencies* of each of the events you care about (successes and failures when it comes to sampling a lucky orange ball).

f_e refers to the *expected frequencies* for each of these same events.

You could think of a χ^2 statistic as a "surprise index." Notice that the most important thing the formula does is to compare expected and observed frequencies. Specifically, expected frequencies are compared with (i.e., subtracted from) observed frequencies, and then a couple of simple transformations are made on these difference scores. The more our observed frequencies depart from what we'd expect if chance alone were operating (that is, the more surprising our results are), the bigger our χ^2 statistic will become. And as our χ^2 statistic grows, it will be telling us that it's less and less likely that we're observing a chance process (and, in this case, more and more likely that we're observing cheating).

The χ^2 value for ten winners (out of 50) when only five were expected is computed as follows:

$$\chi^2 = \frac{(10 - 5)^2}{5} + \frac{(40 - 45)^2}{45}$$

The 10 in the first half of the equation is the *observed* number of successes, and the two 5s refer to the *expected* number of successes. The 40 in the second half of the equation is the *observed* number of failures, and the two 45s refer to the *expected* number of failures. (This has to be the sample size, which is 50, minus the expected number of successes.) When we do the math, we get 25/5 + 25/45, which works out to 5.55. Notice that this *is not* a probability. The way most inferential statistics work is that you generate both the statistic itself (e.g., a correlation coefficient, a *t*-value, an *F*-ratio), and then use the exact value of the statistic to determine a probability value (one that corresponds to the value of your statistic). If you are doing your calculations on a computer, your software program will always do this for you. That is, it will give you the exact *p*-value (i.e., the exact probability) that corresponds to your results after they have been converted to the unambiguous language of your statistic. However, if you are doing your calculations by hand, as we have here, you will need to consult a statistical table to find the *critical values* for your statistic. In the case of our study of cheating, the critical χ^2 value that corresponds to an alpha level of .05 is 3.841. Any χ^2 value that exceeds this score will have an associated *p*-value that is lower than .05, and thus it will be significant when alpha is set at .05. If we were a little bit more stringent, we might set alpha at .02 or .01. Our χ^2 table happens to include critical values for each of these alpha levels (i.e., for each of these probability values). In a study such as ours, the critical $\chi2$ value for an alpha of .02 is 5.412, and the critical χ^2 value for an alpha of .01 is 6.635. By these criteria, our result is still statistically significant even if alpha is set at .02. However, if we move to the still more stringent alpha level of .01, the number of winners we observed would no longer be significant (because we're effectively saying that it'd take more than ten winners to convince us).

Suppose, instead, we followed standard practice and set alpha at .05. We'd then have to conclude that some people cheated. Notice, however, that we couldn't draw any safe inferences about exactly *who* cheated. Presumably about five of our ten winners just got lucky, and about five cheated. Realizing that *only* about five people cheated provides a different perspective on our findings. Specifically, it highlights the fact that there is often more than one way to look at a set of observations. Notice also that an alternate, and equally correct, perspective on our observation is that people are significantly honest! It appears to be the case that about 45 of our 50 students were completely honest—even in a situation that allowed rampant cheating. Why did we say 45? Because we just decided that only about five people are likely to have cheated. In light of how hard it is to win the game by playing fairly, these five or so cheaters led to a significant amount of cheating. However, if we had started out with the hypothesis that 49 out of 50, or 98 percent, of all people should be expected to cheat under these conditions, and if we had taken 49 (nearly absolute dishonesty) as our standard of comparison rather than five (absolute honesty), we would have obtained an *extremely* large χ^2 value. It would have been

$$\chi^2 = \frac{(10 - 49)^2}{49} + \frac{(40 - 1)^2}{1}$$

which is 1552.04, and which corresponds to an infinitesimally small *p*-value. Even if we set alpha at a very, very, very low level (say one in one billion, or .000000001), it would still be significant. In other words, it's important to keep in mind that we appear to have observed a lot more honesty than cheating.[6]

A final aspect of this exercise about drawing Ping-Pong balls from a bag is that it provides a useful metaphor for thinking about what researchers do when they draw inferences about people. Notice that in the lottery involving Ping-Pong balls, we could not directly observe the phenomenon in which we were interested. The activities we cared about were shrouded behind a black curtain—just as the activities that psychologists often care about (e.g., dissonance reduction, feelings of passionate love, parallel distributed representations of language) are hidden inside the black box of people's minds. Inferential statistics work hand in hand with things like operational definitions to allow us to make scientific inferences. Operational definitions allow us to draw inferences about processes that we cannot observe (those that occur inside the person), and inferential statistics allow us to draw inferences about people we can't observe (those we didn't sample in our study). When we conclude that a research finding is significant, we are concluding that it is real and thus that it applies to people who did not take part in our study. This is one sense in which the Ping-Pong ball demonstration is a little different from most significance tests. Although it would probably be safe to generalize our findings about cheating to other college students, what we really cared about most in this particular test was finding out what was going on in our particular sample. Virtually every inferential statistic that you will ever come across will be based on the logic that was explicated here. Of course, the particular distributions of responses that researchers examine vary enormously from one study to the next, and this, among other things, influences the particular statistics that researchers use to summarize and draw inferences about their data. Moreover, once a researcher has chosen a particular statistic, the specific calculations that she or he will have to carry out (or get a computer to carry out) will typically be a good bit more involved than those you have seen here. For example, a two-way ANOVA requires separate calculations (and separate degrees of freedom) for each of the two possible main effects as well as for the two-way interaction. No matter what statistics they calculate, however, researchers will always rely on the logic of probability theory to help them make their case that something significant is at the root of their empirical observations.

THINGS THAT GO BUMP IN THE LIGHT: FACTORS THAT INFLUENCE THE RESULTS OF SIGNIFICANCE TESTS

Alpha Levels and Type I and II Errors

Now that you have a better feel for what it means for a research finding to be statistically significant, it is our duty to warn you that when we look at significance testing in the cold, hard light of day, it has a couple of limitations. In other words, a few things can go wrong when people conduct statistical tests. First of all, it is important to remember that when a researcher conducts a statistical test and obtains a significant result, it does not *always* mean that his or her hypothesis is correct. Even if an experiment is perfectly executed with no systematic design flaws, it is always possible that the researcher's results *were* due to chance. In fact, the *p*-value we observe in an experiment tells us exactly how likely it is that we would have obtained results like ours even if nothing but dumb luck was operating in our study. Statisticians refer to this worrisome possibility—incorrectly rejecting the null hypothesis when it is in fact correct—as a **Type I error**. The likelihood of making a Type I error is a direct function of where we set our alpha level. As suggested earlier, if we think it would be a practical or scientific disaster to reject the null hypothesis falsely, we might want to set alpha at a very conservative level, such as .001. Then we would be taking only one chance in a thousand of falsely rejecting the null hypothesis.

So why not set alpha at .001 (or beyond) all the time? Because we have to strike a balance between being cautious and being so cautious that we become downright foolish. In statistical terms, if we always set alpha at an extraordinarily low level, we would decrease the likelihood of committing a Type I error at the expense of increasing the likelihood of committing a **Type II error**. A Type II error occurs when we fail to reject an incorrect null hypothesis—that is, when we fail to realize that our study has revealed something meaningful (usually that our hypothesis is correct). The reason it is useful to know about Type I and Type II errors is that we can do certain things to minimize our chances of making both of these troublesome mistakes. As suggested above, one of the easiest ways to minimize Type I errors is to set alpha at a fairly low level. Over the years, most researchers have pretty well agreed that .05 is a reasonable level for alpha (i.e., a reasonable risk for making a Type I error). And of course, if we want to be a little more cautious but don't want to ask anyone to adjust any alpha levels, we can always insist on seeing a replication. In the grand scheme of things, replications are what tell us whether an effect is real.

Effect Size and Significance Testing

Although no one wants to make a Type I error, no one really wants to make a Type II error either. Several things influence the likelihood that a researcher will make a Type II error (and fail to detect a real effect). Researchers have little or no control over some of these things, and they have almost complete control over others. One thing that researchers can't do too much about is their **effect size**, the magnitude of the effect in which they happen to be interested. If you collect a sample of 20 people and measure their heights and their foot sizes, you would probably expect to observe a statistically significant correlation between height and foot size, even though your sample is rather small. This is because there is a pretty robust tendency for big people to have big feet. Of course there are exceptions, but they are relatively rare. We doubt that you will ever meet a gymnast who squeezes into a size 14 or an NBA center who slips comfortably into a size 9. On the other hand, if you give a sample of 20 people a measure of extraversion and a measure of self-esteem, you might not necessarily observe a significant correlation. Although self-esteem and extraversion do tend to go hand in hand, this correlation is much more modest than the substantial correlation between height and foot size. To return to our example about peeking and Ping-Pong balls, it would have been much easier to detect an effect of cheating if cheating had been much more rampant. In fact, notice that in this study it was quite easy to detect an effect of honesty—precisely because honesty was so rampant.

Measurement Error and Significance Testing

Although it's obviously impossible to change the true size of an effect, one thing that researchers can sometimes do to maximize their chances of detecting a small effect is to conduct a within-subjects or repeated measures study. As suggested in Chapter 9, within-subjects designs are usually more sensitive than between-subjects designs. One of the reasons this is the case is that within-subjects designs cut down on extraneous sources of variability that can mask an effect. A person in a cool room might deliver high levels of shock to a confederate just because he or she happens to be an unusually aggressive person. However, if we could observe the behavior of the same person in both a hot and a cool room (and if we could make sure the person doesn't know that she or he is being studied), we would presumably see that the person would deliver even higher levels of shock when the temperature was cranked up a bit. Of course, another reason within-subjects designs are more powerful than between-subjects designs is that they simply increase the number of observations in a study. If we measure the aggressive behavior of each of our 20 participants in both a hot and a cool room, it is almost as if we had 40 participants in our study rather than 20. (For a further discussion of the advantages of within-subjects designs, see Pelham, 1993, but remember the disadvantages we discussed in Chapter 9.)

Sample Size and Significance Testing

When researchers are unable to make use of within-subjects designs, they can still do a couple of things to maximize their chances of detecting a real effect. One simple, albeit potentially expensive, thing that researchers can do is to conduct studies with a lot of participants. Increasing your sample size in a study (whether it be an experiment, a quasi-experiment, or an archival study) can greatly increase the chances that you will detect a real effect. For example, suppose that the true correlation between extraversion and self-esteem among American adults is exactly .32. And suppose that you conduct a survey of 27 randomly sampled American adults and observe a correlation of exactly .32 in your study. Would this be statistically significant? Unfortunately not. In a sample of only 27 people, a correlation of .32 would have a p-value slightly greater than .10—at best a marginally significant value. On the other hand, if you sample 102 people rather than 27, and if you happen to hit the nail on the head again by observing another correlation of exactly .32, this result would be significant even if you had set alpha at .001. That's because when you have a sample as large as the second, it's quite unusual to observe a correlation as large as .32 when the two variables in question are actually unrelated. If this doesn't quite seem right to you, consider your own intuitive conclusions when we asked you earlier what you'd think if Hartini were able to correctly predict six heads in ten coin tosses. If he produced exactly the same proportion of heads (600) in 1000 tosses, you should be much more impressed.

Restriction of Range and Significance Testing

Limits in the range or variability of the variables you measure or manipulate (i.e., restriction of range) can also limit your ability to detect a true effect. Wording your dependent measures carefully, choosing the right population, or making sure that your independent variable is as potent and meaningful as possible (which means not shooting yourself in the foot by artificially diminishing your real effect size) are all potential solutions to the problem of restriction of range. Thus, they are all potential solutions to the problem of avoiding Type II errors. The particular statistical analysis that you conduct can also play an important role in whether your research findings are significant. When you have a choice between conducting a powerful test (one that can detect even relatively small effects) and a less powerful test, you should always perform the more powerful of the two. For example, performing a correlation between two continuous variables (e.g., self-esteem and the number of minutes people spend reading positive feedback about themselves) is usually more powerful than performing a median split (e.g., on self-esteem) and then conducting an ANOVA or *t*-test to see if the mean difference between the low group and the high group is significant. Similarly, making use of continuous ("how much did you like your partner?") rather than dichotomous ("did you like your partner?") dependent measures usually allows for more powerful statistical tests. As a second example, when you have a choice of conducting more than one separate between-subjects analysis (e.g., three different between-subjects ANOVAs, one on each of your three different dependent measures) versus a single within-subjects or mixed-model analysis on the same set of research findings (e.g., because you asked people to rate a target person on positive, neutral, and negative traits), you are usually better served by the analysis that incorporates the within-subjects aspect of your design.

The issues discussed here can help you to conduct better research studies. Just as important, they can also help you to better interpret the findings of other people's studies. For example, if a team of researchers claims that they failed to replicate an important effect, you would do well to ask a few questions about the nature of their

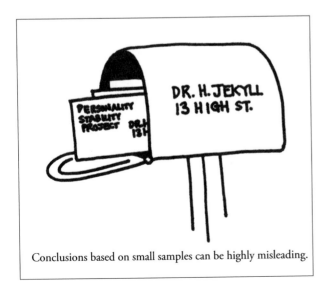

Conclusions based on small samples can be highly misleading.

manipulation, the nature of their sample, the wording of their dependent measures, and the number of participants they included in their between- or within-subjects study before you abandon your own research on the same topic. If Dr. Snittle noted that he failed to replicate Phillips's archival research on suicide because none of the 23 people in his small Nebraska farming community committed suicide after reading about a front-page suicide, it wouldn't be much cause for concern. However, if Dr. Snittle learned to speak fluent Mandarin, traveled to China, gained access to media and suicide records in several very large Chinese provinces, duplicated Phillips's analytical strategies perfectly, and failed to replicate some aspect of Phillips's findings, we'd want to figure out why. Perhaps some aspect of Chinese culture (or Chinese media coverage) is responsible for the difference. This way of thinking about how to interpret statistics is consistent not only with common sense but also with the logic of the scientific method. It is important to remember that statistics are simply a tool. When effectively applied to an appropriate problem, statistics can be incredibly powerful and effective. However, when misapplied or misinterpreted, statistics—like real tools—can be useless or even dangerous.

THE CHANGING STATE OF THE ART: ALTERNATE PERSPECTIVES ON STATISTICAL HYPOTHESIS TESTING

As you may recall from our discussion of the experimental paradigm in Chapter 2, statistical hypothesis testing has become a methodological touchstone for evaluating specific research findings. When a provocative research finding proves to be statistically significant, it is considered scientifically meaningful. When an equally provocative research finding proves to be nonsignificant, it is not taken seriously in scientific circles. As we have just seen, however, an absolute reliance on significance testing, when divorced from basic considerations involving things like effect size or sample size, can lead researchers to inappropriate conclusions. Another way of putting this is that there is more to hypothesis testing than simple significance testing. Critics of significance testing have pointed out, for example, that even when a study is well designed, basing a decision about whether an effect is real solely on the basis of statistical significance is not always advisable. In actual practice, for example, when a researcher conducts a study with promising but not significant results, the researcher will often run additional participants (or modify the design and run the study again) rather than concluding that the original hypothesis is incorrect. In fact, some researchers have argued that the traditional use of significance testing is an inherently misleading process that should be abandoned in favor of other approaches (Cohen, 1994).

Although it seems unlikely that significance testing will be abandoned anytime in the near future, most researchers probably agree that it is often useful to complement significance testing with other indicators of the validity, meaningfulness, or repeatability of an effect. A complete review of the pros and cons of alternate approaches to significance testing is beyond the scope of this book. However, it is probably worth noting that researchers have recently begun to complement significance testing by making use of special statistics to assess the practical or theoretical meaningfulness of research findings. One way researchers have done this is to compute estimates of effect sizes, that is, indicators of the strength or magnitude of their effects. A second way is to compute estimates of (a) the overall amount of existing support for an effect or (b) the consistency or repeatability of the effect. The statistical approach most suited to this second category of questions is referred to as **meta-analysis.**

Estimates of Effect Size

When researchers want to assess the practical or theoretical rather than the statistical significance of a specific research finding—that is, when they want to know how big or meaningful an effect is—they typically calculate an effect size. Although there are many useful indicators of effect size, the two most commonly used are probably r and d. The statistic r is the familiar correlation coefficient, and thus you already have some practice at interpreting one frequently used indicator of effect size. Psychological effects that are considered small, medium, and large correspond respectively to correlations of about .10, .30, and .50. The less familiar statistic d is more likely to be used to describe effect sizes from experiments or quasi-experiments because d is based on the difference between two treatment means. Specifically,

$$d = (\text{mean } 1 - \text{mean } 2)/\Delta$$

where Δ is simply the overall standard deviation of the dependent measure in the sample being studied (see Rosenthal & Rosnow, 1991, p. 302). Thus, d tells us how different two means are in standard deviation units (or fractions thereof). Because two means in a study can sometimes be more than one standard deviation apart, this means that d, unlike r, can sometimes be larger than 1. Otherwise, the interpretation of d is pretty similar to the interpretation of r. The respective values of d that correspond to small, medium, and large effects are about .20, .50, and .80 (see Rosenthal & Rosnow, 1991).

Notice that we used the word "about" when we listed the specific values of r and d that correspond to different effect sizes. We did so because what makes an effect big or small is partly a judgment call. Moreover, how "big" an effect must be to qualify as meaningful varies quite a bit from one research area to another. If a cheap and easy-to-administer treatment (e.g., a daily vitamin C tablet) could reduce the risk of cancer and turned out to have a "small" effect size (e.g., $r = .10$ or less), this could easily translate into millions of saved dollars in medical expenses (and thousands of saved lives). Moreover, as you learned earlier, the size of an effect that researchers observe in a particular study is as much a function of how carefully the study is crafted as it is a function of the state of the world. Thus, considerations of effect size, like considerations of statistical significance, should reflect the theoretical or practical significance of a given finding—regardless of its absolute magnitude. If our easy-to-administer experimental treatment gets blood from only 10 percent of the turnips that we treat, we have to consider the relative value of blood and turnips before deciding how meaningful the treatment is.

For many years, when researchers wanted to know how strongly two variables were related, they would compute a **coefficient of determination** by squaring the correlation associated with a particular effect. So if researchers learn, for example, that people's attitudes about a politician correlated .40 with whether people vote for that politician, the researchers might note that attitudes about candidates account for only 16 percent of the variance in voting behavior (.40 × .40 = .16, or 16 percent). Although this is a technically accurate way of summarizing the association between two variables, some researchers have noted that it provides a misleading picture of the true strength of the relation between two variables. In particular, Rosenthal and Rubin (1982) developed the **binomial effect-size display** as a more intuitive way to illustrate the magnitude and practical importance of a correlation. The binomial effect-size display is referred to as binomial because it makes use of variables that can take on only two values (success or failure, survival or death, male or female) to illustrate effect sizes. As matters of convenience and simplicity, Rosenthal and Rubin demonstrate effect sizes using two dichotomous variables whose two values are equally likely. To simplify matters further, they express binomial effect sizes using samples in which exactly 100 people take on each of the two values of each of the two dichotomous variables.

Consider a hypothetical example involving attendance at a review session and performance on a difficult exam. Assume (a) that exactly 100 of 200 students attend the review session and (b) that exactly 100 of 200 students pass the exam. If we told you that the correlation between attending the review session and passing the exam was .20 (meaning that attendance at the review session accounts for only 4 percent of the variance in exam performance), you might not bother to attend the review session. However, if you examine the binomial effect-size display that appears in Table 10.2, you can see that a correlation of .20 corresponds to 20 more people passing than failing the exam in the group of attendees (and 20 more people failing than passing the exam in the group of nonattendees). More generally, when summarized in a binomial effect-size display, a correlation coefficient corresponds to the difference in success rates that exists between two groups of interest on a dichotomous outcome. If the correlation summarized in Table 10.2 had been .40, we would have seen that 70 percent of those attending the review (and only

Table 10.2 Performance on an exam as a function of attendance at a review session

Attendance at Review	EXAM PERFORMANCE		
	Passed	Failed	Total
Attended	60	40	100
Did not attend	40	60	100
Total	100	100	200

30 percent of those failing to attend) passed the exam ($70 - 30 = 40$). Similarly, if we observed a potential cookie thief for 200 days, if the person was present in the kitchen for exactly 100 of the 200 days, and if cookies disappeared on exactly 100 of the 200 days, then a correlation of .66 would mean that when the potential thief visited the kitchen, cookies disappeared on 83 out of 100 days ($83 - 17 = 66$). Even though the presence of this person accounts for only about 44 percent of the variance in cookie thefts ($.66^2 = .436$), notice that cookies are almost five times more likely to disappear when the person is present than when the person is absent ($.17 \times 5 = .85$). Notice also that the binomial effect-size display can be easily translated into the formula for r that was discussed in the exercise on partial correlation ($r = $ matches $-$ mismatches/n).

Regardless of what format researchers use to illustrate effect sizes, reporting effect sizes provides a very useful complement to traditional significance testing. For example, suppose we know that the effect size for a specific research finding corresponds to a d of .43. If a researcher claims that he or she failed to replicate this finding, it would be useful to consider the effect size the researcher observed (rather than focusing solely on his observed p-value) before concluding that his finding is different from the original (see Rosenthal & Rosnow, 1991, for a much more extensive discussion). In some cases, researchers have claimed that they failed to replicate findings when they observed effects that were just as large as those observed by previous researchers (e.g., when the second group of researchers had a much smaller sample than the first).

Meta-Analysis

Estimates of effect size, such as r or d, provide a useful metric for describing and evaluating the magnitude of specific research findings. Regardless of how big a specific finding is, however, researchers are often interested in questions that have to do with the consistency or repeatability of the finding. Questions about the repeatability of a finding almost always have to do with a *group* of studies (and perhaps even an entire literature) rather than a single specific study. How many failed studies would have to exist to indicate that a set of findings is a statistical fluke rather than a bona fide phenomenon? If a phenomenon is bona fide, how consistently has it been observed from study to study? Even more important, what are the limiting conditions of the effect? That is, when is the effect most and least likely to be observed? Questions such as these can rarely be answered by any single study. Instead, researchers need systematic ways to summarize the findings of a large number of studies.

Fortunately, researchers have developed a special set of statistical techniques to summarize and evaluate entire sets of research findings. Not surprisingly, R. A. Fisher (1938) was one of the first researchers to address the question of how to combine the results of multiple studies. In the days since Fisher offered his preliminary suggestions, researchers have developed a wide array of techniques for summarizing and evaluating the results of multiple studies (see Rosenthal & Rosnow, 1991, for an excellent conceptual and computational review of such techniques). Statistical techniques that are designed for this purpose are typically referred to as meta-analytic techniques. The more commonly used term meta-analysis thus refers to the use of such techniques to analyze the results of studies rather than the responses of individual participants. From this perspective, meta-analyses are to groups of *studies* what traditional statistical analyses are to groups of specific *participants*. Literally, meta-analysis refers to the analysis of analyses.

Prior to the development of meta-analysis, the only way researchers could summarize the results of a large group of studies was to logically analyze and verbally summarize all the studies. Meta-analyses complement such potentially imprecise analyses by providing precise mathematical summaries of different aspects of a set of research findings. For example, a meta-analysis of effect sizes can provide a good estimate of the average effect size that has been observed in all the published studies on a specific topic. Other meta-analytic techniques can be used to indicate how much variability in effect sizes has been observed from study to study on a specific topic (see Hedges, 1987). Finally, meta-analysis can be used to determine the kinds of studies that tend to yield especially large or small effect sizes (e.g., studies that did or did not make use of a particular control technique, studies conducted during a particular historical era, studies conducted in a particular part of the country). This final kind of meta-analysis can provide very useful theoretical and methodological information about the nature of a specific research finding.

As an example of this third approach, consider a couple of meta-analyses conducted by Alice Eagly. Eagly (1978) analyzed findings from a large number of studies of the effects of gender on conformity and social influence. Many researchers had argued that women are more easily influenced than men are. When Eagly looked at studies published prior to 1970 (i.e., prior to the beginning of the women's movement), this is exactly what she found. However, when she focused on studies published during the heyday of the women's movement (during the early to mid-1970s) Eagly observed very little evidence that women were more easily influenced than men. Furthermore, in a second meta-analysis, Eagly and Carli (1981) found that (a) the gender of the researcher conducting the study and (b) the specific influence topic under investigation were good predictors of whether women were more conforming than men. When studies were conducted by men or when the topic of influence was one with which women were likely to be unfamiliar, most studies showed that women were more conforming than men. However, when studies were conducted by women or when the topic of influence was one with which men were likely to be unfamiliar, men often proved to be more conforming than women.

Although meta-analysis may be used for many different purposes, the biggest contribution of meta-analysis to psychological research is probably an indirect one. The growing popularity of meta-analytic techniques has encouraged researchers to think about research findings in more sophisticated ways. Specifically, instead of treating alpha as an infallible litmus test for whether an effect is real, contemporary researchers are beginning to pay careful attention to the question of *when* a given effect is most (and least) likely to be observed. Ideally, when a meta-analysis suggests that an effect is magnified or diluted under certain conditions, researchers should conduct a study in which they directly manipulate these conditions. Doing so boils down to designing factorial studies in which at least two independent variables are completely crossed. As it turns out, then, researchers who have developed and promoted meta-analytic techniques have encouraged a perspective on research that is very similar to McGuire's contextualist perspective reviewed in Chapter 2. It is difficult to fault anyone for adopting this kind of sophisticated approach.

SUMMARY

This chapter provides a very brief overview of statistics. Statistical procedures can be broken down into descriptive statistics and inferential statistics. As the name suggests, descriptive statistics simply describe (i.e., illustrate, summarize) the basic properties of a set of data. Along these lines, measures of central tendency describe the typical or expected score in a given data set. In contrast, measures of dispersion reveal how much the entire set of scores varies around the typical score. The most common measures of central tendency are the mean, the median, and the mode, and the most common measures of dispersion are the range and standard deviation. Of course, psychologists interested in testing psychological theories are typically interested in inferential statistics as well as descriptive. This branch of statistics applies probability theory to determine whether and to what degree an observed data pattern truly differs from a chance pattern. Inferential statistics thus provide a basis for determining whether an observed research finding reveals a systematic association, or whether it merely reflects noise or error. For instance, if a treatment group differs from a control group to a degree that would not be expected by chance alone, researchers will view this as evidence that the treatment is actually causing changes in the outcome. As another example, if people who tend to score high in self-esteem also tend to score high on a measure of aggression, inferential statistics can tell us whether this tendency for the scores to go hand in hand could have happened easily by chance or whether the tendency is strong and consistent enough that it probably reflects a true association between these two variables. Both of these examples reveal the logic of significance testing. More recently, statisticians have begun to complement traditional statistical tests with indicators of effect size. Whereas statistical significance tells you whether an effect is likely to exist, effect size estimates tell you how large an effect is likely to be.

STUDY QUESTIONS

1. What is the difference between descriptive and inferential statistics? Classify each of the following categories of statistics as descriptive or inferential: (a) means, (b) standard deviations, and (c) p-values. Make an argument that one could categorize effect size indicators such as d or r either way.

2. How does the statistical concept of the null hypothesis relate to Popper's point that researchers should try to falsify theories (as discussed in Chapters 1 and 2)?

3. What is an alpha level, and how does it affect how you interpret a p-value? How does the choice of a specific alpha level affect the chances of making a Type I error? How about a Type II error?

4. What is the difference between an effect-size estimate and a test of statistical significance? Are effect-size indicators influenced by sample size? What about tests of statistical significance?

NOTES

1. For more details see http://www.news.com.au/business/story/0,27753,25515799-462,00.html

2. See the *Time* magazine story at http://www.time.com/time/magazine/article/0,9171,1889153,00.html

3. We adapted this example of men of varying heights from an illuminating statistics lecture by Daniel Gilbert.

4. http://imgs.sfgate.com/cgi-bin/article.cgi?f=/c/a/1998/12/28/MN9307.DTL&type=printable

5. Computing the probability of an event as extreme as or more extreme than an observed event (or set of events) is standard practice for most statistical tests. At first blush, paying attention to events even more extreme than an observed event may seem a little odd. However, if we care about events as unusual as or more unusual than our observed event (which we almost always do), it makes a lot of sense. If you think of the unusualness of a set of observations (e.g., a lot of heads tossed, a pair of means that are noticeably different) as a standard of experimental performance that a researcher hopes to meet or exceed, this may help make sense of this practice. If we set a high-jump bar at exactly six feet and Amanda clears it, the set of outcomes that Amanda, the judges, and the fans all care about is jumps of exactly six feet *or higher*. Furthermore, if we try to calculate the probability of a specific observation or event, probabilities would almost always be pretty low—because the probability of any specific event is always quite low. For example, the probability of tossing a fair coin 20 times and observing *exactly* ten heads is .176, even though this is the *most* likely of all the possible outcomes. Once we move to continuous rather than discrete events, this is even more true. The probability that a particular high jump will be *exactly* six feet—even for a very good jumper who is trying to jump exactly six feet—is extremely low.

6. Speaking of cheating, we cheated. Unless we increase our sample size to about 250 people, we couldn't actually conduct this second χ^2 analysis. That's because we're allowed to use the χ^2 statistic only in situations in which all our expected frequencies have a value of at least 5.0. With values lower than 5, the χ^2 values that are generated can be pretty unstable and pretty inaccurate. In an extreme case such as this one, however, it's safe to say that people were significantly honest. If nothing else, we could always choose to make a very conservative comparison and set 90 percent (instead of 98 percent) dishonesty as our standard of comparison. This would yield five rather than one as the expected number of nonwinners. In case you want to practice your calculations, the value you should get if you do the analysis this more conservative (but legal) way is $\chi^2 (1, n = 50) = 272.22$. The 1 in the parenthesis indicates the *degrees of freedom* you'd report in an actual research report in which you conducted this analysis. We discuss this again in the section on reporting commonly used statistics.

Telling the World About It

In this … chapter, there is nothing new to be said and it will not be possible to avoid repeating what has often been said before.
—Sigmund Freud

Never speak more clearly than you think.
—Jeremy Bernstein

One of the most gratifying aspects of the research process is publishing a research paper in a scholarly journal or giving a research talk to one's peers. Publishing papers and giving talks are public signs that the long weeks and months you have devoted to a research project were not spent in vain. Your work means something. In the case of a talk, someone invited you to tell other people about it. In the case of a publication, an editor and several expert reviewers voted to publish your work, and researchers in your area of investigation will presumably read about it. To focus on writing papers for the moment, we are also of the opinion that, even if you do not intend to publish a paper in a scholarly journal, the exercise of writing up a research report can be an inherently gratifying experience. Writing is a complex skill that most people can master only through great dedication and effort. We realize that this may sound a little like something your grandparents would tell you, but there is something inherently satisfying about mastering any complex skill.

The best metaphor we can offer for either writing research papers or giving academic talks is that these activities are a lot like juggling or playing a musical instrument. First, almost no one can honestly say that he or she wouldn't like to be able to do these things and do them well. Second, a few people are so good at these activities that they can do them for a living. Third, for the most part, the people who do these things beautifully and make them look easy are those who have spent countless hours practicing. Of course you can't work at "Cirque du Soleil" or sign with a major record label by showing off your beautiful prose, but you can do equally important things like impressing the professors who provide your letters of reference for graduate school (or writing memos that your co-workers actually understand). From the perspective of this metaphor, the purpose of this chapter is to help beginning writers and speakers turn themselves into the literary equivalents of reasonably competent three-ball jugglers: people who don't make too many drops—and who don't hurt anyone along the way.

Like the introduction to Freud's *The Ego and the Id* (quoted at the beginning of this chapter), much of what we say in this chapter has already been said before. Of course in Freud's case, he could at least take credit for having said it *himself* the first time. In contrast, many of the ideas we present here are borrowed from others. To be more specific, about half of this brief chapter deals with general points about writing empirical research papers and has been inspired heavily by Daryl Bem's (1987) excellent treatment of this topic. Most of what little we have added to Bem's analysis is simply a description of what we have observed among the best writers in social psychology and social cognition (including Bem). In keeping with the hands-on approach we have adopted in this text, we have supplemented this chapter on writing with Appendix 4, which contains the manuscript version of an entire American Psychological Association (APA)-style research paper written by Paul Stermer and Melissa Burkley. The paper provides a complete model of an APA-style paper in draft form. More importantly, it also provides you with a complete model of clear, concise, scholarly, and provocative writing. We suspect that when you are composing your own research papers, you will find yourself referring to this model manuscript much more often than you find yourself referring to this chapter. For example, if you write an APA-style paper yourself, and you forget whether to indent the first sentence of your abstract, you can refer to this sample paper to see that abstracts are *not* indented. To complement both this sample paper and the first two-thirds of this chapter, we have also included a table in this chapter (Table 11.1) summarizing what goes into a good research paper. Also, in Appendix 4, we address a very specific but important aspect of writing that is typically neglected in research methods texts—namely, how to report the results of some commonly used statistical tests. Because the material about reporting statistics is a little more technical than the material reported here, we have set this special discussion of writing aside as a brief lesson unto itself.

The last part of this chapter describes how to give a good research talk in psychology. In the case of this discussion, we demoted ourselves from the role of inspired borrowers to the role of inspired typists. That is, instead of trying to give you advice about giving talks, we have simply provided you with a verbatim account of someone else's advice on giving talks. This advice comes in the form of an informal paper by Dan Gilbert, and the paper is included with his permission. As you will see, Gilbert has also contributed to this chapter in a second way: by providing an excellent example of someone who follows the rules of good writing.

THE HOURGLASS APPROACH TO EMPIRICAL RESEARCH PAPERS

The most important thing for you to know about writing an empirical research report is to structure your report in an *hourglass* form. For example, in the Introduction, open broadly by asking a general question or making a general statement about people. Then work your way toward your specific research hypothesis by reviewing previous research and making a logical case for the study or set of studies that you are reporting. In the Method and Results sections, you become even more specific. In this section, you focus on the important details of your design and analysis and stick very, very close to your data when interpreting your findings. Finally, in the General Discussion section, you begin to broaden your scope again by offering some theoretical and practical insights about what your findings mean (e.g., how they complement or invalidate the theories that you reviewed in the Introduction). Finally, end your paper as broadly as you began, by summarizing the implications of your research in a very general way.

To see an hourglass approach at work, consider some excerpts from a paper by Gilbert, Krull, and Malone (1990). Gilbert et al. were interested in an idea that goes all the way back to the 17th century, when it was discussed by such luminaries as René Descartes (1644/1984) and Baruch Spinoza (1677/1982). The idea is a little slippery; it has to do with whether it is possible to comprehend something without briefly believing it (i.e., considering it to be true). Descartes considered it patently obvious that we can consider newly encountered ideas as abstract possibilities—that is, that we can represent ideas without reference to whether the ideas are true or false. Spinoza, on the other hand, believed that the act of thinking about something was tantamount to thinking it so (at least momentarily). Of course, Spinoza realized that we can identify what is true and what is false, but his position was that to consider an idea is first to accept it, and then to reject it if it proves to be unsupportable. Perhaps because their research problem began with Descartes, Gilbert et al. (1990) open their paper with a quotation from Descartes. Here is that quotation along with their first few sentences:

> That we have the power ... to give or withhold our assent at will, is so evident that it must be counted among the first and most common notions that are innate in us.
>
> —Descartes (1644/1984, p. 205)

René Descartes was right about so many things that he surely deserved to be wrong about something: How people come to believe certain ideas and disbelieve others may be the something about which he was mistaken. Descartes insisted that ideas are initially represented in the mind without reference to their veracity. Thus, upon hearing the utterance "Armadillos may be lured from a thicket with soft cheese," Descartes suggested that the listener's mind simply held that proposition *in aequilibrio*, and only later submitted the proposition to a rational analysis by which it was determined to be true or false....

After reviewing the basics of the Spinozan alternative to Descartes's hypothesis, Gilbert et al.'s report gradually becomes more specific. By the end of the introduction they report:

> The Spinozan hypothesis asserts that rejecting an idea requires the extra step of unaccepting or "tagging" a mental representation as false. If this is so, then people should initially accept both true and false ideas upon comprehension but, when the processing of the idea is interrupted, should not be able to go on and unaccept (or tag) false ideas. As such, interruption should cause Spinozan systems to mistake false ideas for true ones, but not vice versa.

After offering a competing description of mental representation suggested by Descartes's analysis, the authors become more specific still by reporting that:

> Study 1 was an initial attempt to test these competing predictions.

One paragraph later, the authors provide an overview of their first experiment:

> In the context of a language-learning experiment, subjects were presented with novel propositions on a computer screen. On most trials, subjects were subsequently informed that the preceding proposition was either true or false. On some of these trials, subjects' processing of the proposition was interrupted by having them quickly perform an unrelated task (namely, pushing a button in response to a tone). Finally, subjects were presented with the original propositions (in question form) and were asked to determine whether they were true or false.

The ensuing body of the Method section is even more detailed than this thumbnail sketch. It provides details about the research participants, the instructions, the procedure, and the dependent measures that would allow theoretical friends or foes to attempt an exact replication of their experiment. For example, because the authors presented their participants with some pretty unusual stimuli that had never been used in previous research (sentences like "A trica is a weasel," "A nasli is a snake," and "A suffa is a cloud"), they include all these stimuli in a table. The Results section is equally detailed, and equally concise. It provides a summary of the relevant findings in both verbal and graphical form, and it briefly addresses some potential criticisms of the observed findings (which, by the way, supported the position of Spinoza rather than Descartes).

After providing equally precise descriptions of the methods and results of two additional experiments, the authors come to their General Discussion, where their writing begins to take on the same broad form it took in the Introduction. Instead of repeating the specific statements they made in their Results sections ["Subjects responded much more rapidly on comprehension trials ($M = 1,336$ ms) than they did on assessment trials ($M = 1,899$ ms), $F(1, 28) = 65.9$, $p < .001$."], they quote Scottish philosophers, mention rhinoceroses, and discuss research in psycholinguistics—in much the same way that they had originally quoted Descartes, mentioned armadillos, and discussed research on automatic versus controlled information processing. After reiterating the basic theme of their report—that propositions are initially coded as true and must later be recoded as false when they prove to be logically untenable—they end their report as broadly as they began it:

> On occasion, of course, such attempts to recode false information will fail, and when this happens, a Spinozan system will find itself believing what it should not. This method of initially presenting ideas as true may be economical and it may be adaptive, but any system that uses it will err on the side of belief more often than doubt. That human beings are, in fact, more gullible than they are suspicious should probably "be counted among the first and most common notions that are innate in us."

In our usual style of taking back a little bit of what we have just told you, we should let you know that writers who have just been introduced to the hourglass approach often take this advice a bit *too* seriously. They open too broadly, they narrow too narrowly (especially in the Method section), and they close even more broadly than they opened. If your opening or closing paragraphs say anything about the origins of life on earth, the entire field of psychology, or even the entire field of interpersonal relationships, you may have overdone it. An intelligent reader who has read only your opening paragraph should be starting to get some idea of the exact research hypothesis you tested. An intelligent reader who has read only your closing paragraph should have about the same kind and amount of information. If these things are not the case, you need to become a little more focused. The litmus test for the right level of specificity in your Method section has already been provided above. A reader who wishes to replicate your study should be able to get all the information needed to do so by reading your Method section. However, the reader shouldn't be distracted by details that weren't an important part of your study. Unless you are studying the effects of paper color and survey length on people's survey responses, telling readers exactly how many pages were in your survey, or the color of paper on which it was printed, is likely to be distracting rather than enlightening. On the other hand, providing people with the exact phrases that anchored the endpoints of your dependent measure or telling them exactly what your confederate did to be annoying are both highly specific and highly relevant.

At the end of this chapter, in Table 11.1, we provide a checklist of important things to include in a research paper. That checklist serves as a final reminder to organize research papers like an hourglass. If you do so, there is no guarantee that your paper will be as seamless as Gilbert et al.'s paper on Spinozan belief systems, but we can guarantee that it will be better than it otherwise would have been.

SOME RULES TO WRITING RESEARCH PAPERS

If you have crafted your paper in the design of an hourglass and you wish to polish your hourglass up a bit, you can still do quite a few things to improve the quality of your writing. In this section, we briefly summarize some of these things.

Rule 1: Be Correct

Reading an otherwise beautifully written paper that turns out to be filled with mistakes is like opening a beautiful silk purse and finding it stuffed full of sow's ears. Whether it is typographical, grammatical, or factual, any kind of error in a research paper is an embarrassing sign that the author hasn't done his or her homework (because part of an author's homework is double-checking his or her paper for errors). Misinterpreting or misquoting the work of another researcher is probably the most serious error a writer can make. When writers do this, they run the risk of embarrassing those they have miscited and those they have misled as well as themselves. Similarly, reporting a statistic incorrectly or getting a crucial result backward is an easy way either to lose credit with the instructor who is reading your assignment or to lose credibility with the colleagues who are reading your submission to a journal. After you have carefully proofread a draft of your paper once, the second-best way to find additional mistakes is to let the paper sit for a couple of days and to read it again. The *best* way is to show your carefully rewritten second or third draft to a friend or colleague who is willing to play the role of copy editor and identify the mistakes that you and your computer's spell-check program never caught.

Rule 2: Be Clear

On the other hand, if you do prove to be wrong about something, the least you can do is to try to be clear about it. There is no greater virtue in writing than clarity. When an author's writing is not clear, most readers will take it as a sign that the writer's *thinking* isn't clear either. That being said, some writers do seem to subscribe to an opposite theory of writing. Some writers seem to try very hard to be vague and imprecise, perhaps based on the theory that it's hard to be wrong when you're vague. As suggested in the quote from the physicist Jeremy Bernstein at the start of this chapter, an unclear writer might occasionally succeed in hiding unclear thinking. If your ideas are truly horrible, perhaps you should work hard to cover this up by using obtuse, unclear language. However, if you ever wish to say something important, you would be better off reworking your ideas so that they are solid. Solid ideas should never be shrouded in the mystery of confusing prose.

Although it is hard to give general advice about how to be clear, one thing that authors can try to do is to put themselves in the shoes of the smart and motivated reader who is nonetheless ignorant about the topic of a research paper. This is difficult. Once you have thought long and hard about your research problem, it is hard to get back in touch with all the subtle but important things you didn't know before you started it. But you should and must tackle this problem. As a writer, it is your task to do the hard work that makes reading your papers easy. Try to take the perspective of a person who has never seen your survey, your apparatus, or your laboratory, and then tell this person exactly what he or she needs to know to understand the details of your study.

"Yes, Helen, get me the #@*!% employment agency again. And tell them
I asked for ELVES, tiny little ELVES!"

*Choose your words and check your spelling carefully. Seemingly small mistakes
can sometimes lead to serious misunderstandings.*

You can also do a few technical things to ensure that your writing style is
as clear as possible. One thing is to use parallel constructions. Just as parallel
parking strategies are counterintuitive to most beginning drivers, parallel construction strategies are counterintuitive to most beginning writers. If you are
wondering what parallel constructions are, you were just exposed to one in
the last sentence. It was easy to write it, and it was easy to read it. There!
You were just exposed to one again. We bet you're starting to notice them,
and we bet you're starting to like them. Whenever you have to express two
logically related ideas, the use of parallel constructions makes it easy for
your reader to see whatever logical relation you are trying to point out.
Opposites become clearly different. Similarities become clearly the same. As
Bem (1987) noted:

> Inexperienced writers often substitute synonyms for recurring words and
> vary their sentence structure in the mistaken belief that this is more creative,
> stylish, and interesting. Instead of using repetition and parallel construction,
> as in "Men may be more expressive than women in the domain of negative
> emotion, but they are not more expressive in the domain of positive

emotion," they attempt to be more creative: "Men may be more expressive than women in the domain of negative emotion, but it is not true that they are more willing and able to display the more cheerful affects." Such creativity is hardly more interesting but it is certainly more confusing.

If you have developed the bad habit of avoiding parallel constructions in your writing and you don't know how to break it, consider writing the way you speak. Spoken language has to be produced and comprehended on the fly, and for this reason we often speak using parallel constructions. We say things like "I love him a lot, but I don't like him very much." Similarly, our friends and grandparents express their sympathy for our situation by reminding us that "You can't live with 'em, and you can't live without 'em." Anyone who says "I love him a lot, but my level of liking for him is definitely on the low side" runs the risk of slowing down the conversation. Anyone who responds with "You can't live with 'em, and yet it's pragmatically and emotionally untenable to go about your life in their absence" runs the risk of bringing the conversation to a screeching halt. If you want to be a good scientific writer, you can't live without parallel constructions.

Another technical thing writers can do to improve the clarity of their research reports is to avoid the use of abbreviations, jargon, and grandiose phraseology (fancy language). Abbreviations save space, but they can also lead to confusion. Because many readers read papers in bits and pieces, they may reach the second half of your paper having forgotten whether your AAA condition had to do with the size of a battery or the name of a motor vehicle club. Even when you use commonly understood (and thus acceptable) abbreviations, be sure to define them the first time you use them. In an empirical research paper, the first time readers learn that your participants are from UCLA or USC, they should see it in parentheses: "Participants were 20 undergraduates enrolled in an advanced juggling workshop at the University of California, Los Angeles (UCLA)." Similarly, the first time you reveal that you conducted an ANOVA write out the complete term, and put the abbreviation in parentheses: "an analysis of variance (ANOVA)." Once you have done this, you are free to use the abbreviation throughout the rest of your paper. For similar reasons, technical jargon should be used only when it clarifies rather than mystifies. Whenever technical but potentially unfamiliar terms do impart a more precise meaning than informal terms, you should definitely use them but be sure to define them the first time they come up: "In this report, we focus on implicit self-regard, that is, on people's overlearned—and presumably unconscious—positive and negative evaluations of themselves."

Finally, a common mistake that novice writers sometimes make is to try to write in what might be called "Scientese." That is, novice writers often adopt an overly formal style in an effort to sound scientific. This can be seen when writers start using words, like "phraseology," which they would never use in normal everyday phraseology. Along similar lines, words such as "thusly," "shall," and "hitherto" are probably better abandoned in favor of such words as "thus," "will," and "previously." Another common form of overly scientific writing is to name one's hypotheses using numbers and then to compound this error by creating numbered abbreviations. For instance, a writer might state, "Hypothesis 1 is

Original Version	English Translation

Some writers couch their meanings in obscure language, perhaps on the assumption that it's hard for readers to criticize what they can't understand. Avoid this temptation. If you're going to be wrong, at least be clear about it.

that implicit self-regard will be positively correlated with explicit self-esteem, and Hypothesis 2 is that implicit self-regard will be positively correlated with extraversion." The writer then resurrects these hypotheses later on in the paper, assuming that they are still fresh in the minds of most readers. Pages later, the same author might write, "Our findings did not support Hypothesis 1, but they did support Hypothesis 2." This strategy of labeling makes it easier for writers to write, but it does so at the expense of making it harder for readers to read. It is hard enough to find readers who will even *try* to make it through an entire research paper. Don't scare your potential fans away by bombarding them with numbered hypotheses. Thusly, we implore ye to endeavour for limpidity in thine composition, lest ye embrace too ceremonious a timbre.

In other words, be clear.

Rule 3: Be Comprehensive (but Discerning)

This rule is closely related to the rule about being correct, but it refers mainly to the breadth of topics you discuss. It's important to cover all of your important results, to discuss your manipulation checks, and to include the references for all the work you cite. Including all your references is so important that when copy editors are proofreading an accepted paper to get it ready for publication, they go through the entire paper, marking and numbering every reference in the paper and cross-checking it against the reference list. Of course, you won't have that kind of assistance before you submit your paper for consideration in the first place, and so you should do the same kind of thing yourself. When we have read drafts of papers that were not yet published, we have occasionally become pretty upset at the authors for citing and describing a really interesting study and then failing to include the citation in the reference list. This is particularly annoying when the author's last name is Pelham and the reader's last name is Blanton.

This rule about covering all the important bases also applies to theoretical comprehensiveness. Unless you are already a true expert in the area of your paper topic, you should probably perform a literature search (or update your old one) before you even begin to compose your paper. Although you do not need to cite everything that has ever been written on your topic, there will usually be a number of published papers that have changed the way people think about the issue you are studying. You should know the relevant research literature well enough to identify any studies that are directly relevant to the topic of your paper. Be sure to cite these studies—not only to help tell a coherent story but also to give credit where credit is due.

Although it is important to cast a wide net, it is equally important not to cast your net where it does not belong. Believe it or not, it is possible to cite *too many* published papers in your own research paper. Scientific thinking has to be precise and direct, and if you cite a study, it should mean that the study has some kind of precise, direct relevance to your paper. Although this is often a judgment call, the key reason to cite a paper is that it makes a theoretical point or summarizes an empirical finding that supports (or stands in opposition to) the point that you wish to make. Thus, if there is no logical connection between established research on how children learn to do arithmetic and your own research on how children learn to read, you have no business citing your aunt Rochelle's brilliant research on how young children learn to do arithmetic (no matter how brilliant it is, and no matter how much you happen to know about it). On the other hand, if research in both areas shows that young children learn these new academic skills by capitalizing on their previously established skills (i.e., their ability to speak and to estimate quantity), a citation of your aunt's work might be very appropriate.

Rule 4: Be Concise

When the first author of this text was an undergraduate, he was selected for an award that meant he not only got his photo printed in the college yearbook but was also allowed to include a statement regarding his philosophy of life, school, or anything else he wanted to write about. He wrote a *very long* essay. To make matters worse, it wasn't very coherent, and it certainly wasn't very concise. Beneath the essay, a photo of this person dressed in some bizarre clothing seemed to complement his obtuse points about communicating with other people, marching to the beat of a different drummer, and walking the fine line between genius and mental illness. If he had followed the example of some of the people who had won the award before he did, he probably would have written a very different essay. A year or so before he graduated, his college yearbook included a photo of T. Mack Brown, wearing a suit and tie, and making a much subtler point about how to communicate with people. His essay was much shorter than the first author's. The essay was so inspiring that the first author committed it to memory. The essay read as follows:

Be concise. Don't bore people.

Being concise is another tricky aspect of good writing. It is often hard to be concise without sacrificing clarity, correctness, or comprehensiveness. Nonetheless, the solution to the problem is pretty straightforward. As Bem (1987) put it, "Omit needless words." This often means writing and rewriting a passage until you have squeezed the maximum meaning out of every word. Consider what Bem had to say about the importance of being concise:

Virtually all experienced writers agree that any written expression that deserves to be called *vigorous writing*, whether it is a short story, an article for a professional journal, or a complete book, *is* characterized by the attribute of being succinct, *concise*, and to the point. *A sentence*—no matter where in the writing it occurs—*should contain no unnecessary* or superfluous *words*, words that stand in the way of the writer's direct expression of his or her meaning and purpose. In a very similar fashion, *a paragraph*—the basic unit of organization in English prose—should contain *no unnecessary* or superfluous *sentences*, sentences that introduce peripheral content into the writing or stray from its basic narrative line. It is in this sense that a writer is like an artist executing a drawing, and it is in this sense that a writer is like an engineer designing a machine. Good writing should be economical *for the same reason that a drawing should have no unnecessary lines, and* good writing should be streamlined in the same way that *a machine* is designed to have *no unnecessary parts*, parts that contribute little or nothing to its intended function.

This prescription to be succinct and concise is often misunderstood, and *requires* judicious application. It certainly does *not* imply *that the writer* must *make all of his* or her *sentences short* or choppy *or* leave out all adjectives, adverbs, and qualifiers. Nor does it mean *that he* or she must *avoid* or eliminate *all detail* from the writing *and treat his* or her *subjects* only in the barest skeleton or *outline* form. *But* the requirement does imply *that every word* committed to paper should *tell* something new to the reader and contribute in a significant and non-redundant way to the message that the writer is trying to convey.

Bem then asks the reader to take the advice offered in this essay and to omit all the nonitalicized words. The result is an original remark by Strunk and White (1979), through which Bem intentionally wove his much longer statement:

> Vigorous writing is concise. A sentence should contain no unnecessary words, a paragraph no unnecessary sentences, for the same reason that a drawing should have no unnecessary lines and a machine no unnecessary parts. This requires not that the writer make all his sentences short, or that he avoid all detail and treat his subjects only in outline, but that every word tell.

To see an example of concise writing in research (as well as another example of the hourglass model), we spare you the wordier version and go directly to the opening and closing paragraphs of a paper by Swann, Stein-Seroussi, and Giesler (1992). The paper is succinctly entitled "Why People Self-Verify."

> Nearly half a century ago, Prescott Lecky (1945) proposed that people strive to confirm their self-conceptions, even if those self-conceptions are negative. Over the years, his proposal has provoked considerable controversy. Initially, critics questioned the assumption that self-confirmation strivings were powerful enough to override a desire for positive, self-enhancing information. Their skepticism grew stronger when the first widely cited study to support Lecky's claim (Aronson & Carlsmith, 1962) proved difficult to replicate (for reviews, see Dipboye, 1977; Shrauger, 1975). By the mid-1970s, even those who sympathized with Lecky reluctantly concluded that his hypothesis referred to a relatively circumscribed phenomenon (e.g., Shrauger, 1975).

In the next paragraph, Swann et al. discuss how the tables have begun to turn, and they review research suggesting that people *will* sometimes forgo positive feedback out of a concern for self-confirmation. They then discuss the results of two studies designed to figure out *why* people engage in self-confirmation. They end their paper with a paragraph even more concise (and just as broad) as their opening paragraph:

> Our findings therefore bring us closer to understanding the phenomenon that Prescott Lecky (1945) introduced so long ago: the tendency for people with negative self-views to embrace the very persons who think poorly of them. Apparently, people enact such paradoxical behaviors because negative evaluations bolster their perception that their social worlds are predictable and controllable. From this vantage point, people go to great lengths to maintain the perception that they are in touch with social reality, however harsh that reality might be.

Enough said. Be concise: don't run on and on about being concise.

Rule 5: Be (Somewhat) Cautious

Caution is not always a desirable quality in writing. A cautious romantic adventure is probably a bad romantic adventure. However, caution in scientific writing is a very desirable feature. This applies not only to the logical leaps you expect readers to make to get to your research hypothesis but also to the interpretations you expect readers to accept for your research findings. If your hypothesis has little or no previous support, say so in your introduction. If your findings provide only partial support for your hypothesis, say this as well—before your critics do. This doesn't mean selling yourself short or downplaying what is important about your research. Instead, it means expressing your excitement about your findings while sticking to the rules of careful interpretation. If you have demonstrated a significant amount of cheating in a context in which cheating has never been previously demonstrated, point out that you also observed significant levels of honesty—and if it is possible, document this alternate perspective with a statistical analysis. In your General Discussion be sure to say something about the important practical and theoretical implications of your findings. But be sure to say something about their practical and theoretical limitations as well.

If it is appropriate, offer some speculations about what your findings tell us about models of moral development, but make it clear that your speculations are just that (and await empirical scrutiny). Most importantly, do not conclude your paper with grandiose statements about whether people are inherently good or evil. That topic is appropriate for a lunchtime debate with your lab group, but it strays too far from your data to make its way into your written research report. We know of some pretty good examples of a researcher who has occasionally violated this rule by drawing sweeping conclusions in his General Discussion section. Understandably, however, this researcher was unwilling to allow us to quote the offenses directly. If you want to find them yourself, you'll have to track down the actual papers (Pelham, 1991b, is a good place to start). Of course, it's also important to avoid the opposite mistake. We know of another author whose editor once told him (during the process of submitting the paper for publication) that his discussion section read "like a Mea Culpa." (That's the editor's way of saying the author spent most of the discussion section apologizing for and criticizing his work.) Of course, the author was happy to correct his mistake of being overly modest. To see how he did it, check out Blanton, Christie, and Dye (2002; see also Blanton, Rollover, and Dye, 2005).

Rule 6: Be Assertive

Although you should be appropriately cautious about drawing scientific conclusions, you should also be confident and assertive in your writing style. Good writers do not need to be forceful or antagonistic, but they do need to assert themselves and tell a compelling story. For instance, good writers do not sit back and let the authors of past papers do their writing for them (even if these authors are masterful writers). Suppose, for instance, that you hypothesize that people are more threatened when they are stereotyped by members of their own group (an ingroup) than when they are stereotyped by members of a different group (an outgroup). You perform a literature review and discover two published studies that are highly relevant to your hypothesis, a study by Boggs (1999) and a study by Symons (2002). A not so assertive version of your write-up might look like this:

> Evidence for this in-group stereotyping preference can be found from a study by Boggs (1999). She had a group of male and female participants receive success or failure feedback from either a confederate who was the same gender or the opposite gender, and she measured self-esteem before and after this feedback. She found that those participants who received failure feedback from someone who was the same gender experienced a larger drop in self-esteem than did those who received failure feedback from someone of the opposite gender. Interestingly, Boggs also found that those who received success feedback experienced a larger increase in self-esteem if this person was from the same gender, and so it appears that the "in-group gender" was the one who exerted the greatest influence with both success and failure. This is consistent with our hypotheses regarding stereotyping, as stereotyping is much like receiving failure feedback. A second study, conducted by Symons (2002), showed a similar effect with race rather than gender, but their study did not focus on success and failure feedback. Their study looked at the influence of social rejection and mood. Researchers in this study found that it was most damaging to mood to be rejected by someone who was of the same race. This study did not look at acceptance, but the results from Boggs would suggest that acceptance from same-race others might have led to a positive mood if Symons had investigated this issue. Regardless, both studies support our general hypothesis, that stereotyping from an in-group member will be more damaging to self-esteem than stereotyping from an out-group member.

A more assertive version of this write-up might look like this:

> Suggestive evidence for the primary hypothesis can be found in two studies that looked at people's reactions to rejection. Boggs (1999) found that people are more threatened by negative feedback from same-gender than opposite-gender

individuals, and Symons (2002) found that rejection from same-race individuals was more damaging to mood than rejection from different-race individuals. Together, these studies support our view that negative stereotypes will damage self-esteem to a greater extent when they come from members of the in-group.

Notice how the second author did not let Boggs and Symons write his paper. Another way to put this is that good authors engage in *telling* rather than *listing*. Papers that are written by less assertive authors often read like a list of previous findings, or they read like a long list of quotations. An otherwise skillful author who makes this mistake might summarize Dr. Snittle's study beautifully in paragraph three, and summarize Dr. Nettle's study beautifully in paragraph four, but the two studies would be described as if they existed in isolation. Good authors avoid "quarantining" their studies in this way. If the studies (or areas of research) that you review build upon one another by representing successive approximations to your hypothesis, arrange them in an order that brings readers progressively closer to your conclusion. If two studies make similar points, find a way to integrate them and discuss them in the same breath.

The last way for authors to be assertive has to do with tone or "voice." Scientific papers should be written in the active voice, meaning that they should state something directly or describe a subject performing an action. As an example, it is better to use the active voice and say, "The experimenter gave participants a questionnaire," or "Participants completed a questionnaire," rather than to use the passive voice and say "Participants were given a questionnaire by the experimenter." This may seem like a subtle difference, but the active voice asserts a point more emphatically than a passive voice. To illustrate, consider the following wishy-washy description of a theory:

> The idea that people give greater weight to negative than positive information when they form impressions is the primary prediction of this theory.

Contrast that to this more definitive description:

> This theory predicts that people give greater weight to negative than to positive information when they form impressions.

In the case of the more definitive description, readers are put on notice that the author has a theory and that this theory makes predictions. In the case of the first description, readers learn that the author has a theory worth mentioning, if it's not too much of a bother.

Rule 7: Be Predictable

One of the most common mistakes that novice writers make is to confuse writing a research paper with writing good fiction (e.g., a clever poem or a captivating novel). Although there are many differences between good fiction and good scientific writing, the most important one is that, unlike good fiction, good scientific writing is *much* more predictable. For instance, whereas the story line in a good novel unfolds over time and may contain numerous plot twists, good scientific writing cuts right to the chase. In fact, good scientific writing often goes a step further by telling readers where the chase is likely to end before it has even begun! By the time savvy readers have finished the introduction to a good research paper, they usually have a very good idea of what the results will look like. To illustrate how this type of writing differs from an interesting novel, consider how a psychological scientist might have opened up a story such as J. R. R. Tolkien's fantasy trilogy *The Lord of the Rings*:

> This is the story of a Hobbit named Frodo who saves the world from the clutches of an evil wizard named Sauron. Frodo does this by destroying a ring that would have dramatically increased Sauron's power. Moreover, he does this despite the fact that Frodo's mentor and guide, Gandalf, is killed early on in the story. That said, Frodo's success isn't quite as remarkable as it might seem because Gandalf eventually returns from the dead. Ironically, the individual who is of greatest help in Frodo's quest to destroy the ring is Gollum....

Clearly, *The Lord of the Rings* would not have captivated nearly as many readers if Tolkien had given away his major plot twists early in the first book of his trilogy. But good science writers do exactly this. They remove the mystery from their "stories" because they realize that readers may have trouble digesting or interpreting their findings if they have no idea where these findings are likely to lead. Unlike fiction, which is designed to entertain, scientific writing is designed to *inform*. The best way to be informative is to be predictable. In scientific writing, predictability usually means telling your readers why they should expect to see support for your hypothesis, telling them how you tested the hypothesis, and then telling them that you found support for it—even if the support was limited. Of course, if you are faced with the painful job of writing results that clearly oppose your hypothesis—or fail to support any hypothesis—it is a little harder to be predictable. Nevertheless, it is still preferable to set up an expectation in your readers' minds and to present your findings in light of this expectation. If you are wondering where such expectations come from, they come from theories. Good writers make their papers predictable (and thus easy to follow) by providing readers with a good theory that serves as a window or lens on these findings. Of course, there are exceptions to every rule. For example, some excellent papers do create a bit of drama by pointing out that two opposing theories make competing predictions about the likely results of a study. True, some scientists probably disagree with our advice to be predictable, on the basis that the predictable approach can lead to confirmatory biases of the sort that Karl Popper so strongly opposed (see Chapter 2). Regardless, there can be no doubt that whereas most novelists search for ways to create interesting plot twists, most scientists search for ways to avoid them.

If you think we are exaggerating the value of predictability in scientific writing, and if you have never read a journal article before, just get your hands on almost any psychological research article and take a look at how the article begins. The first section in almost any research article is the abstract. In that section, authors succinctly summarize the entire paper, including what theory they tested, how they tested it, what they found, and what conclusions they drew. The abstract thus helps makes an article predictable. Although a novelist might argue that the convention of including abstracts in scientific journal articles ruins all the "drama" of psychological research, most scientists gladly accept this sacrifice in the interest of being informative.

Rule 8: Be Creative

Although you should write predictably, do not become so predictable that doctors recommend your papers as a cure for insomnia. Humor, flair, and some thoughtfully turned phrases can add vigor to otherwise mundane writing. Finding a provocative but succinct way of making a predictable point takes a little skill. Consider the first sentence of this paragraph. We started with, "Although you should write predictably, do not become so predictable that doctors recommend your papers as a cure for insomnia." We do not suggest that this sentence will ever make it into *Bartlett's Familiar Quotations*, but we certainly hope you did not fall asleep reading it. Even though the point we want to make could be predicted completely from the subject header of this section ("Be Creative"), we still tried to make this point in an engaging manner. You, too, should strive to find creative ways to jazz up your writing. Speaking of jazz, consider a comparison between scientific writing and jazz music. Traditional jazz is a highly structured form of expression. In this way, it is highly predictable. In fact, many excellent performances are nothing but slight variations on old standards. Does this mean that jazz musicians are never creative? Certainly not. Jazz is a well-structured form, but it also allows individual artists to improvise within the constraints of the musical structure. Real creativity can be found in how new artists generate provocative ways to express themselves within the broad constraints of a familiar tune. Although one could argue that traditional jazz does not encourage quite as much creativity as modern jazz (which has fewer rules and constraints than traditional jazz), it certainly allows more creative license than traditional takes on classical music (where musicians are completely bound by structure). You don't have to be a scientific Miles Davis or John Coltrane to be a good scientific writer, but you don't have to limit yourself to being a piano tuner either. Although you should observe scientific conventions, you should also feel free to express yourself.

Rule 9: Be Original (and Cite Your Lack of Originality)

As we approach the end of our list, we turn to a sensitive issue—originality. More specifically, we look at a form of highly unoriginal writing known as **plagiarism**. For now, we define plagiarism pretty broadly: *to use (and pass off the ideas or writings of another) as one's own.* If you use someone else's words or ideas, you should not give anyone the impression that these words or ideas are your own. You also should place other people's exact statements safely inside a set of quotation marks to give credit where credit is due. It can be easy to forget this. At times, well-intentioned writers may confuse their own personal notes with notes taken while reading someone else's work. To make matters worse, it is not always easy to spot plagiarism. Consider, for example, our beautifully phrased definition of plagiarism. We plagiarized it—but only to make a point. "Our" definition of plagiarism was taken from the *American Heritage Dictionary*. So let's try that sentence again, to give credit to the hardworking lexicographers who are the true wordsmiths behind this useful definition. The fourth edition of the *American Heritage Dictionary of the English Language* (2000) defines the act of plagiarizing as "to use (and pass off the ideas or writings of another) as one's own" (p. 1340). In this revision, notice how we clearly state that this is not our own "personal" definition and that we use quotes around the original words. We also give the full reference for the dictionary (and see the reference section in this book), and we provide readers with the exact page number for the quotation. This way, someone who wants to read the definition in full or check the accuracy of our quote can go right to the original source.

Occasionally, novice writers who realize that it's a mistake to pack a paper full of quotations attempt to avoid quotations by doing extensive paraphrasing. This, too, can easily constitute plagiarism, even when authors do not cite his or her original sources. Recall that the *American Heritage Dictionary* defines acts as plagiarism, even if they simply used another person's *ideas*. It is hard to avoid plagiarizing altogether if your only strategy for reporting someone else's ideas is to paraphrase their reports.

So, how do you review past material while avoiding plagiarism? The best way is probably to write from memory. If you find yourself constantly checking your own sentences against your original source, then you are probably plagiarizing. This might be true even if you cite the authors whose paper you used to generate your own mildly novel sentences. Of course, after you have written sections of your paper from memory, it is usually a good idea to check your writing for accuracy (see rule 1 on being correct). After all, your memory can sometimes fail you. And if your memory rarely fails you, you might still run the risk of remembering another author's words but forgetting where the words came from, so it is always a good idea to check any sources on which you relied heavily when drafting your own research paper. As we suggested earlier in this chapter, you should be assertive, meaning that you shouldn't rely on others to do your writing for you. In a sense, plagiarism is the most extreme form of failing to adhere to this earlier rule. Just as it is a bad idea to frequently borrow money but downright illegal to steal it, it is a bad idea to rely too heavily on the words or ideas of others but downright unethical to steal them. From this perspective, it may not be too surprising that one of the best ways to avoid stealing others words or ideas is to be familiar with them but to keep them safely out of reach.

Rule 10: Be Gender Neutral

The final rule of good writing in research is more like an ironclad law than a rule. The APA clearly dictates that writers must avoid the use of sexist language. If you submit a paper in which you use the generic masculine "he" to mean people in general rather than one of your 43 male participants, the editor may very well send it back and ask you to correct your mistake before even reviewing it. At the very least, you will be embarrassed when the three female and two male reviewers of your paper all comment on your use of sexist language. For reasons such as this, we have tried to use gender-neutral language throughout this book. In addition to resorting to an occasional use of "he or she" (e.g., "If an author is citing both studies, he or she must have some reason for thinking the two studies are related"), whenever possible we have tried to solve this problem more elegantly by using plural words when speaking about people, as in "According to Aristotle, just as people with thick necks were strong in character and fierce tempered (like bulls), people with long, thin necks were backward and cowardly, like deer." Of course, when you quote someone verbatim or when you really are *just* talking about men, women, or a particular man or woman, it is perfectly appropriate to use gender-specific pronouns. Thus, instead of correcting Aristotle's gender-biased language, we quoted him verbatim (through his translators). Thus we wrote, "Similarly, it seemed self-evident to Aristotle that 'men with small *ears* have the disposition of monkeys' and that 'those with large ears [have] the disposition of asses.'"

Although it may not be an explicit part of the APA's publication guidelines, most researchers agree that the rule about not being sexist also extends to not being racist, classist, fascist, or *hetero*sexist. For example, when we were writing about how a person might choose a date from a pool of men who did or did not vary enormously in their heights, we asked you to "suppose you are a heterosexual woman of average height, and you need to choose a blind date by drawing names from one of two hats." We needed our example of women choosing male dates to make a point about variability, but we didn't need to assume that *all* women always choose male dates. Of course, we could have been even more explicitly nonheterosexist by specifying that the men in the two groups all happened to be heterosexual—but we assumed that one reminder about sexual orientation was enough to make the point.

Rule 11: Be Easy on the Eyes

Scientific papers often contain a lot of technical material. In particular, they often contain a lot of statistics. In Appendix 4, we provide some advice on how to present and discuss the results of some specific statistical tests, but here we discuss a more general issue about how to incorporate statistics into your writing. Good writers write about statistics in ways that make them fade into the background. Along the same lines, they also place their statistics carefully in a sentence in such a way as to minimize the amount of looking that readers have to do to decode the statistics. More specifically, good writers write about statistics in ways that minimize the number of times readers have to move their eyes.

Let's consider a simple example. Suppose a research study compares the self-esteem levels of sociologists and psychologists. The researcher wants readers to know that the sociologists sampled had a mean self-esteem score of 4.34 and a standard deviation of 1.51 and that the psychologists sampled had a mean self-esteem score of 5.29, with a standard deviation of 1.57. The researcher also wants to report the results of a *t*-test that was performed on these two means. This *t*-test had 119 degrees of freedom, and it yielded a value of 14.84, which indicated a statistically significant difference between the two groups, with a *p*-value of less than .001. (See Chapter 10 for explanations of these statistics.) To report all of this information, the author could use some simple statistical notation. For instance, he or she could report the mean and standard deviation for the self-esteem level of the sociologists by reporting $M = 5.29$, $SD = 1.57$. In APA format, the symbol for the mean (M) and the symbol for the standard deviation (SD) can be italicized and put in parentheses. (See Appendices 3 and 4.) APA format also allows authors to report the t-test, its degrees of freedom, and the associated p value in a concise format such as, $t(119) = -14.84$, $p < .001$. Notice also that the t and the p are italicized. APA format requires all statistical symbols to be italicized.

This all seems simple enough, but there are many ways to report these statistics in a results section. Some ways are easy on the eyes, and some are not. Consider this version:

> Results revealed that the sociologists ($M = 4.34$, $SD = 1.51$) were lower than the psychologists ($M = 5.29$, $SD = 1.57$) in terms of self-esteem, $t(119) = -14.84$, $p < .001$.

Although this text is technically correct, it creates some eye work. When readers encounter this text for the first time, they do not know what the two means refer to until they finish reading the entire sentence. Someone reading this sentence would encounter a mean and a standard deviation, followed by another mean and another standard deviation, but this person would not know that these values pertain to self-esteem until reading the last word of text in the sentence. After finally seeing this word, interested readers would have to look back to compare the statistics for the two groups. (That is, they would shift their eyes back and reread the statistics.) Seeing that the two groups do indeed appear to differ, the reader might then look back at the t-statistics at the end of the sentence—to confirm that the means truly are statistically different from one another. That's a lot of eye work!

Similar problems arise in each of these sentences:

> The sociologists ($M = 4.34$, $SD = 1.51$) were lower than the psychologists ($M = 5.29$, $SD = 1.57$) in terms of self-esteem, $t(119) = -14.84$, $p < .001$.

> There was a significant difference, $t(119) = -14.84$, $p < .001$, such that the sociologists ($M = 4.34$, $SD = 1.51$) were lower than the psychologists ($M = 5.29$, $SD = 1.57$) in terms of their self-esteem.

> This t-test, $t(119) = -14.84$, $p < .001$, on the self-esteem of the sociologists and psychologists was significant ($M = 5.29$, $SD = 1.57$ vs. $M = 4.34$, $SD = 1.51$).

In all of these cases, readers' eyes have to do a lot of work to put all of the pieces of the puzzle together and comprehend what is being said. In contrast, consider three different ways of saying the same thing while making it easier on readers' eyes:

> The sociologists had lower levels of self-esteem ($M = 4.34$, $SD = 1.51$) than did the psychologists ($M = 5.29$, $SD = 1.57$), and this difference was significant, $t(119) = -14.84$, $p < .001$.

> The sociologists had lower self-esteem ($M = 4.34$, $SD = 1.51$) than did the psychologists ($M = 5.29$, $SD = 1.57$), $t(119) = 14.84$, $p < .001$.

> An analysis of the self-esteem scores for the two groups revealed a significant difference, $t(119) = -14.84$, $p < .001$, such that the sociologists had lower self-esteem ($M = 4.34$, $SD = 1.51$) than the psychologists ($M = 5.29$, $SD = 1.57$).

In each of these examples, the author holds off on reporting each statistic until readers know what the statistic means. These three examples reveal ways of presenting just one analysis, but they highlight the care you should take when you embed the results of your analyses into your text. Good writers try to be easy on their readers' eyes. In so doing, of course, they usually take it easy on their readers' brains as well, and most readers appreciate both of these efforts.

No More Rules

That's it. We don't have a lot more to say about how to write good empirical research papers. To summarize the basic structure of empirical research papers, and to point out some of the important things that should always be included, a checklist of important things appears in Table 11.1. Although this checklist complements much of what we have said about writing, we should add that writing good papers is not the end of the story when it comes to scientific communication. Giving good talks is also an extremely important

"Why won't you give me feedback about my research paper?
I thought you said we had a **mentor-mentee** relationship."

One of the best ways to improve your scientific communication skills is to get feedback on your work from a seasoned expert (which isn't always easy).

Table 11.1 A checklist of concerns for empirical research papers

1. Abstract
    - ☐ Does it provide a clear and simple description of the theory?
    - ☐ Does it provide a summary of the hypotheses?
    - ☐ Does it correctly describe the study or studies?
    - ☐ Does it describe the conclusions that were drawn?
2. Introduction
    - ☐ Theory: Do the readers know the theory you are proposing?
    - ☐ Theoretical justification: Do you provide a comprehensive literature review?
    - ☐ Justification of hypotheses: Do readers know the specific predictions being tested and what these tests will tell us?
    - ☐ Explanation of hypotheses: Do readers know exactly what you expect to find (or find out) in the study?
3. Method
    - ☐ Participants: Is the sample identified and described correctly?
    - ☐ Materials and procedure: Are the procedure and design of the study clear?
    - ☐ Dependent measures: Are the measures—what they were and how they were worded—made exactly clear?
    - ☐ Control procedures: Are any special control procedures discussed appropriately? Examples: random assignment, experimenters /participants kept blind to hypothesis, anonymity of responses, counterbalancing in within-subjects designs.
4. Results
    - ☐ Statistical tests: Are the statistical tests (e.g., ANOVAs, correlations, etc.) described correctly?
    - ☐ Results: Are all the correct results reported (including results for any manipulation checks)?
    - ☐ Statistics: Are the statistics presented in a way that is easy on the eyes?
    - ☐ Interpretations: Are the findings interpreted correctly?
5. Discussion
    - ☐ Limitations, clarifications, and/or interpretations of results: Are they discussed?
    - ☐ Practical implications of results: If appropriate, are they discussed?
    - ☐ Theoretical implications of results: Are they discussed? Were the conclusions appropriately cautious?
6. Paper as a whole
    - ☐ Coherence: Are the arguments developed in a logical, orderly fashion, and are key themes reinforced throughout?
    - ☐ Writing: Is the writing clear, gender neutral, active voice, and concise?
    - ☐ Originality and accuracy: Are others given credit (citations) for their ideas, and are all citations and statements about others correct?
    - ☐ Predictability: Are the main points established early and used to organize all that follows?
    - ☐ Are you ready to get comments from someone so that you can begin revising?

research skill. Although some overlap obviously exists between writing well and speaking well, these two forms of communication are more distinct than many people realize. With this in mind, savor the advice of someone who has learned to do both of these things extremely well.

HOW TO GIVE A GOOD TALK IN PSYCHOLOGY (BY DANIEL T. GILBERT)

Gilbert wrote this guide for people who were preparing to give a 45- to 50-minute job talk or invited colloquium. Obviously, you will need to adjust the time periods of different aspects of the talk to match the amount of time you have for *your* talk. For example, Gilbert indicates that you should be talking about your specific research hypotheses within the first ten minutes of a 50-minute talk. In the case of a 15-minute talk, for example, this roughly translates into talking about your specific hypotheses within the first three minutes.

Have a Plan

Nothing else is as important as having a cohesive organizational plan in which one point leads naturally to another. Usually this begins with (1) some background about the area of research, which leads into (2) background on the specific hypothesis, which leads into (3) the specific research question you want to address, which leads into (4) the procedures you followed, which leads into (5) your findings, which leads into (6) their interpretation, which leads into (7) the relevance of your findings for the problem you are addressing, which leads into (8) implications for "the big picture." In addition, each of these sections must be logically organized in and of itself. A logical argument is the basis for communicating with your audience. If you don't have one (a logical argument) you won't have one (an audience). Write your plan in (at least) outline form, and use these notes during your talk. If you must, you can write the talk out word for word. If you must have a canned talk, memorize it! Then use your notes as a prop. Ultimately, reading a talk is better than giving a terrible talk—but only a little better.

Tell the Plan

It is often useful to give listeners a road map for the terrain you wish to cover. Tell them the organizational plan in just a sentence or two. For example:

> I'd like to talk today about the effects of alcohol on reasoning; specifically, how alcohol enhances some cognitive performances and impairs others. I'll start with some general background information about research in this area, and then I'll present to you some research that professor Snorkwerth and I have conducted on alcohol use and motor performance. Finally, I'll try to show you how this research addresses the important question of whether motor systems can function independently.

On occasion, you may wish to use suspense, and thus this "tell the plan" heuristic will be inappropriate. Generally, however, you should forego suspense in favor of comprehension. Also, you should use speech markers as transitions to tell your audience where you currently are in the organizational plan (e.g., "Having briefly outlined the past research in this area, let me now turn to the experiment that we recently conducted ...").

Start at the Beginning

Every study is part of a long story that begins with an idea by Aristotle. There are two things you can do wrong in choosing a point in the story at which to begin your talk.

First, you can start too late. You have started too late if you are not talking about your specific hypotheses within ten minutes. You are starting too late if you mention Aristotle anytime after the first sentence. You must know the audience and try to figure out what they already know. You can refresh their memories briefly, but get to the point as quickly as your audience's knowledge will allow.

Second, you can start too early. You have started too early if your first sentence has anything to do with an experimental manipulation (or any other aspect of your method). An introduction sets the stage and explains *why* you did the study you did. Don't say, "I did an experiment on alcohol and reasoning because alcohol abuse is a real problem in society," but say:

> For centuries, people have been using substances that affect their ability to think, feel, and act. Alcohol is one such substance. Yet we still don't know precisely how alcohol affects performance ...

Don't relate the entire history of psychology, but don't act as though there were no history. Even if your study is completely novel and revolutionary, you must tie it into something your audience already knows and cares about. The introduction of a talk locates your work in the body of other work.

Before you can tell what you did, you must tell why. You must make the audience realize that your study is potentially an important one. You must intrigue them by showing the hole in the body of knowledge that your study serves to fill. It is wrong to assume that everyone shares your interests or that any study is worth doing. In the introduction, you must impress your audience with what needs to be done. (And later you'll impress them even more by having done it.) Thus, a rationale like "Emotions are important because everybody has them" does little to make the audience ready for your contribution. On the other hand, you might intrigue the audience with something like:

> Emotions lie at the heart of social behavior—from altruism to aggression, the emotions we feel compel us to act toward each other in a variety of ways. Yet very little is known about the physiological basis of emotion ...

You must have had a reason for doing the research you want to talk about, so tell the audience what it was in the most interesting way possible.

Be Painfully Clear

Once you are talking about your study, you should strive for three things: clarity, clarity, and clarity. Nothing matters if the audience doesn't understand what you did and why. A few points to remember:

1. When you describe your study, explain first what conceptual variables you examined: "To test this hypothesis, we manipulated the anxiety level of our participants." Only then should you explain the operational variables:

We did this by exposing half of our participants to an uncaged lion. These participants were in the "high anxiety" group. We exposed the other participants to an uncaged rabbit. These participants were in the "low anxiety" group.

2. Be redundant. Say the same thing several different times in different ways. Be repetitive. Remember that your audience cannot process your speech nearly as well as they can process your writing because they cannot go back and reread something you have said and because they cannot listen at their own pace. Any important point should be stated twice:

   > We think alcohol impairs some cognitive processes but not others. More specifically, whereas some performances suffer after alcohol consumption, others actually benefit.

3. It is generally unprofessional to say, "Is all of this clear so far?"—but it is better to do this than to lose the audience. If you think the audience is lost, you can ask. But ask someone whom you expect to tell you the truth. Most audience members will be too embarrassed to tell you that they are lost, but they will look around, exchange glances, and make you feel foolish.

4. Make use of visual aids (e.g., a drawing of your 2×2 design). A picture is worth 1,234 words. Supplement your speech with pictures. But remember that a complicated picture is worthless and causes the audience to stop listening to you while they figure out your picture. Thus, when you use a picture, use a simple one with big letters. Also, give the audience a moment to read all of the words on a slide before you start talking again; otherwise, they may miss what you're saying as they scrutinize the slide. Remember also to get rid of a slide when you're done with it. It can prove distracting when left up too long. Last, you should note that handouts are usually a bad idea, because you cannot determine where the audience will focus their attention at any given time. People always look ahead with handouts, and may miss your preliminary comments while they peruse the handout. Use slides or overhead transparencies instead.

5. Present data kindly. If you must present a lot of data, present each piece separately on a different slide. Nothing is worse than a slide full of numbers. Use figures instead of tables wherever possible. Present the most important data first! Don't present the manipulation checks first unless it is absolutely necessary to your argument. What the audience wants to know is "Did your study support your primary hypothesis?" So answer this question before they start asking, "Can I go home yet?"

6. Take the audience's perspective. This is true in every facet of the talk. Try to see your ideas as a naive audience member would. Of course, *you* know that exposure to lions is a way of manipulating anxiety, but does the audience? If not, did you say it? Don't leave anything important unsaid. The best way to get the audience's perspective is to get a practice audience (intimate others and friends are traditional victims) and give your talk to them. Did they follow? You shouldn't have to be a psychologist to understand the talk; any reasonably bright person should follow it. Address your talk to a bright colleague in the art history department. And listen to the practice audience's advice! Think about this: when listeners tell you that something is confusing, they are always, by definition, correct.

Talk about One Interesting Thing

A good talk must have substance. You can't give a great talk on a dull, stupid, or boring idea. However, the converse is not necessarily true. A brilliant and exciting idea can easily be the topic of a very bad talk. Thus, the first rule for giving a good talk is "Have something interesting to say." In his *Rules for Writing*, M. Polya added an important second rule: "Have something to say. If by chance you have two things to say, control yourself." A talk must have a central theme—people can handle one major idea per talk. Ask yourself: "What is the major, take-home point here?" That is, what is the one-sentence summary that you hope a listener will give to his or her friends when they ask, "What was the talk you heard today about?" Of course your study has complexities and nuances of great beauty. Go home and write a poem about them. But give your audience one and only one message, and give it clearly.

Talking clearly means not doing certain stylistic things that distract your audience. Do you pace? Chain yourself to a chair. Do you say "uh" between every sentence? Get therapy. Do you touch your nose or your chin all the time? Cut off your hand. All of these things can be very distracting, because when you are anxious you will do them very fast. As a result, you will not pace in a relaxed and professional manner; you will actually run from one end of the room to the other. (A note on pacing: if you pace you will often find that you need to look at your notes and that they are on a different side of the room than you are.) To find out what annoying stylistic nuances you have, videotape yourself.

Humor can be useful. A light remark puts the audience at ease and shows them that you are relaxed and confident. However, too much humor is probably worse than none at all. People will only consider your work to be as serious as you seem to think it is. If you think of it as a big joke, they will come to agree with you. In addition, nothing is worse than a joke that just doesn't cut it. Here's a good rule: if you don't know how much humor is too much, don't use humor. Not everyone can or should. And never, under any circumstances, tell a long joke that sidetracks you.

Take Charge of the Interaction

This is *your* talk. Don't let someone else take control of it by forcing you to deviate from your organizational plan. If someone requires clarification ("Were the anxious people ever eaten by the lion?"), then answer them briefly and continue. If someone wants to argue philosophy ("But don't you think psychology errs when it thinks of people as real?"), don't take the bait. Audience members may try to throw you off track, and you must not let them—but you must stop them with tact. Anyone can say, "Shut up please, I'm trying to give a talk here." But the expert can say this in other words and still maintain an air of confidence and professionalism. A good standby is something like:

> That's an interesting question to which I've given much thought. I'll be addressing just that issue in a few minutes, but if I don't answer your question, please remind me at the end of the talk.

Of course, you better damn well be prepared to answer it at the end of the talk. If you can't even understand the question, you can always resort to something like:

> To be honest, I'm not quite sure I see the full implications of what you've said, but if I'm going to cover all the ground that I've set out to cover, I think I'd best delay a discussion of that until later.

You may be scared to interrupt a questioner who is persistent, but remember what Ann Landers would say: the interrupting questioner is acting impolitely. You have every right to get the exchange back on track by taking charge. In fact, you owe it to the rest of the audience who have come to hear *you*, not the questioner.

Novices often make the mistake of agreeing with criticisms they can't understand, because they think they will look foolish otherwise, and they think that the questioner will get off their backs if they just agree with him or her. By no means should you verbally agree with any critic unless you really understand her or his point and agree with it. If you do, you will find yourself backed into a corner later on. ("But earlier you agreed when I said people weren't real, so how can you maintain that your data tell us anything about people?")

Novices often make the opposite mistake: they are sometimes too defensive. If a person attacks your study, she or he is not attacking you. If people have a valid criticism of a bad (or a good) study, your refusal to acknowledge their point will make you look both stupid and immature. If you acknowledge their point, you'll just look stupid. The best way to avoid damning criticisms is by letting others hear your talk first. Let a practice audience member (who loves and adores you) find the weaknesses in your argument, and then repair them before you speak in front of people who don't even love you a little. This is another benefit of writing an organizational plan (see "Have a Plan"). When you try to write your argument, you will see most of the flaws in your own logic. Better you than your audience.

End at the End

The same sins that pertain to starting also pertain to ending. You have ended too soon if, after presenting your results, you say, "So that's what we found. Any questions?" You must summarize in two steps. First, summarize your findings (e.g., "So these data show that people who are made anxious tend to show substantially more interest in sex than do people who are not made anxious ..."). Second, show the meaning of your findings for the "big picture" (e.g., "Theorists have always construed anxiety as a deficit, but our findings show that it can indeed have positive consequences ..."). Finally, it is nice if you can point out what other provocative questions your findings suggest (e.g., "It would be interesting to know if the anxious person's increased interest in sex is accompanied by an increased ability to perform. We have several field studies in the works that attempt to show ...").

You have ended your talk too late if (1) the clock tells you so, (2) the audience is yawning, or (3) you are spinning your wheels. Part of being a good teacher is knowing how to pace yourself, and at a job talk, people will be watching to see if you can end on time. If you have a one-hour talk, plan a 45-minute presentation. If you run over your limit by more than ten minutes, look for another job. In any context, a verbose speaker may lose all the points he or she has won by going on and on and on and on. Don't leave the audience with a "bored taste in their mouths"—even if the talk was good, all good things must come to an end. So make your point, make it clearly, show why it's important, and shut the hell up. Like this.

SUMMARY

This chapter provides tips on how to tell the world about your ideas. Thus, it also provides a lot of details that are designed to improve both your written and your spoken communication. If your head is spinning after trying to organize all the specific points in this chapter, you might be interested to know that almost everything in this chapter boils down to one important point: *put yourself in the position of your audience.* When you read a scientific article, you obviously want it to be clear and well organized. Along the same lines, you probably prefer simple direct statements to technical jargon, you don't want to memorize long lists of abbreviations, and you don't want to read every sentence twice to know which group of participants is connected to every mean or standard deviation reported. And, again along the same lines, Dan Gilbert's piece tells you how to put the needs of the reader before your own. When you attend a talk, you want the speaker to be clear, you want the speaker to entertaining, and you appreciate having a manageable number of "take away points" that you can remember after the talk is done. In the case of both writing and speaking, effective communicators work hard to meet the needs of their audiences. For most people, learning the skills to do this takes hard work. However, it is hard work that pays rich dividends. If you build a better manuscript (or a better talk), the world may not beat a path to your door, but they'll be much more likely to leave the door open long enough to hear your message—and they might even enjoy what they hear.

STUDY QUESTIONS

1. How does scientific writing differ from fiction writing? What is the primary goal of scientific writing?

2. Summarize the hourglass approach to writing empirical research papers.

3. What are the 11 rules of writing good research papers? Identify as many specific rules as you can that are highly compatible with one another. Now identify as many specific rules as you can that are potentially incompatible with one another. For example, is it easy to be both comprehensive and concise?

4. List and describe Daniel Gilbert's tips for giving effective research talks.

Putting It All Together: Maximizing Validity with Multi-Method (and Highly Creative) Research

TRADE-OFFS IN RESEARCH

As kids, the authors of this book each grew up loving comic books. Both authors were particularly big fans of DC comic book superheroes (but see the authors' notes about our appreciation of Marvel's *Spiderman*). Both spent many childhood hours reading about *Superman*, the *Flash*, *Batman*, and the *Green Lantern*. Superman was an early favorite for each of us. As we grew older, however, we each became a bit annoyed with Superman, especially as the superpower equivalent of grade inflation began to set in during the 1970s and 1980s. How could *one* Superhero be as fast as the Flash (who was as fast as the speed of light), stronger than the Green Lantern (whose strength was, in principle, unlimited), and smarter than the super-genius Lex Luthor (who made Einstein seem like a doofus)? In real life, Sumo wrestlers never qualify for the 4 × 100 meter relay team and super-geniuses almost never appear on the *World's Strongest Man* competition. In real life there are almost always trade-offs between different abilities.

One of the most important ideas we have emphasized in this text is that research is full of trade-offs. There is no such thing as a perfect research design. The beauty of laboratory experiments is that they can uncover precise information about causes—but only at the risk of being generalizable to a narrow range of (often contrived) situations and a specific group of people (often college students). The beauty of well-conducted population surveys is that, by capitalizing on random sampling, they can identify a small sample of people who are highly representative of the diverse population that is of interest. However, as you know, survey studies are almost always cross-sectional, and thus they rarely allow researchers to make any causal statements about *why* two or more variables are associated with one another. Along similar lines, case studies can document that something previously considered impossible can happen, but they rarely tell us exactly *why* it can happen. Because of Jane Goodall's careful observational research, we now know that chimps can use and even make tools. But this fact alone does not tell us exactly what cognitive and/or motivational processes are the essential ingredients of tool use or which factors influence the timing and nature of tool use in a chimp's life.

About 30 years ago, Joseph McGrath (1982) described this research problem as a **"three-horned dilemma."** Specifically, he argued that research varies on three desirable dimensions: precision, generalizability to situations, and generalizability to people. The researcher's dilemma lies in the fact that efforts to maximize any one of these three desirable things usually results in an unwanted reduction of at least one of the other things, and possibly two. Teach chimps to use sign language in the laboratory and reasonable people will ask why chimps didn't invent sign language on their own out in the forest. Conduct more naturalistic studies to show that chimps spontaneously deceive one another, and skeptics may reasonably accuse you of overinterpreting chimps' highly ambiguous social behavior. McGrath argued that it is impossible for any one study to succeed on all three of the admirable dimensions that are at the heart of his three-horned dilemma.

As it turns out, there is a pretty simple solution to the dilemma, but that solution often requires a combination of clever insights and a great deal of hard work. To address this dilemma, the good researcher must often engage in a research program that includes multiple studies employing different designs, each of which maximizes only some of the desirable qualities of research. No one forms a track team full of sprinters, a hospital full of anesthesiologists, or a high school faculty full of history teachers. The solution to the three-horned dilemma is usually a program of multi-method research. The essence of a **multi-method approach** to research is to employ a variety of different methods, each of which addresses the same research question while operationalizing the independent and dependent variable(s) in different ways. Some specific studies may provide superior information about causality, for example, while others document that there is support for the hypothesis among different samples of people and in different situations.

The view we promote in this chapter is that there is no one perfect research method. Therefore, a good researcher will (1) know the unique advantages and disadvantages of a given method, (2) conduct studies that maximize a method's advantages while minimizing its disadvantages, and (3) carefully construct a research program using multiple studies that compensate for one another's weaknesses. We illustrate this process by making two passes on programmatic research.

We call the first pass "Straight, No Chaser" because this first pass focuses on a single research question and lays out four basic methods (which you have already learned about) that can all be used to address it. This simple framework can help you a pick a specific method to address a specific type of methodological concern. This section builds on a chapter by Burkley and Blanton (2008), and it focuses on the four research methods most commonly used by psychologists: true experiments, correlational (field) studies, quasi-experiments, and population surveys. We highlight both the strengths and weaknesses of each of these four designs and discuss the role that each method will typically play in a program of research. This section thus reviews material we covered in earlier chapters, but it seeks to integrate that earlier material by showing how different chapters pointed to different pieces of a single puzzle—one that can be pieced together to answer a specific research question as definitively as possible. The picture we work to reveal in this first pass draws on the literature on violent video games and aggression conducted by Craig Anderson, along with his colleagues. (We had hoped to discuss the literature on violent comic books and aggression, but we kept fighting about who'd get to write the first draft.)

We should warn you right now that this first pass will be an oversimplification of the rich and sometimes subtle ways in which a real program of research develops. However, as we show in the next section of this chapter (appropriately dubbed "Creative Solutions"), creative researchers often find ways to address questions of interest to them by finding novel uses of traditional methods. In this second section, we review research on a wider range of topics to illustrate the role that creativity and knowledge of a specific topic play in helping to make experimental research more relevant—or making field research more rigorous. Unlike the first section, then, the second section will focus on how a single specific study can sometimes minimize McGrath's concerns. We hope that, taken together, the two sections of this chapter will document two very different ways to maximize the validity of any kind of research.

Straight, No Chaser: Video Game Violence

Since their debut in video arcades in the 1970s, video games have become increasingly violent. A review in 1998 indicated that 80 percent of video games on the market were violent (Dietz, 1998). This has seriously worried that famous group of "applied psychologists" known as parents. The news media has also expressed concerns about video game violence, with some journalists arguing that violent video game content may have contributed to school shootings such as those at Columbine High School in 1999 and at Virginia Tech in 2007. But does exposure to violent video games really ever cause people to become violent? Before we address this question, we should begin by reminding you why we might expect exposure to violent video games to make people behave aggressively in the first place. Bandura's (1977) *social learning theory* states that one of the most potent forms of human learning is *observational learning*. According to social learning theory, that is, there is a powerful human urge to copy what we see others do. This urge is presumably powerful enough that it fuels the kind of copycat homicide you read about in earlier chapters. There has been some debate, however, about whether people copy the behavior of fictional (sometimes non-human) characters that populate violent video games. Without belaboring the details of social learning theory, many proponents of this "monkey see—monkey do" theory have argued that exposure to violent actions in video games should make people more prone to behave violently themselves in real life. So this is the theory behind the research program upon which we are about to focus.

Now even if we limit ourselves to the potential consequences of exposure to violent video games, consider the range of specific research questions one might wish to address and how these specific questions might require different research methods. First, some questions might emphasize causality. It would be useful, for instance, to know if exposure to violent video games can truly cause aggressive behavior, under any circumstances. If a causal link is established in at least some instances, it would further be useful to know the types of situations under which, and the types of people for whom, this causal link is strongest. Finally, it would be helpful to get some estimate of the magnitude of the problem as it unfolds in the real world. How many people are being influenced by the violent content of video games and to what extent? A program of research that addressed all of these questions could help psychologists make informed comments about whether video game violence is merely child's play or whether it is a social epidemic worthy of serious attention.

To get some sense of how each question might be addressed, consult Table 12.1. Here we list the traditional strengths and weaknesses of four basic research methods. We begin with true experiments. Recall that a true experiment uses random assignment to conditions to eliminate person confounds and uses the careful manipulation of independent variables to minimize or eliminate procedural and operational confounds. Thus, when used properly, experiments offer a tremendous amount of precision. With this in mind, video game researchers can employ true experiments to conduct a precise analysis of the causal mechanisms linking video game exposure to aggression.

Anderson and Dill (2000) adopted exactly this approach. They did so by bringing 210 undergraduates into their lab and randomly assigning them

Table 12.1 Research methods and goals

	Research Goals		
Method	Precision	Generalizability to Situations	Generalizability to People
True (Laboratory) Experiment	Strength	Weakness	Weakness
Correlational (Field) Study	Weakness	Strength	Moderate
Quasi-Experiment	Moderate	Moderate	Moderate
Population Survey	Weakness	Weakness	Strength

to play several sessions of either a violent or a nonviolent video game. Following this manipulation, they told all participants they would be competing against another student on a computer-based racing task. When participants lost a trial, they were "hit" with a noise blast at a level that ostensibly had been set by their opponent (but which, in fact, had been set in advance by the experimenters). When participants won trials, they delivered a noise blast in return to "hit" their opponents. Aggressive behavior was then measured based on the intensity and duration of the noise blasts that participants delivered to their phantom opponents. The results of this experiment were straightforward. Those who had played the violent game delivered longer and louder noise blasts to opponents than those who played the nonviolent game.

This elegant study nicely demonstrates the precision one can gain from lab experiments. Unfortunately, however, this same elegant study also illustrates some of the limitations of experiments. This high level of internal validity unfortunately came at the cost of external validity. Compared with other research designs, true experiments often do not allow us to generalize either to other people or to other situations (see Table 12.1). Anderson and Dill cannot be sure at all that the effects they documented ever occur in the "real world." Thus, they don't know if third graders who play violent video games will be more likely to behave aggressively on the playground or while at the beach on vacation. The artificial nature of the dependent variable is also a problem. When is the last time you harmed others by blasting them with noise? This study is also limited in that the researchers cannot even say for sure that the effects they observed with this particular group of college students would generalize to other college students. This is because these participants were not randomly selected from the total population of college students.

The limitations of this elegant study are too great to be addressed by a single additional study. But inspection of Table 12.1 suggests how one might proceed. Suppose, for instance, that you wanted to assess the long-term effects of violent video game play on actual behavior. Perhaps you'd like to see if adolescents who play video games a lot are more likely than those who don't to behave aggressively in their daily lives. Based on Table 12.1, we hope you'd consider some kind of field study; using correlational (i.e., passive observational) methods. As noted in Chapter 6, one of the advantages of correlational methods is that they are often high in generalizability with respect to situations. Real behaviors that occur in a person's daily life can be measured with simple interview or survey questions. Suffice it to say that survey questions about violent behavior would not focus on people's recent or habitual use of noise blasts.

With this in mind, Anderson and Dill (2000) conducted a second study that employed correlational methods to examine the potential long-term effects of violent video game play on real-world aggressive behavior. They had 207 college students answer questions regarding their use of video games and also their tendencies to engage in physical aggression (e.g., "If someone hits me, I hit back"), verbal aggression ("I can't help getting into arguments when people disagree with me"), and their levels of anger and hostility. Participants were also asked to report whether they had engaged in specific acts of delinquency (e.g., "purposely damaged or destroyed property belonging to a school") and whether they had used illegal drugs. As would be expected if violent video games influence aggression, these researchers found that self-reported, long-term exposure to violent video games was positively correlated with aggressive behavior, hostile emotions, delinquency, and drug use. This study thus fills some big gaps left by the first study. Specifically, it linked past real-world exposure to violent video games with current instances of real-world aggression, hostility, and delinquency.

Are you convinced that you should stay away from violent video games—lest they lead you down a path of self-destruction and ruin? We suspect you may have some suspicions, many of which might involve the third-variable problem. Anderson and Dill were aware of such concerns, and so they measured some serious potential confounds and controlled for them statistically. When they did this, they found that their original findings were weakened somewhat but remained significant even after removing the influence of participants' aggressive personality, gender, and time spent playing nonviolent video games. Of course, you could probably list other confounds for which Anderson and Dill did *not* control (e.g., poverty level). You might also point out that controlling for confounds does nothing to eliminate reverse causality. Maybe there is something about behaving aggressively that attracts people to aggressive video games. Although these are reasonable criticisms, Anderson and Dill would probably respond by reminding us that their true experiment addresses both the third-variable problem and the problem of reverse causality. By doing so, Anderson and Dill would be responding to our criticism in precisely the way we advocate in this chapter. They would build a strong argument by conducting multiple studies, rather than trying to make a strong claim on the basis of any single study.

So our point is that two highly imperfect studies, when taken together, are much stronger than either study taken alone. At the same time, these two clever studies are only two studies. More convincing evidence that exposure to violent video games promotes aggressive behavior might come by expanding our methodological arsenal (err ... um, toolbox) even further. Let's consider what a quasi-experiment and a population survey can do to strengthen the empirical case Anderson and Dill wished to make. Let's begin with a quasi-experiment.

Recall that in most quasi-experimental designs, the researcher has only partial control over the independent variables. Typically something that occurs naturally determines people's assignment to different quasi-experimental conditions. Thus quasi-experiments are hybrid designs that sit somewhere between lab experiments and observational field studies. A nice illustration of the utility of quasi-experiments in this program of research can be found in Bartholow and Anderson's (2002) person-by-treatment quasi-experiment. The person variable on which Bartholow and Anderson focused was gender. They focused attention on this variable to see if the relation between exposure to video game violence and aggression would be stronger for men than for women. The procedures in this study were very similar to the procedures of Anderson and Dill's true experiment. This time, however, they *block randomized* (i.e., randomly assigned people to experimental conditions within each gender group), so that approximately half of the men and half of the women were in each manipulated condition. They had 43 students (22 men and 21 women) play a violent video game (*Mortal Kombat*) or a nonviolent video game (*PGA Tournament Golf*) for ten minutes. Participants then completed the same competitive reaction time task as before, and Bartholow and Anderson recorded the average intensity of the noise blasts people delivered to their phantom opponents. As shown in Figure 12.1, men in the violent video game condition delivered more intense noise blasts than did men in the nonviolent video game condition. Women showed no such effect. Notice that this study can speak to the issue of generalizability to people in a way that the original experiment could not, because this new study incorporated a naturally occurring difference (gender) into the factorial design. Other factors one might consider are age differences (Browne & Hamilton-Giachritsis, 2005) or cultural differences (Anderson et al., 2010). Alternatively, if researchers wanted, they could have examined questions related to the generalizability with respect to situations by, say, studying the influence of video games on aggression on hot days versus cold days (see Anderson, Deuser & DeNeve, 1995). It is because of the flexibility of quasi-experimental procedures that in Table 12.1, we argued that on the whole they have "moderate" ability to address all three of the stated research goals.

Perhaps your deep and abiding affection for *Mortal Kombat* is so strong that you are still unwilling to accept the implications of these three quite varied studies. After all, none of these studies can really allow us to generalize to an entire population. As described in Chapter 6, the strongest method for allowing one to generalize to a broad population is a population survey. Population surveys use random selection methods (e.g., true random sampling,

Figure 12.1

Gender differences in aggression, from 1 = low aggression to 10 = high aggression following violent or nonviolent video game play (Bartholow & Anderson, 2002).

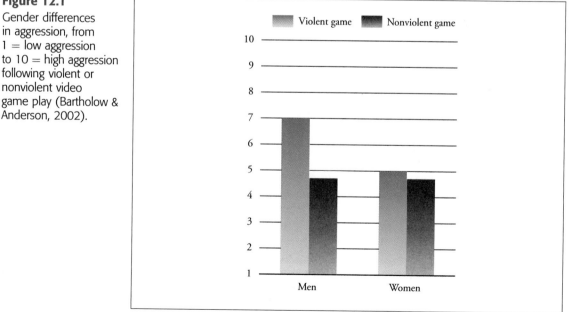

cluster sampling) to obtain a sample that is representative of the larger population. Population surveys can yield many useful descriptive facts about groups one hopes to study. For this reason, they are employed heavily by researchers who are in a position to shape public policies that influence all members of society or members of specific groups. At the same time, precisely because population surveys focus on highly diverse samples, there can be a lot of noise or natural variation in the outcomes measured. Precision is low. Because of the high costs (financial and otherwise) of population surveys, no researchers seem to have exposed random samples of the U.S. population to violent or nonviolent video games to measure their impact on aggressive behavior. However, a few population surveys have focused on the simple question of just how much time kids spend playing video games. For instance, Roberts, Foehr, Rideout, and Brodie (1999) analyzed the results of two national population surveys examining media habits of a total 3,155 U.S. children, ages 2–18. They found that, although television was still the most frequently used form of media at that time, video games were becoming increasingly popular, with 30 percent of the sample playing video games. For children aged 8–13, the average daily use translated into 32 minutes of game play a day. Roberts et al. also observed big gender differences. Specifically, 44 percent of boys versus only 17 percent of girls reported playing video games. Among game players, boys also played games longer (an average of 31 minutes daily) than girls did (eight minutes daily). The overall results thus suggested that video games were extremely popular during middle-childhood (ages 8–13), especially for boys. Recall that it was only among boys that Anderson and Bartholow found a large experimental effect of exposure to video game violence. When you add to this the fact that the games boys do play seem to be more violent than those that girls play, this would appear to be cause for concern. Further, it is hard to imagine that things have gotten better since 1999. Nintendo's *Wii*, Nintendo's *DS*, and Microsoft's *Kinect* products did not yet exist when Roberts et al. published their findings.

From this population survey, then, we get a final piece of the picture—descriptive evidence that video game use is extremely common, especially among boys. We can further infer from national sales figures that at least some of these videos are violent in nature. In December of 2010, for example, *Forbes Magazine* reported that the two top selling video games in the U.S. were *Call of Duty: Black Ops* and *Assassin's Creed Brotherhood*. We're guessing from the titles that neither of these games focuses very heavily on promoting compassion and empathy. Taken together, then, the full set of studies on violent video games strongly suggests that violent video games may contribute in a serious way to aggressive behavior in the U.S. Although no single study in this program of research nailed down the argument, the entire program of research minimized our concerns about McGrath's three-horned dilemma. No one researcher could grab the bull by all three horns at once. Working together, however, teams of researchers could tie the bull down by lassoing one horn at a time (and holding on tight while waiting for help).

Creative Solutions

Research on violent video games offers a compelling example of programmatic research in part, we think, because researchers who study violence are working in an applied area where there is pretty clear consensus about what we'd like to know. Almost anyone conducting research in this area wants to know if exposure to violent video games increases aggression and, if so, to what extent and for which specific groups of people. However, when it comes to basic rather than applied research questions, there is sometimes less consensus about the best way to go about programmatic research. One laboratory may focus on one aspect of a research question using one set of methods while another laboratory focuses on another aspect of the same research question using overlapping but not identical methods. A third lab might use a completely different set of methods, but the research question they address might be somewhat different than the question addressed in the first two labs. All this means that truly programmatic research on one specific research question is not always as common as you might expect from the previous example.

On the other hand, it is our experience that many researchers find creative ways to minimize the trade-offs that lie at the heart of the three-horned dilemma, even when they can only conduct an individual study. For example, you may recall from Chapter 7 that experimental realism can often increase the external validity of lab experiments. Sometimes clever researchers also find ways of maximizing the external validity of laboratory experiments by selecting diverse, out of the ordinary, or highly representative samples of research participants (rather relying on convenience samples of college students). Similarly, researchers can sometimes address concerns about precision with clever field experiments that measure and statistically control for known confounds. With these kinds of ideas in mind, we'd like to review some of the creative examples of research that minimize the trade-offs inherent in different research designs in sometimes surprising ways.

USING PERCEIVED ALIEN ABDUCTIONS TO BETTER UNDERSTAND MEMORY BIAS

One of the most interesting things about human beings is that we are pretty easy to fool, and not just by others but even by ourselves. For example, we sometimes convince ourselves that we have made progress on our diets, our poker playing skills, or our Spanish language skills—by falsely remembering that we used to suck even worse than we do now (Ross et al. 1986). Fifty years of research on cognitive dissonance has also shown that, without realizing we have done so, we often change our attitudes to become more consistent with our recent behavior. In the 1970s, Elizabeth Loftus's laboratory experiments on memory also revealed that our memories are highly imperfect and open to sometimes unwanted suggestions. Dozens of lab experiments using the DRM (Deese, Roediger & McDermott) paradigm yielded a similar insight. Assuming you're not already highly familiar with the DRM paradigm, let's take a quick peek at it. Rest assured, however, that this is *not* one of those annoying memory demonstrations where we'll expect you to remember everything you heard. With that in mind, please indulge us for a minute, and turn this page upside down so that you can read the list of 15 words that follows. Just read the list of words once and then turn your book right side up again.

sour, candy, sugar, bitter, good, taste, tooth, nice, honey, soda, chocolate, heart, tart, cakes, pie

Now if you would indulge us a bit further, please put down that candy bar, pick up a pen or pencil, and write down the name of the five U.S. states you would most enjoy visiting in the next year. Are you done? It's very important that you complete this second task and write down the names of the five U.S. states (either here or on a separate sheet of paper).

Five States I'd Love to Visit

1. _____
2. _____
3. _____
4. _____
5. _____

OK, now that you are done, take a look at the five target words that follow and—*without consulting the list*—circle (or write down on a separate page) any of the five target words that you remember from the original list of 15 words.

Circle the target words you saw on the list

halo   *sugar*   *table*   *tattoo*   *sweet*

If you are like most other people (who haven't yet had a course in cognitive psychology), you had no trouble eliminating the words "halo," "table," and "tattoo." You are correct so far; these words did *not* appear on the list. Further, you probably had no trouble remembering the two words "sugar" and "sweet." The large majority of people who read this list of 15 words, and then perform a very brief distracter task, remember reading both "sugar" and "sweet" (e.g., see Roediger & McDermott, 1995; Schacter, 1996). But here's the problem: the often-remembered word "sweet" is *not* on the list. Go ahead and check it out. If you *have* taken that course in cognitive psychology, you probably know that many people think they read the word "sweet" because it is a close semantic associate of those other 15 words. It is difficult to read those words without activating the word "sweet" in memory. Apparently, we human beings are not as good as we might hope at knowing the difference between *thinking* something and *seeing or hearing* that something. That turns out to be a very important point because it is related to a huge controversy about the malleability of human memory.

As we hope we have demonstrated with this exercise, the DRM paradigm offers a convenient method for creating and studying false memories. It is for this reason that it has been used many times over by cognitive psychologists to help them better understand the cognitive mechanisms underlying memory encoding, storage, and retrieval. Psychologists love tools like this one because such tools give them the experimental precision they crave. But to what end?

As you might have guessed, interest in the DRM stems not just from its usefulness in the laboratory but also for its potential to help psychologists understand false memories that influence the real-world decisions and experiences of everyday people. With a tool for studying false memories, cognitive psychologists have a procedure that might help them weigh in on hotly contested debates of tremendous importance. For instance, whereas memory experts have maintained for decades that human memory is highly imperfect, our legal system (often reliant on eyewitnesses) and many psychotherapists (often reliant on childhood memories) have historically put a great deal of faith in the accuracy of human memory (see Loftus, 1993). Thus, when adults claimed to have unearthed repressed memories from their early childhoods (sometimes of relatives committing heinous crimes), jurors and psychotherapists sometimes took these reports at face value. In the 1970s and 1980s, quite a few people were convicted of crimes based solely on what is now considered highly questionable "recovered" memories. It is certainly a fact that we all possess imperfect memories of our childhoods. Furthermore, it is certainly possible for people to bury unwanted memories for years and retrieve them as adults. However, it is now very well established that well-intended but misguided interrogators or psychotherapists can sometimes convince people that they remember things that simply did not happen. As public, scientific, and legal debate swirled about the reality of repressed memories, however, one argument that was raised repeatedly was the idea that it can't possibly be so easy to fool people into believing that they remember something bizarre or heinous unless it really did happen.

Notice that the controversial issue of the malleability of human memory is a great example of McGrath's three-horned dilemma. Dozens of precise, carefully crafted lab experiments—usually conducted on convenience samples of college students and at times using the DRM procedure we just described—suggested to memory experts that the human memory system is malleable enough that a psychotherapist or police detective with a powerful agenda might unknowingly plant false memories in clients or witnesses in a court case. All kinds of things that once seemed crazy or inexplicable could now be seen as specific examples of malleability and/or suggestibility in human memory. However, to critics of artificial laboratory research, the leap from the psychologist's lab to the psychotherapist's couch or the police interview room seemed outrageous. The precision that allowed memory researchers to document false memories right and left in the lab was an argument against the external validity of the findings. Both the content of the memories (harmless words versus heinous actions) and the people doing the remembering (e.g., college students versus psychotherapy patients) were radically different.

What advice would you give to psychologists based on Table 12.1? It would seem that your best approach would be to run a series of field studies and population surveys, perhaps with a sprinkling of quasi-experiments to round things out. What would these studies look like, however? On the face of it, you would encounter considerable difficulties studying the types of false memories that have meaningful consequences in daily life. It seems more than a little impractical to follow a sample of participants in a longitudinal study to determine what factors can produce false memories about the past. The false memories of greatest concern (that relate to traumatic experiences and crimes) are probably very low frequency events (although too frequent in another sense). Many ethical issues also arise. These same complications, and more, also stand in the way of population surveys. Imagine an opinion pollster calling a nationally representative sample to ask them to estimate the percentage of their memories that are false.

So here's a dilemma that Table 12.1 cannot very readily help us resolve. What's a researcher to do? One group of researchers, Clancy, McNally, Schacter, Lenzenweger, and Pitman (2002) found a remarkably simple way to broaden the likely applicability of their findings. In this case, they chose to stay in the laboratory but they designed a quasi-experiment. Although this study lacked some of the features of good field studies or population surveys, it nonetheless provided us with some traction on the issue of generalizability with respect to people.

Clancy et al. began by posting classified ads targeting research participants who believed they had been abducted by space aliens. They then brought these people (along with two demographically similar comparison groups) into the lab. To be more specific, Clancy et al.'s (2002) quasi-experimental groups were (A) a recovered memory group, who believed that they had recovered repressed memories of alien abduction, (B) a repressed memory group, who believed that they had been abducted by aliens but did *not* claim to have recovered any specific memories of the experience, and (C) a demographically matched control group, who did not believe they had ever been in contact with aliens. All of the participants then took part in a sophisticated memory experiment based directly on the DRM paradigm. Clancy et al. found a robust false memory effect in the control group, comprising individuals who, like the second author, did not think they had ever been abducted by aliens. This finding is not all that surprising because the DRM paradigm established the phenomenon in many samples drawn from populations that probably did not possess alien abduction memories. The control group was important, however, because they provided a baseline for measuring the level of false memory production expected, in general. With this group as a comparison, Clancy et al. found that the false memory effect was larger than usual in the repressed memory group, and largest of all in the crucial group who believed they had recovered repressed memories of having been abducted by aliens!

What does this finding suggest? It suggests that perhaps the type of false memories studied (precisely) using the DRM paradigm have a meaningful connection to the kind of false memories that happen in the real world. Of course, no one study ever *proves* anything, and studies confined to the research laboratory will always introduce questions of external validity. It is *possible*, for example, that aliens are particularly interested in the DRM false memory paradigm. Maybe they selectively abduct earthlings who are especially prone to this particular memory bias as a way of covering their trails. It also is possible that alien abductees do have more false memories on the DRM paradigm but that this process had no true causal link to their abduction memories, false or real. And, even if the DRM pattern is causally linked to this type of false memory, it may have little or nothing to do with other forms of false memories that are of larger societal concerns (e.g., those related to childhood trauma or eyewitness misidentification). But this study does add something beyond precision. This study now makes it seem more plausible that people who are especially susceptible to normal false memory biases, as demonstrated with the DRM paradigm, may be more likely than the general population to become convinced that something they imagined, dreamed, or otherwise observed indirectly could have actually happened to them (e.g., see Johnson, Hashtroudi, & Lindsay, 1993; Johson & Raye, 1981). Sometimes the way to address the three-horned dilemma is to try things you wouldn't ordinarily try—while holding tightly onto a single horn.

RACIAL BIAS AND THE POLICE OFFICER'S DILEMMA

Laboratory researchers who study other controversial topics have taken similar approaches to minimizing concerns about generalizability to persons. One such example involves the controversial question of unintended racism. In the past two decades many researchers who study racism and stereotypes have focused their sights on the unconscious roots of racism (see Banaji & Hardin, 1996; Devine, 1989; Fazio, Jackson, Dunton, & Williams, 1995). The concern with this research is that many individuals who report egalitarian attitudes might nonetheless form impressions of others based on their stereotypes or discriminate against others based on prejudicial attitudes that they cannot report consciously (cf., Blanton & Jaccard, 2008). This hypothesis is provocative, but from the perspective of the second author, research in the domain of "implicit" racial bias has not fully embraced the multi-method approach advocated in this chapter. Early reviews of the literature on prejudice (Sears, 1986) and more recent reviews (Henry, 2008) have arguably shown that research on racial bias has largely been limited to the study of how college students respond to artificial laboratory situations designed to evoke prejudice. Many have argued that until researchers in this tradition move to the "real world," they will be limited in their ability to comment on the nature of prejudice in everyday settings (Blanton & Jaccard, 2008; Tetlock & Mitchell, 2006). Although the first author is more willing than the second to draw pretty broad inferences based on such convenience samples, even he has to admit that all of the usual criticisms of laboratory research apply to laboratory research on stereotyping.

There is one area of research, however, where a focus on laboratory methods seems justified because of the difficulty of studying it definitively in the field. This behavior is the mistaken shooting of unarmed suspects by police. This event, though rare, can be studied in the field, and large-scale studies by the Department of Justice (2001) have shown that Black suspects (armed or not) are, in fact, much more likely than White suspects to be killed by police officers. However, critics have noted that these results are not definitive because of both person and environmental confounds. For example, compared with Whites, Blacks are disproportionately likely to live in (and be confronted by police in) poor, high crime neighborhoods. You might think traditional lab experiments would help resolve this problem, but it would obviously be unethical to manufacture opportunities for participants to shoot anyone in a research laboratory. The social importance of this research question came to national attention in 1999 when four White New York City police officers shot the unarmed Amadou Diallo. In fact, after learning about this tragic incident, several social psychologists became interested in the possibility that White Americans' tendencies to stereotype Black men as violent may have played a role in Diallo's death. Of course, there is no way to know what makes any one specific officer shoot an unarmed person, but this does not mean that this behavior cannot be studied systematically.

The first researcher to investigate this possibility was Keith Payne, one of whose priming experiments we discussed in Chapter 7. In Payne's original (2001) priming experiments he showed that participants (a) identified guns more quickly than usual when primed with a Black face and (b) identified tools more quickly than usual when primed with a White face. So Payne showed that people tend to associate Black versus White faces with different objects. It may have dawned on you, however, that there is really nothing "wrong" with taking a little longer to realize that a gun is a gun because you have just been primed with a White face. Ultimately, the same decision is being made. To examine error rates rather than just response latencies, Payne turned up the heat in a follow-up experiment. In this new experiment the primes did not differ but participants now had only 500 ms. (1/2 second) to identify the targets (as tools versus guns). Not surprisingly, error rates shot up dramatically under this kind of serious time pressure. More important, the errors followed a predictable pattern. Participants who had just been primed with a White face falsely judged a tool to be a gun fully 31 percent of the time. This error rate increased significantly, to 37 percent, when the same participants judged the same tools after having just been primed by a Black face. As interesting as these findings are, however, you may have noticed that these carefully crafted laboratory experiments are pretty far removed from the alleys of New York City. Consistent with McGrath's three-horned dilemma, there is no guarantee that the robust priming effects at work in these experiments would translate into shooting errors made by real police officers.

As it turns out, Payne was not the only social psychologist who took note of the Amadou Diallo shooting. At about the same time that Payne was conducting his experiments, a different team of social psychologists was taking a somewhat different approach to the same basic research question. From our perspective, the nice thing about this is that whereas Payne focused steadfastly on experimental precision, this group developed a judgment task that was potentially higher in mundane realism (though the procedure was still an artificial experimental task). Instead of asking people to focus on

Black versus White faces and identify weapons versus tools, this group asked people to quickly scan an entire computer screen for an entire Black or White man—in urban images that resemble those in which real police officers sometimes have to make real shooting decisions. To be more specific, Correll, Judd, Park, and Wittenbrink (2002) developed a laboratory video game to see if a target person's apparent ethnicity would influence the likelihood that people playing the role of a police officer would erroneously "shoot" the person (by pressing a "shoot" button rather than a "not shoot" button). So in a sense this study brings us back to where we started, at the intersection of video games and violence. However, in this case Correll and colleagues used a video game as a research tool—to gain a better understanding of real-world choices.

Unlike *Mortal Kombat*, this video game is extremely simple. Trial after trial, different target people appear on a computer screen (see Figure 12.2). On some trials the target person is Black; on others he is White. In addition, whether Black or White, the target might be holding a cell phone, a wallet, a Coke can, or a gun. Because this was a lab experiment, Correll et al. could measure not only how often people mistakenly shoot the guy who is holding,

Courtesy of Josh Correll

Figure 12.2

An image from Correll et al.'s (2002) original video game designed to assess racial bias in shooting decisions.

say, a cell phone but also how quickly people make either the correct or the incorrect decision to shoot. Correll et al.'s first experiment on this topic involved college students at the University of Colorado. As the experimenters expected, if the guy holding a gun happened to be Black rather than White, participants were quicker to shoot. In a follow-up experiment, the experimenters increased the time pressure to make the shoot/don't shoot decision. They found, as expected, that participants were more likely to mistakenly shoot an unarmed target if he was Black. In a follow-up quasi-experiment, the authors showed that the bias toward shooting a Black target was stronger than usual for people who reported having had greater exposure to Blacks. In yet another follow-up experiment, Correll et al. recruited a community sample (rather than college students; thus increasing generalizability to people). They found that the racial bias in their shooter task was not limited to White shooters. African American participants showed the same evidence of racial bias in their shooting decisions as did White participants.

Despite both the fact that the stimuli in this video game resemble real people in real-world settings, and despite Correll et al.'s use of a community sample, we hope you can see that the precision of these lab studies still raises questions about generalizability to real people (e.g., real police officers) facing the real situations (e.g., real alleys, real guns). Again, due to the low frequency of the criterion of interest (fatal shooting of civilians) it simply would be difficult to conduct a definitive correlational field study to determine what factors predict faulty shooting. However, Correll et al. (2007) did do one more unusual thing to address concerns about the generalizability of their results with respect to people.

Specifically, they conducted a follow-up study that again relied on quasi-experimental methods. In this study, they compared the strength of the racial bias in shooting decisions between real police officers and untrained members of a community sample. The results of this study were both reassuring and distressing. First, there was evidence that police officers generally set their threshold for shooting a bit higher than did people in the community sample. Across the board, police officers were both more accurate in their shooting decisions and more reluctant to shoot than were regular citizens. Like regular citizens, however, real police officers showed a robust racial bias in terms of their reaction times. For example, police officers were both quicker to shoot an armed target if he was Black and quicker to make a "no shoot" decision for an unarmed target if he was White. This finding suggests that police officers are quicker to make the "correct" decision when it is consistent with racial stereotypes. However, it also suggests that if you are a criminal who wishes to shoot a police officer before he or she shoots you, there may be an advantage to being White. The one bit of good news in this research, though, is that the police officers did not make the "wrong" decision of whether to shoot based on stereotypes. Specifically, they ultimately did *not* shoot unarmed Black targets any more often than unarmed Whites. Further they did not fail to shoot armed Whites more often than armed Blacks. This finding suggests that police training might have some beneficial effects in real-world settings, but even here caution is needed. This clever game is still just a game, and it cannot tell us for sure if police training is usually sufficient to override shooter biases. Coming at this from a completely different angle, it is also possible that selection bias played a role in this study. Specifically, it is possible that the officers who were willing to undergo this kind of careful scrutiny in the lab were particularly conscientious, open-minded, or well trained.

Putting it all together, this study suggests that the earlier work on college students can be useful for studying this type of racial bias. At the same time, it also suggests that one must be cautious when trying to generalize to other groups (e.g., trained police officers) in some instances. Our conclusion? We need more (programmatic) research, conducted both in the lab and in the field.

UNDERSTANDING WHEN PEOPLE ARE TOO SEXY FOR THEIR STINKY T-SHIRTS

To this point, we have considered ways in which researchers might expand the diversity of their sample to include novel groups (self-perceived alien abductees and police officers) to try to connect laboratory findings to the real world. However, diversity is not just found using the kind of *people* we'd like to draw inferences about. It is also found using the kind of *situations* we'd like to draw inferences about. Generalizability to situations is important to consider as well because, to be honest, the kinds of situations psychologists study are usually even more contrived than the kinds of people they study. After all, college students really are one kind of real people. However, laboratory experimenters routinely put their research participants in highly unusual and artificial situations that sometimes bear no resemblance to real-world situations. As we noted in Chapter 7, for example, Asch's famous conformity studies bore little resemblance to the playgrounds or boardrooms where most real social influence happens. And as we may have neglected to note previously, people rarely go around judging other people by smelling those other people's stinky t-shirts. However, evolutionary psychologists who are interested in the cues that people find sexually attractive are quite fond of having people judge other people on the basis of nothing else. Let's take a closer look at exactly how this is typically done.

But first let's examine *why*. In the past two decades a growing body of research on evolutionary psychology has begun to suggest that human beings are not as different from animals as we once thought (e.g., see Buss et al., 2010). For example, 20 years ago most researchers probably assumed that natural body smells play little role in human sexual behavior. Likewise, until very recently, most researchers probably assumed that, unlike other animals (including other great apes) women's sexual receptiveness had nothing to do with ovulatory cycles. From an evolutionary perspective this would be a remarkable break from millions of years of successful mammalian evolution (e.g., see Shubin, 2009). As Haselton and Gildersleeve (in press) put it, "Like other mammals, women can only conceive by having intercourse on the day of ovulation ... Throughout evolutionary history, these were the crucial few days when women's sexual decisions had the greatest reproductive consequences and the only days when men could produce offspring by having sex."

From an evolutionary perspective, it would be surprising if, unlike almost any other animal on the planet, human beings were so ovulationally clueless that heterosexual males never have any idea whatsoever when women of childbearing age are at their most fertile. In keeping with this notion, Haselton and Gildersleeve reviewed research in several different areas that all converge to suggest that women do, in fact, emit cues to their ovulatory status. Moreover, on average, heterosexual men seem to be pretty receptive to these cues. Before we borrow liberally from Haselton and Gildersleeve's review of men's ability to detect women's ovulatory cues, it might be useful to remind you that, in principle, there are many cues women could give off to advertise (unconsciously, we assume) that they are about to ovulate. In a sense each cue is relevant to a different set of situations. How a woman dresses, for example, is different than how she smells or how she wears her hair. Furthermore, some of these cues (e.g., clothing cues) are likely to be observable by almost anyone whereas others (natural body odors) are likely to be available only to a woman's very close relationship partners (and perhaps not even to them if the woman strongly wishes to hide them).

Let's begin with the stinky t-shirt studies. Thornhill et al (2003) convinced 48 female donors to go to bed wearing a clean, odorless t-shirt without doing anything that could influence their natural body odors during sleep. The women were forbidden, for example, from applying perfume, anti-perspirant, or deodorant. They then recruited 77 male judges to come into their lab, sniff the recently-slept-in t-shirts, and judge how pleasant and "sexy" the shirts smelled. If you recognize how powerfully Americans have been socialized to think that human body odor is undesirable, you might not be surprised to learn that the men were not generally too crazy about the smells of these t-shirts. However, the question is not whether dirty t-shirts smelled good, it is whether they smelled better than usual when they had just been worn by women on the most fertile days of their ovulatory cycles. Another way of putting this is that the researchers wanted to know if the pleasantness of the smell (as rated by men in the research laboratory) of the carefully prepared t-shirts would be correlated with the fertility of the women who wore the shirts (in the comfort of their own beds). This is exactly what Thornhill et al. (2003) found. Specifically, the t-shirts that had been worn by women who were at their most fertile were rated as both more "pleasant" and more "sexy" than the t-shirts worn by women who were not at their most fertile (see also Doty, Ford, Preti, & Huggins, 1975).

This is one of those interesting studies that could be categorized either as a correlational study or a quasi-experiment. The study *was* correlational (passive observational) in the sense that the researchers merely correlated a judgment made by male participants with the time of month at which some t-shirts were collected from different women. However, the study was also a natural experiment that the researchers happened to conduct in the laboratory. To be more specific, the researchers capitalized on the fact that different women happened to be at different points in their ovulatory cycles when they generated the t-shirts under highly controlled conditions. In fact, from this perspective, the only reason we might consider this a quasi-experiment rather than a true experiment is that it is possible that something else that is highly correlated with ovulatory status might be driving the results. In other words, unlike true experimenters, these quasi-experimenters had only partial control over the nature of their stimuli. Having said this, let us add that their careful stimulus-generation procedures did give them a lot of experimental control. At any rate, this unique study employed precise laboratory presentation of the crucial stimuli (stinky t-shirts). It was this feature that allowed researchers to study very precisely the phenomenon they wished to understand.

So the t-shirt study provides one creative thread of evidence that women may smell better than usual to heterosexual men when women are at the peak of their fertility cycles. There is also evidence that women may *sound* better than usual when they are at their most fertile. Pipitone and Gallup (2009) recorded 38 women counting to ten at four different points in their ovulatory cycles. Both male and female judges who were kept blind to the women's ovulatory status agreed that the women sounded more attractive when recorded during the high fertility phases. Bryant and Haselton (2009) replicated this effect having 69 female UCLA undergrads record the simple phrase "Hi, I'm a student at UCLA." Objective acoustical analyses revealed that the pitch of women's voices became higher (i.e., more stereotypically feminine) when they were recorded closer to the windows of greatest fertility. These studies, too, could be considered either correlational (passive observational) studies or quasi-experiments depending on how much control you feel the researchers had over the stimuli (women's voices) that served as their independent variables. In this case, for example, the researchers did not need to ask the women not to wear perfume or make-up. Instead, by focusing solely on the human voice, the researchers presumably eliminated the effects of any visual, tactile, or olfactory cues that may covary with a woman's ovulatory status. Further, both studies controlled perfectly for the content of women's speech, which would be a huge source of natural variation if they had simply asked the women to engage in a getting-acquainted conversation with a male stranger. Further, notice that regardless of how we categorize this study, the researchers were taking real things (human odors or voices) that normally exist only in the real world and bringing them to the lab for careful, precise examination. Sometimes you *can* apparently bring some carefully selected components of the mountain (i.e., the situation) to Mohammed.

In yet another study along these lines, researchers have also examined whether women *look* sexier than usual when they are at their most fertile. Haselton, Mortezaie, Pillsworth, Bleske-Rechek, and Frederick (2007) took full-body photographs of 30 women when (according to a hormonal test) the women were either highly fertile or not fertile. Male and female judges who were kept blind to hypotheses viewed the photo pairs with the women's faces covered. Judges simply picked the photo in which the woman was "trying to look more attractive." About 60 percent of the time they chose the photos taken when women were highly fertile. In a follow-up study, Durante, Li, and Haselton (2008) replicated these findings when they asked women who were either at the most or least fertile window of their ovulatory cycle to draw a picture of what they would like to wear to a party that evening. Women who were ovulating drew sexier and more revealing outfits.

So these studies essentially brought something from the real world into the lab. But they were still lab studies, after all, and some of them (e.g., the study in which women drew sexy or not-so-sexy outfits) seem particularly vulnerable to criticisms regarding a potential lack of external validity. Is there any evidence that these kinds of findings replicate outside of the laboratory? There is. Gueguen (2009) conducted a field study that examined the behavior of women in a real-world setting in which they arranged for all women to be exposed to the same carefully controlled stimulus (an attractive man who asked the women to dance). Specifically, Gueguen sent attractive male confederates to a dance club. Their task was to ask women to dance with them (using a standardized, well-rehearsed protocol). Women who were in the fertile phase of their cycles were substantially more likely to say yes to the same standardized request (see also Haselton & Gangstead, 2006; Miller & Maner, 2010).

Field studies have also been used to study the responses of men, much as in the t-shirt studies that started our discussion. Miller, Tybur, and Jordan (2007) convinced exotic dancers at a Dallas strip club to participate in an online daily diary study in which the women recorded exactly how much money they earned in tips for 60 straight days (minus their days off). Because Miller et al. studied the women using a time-series design (see Chapter 8), they were able to count backwards from the point of the dancers' periods to identify (retrospectively) the days at which the dancers were at the peak of their fertility cycles. Further, they were able to make separate comparisons for dancers who were on the pill (whose hormones were being artificially regulated) and dancers who were not. Their study thus employed a method of "patching" and internal analyses to gain insight into the precise mechanisms at play to influence tipping. (Compare their design with the design in Figure 8.9, comparing the role of study habits on grades across time.)

Their key finding was that dancers who were not on the pill earned an extra $15 per hour in tips on high fertility days as compared with low fertility days. Because these are the same dancers working at the same club with the same motivation to make as much money as possible on any given night, it is hard to come up with too many alternative explanations for these findings. Thus, although this was a field study, precision was unusually high. Further, it is precisely because this unusual real-world situation (with such an unusual population of research participants) is so far removed from the more precise laboratory studies of college undergraduates counting from one to ten, or diligently drawing party dresses, that it becomes hard to dismiss the controversial hypothesis that human beings are more like other mammals than we might like to think.

SUMMARY

In this chapter we have argued that there is no perfect research design and thus no perfect study. In any study, it would be nice to maximize precision while at the same time maximizing generalizability to both people and situations. However, any given study will involve trade-offs. Throughout this book we have focused attention on one of these trade-offs, between internal validity (precision) and external validity (generalizability). The current chapter expands on this theme by showing how the limitations of any given study might be addressed by complementing it with a very different kind of study that addresses the same basic research question. We introduced Table 12.1 as a useful guide for how to combine research studies using multiple methods to create a program of research that addresses multiple concerns. The research examining the influence of video game violence on aggression illustrates the utility of this table. However, when we considered other research areas (false memories, shooter biases, and human responses to ovulatory cycle cues), we also considered some creative ways in which researchers might maximize both precision and at least one kind of generalizability in a single study. We thus offer Table 12.1 as a useful guide rather than a fixed set of rigid methodological rules. As we have argued throughout this text, creativity is often the best solution to any methodological problem. We hope some of the studies we reviewed here have helped you appreciate both the programmatic and creative solutions to McGrath's dilemma.

STUDY QUESTIONS

1. What are the three horns of the dilemma faced by researchers? How do they relate to the trade-off between internal and external validity?

2. What are the limitations of a population survey? Which of these limitations might be addressed by a true experiment, conducted in the laboratory, and why? Which of these limitations might be addressed by a correlational study conducted in the field, and why?

3. Sometimes it is difficult to combine methods in a single study. What obstacles typically prevent researchers from getting the full benefit of population surveys and true experiments in a single study? What obstacles typically prevent researchers from getting the full benefit of correlational studies and true experiments in a single study? What about surveys and correlational studies?

4. Which method would you employ if you were most worried about person confounds? Situation confounds? External validity with respect to people? External validity with respect to situations? Internal validity?

5. This chapter did not focus on artifacts (from Chapter 5), but in a way multi-method research is pursued to guard for hidden artifacts. What is an artifact and how does it differ from a confound or from noise? In what way does the multi-method question highlight the problem of artifacts, and how does the pursuit of programmatic research try to address it?

Putting Your Knowledge to Work: 20 Methodology Problems

This chapter contains 20 methodology problems designed to allow you to exercise the methodological skills you have developed by reading this text. Most of these problems provide a specific interpretation of some kind of empirical observation (e.g., the claims made in a commercial, the findings of a laboratory experiment). Your job is usually to provide an alternate interpretation for the same empirical observation. Many of these problems also ask you for advice about improving the way in which the observation was made (e.g., correcting potential design flaws in an experiment). Finally, a couple of the problems ask you to design your own study to test a particular research hypothesis. The common thread that unites these problems is the fact that they all provide you with a chance to demonstrate your methodological expertise. We have found that students usually enjoy working on these problems with other students. In fact, we usually ask students to work on the problems in groups of five to eight people (during class—so that it is possible to monitor students' progress and make suggestions as they work). Regardless of how you approach the problems, however, we hope you will find it as gratifying to solve them as we did to pose them.

Except where otherwise indicated, the problems in this chapter are based on real studies or real claims made by advertisers, laypeople, or trained researchers. In some cases, however, we have consolidated several closely related studies into a single study or changed unimportant details of a study (often to protect the identity of the party who made the original claim). Although our inspiration for each individual problem was always a specific empirical claim or research finding, our main inspiration for creating this set of methodology problems was a scholarly and engaging text by Huck and

Sandler (1979). If you would like some additional practice flexing your methodological muscle, we heartily recommend their text.

1. IN SEARCH OF A DELICIOUS, LOW-FAT TV SHOW

In late July of 1992, a Los Angeles TV station reported the results of a surprising and alarming medical study. The reporter covering the story stated that watching too much TV may be bad for children's hearts as well as their heads. In particular, he said that a study of television viewing and blood cholesterol revealed that, relative to kids who watched very little TV, kids who watched a lot of TV have especially high cholesterol levels. The reporter implied that TV watching actually increases blood cholesterol levels, but we are skeptical of this interpretation. Can you come up with a more reasonable explanation for the results of the study?

2. LET'S GET SUPERNATURAL

Despite the efforts of many to debunk astrology and parapsychology, many people believe that you can predict a person's personality or future from the motion of stars and planets to which the person has never even traveled. Others believe that although the stars cannot predict your future, other people can do so using their psychic powers. If you wanted to conduct a study to test the validity of either (1) astrology and horoscopes or (2) a specific person's claim that he or she can predict future events, how would you do so? In answering this question, try to think of a test that is both simple and fair (i.e., scientific). In doing so, pay special attention to the closely related issues of (1) coming up with a good operational definition of a correct prediction and (2) choosing a good dependent variable or variables.

3. FLY AWAY HOME

We believe that notices on milk cartons can help authorities to recover missing children. We also believe that the television show *America's Most Wanted* has helped law enforcement agencies put away some very dangerous criminals. Similarly, we think it's likely that flyers such as the ones the first author used to receive in the mail on a regular basis can help people recover missing children. The problem is that we'd like to know exactly *how* effective these approaches are. After all, if we can find out which approaches are most effective, we can rescue more children and capture more criminals for the same amount of effort. A flyer that the first author often received in the mail (from an organization called ADVO) seems to answer this question in clear and simple terms. In this flyer, ADVO claimed, "Over 55 children featured have been recovered." The implication of ADVO's claim is that their treatment (the flyers) caused the recovery of over 55 missing children. What are some potential problems with this claim? If ADVO hired you to perform a large-scale study to evaluate the effectiveness of their flyer, how would you go about doing so? In other words, if you had sufficient resources at your disposal, how would you correct any potential threats to the validity of ADVO's implicit claim about the flyers?

4. IMPRESSIVE PICKUP LINES

Vacuum cleaner companies often distribute advertisements that promote the amazing cleaning powers of their particular model of vacuum cleaner. For example, some ads show vacuum cleaners picking up heavy objects such as nails, bolts, or ball bearings. However, an advertisement that each of us has received in the mail many times seems to top them all by showing that the compact version of a particular canister vacuum can pick up a 16-lb. bowling ball! (See Figure 13.1.) One of us happens to know a couple of excellent homemakers who insist that this particular vacuum cleaner really does do an excellent job, and thus we are not necessarily disputing this manufacturer's claim. However, as skeptical consumers (and even more skeptical scientists), we would like to know more before we decide that this vacuum is one of the best on the market. For the purposes of this exercise, we would like you to assume that the compact canister vacuums produced by this particular company really *can* pick up a 16-lb. bowling ball (as we believe they can). However, even if you make this assumption, it is still possible to criticize this specific demonstration of the superior performance of this vacuum. What are your criticisms? As a clue, we think that a consideration of the first three basic forms of validity discussed in Chapter 3 suggests a different methodological critique of this claim (and a way of improving the demonstration).

Figure 13.1

Is the vacuum cleaner the first author is using to pick up this 15-lb. bowling ball the best vacuum money can buy?

5. CLEVER WHO?

As statistics instructors who have frequently seen math anxiety at work among extremely bright and motivated college students, we can easily relate to high-school math teachers who become frustrated trying to get kids interested in math. About 100 years ago, a German math teacher named Mr. von Osten appears to have become so frustrated that he gave up on his regular students and turned his teaching attention to his horse! Interestingly, Mr. von Osten seems to have had better luck with his horse than he had with many of his human students. In fact, he taught his horse to perform such a wide array of intellectual feats that the horse eventually became known as Clever Hans. Not only could Clever Hans perform routine mathematical tasks such as addition, subtraction, and multiplication, but he could also perform more complex tasks such as finding the square root of a number, raising a number to a power, or telling the day of the week that corresponded to a particular date. As if this wasn't enough, Hans could also identify musical tones and answer general-knowledge questions about history, geography, or the arts.

Of course, even Clever Hans had his limits. For example, he couldn't write or speak. However, his owner prepared a special tablet containing all the letters of the alphabet, and Clever Hans could tap out his answers to most questions by using this tablet. Similarly, to give his answers to mathematical questions, Hans would tap his hoof a certain number of times to indicate a certain number. Hans was studied by a wide variety of experts who initially concluded that his amazing abilities were genuine. However, further investigation eventually revealed that Hans wasn't quite as clever as people had originally thought. How do you suppose people eventually discovered the secret behind Hans's performances? What was this secret?

6. LIFE SUCKS AND SO YOU DIE

A large body of research in health psychology suggests that negative life events (such as the death of a loved one or the loss of one's job) can have negative consequences for people's physical well being. One common way of studying the relation between negative life events and illness involves making use of retrospective survey designs. In studies making use of such designs, people who are physically ill and people who are physically healthy are asked to report the number of negative life events they have experienced in the recent past (e.g., the past month). Such studies typically reveal that people who are ill report having experienced a greater number of negative life events. Although such findings are consistent with the possibility that negative life events contribute to physical illness, these findings are open to alternate interpretations. What kinds of alternate interpretations can you suggest? If you wanted to gather more rigorous support for the idea that life events can contribute to illness, how might you improve this kind of retrospective design?

7. ON THE DRAWBACKS OF LIKING YOURSELF

Researchers who study self-concept have identified numerous advantages of high self-esteem. Relative to people low in self-esteem, for instance, people high in self-esteem appear to be happier, better adjusted emotionally, more successful, less lonely, and more likely to succeed at work. Although we believe that all these things are true, the first author once conducted a preliminary study in which he examined the potential *disadvantages* of high self-esteem. After giving people an established, well-validated measure of self-esteem at the beginning of the quarter, he asked them a few questions about their driving behavior two months later. His most important findings were that, in comparison with people low in self-esteem, those high in self-esteem (1) were more likely to report owning a motorcycle or scooter, (2) reported having received more speeding tickets during the last year, and (3) reported a greater frequency of driving while under the influence of alcohol. All these findings were statistically significant, and we hope you will agree that they can all have very serious negative consequences. At least one of us would like to conclude that self-esteem has negative consequences (at least in the area of driving behavior). However, we each have to admit that there are some problems with this claim. How many can you think of? How might you try to fix them?

8. THE EARLY BIRD GETS THE WIN?

When the first author was a freshman in high school, his wrestling coach claimed that his careful analysis of high-school wrestlers indicated that you could usually predict who would win a wrestling match by noticing who got the takedown at the beginning of the match (loosely speaking, by noticing which wrestler was the first to score points for controlling the other wrestler during the opening seconds of a match). The coach claimed that wrestlers who got the takedown won more than 80 percent of the more than 100 matches that formed the basis of his informal study. On the basis of this observation, this coach concluded that if he could teach all his wrestlers to master the basic moves involved in a takedown, his team could greatly improve its win-loss record from the previous year. Thus, the coach had his wrestlers spend a disproportionate amount of training time learning about takedowns. Because the first author was a mediocre wrestler, he really wanted to believe that he could greatly improve his winning percentage by simply improving his skills at the takedown. Of course, the coach was wrong. The first author did improve his takedown skills (perhaps due to sheer regression toward the mean), but doing so didn't do very much for his win-loss record. Moreover, the overall team record that year was far from stellar. What was wrong with this coach's conclusion about takedowns?

9. TESTOSTERONE MAKES BETTER DIVE-BOMBERS

A researcher recently argued that, because of our culture's emphasis on competition among boys and men, men should perform better than women under the pressure of competition. To test his hypothesis, he gave 20 women and

20 men the task of assembling a model airplane as quickly as possible. To create a competitive atmosphere, the researcher promised that the person who assembled his or her plane most quickly would win four tickets to the Super Bowl (and you can assume that his participants believed him). As a group, the men assembled their planes in about half the time required by the women, and a statistical test showed that this difference was highly significant. The researcher concluded that men do indeed work better than women under competitive conditions. We can think of at least three problems with the researcher's study that might render this conclusion suspect. How many can you think of? How would you correct them?

10. WORKING YOUR FINGERS TO THE DEAN'S LIST

As an undergraduate, one of us worked part-time jobs 20–30 hours per week, and he sometimes wished that he had more time to devote to his studies. However, an ad that used to appear frequently in UCLA's student newspaper (the *Daily Bruin*) suggests that we should all take on as many part-time jobs as possible. The ad depicts an attractive young woman who claims, "Last quarter, I earned $3,000 and a 3.5." The ad implies that being employed by UPS can actually improve one's GPA. "Think of it—great pay, flexible hours, and maybe even better grades." Although UPS may run the tightest ship in the shipping business, it appears to run one of the loosest ships in the methodology business. What are some of the problems with its claim?

11. TO THINE OWN SELVES BE TRUE

One of the most fascinating phenomena in psychology is *dissociative identity disorder* (more commonly known by laypeople as "multiple personality disorder"). According to some psychologists, some people possess several distinct personalities, each of which is as rich and elaborate as the single personality that you yourself possess. As an example, at different times, a person with dissociative identity disorder might possess (1) a friendly, easygoing, and confident personality; (2) a shy, self-critical, and withdrawn personality; and (3) a grandiose, self-absorbed, manipulative personality. According to some psychologists, the different personalities of people with dissociative identity disorder may differ dramatically in their skill at particular tasks, their intelligence, or even their biological reactions to different allergens! To provide some empirical evidence for the existence of dissociative identity disorder, one psychologist repeatedly gave a standard intelligence test to a patient believed to be suffering from this problem. In particular, the psychologist asked a colleague who was blind to his hypothesis to administer the revised version of the Wechsler Adult Intelligence Scale (the WAIS-R) to one of his clients on four different occasions. This particular client, whom we will call Cari, appeared to have 11 distinct personalities, and each time she took the test she identified herself as a different person.

The first personality to take the test was "Wanda," who received a score of 114 (somewhat above average) on the WAIS-R. A week later, "Melanie" took the same test and received a score of 123 (clearly above average). The third week, "Jasmine" received a score of 140 (approaching the genius range). Finally, on the fourth week, "Bassandra" received a high but not amazing score of 131. The psychologist who had been treating Cari concluded that each of Cari's personalities has a different IQ and that this finding supports the validity of dissociative identity disorder. Although there now appears to be some pretty solid evidence for the existence of dissociative identity disorder, we would not place the evidence about Cari in that category. Critique this researcher's conclusion. Can you suggest some things the researcher could do to improve upon the design of his study?

12. A ROSY MOOD BY ANY OTHER NAME?

Some people claim that whenever we are in a bad mood, we tend to see ourselves through mud-colored lenses. In particular, it appears to be the case that being in a negative mood causes people to evaluate themselves more negatively than usual. For example, being in a negative mood apparently causes people to focus selectively on negative self-relevant memories—due to a "spreading activation" process in memory. The crucial point is that affect (people's feelings) influences cognition (people's thoughts about themselves). To demonstrate this point, a researcher recently used a mood-induction procedure to put participants into happy versus sad moods. In particular, participants were asked to "relive" (i.e., to focus on and write about) a significant positive or negative experience from their past. After participants experienced the positive or negative mood induction to which they had been randomly assigned, they were given a well-validated measure of their self-perceived abilities in many different areas. The results were clear. Participants in the negative mood condition reported much more negative mood than did those in the positive mood condition, and they also reported significantly more negative self-evaluations (e.g., less self-perceived competence) than those in the positive mood condition. In fact, the effects of the mood manipulation on self-perceived competence were even more dramatic than the effects on mood itself! The researcher concluded that mood causes people to change their beliefs about themselves. Can you think of any problems with this conclusion? A clue: manipulation check versus dependent measure. Another clue: manipulation.

13. OLD GENIUSES NEVER DIE YOUNG?

A recent study appeared to provide good news for geniuses. Compared with people in "regular" occupations that do not require any special form of genius, people like Nobel prize–winning scientists and orchestra conductors appear to live especially long lives. One recent study revealed that Nobel Prize–winning scientists appear to live noticeably longer than either cooks or plumbers and that orchestra conductors lived even longer than Nobel Prize winners. There are many possible explanations for these findings. For example, one could conceivably argue that geniuses can afford superior health care. However, if we assume that there is nothing about being a genius per se that predisposes a person to living a long life, can you think of any additional confounds that could explain why maestros and Nobel Prize winners live longer than cooks, plumbers, and other blue-collar workers? In addition to any confounds involving the life experiences of these two different groups, can you think of a more sweeping methodological critique that might completely invalidate this claim about genius and longevity? A clue: great-grandmothers.

14. SAMPLING STUDENT OPINION

The survey below in Figure 13.2 appeared in the basketball supplement (NCAA Tournament Issue) of the *Daily Bruin* on March 14, 1991. As you can see from reading the survey, it was designed to give the editors of the *Bruin* some objective feedback about student attitudes toward the special basketball supplement appearing in that particular issue of the *Bruin*. Although we commend their efforts to be sensitive to student needs, we do not think

Figure 13.2

Survey from the *Daily Bruin* basketball supplement.

WIN $50! Fill out the survey below and return to the Daily Bruin by TODAY at 4pm. Positive and negative feedback are equally welcomed. Look in the April 1 Issue of the Daily Bruin for the Names of the 3 lucky $50 winners! **WIN $50!**

TELL US ABOUT YOURSELF

1. Name:_____ 2. Phone #:_____
3. Personal Information: (to better understand who is giving us feedback) **sex:** M☐ F☐ **age:** _____
   UCLA status: Student   Faculty   Staff   How many Football games did you attend this year? _____
   How many Basketball games?_____ How many Daily Bruin Sports Supplements did you read this year? _____

GIVE US SOME FEEDBACK!

Rate the following on a scale of 1-5 (1=poor/never, 5=GREAT!/ALWAYS!)
Feel free to give us extra info under your rating.   WHY? (give us some details...)

1. Did you enjoy the Sports Supplement? 1 2 3 4 5 NA _____
2. Was game day coverage thorough?   1 2 3 4 5 NA _____
3. Was coverage as informative as
   other game day media?   1 2 3 4 5 NA _____
4. How was the design & use of color?   1 2 3 4 5 NA _____
5. Were you aware of them in advance?   1 2 3 4 5 NA _____
6. Did you look forward to reading them? 1 2 3 4 5 NA _____
7. Were they easily accessible at games? 1 2 3 4 5 NA _____
8. Did you like having them at games?   1 2 3 4 5 NA _____
9. Did you respond to any of the ads?   1 2 3 4 5 NA _____

10. How can the Sports Supplement be improved? _____
_____

11. Would you like to see the Sports Supplement again next year? YES☐ NO☐ I don't care ☐
    Why or Why not? _____
_____

the approach used by these researchers gave them an accurate view of students' feelings. Why should we be skeptical about the validity of the survey?

15. I'M SPEECHLESS

One of the most controversial debates in psychology has to do with the language capabilities of higher primates such as gorillas and chimpanzees. Although a number of researchers claim that they have taught gorillas and chimps to use symbolic language systems such as American Sign Language, many researchers would argue that the case for higher language capacities in non-human primates has yet to be made. Imagine that an extremely well-funded researcher decided to take a novel approach to this problem by randomly sampling ten normal, healthy American adults and ten normal, healthy adult chimpanzees. The researcher decided to expose the people and the chimps to the same training program in an effort to teach them an artificial language—a language that required "speakers" to communicate by placing arbitrary plastic shapes on a magnetic communication board. The basic idea behind the study was to provide the people and the chimps with an equal amount of exposure to the artificial language and to compare the performance of the two groups.

In an effort to make the training identical for the people and the chimps, the research assistants who attempted to teach participants (i.e., the people and the chimps) the artificial language were forbidden from ever speaking to the human participants (as this would have given the human participants an obvious advantage over the chimps). Moreover, in an effort to minimize experimenter bias, the research assistants were carefully trained to present their language lessons in a highly standardized fashion. Both groups of participants were given three hours of daily training in the artificial language, and this training lasted for 30 days. Every five days, the participants were tested extensively in several aspects of language comprehension and production. For example, there were separate tests for vocabulary and for understanding of grammar or syntax. Importantly, these tests were scored by blind raters who were shown only the responses the participants had made on their magnetic boards (i.e., the raters did not know whether a given set of responses had been produced by a person or a chimp). When asked to summarize the primary findings of the study, the principal investigator reported three important findings. First, at each of the six testing sessions, the human participants performed significantly better than the chimps. Second, the advantages displayed by the humans were larger for the tests involving grammatical rules than they were for the tests involving simple vocabulary. And third, the advantages displayed by the human participants generally grew larger over the course of the six testing sessions. On the basis of these findings, the researcher concluded that, unlike people, chimpanzees do not have the ability to learn and use language.

Critique this interpretation of the study and formulate a more "pro-chimp" interpretation. First, in light of the primary findings, is the researcher's conclusion justified? What else might you want to know about the details of these findings before you decide whether or not you agree with the researcher's interpretation? Second, are there any additional control procedures you would like to see included in the study before you conclude that the overall learning situation was really equal for the people and the chimps? Third, even if you included every imaginable control procedure during the administration of the study itself, can you think of any preexisting differences between the ten people and the ten adult chimps (i.e., any confounds) that would be virtually impossible to control in a study such as this?

16. HE MAY BE SMALL BUT HE'S SLOW

The similarity hypothesis in interpersonal attraction suggests that "birds of a feather flock together"—that is, people are attracted to similar others. Both correlational and experimental studies suggest that this is true. For example, married couples tend to be similar at a much greater than chance level on dimensions as diverse as age, religion, eating habits, and shoe size. Thus, we know that similar people tend to pair off together. But once people are together, does similarity predict happiness? That is, if some couples are *more* similar than others, will those same couples be more satisfied than others? To address this question, a researcher classified married couples as high versus low in similarity by using established methods. He then assessed various aspects of each couple's level of relationship satisfaction by asking them 50 different questions in a confidential survey. He found that on two of the 50 items ("in love" and "committed") the high-similarity couples scored significantly higher than the low-similarity couples (both p's $< .05$). In addition, on one of the remaining questions ("sexually attracted") the low-similarity couples actually scored higher ($p < .05$). He concluded that "among married couples, a high degree of attitudinal similarity appears to lead to love and commitment but may simultaneously reduce sexual attraction." Besides pointing out that correlation does not guarantee causation, how would you criticize his findings? How might you remedy the problem(s) you see?

17. EVERYONE'S A WINNER

If you are familiar with grocery stores in southern California, and if you've heard the results of Lucky's price surveys, you have heard that Lucky is the "low-price leader" among southern California grocery stores. Of course, if you've heard the results of surveys conducted by Ralphs' or Von's grocery stores you have also heard that *these* grocery stores have the best prices in southern California. We haven't bothered to conduct our own price survey, but we feel certain that when several stores all claim to be the least expensive store around, they can't *all* be correct. To add to the confusion, however, we feel pretty sure that the researchers who conducted many of these price surveys had some training in statistics and methodology. For example, most of the price surveys we've heard about involve randomly sampling a large number of items at different grocery stores and simply comparing the price totals of these same items (brand for brand) at two or more stores. At first blush it seems that nothing could possibly be more fair or scientific. After all, no known sampling technique is better than simple random sampling. We may never get to the bottom of who is correct, but we can think of an important change these researchers should make in their sampling procedures if they really want to get things right. If the stores really want to know who's the cheapest, what advice would you give them about improving their sampling procedure?

18. CAN A COUPLE OF BEERS REALLY GO STRAIGHT TO YOUR BELLY?

The results of a recent study of 12,000 people conducted by a group of researchers in North Carolina (reported in the *News of the Weird*—we're not making this up) showed that people who drink a lot of beer tend to put on a lot of weight in their bellies. In contrast, people who drink a lot of wine do not. Thus, there appears to be empirical support for the existence of "beer bellies." We know that alcohol has a lot of useless calories, but we are skeptical of the claim that different alcoholic beverages turn into fat that goes to different parts of our bodies. Can you think of any factors that should be controlled before we conclude that beer bellies are truly a direct consequence of beer consumption?

19. WHAT'S IN A NAME?

In a classic experiment published in 1968, Goldberg devised a simple and elegant way to study gender discrimination. Goldberg simply asked people to evaluate an essay. However, he gave some people the impression that the essay had been written by a man but gave others the impression that the essay had been written by a woman. He did this by merely providing bogus, sex-typed author names on otherwise identical versions of the essay. For example, people asked to evaluate an essay could learn that the essay had been written by John or Joan McKay, Stephen or Stella Hamilton, or Paul or Pauline Conger. Goldberg found that people evaluated the essay more favorably when they thought it had been written by a man. Following the publication of Goldberg's findings, the use of sex-typed names became a very popular way to study topics such as gender discrimination and stereotyping.

Although there is ample evidence that gender discrimination is alive and well in our culture, it now seems pretty clear that there was a problem with Goldberg's original study—and with many of the studies that followed in its footsteps. Although you may wonder how an experiment as simple and elegant as Goldberg's could possibly involve a serious confound, consider the ratings of essay quality provided by participants in the hypothetical study

Table 13.1   Judged quality of essay and gender of essay writer

Brian	Gary	David	Harry	Male Average
4.93	4.24	5.43	3.11	4.43
Louise	Ruth	Lisa	Dorothy	Female Average
3.97	3.68	4.62	2.79	3.77

Note. Each pair of names (i.e., each of the first four columns) reflects the findings of a different experiment. Higher values correspond to higher ratings of essay quality, and you may assume that differences of a quarter of a point or greater are statistically significant.

summarized in Table 13.1. These ratings should provide you with a clue about the confound that appears to have existed in Goldberg's study. In case this clue isn't very helpful, you might want to take a peek at Kasof's (1993) insightful review of research using sex-typed names. In fact, as an additional clue, we should confess that we used Tables 4 and 5 of Kasof's paper to generate the means that appear in Table 13.1. Finally, as a really big clue, you might recall that we reviewed this specific research topic in your text. Can you remember what we had to say?

20. ARE YOU THREATENING ME?

In case you may have drawn the inappropriate conclusion that our culture is relatively free of gender bias, we should remind you that regardless of how people evaluate hypothetical male and female essay writers, there is plenty of solid evidence that people are predisposed to see women (and men) in ways that are consistent with culturally shared sex-role stereotypes. In fact, as you may recall from the discussion of meta-analysis in Chapter 10, gender stereotypes are so pervasive that even scientists who study gender sometimes allow their assumptions about gender to get the better of them. Specifically, recall that early studies of conformity and persuasion appeared to show that women are more easily persuaded than men. However, subsequent research demonstrated that when the topic of influence is one with which men happen to be less familiar than women, men are more easily persuaded than women. Early research on gender and persuasion was misleading.

A great deal of contemporary research on gender, ethnicity, and intellectual potential may also be misleading. Specifically, researchers interested in intelligence and academic performance have sometimes tried to develop socioeconomic status (SES)-free," "culture-free," or "gender-neutral" tests of general intelligence, mathematical ability, etc. For example, in the case of tests aimed at identifying ethnic differences in intelligence, researchers might present people with problems to which neither highly educated nor highly uneducated people are likely to have ever been exposed. Similarly, researchers interested in gender and mathematical ability might present sixth- or seventh-grade kids with math tests that focus on questions that even well-educated sixth and seventh graders have yet to learn about (e.g., by giving seventh graders math questions from the SAT or GRE). Many such studies have revealed that boys (or men) outperform girls (or women). Other studies have revealed that whereas boys and girls perform at about the same average level, many more boys manage to earn extremely high scores on such inappropriately difficult tests. In addition to problems such as experimenter bias or participant expectancies, we can think of at least two very serious confounds that appear to plague studies such as these. Because these confounds are both rather subtle, we will tell you that one confound has to do with the question of whether these difficult tests are, in fact, equally unfamiliar to boys and girls who come from the same schools. The other confound is sort of a cousin of participant expectancies, and it has to do with the inherently social nature of achievement tests. For a further clue about this second confound, you might want to take a look at the research of Steele and Aronson (1995) on "stereotype threat."

Coda

We began this book by saying that we wish to depart from traditional treatments of research methods by making this text both interesting and easy to understand. Although it is hard for us to know how close we have come to achieving this difficult goal, we hope that we have achieved the more modest goal of emphasizing what is logical and intuitive about research methods—thus minimizing some of the discomfort that is part of any learning process. We also hope that we have communicated some degree of enthusiasm for research. In short, we hope that you have learned that psychological research is *fun*.

In the process of writing this book, we have learned a few things ourselves. Although this may sound heretical, the most important thing we learned about research methods is that, prior to writing this text, we probably overestimated the importance of using "correct" methods. As we worked on this book, we increasingly came to realize that a high level of methodological expertise, by itself, does not always allow researchers to conduct intriguing and informative studies. Instead, such studies usually emerge when researchers blend the use of sophisticated research techniques with logical arguments about why the methods they have chosen are well suited to a problem, with clever designs that grab readers' attention, and with a certain artistic flair that is hard to define but usually easy to recognize. From this perspective, if our goal as researchers is to move from vague guesses about psychological truths to closer and closer approximations of the real thing, we will probably get closer to our goal by paying attention to both the mechanical aspects of the scientific method and the powerful sense of curiosity that motivates most good research. This does not mean becoming armchair philosophers. Instead, it means complementing laboratory experiments with thought experiments or naturalistic field studies. Along the same lines, it means supplementing statistical analyses with logical analyses of the boundary conditions of a phenomenon. Although the scientific method is an incredibly powerful tool for understanding human nature, this tool, like almost any other tool, is usually used most effectively when it is combined with other tools. Because we are in the business of trying to understand things as ephemeral and elusive as the weight of smoke, we must learn to make careful use of every tool at our disposal.

Hands-On Activities

HANDS-ON ACTIVITY 1

Galileo's Dice

One of the points emphasized in Chapter 1 is that scientists and nonscientists typically rely on different "ways of knowing." Although Chapter 1 emphasizes the idea that the different ways of knowing may lead to different conclusions, this is not a hard and fast rule. In fact, we suspect that more often than not, the four different ways of knowing (intuition, logic, authority, and observation) lead people to the same conclusion. To give you some direct experience with different ways of knowing, and to demonstrate that they may sometimes diverge and sometimes converge, your instructor will divide you up into three or four groups. Each group will adopt a different approach to answering the question that a group of gamblers once posed to Galileo. Readers who want a little more detail about this problem should consult Freedman, Pisani, Purves, and Adhikari (1991), whose discussion of this problem provides most of the factual basis for this activity.

About 400 years ago, some gamblers were playing a popular game involving three standard, six-sided dice. The game involved betting on how many spots would appear when the three dice were rolled, and most of the gamblers believed that the probability of rolling a nine (a total of nine spots) was the same as the probability of rolling a ten. However, some gamblers had the gut impression that a ten was slightly more likely than a nine, and their casual observations seemed to confirm this intuition. The gamblers who believed that a nine and a ten were equally likely made a simple, logical argument in favor of their position. They noted that when rolling three six-sided dice, *exactly six* different combinations of numbers add up to nine:

1, 2, 6   1, 3, 5   1, 4, 4   2, 2, 5   2, 3, 4   3, 3, 3

Also, *exactly six* different combinations add up to ten:

1, 3, 6   1, 4, 5   2, 2, 6   2, 3, 5   2, 4, 4   3, 3, 4

Thus, it seemed logical to these gamblers that the chances of rolling a nine and the chances of rolling a ten are equal. Because the gamblers could not reconcile their intuitions, their observations, and their logical analysis, they did what any reasonable person would do—they consulted an authority. In particular, they took their puzzle to Galileo, and he was able to solve it to everyone's satisfaction. Before you learn about Galileo's solution, we would like you to directly experience some of the different ways of approaching this problem to see what kinds of conclusions you would generate if you were using only one particular way of knowing to answer the question. Before you learn which group you are in, take a look at the different approaches to the problem that will be adopted by the different groups.

Group 1 (the Logical Counters of Ways)

If you are assigned to this group, you will be asked to adopt a specific logical approach to the problem. It will be your job to work through the logical problem, come to a conclusion about the problem, report your degree of confidence in your conclusion, and defend your answer to the members of the other groups.

Group 2 (the Logical Expected Evaluators)

There is more than one logical approach to solving this problem. If you are assigned to this group, you will be given some clues about a different logical approach to the problem. This particular approach will involve applying the logic of expected values to the problem to see whether a nine or a ten comes closer to the expected value (the long-run average) of all possible rolls of three dice. Like the members of the other two groups, you will draw a conclusion, report your confidence in the conclusion, and defend your answer to the other groups.

Groups 3 and/or 4 (the Empiricists)

If you are assigned to this group or groups, you will have the painstaking but important task of making a series of observations to try to answer the question. Specifically, you will be given a set of three dice and asked to roll them as many times as possible (e.g., 200 times) while the other groups work on their approach to the problem. By recording (1) the total number of rolls you make, (2) the number of nines you roll and (3) the number of tens you roll, you should begin to get some sense of how likely these two rolls are in general. Also, this should give you some sense of which, if either, of the two is *more* likely. Be ready to draw a conclusion, state your confidence in the conclusion, and defend it to the other groups. If you are a member of one of two different groups of empiricists, you should probably take note of how well the other group of empiricists "replicates" your group's findings.

What About Intuition and Authority?

Finally, notice that you were not asked to create a group of people who approach the problem by consulting either their intuitions or their local authority. We suspect that you'd have a very hard time solving the problem intuitively. Even if you did, we suspect that you wouldn't be all that confident in your answer. The reason we didn't ask anyone to consult an authority is that this would take only a few seconds. You'd simply ask your instructor for the correct answer and record it without necessarily knowing why this answer is correct.

When all of the groups have completed their work, we hope you will have solved this problem.

More Detailed Instructions for Groups 1 and 2

There are no special instructions for groups 3 and 4 other than those given above. Here are the detailed instructions and clues for groups 1 and 2. For now, *only* read the instructions for your specific group. After the activity is done, everyone should read the instructions that were provided to every other group to gain a fuller appreciation of the different ways of knowing that are a part of this activity. Alternately, some instructors may wish to have everyone to try *all* the approaches, to allow people to appreciate more fully each way of knowing.

Group 1 (the Logical Counters of Ways)   Galileo's insight into this problem was quite simple—at least in retrospect. Whereas it is true that there are exactly six *general* ways to roll a nine or a ten with three dice, Galileo realized that there could be different numbers of *exact* ways to roll each of these values. To illustrate what he meant by exact ways, Galileo recommended that people keep track of the three separate dice by making each die a different color (see Figure A.1). Galileo made a careful list of (1) all the specific ways of rolling a nine and (2) all the specific ways of rolling a ten. For example, one specific way to roll a nine is to roll a one, a two, and a six (a one on the die arbitrarily designated as the first, a two on the die arbitrarily designated as the second, and a six on the die arbitrarily designated as the third). But of course there are other ways to roll a nine, including other specific orders for the combination one, two, and six. Your job is to make an exhaustive list of all the specific possible ways to roll both nines and tens. One good way to do this is to copy down the six combinations that yield a

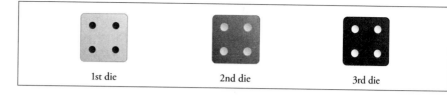

 Figure A1.1

1st die   2nd die   3rd die

nine and then list all the specific ways that you could possibly observe each combination (e.g., exactly how many ways [orders] are there in which to roll a one, a two, and a six?). Finally, note that if you want to state your conclusions in terms of probabilities (the number of unique ways to observe the outcome you care about divided by the total number of possible outcomes), you will need to divide your values by the total number of unique ways to roll three dice. This is 6 × 6 × 6. Do you see why it is 6 × 6 × 6?

Group 2 (the Logical Expected Evaluators) If you have had much experience rolling a pair of six-sided dice, you know that some rolls are much easier to get than others. As it turns out, the most common roll for a pair of standard dice is a seven (a total of seven spots). This should make a lot of sense. If you think about the expected value of a single die (the value you'd expect to see if you rolled the die an infinite number of times under ideal conditions) you should realize that it's the average of all the six possible equally likely rolls [(1 + 2 + 3 + 4 + 5 + 6)/6 = 3.5]. If the expected value (the long-run average) of one die is 3.5, it should not be surprising that the expected value of two dice is 2 × 3.5, or 7.0. If you remember that the probability of different dice rolls forms a very loose approximation of the normal distribution, you should see another reason why seven is the most common roll. It's the mean, and the mean in a nearly normal distribution (like the one describing dice rolls) is the single most likely outcome. An illustration of the distribution of all possible rolls of two dice appears in Figure A.2. This figure shows how the mean outcome is also the most likely

Figure A1.2

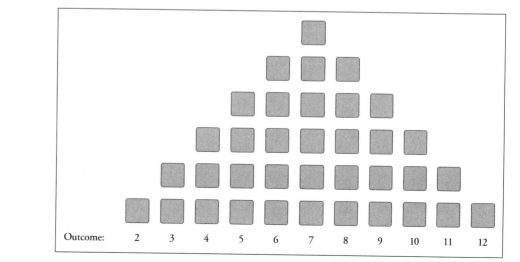

Outcome: 2   3   4   5   6   7   8   9   10   11   12

outcome, and how the probability of each roll tapers off as it departs further and further from seven (e.g., a six is more likely than a five, which is more likely than a four, etc.). In this frequency distribution, each square represents a single specific outcome among the 36 possible outcomes. For example, the figure shows that there are exactly six ways out of 36 to roll a seven and only one way to roll a 12 (rolling a six on each of the two dice).

If you are wondering what this two-dice example has to do with the problem with three dice, ask yourself (1) whether a nine or a ten (rolled with three dice) should be closer to the expected value of three dice and (2) what approximate shape you would expect the distribution of three dice to take. This should lead you to the answer to this question.

Questions

Here are some questions for all three groups (to be answered at the conclusion of your own group activity, before learning anything about the details of what the other groups concluded):

1. Which roll do you think is most likely, a nine, a ten, or neither?
2. How confident are you of this answer? Answer using a single number from the following scale:

0	1	2	3	4	5	6
not at all confident		slightly confident		quite confident		extremely confident

3. What is your best guess as to the *exact* probability of rolling a nine with a fair set of three dice? _____
4. How confident are you in the guess you made in question 3?

0	1	2	3	4	5	6
not at all confident		slightly confident		quite confident		extremely confident

5. What is your best guess as to the *exact* probability of rolling a ten with a fair set of three dice? _____
6. How confident are you in the guess you made in question 5?

0	1	2	3	4	5	6
not at all confident		slightly confident		quite confident		extremely confident

Class discussion should focus on the advantages and disadvantages of each approach, along with the advantages of treating one technique as a check on the others. If there are two groups of empiricists, it is usually interesting to compare the scores. How these two groups of scores compare should tell you something about issues such as sampling error, effect size, and sample size in research.

HANDS-ON ACTIVITY 2

Regression Toward the Mean

As discussed in Chapter 5, one common threat to the validity of many research claims (and a source of many naive theories about human behavior) is regression toward the mean. As you probably recall, regression toward the mean refers to the tendency for people who obtain high or low scores on a particular measure to score closer to the mean when they are retested on the same measure. Many people who understand the definition of regression toward the mean have a great deal of trouble seeing exactly *why* this should be the case. What is it, exactly, that causes extreme scores to become less extreme the second time around? The simple answer is chance. To the degree that people's scores on a particular measure are partly determined by chance as well as by stable properties of people, we would expect high scorers on a measure (as a group) to have been somewhat luckier than low scorers (as a group). Because luck isn't something that people carry around with them, it is reasonable to expect that people who have recently had good or bad luck will have average luck the next time we test them. So long as luck or chance plays a substantial role in determining people's performance on a measure, people's high or low scores on that measure will typically regress toward the mean on a subsequent testing.

To give you a concrete example of how this works, we would like you to engage in a simple group activity that will allow you to see how chance factors combine with stable properties of people to produce regression toward the mean. After randomly assigning you to one of two groups (a group of "high rollers" and a group of "low rollers"), your instructor will give you either two or three standard six-sided dice. In particular, the high rollers will receive three dice, but the low rollers will receive only two. Notice that in this activity the number of dice you are allowed to roll is a stand-in for some stable property of people such as skill or ability at a task (in this case, the task of rolling a lot of spots with two or more dice). Thus, we know that if we asked each of the high rollers and each of the low rollers to roll the dice a thousand times, the average score (i.e., the "true score") of each of the high rollers would be about 10.5, and the average score of each of the low rollers would be about 7.0. You can think of the number of dice you get to roll as a stand-in for your true ability at this game. But suppose we asked each of you to roll your dice only once. In this case, each person's score (i.e., the total number of spots each person rolled) would be influenced not only by the number of dice he or she was rolling but also by the luck of the particular roll. (That is, by chance or measurement error.) To see how chance events can produce regression toward the mean, let's play two rounds of a very simple dice game. Round 1 will be a stand-in for a pretest, and round 2 will be a stand-in for a posttest.

After you have been randomly assigned to be either a high or a low roller, your instructor will ask you to roll the dice, and she or he will publicly record your score. After each person in the class has rolled his or her dice on the first round of the game, each person will be assigned to a *new* group according to the value of his or her roll. Unlike the ability grouping based on people's true scores (i.e., the number of dice people are allowed to roll), this new grouping will be based on performance (i.e., the total number of spots people actually rolled during round 1). In particular, your instructor will perform a median split (i.e., a "split down the middle") on your round 1 scores and place each person in either the upper or the lower half of the class according to this measure of performance. The easiest way to do this is to tally up all the scores at the end of round 1 and to physically place people on opposite sides of the room based on their performance during round 1. Finally, after sorting people into the two groups, you and your instructor should compute and publicly record an average pretest score for each of the two groups. Of course, by necessity, the score for the high performers will be quite a bit higher than the score for the low performers.

Once the pretest scores have been computed, each person will roll the dice again during round 2. The scores people receive during round 2 can be thought of as posttest scores, and it is important that each person generate a posttest score by rolling the *same number of dice* that he or she rolled during round 1 (because truly being a high or low roller is a stable property of each person). As each person rolls the dice again, your instructor will publicly record the scores for round 2. When everyone has rolled the dice a second time, it will be time to compute the average posttest score for the two performance groups. Unless something very unusual happened, you should observe regression toward the mean. That is, the average score for the high performers should have decreased, and the average score for the low performers should have increased.

Questions for Group Discussion

1. First, assuming that you observed at least some evidence of regression toward the mean, why exactly did this happen?
2. Notice that one difference between this demonstration and real life is that in the demonstration it is possible to observe directly the stable properties of people (in this case people's "dice-rolling ability"). When we can't look inside people and see their true scores, we are forced to rely solely on measures of performance as proxies for ability. However, suppose we developed a measure so valid and reliable that it allowed us to categorize people perfectly on the basis of their true scores (e.g., their true ability at a task). Would we expect to see any more or any less evidence of regression toward the mean in a case such as this? If you are uncertain, notice that the observations you generated in this demonstration could be used to answer this question. That is, if you assigned people to groups on the basis of their *true* status as a high or low roller and then computed pretest and posttest scores for the true high and low rollers, what would you be likely to observe?
3. Finally, notice that the degree to which chance plays a role in people's scores on a measure can be thought of as a proxy for the reliability of

that particular measure. What is the general relation between the reliability of a measure and the amount of regression toward the mean that you'd expect to observe on this measure? For example, if a measure involved an even larger component of chance than the measure we used today (e.g., suppose everyone rolled only a single die but some people rolled a six-sided die and some people rolled a seven-sided die), would you expect to see more or less evidence of regression toward the mean?

Special Notes to the Instructor

This demonstration works best with a group of exactly 20 students. Using 20 students will create two groups of exactly ten participants, making it very easy to compute the means that serve as the basis of the demonstration. There are likely to be some ties when you are trying to perform your median split. To increase the chances that you will observe regression toward the mean, you might want to break any ties by sending people to performance groups that are at odds with their true scores. Alternately, of course, you could allow tied participants to take part in a "roll off" to determine their assignment to one of the two performance groups. Finally, if you would like to try a simpler and more dramatic demonstration of regression toward the mean, you might consider having students play two rounds of some kind of psychic guessing game. Because performance on this test will consist solely of error or luck, you will typically see a tremendous amount of regression toward the mean on the second round of this game. (The authors thank Dr. Tara MacDonald for suggesting this last demonstration.)

An alternate version of this game can also be played by creating groups using procedures based largely, if not completely, on chance. As an example, students could be arbitrarily paired up to play a single game of "scissors, paper, rock." This should yield a group of "winners" and a group of "losers." The winners, of course, would have a 100 percent rate of winning, and the losers would have a 0 percent rate of winning. During the second round of the same game, the two groups should presumably move to the mean expected win rate for a game of chance (i.e., 50 percent). The degree to which this outcome does not happen (i.e., to the degree that the winners continue to outperform the losers) would suggest that there truly is some degree of skill involved in this classic game.

HANDS-ON ACTIVITY 3

A Double-Blind Taste Test with Popular Colas

One good way to familiarize yourself with research methods is to ask yourself how you might go about answering a simple, everyday question the way a research psychologist would go about doing so. For example, suppose you want to know which of two nationally advertised soft drinks people really prefer. Specifically, what if you want to find out whether people prefer Coca-Cola or Pepsi-Cola? You might start by assuming that people have no preference. In fact, you might start by assuming that, if the two drinks weren't labeled, people couldn't even tell them apart. In this hands-on activity, you and your classmates will take part in a blind taste test designed to address two simple questions. First, can people correctly identify Coke and Pepsi in a blind taste test? Second, regardless of whether people can correctly identify the two colas, do people prefer one cola over the other? Because we think it will be useful for you to see what is taking place behind the scenes while you serve as a taster in this activity, we have summarized the procedures here from the experimenter's perspective. Also, a set of instructions for tasters and a brief survey for indicating your responses to the test are included following the instructions to the experimenter. (Those interested in seeing a published study that used this actual procedure should see Blanton, Pelham, Dehart & Carvallo, 2001, Study 1).

Information for the Experimenter

For this activity, you will need (1) some chilled two-liter bottles of Coca-Cola and Pepsi-Cola (2 to 2½ ounces of each cola for each of your participants), (2) two three-ounce paper cups for each of your participants, (3) a box of saltine crackers (at least one cracker per participant), (4) some napkins, (5) some stickers or tape that you can use to number the paper cups, and (6) a large partition that permits you to pour the colas at the front of the room without allowing students to see which cola is being poured into which cup. (A partition can be readily assembled from cardboard or foam board.) Before beginning the taste test, set up your materials by numbering the cups consecutively (e.g., from one to 60 if you have 30 students). In addition, before beginning the tasting, participants will answer a few background questions about their cola-drinking behavior and their established preferences for the two colas (see the rating surveys). Once you have set up all your materials, recruit an assistant to serve the colas. To minimize the possibility of experimenter bias and participant expectancies, you will use a double-blind procedure in which neither the server nor the participants are informed of the content of the cups.

The basic procedure involves filling one of each pair of cups with Coke and the other one with Pepsi. For example, if you pour Coke into cup 17, you will pour Pepsi into cup 18. This will guarantee that each participant receives one serving of each cola. After you have filled each consecutively numbered set of cups using a chart that contains a list of random serving orders, your research assistant (the server) will give each participant two consecutively numbered cups of cola along with a napkin and a saltine cracker. As noted in the instructions below, participants will take a bite of the saltine cracker, drink the first cup of cola, take another bite of the saltine cracker, and then drink the second cup of cola. Tasting the cracker prior to tasting each cola should minimize contamination effects. After finishing both of the colas, participants will (1) try to identify each of the two colas and (2) report their degree of liking for each cola. To maintain the integrity of the counter-balancing procedure, it is important that participants taste the cups of cola in *numerical order* (e.g., the fifth participant should drink the cola in cup 9 before drinking the cola in cup 10). You can use the following table to determine the order in which the colas are served. Before beginning the taste test, flip a coin to determine which of the two charts you will use. Because the charts (order 1 and order 2) represent "opposite" orders, even a participant who memorized the two charts would have no way of knowing which cola he or she received first.

Instructions for Participants in the Cola Taste Test

Before beginning the blind taste test, fill out the top half of the Cola Rating Sheet. During the blind taste test itself, you will be asked to taste each of the two numbered colas (in numerical order). You will then try to identify the brand name of each cola and report how much you liked each one.

1. Fill out the top half of your Cola Rating Sheet. Once you have received your cola samples, notice that you received two consecutively numbered cups of cola (e.g., cups numbered 31 and 32).
2. Eat a bite (about half) of the saltine cracker.
3. Drink all the cola in the cup with the *lower* number.
4. Eat the remaining half of the saltine cracker.
5. Drink all the cola in the cup with the *higher* number.
6. Fill out the remaining portion of your Cola Rating Sheet.

Questions for Students

1. You will notice that there are two versions of the Cola Rating Sheet—see pages 000-000. Why are there two versions? After you have taken part in the blind taste test, your instructor will probably summarize the primary results of the test for you. To get in the habit of thinking like a statistician, you should give some thought to what kind of comparisons you would make to answer the basic questions that are addressed in this study.
2. Specifically, how would you determine whether people are able to tell the two colas apart? For example, to see if people are able to label the colas correctly, you will probably want to make a statistical comparison of (a) your class's overall performance with (b) some kind of reasonable performance standard. What should that performance standard be?
3. What kind of comparison(s) should you make to see which of the two colas people prefer (before taking part in the study and in the actual taste test)?

Two Possible Orders (Counterbalancing Schemes) for Serving the Colas

Order 1		Order 2	
001 = Coke	002 = Pepsi	001 = Pepsi	002 = Coke
003 = Pepsi	004 = Coke	003 = Coke	004 = Pepsi
005 = Pepsi	006 = Coke	005 = Coke	006 = Pepsi
007 = Pepsi	008 = Coke	007 = Coke	008 = Pepsi
009 = Coke	010 = Pepsi	009 = Pepsi	010 = Coke
011 = Coke	012 = Pepsi	011 = Pepsi	012 = Coke
013 = Coke	014 = Pepsi	013 = Pepsi	014 = Coke
015 = Pepsi	016 = Coke	015 = Coke	016 = Pepsi
017 = Pepsi	018 = Coke	017 = Coke	018 = Pepsi
019 = Pepsi	020 = Coke	019 = Coke	020 = Pepsi
021 = Pepsi	022 = Coke	021 = Coke	022 = Pepsi
023 = Coke	024 = Pepsi	023 = Pepsi	024 = Coke
025 = Coke	026 = Pepsi	025 = Pepsi	026 = Coke
027 = Coke	028 = Pepsi	027 = Pepsi	028 = Coke
029 = Coke	030 = Pepsi	029 = Pepsi	030 = Coke
031 = Coke	032 = Pepsi	031 = Pepsi	032 = Coke
033 = Coke	034 = Pepsi	033 = Pepsi	034 = Coke
035 = Coke	036 = Pepsi	035 = Pepsi	036 = Coke
037 = Pepsi	038 = Coke	037 = Coke	038 = Pepsi
039 = Coke	040 = Pepsi	039 = Pepsi	040 = Coke
041 = Pepsi	042 = Coke	041 = Coke	042 = Pepsi
043 = Coke	044 = Pepsi	043 = Pepsi	044 = Coke
045 = Coke	046 = Pepsi	045 = Pepsi	046 = Coke
047 = Pepsi	048 = Coke	047 = Coke	048 = Pepsi
049 = Pepsi	050 = Coke	049 = Coke	050 = Pepsi
051 = Coke	052 = Pepsi	051 = Pepsi	052 = Coke
053 = Pepsi	054 = Coke	053 = Coke	054 = Pepsi
055 = Pepsi	056 = Coke	055 = Coke	056 = Pepsi
057 = Coke	058 = Pepsi	057 = Pepsi	058 = Coke
059 = Pepsi	060 = Coke	059 = Coke	060 = Pepsi
061 = Pepsi	062 = Coke	061 = Coke	062 = Pepsi
063 = Pepsi	064 = Coke	063 = Coke	064 = Pepsi

Note: If you have more than 32 participants, you can simply start over (at the top of a chart) for your 33rd participant. To minimize errors, it is wise to cover up the unused order (the right half or the left half of the table) while pouring the colas.

1   **Cola Rating Sheet**   Gender: M F

1. About how many 12-oz. servings of cola do you currently drink on a typical day? (Enter a whole number.) _____

2. What percentage of the cola you drink is regular cola (rather than diet cola)? (Enter a whole number.) _____

3. In the last six months …

   _____ percent of the cola I've consumed has been Coca-Cola.

   _____ percent of the cola I've consumed has been Pepsi-Cola.

   _____ percent of the cola I've consumed has been other brands.

   (Please be sure that these three values add up to 100 percent.)

4. How much do you like Coca-Cola? (Circle one number.)

0	1	2	3	4	5	6
not at all		slightly		quite a bit		extremely

5. How much do you like Pepsi-Cola? (Circle one number.)

0	1	2	3	4	5	6
not at all		slightly		quite a bit		extremely

6. Which of these two brands do you prefer? _____

STOP: PLEASE WAIT FOR INSTRUCTIONS ON THE TASTE TEST.

7a. The cola I tasted first was labeled with the number _____.

7b. I think this cola was (circle one): Coke Pepsi

7c. I liked this cola:

0	1	2	3	4	5	6
not at all		slightly		quite a bit		extremely

8a. The cola I tasted second was labeled with the # _____.

8b. I think this cola was (circle one): Coke Pepsi

8c. I liked this cola:

0	1	2	3	4	5	6
not at all		slightly		quite a bit		extremely

9. Of the two colas I tasted, the one I preferred was:
   (a) the first
   (b) the second

2   Cola Rating Sheet   Gender: M F

1. About how many 12-oz. servings of cola do you currently drink on a typical day? (Enter a whole number.) _____

2. What percentage of the cola you drink is regular cola (rather than diet cola)? (Enter a whole number.) _____

3. In the last six months …

    _____ percent of the cola I've consumed has been Pepsi-Cola.

    _____ percent of the cola I've consumed has been Coca-Cola.

    _____ percent of the cola I've consumed has been other brands.

    (Please be sure these three values add up to 100 percent.)

4. How much do you like Pepsi-Cola? (Circle one number.)

0	1	2	3	4	5	6
not at all		slightly		quite a bit		extremely

5. How much do you like Coca-Cola? (Circle one number.)

0	1	2	3	4	5	6
not at all		slightly		quite a bit		extremely

6. Which of these two brands do you prefer? _____

STOP: PLEASE WAIT FOR INSTRUCTIONS ON THE TASTE TEST.

7a. The cola I tasted first was labeled with the number _____.

7b. I think this cola was (circle one): Pepsi Coke

7c. I liked this cola:

0	1	2	3	4	5	6
not at all		slightly		quite a bit		extremely

8a. The cola I tasted second was labeled with the number _____.

8b. I think this cola was (circle one): Pepsi Coke

8c. I liked this cola:

0	1	2	3	4	5	6
not at all		slightly		quite a bit		extremely

9. Of the two colas I tasted, the one I preferred was:
   (a) the first
   (b) the second

HANDS-ON ACTIVITY 4

The Stroop Interference Effect

The next hands-on activity is a bit different than the others in this text. Unlike the other hands-on activities, each of which allows you to explore a single methodological concept, this activity is designed to give you a sense of what it is like to actually conduct a very simple experiment. In fact, it not only allows you to play the role of experimenter, but it also allows you to play the role of participant. This activity requires you to trade places with a partner—who will *also* serve as both experimenter and participant in the activity. Different instructors may wish to use this activity in different ways. In our classes, for example, we often ask each student who takes part in the activity to report his or her data for aggregation and statistical analysis. Regardless of whether your instructor collects and analyzes (or asks you to analyze) your data, it is important to read the instructions for this activity as carefully as possible. Your main goal should be to follow these instructions to the finest level of detail possible. When you are done, we hope you will have some questions of your own about what happened during the activity. We also hope you'll have some sense of what it's like to play the role of experimenter.

In 1935, J. Ridley Stroop conducted a clever and elegant experiment that had a powerful influence on a great deal of psychological research (Stroop, 1935, Experiment 2). Stroop was interested in the fact that many forms of knowledge come at a cost. Specifically, he noticed that in a wide range of situations, well-learned habits often interfere with the production of competing responses. For example, if you emigrated to a culture in which green traffic lights indicated that you should stop at an intersection, your established associations about traffic lights could get you into quite a bit of trouble. Similarly, if you tried to learn to speak Spanish as an adult, you could be guaranteed that the habits of pronunciation you had learned in English would interfere with the quality of your pronunciation of many Spanish words and phrases.

Effects such as these are typically referred to as interference effects, and Stroop developed an elegant procedure for studying them. Specifically, in the experimental condition of his study, Stroop presented participants with a long list of color words ("red," "blue," "green," "brown," and "purple") that were always printed in an ink color that differed from the color named by the word (e.g., the word "red" was printed in blue, green, brown, and purple ink at different places in the list; the word "blue" was printed in red, green, brown, and purple ink at different places in the list). Participants were instructed to work their way through the list as quickly as possible by correctly naming the ink color that printed each individual word. In the control condition of this same experiment, the ink color identification task was very similar except that the ink colors didn't print any words—they simply printed little squares. Stroop compared (1) the length of time it took people to name the ink colors in a list of 100 "mismatched" color words with (2) the length of time it took people to name the same 100 ink colors when the ink colors printed the squares. If you are having difficulty picturing this situation, the inside front cover of this book has an abbreviated version of Stroop's stimuli. When Stroop compared people's performance in the two conditions, he found that it took the average person almost 75 percent longer to name all the ink colors in the mismatched condition. This finding—increased naming latencies for ink colors when the ink colors spell color words that are different from the color of the ink—has been appropriately dubbed the Stroop interference effect.

In this hands-on activity, you will serve as an experimenter in an abbreviated version of Stroop's classic experiment. Of course, this means that you will need a partner to serve as a participant. However, one of the interesting aspects of the Stroop interference effect is that even people who are fully aware of the effect cannot usually avoid falling prey to it. This means that after you have served as an experimenter in this demonstration, you can reverse places with your partner and serve as a participant as well. We are assuming that your instructor will want you to conduct this demonstration during a class session with a classmate or classmates. However, in case you have to conduct the experiment outside class, we have written the instructions for the task as if you were planning to conduct the experiment on a naive volunteer.

Advance Preparation

The materials you will need for this activity are (1) the inside front cover of your textbook, (2) a stopwatch (a wristwatch that indicates seconds will do in a pinch), (3) a piece of paper and a pencil, (4) a fair coin, (5) one or two half-sheets of thick paper or cardboard (to hide the upper and lower halves of the Stroop page prior to the beginning of the activity), and (6) the data recording sheets that are included on a separate page, at the end of this activity. Notice that your data recording sheet includes an answer key that consists of a numbered list of the correct ink colors for each of the 20 stimuli. *This sheet is very important because it will be impossible for you to check your participant's performance if you can't see the correct answers while he or she does the task.* Of course, you should have all your Stroop materials in hand and be ready to begin the task before you recruit your participant. In addition, you should probably review the instructions below at least twice before you attempt to do the actual Stroop activity.

Task Instructions

Once you and your participant are ready to begin, allow your participant to take a quick peek at the inside front cover of the book and explain that he or she will be trying to name the colors of 20 inks as quickly as possible, without making any errors. To be certain that your participant is familiar with the appropriate labels for the five colors, direct his or her attention to the five color words printed at the very top of the page. In fact, ask your participant to name these five ink colors as quickly as possible as a warm-up for performing the real experimental task. You should also explain that the experiment has two separate trials—one involving the list of squares and one involving the list of color words. When you are certain that your participant understands the task, place the Stroop page in front of your participant. However, before doing so carefully cover up the top *and* bottom halves of the page (except for the color labels at the very top) with your half-page cover sheets.

Before your participant begins the task, flip a fair coin to determine which list your participant will use first. If the coin comes up heads, announce that your participant will begin by naming all the colors in the *top* list. If it comes up tails, announce that your participant will begin by naming all of the colors in the *bottom* list. Of course, your participant will have little choice about following these instructions because you will uncover only *one* of the two lists when you give the signal to begin. On your signal (Stroop used "Ready! Go!"), uncover the appropriate list and start your stopwatch while your participant tries to name the 20 ink colors *by number* as quickly as possible (e.g., "One red, two brown, three green," etc.). As soon as your participant announces the 20th color, stop your watch and record the time. After a brief pause, you will repeat the activity, but this time you will uncover the *other* list. This will allow you to compare your participant's performance in the two different conditions. You should record your participant's time for each task and also make a note of which task your participant completed first. If your participant is like the large majority of Stroop's participants, he or she will take longer to name all the ink colors in the mismatched list. To familiarize you with the way these data would be analyzed in a formal research paper, your instructor may wish to collect and aggregate your data for analysis. Regardless of whether your instructor aggregates your data, however, consider the following questions.

1. Which list took you longer to complete? Did your partner's data show the same pattern?
2. Imagine that, for a large group of participants, performance was slower in the "words" condition than in the "squares" condition. How easily could a critic explain this finding in terms of (a) individual differences, (b) practice effects, (c) fatigue, or (d) demand characteristics?
3. Can you think of *any* potential procedural confounds at work in this activity? (We can see one—a very subtle one.)
4. The first author once asked a very large group of students ($N = 187$) to do this activity. When he analyzed all of their data, he found that 121 of them reported that they had run the top condition first whereas 66 of them reported that they had run the bottom condition first. What did he begrudgingly have to conclude about how well the students were following the exact instructions for this activity?

Methodological Notes

In this activity we presented an abbreviated version of Stroop's original interference task. Most contemporary psychologists who are interested in the Stroop effect present their stimuli one at a time on a computer monitor and assess participants' response latencies to each individual stimulus. In Stroop's day the technology wasn't available to do this, and thus part of Stroop's ingenuity was to make small differences in response latencies measurable by stringing a lot of them together. Refinements in our measurement techniques have led to some interesting developments that Stroop would have had difficulty uncovering. For example, by assessing interference effects on a stimulus-by-stimulus basis, Klopfer (1996) demonstrated that Stroop interference effects get larger as ink colors and color words get more similar. For example, larger interference effects are observed when green ink is used to print the word "blue" than they are when green ink is used to print the word "red." Another advantage of assessing Stroop effects using a computer is that computers do not have expectancies. Thus, in most computerized versions of the Stroop task, there is not much need to worry about problems such as experimenter bias. (Incidentally, if you were worried about experimenter bias, you could have recruited a third experimenter who held the answer key, gave the start command, and controlled the stopwatch—but who wasn't informed of which list your participant was working on during the two experimental trials.)

Contemporary psychologists have put the Stroop task to a wide variety of uses. For example, clinical psychologists have made extensive use of the Stroop technique to investigate whether emotionally threatening words (e.g., "spider," "death") can produce interference in ink naming, especially among people with certain clinical disorders (e.g., spider phobics, people who are unduly anxious about death). They can (see Williams, Mathews, & MacLeod, 1996). Similarly, social and personality psychologists have adapted the Stroop interference effect to study phenomena such as thought suppression (see Wegner, 1994) and emotional regulation (see Rusting, 1998). Stroop would be happy to know that his simple color-naming task has contributed greatly to our understanding of how people process many different kinds of information.

Data Recording Sheet for Stroop Interference Task

If you flip HEADS, your partner will do the top task first.

If you flip TAILS, your partner will do the bottom task first.

Your partner's job will be to call out each number followed by the ink color corresponding to that number (e.g., "one, blue, two, green," etc.).

1. blue	2. green	3. red	4. brown	5. purple
6. blue	7. red	8. green	9. purple	10. brown
11. green	12. blue	13. red	14. purple	15. brown
16. blue	17. purple	18. brown	19. red	20. green

Which task did your partner do first? TOP   BOTTOM

Did your partner serve as the experimenter first, or did your partner serve as the experimenter first? My partner was the _____ (1st, 2nd, 3rd, etc.) person in our group to do the Stroop task.

1a. Time your partner took to complete the top list, in seconds: _____

1b. Number of errors your partner made on the top list: _____

2a. Time your partner took to complete the bottom list, in seconds: _____

2b. Number of errors your partner made on the bottom list: _____

Methodology Exercises

METHODOLOGY EXERCISE 1

Partial Correlation

After Galton's development of the correlation coefficient, the most dramatic and useful development in nonexperimental statistics has probably been the development of covariance techniques such as partial correlation. A partial correlation is a lot like a regular correlation. For example, like a regular correlation, a partial correlation always ranges in value from –1 to +1, with higher absolute values indicating a stronger linear relation between two variables of interest. Instead of reflecting the simple (descriptive) relation between two variables, however, a partial correlation reflects the unique relation between two variables when the effect of a third variable is (mathematically) taken into account. Thus, partial correlation is very useful because it takes you a step closer to seeing the causal relation between two variables. For example, suppose a researcher randomly sampled 1,000 Los Angeles-area residents, weighed them, gave them a test of verbal ability, and correlated the two scores. Would you be surprised to learn that the correlation between weight and verbal ability was +.60? (You should be. If weight and verbal ability truly went hand in hand, professional wrestlers would be among the most articulate members in society.) What if you then learned that the researcher had sampled children ranging from early infancy to middle school? In this case, you would probably realize very quickly what was going on. Weight just happens to be associated with age, and age is, for obvious reasons, strongly related to the "verbal ability" of young children. What the researcher would really like to know, then, is whether there is any relation between weight and verbal ability when age is held constant. To find out the answer, the researcher would need to conduct a partial correlation. If the partial correlation between weight and verbal ability remained positive and significant after controlling for age, you could put aside one possible third variable (age) as an explanation for the researcher's findings.

Although hypothetical examples like this are useful, it is probably easiest to see how a partial correlation works by computing one in your head—using the reasoning skills you have been honing since you weighed only a few pounds. This is your assignment, and we are betting that it is much easier than you might think. The data you will evaluate come from an unobtrusive observational study we recently conducted. To test the suspicion that a colleague's daughter, Lisa, was stealing cookies from the psychology department cookie jar, we made observations on 12 different days. At the end of each day we recorded (1) whether Lisa had visited the psychology department and (2) whether any cookies were missing from the cookie jar. To convert the data to numerical form, we coded them as follows: For Lisa's presence in the department, a "0" meant that she *had not* and a "1" meant that she *had* visited the department on a given day. For cookie thefts, a "0" meant that cookies *had not* been stolen and a "1" meant that cookies *had* been stolen on a given day. A summary of the data appears below.

Hypothetical Data From Observational Study of Cookie Thefts

	Cookies Stolen?	Lisa Visited?
Day 1:	No (0)	No (0)
Day 2:	No (0)	No (0)
Day 3:	No (0)	No (0)
Day 4:	No (0)	No (0)
Day 5:	No (0)	No (0)
Day 6:	No (0)	Yes (1)
Day 7:	Yes (1)	No (0)
Day 8:	Yes (1)	Yes (1)
Day 9:	Yes (1)	Yes (1)
Day 10:	Yes (1)	Yes (1)
Day 11:	Yes (1)	Yes (1)
Day 12:	Yes (1)	Yes (1)

A Question

1. We conducted an analysis of these data and recorded the correlation. Which of the five answers below do you think it was?
   a. $r(10) = -.67, p = .018$.
   b. $r(10) = -.13$, n.s.
   c. $r(10) = 0.00$, n.s.
   d. $r(10) = +.13$, n.s.
   e. $r(10) = +.67, p = .018$.

To check your intuitions about this answer, you can actually calculate the correlation coefficient by using the following formula:

$$r = (\text{matches} - \text{mismatches})/p$$

where "matches" refers to observations for which the two variables take on the same value and "mismatches" refers to observations for which the two variables take on different values. For example, if there were ten matches and four mismatches in a set of 14 observations, the correlation would be $(10 - 4)/14$ or about .43. (Incidentally, this simple formula works only when you are correlating two dichotomous variables whose outcomes are equally likely—as they are here.)

Assume that these are the only data you have at your disposal. What conclusion would you draw based on the magnitude and significance of this test? Based on the data you have so far, how likely is it that Lisa is guilty of at least some of the cookie thefts?

More Data

Now suppose that we had conducted a more complete study—one in which we also observed the behavior of a second child, Bart, on the same 12 days. Because Lisa and Bart are both children of our colleague Homer, they tend to come as a package (i.e., their presence in the department is positively correlated). Because this is the case, you could think of Bart as a third variable or confound. It is obviously possible that Bart is the true culprit. Statistically, it is possible to conduct a partial correlation to get a better idea of who is responsible for the cookie thefts. In fact, not only could we compute a partial correlation between Lisa's presence and cookie thefts (controlling for Bart's presence), but we could also compute a partial correlation between Bart's presence and cookie thefts (controlling for Lisa's presence). In other words, we could try to see who is the true cause of the cookie thefts. The complete data for this study appear below.

Complete Data for Observational Study of Cookie Thefts

	Cookies Stolen?	Lisa Visited?	Bart Visited?
Day 1:	No (0)	No (0)	No (0)
Day 2:	No (0)	No (0)	No (0)
Day 3:	No (0)	No (0)	No (0)
Day 4:	No (0)	No (0)	No (0)
Day 5:	No (0)	No (0)	No (0)
Day 6:	No (0)	Yes (1)	No (0)
Day 7:	Yes (1)	No (0)	Yes (1)
Day 8:	Yes (1)	Yes (1)	Yes (1)
Day 9:	Yes (1)	Yes (1)	Yes (1)
Day 10:	Yes (1)	Yes (1)	Yes (1)
Day 11:	Yes (1)	Yes (1)	Yes (1)
Day 12:	Yes (1)	Yes (1)	Yes (1)

More Questions

2. If we gave these data to a computer, the computer would give us a very clear idea of who is responsible for the cookie thefts (in the form of a couple of partial correlations). Based on the additional data provided above and your intuitions about how the data look, who would you blame? In answering this question, be sure to report whether you think you now have a better grip on who was responsible for the cookie thefts. In your answer include:

   a. Your estimate of the partial correlation between Bart's presence and cookie thefts. A good way to think about this is to ask yourself what portion of the blame for the cookie thefts should most reasonably be placed on Bart—given what you know about everything that is going on. If Bart seemed to deserve about half of the blame, for example, you might estimate his correlation at about .50 (or about .71, but this is a detail you don't need to worry about). (You do not necessarily have to hit the answer to the partial correlation right on the head, but you must logically defend your answer.)

   b. Your estimate of the partial correlation between Lisa's presence and cookie thefts. That is, how uniquely responsible is Lisa for the cookie thefts? (Be sure to defend your answer.) *Hint:* Some days are much more informative than others. Be sure to tell *which* days and why.

3. The power of partial correlation might lead some people to conclude that we no longer need laboratory experiments to assess causal relations between variables. Attack or defend this position. *Hint:* Recall the problem of induction from Chapters 2 and 6. What if Lisa had a great number of siblings and you could observe only one or two of them at once? Alternately, what if Homer occasionally trusted Lisa to come to the department by herself, but always accompanied Bart? *Second hint:* In the cookie example, it is obvious that causality can run in only one direction (i.e., it seems unlikely that disappearing cookies can cause Bart or Lisa to appear in the department), but what if you were trying to assess the relation between income and education, controlling for personality? Would partial correlation be any more or less informative than it was in the case of missing cookies? *Final hint:* Partial correlation controls for any confounding variable or variables that you were insightful enough to measure and add to your statistical analysis. For which variables does random assignment control?

METHODOLOGY EXERCISE 2

Random Assignment

As you know, random assignment is one of the defining features of true experiments. To see how well random assignment works, why not try

Condition	Age	IQ	Height	Surgency	Self-esteem
1 C E	16	145	73	10	42
2 C E	17	73	64	12	48
3 C E	21	86	70	9	30
4 C E	39	108	71	1	36
5 C E	18	58	72	5	38
6 C E	37	109	70	9	42
7 C E	31	91	68	7	28
8 C E	25	124	73	9	39
9 C E	23	64	66	6	40
10 C E	21	121	61	6	36
11 C E	28	93	71	5	45
12 C E	21	107	74	6	44
13 C E	26	94	64	4	43
14 C E	25	114	72	9	35
15 C E	31	78	68	7	40
16 C E	15	104	71	6	45
17 C E	25	128	68	7	42
18 C E	17	81	66	7	41
19 C E	21	136	65	9	38
20 C E	23	97	75	6	42

Experimental Group ($n = $ _____)   Control Group ($n = $ _____)

#	Age	IQ	Height	Surg.	Self-esteem	#	Age	IQ	Height	Surg.	Self-esteem
—	—	—	—	—	—	—	—	—	—	—	—
—	—	—	—	—	—	—	—	—	—	—	—
—	—	—	—	—	—	—	—	—	—	—	—
—	—	—	—	—	—	—	—	—	—	—	—
—	—	—	—	—	—	—	—	—	—	—	—
—	—	—	—	—	—	—	—	—	—	—	—
—	—	—	—	—	—	—	—	—	—	—	—
—	—	—	—	—	—	—	—	—	—	—	—
—	—	—	—	—	—	—	—	—	—	—	—
—	—	—	—	—	—	—	—	—	—	—	—
—	—	—	—	—	—	—	—	—	—	—	—
—	—	—	—	—	—	—	—	—	—	—	—
—	—	—	—	—	—	—	—	—	—	—	—
—	—	—	—	—	—	—	—	—	—	—	—
—	—	—	—	—	—	—	—	—	—	—	—
M_e	—	—	—	—	—	M_c	—	—	—	—	—

it yourself? The table on p. 420 describes 20 people who differ on all kinds of variables, from height to self-esteem. What would happen if you randomly assign each person to an experimental or a control condition for a hypothetical experiment? Would your experimental and control groups be similar on all the dimensions listed? To find out, start at the top of your list and flip a fair coin to determine each person's condition. If the coin lands on heads, circle the **e** next to that person's participant number to indicate that you have assigned that particular person to your experimental group (and enter that person's scores in the appropriate set of blanks below the list). If the coin lands on tails, circle the **c** next to that person's participant number to indicate that you have assigned that person to your control group (and enter the person's scores in the other set of blanks). When you have worked your way through the entire list of 20 people, compute group means on each of the variables listed and enter them (rounded to the nearest hundredth of a point) in the spaces provided at the bottom of the table.

Questions

1. On the whole, are the two groups as similar as you expected? (This question could be answered correctly with either a yes or a no. The important thing is to explain your answer.)
2. Do the two groups differ meaningfully on any of the variables measured? That is, did random assignment appear to work better for some variables than for others? (This question isn't as easy as it may seem. Be sure you give some thought to the fact that the different variables are scored in very different ways. For example, IQ scores of 101 and 107 are pretty similar. Is a six-point difference in age equally small? This observation gives you some insight into the meaning of a standard deviation.)
3. Remembering (a) that any differences you observed must have been the result of chance and (b) that researchers typically take it for granted that their experimental and control groups are identical prior to any manipulations, imagine that your participants differed noticeably on only one variable—self-esteem. Briefly describe an experiment or kind of experiment in which this preexisting difference between your groups might have disastrous consequences. Describe a different kind of experiment in which this particular difference would be unlikely to pose any problems. (Hint: Is a confound involving self-esteem always a concern?)
4. Next, assume that you have a group of 40 people at your disposal rather than 20. What advantages and disadvantages would the extra 20 people pose? Make sure you frame at least one of your answers to this question in terms of the goal of random assignment.

METHODOLOGY EXERCISE 3

Interactions

Does your dog bite? Will this pain reliever make me feel better? Are people attracted to those who say good things about them? When people ask important questions such as these, they usually want straightforward answers. That is why people typically become frustrated when they pose questions such as these to psychologists (especially social psychologists). That's because many psychologists give the same answer to every question: "It depends." "Spot usually bites men, but he almost never bites women." "Sodium salycarbanol is a great pain reliever, but it'll kill you if you take it with antihistamines." "Most people like to be flattered, but people who are very low in self-esteem prefer to be viewed negatively rather than positively."

Experimenters (especially experimental psychologists) are so intrigued with the "it depends" notion that they have developed a special statistical analysis to tell us when it depends. They have developed techniques, that is, for detecting interactions. Technically, an interaction means that a particular independent variable has different effects on a dependent variable at different levels of some other independent variable. It means, in short, that we cannot predict the effects of A on C without knowing something about variable B. The key is that the two independent variables work *together* to determine behavior. Information about one variable by itself tells you very little, but information about both variables tells you a lot.

To test for an interaction between two variables, you have to independently manipulate both of the variables in a factorial design. In its simplest form a factorial design is an experimental design that includes every possible combination of two independent variables. It is easiest to illustrate both an interaction and a factorial design with an example. Medical doctors often use the phrase "drug interaction precaution." Although they may not realize it, they are using the term "interaction" exactly the way a methodologist or statistician would. What they mean is that drug A by itself is good, and drug B by itself is good, but drugs A and B together are bad. The table below shows the results of a hypothetical study that illustrates this point. The study makes use of a 2 (drug A: placebo versus treatment) 3 2 (drug B: placebo versus treatment) factorial design (remember, the "3" is pronounced "by"), and the dependent variable is the amount of pain that migraine sufferers reported 30 minutes after receiving their specific combination of treatments (higher numbers mean more self-reported pain on a 7-point scale).

	Level of Drug A	
Level of Drug B	Placebo	Treatment
Placebo	5.8 (ouch!)	1.2 (aaah …)
Treatment	1.5 (aaah …)	6.3 (ouch!)

Notice, first of all, that the design includes every possible treatment combination of the two drugs. According to their random assignment to one of four experimental conditions, (1) some patients got drug A only (along with a placebo that they thought was drug B), (2) some got drug B only (along with a placebo that they thought was drug A), (3) some got neither drug (they got two placebos), and (4) some got both drugs. By the way, all the patients *thought* that they got both drugs; the manipulation had to do with what the patients actually got. If we had a large sample in this hypothetical study, a statistical test would definitely indicate that there was an interaction between the two treatments. When given alone, each drug was very effective, but when given together, the two drugs canceled each other out (in this case, however, they did not produce death).

Of course, interactions do not always take the form described above. For instance, some drugs probably work better in combination than they do alone. An interaction means that the effects of variable A are *different* at different levels of variable B. The effects of A could be strengthened, weakened, or totally reversed at a particular level of variable B, and you would still say that there was an interaction between the two variables.

If all these different patterns qualify as interactions, does this mean that factorial designs always reveal some kind of interaction? Definitely not. Some drugs are absolutely unaffected by the presence of other drugs, just as some dogs are equally likely to bite people of either sex. According to self-enhancement theory, it should also be the case that everybody (whether high or low in self-esteem) prefers positive feedback rather than negative feedback. In statistical terms, straightforward ideas and theories such as these would be reflected by main effects rather than interactions. The presence of a main effect in a factorial design (without an interaction) means that you don't need to know anything about B to describe the effect of A on your dependent variable. If the drug experiment just described had yielded only a main effect of drug A (no main effect of B and no interaction), the results might look something like those tabled below.

| | Level of Drug A | |
Level of Drug B	Placebo	Treatment
Placebo	6.2 (ouch!)	1.4 (aah …)
Treatment	6.3 (ouch!)	1.5 (aah …)

This result would mean that the effects of drug A had nothing to do with drug B. People who got drug A felt better. Period.

To give you a better feel for how interactions work, we would like you to consider some data from a hypothetical study involving feedback and self-esteem. In this quasi-experiment (see Chapter 8), ten high-self-esteem participants and ten low-self-esteem participants were randomly assigned to receive either negative feedback from a confederate (e.g., "You don't seem to be very good at this task; it seems like the kind of thing you're just not cut out for") or positive feedback from a confederate (e.g., "You did a really great job on this task; you really seem to have what it takes"). The dependent variable was participants' liking for the confederate measured on a 9-point scale (on which higher scores indicated greater liking). Thus the design was a 2 (self-esteem: low versus high) × 2 (feedback: negative versus positive) factorial. The raw data (not the means) are as follows:

	Self-Esteem	
Feedback	Low	High
Negative	7, 8, 7, 9, 9	3, 2, 3, 4, 3
Positive	2, 3, 4, 5, 1	6, 9, 9, 7, 9

After computing the mean liking score in each cell of this design and comparing these means, you should have a pretty clear idea of whether you observed (1) a main effect of self-esteem, (2) a main effect of feedback, and (3) an Esteem × Feedback interaction.

1. Which of these effects did you observe? Be sure to defend your answers by describing the findings with whatever mean comparisons are appropriate.
2. What do these results tell you about the nature of self-esteem? For example, is there evidence for self-enhancement theory (the theory that people always prefer positive feedback)?
3. In addition to checking for main effects and an interaction, are there any additional (follow-up) analyses you might want to conduct on these data?
4. Finally, if you had failed to include self-esteem as a factor in this study, and you had simply run a *t*-test to see if people preferred positive or negative feedback, what would you have found? Would these results have been misleading in any way?

METHODOLOGY EXERCISE 4

Repeated Measures Designs

In the first methodology exercise, we learned that matching is very bad. In fact, matching isn't *all* bad; it just has a few drawbacks (like being imperfect and impractical). However, if matching worked perfectly (and if it were practical), it would be pretty wonderful. Imagine, for example, that you can somehow create perfect clones of ten people and assign one member of each pair of clones to one of two conditions in an experiment. Notice, first of all, that you no longer need random assignment. If the clones are truly *perfect* clones, there is no need to worry about which member of a pair of clones goes into which condition. Now suppose you run your experiment and find that the clones in your experimental group behave differently from those in your control group. How confident would you feel that the behavioral differences you observe are the result of your experimental manipulation? You should feel extremely confident, because a major source of behavioral variability (individual differences) has been completely eliminated from your study (remember that random assignment controls pretty well for individual differences but it never eliminates them entirely).

Given the recent media attention paid to cloning, it has probably occurred to you by now that cloning for experimental control has some pretty serious ethical and practical drawbacks. Even though we can't clone people to serve in research experiments, we can come pretty close. How? By allowing each person in an experiment to serve in more than one condition of the study and thus to serve as his or her own control. This is exactly what repeated measures or within-subjects designs do. They place each participant in more than one condition of an experiment to see if the same person's thoughts, feelings, or behavior will be different under different experimental conditions. Besides giving you a great deal of control in your experiment, repeated measures designs can also increase the impact of certain manipulations. Suppose you want to vary either (1) the strength of two electric shocks people have to rate for painfulness or (2) the physical attractiveness of a woman whom participants have to rate for friendliness. Wouldn't your manipulations be more salient if each participant is exposed to both levels of shock or attractiveness? In addition to the advantages of control and impact, repeated measures designs have a final practical advantage. In comparison with traditional (between-subjects) designs, they typically require less of the two most valuable resources any experimenter has: time and research participants.

To give you a feel for how repeated measures designs work, this exercise will allow you to analyze a hypothetical data set from an experiment on the self-concept. One of the most widely accepted theories of the self is self-enhancement theory, which states that people have a strong need to think well of themselves and usually try to boost their own egos in any way that they can. Suppose two experimenters each run a study in an effort to gain support for self-enhancement theory. In particular, suppose they both decide to see if people are more likely to endorse positive rather than negative traits as self-descriptive. Suppose further that in an effort to gain evidence that self-enhancing self-ratings exist independent of potentially accurate self-knowledge, the researchers decide to study experimentally generated positive versus negative beliefs. That is, they examine people's tendencies to endorse *nonexistent* positive or negative traits as self-descriptive.

For example, one researcher (Dr. Craig) gave half of her ten participants the following "personality measure" and asked them to place a "yes" or a "no" next to each trait to indicate whether they consider it self-descriptive:

Negative Traits	Positive Traits
_____ immature	_____ considerate
_____ humorless	_____ hardworking
_____ untruthful	_____ friendly
_____ boring	_____ open-minded
_____ **casortic**	_____ creative
_____ disagreeable	_____ talented

She gave the other (randomly assigned) half of her participants a different version of the same measure:

Negative Traits	Positive Traits
_____ immature	_____ considerate
_____ humorless	_____ hardworking
_____ untruthful	_____ friendly
_____ boring	_____ open-minded
_____ unreliable	_____ **gamant**
_____ disagreeable	_____ talented

If you examine the two personality scales carefully, you will see that people who receive the first scale will probably assume that being "casortic" isn't very good. People who receive the second scale, however, will be likely to assume that "gamanticity" is pretty wonderful.

Although we think that Dr. Craig has designed a pretty clever experiment, we don't think her experiment was quite as nice as a similar experiment run by Dr. Henderson. Dr. Henderson took a within-subjects approach and presented _each_ of her ten participants with a measure that looked like this:

Negative Traits	Positive Traits
_____ immature	_____ considerate
_____ humorless	_____ hardworking
_____ untruthful	_____ friendly
_____ boring	_____ **gamant**
_____ **casortic**	_____ open-minded
_____ disagreeable	_____ talented

Notice that Dr. Henderson's design is essentially the equivalent of giving ten people the first scale devised by Dr. Craig and then giving ten clones of the original participants the second scale, also devised by Dr. Craig. For the sake of this exercise, assume Dr. Henderson was able to travel to an alternate universe that is one day behind our own. Thus Dr. Henderson was able to conduct her within-subjects study on _exactly the same ten people_ studied by Dr. Craig (but who had no knowledge of having been in the original study). Like Dr. Craig,

Dr. Henderson was interested in the hypothesis that people would be more likely to endorse a bogus trait (i.e., to say that it was self-descriptive) if it happened to be positive rather than negative. The data from both studies appear below:

	Dr. Craig's Experiment		Dr. Henderson's Experiment		
Participant	Valence of bogus trait	Endorsed?	Participant	Endorsed − trait?	Endorsed + trait?
01	−	N	01	N	Y
02	−	Y	02	Y	Y
03	−	N	03	N	Y
04	−	Y	04	Y	N
05	−	N	05	N	Y
06	+	Y	06	N	Y
07	+	Y	07	N	Y
08	+	Y	08	N	Y
09	+	Y	09	N	Y
10	+	N	10	N	N

Note: Valence of bogus trait refers to whether the bogus trait was negative (−) or positive (+).

Questions

1. Compare scores from the same participants if they live in Dr. Craig's universe or Dr. Henderson's alternate universe. How do the responses of participants 1–5 compare with the responses of the same participants from the alternate universe? How about participants 6–10? Be specific by making it clear which responses can be compared and which ones can't.

2. Summarize the results of Dr. Craig's between-subjects experiment. What percentage of participants endorsed the bogus trait in the positive and negative trait conditions? Do the results provide any support at all for the hypothesis? Suppose you were to conduct a traditional ANOVA on the data from experiment A. Which of the following F ratios and p values do you think you would obtain? (Recall that only p values of less than .05 are significant.)
   a. $F(1, 8) = 1.60$, $p = .2415$.
   b. $F(1, 9) = 7.36$, $p = .0239$.

3. Summarize the results of Dr. Henderson's within-subjects experiment. If you conducted a repeated measures ANOVA on both sets of scores in experiment B, which of the following F ratios and p values do you think you would obtain?
   a. $F(1, 8) = 1.60$, $p = .2415$.
   b. $F(1, 9) = 7.36$, $p = .0239$.
   Answer questions 2 and 3 by trying to decide which experiment (the first or second) would yield significant results (only one would). Now explain why you think one study would yield more significant results than the other. (There is more than one reason.)

4. The results of this exercise might suggest that we should always use repeated measures designs, but despite all of their advantages, repeated measures designs also have some drawbacks. Can you think of any? First, can you think of a potential confound or problem that could "spoil" repeated measures designs (as they are conducted in a single universe)? How do researchers typically deal with this problem? (You should be able to answer these two questions from material in Chapter 9.) Second, can you think of any experiments or types of experiments that would be difficult or impossible to run using a repeated measures design?

How to Describe the Results of Statistical Analyses

Although we hope that Chapter 11 provided you with useful information about writing empirical research papers, it is missing something very important. It is missing a category of information about how to write the trickiest and most unfamiliar part of a research report—namely, reporting statistical analyses. If anything is harder than understanding the ins and outs of statistics, it is knowing how to describe them in written research reports. We find that even students who understand a particular statistic perfectly well often have little idea how to describe the outcome of the statistical analysis. When we have learned a new statistical test—because we have used it in our research—we may still be at a loss when we have to write about it for the first time in a research paper. With this in mind, we have devoted this appendix to a discussion of how to report some commonly used statistics.

The particular statistics that a researcher uses to summarize and analyze his or her data are dictated partly by the designs the researcher has adopted (e.g., whether it's a within- or a between-subjects design), partly by the kind of measurement scale the researcher has used (e.g., whether it's a nominal or an interval scale), and partly by the particular question the researcher wants to answer about the data (e.g., whether a particular scale is internally consistent or whether two means are significantly different from one another). To facilitate direct comparisons between different statistical tests (and how they are reported), we will report the results of some fictional statistical tests that were all conducted to address some aspect of the same basic research question: a question about mysterious colorful spheres. Finally, although this is primarily a chapter about reporting statistics, a secondary goal here is to provide you with a fictional example of how different research techniques may be brought to bear on the same basic research question.

THE MYSTERIOUS SPHERES

Imagine that you are relaxing in front of the TV and your favorite program is interrupted by a special news bulletin. A newscaster reports that several dozen strange, colorful spheres have appeared here and there throughout the city. The spheres aren't very big. They range in diameter from about four to ten inches (in fact, careful descriptive studies eventually reveal that the spheres are normally distributed in size, with an average diameter of exactly seven inches and a standard deviation of exactly one inch—meaning that exactly 99.74 percent of them are between four and ten inches in diameter). However, the spheres are getting a lot of attention. Early speculations about the origin of the spheres range from theories about government conspiracies or alien invasions to theories that the spheres are simply a large-scale practical joke. You eventually learn that the spheres have made sporadic appearances across the country and possibly across the globe.

The strange spheres are collected and analyzed by dozens of experts ranging from military experts and bomb-squad specialists to physicists, chemists, and electrical engineers. The spheres are a scientific mystery. It is impossible to determine their mass because they defy gravity, always hovering a few inches above the ground. Most interesting, and perhaps most disturbing, the spheres are completely indestructible. They defy all attempts to bend, break, crush, or otherwise reshape them, and they cannot be taken apart. They also cannot be x-rayed, sonographed, magnetically imaged, thermoscanned, or otherwise analyzed internally. In short, no one has a clue about what's up with the spheres. They also happen to be completely immovable, which makes them a bit of a hazard when they settle down in places such as airport runways and major freeways. The only thing certain about the spheres is: (1) they come with equal frequency in two colors (green and yellow) and (2) they appear to have a strange influence on human behavior.

Study 1: The Murder Rate Study

Although everyone agrees that the spheres have a strange influence on human behavior, no one can seem to agree on exactly what this influence is. One of the first clues comes from a team of applied social psychologists who conducted a large-scale archival study of the influence of the spheres. The study compared police reports of murders in two large American cities known to have had nearly identical murder rates prior to the arrival of the spheres. Importantly, the researchers noted that it happens to have been the case that a preponderance of spheres of a *particular color* landed in each of the two cities. In one city a disproportionate number of green spheres fell (86 percent, to be precise), and in the second city a disproportionate number of yellow spheres fell (83 percent, to be equally precise). The researchers examined

Table A3.1   Estimated number of people who did and did not commit murder in a one-year period in two cities with previously comparable murder rates

	Predominant Color of Spheres Observed	
	Green	Yellow
Murderers	83	10
	(62)	(31)
Nonmurderers	1,999,917	999,990
	(1,999,938)	(999,969)

Note: Expected frequencies appear in parentheses below observed frequencies. Despite the assumption of identical murder rates, the expected numbers of murders differed for the two cities because the population of the "green" city was twice that of the "yellow" city.

murder rates in the two cities as a function of the color of the spheres that predominated in each particular city. Because murders are categorical events (either a murder occurs or it doesn't), the researchers simply counted up the murders in each city during a one-year period and checked this number against the official population of each city. This gave them an estimate of the number of people who had and had not committed a murder in each city in a given year. This became a little tricky, by the way, because it is possible that some people were responsible for more than one murder in a given year. (If 20 murders occurred, it doesn't guarantee that 20 different people committed murder. In principle, a single person could have committed them all.) However, the researchers addressed this critique very carefully in a footnote—a footnote that we will conveniently ignore.

Without getting too enmeshed in the researchers' exact methods, notice that their dependent measure is a categorical variable. This means that their study is a good candidate for a χ^2 analysis (similar to, but a bit more complex than, the one we did with the Ping-Pong balls). With this in mind, let's look at some hypothetical results (depicted in Table A3.1) and see how the researchers might have described them in the Results section of their groundbreaking paper.[1]

> Our findings revealed a clear and significant association between city status and observed murder rates over the one-year period. As suggested by the pattern of observed and expected frequencies that appear in Table A3.1, murders were not equally distributed between the two cities, χ^2 (1, N = 3,000,000) = 21.34, $p < .001$, equivalent ϕ^2 = .00267. In the absence of any differences associated with the spheres, we would have expected exactly twice the number of murders in the city in which most of the spheres were green. Instead, we observed that the number of murders committed in this city was more than eight times as high as the number of murders committed in the city in which most of the spheres were yellow. It is possible that green spheres act as a green light to murder.

There are several things to note about this description. First, notice that the statistics took a backseat to the verbal description of what was going on. The information about the χ^2 test is extremely important. Without it, we don't know whether to make much of the observed differences. As important as it is, however, it is not nearly as important as a simple description of what happened in the study. Second, notice that, for the most part, the researchers avoided the use of causal language. Instead of saying that the spheres caused the observed differences, they said that they observed an association between the preponderance of the spheres and murder rates. The only suggestion of causality was the little flourish thrown in at the very end (and it was qualified by the word "possible"). Later in the paper, the authors may choose to make arguments about causes, but in the primary part of the Results section, it is best to be cautious. Finally, notice that the researchers supplemented their χ^2 statistic with a ϕ (phi) value. This is the conceptual and mathematical equivalent of r (a correlation coefficient), and it is typically reported instead of r when the two variables being correlated are both dichotomous. You might also have noticed that the value of ϕ is extremely small. Whenever scores on a variable are highly skewed (e.g., when there are many, many more nonmurderers than murderers), this places some extreme limits on the size of a contingency coefficient. To steer readers away from the inappropriate assumption that the effect they observed in their study was extremely small, the authors expressed their findings in terms of observed versus expected murder rates.

Study 2: The Survey Study of Apathy and Energy

The first group of researchers made a breakthrough discovery. They were the first people to document the possibility that the *color* of the spheres might be a significant marker of what the spheres do. As is often the case with real research, however, this early breakthrough turned out to represent only an imperfect truth. A second group of researchers felt that the color of the spheres was very informative, but they also noticed that the spheres seemed to influence much more than just murder rates. In the green city, for instance, they noticed that several unusually impressive sports records had been set during the same year as the archival study of murder. The researchers' casual observations also suggested that certain kinds of heroic behaviors (e.g., jumping into a freezing river to save a drowning child) had increased in the green city. Finally, during the summer of the first year of the spheres, ice cream sales had tripled in the green city! The researchers had difficulty getting hold of ice cream sales records in the yellow city, but it seemed to be the case that ice cream sales had actually decreased there during the same period. In short, a mixture of formal and informal observations convinced the second team of researchers that the green spheres might act as some kind of general energizer, increasing the vigor with which people pursue any kind of activity (whether it be murdering one's enemies, competing with one's opponents, or rescuing someone else's enemies). They were less certain about the yellow spheres, but they suspected that they simply mellowed people out, making people's psychological responses to stimuli less intense.

   To test their hypotheses, the second team of researchers conducted a large-scale survey study in which they asked a randomly sampled group of participants to recall the last time they had come into close contact with one of the spheres, to report whether the sphere had been green or yellow, and to answer a series of questions about their experience in the presence of the sphere. In particular, they created multiple-item measures of what they called apathy and energy (without labeling them as such), and they asked their participants to report the degree to which they had felt apathetic or energized the last time they had come into close contact with one of the spheres. The researchers expected to find that the color of the sphere people reported having most recently come into contact with would be strongly correlated with people's self-reported experiences of apathy and energy while in the sphere's presence. Because the researchers realized that numerically coding for nominal data is arbitrary, they simply coded reports of yellow-sphere experiences as -1 and reports of green-sphere experiences as $+1$. (They could have just as readily used values of -17 and $+142.68$; the only important thing would be to remember which color got the higher of the two arbitrary values.) The researchers tested their hypotheses by simply computing point-biserial correlations between people's color codes and their reported experiences on the apathy and energy scales.

Because the researchers had developed their own measures of apathy and energy, they wanted to show that these measures were reliable before showing that they correlated as expected with people's self-reported exposure to a particular kind of sphere. As you may recall, in the case of multiple-item survey measures, the most relevant form of reliability is usually internal consistency. Before we take a look at how the researchers might have discussed the reliability of their measures, we should note that they probably *wouldn't* have presented information about reliability in their Results section. Because reliability is a property of survey measures, information about reliability is most likely to be found in a paper's Method section. Here is an example of what this paragraph of the authors' Method section might have looked like:

> *Measures of Apathy and Energy.* Because we were unable to find any existing measures of apathy and energy, we developed a new measure of each of these constructs. Based on pilot tests, we selected a set of ten items for each scale. The apathy scale included items such as "When I was in the presence of the sphere, I didn't feel much like doing anything," and "When I was in the presence of the sphere, things that usually seemed important just didn't seem to matter." The energy scale included items such as "When I was in the presence of the sphere, I felt all revved up," and "When I was in the presence of the sphere, my feelings were more intense than usual." Participants answered the items in both scales using Likert scales that ranged from 1 *(not at all true)* to 9 *(extremely true)*. Coefficient alpha for the resulting measures of apathy and energy was high (.88 and .91, respectively).

Although there are many other ways to describe a set of measures, this description summarizes the important characteristics of the scales. If it were important for readers to see all the items in these scales (as it usually is for new scales), the authors would want to include all of the items in the scales, along with any important instructions, in an appendix. The final sentence in the paragraph provides the crucial information about the reliability of the scales. There are many other ways to state this (and you should develop your own). Another way to have said this is: "The items in both scales proved to be internally consistent (respective as for the measures of apathy and energy were .88 and .91)." Incidentally, the Greek character alpha is short for Cronbach's alpha, and it is very different from an alpha level for statistical testing.

Measures of temporal consistency wouldn't make much sense for the kinds of items included in these two measures, but if they did, and if they were available, the researchers would probably want to present this information too. They might add: "In a separate sample of 100 participants, these scales also proved to be stable over time. The respective test-retest correlations for a 2-week period were r (98) = .77 and .84 for apathy and energy respectively." (Given both the magnitude of these correlations and the size of their sample, the researchers might not bother to report the obvious fact that these correlations are significant at $p < .001$.)

What about the results themselves? This part would be pretty straightforward. Given that there are only two correlations to report, reporting them in a table would be unnecessary. The researchers' description might look something like this:

> The correlations we observed provided strong support for our predictions. First, there was a moderately strong negative association between reports of sphere color and reported experiences of apathy, r (134) = −.46, $p < .001$. Because reports of having been in the presence of the green sphere were coded with higher values, this negative correlation means that participants who reported having been in the presence of the yellow sphere were substantially more likely to have reported overall feelings of apathy. Second, there was a very strong positive association between reports of sphere color and reported experiences of energy, r (132) = .71, $p < .001$. Participants who reported having been in the presence of the green sphere were especially likely to report having experienced high levels of energy and excitement. One participant who reported having been exposed to the green sphere spontaneously wrote on his survey: "Yellow spheres suck but green spheres our [sic] great! I wish I could can that stuff and sell it!" One wonders how long it had been since he had last been exposed to a green sphere.

There are a few things to note about this description. First, the value in parenthesis after each r indicates the degrees of freedom associated with that correlation. It's always $n - 2$, and so the researchers must have had 136 people in their sample. We intentionally made the degrees of freedom a little different for the second correlation. That kind of thing could easily happen if a couple of people completed the apathy measure but left part of the energy measure blank. If this did happen, the authors would probably want to point it out in a footnote so that readers didn't get the impression that the authors had made some kind of mistake. Second, notice that these authors, too, were pretty cautious about their language when describing the correlations (though they, too, may have been guilty of waxing a little causal in their final sentence). Finally, although we presented these data in the form of two correlations, it would have been equally reasonable to have divided participants into two groups based on sphere color and to have conducted a simple one-way ANOVA (or a t-test) on the data. The statistics would have been a little different, but the probability values would have been exactly the same. So in this particular case, the choice of which statistic to conduct (and report) is largely a matter of taste. One possible advantage of running an ANOVA or *t*-test is that experimentally inclined researchers (who are more accustomed to seeing means) would probably get a better sense of the nature of your findings if each finding were presented in the form of two means rather than a single correlation.[2]

Study 3: The Newlywed Marriage Study

One limitation of the second study is that the participants' expectancies (or naive theories) about the spheres could have biased what they were reporting. Of course, expectancies are grounded in folk wisdom, and folk wisdom often proves to be correct. On the other hand, it would be nice to have some evidence about the operation of the spheres that was less susceptible to this criticism. A third group of researchers was sympathetic to the view of the second group, but they wanted to address this criticism and broaden the empirical basis for the other researchers' conclusions. They obtained records from marriage licenses in Los Angeles County over a one-year period. Except in the case of confidential licenses, marriage licenses always provide the mailing address of the newlywed couple. The researchers used these addresses to locate the single-family dwellings of a very large group of newlyweds, and then they sent interviewers into the field to identify couples on whose lawns either a green or a yellow sphere had landed. Whenever the researchers identified such a home, they recorded the color of the sphere and attempted to secure an interview with one of the newlyweds. If no one was home, the interviewers returned to the dwelling on as many as three different occasions before giving up on a particular couple.

When the interviewers found someone at home and were able to secure an interview, they began by asking questions on a number of mundane topics (such as who was responsible for what chores and how much time participants spent watching television each week). However, these questions were really just warm-up questions. When the interviewers had finished these questions, they told the interviewees that they also had a few questions that most people felt more comfortable about answering in a confidential survey. They then gave participants a small survey card and an envelope and asked them if they would be willing to conclude the interview by privately answering the questions on the card and sealing the card in the envelope. Everyone who agreed to the initial interview also agreed to fill out the card. The card asked people to think about their relationship for the last month and to report: (1) how happy they were with their marriages, (2) how many times in an average week the couple had an argument, and (3) how frequently (i.e., how many times per week) the couple had engaged in sexual intercourse. During the interview, the researchers made it a point *not* to mention anything about the spheres. In those few cases in which interviewees spontaneously mentioned the spheres, the researchers remarked that they hadn't really noticed them and politely moved on with the interview. At the conclusion of the interview, however, the researchers always made a record of this comment on the participant's data-record sheet. This way, they could later check to see if the responses of these participants were different from those of the rest of the group.[3]

The three primary questions answered on the card constituted the researchers' dependent variables, but the researchers also measured a couple of other variables that they expected to be related to the dependent measures. The most important one, how many months the couple had been married, served two purposes. First, it allowed the researchers to be sure that they had, in fact, sampled who they were after (because participants' reports could be compared with the date of the marriage given on the actual marriage license). Second, if this measure agreed with the researchers' records (which it almost always did), it could serve as an additional predictor of people's responses to the three questions on the card. In other words, because the researchers were unable to get an extremely large sample, they wanted to minimize noise or unpredictable fluctuations in their participants' responses. For example, one pretty good predictor of how happy people report being with the quality of their marriages is how long they have been married. During the first year of a marriage (and beyond), you often see a gradually dwindling "honeymoon effect." People are extremely happy at first, but their level of reported happiness gradually tapers off over time. By measuring how long people had been married, researchers were able to use statistical procedures to determine how length of marriage resulted in systematic differences between the couples.

Because the researchers measured more than one variable that they expected to influence their participants' responses and because at least one of these predictors (length of marriage in months) was a continuous variable, the researchers decided to test their hypotheses by conducting a multiple regression analysis. Multiple regression is essentially a souped-up version of partial correlation. Thus, if you took part in the methodology exercise on partial correlation (in Chapter 5) you should have at least a cursory idea of what multiple regression is about. For the time being, however, the most useful thing about multiple regression is that it allows researchers to control for one variable when they're examining the potential effects of a second variable. The controlled-for variable could be a suspected confound—like Bart when we really care about Lisa—or it could merely be a source of noise that the researchers wish to minimize, like how long people have been married in months when we really care about green and yellow spheres. Because there are many specific kinds of multiple regression analyses, researchers who use multiple regression have to be very clear about which particular kind of regression they conducted when they report their findings. Here is an example of what the researchers might have reported had they conducted a multiple regression analysis on their data. Before you check it out, however, here are a couple of important pieces of vocabulary. In multiple regression, the variables that researchers treat as independent variables are referred to as **predictors,** and the variable that researchers treat as the dependent variable is referred to as the **criterion.** Regression analyses also yield the logical equivalent of partial correlations. These measures of association are referred to as

regression coefficients, and they are conceptually identical to partial correlation coefficients.

As noted earlier, we tested our hypothesis by conducting three separate simultaneous multiple regression analyses. Our criterion variable in each of these analyses was always one of the three different measures of marital quality (happiness, arguments, and sex). Our predictors were always (1) the dummy coded sphere variable and (2) the number of months that participants had been married. Table A3.2 summarizes the results of each of these regression analyses. As suggested by the pattern of correlations and standardized regression coefficients shown in Table A3.2, marital length was related in the expected ways with each of the three criterion variables. The longer participants had been married, the less happy they reported being, the more they reported arguing, and the less frequently they reported engaging in sexual intercourse (though the significant zero-order correlation observed for happiness fell somewhat short of significance in the simultaneous regression). More importantly, however, all three of the regression analyses revealed strong and significant effects of the color of sphere. Moreover, unlike the measure of length of marriage, the presence of the green as compared with the yellow sphere was not simply associated with an across-the-board increase or decrease in reported marital quality. Instead, the green sphere seemed to magnify all three of these (self-reported) marital experiences—including both the two positive experiences (happiness and sex) and the one negative experience (arguments). In fact, the largest effects of the sphere appear to have occurred for arguments. Relative to the yellow spheres, the green spheres appear to have magnified couples' tendencies toward arguments even more than they magnified their tendencies toward happiness and sex.

Table A3.2 Marital happiness, frequency of arguments, and frequency of sexual intercourse as a function of length of newlywed marriage in months and proximity to green versus yellow spheres

Predictor	*r*	*t*	*β*	*p*
Results for Happiness				
Length of Marriage	−.230	−1.82	−.186	.078
Sphere Type	.612	11.47	.587	< .001
Results for Frequency of Arguments				
Length of Marriage	.356	2.48	.256	.023
Sphere Type	.740	14.29	.853	< .001
Results for Frequency of Sexual Intercourse				
Length of Marriage	−.400	−6.49	−.393	< .001
Sphere Type	.553	9.02	.540	< .001

Note: Beta weights and *t* values have the same probability values. Respective *r*'s with absolute magnitudes greater than .217, .283, and .357 are significant at *p* <.05, .01, and .001. The yellow and green spheres were dummy coded −1 and +1, respectively.

One thing you may have noticed about this description is that it is chock-full of technical terms like "dummy coded" and "standardized regression coefficient." Multiple regression analyses yield a great number of statistics, including many (such as R^2 and adjusted R^2 values) that we chose not to include here. Researchers in training who want to become comfortable with multiple regression techniques usually take one or more courses in multiple regression, and regression techniques are continuously being refined and developed (see Edwards, 1976, for an excellent introduction, and see both Aiken & West, 1991, and Pedhazur, 1982, for excellent treatments of more advanced topics). Although a detailed treatment of regression is well beyond the scope of this text, you can easily do one thing to become a little more familiar with multiple regression. Later in this appendix, we take a look at how the researchers who conducted this hypothetical study might have described exactly the same set of findings using the analysis of covariance (ANCOVA). By making a comparison of these two techniques, you can probably get a slightly better feel for how to think (and write) about regression.

A second thing you may have noticed about this description is that the authors avoided the use of causal language when it came to the association for marriage length, but they sometimes indulged in causal descriptions when it came to the naturalistic manipulation of sphere type (e.g., by using words like "effect" and "magnify"). Because the study in question was a natural experiment rather than a true experiment, many researchers would have been a little more cautious about the use of causal language. Some researchers might also have been a little more cautious about making any relative statements about the *size* of the sphere effect for the different criterion variables (strong statements of this sort should really be supported by a special significance test). Finally, even though this write-up was a little on the bold side, notice that the researchers were generally pretty cautious when it came to making direct statements about behavior. Because the researchers didn't actually measure any behavior, they didn't speak directly about arguing and having sex. Instead, they wrote that people who had been married longer *reported* having had more arguments (and less sex).

Study 4: The Stereotyping Study

So far, the evidence is starting to suggest that the green and yellow spheres respectively magnify and water down normal human psychological responses. However, all the evidence we have seen so far is either correlational or quasi-experimental. It'd be nice to see what the spheres do to people in the carefully controlled confines of the laboratory. Another limitation of the existing studies is that they tell us the two kinds of spheres are different but don't necessarily guarantee that *both* of the spheres are having an effect on people. Are the yellow spheres really mellowing people out, or are they simply failing to rev people up the way the green spheres do? To answer this question, we'd need some kind of control group of people who are not exposed to the spheres at all. To address concerns such as these, and to extend studies of the effects of the spheres to yet another area of human experience, a fourth group of researchers decided to conduct a laboratory experiment on the influence of the spheres. In the early days of spherical research, no one considered trying to conduct any experiments on spherical issues because of the simple fact that the spheres were immovable. It's pretty hard to bring an immovable object to the lab. A few enterprising psychologists solved this problem by bringing their laboratories to the spheres! In particular, they simply identified spheres that had fallen in open (though usually inconspicuous) areas on college campuses, and built small laboratories around them. It was well established that the range of influence of the spheres was about 40 feet, and thus it was easy for researchers to disguise the fact that their new labs had been built next to or around the spheres. Of course, participants in different conditions of the experiments had to be herded off to different parts of campus, but this was easy to arrange.

One particularly fortunate, and well-funded, pair of researchers was even able to set up a 2 × 2 factorial experiment on their campus. In particular, the researchers independently manipulated whether people were exposed to each of the two spheres. The design of their study was a 2 (yellow sphere: absent or present) × 2 (green sphere: absent or present) completely between-subjects factorial. This meant, by the way, that there happened to be an accessible spot on these researchers' campus where a green and a yellow sphere had landed in close proximity to each other (which allowed them to create the present/present cell in all their 2 × 2 experiments). By simply creating the same psychological situation in the four laboratories they had set up across campus, the researchers could investigate any topic in which they were interested to see how the spheres influenced different kinds of behaviors.

In their first study, the researchers decided to study ethnic stereotyping. Normally, they might have studied stereotyping by manipulating the apparent ethnicity of a target person (e.g., by describing a protagonist as "Robert Gardner" or "Roberto Garcia") and examining stereotype-relevant judgments of this person (for a real example of how this might work, see Bodenhausen, 1990). However, for their study of the spheres, the researchers merely described a case in which an eyewitness who wasn't wearing his eyeglasses claimed to identify the defendant, Roberto Garcia, as the person who had stolen his new sports car. (Notice that including a "Robert Gardner" condition would have required a more complex 2 × 2 × 2 design.) The researchers' dependent measure was simply the length of the prison sentence that participants recommended for the defendant. From their informal observations of people's behavior when they were exposed to both spheres at once, the researchers predicted that the presence of the two spheres together would lead to a different pattern of judgment than would be expected based on observations of how each sphere influenced people in isolation. In other words, the researchers predicted an interaction between the presence of the yellow sphere and the presence of the green sphere. Here is how the researchers described their results:

> The sentencing measure was submitted to a 2 (yellow sphere: absent or present) × 2 (green sphere: absent or present) completely between-subjects ANOVA. This analysis revealed both a main effect of the presence of the yellow sphere, $F(1, 40) = 12.84$, $p < .001$, $d = 1.113$, and a main effect of the

presence of the green sphere, $F(1, 40) = 7.32$, $p = .010$, $d = 0.856$. The first main effect reflected the fact that those exposed to the yellow sphere recommended shorter-than-average prison sentences. The second main effect reflected the fact that those exposed to the green sphere recommended longer-than-average prison sentences. Each of these main effects was consistent with the effects of the spheres observed in previous studies. However, the analysis also revealed that these main effects were qualified by a significant Yellow Sphere × Green Sphere interaction, $F(1, 40) = 8.31$, $p = .005$, $d = 0.911$. As suggested by the means appearing in Table A3.3, the nature of this interaction was consistent with predictions. Specifically, when the yellow sphere was absent, the presence of the green sphere had a large effect on sentencing. Those exposed to the green sphere recommended sentences almost three times as long as usual, $t(20) = 5.03$, $p < .001$, $d = 2.250$. However, when the yellow sphere was present, the presence of the green sphere had no effect whatsoever on participants' judgments. Participants recommended equal (and equally lenient) sentences for the defendant regardless of their level of exposure to the green sphere, $|t| < 1$, n.s., $d = -0.081$. Apparently, the yellow spheres not only minimize people's normal psychological responses to a situation but also neutralize any effects of the green spheres. At any rate, it is clear that the spheres do not simply cancel each other out. If they did, participants' responses in the present/present cell would have looked more like their responses in the absent/absent cell.

Interestingly, extensive discussions with participants in the yellow-sphere condition (during debriefing) revealed that they typically reported feeling little sympathy for Roberto. Instead, most of them reported that they just didn't see why it was such a big deal to steal a car or two every now and then. Two separate participants in the yellow-sphere condition also insisted on referring to the defendant as "Rob," and when queried about this habit reported that they simply hadn't bothered to read the rest of his name. Finally, the few participants in these conditions who did report that they felt it was wrong to steal cars all reported that it just wasn't worth the trouble to incarcerate hardened criminals. In the yellow-sphere-absent condition, however, not a single participant reported any of these apathetic responses. In fact, a few participants who were exposed to the green sphere and nothing else spontaneously reported that in the case of particularly heinous crimes such as Roberto's, they were strongly in favor of capital punishment (preferably by pressing, breaking on the wheel, burning, hanging in chains, bludgeoning, or gibbeting; see Sidanius & Pratto, 2000).

Table A3.3 Length of recommended prison sentence for Roberto Garcia as a function of exposure to green and yellow spheres

Green Sphere	Yellow Sphere	
	Absent	Present
Absent	2.21	0.45
Present	6.58	0.32

Note: Means are recommended sentences in years (theoretical range = 0–10). There were 11 participants in each condition.

The first paragraph is a standard discussion of main effects, interactions, and the ensuing simple effects tests that are conducted to clarify the nature of an observed interaction (along with some supplemental reports of effect sizes). The second paragraph is a slightly exaggerated version of the kind of thing researchers might add to their Results section (or possibly their General Discussion) to give readers some added insights into the experiences of their participants. In a real experiment, of course, participants' responses wouldn't normally be quite this colorful, but they might be just as telling.

Study 5: A Brief Return to Roberto and to the Newlywed Study

Imagine that the researchers who conducted the last study had pretested all of their participants a few weeks before their experiment to determine the strength of their participants' stereotypes about Latinos. If the spheres hadn't proven to have such a potent effect on people's behavior, these pretest scores might have come in very handy in such a study because we might expect these scores to be correlated with people's tendencies to recommend harsher sentences for Roberto Garcia. If this were true, the researchers in question could conduct a more sensitive experimental test of their hypotheses by conducting an ANCOVA—rather than a regular ANOVA—on their participants' recommended sentences. ANCOVA is very similar to ANOVA except that before the scores are analyzed, they are statistically adjusted for any effects of the covariate (the measured variable that is expected to covary with the researcher's dependent measure). Thus, ANCOVA is a hybrid analysis that incorporates desirable features of both multiple regression and the analysis of variance. Like regression techniques, ANCOVA can statistically adjust for variables that may be confounded with a researcher's independent variables. In addition, it can reduce what would otherwise be random noise or error in a set of scores—to make it easier to detect the effects of the variables in which researchers are most interested. In this second case, ANCOVA is the loose experimental equivalent of a noise-reduction system (such as a Dolby noise-reduction system in a stereo). It allows researchers to bypass a good deal of noise to get a better idea of whether a set of data has anything beautiful to tell us.

The main difference between reporting the results of an ANOVA and reporting those of an ANCOVA is that researchers typically report the effects of any covariates first (much like main effects—because both conceptually and mathematically they *are* main effects) and then report all the usual things that are reported in a typical ANOVA. The only other notable difference in how the results are discussed is that the resulting means are referred to (quite appropriately) as *covariate-adjusted means*, both in the body of the results and in any tables that might refer to them. If the researchers who conducted the interview study of newlyweds had decided to analyze their data by using

ANCOVA, their first set of results (for happiness) might have been reported like this:

> Our primary analyses consisted of three separate one-way (sphere type: yellow or green) analyses of covariance ANCOVAs in which length of marriage was treated as the covariate (and thus statistically controlled). Each ANCOVA focused on one of our three separate dependent measures (happiness, arguments, and sexual intercourse). The analysis of participants' reported happiness with their marriage revealed that the covariate (length of marriage) was only marginally associated with participants' reports of being happily married, $F(1, 102) = 3.20$, $p = .078$. Nonetheless, because of its *a priori* importance (and because it was significant in the other two ANCOVAS) the covariate was retained in the analysis. More importantly, the analysis also revealed a very large effect of sphere type, $F(1, 102) = 131.56$, $p < .001$. As suggested by the covariate-adjusted means for marital happiness, newlyweds whose lawns contained green spheres ($M = 8.53$) rather than yellow spheres ($M = 4.88$) reported much higher levels of marital satisfaction. In fact, the modal response in this condition was 9, which was the upper endpoint of our scale. Whereas green spheres appear to intensify feelings of marital happiness, yellow spheres appear to minimize these same feelings.

Similar descriptions should be provided for the other two dependent measures, and the psychological interpretation of the observed findings should obviously be the same as it was in the case of the discussion of the regression analyses. In fact, if you were minding your *p*-values carefully, you may have noticed that the two *p*-values reported here were identical to the two *p*-values reported in the upper section of Table A3.2. Although the results for both the regressions and the ANCOVA are fictional, this aspect of the results is not an accident. If we had provided the results of an ANCOVA for a variation on the stereotyping study and we had run a regression to analyze the same data, the results of both the ANCOVA and the regression would be more complex than those reported here (because there would be two main effects and an interaction to report, not to mention simple effects tests). However, the *p*-values from the regression and the ANCOVA that corresponded to the same effects (e.g., the *p*-value for the main effect of the green sphere) would be identical in the two analyses.

Study 6: The Duck in the Drugstore Study

So far we have seen that the mysterious spheres appear to influence a wide range of responses, including aggression, stereotyping, general feelings of apathy and energy, and specific feelings and behaviors related to interpersonal relationships. However, figuring all this out has been a laborious and time-consuming enterprise. To answer questions about the spheres, the researchers you've read about thus far were looking at reams of police records, sending teams of people out into the field to conduct interviews and, when they had to, even building new laboratories. In addition, the researchers generally had access to pretty large samples of participants. What would the researchers have done if they hadn't had so much time or money, or so many research participants? Presumably, they might have been forced to design more economical studies. It's pretty likely that such studies might have made use of within-subjects manipulations. It's also pretty likely that you, too, will someday have to design a pretty economical study. With this in mind, let's look at a final study that investigated the effects of the spheres (one of them at least) on a shoestring budget.

In this study, a group of students wanted to conduct an experiment on the effects of the spheres without having to build their own laboratory or run dozens and dozens of research participants. The students had located a relatively inconspicuous green sphere near a commonly used campus thoroughfare, and they decided to focus solely on the effects of the green sphere in their study. Knowing that they would have to take their study to the sphere, they decided to conduct an experiment in which they could present people with their stimuli using nothing more than a portable stereo (with headphones) and a clipboard. One of the students had long been interested in the psychology of humor, and she convinced the others to conduct a study of how the green sphere influences people's perceptions of the humorousness of jokes.[4]

To minimize the number of participants they would need to run, the students designed a study with a mixed-model design. They had one between-subjects variable (whether participants responded to some audiotaped jokes in close proximity to the green sphere—which the students covered with a backpack and a jacket—or whether they responded to the same jokes in an area devoid of any spheres). They also had one within-subject variable—whether the jokes their participants heard did or did not contain canned laughter (i.e., a dubbed-in laugh track). Because the students obviously couldn't expect people to respond to the same joke twice (with and without a laugh track), they pilot-tested a large group of jokes (on 14 of their friends) to identify two equally, and only moderately, funny jokes. The first joke was about a duck in a drugstore: A duck walks into a drugstore and asks for some ChapStick. When the cashier asks him if he'll be paying in cash, the duck says, "No, I was hoping you could just put it on my bill." The second joke was also an animal joke. Question: What do you get when you cross an elephant with a rhinoceros? Answer: Elephino. (It's pronounced "Ell-if-I-know.")

Because the students had been well trained in research methods, they prepared four different versions of their joke tapes. These four versions are summarized below:

Tape A: (1) duck joke without laugh track followed by (2) elephino joke with laugh track

Tape B: (1) duck joke with laugh track followed by (2) elephino joke without laugh track

Q: What's the difference between a duck? A: Eliphino.

Tape C: (1) elephino joke without laugh track followed by (2) duck joke with laugh track

Tape D: (1) elephino joke with laugh track followed by (2) duck joke without laugh track

In other words, the students counterbalanced both (1) the particular joke that came first, and (2) whether the laugh track was paired with the first or the second joke. In so doing, they unconfounded their within-subjects laugh track manipulation with (1) any potential differences in the humorousness of the two jokes, and (2) any effects of whether a joke came first or second. For reasons that should become clear below, the students predicted an interaction between the sphere manipulation and the laugh track manipulation. Here is how the students summarized their findings:

> Because our experiment had both a between-subjects and a within-subjects manipulation, we submitted the data to a 2 (green sphere: absent vs. present) × 2 (laugh track: absent vs. present) mixed-model analysis of variance (ANOVA). The ANOVA revealed main effects of both the sphere manipulation, $F(1, 23) = 18.97, p < .001$, and the laugh track manipulation, $F(1, 23) = 7.86, p = .011$. Both the presence of the sphere and the presence of the laugh track increased people's ratings of the humorousness of the jokes. The ANOVA also revealed the predicted Sphere × Laugh Track interaction, $F(1, 23) = 11.41, p < .001$. As suggested by the means in the left half of Table A3.4, when there was no laugh track, the sphere still intensified people's responses to the jokes, $F(1, 23) = 4.35$, $p = .048$. However, as suggested by the means in the right half of the table, the effect of the sphere was noticeably greater when the jokes were accompanied by a laugh track, $F(1, 23) = 27.67, p < .001$. It appears that the green sphere not only magnified people's responses to the jokes themselves but also magnified people's responses to the laugh track manipulation.

Notice that very little is special about how to discuss the results of a mixed-model ANOVA. The students duly mentioned that they had conducted a mixed-model ANOVA to analyze their data, but except for this fact, the students could just as easily have been describing the results of a completely between-subjects factorial. The same thing would be true if the students had somehow been able to conduct a 2 × 2 completely within-subjects design (in which every participant served in every condition of the study). The only exception to this rule is that when you are reporting the results of studies that have within-subjects manipulations, you will sometimes want to report

Table A3.4 Judged humorousness of jokes as a function of the presence of green spheres and laugh tracks

	Laugh Track	
Green Sphere	Absent	Present
Absent	5.25	5.84
Present	6.80	8.92

Note: Means reflect the rated humorousness of the jokes (theoretical range = 1–10). There were 12 participants in each of the two sphere conditions.

any effects of your counterbalancing procedures (i.e., you may want to report whether you observed any order effects). Of course, if there were any order effects, you took care of them by balancing them out across your within-subjects conditions. Thus, most readers don't really care that much about seeing this kind of discussion. On the other hand, if order effects would be interesting in their own right, or if you observe an interaction between order and an experimental manipulation, you should always report such effects.

Because the hypothetical studies discussed here span the range from archival to experimental studies, you may be wondering if we have spanned the entire range of statistical tests that researchers might need to report. We haven't. Although the tests reviewed here are some of the most commonly conducted statistical tests, there are literally hundreds of statistical tests. However, a good portion of these other tests will bear at least a passing resemblance to the tests reported here. For example, if you had measured a lot of separate dependent measures that weren't organized along any kind of continuum (i.e., that didn't really represent levels of a within-subjects manipulation), you might want to conduct a MANOVA (a multivariate analysis of variance) on your data. However, the basic approach you adopted to describe the results of your MANOVA would be very similar to the approach adopted here. Of course, your writing style is probably very different from either of ours, and thus even if your analysis was exactly like one of those we have reported here, you would never say things *exactly* the way we have said them. (In fact, if you did, we would be forced to report you for plagiarism.) Regardless of your writing style, however, if you were writing about your results *well*, you would do three important things: you would focus primarily on the meaning of your findings, you would organize these findings in a coherent way, and you would document all of your findings by mentioning the statistical tests that made them scientifically meaningful. That, in a nutshell, is how to write about results.

NOTES

1. To compromise between simplicity and the real differences you'd see in the sizes of different real cities, we computed the statistics in this hypothetical example based on populations of 2 million and 1 million, respectively, for the green and yellow cities. Given that we started out with 93 total murders to split between the two cities, and given that the green city was twice as big as the yellow city, our expected frequency for murders in the green city had to be twice the expected frequency of murders in the yellow city. This works out to exactly 62 and 31 murders, respectively. Although it now requires more calculations, the χ^2 formula used to compute this statistic was exactly the same one you saw in Chapter 10.

2. Because participants in this study responded to two different kinds of questions that were measured on the same scale, the researchers could also have conducted a 2 × 2 mixed-model ANOVA in which the between-subjects variable was the color of the sphere and the within-subjects variable was the measure of apathy versus the measure of energy.

3. Except for the part about the spheres, this fictional study is loosely inspired by a project on newlywed marriage conducted by Bradbury and colleagues (see Davila, Bradbury, Cohan, & Tochluk, 1997; Karney & Bradbury, 1997).

4. The student also happened to be familiar with the research of James Olson. The study described here is partly inspired by Olson's (1992) experiment on the effects of laugh tracks on people's perceptions of humor.

XXX-Box: The Effect of Sexualized Video Games on Players' Rape Supportive Responses

S. Paul Stermer
Oklahoma State University

Melissa Burkley
Oklahoma State University

XXX-Box: The Effect of Sexualized Video Games
on Players' Rape Supportive Responses
S. Paul Stermer and Melissa Burkley
Oklahoma State University

Author Note

S. Paul Stermer, Department of Psychology, Oklahoma State University; Melissa Burkley, Department of Psychology, Oklahoma State University.

Correspondence concerning this article should be addressed to S. Paul Stermer, Department of Psychology, Oklahoma State University, Stillwater, OK, 74078. Contact: paul.stermer@okstate.edu

Abstract

The present investigation examined the consequences of playing violent video games containing sexualized depictions of women. In this study, video game content was manipulated to determine the causal relationship between playing violent sexualized video games and rape supportive responses. Results showed that men who played the sexualized video game judged a rape victim more negatively than men who played the non-sexualized video game. This effect was especially pronounced among men who did not regularly play video games and therefore were more sensitive to the video game manipulation. This work suggests that playing sexualized video games encourages men to trivialize and justify sexual violence against women.

Keywords: video games, sexualized media, rape, gender differences

XXX-Box: The Effect of Sexualized Video Games
on Players' Rape Supportive Responses

Much debate has occurred surrounding the potential negative consequences of playing video games. The majority of research on this topic
has focused on video games' propensity for violence, demonstrating
a causal link between playing violent video games and aggressive
responses (see Anderson et al., 2010, for review). Violence, however, is
not the only potentially harmful aspect of modern video games—these
games also depict women in overly sexualized ways.

Content analyses indicate that video games consistently portray women
as scantily clothed, large-breasted sex objects that are treated as rewards for
male characters (Burgess, Stermer & Burgess, 2007; Dietz, 1998; Dill &
Thill, 2007). However, the question that remains is what impact this sexualized content has on players' behavior. Such sexualized content may produce a number of negative outcomes but a major concern is that when this
sexualized imagery is combined with the violence prevalent in video games,
it may encourage and perpetuate aggression towards women. The present
investigation sought to fill this void in the literature by examining if violent
sexualized video games promote beliefs that trivialize and justify rape.

Video games contain the most blatantly sexualized depictions of women
to be found in popular mass media today (Dill & Thill, 2007). It is therefore
surprising that only a few empirical studies have been conducted on this
potentially harmful aspect of video games (Yao, Mahood & Linz, 2010).
However, a number of studies have examined the impact of sexualized
female imagery in more traditional forms of media. Much of this work

explored how sexualized media (e.g., R-rated movies, pornography) impacts men's reactions to and propensity towards sexual violence. For instance, in a classic study by Donnerstein and Berkowitz (1981), men viewed neutral, erotic, or violent-erotic films and were later placed in a Milgram-type situation where they were given the opportunity to deliver painful shocks to a male or female confederate. Results showed that men who watched the violent-erotic film delivered twice the intensity of shocks to their female partner, compared to the other film conditions. Thus, it is clear that viewing sexualized media depicting real women can increase men's rape supportive responses. However, what is not known is if such effects extend to video games, where the sexualized imagery involves *virtual* women.

The purpose of the present investigation was to examine if playing video games that contain sexualized female imagery impacts players' rape reactions. We used an experimental design to assess the impact of short-term violent and sexualized video game (VSVG) exposure on rape supportive responses. We expected VSVG to be associated with greater rape supportive responses. We also expected that this effect of VSVG would be most evident among participants who rarely play video games. This is because people who frequently play video games have had greater exposure to such content overtime and therefore have become desensitized to the effects of an acute experimental manipulation (Bartholow, Bushman & Sestir, 2006). In sum, we predicted that men who played a game with sexualized content would demonstrate greater rape supportive responses than men who played the same game with non-sexualized content, and that this difference would be most evident among men who rarely play video games.

Method

Participants

Forty-nine men from a large Midwestern university participated for course credit (mean age was 19).

Materials and Procedure

Participants were told they were participating in two unrelated studies that were investigating memory for video game content and impression formation. All participants first played a fighting scene from the video game *Dead or Alive 4* on an *X-Box 360* for 10 minutes.

Video game characters. Participants were randomly assigned to play the video game with sexualized or non-sexualized female characters. The sexualized female characters wore provocative, revealing clothing and were portrayed in a way that emphasized their body (e.g., bikini top, fishnet stockings). The non-sexualized female characters were fully clothed (e.g., long sleeve shirts, jeans). Next, participants reported how many hours per week on average they played video games. They were then guided to another room for the second portion of the study where they were greeted by a new experimenter.

Rape supportive responses. Next, participants read a vignette describing an acquaintance rape scenario and were asked to rate the appropriateness of the rape victim's behavior (Abrams, Viki, Masser, & Bohner, 2003). Participants rated the rape victim's behavior on five semantic differential items: *Unladylike vs. ladylike, impure vs. pure, undignified vs. dignified, indecent vs. decent,* and *improper vs. proper.* Responses were made on a 1 to 7 rating scale, with each pair of adjectives serving as end points. These

SEXUALIZED VIDEO GAMES   6

ratings were averaged to create a composite score ($\alpha = .90$), with lower values indicating a more negative evaluation of the rape victim's behavior.

Results

Means and standard deviations for all variables can be seen in Table 1. In line with our hypothesis, men who played the sexualized game evaluated the rape victim's behavior as less appropriate ($M = 3.53, SD = .88$) than men who played the non-sexualized game ($M = 4.05, SD = 1.03$), although this effect was only marginally significant, $B = -.51, t(45) = -1.86, p = .06, d = .54$.

However, as predicted, this main effect was qualified by a significant Condition $\times$ Hours per week spent playing video games interaction, $B = .11, t(45) = 2.15, p = .04, d = .64$. To reveal this pattern of data, we examined the effect of video game condition on rape reactions at 1 SD above (10 hours weekly) versus 1 SD below (0 hours weekly) the mean of average hours a week spent playing video games ($M = 4.66, SD = 5.13$; Aiken & West, 1991). This analysis revealed that video game condition had little impact on rape responses for men who often played video games, $t(45) = .21, p = .84, d = .45$, but significantly impacted rape responses for men who rarely played video games, $t(45) = -2.88, p = .006, d = .86$ (Figure 1). That is, when men who rarely played video games played the sexualized game, they evaluated the rape victim's behavior as less appropriate, or more deserving, than men who played the non-sexualized game.

Discussion

The present study demonstrated a relationship between sexualized video games and rape supportive responses. Men who played a VSVG evaluated a rape victim more harshly than men who played a non-sexualized game, and

SEXUALIZED VIDEO GAMES   7

this was especially the case when the men rarely played video games. These results are important because they are the first to demonstrate a causal relationship between sexualized video games and rape supportive responses.

This research also provides an important contribution to the video game literature more generally. Video game researchers have focused on certain video game qualities, such as level of violence (Anderson & Bushman, 2001) and amount of blood (Barlett, Harris & Bruey, 2008), but have largely neglected the type of character played. The present work shows that even when all other qualities of the game are held constant, the type of character played can have a substantive impact on psychological responses.

One limitation of the present study is that we only examined men's responses. Future research should determine if similar effects are found among female video game players. Another limitation was that we held constant the level of violence in this study, such that all participants played a fighting video game. Future research could examine if the level of violent content moderates the impact of sexualized content by incorporating a sexualized non-violent game (e.g., bikini volleyball game).

Overall, these results advance current theories of sexualized media by extending these concepts into the realm of video games. The present study demonstrated that even sexualized *virtual* images of women can lead individuals to adopt beliefs that trivialize or justify rape. To our knowledge, our study provides the first empirical demonstration that these effects can be extended to the realm of virtual imagery. Such an extension is greatly needed, given the increasing popularity of computer-generated characters in video games, film, and television.

SEXUALIZED VIDEO GAMES   8

References

Abrams, D., Viki, G. T., Masser, B., & Bohner, G. (2003). Perceptions of stranger and acquaintance rape: The role of benevolent and hostile sexism in victim blame and rape proclivity. *Journal of Personality and Social Psychology, 84,* 111–125. doi:10.1037/0022-3514.84.1.111

Aiken, L. S. & West, S. G. (1991). *Multiple regression: Testing and interpreting interactions.* London: Sage Publications.

Anderson, C. A., & Bushman, B. J. (2001). Effects of violent video games on aggressive behavior, aggressive cognition, aggressive affect, physiological arousal, and prosocial behavior: A meta-analytic review of the scientific literature. *Psychological Science, 12,* 353–359. doi:10.1111/1467-9280.00366

Anderson, C. A., Shibuya, A., Ihori, N., Swing, E. L., Bushman, B. J., Sakamoto, A., Rothstein, H. R., & Saleem, M. (2010). Violent video game effects on aggression, empathy, and prosocial behavior in Eastern and Western countries: A meta-analytic review. *Psychological Bulletin, 136,* 151–173. doi:10.1037/a0018251

Barlett, C. P., Harris, R. J., & Bruey, C. (2008). The effect of the amount of blood in a violent video game on aggression, hostility, and arousal. *Journal of Experimental Social Psychology, 44,* 539–546. doi:10.1016/j.jesp.2007.10.003

Bartholow, B. D., Bushman, B. J., & Sestir, M. A. (2006). Chronic violent video game exposure and desensitization to violence: Behavioral and event-related brain potential data. *Journal of Experimental Social Psychology, 42,* 532–539. doi:10.1016/j.jesp.2005.08.006

SEXUALIZED VIDEO GAMES 9

Burgess, M. C. R., Stermer, S. P., & Burgess, S. R. (2007). Sex, lies, and video games: The portrayal of male and female characters on video game covers. *Sex Roles, 57*, 419–433. doi:10.1007/s11199-007-9250-0

Dietz, T. L. (1998). An examination of violence and gender role portrayals in video games: Implications for gender socialization and aggressive behavior. *Sex Roles, 38*, 425–442. doi:10.1023/A:1018709905920

Dill, K. E., & Thill, K. P. (2007). Video game characters and the socialization of gender roles: Young people's perceptions mirror sexist media depictions. *Sex Roles, 57*, 851–864. doi:10.1007/s11199-007-9278-1

Donnerstein, E., & Berkowitz, L. (1981). Victim reactions in aggressive erotic films as a factor in violence against women. *Journal of Personality and Social Psychology, 41*, 710–724. doi:10.1037/0022-3514.41.4.710

Murphy, S. (2007). A social meaning framework for research on participation in social on-line games. *Journal of Media Psychology, 12*, Retrieved from: http://www.calstatela.edu/faculty/sfischo/A_Social_Meaning_Framework_for_Online_Games.html

Yao, M. Z., Mahood, C., Linz, D., (2010). Sexual priming, gender stereotyping, and likelihood to sexually harass: Examining the cognitive effects of playing a sexually explicit video game, *Sex Roles, 62*, 77–88. doi:10.1007/s11199-009-9695-4

SEXUALIZED VIDEO GAMES   10

Footnotes

[1]This paper has no footnotes, but your own papers may. Thus, we inserted this otherwise useless footnote to show you that the Footnotes page comes after the References and before any Tables.

[2]This second note is even more meaningless than the first, but if you had two real notes you'd want to number them as we have done here.

[3]OK, that's enough. Comedy may come in threes, but so does annoyance. Don't you agree that Brett is really annoying?

[4]I know you are, Hart, but what am I?

SEXUALIZED VIDEO GAMES 12

Table 1 Mean and Standard Deviations (N = 49)

Variables	M	SD
Age	18.96	3.26
Hours per week playing video games	4.66	5.13
Ladylike	3.55	1.24
Pure	3.57	1.12
Dignified	3.84	1.01
Decent	4.20	1.22
Proper	3.76	1.22
Averaged Appropriateness	3.78	0.98

Note. Means and standard deviations for the five semantic differential items (unladylike vs. ladylike, impure vs. pure, undignified vs. dignified, indecent vs. decent, and improper vs. proper) were made on a 1 to 7 rating scale, with high scores indicating stronger endorsement. Averaged appropriateness is computed as the average of the five semantic differentials, with higher scores indicating less negative (more positive) evaluation of the rape victims' behavior.

SEXUALIZED VIDEO GAMES   13

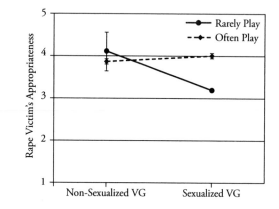

Figure 1

Ratings of rape victim's appropriateness as a function of type of video game and frequency of video game play. Rarely play video games = 0 (1 *SD* below mean); Often play video games = 1 (1 *SD* above mean).

Glossary

absolute scales: Rating scales that use readily observable physical referents as opposed to scales that use psychological referents that are based on subjective experiences. As examples, absolute scales might ask respondents to rate how many cigarettes they smoke each day, how tall they are, and how many hours they sleep each night as opposed to asking people to rate whether they feel healthy, tall, or well rested.

accounting for conflicting results: Attempting to come up with theoretical reasons why different studies on the same topic have yielded different findings. McGuire noted that this is a good way to generate research hypotheses.

accounting for exceptions: Attempting to generate exceptions or limiting conditions to well-established psychological principles or empirical findings. McGuire noted that this is a good way to generate research hypotheses.

alpha level: The probability value that serves as the standard for rejecting the null hypothesis in a statistical test. Alpha is most commonly set at .05, meaning that researchers typically conclude that their findings are "real" only if findings as extreme as or more extreme than theirs would have occurred fewer than five times in 100 based on chance.

alternative hypothesis: The statistical assumption that there is a relation between the independent and dependent variables of interest in an investigation (i.e., the assumption that the researcher's prediction is true).

analyzing the practitioner's rule of thumb: Analyzing things that experts in a specific area do to achieve certain outcomes. McGuire noted that such an analysis might serve as a means of generating research hypotheses.

anchor: A verbal label included in a ratings scale to lend meaning to numeric ratings. For example, the unipolar version of the **EGWA** scale typically centers the anchors "not at all," "slightly," "quite a bit," and "extremely" under the numbers 0, 2, 4, and 6.

animism: The belief that natural phenomena are alive and influence behavior. This is the earliest category of metaphysical explanations for human behavior. See also **astrology** and **mythology and religion**.

applying a functional or adaptive analysis: Analyzing what an organism has to do to successfully master an environment or achieve a desired end state.

McGuire noted that this is a good way to generate research hypotheses.

archival research: Research in which investigators examine naturally existing public records to test a theory or hypothesis.

artifact: A variable that is held constant in a study but which influences the relation between the independent (or predictor) variable and the dependent variable. Consider a drug study that includes only male participants. If the drug being studied works for men but not for women, gender would be an artifact. This is a threat to **external validity**. Contrast with **confound** and **noise**.

astrology: The belief that human behavior and personality are influenced by the positions of celestial bodies such as planets and stars. This is one of the three categories of metaphysical explanations for human behavior. See also **animism** and **mythology and religion**.

attrition: See **experimental mortality**.

authority: Expertise or status in a specific area. People often rely on the opinions of authorities or experts as a way of answering questions. Relying on authority is one of the four ways of knowing emphasized in this text.

behavioral confirmation: The tendency for social perceivers to elicit behaviors from a person that are consistent with the perceivers' initial expectations about the person (e.g., expecting a person to be aggressive and being more aggressive than usual with the person, which leads the person to behave in a very aggressive fashion toward you).

between-subjects design: An experimental design in which each participant serves in one and only one condition of the experiment. See also **within-subjects design**.

bidirectionality problem (reverse causality): An interpretive problem that occurs in most forms of passive observational research (e.g., in cross-sectional survey research). When an investigator documents that two variables are related, it is not usually possible to tell which variable is the cause of the other.

bimodal distribution: A distribution of scores in which two distinct ranges of scores are more common than any other scores.

binomial effect-size display: A simple, intuitive way to illustrate the strength of the relation between two dichotomous variables. It involves categorizing participants in terms of their scores on each of the two dichotomous variables and entering the frequencies of these categorizations in a contingency table whose rows and columns sum to 100. See Table 10.2 (page 290).

bipolar scales: Scales that assess a psychological dimension that is anchored at the low and high ends by two opposing concepts (e.g., "disagree" and "agree" or "negative" and "positive") and for which there is a meaningful midpoint (e.g., "neither agree nor disagree" or "neutral"). Bipolar scales typically use numbering systems that range from negative to positive, with the value of zero placed at the midpoint. Contrast with **unipolar** scales.

canon: A fundamental assumption that is accepted on faith. The four canons of science are **determinism, empiricism, parsimony,** and **testability**.

carryover effects: A methodological problem that occurs in within-subjects designs. This occurs when participants' responses in one condition of a study influence their responses in a subsequent condition. See also **order effects, counterbalancing**.

case study: A systematic analysis of the experiences of a particular person or group of people. In addition to serving as studies in their own right, case studies often serve as sources of inspiration for more traditional scientific investigations such as experiments.

categorical scale: See **nominal scale**.

ceiling effect: A methodological problem that occurs when everyone or almost everyone in a sample responds at the same high level on a survey question or dependent measure. A specific example of the problem of **restriction of range**.

census: An exhaustive survey of an entire population of people. Censuses are typically conducted to gather basic demographic information about people and to provide a total head count in a population. The U.S. government conducts a national census every ten years.

central tendency: A statistical term for the average or most representative score in a set of observations.

cluster sampling: A variation on true random sampling in survey research. Researchers who use this technique identify large, usually natural, groups of people (e.g., specific schools, specific cities, people living in specific zip codes) and first randomly sample a limited number of groups (e.g., 30 zip codes from the entire United States) before sampling individual people randomly from each of these groups.

coefficient of determination: The percentage of variance in one variable that is accounted for by a person's score on another variable. This is $r2$, the square of the correlation coefficient describing the relation between the two variables.

complete counterbalancing: A comprehensive form of counterbalancing in which the researcher presents every possible order of the different experimental conditions in a within-subjects experiment.

conceptual validity: One of the four basic forms of validity emphasized in this text. Conceptual validity refers to the degree to which the specific hypotheses that are being tested speak to the validity of the theory that is being studied.

conciseness (in writing): Brevity, efficiency.

confederate: A trained research assistant who pretends to be a research participant by acting out a specific part during an experiment. This is usually done to create a psychological state in the real participant(s) that would otherwise be difficult to achieve.

confound: A design problem in which some additional variable (or nuisance variable) exists that (a) may influence the dependent variable and that (b) varies systematically along with the independent or predictor variable(s). This is a threat to **internal validity**. Contrast with **artifact** and **noise**.

conspecifics: A word that is unfamiliar to most English speakers. It is used in Chapter 4 to illustrate how the meaning of a question can be obscured when unfamiliar words are used. If you want to know what conspecific means, you will need to look it up in a dictionary. The fact that you need to look it up in the dictionary should make it clear why it is not a good idea to use unfamiliar words in questions.

construct validity: The degree to which the independent and dependent variables in a study truly represent the abstract, hypothetical variables (i.e., the constructs) in which the researcher is interested.

contamination effects: A methodological problem that occurs in experiments utilizing within-subjects designs. This occurs when participants' experiences in an earlier condition of the experiment influence their responses in a later condition of the experiment (e.g., because of learning, interference, or insight). This problem can sometimes, but not always, be corrected by the use of counterbalancing.

control group: A group that is used as a standard of comparison for assessing the effects of an experimental manipulation or psychological treatment.

convenience sample: A sample of research participants who are selected into a study because they are readily available to a researcher rather than because they are highly representative of a population.

correlational method: An approach to research in which researchers gather a set of observations about a group of people and test for associations (i.e., correlations) between different variables. Questionnaires, interviews, and archival studies are good examples of correlational studies.

counterbalancing: A method of control in within-subjects studies whereby the researcher varies the order in which participants experience the different experimental conditions (by presenting the conditions in different orders to different participants).

covariation: The principle of correlation, that is, the co-occurrence of or association between two events (e.g., when it is cloudy, it usually rains). According to John Stuart Mill, covariation is the first of three requirements that must be met to establish that one thing (such as clouds) causes something else (such as rain). See also **temporal sequence** and **elimination of confounds**.

cover story: A false story about the nature and purpose of a study. Researchers use a cover story to divert participants' attention from the true purpose of the study when they are concerned about participant reaction bias (i.e., when they believe that participants would not behave naturally if they knew the true purpose of the study). Most forms of deception in research are part of a cover story.

criterion: The outcome variable in a multiple regression analysis (the regression equivalent of the dependent variable in an experimental design).

crossover interaction (disordinal interaction): A specific kind of statistical interaction. This describes the situation in which (1) there are no main effects of either independent variable and (2) the effects of each independent variable are opposite at different levels of the other independent variable.

data: Numerical or categorical facts about specific people or things, especially when such people or things are the objects of systematic investigation.

debriefing: The ethical principle of educating participants about the nature and design of an investigation to be sure that when they leave the study, their frame of mind is at least as favorable as when they arrived. When deception is used in a study, debriefing at the conclusion of the study includes informing , participants about the nature of and reasons for the deception.

deduction: Reasoning from the general to the specific (e.g., drawing a conclusion about human memory by logically deriving it from a set of higher-order principles about human cognition). See also **induction**.

demand characteristics: Aspects of an experiment that subtly suggest how participants are expected to behave. Demand characteristics often contribute to the problem of **participant expectancies**.

dependent variable: The variable in an experiment that is measured by an experimenter. The experimenter expects the dependent variable to be influenced by the independent variable.

descriptive statistics: Statistics used to summarize or describe a set of observations.

determinism: The idea that the universe is orderly—that all events have meaningful, systematic causes. It

is one of the four canons of science emphasized in this text.

disordinal interaction: See **crossover interaction**.

dispersion (variability): A statistical term for the degree to which the typical score in a set of scores deviates from the mean or most representative score. As measures of dispersion increase, the mean becomes progressively less representative of the entire set of scores. The range and standard deviation are common measures of dispersion.

double-barreled question: A question, especially a survey question or dependent measure, that contains two different assertions (e.g., "I like going to movies and eating popcorn."). Such questions are problematic because participants who agree with one assertion and disagree with the other do not know how to respond.

double-blind procedure: A method of controlling for both participant expectancies and experimenter bias by keeping both research participants and experimenters unaware of participants' treatment conditions during an experiment.

effect size: An indicator of the strength of the relation between two or more variables. Two common indicators of effect size are r and d.

EGWA: Empirically grounded, well-anchored scale. Using EGWA scales is likely to increase the reliability and validity of self-report measurements of a wide range of psychological constructs.

elimination of confounds: Ruling out other plausible causes of an event before concluding that one thing (e.g., touching poison ivy) is the cause of another (e.g., developing a rash). This is the third of John Stuart Mill's requirements for establishing causality. See also **covariation** and **temporal sequence**.

empiricism: An approach to understanding the world that involves collecting data or making observations. It is one of the four canons of science emphasized in this text.

environmental confound: A confound that occurs in nonexperimental research when a measured variable (e.g., depression) seems to cause something because people who are high or low on this variable also happen to be high or low on some contextual or situational variable (e.g., the recent loss of a loved one) that is associated with the outcome variable of interest (e.g., physical illness).

epidemiological research (in clinical psychology): Descriptive studies that focus primarily on the prevalence of different psychological disorders within different populations.

epidemiology (general definition): The scientific study of the causes of disease.

equal appearing intervals: A scale has equal appearing intervals whenever the psychological distance implied by a single-unit difference on the rating scale remains constant across the entire range of the scale. When rating self-esteem with a scale that ranges from 1 to 7, the difference in self-esteem implied by a rating of 2 versus 5 would be the same as the difference implied by a rating of 4 versus 7.

equifinality: The notion that the same behavior is often produced by many different causes.

evaluation apprehension: The form of participant reaction bias that occurs when participants attempt to behave in whatever way they think will portray them most favorably. Evaluation apprehension is a threat to internal validity.

expected value(s): The most likely outcome (or the entire distribution of all possible outcomes) in a probabilistic situation that is repeated a great number of times under ideal conditions. For example, the expected value of an 80 percent chance of winning $100 is $80 because if you take this gamble a great number of times, the average amount of money you will gain will be $80 per trial of the gamble.

experiment: A research design in which the investigator manipulates one or more variables and then assesses the impact of this manipulation. An experiment isolates the effect of a variable by holding all other variables constant while this variable is manipulated.

experimental method: The method by which levels of one or more independent variables are systematically manipulated or measured in order to gauge their effects on one or more dependent variables.

experimental mortality (attrition): The failure of some research participants to complete an investigation. In an experiment or quasi-experiment this may include **homogeneous attrition** (when attrition rates are equal across experimental conditions) and **heterogeneous attrition** (when attrition rates are different across experimental conditions). Heterogeneous attrition is primarily a threat to internal validity, and homogenous attrition is primarily a threat to external validity.

experimental paradigm: The approach to research (popularized by R. A. Fisher) in which the researcher randomly assigns participants to different treatment conditions, measures some outcome of interest, and makes use of inferential statistical tests to draw conclusions about the effects of the manipulation(s).

experimental psychology: A branch of psychology that emphasizes the systematic manipulation of variables as a means of learning about human experience and behavior. See **experimental paradigm**.

experimental realism: The degree to which the subjective experiences of research participants are realistic or psychologically meaningful. Well-designed experiments can be high in experimental realism even when they bear little physical resemblance to the real world (e.g., participants can be made fearful or anxious by being convinced that they are about to receive electric shocks to their big toes). See also **mundane realism**.

experimental simulation: An experiment in which participants are randomly assigned to treatment conditions but are asked to play a specific role or act out a part rather than engaging in wholly natural behavior.

experimenter bias: The bias that occurs in research when the investigator's expectations about participants lead to false support for these expectations. One form of experimenter bias occurs when experimenters interpret ambiguous behaviors in ways that are consistent with their expectations. A second form occurs when experimenters actually treat participants differently in different experimental conditions and thus influence participants' real behavior in hypothesis-consistent ways.

external validity: The degree to which a research finding provides an accurate description of what typically happens in the real world. The degree to which the observed relation between an independent and a dependent variable in a specific study applies to people, times, and settings not examined in the study of interest.

extreme groups approach: An approach to selecting people for inclusion in a laboratory study. In the case of this approach, experimenters recruit people to take part in a study only if such people receive extreme (i.e., very high or very low) scores on an individual difference measure of interest. See **prescreening** and **median split**.

factor analysis: A statistical procedure for determining if all of the items on a psychological measure assess the same psychological construct or if different items are influenced by different psychological constructs.

factorial design: A research design containing two or more independent variables that are completely crossed, meaning that every level of every independent variable appears in combination with every level of every other independent variable.

false consensus effect: The tendency to overestimate the proportion of other people whose attitudes and behaviors are similar to one's own.

falsifiability: Openness to disconfirmation. This is closely related to the scientific canon of **testability** and may refer either to a philosophy of science or to a property of a specific theory or hypothesis.

falsification: An approach to scientific hypothesis testing in which a researcher attempts to gather evidence that would invalidate or disprove a specific hypothesis. This is one of the three common approaches to scientific hypothesis testing emphasized in this text.

floor effect: A methodological problem that occurs when everyone or almost everyone in a sample responds at the same low level on a survey question or dependent measure. A specific example of the problem of **restriction of range**.

focus group: A group selected from a population of interest that is used to better understand that population. Information is typically gathered in focus groups using semi-structured interviews. This format allows group members to discuss topics that are of interest to the researcher using their own words. Focus groups are often used in **pilot testing** to help researchers design better questionnaires.

freedom from coercion: The ethical principle of respecting participants' rights to drop out of a study if they choose to do so. This mainly consists of making it clear to participants that they have the right to stop participating without any fear of negative consequences.

Hawthorne effect: The increases in productivity that may occur when workers believe that their behavior is being studied or believe that they are receiving special treatment. Because participants who are receiving an experimental treatment are more likely to believe these things than are participants in a control condition, Hawthorne effects may be mistaken for treatment effects and thus are a threat to internal validity.

heterogeneous attrition: See **experimental mortality**.

history: Changes that occur over time in a very large group of people such as those living in a city, state, nation, or culture. When an investigator conducts a pretest-posttest study in which all participants receive a treatment, changes due to history may masquerade as treatment effects. Thus, history represents a threat to internal validity. See also **maturation**.

homogeneous attrition: See **experimental mortality**.

hourglass approach: A symmetrical approach to writing an empirical research paper in which the writer opens the Introduction broadly, becomes increasingly more focused throughout the Introduction, remains highly focused and detailed in the Method and Results sections, and then becomes increasingly broader in the Discussion or General Discussion section.

hypothesis: A prediction about a specific event or events. Hypotheses are usually derived from one or more theories.

hypothetico-deductive method: Beginning with a working set of assumptions and deriving one or more logical conclusions from these basic assumptions. McGuire noted that this is a good way to generate research hypotheses.

illusory correlation: The false association that people often form between membership in a statistical minority group and rare (and typically negative) behaviors.

incomplete counterbalancing: Any method of counterbalancing in which the researcher using a within-subjects manipulation does not present every possible order of the within-subjects variable(s) across participants (an example is reverse counterbalancing).

independent variable: The variable in an experiment that is manipulated by an experimenter. The experimenter expects the independent variable or variables to influence the dependent variable.

induction: Reasoning from the specific to the general (e.g., drawing a conclusion about human memory by noticing that a certain pattern of findings shows up in many different studies of memory). See also **deduction, problem of induction**.

inferential statistics: Statistics used to make inferences, that is, to interpret or draw general conclusions about a set of observations.

informed consent: The ethical principle of advising participants about any foreseeable risks that are posed by a specific study and getting participants' permission to take part in the research prior to the beginning of the study.

interaction: A statistical term indicating that the effect of an independent variable on the dependent variable is different at different levels of another independent variable. The presence of an interaction means that one cannot make a simple, blanket statement about the independent and dependent variables in a factorial study. See also **main effect**.

interference effect: A problem that occurs in within-subjects designs when people's experience in one within-subject condition disrupts or diminishes their performance in a later within-subject condition. Interference effects are roughly the opposite of **practice effects**.

internal analysis: A specific form of patching in quasi-experiments in which a researcher breaks a group of participants into one or more subgroups to test for subgroup differences that are consistent with the focal theory or with competing theories. As an example, a researcher interested in whether the trauma of being exposed to a tornado leads to anxiety disorders might identify participants who were and who were not physically injured during a tornado to see if those who were injured showed a greater subsequent increase in their level of anxiety disorders.

internal consistency: The degree to which the total set of items or observations in a multiple-item measure behave in the same way. For example, the degree to which each item in a ten-item self-esteem inventory rank orders participants in the same manner.

internal review board (IRB): A committee that is charged with protecting human rights and ensuring that all research studies are conducted in a manner consistent with community, professional, and legal standards. The American Psychological Association only accredits colleges and universities if they have an IRB in place to evaluate all studies using human subjects.

internal validity: The degree to which a research finding provides accurate or compelling information about causality. The degree to which changes in the independent variable in a particular study really do influence the dependent variable in the way suggested by the results of the study.

interobserver agreement (interrater reliability): The degree to which different judges independently agree upon a measurement, judgment, or observation. This is one of the three kinds of reliability emphasized in this text.

interrater reliability: See **interobserver agreement.**

interval scale: A measurement scale that uses real numbers designating amounts to reflect relative differences in magnitude. Interval values can be negative, and adjacent scores on different parts of interval scales (e.g., 10 versus 11, 25 versus 26) are typically, but not always, separated by equal amounts. Temperature, SAT scores, self-esteem scores, and most psychological scales are examples of interval scales. See also **nominal, ordinal, and ratio scales.**

intuition: An implicit understanding of a phenomenon that a person develops in the absence of any formal training on the topic. Loosely speaking, common sense or folk wisdom. It is one of the four ways of knowing emphasized in this text.

judgment and decision making: A kind of scientifically rigorous single-variable research in which participants' judgments or decisions on a specific topic are compared with the judgments or decisions that would be made by a purely rational decision maker.

judgment phase: The cognitive stage at which participants in studies interpret the meaning of questions that are asked of them.

Latin square: A form of partial counterbalancing in a within-subjects experiment in which each condition appears with equal frequency in every possible ordinal position (e.g., 1st, 2nd, 3rd, etc.). For example, an ideal Latin square for a within-subjects experiment with four conditions can be represented (1) A B C D, (2) B A D C, (3) C D A B, and (4) D C B A.

law: A precise, coherent, well-developed account of the relation between two or more variables. A universal statement that allows reliable predictions of future events.

leading questions: Questions that are worded in ways suggesting that some kinds of answers are more appropriate than others (e.g., "What do you like most about this wonderful textbook?").

logic: The formal rules of correct and incorrect reasoning. The use of logic is one of the four ways of knowing emphasized in this text.

logical positivism: The idea that science and philosophy should be based solely on things that can be observed with absolute certainty. Many logical positivists (e.g., Karl Popper) also emphasize falsification as an approach to scientific discovery. See **falsification.**

longitudinal design: A nonexperimental research design (often involving questionnaire, interview, and/or observational techniques) in which researchers track participants' response over time (e.g., to track changes in children's social development or adults' personalities).

main effect: A statistical term indicating that, on the average (i.e., collapsing across all levels of all other independent variables), an independent variable in a factorial design had a significant effect on the dependent variable. Main effects can be taken at face value only when there are no interactions between the independent variables in a factorial study. See also **interaction.**

manipulation: Systematically varying the level of an independent variable in an experiment, with the goal of seeing whether doing so has any effect on the measured level of a dependent variable. Manipulation and **random assignment** are the two defining ingredients of the experimental method.

manipulation check: A measure taken to see if participants in different experimental conditions truly experienced the different levels of the independent variable that the researcher hoped to manipulate.

marketing research: Research designed to assess consumers' attitudes about and preferences for different kinds of products and services. This kind of scientifically rigorous, single-variable research is very similar to public opinion polls.

matching: A method of assigning participants to experimental conditions. Researchers who use matching try to identify similar individuals in order to place them in different conditions. This is done to gain some degree of comparability between experimental conditions (i.e., to minimize the chance of a **person confound**). This strategy is inferior to **random assignment.**

maturation: Changes that occur over time in a specific person or group of people due to normal development or experience (e.g., growth, learning). When an investigator conducts a pretest-posttest study in which all participants receive a treatment, changes due to maturation may masquerade as treatment effects. Thus, maturation represents a threat to internal validity. See also **history.**

median split: An approach to selecting people for inclusion in a laboratory study. In the case of this approach, experimenters recruit people who score in either the top half or the bottom half (i.e., people above or below the median) on an individual difference measure of interest. This approach is usually inferior to the extreme groups approach. See **prescreening** and **extreme groups approach.**

meta-analysis: A set of statistical techniques for summarizing findings from a large set of studies to (1) determine the total amount of existing support for an effect, (2) assess the consistency or repeatability of the effect, and (3) identify determinants of the strength or magnitude of the effect across different studies.

metaphysical systems: An early set of explanations for human behavior and the operation of the physical world. Metaphysical explanations attribute behavior or experience to the operation of nonphysical forces such as deities. Metaphysical explanations include (1) **animism,** (2) **mythology and religion,** and (3) **astrology.**

method of deduction: A method of theory testing in which a specific hypothesis is derived from a broader theory and then tested empirically. This is contrasted with the method of induction because researchers first begin with a theory and then make observations. Logically, this method can be used only to falsify or qualify a theory because support for a theory in one instance never proves that the theory is true in all other instances (see the **problem of induction**).

method of induction: A method of scientific reasoning popularized by Francis Bacon. It refers to making many specific observations in an effort to draw general conclusions (to formulate theories or laws) about the nature of things. This is contrasted with the method of deduction because researchers first begin with observations and then try to formulate theories on the basis of these observations (but see the **problem of induction**).

mixed design: See **mixed-model design.**

mixed-model design: An experimental design in which at least one independent variable is manipulated on a between-subjects basis and at least one independent variable is manipulated on a within-subjects basis.

"more is better" rule of reliability: The idea that, all else being equal, measurements based on a large number of items, events, or observations are usually higher in reliability than measurements based on a small number of items, events, or observations.

multiple-groups design: A one-way experimental design in which there is a single independent variable that takes on three or more levels (e.g., a drug dosage study in which participants receive 0, 50, 100, or 150 mg of an experimental drug). See also **two-groups design.**

mundane realism: The degree to which the physical setting in an experiment is similar to the real-world setting(s) in which the experimenter's independent and dependent variables are most likely to operate. See also **experimental realism.**

mythology and religion: The belief that human behavior and experience are influenced by the operation of spiritual forces such as the wishes of a deity. This is one of the three categories of metaphysical explanations for human behavior. See also **animism** and **astrology.**

name-letter effect: The finding that people like the letters in their own names (1) more than they like other letters of the alphabet and (2) more than other people like these same letters (when these letters do not occur in their names).

natural experiment: A kind of quasi-experiment in which the researcher makes use of archival data documenting the consequences of a natural manipulation such as a natural disaster or a change in traffic laws in a particular state. The best natural experiments typically involve arbitrary or near-chance events that affect a large group of people.

noise: An extraneous variable in an experiment that (a) influences the dependent variable but that (b) is evenly distributed across experimental conditions. This is a not a threat to validity, but it may decrease a researcher's ability to detect the effect in which he or she is more interested. Contrast with **confound** and **artifact.**

nominal (categorical) scale: A measurement scale that uses meaningful but typically arbitrary, and nonnumerical, names or categories. Gender, HIV status, license plate number, favorite color, and pet ownership are examples of nominal variables. See also **interval, ordinal,** and **ratio scales.**

nonparallel lines: What, along with evidence of serious wipeouts, both authors of this book leave in the snow when they try to make it down an intermediate ski slope. In a figure using two or more lines to represent the results of a factorial study, nonparallel lines are also signs of a statistical interaction.

nonresponse bias: The bias that occurs in research when a substantial proportion of those invited to take part in a study refuse to do so. If those who agree to take part are different from those who refuse, the resulting bias is similar to selection bias and represents a threat to external validity. See also **selection bias.**

normal distribution: A symmetrical, bell-shaped distribution of scores in which one distinct score is more common than any other score. Most continuous physical and psychological measures (e.g., height, SAT scores) approximate a normal distribution.

null hypothesis: The statistical assumption that there is no relation between the independent and dependent variables of interest in an investigation (i.e., the assumption that the researcher's hypothesis is false).

observation: The practice of taking measurements of an object or phenomenon to figure out its nature (e.g., looking at something, measuring its weight). This is one of four ways of knowing emphasized in this text. See also **empiricism.**

observational research: Research in which investigators record the behavior of people in their natural environments without influencing people's behavior. Such observations are usually made secretly or unobtrusively.

one-group design: A very simple research design in which all the participants are in a single group that received a natural or experimental manipulation. This is the rough equivalent of a pseudo-experiment. It is usually very difficult to draw any clear conclusions from a study making use of a one-group design.

one-group, pretest-posttest design: A quasi-experimental research design in which measures are taken from a single group of research participants both prior to and after the participants receive a natural manipulation. Because this design does not include a control group, it usually yields findings that are open to many alternative explanations.

one-way design: An experimental design in which there is one and only one independent variable. Importantly, this independent variable may sometimes take on more than two levels. Manipulating whether a person's answers to a question are public or private is an example of two levels; manipulating whether a person received one of four dosages of an experimental drug is an example of four levels.

open-ended questions: Questions that allow people to respond to questions in their own words. Do you like open-ended questions? Feel free to respond in your own words. Contrast with **structured self-report questions.**

operational confound: A confound that occurs when a measure designed to assess a specific construct such as self-esteem, time pressure, or happiness inadvertently measures something else as well. Operational confounds are applicable to both experimental and nonexperimental research designs and are closely tied to the notion of **operational definitions.**

operational definition: A definition of a theoretical construct that is stated in terms of concrete, observable procedures (e.g., defining helping as the number of minutes a child spends assisting a friend with a problem). See also **testability.**

order effects (sequence effects): A methodological problem that occurs in experiments utilizing within-subjects designs. This occurs when participants' responses change over the course of the experiment due to fatigue, boredom, or the simple passage of time. This problem can almost always be corrected by the use of counterbalancing.

ordinal interaction: See **spreading interaction.**

ordinal scale: A measurement scale that uses order or ranking. Birth order, ranking in a foot race, or liking rankings for four different kinds of breakfast cereal are examples of ordinal variables. See also **interval, nominal,** and **ratio scales.**

paradigm: A widely shared set of guiding assumptions and research methods that make up a scientific research tradition.

paradoxical incidents: Puzzling, counterintuitive, or nonsensical observations. McGuire noted that such observations are a rich source of research hypotheses.

parsimony (parsimonius): The idea that, all else being equal, one should prefer simple theories or explanations over complex ones. It is one of the four canons of science emphasized in this text.

partial correlation: A statistical technique for determining the unique (i.e., nonredundant) relation between two variables when the relation between an additional variable (i.e., a potential confound) and each of the first two variables is taken into account. This also refers to the result of such an analysis.

partial counterbalancing: A category of incomplete counterbalancing in which several different orders are presented and in which each condition appears with equal or roughly equal frequency in every possible ordinal position in the experiment (e.g., 1st, 2nd, 3rd, etc.). The two most common forms of partial counterbalancing include (1) choosing several orders at random from the pool of all possible orders and (2) making use of a **Latin square** procedure.

participant expectancies: The form of **participant reaction bias** that occurs when participants consciously or unconsciously try to behave in ways they believe to be consistent with the experimenter's hypothesis. Participant expectancies are a threat to internal validity. See also **demand characteristics.**

participant reactance: The form of **participant reaction bias** that occurs when participants attempt to assert their sense of personal freedom by choosing to behave in ways they believe to be in opposition to the experimenter's expectations. Participant reactance is a threat to internal validity.

participant reaction bias: The bias that occurs when research participants realize they are being studied and behave in ways in which they normally not behave. The three forms of participant reaction bias emphasized in this text are (1) **participant expectancies,** (2) **participant reactance,** and (3) **evaluation apprehension.** Most forms of participant reaction bias threaten the internal validity of an investigation.

patched-up designs: The term Campbell and Stanley (1966) used to refer to a set of quasi-experimental findings in which a researcher has made repeated use of patching (the addition of control groups) to refine and strengthen the design. See **patching.**

patching: A research method in which a researcher adds new conditions to a quasi-experiment to help establish the size of an effect, to test for the influence of conceivable confounds, or both.

person-by-treatment quasi-experiment: A research design in which the researcher *measures* at least one independent variable and *manipulates* at least one other independent variable. Person-by-treatment designs are always **factorial designs**.

person confound: A confound that occurs in nonexperimental research when a variable (e.g., income level) seems to cause something because people who are high or low on this variable also happen to be high or low on some individual difference variable (e.g., education level) that is associated with the outcome variable of interest (e.g., scores on an IQ test). True experiments eliminate person confounds by virtue of their use of **random assignment**.

philosophy: The systematic study of human behavior and experience by means of logic, intuition, and empirical observation. Philosophers are interested in the nature of knowledge, ethics, aesthetics, logic, etc. Along with physiology, philosophy was one of the two most important precursors of psychology.

physiology: A branch of biology focusing on the functions, operations, and interrelations between different parts of the brain and body. Along with philosophy, physiology was one of the two most important precursors of psychology.

pilot test (pilot study): A preliminary study or "practice study" conducted by researchers before they conduct the full-blown version of the study in which they are interested. Pilot tests often allow researchers to refine their experiments and/or hypotheses by revealing errors or problems in the design of the study.

placebo: A pill or other fake drug that contains no active ingredients. Placebos are often used in medical research to control for patient expectancy effects. The goal is usually to see if a real drug produces greater benefits than the placebo (which often produces substantial medical benefits).

population survey: A survey designed to provide a description of the members of a population by sampling a representative portion of that population. If researchers make use of random sampling, they can typically provide accurate estimates of the characteristics of a very large population based on a relatively small number of people.

positive test bias: The tendency for hypothesis testers to attempt to confirm rather than disconfirm a hypothesis. This bias in hypothesis testing is similar to (1) behavioral confirmation in social interaction and (2) validation as an approach to scientific hypothesis testing.

positivism: The idea that sense perceptions are the only basis for knowledge or certainty (also known as logical positivism).

posttest-only design with nonequivalent group: A quasi-experimental design in which a researcher compares two similar but nonidentical groups after one and only one of the groups experiences a treatment condition.

practice effect: A problem that occurs in within-subjects designs when people's experience in one within-subject condition facilitates their performance in a later within-subject condition. Practice effects are thus very similar to **testing effects** and are roughly the opposite of **interference effects**.

predictor(s): The variable(s) used to predict an outcome of interest in a multiple regression analysis (the regression equivalent of the independent variables in an experimental design).

prescreening: A procedure for identifying the participants who will take part in a laboratory study (usually a **person-by-treatment quasi-experiment**). Researchers who use this technique give an individual difference measure to a large group of people prior to the time that they run their laboratory studies. People who receive specific scores (usually extreme scores) on the individual difference measure are then recruited to take part in the laboratory study.

pretest-posttest design with nonequivalent groups: A quasi-experimental research design in which data are collected from two presumably comparable groups of research participants both prior to and after one of the groups receives a natural manipulation. To the degree that one can safely assume that the two groups were truly similar prior to the time that they experienced different levels of the manipulation, this is a relatively strong quasi-experimental design.

probability: The number of specific outcomes that qualify as an event divided by the total number of all possible outcomes (e.g., the probability of drawing an ace from a fair deck of cards is 4/52 or 1/13). Probabilities can never be lower than 0 or higher than 1.0.

problem of induction: A shortcoming of the method of induction. The problem, pointed out by David Hume, is that one can never safely infer anything with absolute certainty on the basis of induction (reasoning from specific observations to general principles). The problem exists because a single disconfirming instance can invalidate a principle that has received consistent support in hundreds of previous observations.

procedural confound: A confound that occurs in a laboratory experiment or quasi-experiment when a researcher mistakenly allows a second variable to vary along with a manipulated variable. See also **environmental confound**.

protection from physical and psychological harm: The ethical principle of taking steps to eliminate or minimize any physical or psychological risks to the participants taking part in an investigation.

pseudo-experiment: A "false" experiment. A research design in which the investigator exposes one or more people to a variable of interest and notes that the people exposed to this treatment felt, thought, or behaved as expected.

psychology: The scientific study of human behavior.

public opinion poll: A survey study designed to determine the attitudes, opinions, or preferences of large groups of people such as voters or consumers. This is one kind of scientifically rigorous single-variable research. See also **marketing research.**

qualification: An approach to scientific hypothesis testing in which a researcher attempts to identify the conditions under which a hypothesis is and is not true. This is one of the three common approaches to scientific hypothesis testing emphasized in this text.

quasi-experiment: A research design in which the researcher has only partial control over his or her independent variables. Quasi-experiments include both natural experiments that are typically based on archival data and person-by-treatment quasi-experiments that are typically conducted in the laboratory.

questionnaire research: Research in which an investigator asks participants to respond to a standard set of written questions about their attitudes, moods, experiences, and/or background characteristics.

random assignment: A technique for assigning participants to different conditions in an experiment. The use of random assignment means that every person in the study has an equal chance of being assigned to any of the conditions of the study. The use of random assignment makes it highly likely that the groups of participants in different experimental conditions are highly similar to one another.

random sampling (random selection): A technique for deciding which participants in a population are selected for inclusion in a study. When true random sampling is used, every person in a population (e.g., American adults) has an equal chance of being selected into the study. The use of random sampling makes it highly likely that the participants who take part in an investigation are highly similar to the entire population of people from whom they were sampled.

random selection: See **random sampling.**

randomization: Random sampling and random assignment. See also **experimental paradigm.**

range: A statistical term for the difference between the highest and the lowest score in a set of scores. The range is a measure of dispersion.

ratio scales: Measurement scales that use real numbers designating equal amounts to reflect relative differences in magnitude. Ratio scales have all the properties of interval scales except that ratio scales always have a true zero point (at which none of the quantity under consideration is present). Thus, ratio scales literally allow researchers to designate ratios

(e.g., David is 6.1 times as heavy as Alisa; Faith solved 3.4 times as many anagrams as David did), and ratio scores cannot be negative. See also **nominal, ordinal,** and **interval scales.**

reasoning by analogy: Analyzing similarities or concordances between different phenomena to shed light on the less well understood of the two phenomena. McGuire noted that this is a good way to generate research hypotheses.

rectangular distribution: A distribution of scores in which all of the scores occur with equal frequency or likelihood (e.g., the distribution of the probabilities of drawing cards of different values from a fair deck).

redundancy (in writing): A stumbling block, problem, flaw, error, mistake, quandary, hitch, mess, snag, or fault in writing (i.e., composition, inscription, written communication, prose production) that often or frequently, if not typically, involves unnecessarily, without useful purpose and for no good reason, repeating, restating, duplicating, saying over again, replicating, or reiterating oneself to the point of causing, producing, or creating suffering, distress, pain, and unhappiness (not to mention boredom or monotony) on the part of the reader or consumer of written prose rather than enlightening, edifying, educating, or informing said same reader or consumer of written prose. Contrast with **conciseness.** See **repetitive.**

regression coefficients: The statistical measures of association between variables that are generated when one conducts a multiple regression. They are conceptually identical to partial correlations.

regression toward the mean: The tendency for people who receive extreme scores on a specific test or measure to score closer to the mean when given the test or measure at some point in the future. Regression toward the mean occurs because performance is influenced by error or luck as well as by a person's true score. When an investigator conducts a pretest-posttest study in which all participants receive a treatment, regression toward the mean may masquerade as a treatment effect. Thus, it is a threat to internal validity.

reliability: The consistency, coherence, or repeatability of a measure or observation. The three kinds of reliability emphasized in this text include (1) interobserver agreement or interrater reliability, (2) internal consistency, and (3) temporal consistency or test-retest reliability.

repeated measures design: See **within-subjects design.**

repetitive: See **redundancy.**

replication: A follow-up experiment that tests the idea behind the original experiment again—often by making use of different operational definitions of the independent and dependent measures and sometimes by testing the idea on a different kind of research participant (e.g., adults versus children).

response translation phase: The cognitive stage at which participants in studies "translate" the answer they generated to a question (during **judgment phase**) into the responses that a researcher has provided on a rating scale or other response format.

restriction of range: The methodological problem of a lack of variability in participants' response to a survey question or dependent measure. This includes both floor effects and ceiling effects.

reverse causality: See **bidirectionality problem**.

reverse counterbalancing: A form of counterbalancing the order of presentation of the experimental conditions in a within-subjects experiment. Some participants are presented with one specific order, and other participants are presented with the opposite order.

risk-benefit analysis: A comparison of the potential negative effects (or risks) in a study to its potential positive effects (or benefits). To receive accreditation by the American Psychological Association, colleges and universities must have an internal review board perform a risk-benefit analysis of all studies involving human subjects.

risk-benefit rule: The ethical principle of weighing (1) any potential risks to research participants taking part in an investigation against (2) the benefits to participants or to society as a whole that are likely to accrue from the research. The benefits must outweigh the risks.

sample: A subgroup drawn from a population that is being studied.

sampling error: The likely discrepancy between the results one obtains in a specific survey sample and the results one would have been likely to have obtained from the entire population. This estimate of a survey's potential inaccuracy is also known as the margin of error. All else being equal, surveys taken from larger samples usually suffer from less sampling error.

selection bias: Choosing research participants from a nonrepresentative sample by using imperfect (i.e., biased) sampling techniques rather than true random sampling. This typically represents a threat to external validity.

semantic priming: The finding that people recognize most words more quickly than usual when they have just been exposed to words that have a similar meaning. For instance, people are usually able to identify the word "smile" more quickly than usual if they have just been exposed to the word "happy." Semantic priming also refers to the experimental procedures used to demonstrate this effect.

sequence effects: See **order effects**.

serendipity: Luck or good fortune. B. F. Skinner noted that many important scientific discoveries are partly the result of serendipity.

simple effects tests (simple main effects tests): A set of follow-up tests that are conducted when the statistical analysis in a factorial design yields a significant interaction. Simple effects tests clarify the precise nature of an interaction.

simple main effects tests: See **simple effects tests**.

spreading interaction (ordinal interaction): A specific kind of statistical interaction. This describes the situation in which an independent variable has an effect at one level of a second independent variable but has a weaker effect, or no effect, at a different level of the second dependent variable.

standard deviation: A statistical term for the average amount that each of the scores in a sample differs from the sample mean. The standard deviation is a very commonly used measure of dispersion.

statistical significance: The likelihood that an observed effect would occur by chance alone. This number is typically expressed with a p-value to indicate the number of times out of 100 that the observed effect would occur by chance.

statistical testing: A technique, popularized by R. A. Fisher, for drawing conclusions about the results of empirical studies. It involves considering the likelihood that the observed findings would have occurred by chance. If the results are unlikely to have occurred by chance, researchers conclude that the results support the hypothesis being investigated.

statistics: A set of mathematical procedures for summarizing and interpreting observations. See also **descriptive statistics** and **inferential statistics**.

structured debriefing: An interview conducted with participants immediately after they have completed a study to determine exactly what participants thought the researcher expected to find. This always occurs prior to the point at which the experimenter conducts a full debriefing in which he or she explains the true purpose of the study. Conducting a structured debriefing is more important than usual when researchers make use of **within-subjects designs**.

structured self-report questions: Questions that require participants to respond to questions in a specific self-report format. Do you like structured self-report questions? Answer using a scale from 0 to 6, where 0 represents "not at all" and 6 represents "extremely." Contrast with **open-ended questions**.

superstitious conditioning: The "false" conditioning that often occurs when an organism is provided with reinforcements at random intervals. It occurs because the organism comes to associate an arbitrary response with the delivery of the reinforcement and repeats the response until a reinforcement is eventually delivered.

survey research: Research in which investigators ask people to respond to written or verbal questions about their thoughts, feelings, and behavior. This includes pencil-and-paper questionnaires, face-to-face or telephone interviews, and—increasingly—electronic surveys filled out by email or on the Internet.

temporal consistency: See **test-retest reliability**.

temporal sequence: Establishing that a potential cause of an outcome occurs prior to the outcome in question. This is the second of John Stuart Mill's requirements for establishing causality. See also **covariation** and **elimination of confounds**.

testability: The idea that scientific theories should be confirmable or disconfirmable using currently available research techniques. It is one of the four canons of science emphasized in this text.

testing effects: The tendency for most people to perform better on a test or personality measure the second time they take the test or measure. When an investigator conducts a pretest-posttest study in which all participants receive a treatment, testing effects may masquerade as treatment effects. Thus, testing effects represent a threat to internal validity.

test-retest reliability: The degree to which a test continues to rank order participants' scores in a stable manner over time. This is ideally assessed by correlating participants' responses on a measure at time 1 with their scores on the same measure assessed at time 2 (some later date).

theory: A general statement about the relation between two or more variables. A good theory should be testable or falsifiable. See also **hypothesis** and **law**.

third-variable problem: The problem of confounds, especially as it applies to passive observational research.

time-series design: A quasi-experimental research design in which researchers collect multiple waves of data from two presumably comparable groups of research participants. If the two groups of participants receive highly similar scores on a dependent measure prior to a natural manipulation but begin to receive different scores immediately after the natural manipulation, this strongly suggests that the manipulation may be responsible for the observed post-manipulation differences.

two-groups design: An experimental design in which there is only one independent variable and only two levels of this variable. This is the simplest possible kind of experimental design.

Type I error: Rejecting the null hypothesis when the null hypothesis is actually correct. That is, concluding that a researcher's hypothesis is true when it is false.

Type II error: Failing to reject the null hypothesis when the null hypothesis is actually incorrect. That is, failing to conclude that a researcher's hypothesis is true when it is in fact true.

unipolar scales: Scales that assess a psychological dimension that is anchored at the low and high end by terms that only differ in magnitude or degree (e.g., "not at all happy" to "extremely happy"). Unipolar scales typically use numbering systems that range from either 0 or 1 to some positive integer between 7 or 10. Contrast with **bipolar** scales.

unobtrusive observations: Observations or measurements that are made secretly or surreptitiously (i.e., without asking participants any direct questions and without letting participants know that their behavior is being measured). An example of an unobtrusive measurement is assessing how far a participant sits from a confederate to determine how much the participant likes the confederate.

validation: An approach to scientific hypothesis testing in which a researcher attempts to gather evidence that supports or confirms the hypothesis. This is one of the three common approaches to scientific hypothesis testing emphasized in this text.

validity: The relative accuracy or correctness of a psychological statement or finding. The three kinds of validity emphasized in this text are internal validity, external validity, and construct validity.

variability: See **dispersion**.

within-subjects design (repeated measures design): An experimental design in which each participant serves in more than one condition (typically all of the conditions) of the experiment. See also **between-subjects design**.

References

ABRAMSON, P. R. (1984). *Sarah: A sexual biography.* Albany, NY: SUNY Press.

ABRAMSON, P. R. (1992). *A case for case studies: An immigrant's journal.* Newbury Park, CA: Sage Publications.

AIKEN, L. S., & WEST, S. G. (1991). *Multiple regression: Testing and interpreting interactions.* Newbury Park, CA: Sage Publications.

ALBRECHTSEN, J. S., MEISSNER, C. A., & SUSA, K. J. (2009). Can intuition improve deception detection performance? *Journal of Experimental Social Psychology, 45,* 1052–1055.

ALLOY, L. B., & ABRAMSON, L. Y. (1979). Judgment of contingency in depressed and nondepressed students: Sadder but wiser? *Journal of Experimental Psychology: General, 108,* 441–485.

ALLPORT, G. W. (1954). *The nature of prejudice.* Cambridge, MA: Addison-Wesley.

American Heritage Dictionary of the English Language (4th ed.). (2000). New York: Houghton Mifflin Company.

ANDERSON, C. A. (1987). Temperature and aggression: Effects on quarterly, yearly, and city rates of violent and nonviolent crime. *Journal of Personality and Social Psychology, 52,* 1161–1173.

ANDERSON, C. A. (1989). Temperature and aggression: Ubiquitous effects of heat on occurrence of human violence. *Psychological Bulletin, 106,* 74–96.

ANDERSON, C. A., & ANDERSON, K. B. (1996). Violent crime rate studies in philosophical context: A destructive testing approach to heat and southern culture of violence effects. *Journal of Personality and Social Psychology, 70,* 740–756.

ANDERSON, C. A., DEUSER, W. E., & DENEVE, K. M. (1995). Hot temperatures, hostile affect, hostile cognition, and arousal: Tests of a general model of affective aggression. *Personality and Social Psychology Bulletin, 21,* 434–448.

ANDERSON, C. A., & DILL, K. E. (2000). Video games and aggressive thoughts, feelings, and behavior in the laboratory and in life. *Journal of Personality and Social Psychology, 78,* 772–790.

ANDERSON, C. A., SHIBUYA, A., IHORI, N., SWING, E. L., BUSHMAN, B. J., SAKAMOTO, A., ROTHSTEIN, H. R., & SALEEM, M. (2010). Violent video game effects on aggression, empathy, and prosocial behavior in Eastern and Western countries: A meta-analytic review. *Psychological Bulletin, 136,* 151–173.

ARONSON, E., & CARLSMITH, J. M. (1968). Experimentation in social psychology. In G. Lindzey & E. Aronson (Eds.), *The handbook of social psychology* (pp. 1–78). Reading, MA: Addison-Wesley.

ARONSON, E., WILLERMAN, B., & FLOYD, J. (1966). The effect of a pratfall on increasing interpersonal attractiveness. *Psychonomic Science, 4,* 227–228.

ASCH, S. E. (1955). Opinions and social pressure. *Scientific American, 193,* 31–35.

ASCH, S. E. (1956). Studies of independence and conformity: I. A minority of one against a unanimous majority. *Psychological Monographs, 70,* 1–70.

ASIMOV, I. (1964). *Asimov's biographical encyclopedia of science and technology.* Garden City, NY: Doubleday.

BAILLARGEON, R. (1994). How do infants learn about the physical world? *Current Directions in Psychological Science, 3,* 133–140.

BANAJI, M. R., & CROWDER, R. G. (1989). The bankruptcy of everyday memory. *American Psychologist, 44,* 1185–1193.

BANAJI, M. R., & HARDIN, C. D. (1996). Automatic stereotyping. *Psychological Science, 7,* 136–141.

BANDURA, A. (1977). *Social learning theory.* Englewood Cliffs, NJ: Prentice-Hall.

BANDURA, A., & WALTERS, R. H. (1963). *Social learning and personality development.* New York, NY: Holt Rinehart and Winston.

BARGH, J. A., CHEN, M., & BURROWS, L. (1996). Automaticity of social behavior: Direct effects of trait construct and stereotype activation on action. *Journal of Personality and Social Psychology, 71,* 230–244.

BARGH, J. A., & TOTA, M. E. (1988). Context-dependent automatic processing in depression: Accessibility of negative constructs with regard to self but not others. *Journal of Personality and Social Psychology, 54,* 925–939.

BARNES, J. (ED.). (1984). *The complete works of Aristotle: The revised Oxford translation.* Princeton, NJ: Princeton University Press.

BARON, R. A., & BELL, P. A. (1976). Aggression and heat: The influence of ambient temperature, negative affect, and a cooling drink on physical aggression.

Journal of Personality and Social Psychology, 33, 245–255.

BARON, R. M., & KENNY, D. A. (1986). The moderator-mediator variable distinction in social psychological research: Conceptual, strategic and statistical considerations. *Journal of Personality and Social Psychology, 51,* 1173–1182.

BARTHOLOW, B. D., & ANDERSON, C. A. (2002). Effects of violent video games on aggressive behavior: Potential sex differences. *Journal of Experimental Social Psychology, 38,* 283–290.

BASHAW, W. L., & ANDERSON, H. E., JR. (1968). Developmental study of the meaning of adverbial modifiers. *Journal of Educational Psychology, 59,* 111–118.

BAUMEISTER, R. F. & STEINHILBER, A. (1984). Paradoxical effects of supportive audiences on performance under pressure: The home field disadvantage in sports championships. *Journal of Personality and Social Psychology, 47,* 85–93.

BAUMRIND, D. (1964). Some thoughts on ethics of research: After reading Milgram's "Behavioral Study of Obedience." *American Psychologist, 19,* 421–423.

BEAMAN, A. L., KLENTZ, B., DIENER, E., & SVANUM, S. (1979). Self-awareness and transgression in children: Two field studies. *Journal of Personality and Social Psychology, 37,* 1835–1846.

BECKER, D. V. (2009). Lingering effects of inattention on the recognition of novel forms. *Memory, 17,* 687–694.

BEM, D. J. (1967). Self-perception: An alternative explanation of cognitive dissonance phenomena. *Psychological Review, 74,* 183–200.

BEM, D. J. (1972). Self-perception theory. In L. Berkowitz (Ed.), *Advances in experimental social psychology* (Vol. 6). New York: Academic Press.

BEM, D. J. (1987). Writing the empirical journal article. In M. P. Zanna & J. M. Darley (Eds.), *The compleat academic* (pp. 171–201). Hillsdale, NJ: Erlbaum.

BERGER, J., FISEK, M. H., NORMAN, R. Z., & ZELDITCH, JR., M. (1977). *Status characteristics in social interaction: An expectation status approach.* New York: Elsevier.

BERKOWITZ, L., & LEPAGE, A. (1967). Weapons as aggression-eliciting stimuli. *Journal of Personality and Social Psychology, 7,* 202–207.

BETTLEHEIM, B. (1943). Individual and mass behavior in extreme situations. *Journal of Abnormal and Social Psychology, 38,* 417–452.

BLAIR, I. V., JUDD, C. M., & FALLMAN, J. L. (2004). The automaticity of race and Afrocentric facial features in social judgments. *Journal of Personality and Social Psychology, 87,* 763–778.

BLANTON, H., CHRISTIE, C., & DYE, M. (2002). Social identity versus reference frame comparisons: The moderating role of stereotype endorsement. *Journal of Experimental Social Psychology, 38(3),* 253–267.

BLANTON, H., COOPER, J., SKURNIK, I., & ARONSON, J. (1997). When bad things happen to good feedback: Exacerbating the need for self-justification through self-affirmation. *Personality and Social Psychology Bulletin, 23,* 684–692.

BLANTON, H. & JACCARD, J. (2006). Arbitrary metrics in psychology. *American Psychologist, 61,* 27–41.

BLANTON, H., & JACCARD, J. (2008). Unconscious racism: A concept in pursuit of a measure. *Annual Review of Sociology, 34,* 277–297.

BLANTON, H., JACCARD, J., GONZALES, P. M., & CHRISTIE, C. (2006). Decoding the implicit association test: Implications for criterion prediction. *Journal of Experimental Social Psychology, 42,* 192–212.

BLANTON, H., PELHAM, B. W., DEHART, T., & CARVALLO, M. (2001). Overconfidence as dissonance reduction. *Journal of Experimental Social Psychology, 37,* 373–385.

BLANTON, H., STUART, A. E., & VANDENEIJNDEN, R. J. J. M. (2001). An introduction to deviance-regulation theory: The effect of behavioral norms on message framing. *Personality and Social Psychology Bulletin, 27,* 848–858.

BOGGS, M. B. (1999). Made up article, used in Chapter 11 to illustrate the value of writing assertively. *Journal of Fictitious Findings, 1,* 1–29.

BOOTE, A. S. (1981). Markets segmentation by personal and salient product attributes. *Journal of Advertising Research, 21,* 29–35.

BOWLBY, J. (1977). The making and breaking of affectional bonds: I. Aetiology and psychopathology in the light of attachment theory. *British Journal of Psychiatry, 130,* 201–210.

BREHM, J. W. (1966). *A theory of psychological reactance.* New York: Academic Press.

BROWNE, K. D., & HAMILTON-GIACHRITSIS, C. (2005). The influence of violent media on children and adolescents: A public-health approach. *The Lancet, 365,* 702–710.

BUHRMESTER, M. D., BLANTON, H., & SWANN, W. B., JR. (2010). Implicit self-esteem: Nature, measurement, and a new way backward. *Journal of Personality and Social Psychology.*

BUI, K. V. T. (1997). A model of contrast and assimilation in social comparison. Unpublished doctoral dissertation, University of California, Los Angeles.

BURGER, J. M., MESSIAN, N., PATEL, S., DEL PRADO, A., & ANDERSON, C. (2004). What a coincidence! The effects of incidental similarity on compliance. *Personality and Social Psychology Bulletin, 30,* 35–43.

BUSS, A. (1988). Personal communication, October 1988.

BYLSMA, W. H., MAJOR, B., & COZZARELLI, C. (1995). The influence of legitimacy appraisals on the determinants of entitlement beliefs. *Basic and Applied Social Psychology, 17,* 223–237.

CACIOPPO, J. T., GARDNER, W. L., & BERNTSON, G. G. (1997). Beyond bipolar conceptualizations and measures: The case of attitudes and evaluative space. *Personality and Social Psychology Review, 1,* 3–25.

CAMPBELL, D. T., & FISKE, D. W. (1959). Convergent and discriminant validation by the multi-trait multi-method matrix. *Psychological Bulletin, 56,* 81–105.

CAMPBELL, D. T., & STANLEY, J. C. (1966). *Experimental and quasi-experimental designs for research.* Chicago: Rand McNally.

CAMPBELL, J. D. (1986). Similarity and uniqueness: The effects of attribute type, relevance, and individual differences in self-esteem and depression. *Journal of Personality and Social Psychology, 50,* 281–294.

CANDLISH, A. (1990). *The revised Waite's compendium of natal astrology.* London: Penguin Books.

CARLI, L. L., & EAGLY, A. H. (1999). Gender effects on social influence and emergent leadership. In G. N. Powell (Ed.), *Handbook of gender and work* (pp. 203–222). Thousand Oaks, CA: Sage.

CARVER, C. S., & SCHEIER, M. F. (1990). Origins and functions of positive and negative affect: A control-process view. *Psychological Review, 97,* 19–35.

CEJKA, M. A., & EAGLY, A. H. (1999). Gender-stereotypic images of occupations correspond to the sex segregation of employment. *Personality and Social Psychology Bulletin, 25,* 413–423.

CHAIKEN, S., LIBERMAN, A., & EAGLY, A. H. (1989). Heuristic and systematic information processing within and beyond the persuasion context. In J. S. Uleman & J. A. Bargh (Eds.), *Unintended thought* (pp. 212–252). New York: Guilford Press.

CIALDINI, R. B. (1993). *Influence: Science and practice* (3rd ed.). New York: Harper Collins.

CIALDINI, R. B., & ASCANI, K. (1976). Test of a concession procedure for inducing verbal, behavioral, and further compliance with a request to give blood. *Journal of Applied Psychology, 61,* 295–300.

CIALDINI, R. B., CACIOPPO, J. T., BASSETT, R., & MILLER, J. A. (1978). Low-ball procedure for producing compliance: Commitment then cost. *Journal of Personality and Social Psychology, 36,* 463–476.

CLANCY, S. A., MCNALLY, R. J., SCHACTER, D. L., LENZENWEGER, M. F., & PITMAN, R. K. (2002). Memory distortion in people reporting abduction by aliens. *Journal of Abnormal Psychology, 111,* 455–461.

CLIFF, N. (1959) Adverbs as multipliers. *Psychological Review, 66,* 27–44.

COHEN, J. (1994). The earth is round ($p < .05$). *American Psychologist, 49,* 997–1003.

COLLINS, B. E., & HOYT, M. F. (1972). Personal responsibility-for-consequences: An integration and extension of the "forced compliance" literature. *Journal of Experimental Social Psychology, 8,* 558–593.

CONFER, J. C., EASTON, J. A., FLEISCHMAN, D. S., GOETZ, C. D., LEWIS, D. M. G., PERILLOUX, C., & BUSS, D. M. (2010). Evolutionary psychology: Controversies, questions, prospects, and limitations. *American Psychologist, 65,* 110–126.

CONWAY, M., & ROSS, M. (1984). Getting what you want by revising what you had. *Journal of Personality and Social Psychology, 47,* 738–748.

COOK, T. D., & CAMPBELL, D. T. (1979). *Quasi-experimentation: Design and analysis issues for field settings.* Boston: Houghton Mifflin.

COPI, I. M. (1978). *Introduction to logic* (5th ed.). New York: Macmillan.

CORREL, J., PARK, B., JUDD, C. M., WITTENBRINK, B. (2002). The police officer's dilemma: Using ethnicity to disambiguate potentially threatening individuals. *Journal of Personality and Social Psychology, 83,* 1314–1329.

CORREL, J., PARK, B., JUDD, C. M., WITTENBRINK, B., SADLER, M. S., & KEESEE, T. (2007). Across the thin blue line: Police officers and racial bias in the decision to shoot. *Journal of Personality and Social Psychology, 92,* 1006–1023.

CORREL, J., URLAND, G. R., & ITO, T. A. (2006). Event-related potentials and the decision to shoot: The role of threat perception and cognitive control. *Journal of Experimental Social Psychology. 42,* 120–128.

COX, J. R., & GRIGGS, R. A. (1982). The effects of experience on performance in Wason's selection task. *Memory and Cognition, 10,* 496–502.

CRABTREE, S. (2010). Religiosity highest in world's poorest nations. August 31, 2010, *Gallup World News.* Accessed at http://www.gallup.com/poll/142727/religiosity-highest-world-poorest-nations.aspx on August 2, 2011.

DAMASIO, A. R. (1994). *Descartes' error.* New York: Avon Books.

DAMASIO, H., GRABOWSKI, T., FRANK, R., GALABURDA, A. M., & DAMASIO, A. R. (1994). The return of Phineas Gage: The skull of a famous patient yields clues about the brain. *Science, 264,* 1102–1105.

DARLEY, J. M., & GROSS, P. H. (1983). A hypothesis-confirming bias in labeling effects. *Journal of Personality and Social Psychology, 44,* 20–33.

DARWIN, C. (1859). *On the origin of species by means of natural selection.* London: J. Murray.

DARWIN, C. (1872). *The expression of the emotions in man and animals.* London: J. Murray.

DARWIN, C. (1881). *The formation of vegetable mould, through the action of worms: With observations on their habits.* London: J. Murray.

DAVILA, J., BRADBURY, T. N., COHAN, C. L., & TOCHLUK, S. (1997). Marital functioning and depressive symptoms: Evidence for a stress generation model. *Journal of Personality and Social Psychology, 73*, 849–861.

DEESE, J. (1959). On the prediction of occurrence of particular verbal intrusions in immediate recall. *Journal of Experimental Psychology, 58*, 17–22.

DEHART, T., MURRAY, S., PELHAM, B., & ROSE, P. (2003). The regulation of dependency in mother-child relationships. *Journal of Experimental Social Psychology, 39*, 59–67.

DEHART, T., PELHAM, B. W., & TENNEN, H. (2006). What lies beneath: Parenting style and implicit self-esteem. *Journal of Experimental Social Psychology, 42*, 1–17.

DENNETT, D. C. (1991). *Consciousness explained.* Boston: Little, Brown.

DESCARTES, R. (1984). Principles of philosophy. In J. Cottingham, R. Stoothoff, & D. Murdock (Eds. & Trans.), *The philosophical writings of Descartes* (Vol. 1, pp. 193–291). Cambridge, England: Cambridge University Press. (Original work published 1644)

DESMARAIS, S., & CURTIS, J. (1997). Gender and perceived pay entitlement: Testing for effects of experience with income. *Journal of Personality and Social Psychology, 72*, 141–150.

DESTENO, D. (2011). Personal communication. Using "social" robots as tutors.

DEVINE, P. G. (1989). Stereotypes and prejudice: Their automatic and controlled components. *Journal of Personality and Social Psychology, 56*, 5–18.

DEWAAL, F. (1996). *Good natured: The origins of right and wrong in humans and other animals* (pp. 1–131) Cambridge, MA: Harvard University Press.

DIAMOND, J. (1992). *The third chimpanzee: The evolution and future of the human animal* (pp. 1–136). New York: Harper Collins.

DIENER, E., & WALLBOM, M. (1976). Effects of self-awareness on antinormative behavior. *Journal of Research in Personality, 10*, 107–111.

DIETZ, T. L. (1998). An examination of violence and gender role portrayals in video games: Implications for gender socialization and aggressive behavior. *Sex Roles, 38*, 425–442.

DIJKSTERHUIS, A. (2004). Think different: The merits of unconscious thought in preference development and decision making. *Journal of Personality and Social Psychology, 87*, 586–598.

DIPBOYE, R. L. (1977). A critical review of Korman's self-consistency theory of work motivation and occupational choice. *Organizational Behavior and Human Performance, 18*(1), 108–126.

DOBSON, K. S. (1985). The relationship between anxiety and depression. *Clinical Psychology Review, 5*, 307–324.

DOBSON, K. S., & MOTHERSKILL, K. J. (1979). Equidistant categorical labels for construction of Likert-type scales. *Perceptual and Motor Skills, 49*, 575–580.

DOOLEY, D. (1995). *Social research methods* (3rd ed.). Englewood Cliffs, NJ: Prentice-Hall.

DOOLING, D. J., & LACHMAN, R. (1971). Effects of comprehension on retention of prose. *Journal of Experimental Psychology, 88*, 216–222.

DUFFY, M. (1993). *Occam's razor.* London: Sinclair-Stevenson.

DUNNING, D., & STORY, A. L. (1991). Depression, realism, and the overconfidence effect: Are the sadder wiser when predicting future actions and events? *Journal of Personality and Social Psychology, 61*, 521–532.

DURANTE, K. M., LI, N. P., & HASELTON, M. G. (2008). Changes in women's choice of dress across the ovulatory cycle: Naturalistic and laboratory task-based evidence. *Personality and Social Psychology Bulletin, 34*, 1451–1460.

EAGLY, A. H. (1978). Sex differences in influenceability. *Psychological Bulletin, 85*, 86–116.

EAGLY, A. H., ASHMORE, R. D., MAKHIJANI, M. G., & LONGO, L. C. (1991). What is beautiful is good, but: A meta-analytic review of research on the physical attractiveness stereotype. *Psychological Bulletin, 110*, 109–128.

EAGLY, A. H., & CARLI, L. (1981). Sex of researchers and sex-typed communications as determinants of sex differences in influenceability: A meta-analysis of social influence studies. *Psychological Bulletin, 90*, 1–20.

EAGLY, A. H., & CHAIKEN, S. (1993). *The psychology of attitudes.* Fort Worth: Harcourt-Brace.

EDNEY, J. J. (1979). The nuts game: A concise commons dilemma analog. *Environmental Psychology and Nonverbal Behavior, 3*, 252–254.

EDWARDS, A. L. (1976). *An introduction to linear regression and correlation.* San Francisco, CA: W. H. Freeman.

ERON, L. D., HUESMANN, L. R., LEFKOWITZ, M. M., & WALDER, L. O. (1996). Does television violence cause aggression? In D. F. Greenberg (Ed.), *Criminal careers*, Vol. 2. (pp. 311–321). Brookfield, VT: Dartmouth Publishing Company.

FAZIO, R. H., JACKSON, J. R., DUNTON, B. C., & WILLIAMS, C. J. (1995). Variability in automatic activation as an unobtrusive measure of racial attitudes: A bona fide pipeline? *Journal of Personality and Social Psychology, 69*, 1013–1027.

FAZIO, R. H., & OLSON, M. A. (2003). Implicit measures in social cognition research: Their meaning and use. *Annual Review of Psychology, 54*, 297–327.

FAZIO, R. H., SANBONMATSU, D. M., POWELL, M. C., & KARDES, F. R. (1986). On the automatic activation of attitudes. *Journal of Personality and Social Psychology, 50*, 229–238.

FAZIO, R. H., ZANNA, M. P., & COOPER, J. (1977). Dissonance and self-perception: An integrative view of each theory's proper domain of application. *Journal of Experimental Social Psychology, 13*, 464–479.

FEIN, S., HILTON, J. L., & MILLER, D. T. (1990). Suspicion of ulterior motivation and the correspondence bias. *Journal of Personality and Social Psychology, 58*, 753–764.

FESTINGER, L. (1957). *A theory of cognitive dissonance.* Stanford, CA: Stanford University Press.

FESTINGER, L., & CARLSMITH, J. M. (1959). Cognitive consequences of forced compliance. *Journal of Abnormal and Social Psychology, 58*, 203–210.

FISCHHOFF, B. (1982). Debiasing. In D. Kahneman, P. Slovic, & A. Tversky (Eds.), *Judgment under uncertainty: Heuristics and biases* (pp. 422–444). Cambridge: Cambridge University Press.

FISHER, R. A. (1925). *Statistical methods for research workers.* Edinburgh: Oliver & Boyd.

FISHER, R. A. (1935). *The design of experiments.* Edinburgh: Oliver & Boyd.

FISHER, R. A. (1938). *Statistical methods for research workers* (7th ed.). London: Oliver & Boyd.

FORER, B. R. (1949). The fallacy of personal validation: A classroom demonstration of gullibility. *Journal of Abnormal and Social Psychology, 44*, 118–123.

FREEDMAN, D., PISANI, R., PURVES, R., & ADHIKARI, A. (1991). *Statistics* (2nd ed.). New York: Norton & Company.

FREUD, S. (1962/1923). *The ego and the id* (translated by J. Riviere, revised and edited by J. Strachey). New York: Norton & Company.

GAERTNER, L., SEDIKIDES, C., VEVEA, J. L., & IUZZINI, J. (2002). The "I," the "we," and the "when": A meta-analysis of motivational primacy in self-definition. *Journal of Personality and Social Psychology, 83*, 574–591.

GILBERT, D. T. (1989). Thinking lightly about others: Automatic components of the social inference process. In J. S. Uleman & J. A. Bargh (Eds.), *Unintended thought* (pp. 189–211). New York: Guilford Press.

GILBERT, D. T. (1991). How mental systems believe. *American Psychologist, 46*, 107–119.

GILBERT, D. T., KRULL, D. S., & MALONE, P. S. (1990). Unbelieving the unbelievable: Some problems in the rejection of false information. *Journal of Personality and Social Psychology, 59*, 601–613.

GILBERT, D. T., PELHAM, B. W., & KRULL, D. S. (1988). On cognitive busyness: When person perceivers meet persons perceived. *Journal of Personality and Social Psychology, 54*, 733–740.

GIVON, M. M., & SHAPIRA, Z. B. (1984). Response to ratings scales: A theoretical model and its application to the number of categories problem. *Journal of Marketing Research, 21*, 410–325.

GLENN, J. (1996). *Scientific genius: The twenty greatest minds.* New York: Crescent Books.

GOLDBERG, P. (1968). Are women prejudiced against women? *Trans-Action, 5*, 28.

GREENWALD, A. G., & BANAJI, M. R. (1995). Implicit social cognition: Attitudes, self-esteem, and stereotypes. *Psychological Review, 102*, 4–27.

GREENWALD, A. G., MCGHEE, D. E., & SCHWARTZ, J. L. K. (1998). Measuring individual differences in implicit cognition: The implicit association test. *Journal of Personality and Social Psychology, 74*, 1464–1480.

GREENWALD, A. G., SPANGENBERG, E. R., PRATKANIS, A. R., & ESKENAZI, J. (1991). Double-blind tests of subliminal self-help audiotapes. *Psychological Science, 2*, 119–122.

GRICE, H. P. (1975). Logic and conversation. In D. Davidson & G. Harman (Eds.), *The logic of grammar.* Encino, CA: Dickenson.

HAINES, E. L., & JOST, J. T. (2000). Placating the powerless: Effects of legitimate and illegitimate explanation of affect, memory, and stereotyping. *Social Justice Research, 13*, 219–236.

HAMILTON, D. L., & GIFFORD, R. K. (1976). Illusory correlation in interpersonal perception: A cognitive basis of stereotypic judgments. *Journal of Experimental Social Psychology, 12*, 392–407.

HAMILTON, D. L., & ROSE, T. L. (1980). Illusory correlation and the maintenance of stereotypic beliefs. *Journal of Personality and Social Psychology, 39*, 832–845.

HAMILTON, D. L., & SHERMAN, J. W. (1994). Stereotypes. In R. S. Wyer, Jr. & T. K. Srull (Eds.), *Handbook of social cognition* (2nd ed., pp. 1–68). Hillsdale, NJ: Erlbaum.

HARRÉ, R. (1981). *Great scientific experiments.* Oxford: Phaidon Press.

HASELTON, M. G., & GANGESTAD, S. W. (2006). Conditional expression of women's desires and men's mate guarding across the ovulatory cycle. *Hormones and Behavior, 49*, 509–518.

HASELTON, M. G., & GILDERSLEEVE, K. (2011). Can men detect ovulation? *Current Directions in Psychological Science, 20*, 87–92.

HASELTON, M. G., MORTEZAIE, M., PILLSWORTH, E. G., BLESKE-RECHEK, A., & FREDERICK, D. A. (2007). Ovulatory shifts in human female ornamentation: Near ovulation, women dress to impress. *Hormones and Behavior, 51*, 40–45.

HATFIELD, E., & WALSTER, G. W. (1978). *A new look at love.* Reading, MA: Addison-Wesley.

HEATHERTON, T. F., & POLIVY, J. (1991). Development and validation of a scale for measuring state self-esteem. *Journal of Personality and Social Psychology, 60*, 859–910.

HEDGES, L. V. (1987). How hard is hard science, how soft is soft science? The empirical cumulativeness of research. *American Psychologist, 42*, 443–455.

HEIDER, F. (1958). *The psychology of interpersonal relations*. Hillsdale, NJ: Erlbaum.

HEISENBERG, W. (1955/1958). *The physicist's conception of nature* (translated by Arnold J. Pomerans). New York: Harcourt, Brace & World.

HENRICH, J., HEINE, S. J., & NORENZAYAN, A. (2010). The weirdest people in the world? *Behavioral and Brain Sciences, 33*, 61–83.

HENRY, P. J. (2008). College sophomores in the laboratory redux: Influences of a narrow data base on social psychology's view of the nature of prejudice. *Psychological Inquiry, 19*, 49–71.

HETTS, J. J., SAKUMA, M., & PELHAM, B. W. (1999). Two roads to positive regard: Implicit and explicit self-evaluation and culture. *Journal of Experimental Social Psychology, 35*, 512–559.

HIGGINS, E. T. (1989). Self-discrepancy theory: What patterns of self-beliefs cause people to suffer? In L. Berkowitz (Ed.), *Advances in experimental social psychology* (Vol. 22, pp. 93–136). San Diego: Academic Press.

HOGUE, M. & YODER, J. D. (2003). The role of status in producing depressed entitlement in women's and men's pay allocations. *Psychology of Women Quarterly, 27*(4), 330–337.

HOOKE, R. (1665). *Micrographia or some physiological descriptions of minute bodies made by magnifying glasses with observations and inquiries thereupon*. London: The Royal Society.

HOVLAND. C. I., & WEISS, W. (1951). The influence of source-credibility on communication effectiveness. *Public Opinion Quarterly, 15*, 635–650.

HOWE, E. S. (1962). Probabilistic adverbial qualifications of adjectives. *Journal of Verbal Learning and Verbal Behavior, 1*, 225–242.

HOWE, E. S. (1966a). Verb tense, negatives and other determinants of the intensity of evaluative meaning. *Journal of Verbal Learning and Verbal Behavior, 5*, 147–155.

HOWE, E. S. (1966b). Associative structure of quantifiers. *Journal of Verbal Learning and Verbal Behavior, 5*, 156–162.

HUCK, S. W., & SANDLER, H. M. (1979). *Rival hypotheses: Alternative interpretations of data-based conclusions*. New York: Harper & Row.

HULL, C. L. (1943). *Principles of behavior*. New York: Appleton–Century–Crofts.

ISEN, A. M. (1987). Positive affect, cognitive processes, and social behavior. In L. Berkowitz (Ed.), *Advances in experimental social psychology* (Vol. 20, pp. 203–253). San Diego: Academic Press.

ISEN, A. M., & LEVIN, P. F. (1972). Effect of feeling good on helping: Cookies and kindness. *Journal of Personality and Social Psychology, 21*, 384–388.

JACCARD, J., BLANTON, H., & DODGE, T. (2005). Peer influences on risk behavior: An analysis of the effects of a close friend. *Developmental Psychology, 41*(1), 135–147.

JOHNSON, M. K., HASHTROUDI, S., & LINDSAY, D. S. (1993). Source monitoring. *Psychological Bulletin, 114*, 3–28.

JOHNSON, M. K., & RAYE, C. L. (1981). Reality monitoring. *Psychological Review, 88*, 67–85.

JOHNSON, S. E., RICHESON, J. A., & FINKEL, E. J. (2011). Middle class and marginal? Socioeconomic status, stigma, and self-regulation at an elite university. *Journal of Personality and Social Psychology*.

JONES, E. E., & SIGALL, H. (1971). The bogus pipeline: A new paradigm for measuring affect and attitude. *Psychological Bulletin, 76*, 349–364.

JONES, J. T., PELHAM, B. W., MIRENBERG, M. C., & HETTS, J. J. (2002). Name letter preferences are not merely mere exposure: Implicit egotism as self-regulation. *Journal of Experimental Social Psychology, 38*, 170–77.

JOST, J. T. (1997). An experimental replication of the depressed-entitlement effect among women. *Psychology of Women Quarterly, 21*, 387–393.

JOST, J. T., & BANAJI, M. R. (1994). The role of stereotyping in system-justification and the production of false consciousness. *British Journal of Social Psychology, 33*, 1–27.

KAHNEMAN, D., & TVERSKY, A. (1973). On the psychology of prediction. *Psychological Review, 80*, 237–251.

KARNEY, B., & BRADBURY, T. N. (1997). Neuroticism, marital interaction, and the trajectory of marital satisfaction. *Journal of Personality and Social Psychology, 72*, 1075–1092.

KARPICKE, J. D., & BLUNT, J. R. (2011). Retrieval practice produces more learning than elaborative studying with concept mapping. *Science, 331*, 772–775.

KARPINSKI, A., & HILTON, J. L. (2001). Attitudes and the implicit association test. *Journal of Personality and Social Psychology, 81*(5), 774–788.

KASOF, J. (1993). Sex bias in the naming of stimulus persons. *Psychological Bulletin, 113*, 140–163.

KENRICK, D. T., & MACFARLANE, S. W. (1986). Ambient temperature and horn honking: A field study of the heat/aggression relationship. *Environment and Behavior, 18*, 179–191.

KINSEY, A. C., POMEROY, W. B., & MARTIN, C. E. (1948/1998). *Sexual behavior in the human male*. Philadelphia: W.B. Saunders; Bloomington: Indiana U. Press.

KITAYAMA, S., & KARASAWA, M. (1997). Implicit self-esteem in Japan: Name letters and birthday numbers. *Personality & Social Psychology Bulletin, 23*, 736–742.

KLEIN, S. B., SHERMAN, J. W., & LOFTUS, J. (1996). The role of episodic and semantic memory in the development of trait self-knowledge. *Social Cognition, 14*, 277–291.

KOMORITA, S. S., & GRAHAM, W. K. (1965). Number of scale points and the reliability of scales. *Education and Psychological Measurement, 25,* 987–995.

KOOLE, S. L., SMEETS, K., VAN- KNIPPENBERG, A., & DIJKSTERHUIS, A. (1999). The cessation of rumination through self-affirmation. *Journal of Personality and Social Psychology, 77,* 111–125.

KRULL, D. S. (1993). Does the grist change the mill? The effect of the perceiver's inferential goal on the process of social inference. *Personality and Social Psychology Bulletin, 19,* 340–348.

KRULL, D. S., & ERICKSON, D. J. (1995). Judging situations: On the effortful process of taking dispositional information into account. *Social Cognition, 13,* 417–438.

LECKY, P. (1945). *Self-consistency: A theory of personality.* Washington, DC: Island Press.

LEPPER, M. R., GREENE, D., & NISBETT, R. E. (1973). Undermining children's intrinsic interest with extrinsic reward: A test of the "overjustification" hypothesis. *Journal of Personality and Social Psychology, 28,* 129–137.

LERNER, M. J. (1980). *The belief in a just world: A fundamental delusion.* New York: Plenum Press.

LEVETT, S. D., & DUBNER, S. J. (2005). *Freakonomics: A rogue economist explores the hidden side of everything.* William Morrow (Imprint of Harper Collins).

LIEBERMAN, M. D., OCHSNER, K. N., GILBERT, D. T., & SCHACTER, D. L. (2001). Do amnesiacs exhibit cognitive dissonance reduction? The role of explicit memory and attention in attitude change. *Psychological Science, 12,* 135–139.

LOBEL, M., DUNKEL-SCHETTER, C., & SCRIMSHAW, S. C. (1992). Prenatal maternal stress and prematurity: A prospective study of socioeconomically disadvantaged women. *Health Psychology, 11,* 32–40.

LOFTUS, E. F. (1993). The reality of repressed memories. *American Psychologist, 48,* 518–537.

MACDONALD, T. K., ZANNA, M. P., & FONG, G. T. (1995). Decision making in altered states: Effects of alcohol on attitudes toward drinking and driving. *Journal of Personality and Social Psychology, 68,* 973–985.

MADDOX, K. B. (2004). Perspectives on racial phenotypicality bias. *Personality and Social Psychology Review, 8,* 383–401.

MAJOR, B. (1994). From disadvantage to deserving: Comparisons, justifications and the psychology of entitlement. In M. P. Zanna (Ed.), *Advances in experimental social psychology* (Vol. 26, 293–335). New York: Academic Press.

MAJOR, B., & TESTA, M. (1989). Social comparisons processes and judgments of entitlement and satisfaction. *Journal of Experimental Social Psychology, 21,* 393–405.

MARECEK, J. (1995). Gender, politics, and psychology's ways of knowing. *American Psychologist, 50,* 162–163.

MARKUS, H. R., & KITAYAMA, S. (1991). Culture and the self: Implications for cognition, emotion, and motivation. *Psychological Review, 98,* 224–253.

MARSH, H. W. (1993). Relations between global and specific domains of self: The importance of individual importance, certainty, and ideals. *Journal of Personality and Social Psychology, 65,* 975–992.

MARTIN, L. L., SETA, J. J., & CRELIA, R. A. (1990). Assimilation and contrast as a function of people's willingness and ability to expend effort in forming an impression. *Journal of Personality and Social Psychology, 59,* 27–37.

MATELL, M. S., & JACOBY, J. (1971). Is there an optimal number of alternatives for Likert scale items? Study I: Reliability and validity. *Educational and Psychological Measurement, 31,* 657–674.

MCGRATH, J. E. (1982). Dilemmatics: The study of research choices and dilemmas. In J. E. McGrath & R. A. Kulka (Eds.), *Judgment calls in research* (pp. 69–102). Beverly Hills: Sage.

MCGUIRE, W. J. (1961). Resistance to persuasion conferred by active and passive prior refutation of the same and alternative counterarguments. *Journal of Abnormal and Social Psychology, 63,* 326–332.

MCGUIRE, W. J. (1973). The yin and yang of progress in social psychology: Seven koan. *Journal of Personality and Social Psychology, 26,* 446–456.

MCGUIRE, W. J. (1989). A perspectivist approach to the strategic planning of programmatic scientific research. In B. Gholson, W. R. Shadish, Jr., R. A. Neimeyer, & A. C. Houts (Eds.), *Psychology of science: Contributions to metascience* (pp. 214–245). Cambridge, England: Cambridge University Press.

MCKEARNEY, J. W. (1987–1988). Asking questions about behavior. *Perspectives in Biology and Medicine, 21,* 109–119.

MCKELVIE, S. J. (1978). Graphic rating scales—How many categories? *British Journal of Psychology, 69,* 185–202.

MCKELVIE, S. J. (1990). Student acceptance of a generalized personality description: Forer's graphologist revisited. *Journal of Social Behavior and Personality, 5,* 91–95.

MEDVEC, V. H., MADEY, S. F., & GILOVICH, T. (1995). When less is more: Counterfactual thinking and satisfaction among Olympic medalists. *Journal of Personality and Social Psychology, 69,* 603–610.

MILGRAM, S. (1963). Behavioral study of obedience. *Journal of Abnormal and Social Psychology, 67,* 371–378.

MILLER, G., TYBUR, J. M., & JORDAN, B. D. (2007). Ovulatory cycle effects on tip earnings by lap dancers: Economic evidence for human estrus? *Evolution and Human Behavior, 28,* 375–381.

MILLER, J. (1984). Culture and the development of everyday social explanation. *Journal of Personality and Social Psychology, 46,* 961–978.

MILLER, S. L., & MANER, J. K. (2010). Ovulation as a male mating prime: Subtle signs of women's fertility influence men's mating cognition and behavior. *Journal of Personality and Social Psychology, 100,* 295–308.

MIYAKE, A., KOST-SMITH, L. E., FINKELSTEIN, N. D., POLLOCK, S. J., COHEN, G. L., & ITO, T. A. (2010). Reducing the gender achievement gap in college science: A classroom study of values affirmation. *Science, 330,* 1234–1237.

MONTOYA, R. M., HORTON, R. S., & KIRCHNER, J. (2008). Is actual similarity necessary for attraction? A meta-analysis of actual and perceived similarity. *Journal of Social and Personal Relationships, 25,* 889–922.

MOONEY, C. S., & LEE, M. H. (1995). Legislating morality in the American States: The case of pre-*Roe* abortion regulation reform. *American Journal of Political Science, 39,* 599–627.

MORWITZ, V. G., & FITZSIMONS, G. J. (2004). The mere-measurement effect: Why does measuring intentions change actual behavior? *Journal of Consumer Psychology, 14,* 64–74.

MORWITZ, V. G., JOHNSON, E, & SCHMITTLEIN (1993). Does measuring intent change behavior? *Journal of Consumer Research, 20,* 41–61.

MURRAY, S. L., HOLMES, J. G., & GRIFFIN, D. W. (1996). The benefits of positive illusions: Idealization and the construction of satisfaction in close relationships. *Journal of Personality and Social Psychology, 70,* 79–98.

NATIONAL COMMITTEE ON PAY EQUITY. (2001). *The wage gap: 1999.* Source: U.S. Census Bureau, 1999 Current Population Reports. http://www.feminist.com/fairpay/Retrieved August 2001.

NISBETT, R. E., & WILSON, T. D. (1977). Telling more than we can know: Verbal reports on mental processes. *Psychological Review, 84,* 231–259.

NUTTIN, J. M. (1985). Narcissism beyond Gestalt and awareness: The name letter effect. *European Journal of Social Psychology, 15,* 353–361.

NUTTIN, J. M. (1987). Affective consequences of mere ownership: The name letter effect in twelve European languages. *European Journal of Social Psychology, 17,* 381–402.

OLSON, J. M. (1992). Self-perception of humor: Evidence for discounting and augmentation effects. *Journal of Personality and Social Psychology, 62,* 369–377.

ORNE, M. T. (1962). On the social psychology of the psychological experiment: With particular reference to demand characteristics and their implications. *American Psychologist, 17,* 776–783.

ORTH, B. & WEGENER, B. (1983). Scaling occupational prestige by magnitude estimation and category rating methods: A comparison with the sensory domain, *European Journal of Social Psychology, 13*(4), 417–431.

OSGOOD, C. E. (1952). The nature and measurement of meaning. *Psychological Bulletin, 49,* 197–237.

OSGOOD, C. E., SUCI, G. J. & TANNENBAUM, P. H. (1957). *The measurement of meaning.* Urbana: University of Illinois Press.

OSTROV, J. M., & GODLESKI, S. A. (2010). Toward an integrated gender-linked model of aggression subtypes in early and middle childhood. *Psychological Review, 117,* 233–242.

PATERNOSTER, R. (1983). Race of victim and location of crime: The decision to seek the death penalty in South Carolina. *Journal of Criminal Law and Criminology, 74,* 754–785.

PAYNE, B. K. (2001). Prejudice and perception: The role of automatic and controlled processes in misperceiving a weapon. *Journal of Personality and Social Psychology, 81,* 181–192.

PEDHAZUR, E. (1982). *Multiple regression in behavioral research.* New York, NY: CBS Publishing.

PELHAM, B. W. (1991a). On confidence and consequence: The certainty and importance of self-knowledge. *Journal of Personality and Social Psychology, 60,* 518–530.

PELHAM, B. W. (1991b). On the benefits of misery: Self-serving biases in the depressive self-concept. *Journal of Personality and Social Psychology, 61,* 670–681.

PELHAM, B. W. (1993). The idiographic nature of human personality: Examples of the idiographic self-concept. *Journal of Personality and Social Psychology, 64,* 665–677.

PELHAM, B. W. (1998). Unpublished raw data, University of California, Los Angeles.

PELHAM, B. W. & CARVALLO. M. R (2011). The curious case of Benjamin Benjamin: Moderators of implicit egotism. Under review.

PELHAM, B. W. & CARVALLO. M. R (2011). The surprising potency of implicit egotism: A reply to Simonsohn. *Journal of Personality and Social Psychology, 101,* 25–30.

PELHAM, B. W., & HETTS, J. J. (2001). Underworked and overpaid: Elevated entitlement in men's self-pay. *Journal of Experimental Social Psychology, 37*(2), 93–103.

PELHAM, B. W., JONES, J. K., MIRENBERG, M. C., & CARVALLO, M. C. (2002). *The man who took a wife because of an H: Implicit egotism and marriage.* Under review.

PELHAM, B. W., MIRENBERG, M. C., & JONES, J. T. (2002). Why Susie sells seashells by the seashore: Implicit egotism and major life decisions. *Journal of Personality and Social Psychology, 82,* 469–87.

PELHAM, B. W., & NETER, E. (1995). The effect of motivation on judgment depends on the difficulty of the judgment. *Journal of Personality and Social Psychology, 68,* 581–594.

PELHAM, B. W., SUMARTA, T. T., & MYASKOVSKY, L. (1994). The easy path from many to much: The numerosity heuristic. *Cognitive Psychology, 26,* 103–133.

PELHAM, B. W., & SWANN, W. B., JR. (1989). From self-conceptions to self-worth: On the sources and structure of global self-esteem. *Journal of Personality and Social Psychology, 57,* 672–680.

PETERSON, C., & SELIGMAN, M. E. P. (1987). Explanatory style and illness. *Journal of Personality, 55,* 237–265.

PETTY, R. E., & CACIOPPO, J. T. (1986). *Communication and persuasion: Central and peripheral routes to attitude change.* New York: Springer-Verlag.

PHILLIPS, D. P., & CARSTENSEN, L. L. (1986). Clustering of teenage suicides after television news stories about suicide. *New England Journal of Medicine, 315,* 685–689.

PIPITONE, R. N., & GALLUP, G. G., JR. (2008). Women's voice attractiveness varies across the menstrual cycle. *Evolution and Human Behavior, 29,* 268–274.

POPPER, K. (1974/1990). *Unended quest: An intellectual autobiography.* LaSalle, IL: Open Court.

PYSZCZYNSKI, T., GREENBERG, J., & SOLOMON, S. (1997). Why do we need what we need? A terror management perspective on the roots of human social motivation. *Psychology Inquiry, 8,* 1–20.

REBER, P., & KOTOVSKY, K. (1997). Implicit learning in problem solving: The role of working memory capacity. *Journal of Experimental Psychology: General, 126,* 178–203.

REGIER, D. A., & BURKE, J. D. (1987). Psychiatric disorders in the community: The epidemiologic catchment area study. In R. E. Hales & A. J. Frances (Eds.), *American Psychiatric Association Annual Review* (Vol. 6, pp. 610–624). Washington, DC: American Psychiatric Press.

REIFMAN, A. S., LARRICK, R. P., & FEIN, S. (1991). Temper and temperature on the diamond: The heat-aggression relationship in major league baseball. *Personality and Social Psychology Bulletin, 17,* 580–585.

RENSBERGER, R. (1986). *How the world works: A guide to science's greatest discoveries.* New York: William Morrow.

RIDGEWAY, C. L. (2001). The emergence of status beliefs: From structural inequity to legitimizing ideology. In J. T. Jost & B. Major (Eds.), *The psychology of legitimacy: Emerging perspectives on ideology, justice, and intergroup relations* (pp. 257–277). New York: Cambridge.

RIDGEWAY, C. L., & WALKER, H. A. (2001). Status structures. In A. Branaman (Ed.), *Self and society* (pp. 298–320). Malden, MA: Blackwell.

ROBERTS, D. F., FOEHR, U. G., RIDEOUT, V. J. (COL), & Brodie, Maryanne (COL). (2003). *Kids and media in America.* New York, NY: Cambridge University Press.

ROEDIGER, H. L., III, & MCDERMOTT, K. B. (1995). Creating false memories: Remembering words not presented in lists. *Journal of Experimental Psychology: Learning, Memory, & Cognition, 21,* 803–814.

ROESE, N., & JAMIESON, D. W. (1993). Twenty years of bogus pipeline research: A critical review and meta-analysis. *Psychological Bulletin, 114,* 363–375.

ROMANES, G. J. (1882). *Animal intelligence.* London: Routledge & Kegan Paul.

ROSENBERG, M. J. (1965). *Society and the adolescent self-image.* Princeton, NJ: Princeton University Press.

ROSENTHAL, R., & FODE, K. L. (1963). The effect of experimenter bias on the performance of the albino rat. *Behavioral Science, 8,* 183–189.

ROSENTHAL, R., & JACOBSON, L. (1966). Teachers' expectancies: Determinants of pupils' IQ gains. *Psychological Reports, 19,* 115–118.

ROSENTHAL, R., & ROSNOW, R. L. (1991). *Essentials of behavioral research: Methods and data analysis* (2nd ed.). New York: McGraw-Hill.

ROSENTHAL, R., & RUBIN, D. B. (1982). A simple general purpose display of magnitude of experimental effect. *Journal of Educational Psychology, 74,* 166–169.

ROSNOW, R. L., & ROSENTHAL, R. (1991). If you're looking at cell means, you're not looking at only the interaction (unless all main effects are zero). *Psychological Bulletin, 110,* 574–576.

ROSS, L. (1977). The intuitive psychologist and his shortcomings. In L. Berkowitz (Ed.), *Advances in experimental social psychology* (vol. 10, pp. 173–220). San Diego: Academic Press.

ROSS, L., GREENE, D., & HOUSE, P. (1977). The false consensus effect: An egocentric bias in social perception and attribution processes. *Journal of Experimental Social Psychology, 13,* 279–301.

ROSS, L., LEPPER, M. R., & HUBBARD, M. (1975). Perseverance in self-perception and social perception: Biased attributional processes in the debriefing paradigm. *Journal of Personality and Social Psychology, 32,* 880–892.

ROTHERMUND, K., & WENTURA, D. (2001). Figure-ground asymmetries in the Implicit Association Test (IAT). *Zeitschrift fuer Experimentelle Psychologie, 48*(2), 94–106.

RULE, B. G., TAYLOR, B. R., & DOBBS, A. R. (1987). Priming effects of heat on aggressive thoughts. *Social Cognition, 5,* 131–143.

RUSTING, C. L. (1998). Personality, mood, and cognitive processing of emotional information: Three alternative models. Under review.

SACKS, O. W. (1985). *The man who mistook his wife for a hat and other clinical tales.* New York: Summit Books.

SCHACTER, D. L. (1996). *Searching for memory: The brain, the mind, and the past.* New York: Basic Books.

SCHALLER, M., CRANDALL, C. S., STANGOR, C., & NEUBERG, S. L. (1995). "What kinds of social psychology experiments are of value to perform?" A reply to Wallach and Wallach. *Journal of Personality and Social Psychology, 69,* 611–618.

SCHULTZ, D. (1981). *A history of modern psychology* (3rd ed.). San Diego: Academic Press.

SCHWARZ, N. (1999). Survey methods. In D. T. Gilbert & S. T. Fiske (Eds.), *The handbook of social psychology* (Vol 1, 4th ed., pp. 143–179). New York: McGraw-Hill.

SCHWARZ, N., STRACK, F., & MAI, H. P. (1991). Assimilation and contrast effects in part-whole question sequences: A conversational logic analysis. *Public Opinion Quarterly, 55,* 3–23.

SEARS, D. O. (1986). College sophomores in the laboratory: Influences of a narrow data base on social psychology's view of human nature. *Journal of Personality and Social Psychology, 51,* 515–530.

SHADISH, W. R., COOK, T. D., & CAMPBELL, D. T. (2002). *Experimental and quasi-experimental designs for generalized causal inference.* Boston: Houghton-Mifflin.

SHRAUGER, J. S. (1975). Responses to evaluation as a function of initial self-perceptions. *Psychological Bulletin. 82*(4), 581–596.

SIDANIUS, J., & PRATTO, F. (2000). *Social dominance: An intergroup theory of social hierarchy and oppression.* Cambridge: Cambridge University Press.

SIMON, L., GREENBERG, J., HARMON-JONES, E., SOLOMON, S., PYSZCZYNSKI, T., ARNDT, J., & ABEND, T. (1997). Terror management and cognitive-experiential self-theory: Evidence that terror management occurs in the experiential system. *Journal of Personality and Social Psychology 72,* 1132–1146.

SIMONSOHN, U. (2011). Spurious? Name similarity effects (implicit egotism) in marriage, job, and moving decisions. *Journal of Personality and Social Psychology, 101,* 1–24.

SKINNER, B. F. (1948). "Superstition" in the pigeon. *Journal of Experimental Psychology, 38,* 168–172.

SKINNER, B. F. (1971). *Beyond freedom and dignity.* New York: Bantam Books.

SMITH, E. R., & MACKIE, D. M. (1995). *Social psychology.* New York: Worth.

SNYDER, M., & SWANN, W. B. (1978). Hypothesis-testing processes in social interaction. *Journal of Personality and Social Psychology, 36,* 1202–1212.

SNYDER, M., TANKE, E. D., & BERSCHEID, E. (1977). Social perception and interpersonal behavior: On the self-fulfilling nature of social stereotypes. *Journal of Personality and Social Psychology, 35,* 656–666.

SPELKE, E. S. (1991). Physical knowledge in infancy: Reflections on Piaget's theory. In S. Carey & R. Gelman (Eds.), *The epigenesis of mind: Essays on biology and cognition* (pp. 133–169). Hillsdale, NJ: Erlbaum.

SPINOZA, B. (1982). *The ethics and selected letters.* (S. Feldman, Ed., and S. Shirley, Trans.). Indianapolis, IN: Hackett. (Original work published 1677)

STAATS, A. W., & STAATS, C. K. (1958). Attitudes established by classical conditioning. *Journal of Abnormal Psychology, 57,* 37–40.

STAPEL, D. A. & SCHWARZ, N. (1998). The Republican who did not want to become president: Colin Powell's impact on evaluations of the Republican party and Bob Dole. *Personality and Social Psychology Bulletin, 24,* 690–698.

STEELE, C. M., & ARONSON, J. (1995). Stereotype threat and the intellectual test performance of African-Americans. *Journal of Personality and Social psychology, 69,* 797–811.

STEELE, C. M., CRITCHLOW, B., & LIU, T. J. (1985). Alcohol and social behavior: II. The helpful drunkard. *Journal of Personality and Social Psychology, 48*(1), 35–46.

STEELE, C. M., & LIU, T. J. (1983). Dissonance processes as self-affirmation. *Journal of Personality and Social Psychology, 45,* 5–19.

STEWART, B. D., & PAYNE, B. K. (2008). Bringing automatic stereotyping under control: Implementation intentions as an efficient means of thought control. *Personality and Social Psychology Bulletin 34,* 1332–1345.

STEWART, I. (1989). *Does God play dice? The mathematics of chaos.* Cambridge, MA: Blackwell.

STRACK, F., MARTIN, L. L., & SCHWARZ, N. (1988). Priming and communication: The social determinants of information use in judgments of life-satisfaction. *European Journal of Social Psychology, 18,* 429–442.

STROOP, J. R. (1935). Studies of interference in serial verbal reactions. *Journal of Experimental Psychology, 18,* 643–662.

STRUNK, W., JR., & WHITE, E. B. (1979). *The elements of style* (3rd ed.). New York: Macmillan.

SULS, J., & WILLS, T. A. (1991). *Social comparison: Contemporary theory and research.* Hillsdale, NJ: Erlbaum.

SUTER, W. N., & LINDGREN, H. C. (1989). *Experimentation in psychology: A guided tour*. Boston: Allyn & Bacon.

SWANN, W. B., JR. (1987). Identity negotiation: Where two roads meet. *Journal of Personality and Social Psychology, 53*, 1038–1051.

SWANN, W. B., JR. (1992). Seeking "truth," finding despair: Some unhappy consequences of a negative self-concept. *Current Directions in Psychological Science, 1*, 15–18.

SWANN, W. B., JR., PELHAM, B. W., & CHIDESTER, T. R. (1988). Change through paradox: Using self-verification to alter beliefs. *Journal of Personality and Social Psychology, 54*, 268–273.

SWANN, W. B., JR., PELHAM, B. W., & KRULL, D. S. (1989). Agreeable fancy or disagreeable truth? Reconciling self-enhancement and self-verification. *Journal of Personality and Social Psychology, 57*, 782–791.

SWANN, W. B., STEIN-SEROUSSI, A., & GIESLER, R. B. (1992). Why people self-verify. *Journal of Personality and Social Psychology, 62*, 392–401.

SYMONS, V. L. (2002). Make-believe article, used in Chapter 11 to illustrate the value of writing assertively. *Journal of Bogus Studies, 1*, 1–1543.

TAFARODI, R. W., & SWANN, W. B., JR. (1995). Self-liking and self-competence as dimensions of global self-esteem: Initial validation of a measure. *Journal of Personality Assessment, 65*, 322–342.

TASSINARY, L. G., & CACIOPPO, J. T. (1992). Unobservable facial actions and emotion. *Psychological Science, 3*, 28–33.

TAYLOR, S. E., & BROWN, J. D. (1988). Illusion and well-being: A social psychological perspective on mental health. *Psychological Bulletin, 103*, 193–210.

TAYLOR, S. E., REPETTI, R. L., & SEEMAN, T. (1994). Health psychology: What is an unhealthy environment and how does it get under the skin? *Annual Review of Psychology, 48*, 411–447.

TAYLOR, S. P., & GAMMON, C. B. (1975). Effects of type and dose of alcohol on human physical aggression. *Journal of Personality and Social Psychology, 32*(1), 169–175.

TEDESCHI, J. T. SCHLENKER, B. R., & BONOMA, T. V. (1971). Cognitive dissonance: Private ratiocination or public spectacle? *American Psychologist, 26*(8), 685–695.

TESSER, A. (1986). Some effects of self-evaluation maintenance on cognition and action. In R. M. Sorrentino & E. T. Higgins (Eds.), *Handbook of motivation and cognition: Foundations of social behavior* (pp. 435–464). New York: Guilford Press.

TESSER, A., & VALENTI, A. C. (1981). On the mechanism of thought-induced attitude change. *Social Behavior and Personality, 9*, 17–22.

TETLOCK, P. E. (1985). Accountability: A social check on the fundamental attribution error. *Social Psychology Quarterly, 48*, 227–236.

TETLOCK, P. E. & MITCHELL, G. (2008). Calibrating prejudice in milliseconds. *Social Psychology Quarterly, 71*, 12–16.

THURSTONE, L. L. (1931). The measurement of change in social attitude. *The Journal of Social Psychology, 2*, 230–235.

TOURANGEAU, R., RIPS, L. J., AND RASINSKI, K. (2000). *The psychology of survey responses*. Cambridge: Cambridge University Press.

TRIANDIS, H. C. (1989). The self and social behavior in differing cultural contexts. *Psychological Review, 96*, 506–520.

TULVING, E. (1993). Self-knowledge of an amnesic individual is represented abstractly. In T. K. Srull & R. S. Wyer, Jr. (Eds.), *The mental representation of trait and autobiographical knowledge about the self: Advances in social cognition* (Vol. 5, pp. 147–156). Hillsdale, NJ: Erlbaum.

TURNER, C. W., SIMONS, L. S., BERKOWITZ, L., & FRODI, A. (1977). The stimulating and inhibiting effects of weapons on aggressive behavior. *Aggressive Behavior, 3*, 355–378.

TVERSKY, A., & KAHNEMAN, D. (1982). Evidential impact of base rates. In D. Kahneman, P. Slovic, & A. Tversky (Eds.), *Judgment under uncertainty: Heuristics and biases* (pp. 153–160). Cambridge: Cambridge University Press.

TVERSKY, A., & KAHNEMAN, D. (1983). Extensional versus intuitive reasoning: The conjunction fallacy in probability judgment. *Psychological Review, 90*, 293–315.

UNITED NATIONS. (2000). *The world's women 2000: Trends and statistics*. New York: United Nations Publications. ISBN 92-1-161428-7.

VALDESOLO, P., & DESTENO, D. (2011). Synchrony and the social tuning of compassion. *Emotion, 11*, 262–266.

VARGAS, P. T., VON HIPPEL, W., & PETTY, R. E. (1998). It's not just what you think, it's also how you think: Using measures of biased processing to predict behavior. Under review.

WASON, P. C. (1971). Problem solving and reasoning. *British Medical Bulletin, 27*, 206–210.

WEBSTER, M., JR., & HYSOM, S. J. (1998). Creating status characteristics. *American Sociological Review, 63*, 351–378.

WEGNER, D. M. (1994). Ironic processes of mental control. *Psychological Review, 101*, 34–52.

WEGNER, D. M., ERBER, R., & BOWMAN, R. E. (1993). *On trying not to be sexist*. Unpublished manuscript.

WEGNER, D. M., LANE, J. D., & DIMITRI, S. (1994). The allure of secret relationships. *Journal of Personality and Social Psychology, 66*, 287–300.

WEGNER, D., WENZLAFF, R., KERKER, R. M., & BEATTIE, A. E. (1981). Incrimination through innuendo: Can media questions become public answers? *Journal of Personality and Social Psychology, 40*, 822–832.

WEINSTEIN, N. D. (1980). Unrealistic optimism about future life events. *Journal of Personality and Social Psychology, 39*, 806–820.

WELLS, G. L., & PETTY, R. E. (1980). The effects of overt head movements on persuasion: Compatibility and incompatibility of responses. *Basic and Applied Social Psychology, 1*, 219–230.

WENG, L. J. (2004). Impact of the number of response categories and anchor labels on coefficient alpha and test-retest reliability. *Educational and Psychological Measurement, 64*(6), 956–972.

WILLIAMS, J. E., & BEST, D. L. (1990). *Measuring sex stereotypes: A multination study.* Newbury Park, CA: Sage.

WILLIAMS, J. M. G., MATHEWS, A., & MACLEOD, C. (1996). The emotional Stroop task and psychopathology. *Psychological Bulletin, 120*, 3–24.

WILLIAMS, P., FITZSIMONS, G. J., & BLOCK, L. G. (2004). When consumers do not recognize "benign" intention questions as persuasion attempts. *Journal of Consumer Research, 31*, 540–550.

WILSON, T. D., LINDSEY, S., & SCHOOLER, T. Y. (2000). A model of dual attitudes. *Psychological Review, 107*, 101–126.

WILSON, T. D., & SCHOOLER, J. W. (1991). Thinking too much: Introspection can reduce the quality of preferences and decisions. *Journal of Personality & Social Psychology, 60*, 181–192.

YODER, J. D., & KAHN, A. S. (2003). Making gender comparisons more meaningful: A call for more attention to social context. *Psychology of Women Quarterly, 27*(4), 281–290.

ZAJONC, R. B. (1965, July 16). Social facilitation. *Science, 149*, 269–274.

ZANNA, M. P., CROSBY, F., & LOEWENSTEIN, G. (1987). Male reference groups and discontent among female professionals. In B. Gutek and L. Larwood (Eds.) *Women's career development* (pp. 28–42). Newbery Park, CA: Sage.

Name Index

Subject Index

Note: Page numbers followed by f or t refer to Figures or Tables